Gallaudet Encyclopedia of DEAF PEOPLE AND DEAFNESS

3

S–Z

Index

John V. Van Cleve, Editor in Chief
Gallaudet College

McGraw-Hill Book Company, Inc.

New York • St. Louis • San Francisco • Auckland • Bogotá • Hamburg
Johannesburg • London • Madrid • Mexico • Milan • Montreal • New Delhi
Panama • Paris • São Paulo • Singapore • Sydney • Tokyo • Toronto

GALLAUDET ENCYCLOPEDIA OF DEAF PEOPLE AND DEAFNESS
Copyright © 1987 by McGraw-Hill, Inc.

1 2 3 4 5 6 7 8 9 0 HAHA 8 9 4 3 2 1 0 9 8 7

ISBN 0-07-079229-1

Library of Congress Cataloging in Publication Data

Gallaudet encyclopedia of deaf people and deafness.

  Includes bibliographies and index.
  1. Deaf—Dictionaries.   2. Deafness—Dictionaries.
I. Van Cleve, John V.   II. Gallaudet College.
HV2365.G35   1987   362.4'2'0321   86-15396
ISBN 0-07-079229-1 (set)

Gallaudet Encyclopedia of DEAF PEOPLE AND DEAFNESS

3

S–Z

Index

Gallaudet
Encyclopedia of
DEAF PEOPLE
AND DEAFNESS

3

S–Z

Index

S

SCHOWE, BENJAMIN MARSHALL, SR.
(1893–1979)

Benjamin M. Schowe was a labor economist specialist with the Firestone Tire and Rubber Company of Akron, Ohio. He was also a prominent consultant for deaf employees in industry from the early 1920s to the late 1950s. He was a leader, go-getter, and outstanding advocate for the welfare of deaf employees. He successfully fought big insurance companies and government agencies that banned deaf employees from jobs sponsored by the Work Projects Administration during the Great Depression and World War II.

Schowe was born in Columbus, Indiana, on September 29, 1893. In early years, his hearing slowly deteriorated and he became deaf in his early teens. He had attended the public school near his home in Columbus until his first year of high school. He found it impossible to follow the conversation of others and decided to attend the Indiana School for the Deaf until graduation. In 1913 he enrolled at Gallaudet College in Washington, D.C., and graduated with a bachelor of arts degree in 1918. In the same year he married Dorothy Conover, who also graduated from Gallaudet College. A hard-of-hearing son, Benjamin, Jr., was born in 1920 and later graduated from Gallaudet College too. *See* GALLAUDET COLLEGE.

After graduation, Schowe returned to the Midwest and eventually secured a job with the Firestone Tire and Rubber Company of Akron in March 1919. In his first position at Firestone, he recruited deaf people to work for the company. He also worked on the assembly lines as a tire builder and as a tire inspector from 1921 to 1934. In 1934 he transferred to the labor department where he was responsible

Benjamin M. Schowe. (Gallaudet College Archives)

for researching issues on labor relations, economics, and law. In 1942 he changed over to the economics department as labor economist research specialist. During this time, though, he also continued to counsel deaf employees in the company and interview deaf applicants. He retired in October 1958 from Firestone, for whom he had worked for nearly 40 years.

During his years with Firestone, Schowe became well known for his articles on employment counseling with regard to deaf workers in the factory setting. His publications regarding the topic of deaf employment were distributed to potential employers nationwide. One publication was funded and cosponsored by the Federal Security Agency and the Office of Vocational Rehabilitation. In 1951 Schowe wrote an article, "Guidelines for the Employment of Deaf Workers," for the U.S. Department of Health, Education and Welfare. In this, he discussed the social and psychological adjustments of deaf workers in a hearing environment, and the specific ramifications of their presence in the factory environment. With regard to on-the-job training of deaf workers, for example, he said, "The cardinal principle is simply this: Show them how (Don't try to tell them how.) SHOW is better than to TELL." He also wrote "The Deaf at Work," which was jointly sponsored by the National Association of the Deaf and the Office of Vocational Rehabilitation under a grant from the U.S. Department of Health, Education and Welfare. This publication attempted to encourage all employers to understand the idiosyncrasies of deaf employees and the ramifications of their deafness. In "These Deaf-Mutes Are Good Factory Workers," he argued that segregation of deaf workers in the factory was unproductive and degrading. He suggested also that written communication was simple and practical. *See* NATIONAL ASSOCIATION OF THE DEAF.

Schowe, throughout his career with Firestone, interviewed deaf applicants seeking work with the company. He was always on call with the employment office to help with interviewing new applicants and counseling deaf workers already with the company. The company never established any written policy relating to the employment of deaf workers. Schowe believed, however, that the deaf applicant should fulfill certain minimum requirements. The deaf person, he felt, should possess basic English language skills, should be able to comprehend simple written instructions, and should have enough arithmetic skills to fill out the time card and calculate the pay. He strongly believed that the most accurate and fastest way to communicate with deaf people was in writing rather than lipreading, which he felt was an overrated communication method. He said, "It is easy to get off to wrong assumptions with lip reading."

During World War II, deaf people were barred from joining military service because of their hearing loss. Yet, because the work force had dwindled, large numbers of deaf people were provided the opportunity of acquiring jobs. At the Firestone company, there were between 200 and 250 deaf laborers and skilled crafts people, chemists, and administrators on the payroll. Schowe's philosophy was that this wartime employment afterward provided deaf workers with self-confidence and experience which enabled them to become qualified to enter other areas of private industry.

Though deaf people had better opportunities for getting jobs during the 1940s, there were instances of discrimination. For example, the Work Projects Administration decided to ban employment of deaf workers for a project in Missouri—the reason being that the insurance company refused to insure deaf workers on the government jobs there. As a spokesman of the Industrial Committee of the National Association of the Deaf and the National Fraternal Society of the Deaf, Schowe argued with the Work Projects Administration and the insurance company to rectify the injustice. He maintained that deaf workers would not increase potential for on-the-job injuries. Once convinced of this, the insurance company agreed to cover deaf workers and the Work Projects Administration began hiring deaf employees. *See* NATIONAL FRATERNAL SOCIETY OF THE DEAF.

Schowe participated in many activities and was a member of several organizations. He was a state council member of the Ohio Federation of Organizations of the Deaf, and a member of the board of managers of the Ohio Home for the Aged and Infirm Deaf near Westerville. He served on the President's Committee on Employment of the Physically Handicapped, to which he was appointed in March 1959 in recognition of his leadership in matters concerning employment problems of deaf people. He was first vice-president and then president of the Gallaudet College Alumni Association during 1939–1946 and 1946–1950, respectively. He also was an honorary member of the Conference of Executives of American Schools for the Deaf. Schowe received an honorary doctorate in humane letters from Gallaudet College in 1951. *See* GALLAUDET COLLEGE ALUMNI ASSOCIATION.

On September 26, 1979, Schowe died in Akron.

Bibliography
"The Benjamin M. Schowe Papers," Archives, Gallaudet College, Washington, D.C.

Bowe, Frank: "Ben M. Schowe, Maverick from Akron," *The Deaf American*, vol. 25, no. 1, September 1972.

Schowe, Ben M.: "The Deaf in Industry" and "The Place of the Deaf in the Community," *The Bulletin* (Gallaudet College), vol. 4, no. 2, 1955.

———: *Deaf Workers on the Home Front: Notes on Motivation for Employment in War and Peace*, 1969.
———: "Employment: The Deaf at Work," *American Annals of the Deaf*, vol. 103, no. 2, March 1958.
———: "Guidelines for the Employment of Deaf Workers," *Employment Security Review*, 1951.
———: *Identity Crisis In Deafness: A Humanistic Perspective*, 1979.
———: "The Industrial Potential of the Deaf," *The Silent Worker*, vol. 7, no. 2, October 1954.
———: "These Deaf-Mutes Are Good Factory Workers," *Factory Management and Maintenance*, 1946.

Michael J. Olson

SCHREIBER, FREDERICK CARL
(1922–1979)

In the 15 years he served as its chief executive officer, Frederick Carl Schreiber led the National Association of the Deaf (NAD) from a position of relatively obscurity to one of great influence on the lives of deaf people. He changed the NAD from a social, ceremonial group to an active, political force whose influence has spread throughout the United States and overseas. Schreiber was born in Brooklyn, New York, on February 1, 1922. He died at New York University Hospital in Manhattan on September 6, 1979. In his 57 years, he traveled across the United States and to many foreign countries, including Italy, France, Germany, England, Canada, Mexico, Israel, Thailand, and the Soviet Union (from which his parents had fled seven decades earlier). Wherever he went, he promoted changes in attitudes towards deafness, shifting the public from viewing deaf people as weak-minded and dependent to regarding them as intelligent, self-sufficient persons who ask no more from society than accommodations that enable them to enjoy full citizenship. *See* NATIONAL ASSOCIATION OF THE DEAF.

EARLY YEARS
Schreiber lost his hearing from attacks of spinal meningitis that began when he was six years old. His illnesses also caused a severe curvature of his spine from which he recovered after two years of wearing a plaster cast and then a brace. Despite his deafness, he did not attend a school for deaf children until he was 10 years old, when he entered the Lexington School for the Deaf. At 13 he shifted to the New York School for the Deaf (Fanwood), where he learned sign language. Two years later, he was accepted in the preparatory program of Gallaudet College. He graduated with a bachelor's degree in chemistry at age 20. *See* GALLAUDET COLLEGE.

Schreiber entered Gallaudet College while the United States was in the Great Depression and left it a few months after the country entered World War II. He suffered family tragedies as his father lost his sight and his business. The carefree college boy quickly had to become a responsible contributor to his family by going to work, along with many other deaf people, in war plants in Akron, Ohio. At Firestone Rubber Company, he broke through the prejudice that forced deaf persons to work solely as machine tenders, and became the first deaf machine-shop inspector. He later described his postgraduate years: "I became what might be called a 'gate crasher,' which is to say I was placed in departments in Firestone where no deaf workers had ever been hired, to see if it were possible for deaf people to work in these areas. It was hard, and it was challenging, and you might say I have been doing this ever since."

Schreiber's success in industry led him to consider marriage. He had met Kathleen (Kit) Bedard while they were both students at Gallaudet College. They continued their courtship in Akron, and on September 23, 1944, they married. They had four children.

In 1947 Schreiber left Akron to accept a position as an instructor at the Texas School for the Deaf in Austin. He lasted a year, during which he quarreled with the administration over what he saw as discrimination against deaf faculty members. He returned to New York City, where he joined the International Typographers' Union and started to earn his living as a printer. In 1952 he shifted employment to the *Washington Star* and then to the U.S. Government Printing Office, both in Washington, D.C. He continued to work as a compositor until 1966.

Schreiber attended his first NAD convention in 1949. That convention introduced many themes that were congenial to him: it eliminated all racial bars to membership; it considered a motion to establish a permanent home for the NAD, which narrowly lost; and it reinstituted the NAD's national magazine. As a devoted civil libertarian, Schreiber appreciated the first change; as an astute leader, he realized the importance of the other two changes. He was particularly concerned with communication. In college he had written a column for the student newspaper. Later he became the founder and editor of the District of Columbia Association of the Deaf's newsletter, and as executive secretary of the NAD, he wrote a monthly column. Also, under his direction, the NAD began printing a monthly tabloid, *The Broadcaster*.

NAD ACTIVITIES
The 1949 convention spurred Schreiber's organizational interest. In 1950 he was elected the youngest president in the history of the Hebrew Association of the Deaf in New York City. When he moved to Washington, he joined the District of Columbia

Association of the Deaf (DCAD), the District of Columbia Club of the Deaf, and the Maryland Association of the Deaf. But the DCAD was to become the vehicle that he would ride to power within the NAD. The NAD changed to a federation of state associations in 1960. To be effective in the affairs of the NAD, Schreiber needed a state perch, and DCAD provided it.

All of his preparations finally bore fruit at the 1964 NAD convention. As a delegate, he successfully campaigned for removal of the NAD headquarters from Berkeley, California, to the nation's capital. The move characterized the new role that Schreiber and many other deaf leaders foresaw for the NAD. The government paid almost no attention to the NAD, so the organization had little say in federal legislation affecting deaf people; its lack of full-time personnel and of visibility among the authorities denied the NAD participation in important deliberations about rehabilitation and education—two critical areas of interest to deaf people.

The 1964 NAD convention elected Schreiber as its secretary-treasurer, an unpaid position second in power only to the presidency. In subsequent board meetings, the need for full-time employees was pressed, and at the 1966 convention the position of executive secretary was created. As the convention closed, President Robert Sanderson rose and announced the board's selection to the delegates: Schreiber, a popular choice. He accepted the position along with instructions to find some way to pay his salary, which amounted to a substantial pay cut over his earnings at the Government Printing Office.

ACCOMPLISHMENTS

As a leader, Schreiber accomplished so much that the magnitude of it is clear only in retrospect. The NAD had been established in 1880 to counteract the move to eliminate sign language from the instruction of deaf children and, as a consequence, the loss of teaching positions for qualified deaf adults. He lived to see sign return to the majority of classes for deaf children. *See* HISTORY: Sign Language Controversy.

Until 1964, federal and state authorities seldom consulted deaf leaders about policies specifically directed at their constituents. After Schreiber became executive secretary, he spent a majority of his hours in consultation with government officials and serving on important committees. He frequently testified before Congress and state legislatures, and he appeared frequently on television and at innumerable banquets and conventions.

To be effective in the way that he was, Schreiber had to build the NAD as an organization. He stimulated its membership, sought and received federal grants to perform important projects and earn money for the organization, established a book service and began publishing materials of particular interest to deaf people, and purchased a home office in Silver Spring, Maryland, that houses not only the NAD but also several of the other organizations that work on behalf of deaf people. His vision had encompassed developing a physical center of activities devoted to deafness, and he succeeded. By 1979, the NAD had accumulated an impressive treasury and had set a pattern for the use of its resources that made it the recognized voice of deaf people in the United States.

As with other great leaders, Schreiber did not complete his self-imposed agenda. He wanted deaf people from the United States to assume the major leadership in the World Federation of the Deaf (WFD), not from any chauvinistic feelings but because deaf Americans, unlike many of their foreign colleagues, were largely independent of government interference. In 1983, five years after Schreiber died, Yerker Andersson, a United States citizen, became the WFD's president. Schreiber also wanted to expand the NAD's influence in the United States through a coalition of all organizations serving deaf people. Such a coalition would provide a forum at which all of the interests among deaf people could be aired and from which would emerge a strong, unified front. That dream has not yet been realized. *See* WORLD FEDERATION OF THE DEAF.

Perhaps Schreiber's most enduring legacy will be found in his writings. He had a unique view of the world that enabled him to be both humorous and incisive. He lived in the center of the deaf world, so he had no need to invent stories. He made profound points from everyday incidents; for example, he illustrated one approach to overcoming prejudices against deaf workers with the following anecdote:

"One young lady came to my office for help. She was frustrated because 'When I apply for a job I am usually asked, "Can you read my lips?" and when I say "No," the boss loses interest.' So I told her, 'The next time you are asked that question, say "Yes, if you speak plain." ' Well, she has a job now. She still doesn't read lips, but now her boss thinks it is his fault."

This turning of the tables characterized Schreiber's style. One of his most brilliant essays was entitled "The Idiot—Or Some of My Best Friends Are Hearing." He began by asking, "What's so great about the hearing world anyway?," a startling question for deaf people who are repeatedly told in school that their goal in life should be to act as much like hearing people as they can. He continued:

"The world as we know it is dominated by people who hear. And one can see merely by looking at the headlines in the papers that it is in a hell of a mess. There is hardly a thing to indicate that hearing people are doing a great job in managing the world we live in. In fact, there is a great deal in the papers that leads one to think that one might, if he had a choice, do better than to choose this world. It is safe to say that all the wars in the world were started by people who hear; 99 and 44/100ths of all the crimes are committed by people who hear; and the same is true of all the vehicular homicides."

He did not add, as well he might, that the world would be a much better place if deaf people were in charge of it. He would have been correct in saying it—provided those deaf people were all like him.

Bibliography

Schein, Jerome D.: *A Rose for Tomorrow*, National Association of the Deaf, Silver Spring, Maryland, 1981.

Jerome D. Schein

SCOTLAND

Scotland covers an area of 30,414 square miles (79,076 square kilometers) with a population of more than 5 million. The principal cities are Edinburgh (the capital), Glasgow, Aberdeen, and Dundee.

DEMOGRAPHICS

Unlike statistics of hearing impairment that are available for England and Wales, there are no Scottish equivalents to the registers of persons who are deaf without speech, deaf with speech, and hard-of-hearing. Voluntary societies claim to be in touch with most profoundly deaf adults in their areas, and about 4000 deaf people make use of their services.

In 1982 the annual school census completed for the Scottish Education Department showed that of the special school population of 10,780, there were 352 pupils (3.2 percent) classified as deaf and 227 (2 percent) as partially deaf. Since the Education (Scotland) Act 1981 was implemented on January 1, 1983, the classifications of deaf and partially deaf have been superseded by the generic term "children recorded as having pronounced specific or complex special educational needs."

SOCIAL WORK

Voluntary welfare services or "missions" for adult deaf persons in the United Kingdom originated in Scotland when in 1818 Elizabeth Burnside noticed that deaf men congregated each evening at the corner of Lawnmarket and Bank Street, Edinburgh, because they had no meeting place. With the help of the principal of the Edinburgh Deaf Institution, a mission, the Edinburgh Deaf and Dumb Meeting,

was established, which eventually became the Edinburgh Deaf and Dumb Benevolent Society. Other voluntary missions for deaf people were founded at Aberdeen (1895), Dundee (1893), Glasgow (1882), and Paisley (1880). There are also local societies at Greenock and Kilmarnock and branches of larger societies in other localities.

Today the nine regional and three island local authorities provide social work assistance to hearing-impaired people under the Social Work (Scotland) Act 1968 and the Chronically Sick and Disabled Persons (Scotland) Act 1970. Some local authorities provide these services directly by employing social workers who can communicate with deaf people. Others do so by agency agreements with local voluntary societies for deaf persons.

COORDINATION OF WORK FOR THE DEAF

A conference organized by the then National Institute for the Deaf led to the establishment in 1928 of the Scottish Regional Association for the Deaf as the national coordinating body for all aspects of Scottish work with deaf people. The Scottish Workshop for the Deaf, which attempts to integrate deaf and hearing people by means of total communication, was established in 1976.

Kenneth Lysons

Education

There have been schools for deaf children in Scotland since 1769, when one was opened by Thomas Braidwood in Edinburgh following his success with four deaf children in his school for hearing pupils. *See* BRAIDWOOD, THOMAS.

Scotland's education of deaf children has gone through cycles of fashion. It was formerly centered in large residential schools, but now there are few residential pupils in schools for hearing-impaired students. It has been conducted orally, manually, and in a combined fashion, using total communication where the manual component is either Signed English or the Paget Gorman Systematic Sign System. *See* EDUCATION: Communication.

There were once nursery schools for deaf pupils, but now deaf children under five must attend nursery schools for hearing children. Nursery schools for deaf children in the United Kingdom, as well as schools specially for partially deaf children, were pioneered in Scotland; but units as used in England were very slow to develop in bordering areas of Scotland. *See* ENGLAND, EDUCATION IN.

PRESENT POSITION

In Scotland, more than 2000 children with hearing loss receive annually some form of specialist help in their education. About 75 percent of these students attend hearing schools, and the rest are in special units or schools exclusively for hearing-impaired youth. In addition, many receive preschool support, as do their parents.

Scotland made major strides toward an effective evaluation of the educational needs of its hearing-impaired children as the result of its official report *Ascertainment of Children with Hearing Defects* (1967). A multidisciplinary approach in determining the needs of individual children with a hearing loss led to the recognition that audiograms alone do not prescribe the type of education most suited to each child's needs. Thus, it was recommended that not only hearing loss but emotional, social, intellectual, and linguistic development be considered and records kept. Although not all areas rigorously adhere to the recommendations laid down in the 1967 report, on the whole it has shaped educational provisions. *See* AUDIOLOGIC CLASSIFICATION.

As a result of the Education (Scotland) Act 1981, parents have become aware of their rights. They have often reacted negatively to suggestions that their children be sent to residential schools; for example, hearing-impaired children from the Orkney Isles, the Shetland Isles, and the Western Isles were formerly sent to the mainland to be educated. Now there are some facilities which enable children who can cope with the help available to be educated in their own community. Nevertheless, authorities will send children to a mainland residential school if it is deemed necessary and the parents are willing.

Scotland's scattered population makes it difficult in some areas to gather enough deaf children together to make a viable group. In some areas, too, severe weather impedes teachers who visit the children.

FACILITIES IN SCOTLAND

Over half of the population lives in the large region known as Strathclyde, and the majority of facilities for hearing-impaired children are situated there.

Educational facilities for hearing-impaired children elsewhere in Scotland are outlined below—starting with Edinburgh, the capital city and center of the Lothian Region.

Lothian Region There are two schools in Edinburgh: St. Giles School, belonging to Edinburgh District Council, and Donaldson's School for the Deaf, which is a grant-aided school run by Donaldson's Trust.

St. Giles School is the Lothian Region Center for services to hearing-impaired children. Thus, under one roof are: (1) The school for children who can operate as partially hearing but who cannot cope in an ordinary school for one reason or another. Among these children are some whose hearing loss (in decibels) is profound. (2) The Audiometric Service, which involves a team of qualified teachers of deaf students under an educational audiologist.

They are responsible for testing the hearing of each child in the Lothian Region a minimum of three times in his or her school career. This team is also involved in diagnostic testing and the prescription of hearing aids. (3) The Preschool nursery, and the guidance service for parents whose babies are found to have a hearing loss. This support is based on action by the two following units. (4) The Paediatric Hearing Assessment Unit, where each child's case is judged by a multidisciplinary team consisting of audiologists, medical people, teachers of hearing-impaired children, psychologists, and any other professional whose help is required for a particular child. (5) The Visiting Teacher of the Deaf Service. These fully qualified and experienced teachers of hearing-impaired children give support to hearing-impaired children in schools for hearing pupils, in schools for children with special educational needs, and in further education colleges.

Donaldson's School also has a preschool and parental guidance service. It uses the Paediatric hearing Assessment Unit at St. Giles. Formerly a huge residential school, it now has a much smaller role and very few residential children. The school provides residential facilities for some hearing-impaired young people taking further education in Edinburgh. As with St. Giles, it is a school for children of all ages.

St. Giles uses oral methods with its pupils, whereas Donaldson's School uses total communication methods, Signed English being the manual component.

Also in Edinburgh is Telfora College of Further Education, which supplies a foundation course for hearing-impaired youngsters plus support for those children who are integrated in courses for hearing people.

The fourth educational institute in Edinburgh concerned with hearing-impaired people is the Scottish Centre for Education of the Deaf. It not only offers courses to train teachers of hearing-impaired children, but also courses for those who teach deaf pupils in schools or colleges for hearing people. It acts in a consultancy role to local authorities, schools, parents, societies, social workers, psychologists, medical people, and individuals. Its purpose is to help those who have a hearing loss or who work with and for hearing-impaired people.

The National Library on Deafness was initiated at the Scottish Centre, as was the National Video News Service. There too is a resource center for deaf people, parents, teachers, social workers, and so on, who wish to examine available hearing aids, signal alarms, telephone aids, and teletext televisions. Working closely with the Scottish Centre is the Scottish Association for the Deaf, which is the official coordinating body for all societies and association working for deaf people. Together they provide communicators' and interpreters' courses, and are involved in the training of social workers for deaf clients.

Strathclyde Region The Strathclyde Region has five divisions with facilities for hearing-impaired children, located at Ayr, Renfrew, Lanark, Glasgow, and Dunbarton. The Ayr Division has a school and nursery for children who depend primarily on oral communication, an audiology unit with a peripatetic team and parental guidance, a unit attached to a secondary school, and a special unit for multiply handicapped deaf children.

The Renfrew Division is divided into two sectors, the east end and the west end. The former uses a total communication approach, whereas the latter depends solely on oral communication. East end services include a small primary school, which also functions as the center for the peripatetic service, and a unit attached to a secondary school. The west end has a nursery school, which houses the peripatetic service, and two units in secondary school.

The Lanark Division has services ranging from preschool through further education. On the campus of a comprehensive high school is a total communication unit for deaf children between 8 and 16 years of age. There is also a nursery school housed in a facility for mentally and physically handicapped children, a secondary unit in a secondary school, a three-class primary unit in a primary school, a peripatetic service, and a unit in a college for further education.

The Glasgow Division has, in addition to the usual facilities, a Roman Catholic school. This school for children of all ages is divided into two sections, one that uses the oral method and one that uses total communication. The government services include a nursery and school that uses total communication, a school for children who can communicate orally but who cannot be integrated with hearing pupils, a unit for multiply handicapped deaf children, a peripatetic service, and an audiology unit that does assessment and provides parental guidance.

The Dunbarton Division has comparatively few services; one is a large peripatetic service, and the other is a small total communication unit.

Other Regions The other regions in Scotland—Central, Fife, Tayside, Grampian, Highland, Borders, and Dumfries and Galloway—all have a smaller range of facilities and services for hearing-impaired children than do the Lothian and Strathclyde regions. Each has a peripatetic service and one or more units in nursery, primary, or secondary schools. There is variation in communication methods among the regions, with some depending primarily on oral means, others using total communication, and still others using the Paget Gorman Systematic Sign System.

None of the islands has special units for hearing-impaired children. The Western, Shetland, and Orkney Isles provide only a peripatetic service.

Important Changes There have been two important changes in the education of deaf children in Scotland since the 1970s. One has been the growth of pressure on local authorities to provide educational opportunities close to home. The second has been the resultant decrease in residential school populations and the proliferation of local services. The quality and type of local services vary widely, however, so that a child's birthplace may determine whether he or she attends a school for hearing children, a special unit, a school using oral methods, or one employing total communication. In Scotland, to assure an academic future for a bright hearing-impaired child, one must send the child to the Mary Hare Grammar School in England.

M. Turner

Teacher Training

In 1769 when Thomas Braidwood opened his Edinburgh School for deaf children, there were no college programs to train teachers of deaf pupils. Rather, such teachers were trained in the schools, according to the ideas of the head teacher in each facility. Inservice training, teaching while in the schools, has never been popular with the Scottish Education Department. In 1919, a training course introduced at the Victoria University of Manchester for teachers of deaf pupils was given official recognition by English authorities, it received similar approval in Scotland. There was, however, one additional requirement in Scotland: all teachers of deaf children also had to be qualified teachers of hearing children in either primary or secondary schools. Scottish university graduates who took the training in Manchester were also required to study in a Scottish College of Education before they could be considered qualified to teach in a school for deaf or partially deaf children. That extra training is now of one year's duration. *See* ENGLAND, EDUCATION IN: Teacher Training.

MORAY HOUSE COLLEGE

On several occasions requests were made to the secretary of state for Scotland—in whom lies the ultimate responsibility for education at all levels in Scotland—to set up a course to train teachers for deaf and partially deaf children. These requests were ignored until 1967. Then, as one of the results of the British government's report *Ascertainment of Children with Hearing Defects*, it was decided that a small course be set up in Moray House in Edinburgh. In 1969 the course for training teachers of mentally and physically handicapped children was taken from the department of psychology in that college and placed in a new department, special education.

TEACHERS' TRAINING COURSE

From the outset the policy of this course was to equip teachers to meet the needs of children who were deaf or partially deaf. The program was designed, not to produce strictly oralist or manualist teachers, but teachers who could be realists in assessing the needs of the children in their care.

Another deviation from usual practice was insistence on the significance of the whole child. Teachers were given training in how to include esthetic subjects, how to develop recreational activities, and how to use television in the classroom.

In the beginning, the linguistics component (this was the first training course in the United Kingdom to include such) was supplied by the University of Edinburgh, which also supplied lectures on the physics of sound and on phonetics. Later, however, it became obvious to staff, students, and the external examiner that the university's contributions were too far removed to benefit the classroom. Thereafter, a linguist was shared by the English department and the Scottish Centre for Education of the Deaf, which had grown out of and apart from the department of special education.

The course was reorganized in 1980 in an attempt to meet the varying needs of local authorities. Because of change in the educational structure, some teachers were being put directly into peripatetic work, parent guidance work, audiology clinics, schools using total communication, or schools using oral methods.

The teachers' training course is recognized by both the Scottish Education Department and the Department of Education and Science (in England, Wales, and Northern Ireland). The Scottish Centre also runs a course for students from overseas, and there have been teachers and administrators from more than 30 countries.

The present course lasts for one academic session and is at diploma level. All entrants must be fully qualified teachers with a minimum of three years of experience. Both primary and secondary teachers are accepted.

The structure is such that term one is basic, very theory-based, and taught mainly in the classroom. A few of the lectures are shared with social workers in Moray House College taking the postqualifying course to become Social Workers for the Deaf. Term two contains eight weeks of teaching practice split into two sections. The placements are as different as possible so that teachers may see a wide variety of work with hearing-impaired children. While practice-teaching, depending on the facilities of the Local Authority, students are given the opportunity to see audiology clinics, peripatetic work, and units in hearing schools. In term three, teachers take two of the following modules: teaching of speech and auditory training, peripatetic and parental guidance work, teaching of reading and number, total communication, esthetic subjects, and audiology. All teachers are given the opportunity to visit a famous oral school in England and the large school for deaf children with additional handicaps, also in England.

The teachers' training course includes the following areas.

Practical Work Students do a variety of activities designed to familiarize them directly with the major responsibilities of teachers of deaf students. They visit schools for deaf and partially hearing children, audiology clinics, units in hearing schools, schools for multiply handicapped deaf children, and eventide home for deaf individuals, a rehabilitation unit for deaf adults, a children's hospital, and a hearing aid factory. These visits are followed by tutorials and discussions. In term two, students practice-teach in two schools with pupils of two different age groups and, where possible, with both deaf and partially hearing children. Students also work with individual deaf children, and observe and practice speech teaching of various kinds. Finally, they acquire practical knowledge of audiology at the Scottish Centre for Education of the Deaf. The judgment of practical work is based mainly on continuing assessment by the course tutors. Reports from the schools providing the practice teaching, the teachers' own written records of that work, and their observations while practice teaching also are evaluated. Additionally, there are practical tests in teaching and speech, some or all of which are given in the presence of an external examiner.

Audiology This course teaches students about the nature of sound, hearing, and amplification. They are introduced to the vocabulary of audiology, become familiar with the audiologic equipment used by hearing-impaired children, develop ability to evaluate different auditory speech-training systems, learn to evaluate technical data about hearing-assistance equipment, and consider developments in the audiology field.

Communication Studies Students are introduced to the philosophy of total communication. They also learn the basic skills necessary for the manual component. *See* SOCIOLINGUISTICS: Total Communication.

Drama The emphasis is on encouraging the children to make maximum expressive use of the whole body. Creative mime and movement and drama are employed to aid the child's understanding and communication at both the primary and secondary levels.

Education of Hearing-Impaired Children This course, involving lectures and group tutorials, discusses the problems peculiar to the education of children with a hearing loss, and the provisions to meet the requirements of those children. There are distinct streams within this course, although all streams contribute to the knowledge and understanding of education of hearing-impaired children.

The streams are: classification, auditory training, audiometry, child development, comparative education, curriculum development, effects of deafness on language development and reading, history of education of deaf persons, language schemes, communication methods, numbers (mathematics), parent guidance, peripatetic work, preschool work, provision of facilities, education of multiply handicapped students, and visual aids.

Educational Television   There are two objectives in this course: (1) Working in a cooperative group, the teachers study all aspects of television production. They receive experience in handling television equipment so that they will be able to use it with confidence in schools. (2) They learn to analyze the strengths and weaknesses of different television productions. The teachers become aware of the possibilities of using television creatively and dynamically to meet the particular educational needs of the hearing-impaired child.

Medical Aspects of Hearing and Hearing Loss   Students study the anatomy, physiology, and pathology of the ear.

Music   A great deal of the time spent in the music department is allocated to the acquisition of basic skills in the use of tuned and untuned percussion instruments. This, allied with rhythmic speech work and body movements, is aimed at helping deaf children coordinate and communicate better. Action songs, of a repetitive nature, are very useful with young children. The ability to use these is encouraged especially by the general class teacher rather than the music specialist. Singing as a part of class work is very valuable for the development of speech and proper breathing. Class work can include the use of blow-organs or Melodicas, as well as a wide variety of percussion instruments, and where possible the accompaniments are played on low-pitched tuned percussion instruments or electronic organ. The beginnings of a basic repertoire is the goal, and integration of music into other curricular activities is proposed.

Phonetics, Phonology, and Linguistics   Phonetics and phonology deal with the production and perception of speech, with the phonetics and phonology of English, and, in tutorials, with the application of these studies to the problems encountered in the teaching of speech to deaf and partially hearing pupils. A weekly session in practical phonetics (ear training and performance) is given. The linguistics course is concerned with language study

and contemporary schools of thought. Guidance is given on the analysis of language used by children.

Psychology   This course is concerned with the assessment of abilities and attainments of deaf children, with emphasis on interpretation of these. The effects of having a handicapped person in the family and in the community are discussed.

Physical Education   This course includes the study of a variety of physical activities to assist in developing the rhythmic and skillful awareness of body movement. There are opportunities to observe deaf children participating in physical activity.

Visual Arts   Opportunities are provided for gaining experience in a variety of media, with emphasis on children's needs in expression, communication, therapy, and creative work generally, as well as links with other areas of learning.

M. Turner

Scottish Workshop with the Deaf

An important aspect of all organizations is the informal communication networks which act as counterweights to the formal, often authoritarian, links within the organizations. Formal communication links are usually an impersonal duty, whereas the informal follow more natural personal affinities and friendships. This concept led to the founding of the Scottish Workshop with the Deaf in 1976. The workshop brought together several long-existing trends in deaf affairs throughout Scotland: Maxwell Ridley's multidiscipline seminars in Ninewells Hospital, Dundee; teach-in sessions on deafness with student psychologists, psychiatrists, and social workers at Edinburgh University; and similar liaison work of Stewart Lochrie in Glasgow. At about this time a new hope for improved relationships between hearing and deaf people, total communication, was introduced to Scotland at the British Deaf Association Ayr Conference of 1974. Total communication appealed to many teachers of profoundly deaf pupils in Scotland who resented their inadequate, oralist-biased teacher training and preferred to really communicate with their pupils. Teachers who were eager to improve total communication skills formed an important strand in the multidiscipline workshop. This new communicating community was cemented by the original 16 experienced interpreters who made participation for deaf individuals a pleasure. The purely voluntary, unpaid membership grew rapidly to 200 deaf and hearing professionals working with deaf people, and has now stabilized at around 250–300.

The workshop is a novel attempt to integrate deaf and hearing people by means of total communication. It has shown that communication can be acquired enjoyably, and that informing individuals and, hence, authorities about the realities of deafness can bring enlightenment. Early on, the weekly sessions to teach teachers British Sign Language, for example, became unnecessary when the Scottish teacher of the deaf course began to offer total communication to teachers in training. On the other hand, the attempts to change the "medical rules" excluding deaf persons from courses of teacher training have been unsuccessful, and this injustice is unlikely to be removed while most training colleges and teachers' associations in the United Kingdom continue to be dominated by oralists. *See* SIGN LANGUAGES: British.

Because of the explicitly temporary and nonhierarchical nature of the leadership, deaf members were given the opportunity to practice organizational and executive skills. Within one year the entire secretariat consisted of profoundly deaf officebearers. As a training ground for administrative experience and the exercise of initiative and organizational flair, the workshop maintains a good record as many who learn to handle part-time responsibilities go on to assume full-time executive posts in the larger deaf organizations. Many deaf members become used to expressing their opinions in public and then use this skill elsewhere, thus helping to give deaf people a say in provisions being designed for them. Apart from the English National Union of the Deaf, the Scottish Workshop is the only deaf organization in the United Kingdom led by deaf people. *See* UNITED KINGDOM: Organizations.

Since becoming affiliated to the World Federation of the Deaf at the Twelfth Congress in Bulgaria in 1979, the Scottish Workshop has expanded its activities with the addition of an international element provided by foreign visitors. Current activities consist of day conferences and residential weekend workshops held throughout Scotland, written submissions to authorities making administrative or legal rulings involving deaf people, campaigns aimed at marshalling opinion behind deaf concerns, and publication of lectures presented to workshops and collating the best in book form. *See* WORLD FEDERATION OF THE DEAF.

One strength of the workshop is the diverse background of its members. This enables a real exchange of ideas across professional boundaries and avoids the narrow range of ideas often found in associations consisting entirely of, for example, teachers, parents, or social workers. The workshop does not seek to replace professional associations, but aims to provide them with broader insights into the outlook of other groups.

The multidiscipline nature of the membership is reflected in the wide variety of discussion topics: language and communication, education, mental health, legal matters, deafness and the media, integration, parent guidance, computers in schools and clubs, sex education, sailing, employment, and family guidance.

Wider interest in the Scottish Workshop has resulted in the birth of two sibling workshops, the Northumbrian Workshop with the Deaf and the Yorkshire Workshop with the Deaf. All three workshops are independent, and interrelate only by strong but informal links of common interest and friendships.

Bibliography

Crawford, B.: *SWD Publications List*, SWD Publications Secretary, Donaldson's School. West Coates, Edinburgh, Scotland.

Montgomery, G.: "The Ideal of a Workshop with the Deaf," *The Integration and Disintegration of the Deaf in Society*, chap. 12, SW Publications, 1981.

Report of Scottish Workshop with the Deaf to World Federation of the Deaf, Rome, 1983.

George Montgomery

Scottish Association for the Deaf

During the nineteenth century, voluntary work with deaf individuals in Scotland fell into two categories, education for children and spiritual welfare for adults, all on a very limited scale. Various locally based associations became active, and eventually it was recognized that a national body was needed to coordinate all their efforts. In 1927 the Scottish Association for the Deaf (SAD) was established because "work among the deaf had become too insular and self contained" and a body "should co-ordinate all current efforts, encourage all yet supplant none, become the clearing house of information on the deaf and deafness and . . . be a bond uniting every personal agency labouring for the welfare of the deaf whether in childhood, adolescence, or adult life." (The word "deaf" applies to all persons whose hearing impairment is such as to constitute a handicap.) The early discussions which led to the formation of the association were held under the aegis of the National Institute for the Deaf (NID), now known as the Royal National Institute for the Deaf (RNID) in London. The agreement made then between the National Institute and the Scottish Association is still accepted, and states that the Scottish Association is an independent organization. Although affiliated with the RNID, it is not a regional association of that institute. This agreement was necessary because the legislature in Scotland is separate from that of England and Wales. The Scottish Association, however, is represented on the Council of Management of the RNID, and enjoys a close working relationship with the council.

The Scottish Association has a voluntary membership with constituent bodies and organizations, as well as individuals interested in the welfare of deaf people of all ages in Scotland. Representatives from these groups are members of the executive committee; the groups include: the original nine voluntary societies of the adult deaf in Scotland, the Convention of Scottish Local Authorities, the Association of Directors of Education, the Scottish Region of the British Association of Teachers of the Deaf, the Educational Institute of Scotland, the Scottish Region of the National Association of Schoolmasters/Union of Women Teachers, the Scottish Centre for the Education of the Deaf, the British Deaf Association, the British Association of the Hard of Hearing, the Church of Scotland, the Area Health Boards in Scotland, the Scottish Ololaryngological Society, the Royal National Institute for the Deaf, the Scottish Regions of the National Deaf Children's Society, the Association of Directors of Social Work, the Scottish Region of the National Council of Social Workers with the Deaf, the Scottish Association of Interpreters for the Deaf, the Deaf Advisory Group, and the British Tinnitus Group. Under the constitution of the Scottish Association for the Deaf, it is mandatory for each society for deaf people to appoint at least one deaf person to represent them on the executive committee of the association. Although the executive committee meets regularly in various parts of Scotland, most of the essential discussions and implementation of decisions are carried out by subcommittees specializing in education, social work, medical and technical, the arts, and so on.

By providing a forum for all the aforementioned organizations, the Scottish Association for the Deaf is able to stimulate an interest in the needs of all deaf people in Scotland, and to act on their behalf (especially through the Deaf Advisory Group, consisting entirely of deaf people) in dealings with the government and other statutory bodies. The association, with the cooperation of the representatives of its constituent groups, has initiated many national projects such as (1) the establishment of a recognized training and qualification program for all communicators and interpreters for deaf persons; (2) the supply of television equipment to all societies for deaf people to encourage the exchange of news items and so forth; (3) a complete survey of the quality and quantity of ear molds supplied to deaf children; (4) a survey of public buildings equipped with appropriate aids for the benefit of deaf people; (5) the establishment of the first Library on Deafness in Scotland; and (6) a counseling service for deafened adults.

There are many other areas of activity despite the fact that as a voluntary organization the Scottish Association for the Deaf has no regular income from regional authorities in Scotland. It is a coordinating body and has no direct client contact; such contact is done indirectly through its constituent groups.

Tom McLaren

SEARING, LAURA
(1840–1923)

Laura Catherine Redden Searing was a journalist, poet, and Civil War patriot for the Union cause. She wrote under the pseudonym Howard Glyndon. Born in Somerset County, Maryland, on February 9, 1840, she was the daughter of Wilhelmine Waller and Littleton James D. Redden and a descendant of Sir Edmund Waller, the English poet and member of the British House of Commons. She was described as "gifted at birth with the soul of a poet." She turned her deafness into a blessing and during her lifetime wrote and published over 225 poems. She wrote five books and her poetry appeared in several anthologies.

Laura Searing was deafened by cerebrospinal meningitis when she was 11 years old. By then her family had moved to St. Louis, and she was enrolled at the Missouri School for the Deaf in Fulton, from which she graduated in 1858.

Deafness left her speech with a strained and unnatural sound. Only family members and close friends could understand her when she talked. Embarrassed by the difficulties others had understanding her speech, she ceased using it, relying instead on written communication. As an adult, she studied speech and lipreading at the Clarke School for the Deaf in Northampton, Massachusetts, at the Whipple Home School in Mystic, Connecticut, and under Alexander Graham Bell in Boston. Through these efforts she was able to regain the use of her speech, which was described as "pleasant and distinct," but she never mastered the art of lipreading. *See* BELL, ALEXANDER GRAHAM; CLARKE SCHOOL.

CAREER
Searing began her writing career as a reporter for a St. Louis religious newspaper, *The Presbyterian and Our Union*, following her graduation from the Missouri School, and she began contributing poems and articles to the *St. Louis Republican*. The *Republican* sent her to Washington, D.C., to report on the Civil War. There she interviewed President Abraham Lincoln, General Ulysses S. Grant, General James A. Garfield, members of Congress, and other prominent persons. This resulted in the publication in 1862 of her first book, *Notable Men in the House of Representatives*. She later wrote for the *New York Times* and several other New York news-

Laura Searing. (Gallaudet College Archives)

papers including the *Sun*, the *Evening Mail*, and the *Tribune*. During the Civil War she accompanied General Grant to the front lines of the Union Army, a privilege permitted few women. In 1864 she published *Idyls of Battle and Poems of the Rebellion*. President Lincoln saw the proof sheets of this book, and wrote in a note: ". . . I have glanced over these poems and find them all patriotic and some very pretty."

In 1865 Searing sailed to Europe, where she spent approximately four years writing for American newspapers and magazines and studying languages. She mastered French, German, Italian, and Spanish. While in Italy, she wrote two papers for the U.S. Department of Agriculture on the subject of orange and silkworm culture. On her return from Europe she translated a French story, "Memoir d'un Petit Garçon," which was published by Hurd and Houghton under the title "A Little Boy's Story." She joined the staff of the *New York Evening Mail*, where she wrote a series of articles entitled "Children of Silence," in which she advocated the teaching of speech in schools for deaf people. These articles aroused much interest and are credited by some as encouraging the teaching of speech in many schools.

In 1876 she married Edward W. Searing, a hearing man, in Mystic, Connecticut. He was a well-known attorney and a native of Sherwood, New York, where the couple settled; they had one child, Elsa.

POETRY

Laura Searing started writing poetry while a student at the Missouri School, and became widely published. Her poetry appeared in the *Missouri Record*, the *Silent Worker*, "Facts, Anecdotes and Poetry Relating to the Deaf and Dumb," *Harper's Monthly*, *Harper's Weekly*, *Atlantic Monthly*, *Putnam's Magazine*, *Galaxy*, *Arena*, *Alaska-Yukon Magazine*, and *El Dorado*. Her work also appeared in several anthologies, including John Greenleaf Whittier's, E. C. Stedman's, William Cullen Bryant's, and *The Silent Muse*, an anthology of prose and poetry by deaf writers.

In 1873 a collection of her poetry was published under the title *Sounds from Secret Chambers*. It was described as a book "that makes one feel as if he knew the author, and her readers can hardly help calling themselves her friends." Another volume of her poetry followed a year later. In 1921 Searing's daughter collected and published a complete edition of the poetry under the title *Echoes of Other Days*. Elsa Searing McGuinn observed that the writings "gladdened the hearts of those in sorrow, uplifting the weary and discouraged, and holding aloft the beacon of light to light others on to success, exemplifying to the world that earnest endeavor is not in vain." Deaf biographer Guilbert C. Braddock defined Searing's style as "easy and informal" and noted that she wrote about "people, politics, places, books, and art." Braddock considers "Mazzini" (which she wrote in Italy), "The Battle of Gettysburg," and "The Hills of Santa Cruz" her masterpieces. James E. Gallaher, another deaf author, called her "a literary patriot" for the Union cause. Searing's friend John Greenleaf Whittier was also impressed with her poem about the Santa Cruz hills. He defined it as "fine in conception and felicitous in execution." He predicted the poem would "cling to the Santa Cruz mountain range forever." Her poem "Belle Missouri" was dedicated to the Civil War volunteers from her state and became a popular battle song of the Missouri Union Army. It was written in response to the Confederacy's "Maryland, My Maryland."

Laura Searing received many honors. Glyndon, Minnesota, a small town at the junction of the Northern Pacific and St. Paul and Pacific Railroads in Minnesota's Red River Valley, was named after her pseudonym. In 1889, when the Thomas Hopkins Gallaudet and Alice Cogswell statue was unveiled on the Gallaudet College campus, Searing wrote the dedicatory poem, which she delivered by sign and voice. Her biography was one of four biographies of deaf persons to be included in the *Dictionary of American Biography* published in 1928. (The others were those of educator Laurent Clerc, poet James Nack, and artist Albert Newsam.) In the fall of 1984 Gallaudet College named a building on its Northwest Campus in Searing's honor. *See* CLERC, LAURENT; GALLAUDET COLLEGE; NACK, JAMES; NEWSAM, ALBERT.

In 1886 Searing moved to San Mateo, California, to be near her daughter. She experienced poor health in her later years and gradually stopped writing. "The Hills of Santa Cruz" was her last notable effort. Her final years were spent as an invalid. She died in San Mateo on August 10, 1923, and is buried in the Holy Cross Cemetery there.

Bibliography

Dictionary of American Biography, vol. 8, 1928.

Fanwood Journal, February 1937.

Gallaher, James E.: *Representative Deaf Persons in the United States of America*, James E. Gallaher Publisher, Chicago, 1898.

Gannon, Jack, R.: *Deaf Heritage, A Narrative History of Deaf America*, National Association of the Deaf, Silver Spring, Maryland, 1981.

Glyndon, Howard (pseud. of Laura Searing): *Echoes of Other Days*, Harr Wagner Publishing, San Francisco, 1921.

Hodgson, Edwin: *Facts, Anecdotes and Poetry Relating to the Deaf and Dumb*, Deaf-Mutes Journal Print, New York, 1891.

Johnson, Roy: *Roy Johnson's Red River Valley*, ed. by Clarence A. Glasrud, Red River Historical Society, Moorhead, Minnesota, 1982.

Silent World, August 15, 1876; October 15, 1876; June 1894.

Jack R. Gannon

SENSORY AIDS

Sensory aids are devices to provide sound information to severely or profoundly deaf persons; these aids are designed to present sound via senses other than hearing—through sight and touch. These are distinct from devices that are designed to provide auditory sensation for deaf people, such as cochlear implants. *See* COCHLEAR IMPLANTS.

The substitution of some other sense for hearing has been studied since the mid-1920s. Bell Laboratories developed a vibrating sound analyzer for deaf people in the late 1920s. During World War II, Bell Laboratories developed a visual display of sound, the spectrograph, as an aid to unscrambling coded voice messages; after the war the first instant-display spectrograph, the Visible Speech Translator, was built, and tested with deaf people. Modern versions of these aids are being developed and studied. *See* VISIBLE SPEECH.

The sounds received by the aid must be analyzed into special patterns for presentation to the substitute sense; this is accomplished via microprocessor chips or computer. The analysis is usually adapted to transmit patterns that are related to speech information, such as the occurrence of the different vowels and consonants.

VISUAL SPEECH AIDS

The first wearable visual aid, the Upton Eyeglass Speechreader, emerged from a concept developed in 1965 by Hubert Upton, a hearing-impaired engineer. A microphone and analyzer, worn by the hearing-impaired person, control separate bars of red light from light-emitting diodes (LEDs). The LEDs are mounted in a small projector positioned at the corner of the eyeglass frame. The projector is aimed at a tiny reflecting area located on the rear surface of the eyeglass lens. The images of the bar-lights appear in space between the wearer and the speaker. Each bar, when lighted, indicates a particular type of sound pattern. There are six different bars that are assigned by the analyzer to six different types of speech sound patterns as they are picked up by the microphone. Improved reception over lipreading alone has been demonstrated with this aid.

The Autocuer, which also uses an eyeglass projection display, contains a small computer that carries out a partial speech recognition. It detects vowels and consonants in the speech stream and pairs a consonant with the following vowel to establish a "syllable" as the unit for recognition. The consonant and vowel are not identified precisely—this exceeds the ability of present portable speech recognition techniques. However, the system does identify the category to which the syllable belongs. It then flashes a symbol indicating the category (which usually comprises nine syllable possibilities) on the eyeglasses of the deaf speechreader.

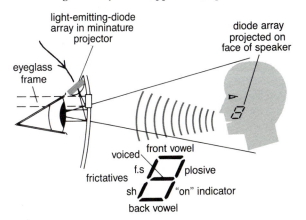

Upton speechreading aid; a detailed description appears in the text. (After J. M. Pickett, "Hearing Through Sight and Feeling," *IEEE Spectrum*, pp. 37–41, April 1982)

The viewer, with this clue to the syllable, can accurately decide, from the speaker's lip and face movements, which syllable was actually spoken.

TACTILE SPEECH AIDS

The presentation of sound patterns on the skin may be preferred by deaf persons who find visual displays distracting. The Boothroyd Portapitch Aid is a tactile device worn on the wrist or arm. It contains eight vibrators, each energized by a different level of the pitch of the voice received. It can operate for six to eight hours on a rechargeable battery. Other types of tactile aids present information related to the vowels and consonants, using arrays of three to a hundred or more tactile stimulators. The results in speech perception training have shown that it is possible to learn a large vocabulary via tactile stimulation.

Several single-vibrator tactile aids are available, and even such a simple aid has been found to be useful to deaf children and adults. Users report benefits of better contact with the environment and with people, and some help in speechreading. A wearable 16-electrode stimulator for tactile speech coding, the Saunder's Tacticon, has been approved by the Food and Drug Administration; field testing with deaf children indicated improvements in their speech development. *See* SPEECHREADING.

SPEECH TRAINING AIDS

Electronic displays of speech have been designed to teach those who cannot hear to use their voices. One display, the Speech Spectrographic Display, presents the complete time-varying spectrum of speech. Other indicators of particular voice features, such as the voice pitch, loudness, vowel quality, or consonant sharpness, have been built. A children's computer-based speech-training system with displays that resemble video games has also been developed.

Cathode-ray-tube displays for a children's computer-based speech training system in which a ball moving from left to right traces voice pitch. (a) Raised voice pitch moves the ball up toward the gap in the "wall." (b) Maintaining the correct pitch moves the ball through the gap and into the score basket. (After J. M. Pickett, "Hearing Through Sight and Feeling," *IEEE Spectrum*, pp. 37–41, April 1982)

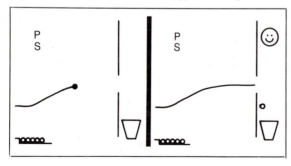

In Kumamoto, Japan, a color TV receiver has been used in an experimental speech trainer. The colors change with changes in the positions of the speaker's lips and tongue as the speaker articulates. Thus the colors of the TV image may be useful as feedback in speech training.

Indicators of the positions and movements of the tongue and larynx have also been studied as speech training aids. Some of these operate from a microphone responding to the voice and others directly from the speaker's articulators. For a voice-operated system, a computer is programmed to transform the voice signal into a moving vocal tract that is displayed for the trainee.

An example of an articulation appliance is the artificial palate. It holds an array of electrical contacts in the mouth; as the contacts are touched by the speaker's tongue, the touches are shown on a display. Thus a trainee can see the areas of tongue articulation, helping to convey how such consonants as *t*, *d*, *s*, and *z*, and vowels *ee* and *ah*, are produced.

Another articulation sensor is the Laryngograph, which monitors the voice action of the larynx via two plates held against the throat. The output is processed to yield a display of voice pitch, coordination of voice with other movements, and voice quality. *See* SPEECH TRAINING.

COMPUTER SPEECH

A computer speech recognition system is utilized in some speech training experiments. Suitable speech patterns are stored in the recognizer so that the trainee can try to pronounce them. A deaf person sometimes pronounces a word or phrase very well, but other times errs. Therefore the word recognizer is programmed with the deaf person's better attempts and then used for feedback during other training sessions.

The electronic synthesis of speech from typed input has been developed to the point where commercial products are available. Some of these are portable speech synthesizers. Other wheelchair-mounted synthesizers are being used by nonvocal, normal-hearing people—for example, those who cannot speak because of a stroke—and might also be used by deaf people to speak with a synthetic but more intelligible voice.

Expectations are that it will become possible to equip central telephone offices with commercially useful speech recognizers. These could support telephone conversations between deaf people and hearing people. The recognizers would convert voice input to written output on a teletypewriter to convey messages to the deaf conversant.

Commercially available recognizers are limited: they encompass only a small vocabulary, they confuse words at times, and speakers must learn to use the devices. However, they could expand the use of telecommunications devices for the deaf (TDDs) to include nondeaf people who lack TDDs but are frequently called on routine matters by deaf people. The system would first be informed, by means of a Touch-Tone code, of the identity of the person with hearing, and the topic to be talked about. The speaker's message would be recognized and printed by the teletype for the deaf person or would be displayed on the screen of a TDD. The deaf person would type replies on the TDD, which would then be converted to sound by the speech synthesizer. Messages would have to be formed within the limits of the vocabulary and adhering to a prearranged set of sentence forms. The vocabulary and grammar of a speech recognizer device can be expanded if the set-up permits the speaker to be visible to the deaf person. The speaker's lip and tongue movements can be used by the deaf viewer to resolve ambiguities. This is also the principle of operation for the Autocuer eyeglass aid mentioned above. *See* TELECOMMUNICATIONS.

Bibliography

Levitt, H., J. M. Pickett, and R. Houde (eds.): *Sensory Aids for the Hearing-Impaired*, IEEE Press, 1980.

Pickett, J. M.: "Hearing Through Sight and Feeling," *IEEE Spectrum*, pp. 37–41, April 1982.

————: "Speech Technology and Communication for the Hearing Impaired," in F. Withrow (ed.), Learning Technology and the Hearing Impaired, *Volta Review*, 83(5):301–309, 1981.

———— and W. F. McFarland, "Auditory Implants and Tactile Aids for the Profoundly Deaf," *Journal of Speech and Hearing Research*, 28:134–150, 1985.

Sherrick, C.: "Basic and Applied Research on Tactile Aids for Deaf People: Progress and Prospects," *Journal of the Acoustical Society of America*, 75:1325–1342, 1984.

J. M. Pickett

SEXUALITY

Little is known regarding sexual adjustment, sexual attitudes, sexual behaviors, and sex education programming for deaf persons. Traditionally, the primary focus of educators of deaf children has been upon the learning of speech, language, and vocational skills, while issues of a psychosexual nature have been largely ignored. Educators have consistently heard that sex education is the parents' right, duty, and responsibility; however, parents often state that they do not have the necessary communication skills, and they hope the school is providing sex education. The result is that the formal sexuality education of deaf youths has been left to chance, which generally means learning from one's peers. Peer sex education is important and necessary. However, efforts to include significant adults in this process are critical for healthy psychosexual development.

What is believed about sexuality and deafness often is based upon outdated and limited studies. Teachers in training years ago were told that deaf people are to be considered as sexually immature and confused from a psychosexual viewpoint, since they do not hear the innuendos and taboos regarding sex, and consequently are more likely to behave in an immature way. A more accurate description would be that deaf people are often extremely deprived of accurate, comprehensive sexual knowledge and understanding about themselves and others. This is due largely to the communication barriers imposed by deafness.

SOCIOSEXUAL DEVELOPMENT

In 1963 J. Rainer and colleagues concluded that sexual delinquency was a more frequent problem in the deaf population than in the hearing population. According to this team of researchers, sex offenders and prostitutes constitute the smallest number of arraignments in the general criminal population. However, 37 percent of the arraignments of deaf persons were for sex offenses, excluding prostitution. It is difficult to conclude the reasons for this difference, although Rainer and colleagues suggest this may be a reflection of general immaturity, a dire lack of sex education and family life education, and the influences of residential school living.

As part of the Rainer studies, a representative sample of deaf adults was interviewed by skilled communicators. Of this sample, 51.8 percent of the respondents reported having had no dates while in school, while only 7.7 percent experienced individual couple dating. None of the deaf women reported any sexual experiences, and a large number of deaf men had no sexual experiences. Of the males, 19.6 percent reported homosexual interaction, while almost 50 percent reported no friendly relationships with the same sex. Moreover, 10 percent had no relationships with the opposite sex. Generally, those who were married experienced some kind of friendly relationships with either the same sex or opposite sex, although 14 percent of the married persons had no dates other than with their spouse.

Formerly, most deaf children grew up in residential facilities where extreme sexual segregation was the rule. Dating in residential schools was traditionally considered a privilege and was permitted only in groups with chaperones. Today, this situation has begun to change. First, more deaf children are now placed in mainstreamed programs which allow more flexibility in dating norms. Second, most residential schools have developed more flexible dating policies, with less traditional sexual segregation. *See* EDUCATIONAL PROGRAMS: Residential Schools.

In 1972 H. Schlesinger and K. Meadow obtained information about sex role behaviors from a sample of deaf children in the San Francisco Bay area. This study found some interesting comparisons between day students and residential students and between children with deaf parents and children with hearing parents. As part of this study, adults were asked to observe and rate deaf children on their appropriateness in sex role behavior. The following results were noted. The day school students were rated highest, the students with deaf parents next, and the residential deaf students with hearing parents lowest. In this study, it was found that family role modeling and communication appeared to make a difference in the development of appropriate sex roles. The significance of the deaf parents' ability to communicate with their deaf children, as well as visual messages in a family, may consequently be very important in sex role development. Unfortunately, the effects of absent family role models is less understood.

Traditionally, formal sex education has been almost nonexistent, and informal opportunities for heterosexual interaction have been extremely limited in most residential situations. Such an environment can create barriers to sociosexual development, that is, the development of role-appropriate behaviors and the ability to interact and form relationships. D. Goslin asserted that social isolation and rate of social interaction are directly related to role learning and effective socialization. Thus, effective socialization is impossible under conditions where the individual is isolated from the system into which he or she is being socialized. The implications of residential placement and communication isolation upon social development surely exist. However, the degree of impact upon deaf people remains to be determined.

Some residential facilities for deaf children continue to segregate students by sex, or constantly chaperone all socializing. Therefore, opportunities for privacy, which most hearing children experience, are minimal. Adult supervision in the form of a teacher, dorm staff, or administrator is generally present day and night. Leisure time for informal communication with the other sex is limited and highly structured. In 1970, for example, the general policy of a "progressive" residential school permitted no dating, but only supervised boy-girl group activities.

There is a paucity of research regarding implications of institutionalization upon deaf persons' sociosexual development. As discussed above, the minimal research tends to indicate that residential life may be less than positive for some aspects of psychosexual development. Rainer and coworkers observed that frustrations, poor adjustment, and sexual delinquency arise within the matrix of the family and the early residential setting, thus rendering the deaf adolescent without adequate knowledge and guidance. The residential school environment is not the same as a child's own home and family. This is not to imply that residential schools should not try to make dormitories homelike. However, making the residential facilities more homelike is only part of the picture—schools have to work more closely with parents as well.

SOURCES OF SEX INFORMATION

In 1963 a New York State sample of deaf adults indicated that for most of them (56 percent) acquisition of sexual knowledge during school years occurred through friends. Some females (10 percent) learned about sex at home, while some males (22 percent) learned by reading or at school.

In the fall of 1977, D. and M. Fitz-Gerald conducted a survey of 75 deaf adults and 75 hearing adults in the metropolitan Washington area in an effort to compare sources of sex information for each group. Ninety-one percent of the deaf sample and 75 percent of the hearing sample indicated that friends were the primary source of sex information. Both the hearing and deaf groups indicated that reading was a significant source of information. The deaf sample also indicated that television and movies were significant sources, while these were not as important for the hearing sample. Parents, teachers, or religious representatives were not viewed as a significant source of sex information for either population. Additional research is needed in order to determine the primary sources of sex information used by deaf persons. Such information could be used in program development and implementation, as well as in enhancing understanding of the impact of deafness upon sexual development and expression.

In the general deaf population there appears to be a scarcity of basic sex information. At the same time, there appears to be an excess of misinformation. Perhaps this paradoxical situation is a result of the communication barriers and social isolation produced by a severe hearing impairment. So much of the information, either correct or incorrect, acquired by the hearing person is acquired effortlessly and without a great deal of thought. This is not true for the hearing-impaired person. The reality of the implications of information deprivation were further validated in 1970, when Steven Grossman used the SKAT (Sexual Knowledge and Attitude Test) to compare students from Gallaudet College and from Pennsylvania State University. According to this unpublished research the Gallaudet deaf students (1) had less sexual knowledge, (2) were more accepting of sexual myths, and

(3) engaged in more sexual activity then the Pennsylvania State first- and second-year students with whom they were compared. Furthermore, the Gallaudet deaf students' level of sexual knowledge did not increase with age. Grossman suggested this reflected the lack of formal sex education programming at Gallaudet. The details of the Grossman study are reflected in the table. *See* GALLAUDET COLLEGE.

Grossman Study Results, in Percent

	Gallaudet Students	Pennsylvania State Students
Dated in past	81.8	76.3
Had intercourse	52.7	41.8
Masturbated	62.7	56.3
Used pill	12.7	16.3
Used condom	25.4	30.9
Used withdrawal	38.1	27.2
Used rhythm	30.0	21.8
Had sex with variety of partners	33.6	18.1

SEX EDUCATION AND POLICIES IN RESIDENTIAL SCHOOLS

One of the first efforts to develop professional awareness of the need for a formal sex education program for deaf children was attempted in the early 1940s, when Stanford Blish published an extensive series of articles on sex education and the deaf child. Blish viewed sex education as imperative for the deaf child and encouraged residential schools to broaden their curriculum.

His articles proposed school and parent cooperation, strict guidelines for sex educators, and the development of an in-school team to organize a program. Results of this first known effort met with limited support of sex education programs within residential facilities. By the late 1950s various individuals had begun implementing a variety of health and hygiene courses in various schools for deaf students. The Illinois School for the Deaf, the Clarke School for the Deaf, and the New Jersey School for the Deaf were among the first. *See* CLARKE SCHOOL.

In 1966 a major effort was made to determine the residential schools' policies and programs with respect to dating and social relationships among deaf teenage students, and to determine the provisions for family life education in the school. Of the 66 residential schools surveyed, 60 schools (90.9 percent) responded to the survey. Responses indicated that 85 percent of the schools permitted dating in some form. Approximately 53 percent allowed students to date off campus. However, in most instances, off-campus dating was limited to group activities. Formal sex education classes were given in 30 of the responding schools. This represented 50 percent of the sample. Details of the kind and content of sex education classes were not determined by this study.

In 1972 a similar survey was conducted in an effort to determine the status of sex education and drug abuse in various residential schools. Surveys were sent to 125 schools with a deaf student population of at least 50. Seventy (56 percent) of the survey forms were returned. Seventy percent of the 56 percent that responded to the survey indicated that they provided a sex education program for the deaf students.

In 1974 a more inclusive study was developed and distributed to 112 residential facilities for deaf students. According to the respondents, minimal programming was provided at the primary level, while most programming existed at the secondary level. Answers to the question of how many hours per school year are devoted to sex education ranged from as low as 1 hour per school year to as high as 720 hours. This supported the reality that even though 66 percent of the residential facilities stated they have a formal sex education program, a great deal of this instruction was meager and crisis-oriented in nature.

This study determined that the classroom teacher was the sex education instructor 70 percent of the time. Physical education teachers, nurses, dormitory teachers, guidance counselors, psychologists, ministers, religious teachers, and department supervisors were also utilized to varying degrees. While only 15 percent of all facilities reported that special training was required for sex education instructors, 45 percent of all instructors were reported to have actually received some special training. This statistic seemed rather high when only 21 percent of 240 responding public teacher-training institutions indicated that they offered one or more courses designed to prepare teachers to teach sex education.

This high statistic prompted a telephone survey of the 71 teacher-training programs for educators of the deaf in January 1977. Of the 71 programs, 69 (96 percent) did not offer a specific course or courses designed to prepare their trainees to teach sex education. However, 39 (57 percent) stated that some effort was made to provide this type of preparation through other courses, although most admitted that these efforts were indeed meager. Sixty (83 percent) of the respondents indicated that they felt there was definitely a need to prepare teachers to assume this type of responsibility.

CURRENT SEXUAL ISSUES

The most frequently asked question by both parents and professionals is whether deafness affects one's sexuality. Deafness per se, it must be said, does not affect an individual's sexuality. Deaf people are born with the same variety of sexual desires, interests, appetites, and curiosities as their hearing peers. However, deaf people do face, from the moment of birth, differences in available ways to learn about their sexuality and that of others.

Learning what it means to be a male or female occurs both informally and formally, through personal experiences, talking, reading, observation, and listening to others. Some or all of these avenues of learning can be affected by deafness. The degree varies with the kind of hearing loss, age at onset, family environment, and school placement.

The potential to talk about or listen to sexual information is impeded to varying degrees for the deaf person. Depending upon the degree of the hearing impairment, verbal exchange of sexual information through interpersonal communication, radio, television programs, and films is minimal or nonexistent. For example, most deaf children are born to hearing parents who generally find verbal communication difficult with their deaf children. Most of these parents do not use sign language with their deaf children. Comments, explanations, and questions about sexuality are difficult and therefore extremely limited.

This fact raises many questions about the kind of sexual information deaf children receive, as well as how this affects the process of value development. Learning about sexuality through reading always hinges on the reading skills of the person. Often, reading does not prove to be a very successful means by which deaf people learn about sexuality. With potential limitations placed upon reading and listening to or talking with others, the deaf person is left with two primary ways of learning about sexuality: by watching others and through direct experiences.

It is often asked if deaf people are oversexed. Deaf people have the same sexual interest and curiosities as other people. However, when deaf children are denied opportunities to learn about their sexuality, they use the only means they have available to them, primarily their personal experience and their chances to observe others. Sometimes the personal experiences occur in inappropriate places. For example, in a residential facility privacy may be limited, but sexual experimentation and learning still occur. With close supervision these behaviors may be discovered more frequently, and thus it may appear that the deaf child is more sexual. However, these behaviors are a very normal response to a desire and need to know about sexuality. Deaf children, being sexually normal, are going to learn about sexuality any way they can.

There is also a significance in watching others as a means of learning about sexuality. Hearing people with sight use their vision as a means of learning. However, most people use their hearing to help them interpret and understand what they are seeing. Deaf people are highly dependent upon their vision. However, the visual picture that is seen can be incomplete, confusing, or even frightening. This confusion was illustrated in the classroom several years ago in a school for deaf children. A deaf boy approximately 12 years old entered the classroom and began to share a package of breath mints with several girls. As the interaction between the students continued, it soon became obvious that he was anticipating a kiss in return for the mints. This was a natural assumption on his part, as that is the nonverbal message that had been communicated by the television advertisement he had seen. As a result of his deafness, he had missed the verbal communication referring to improvement of the user's breath.

This is a humorous example, but other misunderstandings may not result in such a harmless outcome. A very different outcome could have occurred if the instructor had not intervened, and if the young man had tried to force his interests on the girls. The concept of mutuality is often missing in nonverbal messages. This deaf boy could not be expected to understand mutuality from only watching the television commercial. Watching must be supported with language and communication.

The most obvious aspect of whether being deaf affects one's sexuality focuses upon the area of knowledge. Deafness does impede the opportunity for most deaf persons to gain correct, factual information about sexuality. Most people generally do not question this. However, there are perhaps less obvious aspects to deafness, relating to such issues as value development, sex roles, sex identity development, and sexual orientation.

Sexual ignorance, be it about oneself or others, imprisons and debilitates the person, and places limits upon potential for sexual fulfillment and happiness. Good sex will not make a poor relationship work; however, poor sex can destroy what is otherwise a good relationship. People cannot be overprepared or learn too much about sexuality.

EFFEMINATE BEHAVIORS

The second most frequently asked question is why do so many deaf males act in an effeminate way. To answer this, one must first define several terms that are generally confused by most people.

The first of these terms is gender identity or sexual identity. In simplest terms, a person's gender identity is that private, internal feeling of being either a male or a female. The second term, gender role or sexual role, is defined as the public or external expression of one's gender identity, that is, how one acts publicly as a male or as a female. This public male or female role is determined by one's culture. Generally, when a person is born male or female, they feel male or female and behave according to the roles established by their culture.

It is currently believed that the concepts of gender identity and gender role are primarily learned. For instance, research by John Money has established that by three years of age a child can identify his or her sex correctly as well as the sex of others. This statement applies to hearing children, since it is currently believed that a boy's concept of maleness and a female's concept of femaleness are primarily the result of what he or she sees and hears. Currently there is no research on whether the loss of hearing affects the development of gender identity role expression in the deaf child.

Further analysis of the question of effeminacy in deaf males requires examination of their early environment, with particular focus upon role models. Often, young deaf boys are surrounded by female role models in their early educational and home environments. As a result, they often imitate feminine roles, which may later create problems for them among their peers. These males are labeled as sissy, queer, or fag. Thus, these males do not fit the prescribed male role and are therefore at greater risk of being shunned and isolated from their peers. Such treatment is very unpleasant and possibly destructive to a child's psychosexual growth.

If the concepts of sexual identity/role are primarily learned, it is often wondered what is the effect of an environment where one cannot understand the verbal communication of one's parents, or when one's primary role models are feminine. These questions deserve an answer, based on thorough study, not just an opinion.

SEXUAL ORIENTATION

The third most frequently asked question is whether there are more homosexuals among deaf people than among hearing people. It is important to note that no one knows why a person becomes either homosexual or heterosexual. Currently there are theories regarding sexual orientation but no substantial proof for any one theory. The true frequency of homosexuality in the deaf community is unknown. While there may not be a greater number of homosexuals in the deaf community than in the hearing one, there may be greater homosexual activity.

A homosexual may be defined as one who prefers romantic attachments and sexual interaction with the same sex, and typically is maximally aroused by same-sex erotic imagery. Within a residential facility, more frequent same-sex behavior occurs due to opportunity and sexual segregation. Still, engaging in same-sex behavior does not mean a person becomes homosexual.

A great many deaf males have been labeled homosexual because of feminine characteristics and have become involved in same-sex activity as a result of such labeling. They begin to believe the label and act accordingly. Other deaf males have developed high levels of discomfort regarding physical and emotional intimacy with females. Often these deaf males have been involved in homosexual activities but have not had opportunities to interact sexually or socially with females. This is not to argue that all a homosexual male needs is a "good" woman and he would be "straight." However, there appears to be critical developmental stages in development of one's sexual orientation. When these stages are missed, for whatever reason, they are compensated for by the individual. The compensation takes many forms, one of which may be homosexual behavior. These individuals may or may not believe themselves to be homosexual. Some view themselves as heterosexual although their behavior is homosexual. Other view themselves as homosexual and behave accordingly.

SEXUAL ADJUSTMENT

The fourth most frequently asked question by parents, professionals, and deaf people is whether deaf people have more or different marital or sexual problems than hearing people. One of the biggest disadvantages that deaf people face is not having access to someone who can assist them with their sexual concerns or problems. Hearing people have a variety of professional sources to help them when confronting a relationship or sexual problem. This is not true for the average deaf person. Due to the fact that few helping professionals use sign language, opportunities to obtain professional assistance by deaf individuals and couples are extremely limited.

It is difficult to say if deaf people have more or fewer relational and sexual problems than their hearing peers. Observation suggests they do simply because deaf people do not have equal access to information about sexuality compared with hearing people. Ignorance about sexuality often translates into difficulties or problems.

Whether deaf people have more or fewer sexual problems than their hearing peers is really not the issue, however. The real issue is that deaf people must have access to services that are designed to respond to their needs and rights to complete sexual fulfillment.

VALUE DEVELOPMENT

Another frequently asked question is how deaf people develop their sexual values. A value is an idea, a belief about what someone thinks is important in life. All people have values of one kind or another. Values are learned from the environment in which a person participates. Initially, values are learned from one's parents and immediate family members. As a child's environment expands, so does his or her exposure to values different from those held by the family. One of the greatest influences upon early values development, other than the family, is television. In many homes and residential schools, television represents the primary form of entertainment. The potential implications upon hearing viewers of programs depicting sex and violence is being studied and hotly debated. However, no one knows or is studying how this affects deaf people, who view television without the benefit of auditory understanding.

Parents are among the first and most significant conveyors of sexual values to an infant. This fact presents many considerations about value development in deaf children. For example, how is communication of values affected when the child cannot hear the parents express their values? What kind of values does the deaf child develop in such an environment? For the child in the residential school who does not get home very often, where is he or she acquiring values? What kind of values does a child learn from the environment when placed in a residential program at three or four years of age?

Furthermore, deaf children are often sexually segregated in residential programs. During the early years, their primary contact is with female teachers and female dormitory staff—excellent female or mother role models, but what about male or father role models? How does this type of environment affect sexual values, sexual roles, and sexual orientation?

During the spring of 1980, the first National Conference on Sexuality and Deafness was held in St. Louis, Missouri. Approximately 275 professionals in deafness and sexuality met for the first time to exchange ideas. During this conference the issue of sexual value differences between hearing and deaf people was discussed. Hearing and deaf professionals alike began to ask whether deaf and hearing people have different sexual values, and if so, how they are different and why.

With such an issue, the discussion soon turns to the question that if deaf and hearing sexual value systems are different, which is right, which is wrong, or which is best. This kind of thinking is destructive to further inquiry, research, and possible new understanding about value development among deaf people. The result is that people have a great deal of fear and anxiety about the possible answers; thus there are no answers, only more questions.

CONCLUSION

Deaf people are sexual in varying degrees and in various ways. They are no more or less sexual than any other group of people. They do have sexual needs, problems, and worries like everyone else.

Ignorance inhibits professionals' ability to provide the very best in sexuality programs and services for deaf people. As a result, programs and services are limited and far less effective than they could be. Deaf people have the right to develop to their full potential in all aspects of their lives—this includes their sexuality.

Bibliography
Best, Harry: *Deafness and the Deaf in the United States,* Macmillan, New York, 1943.
Blish, Stanford: "Problems Involved in Sex Education in Residential Schools for the Deaf," *Volta Review,* vol. 42, March, April, May, 1940.
Craig, W., and P. Anderson: "The Role of Residential Schools in Preparing Deaf Teenagers for Marriage," *American Annals of the Deaf,* 111:488–498, May 1966.
Fay, E. A.: *Marriages of the Deaf in America,* Volta Bureau, Washington, D.C., 1898.
Fitz-Gerald, D., M. Fitz-Gerald, and C. Williams: "Sex Education: Who's Teaching the Teacher?", unpublished, Gallaudet College, Washington, D.C., 1977.
Fitz-Gerald, M., and D. Fitz-Gerald: "Sex Education Survey of Residential Facilities for the Deaf," *American Annals of the Deaf,* 121:480–483, 1976.
Goslin, D. (ed.): *Handbook of Socialization Theory and Research,* Rand McNally, Chicago, p. 1963, 1969.
Grossman, S.: "Sexual Knowledge, Attitudes and Experience of Deaf College Students," unpublished masters thesis, George Washington University, Washington, D.C., May 14, 1972.
Malfetti, J. L., and A. M. Rubin: "Sex Education: Who Is Teaching the Teachers?", *Teachers College Record,* 69:213–221, 1969.
Masters, William, H., and Virginia E. Johnson: *Homosexuality in Perspective,* Little, Brown, Boston, 1979.
Money, John, and Anke Ehrhardt: *Man and Woman, Boy and Girl,* Johns Hopkins University Press, Baltimore, 1972.
Myklebust, H. R.: "Psychological and Psychiatric Implications of Deafness," *Archives of Otolaryngology,* 1963.
Powell, Jack L., and Joseph Buschmann: "Mixed Marriage . . . It's Not as Simple as Deaf and Hearing," *Deaf American,* pp. 17–19, March 1976.
Rainer, J. D., et al. (eds.): *Family and Mental Health Problems in Deaf Population,* New York State Psychiatric Institute, New York, 1963.
Ramey, J.: *Intimate Friendships,* Prentice-Hall, Englewood Cliffs, New Jersey, 1976.
Schein, J. D., and M. Delk, Jr.: "The Deaf Population of the United States," National Association of the Deaf, Silver Spring, Maryland, 1974.
Schlesinger, H. S., and K. Meadow: *Sound and Sign,* University of California Press, Berkeley, 1972.
Scott, E., and D. Adams: "Sex Education and Drug Abuse," *Proceedings of the Forty-Sixth Meeting of the Convention of American Instructors of the Deaf,* Indiana School for the Deaf, June 24–29, 1973.
Woodard, James: "Sex Is Definitely a Problem: Interpreter's Knowledge of Signs for Sexual Behavior," George Washington University, October 1976.

Della Reaves Fitz-Gerald; Max Fitz-Gerald

SICARD, ABBÉ ROCH AMBROISE CUCURRON (1742–1822)

Roch Ambroise Cucurron Sicard was born in Fousseret, near Toulouse (Department Haute Garonne) on September 28, 1742. His interest in teaching deaf people brought him to Bordeaux, where the archbishop, Champion de Cicé, founded a school for the deaf in 1783. Recognizing Sicard's gifts as an educator, the archbishop sent him to Paris for training at the school of the famous Abbé de l'Epée. In 1786 Sicard returned to Bordeaux as headmaster. Sicard succeeded the Abbé de l'Epée after his death in 1790, and ran the school for the deaf in Paris in an autocratic and Spartan manner until his own death on May 10, 1822, at the age of 80. It is owing to his great political skill that, in 1795, his institution moved into the palatial Magloire Seminary, high on the Montagne Ste. Geneviève, near the Pantheon, a place that the Institution Nationale des Jeunes Sourds occupies to this day. *See* L'EPÉE, ABBÉ CHARLES MICHEL DE.

That the education of handicapped children was pioneered by clerics was a natural development in a Catholic country like France where the clergy had been in charge of education for over a thousand years. Under the Old Regime, an abbé lived a secular life, without obligation to any parish or duties toward any religious community. Sicard was thus free to dedicate himself entirely to deaf people. But during the French Revolution, any abbé was suspect as a potential monarchist and subversive agent. Sicard's pliability, popularity, and array of friends in high places saved his life during the September Massacres, and salvaged his institution. *See* RELIGION, CATHOLIC.

From a political point of view, Sicard's advent as headmaster of the Abbé de l'Epée's school in 1790 was timely indeed. When the National Assembly debated the implementation of the "rights of man," Sicard convinced them that aid for handicapped persons was among their "natural duties." His ally in the legislature, Prieur de la Marne, argued that the National Assembly must repair a "sad mistake of nature." Therefore, the assembly voted "special protection" for deaf people, nationalized the Abbé Sicard's school, and gave it a home and 24 scholarships. A private school became the National Institution for the Congenitally Deaf (*Institution Nationale des Sourds-Muets de Naissance*). France thus established a new principle on July 21, 1791, one that democratic countries have emulated ever since.

Sicard actually owed his fame to Jean Massieu, a deaf-mute boy whom he found in the woods near Bordeaux in the 1780s. He described the boy's education in *Course of Instruction of a Congenitally Deaf-Mute, Intended for the Education of Deaf-Mutes and for Possible Use in the Education of Those Who*

Hear and See (Paris, 1801). It was Massieu's demonstration of his skills that won Sicard the headmastership in 1790, helped convince the National Assembly in 1791, and dazzled visitors to the National Institution where Sicard held weekly public teaching sessions to attract attention. *See* MASSIEU, JEAN.

Sicard used a method of teaching deaf people based on the Abbé de l'Epée's "methodical signs." He supplemented this with written communication. Particularly interested in teaching the logic of grammatical construction, he must have wearied the children endlessly, trying to explain the intricacies of the conditional or the subjunctive, with the aid of fingerspelling and sign language. His teaching led him to write a *Theory of Signs, for the Instruction of the Deaf-Mute* (Paris, 1808). *See* SIGN LANGUAGES; SIGNS: Fingerspelling.

But his main purpose was to inculcate morality and religion. After the revolution, and with the reestablishment of the Catholic Church in 1801, religious teaching occupied a central place at the National Institution. Sicard penned several manuals such as *The Christian Day of a Deaf-Mute, or Exercises for Mass, Confession, Communion, Vespers, Compline, Salve Regina, etc., and Readings for Every Day of the Month* (Paris, 1805).

Sicard's expertise in grammar enhanced his career. In 1794 he was appointed to the faculty of the newly created national Normal School. His course resulted in *Elements of General Grammar, Applied to the French Language* (2 vols, Paris, 1799; 2d ed., 1808). Grammar was also of concern to the newly formed National Institute, where Sicard was elected in 1796 to the Third Class (the former French Academy) section for grammar. He soon headed the committee charged with revising the famous *Dictionary of the French Language*.

All this official recognition created publicity for the National Institution for the Deaf. The many foreign visitors who came to Paris in the early nineteenth century usually included the institution in their rounds. This was particularly true after Sicard brought the "Wild Boy of Aveyron" (a youth of about 12 completely lacking social training when found in the woods of Aveyron Department) to the school in 1800, and hired Jean Marc Itard to care for him. Sicard is thus indirectly responsible for the famous debate over the boy's fate, at the Society of the Observers of Man, between Itard and the well-known alienist Philippe Pinel. Itard went on to found the modern medical specialty of otology that has been crucial in therapy for hearing-impaired persons.

Sicard trained no successor, nor did he tolerate any divergence of opinion, let alone criticism, among his staff. Upon his return from temporary exile in 1800, he dismissed the acting headmaster. The Abbée Roch Ambroise Bébian, Sicard's godson, eventually had to leave the institution, and the Abbé Charles Louis Carton moved to Bruges to head a school for the deaf in newly created Belgium. Sicard remained in charge for 32 years. Emphasis on grammar was law at the National Institution, and training for speech discouraged as time-consuming and unprofitable for deaf people. *See* HISTORY: Sign Language Controversy.

Sicard received medals from Tsar Alexander I of Russia, King Bernadotte of Sweden, and King Louis XVIII of France. The First Spanish Patriotic Society elected him to membership, together with Edward Jenner and Count Rumford. In 1805, when Pope Pius VII visited Paris for the coronation of Napoleon, Sicard received an official visit at the Institution for the Deaf. More than anyone else in the world, at the turn of the nineteenth century, the Abbé Sicard brought deaf people to public attention.

Bibliography

Berthier, F.: *L'abbé Sicard, célèbre instituteur des sourds-muets, successeur immédiat de l'abbé de l'Epée; Précis historique sur sa vie, ses travaux, ses succès, suivi de détails biographiques sur ses élèves sourds-muets les plus remarquables Jean Massieu et Laurent Clerc, et d'un Appendice contenant des lettres de l'abbé Sicard au baron de Gérando, son ami et son confrère à l'Institut*, Douniol, Paris, 1873.

Philip, F., and H. Lane: *Readings in the History of the Deaf*, including translated excerpts of Sicard's *Cours d'instruction d'un sourd-muet de naissance*, 1983.

Dora B. Weiner

SIGN LANGUAGE STUDIES

Sign Language Studies (*SLS*) is the only learned journal devoted entirely to the study of signed languages, especially primary sign language, and their cultural, linguistic, and psychological aspects. (Primary sign languages are gesturally expressed languages developed and used among groups of deaf people as their major or only means of linguistic communication.) *Sign Language Studies* began as a semiannual publication in 1971 and is now a quarterly.

HISTORY

Thomas A. Sebeok, editor of the journal *Semiotica*, suggested in 1971 that William Stokoe edit an international journal on sign language. The new journal would be published by Sebeok's research center in Bloomington, Indiana, along with several other journals in language sciences and semiotics. Both agreed that the availability of material and the numbers of scholars interested in the subject would make semiannual publication best to begin with. By the time the first issue appeared in September

1972, Sebeok had concluded an arrangement with Mouton Publishers. The first five issues of *SLS* (1972–1974) were therefore published under the auspices of the Indiana University Research Center for the Language Sciences (IURCLS), by Mouton Publishers, The Hague, The Netherlands.

Early in 1974, however, Mouton's reorganization led to its decision to cease publication of *Sign Language Studies* at the end of that year. With a growing number of contributors and an active interest in signing and signers, Stokoe was unwilling to see the journal die so soon after its debut. The IURCLS, hard hit by the Dutch publisher's collapse, was unable to continue *SLS* and several other of its journals. In the cessation of Mouton's activities, correspondence, circulation figures, lists of paid subscriptions, and other vital information could not be obtained. Stokoe reasoned that it would therefore be difficult or impossible to convince a university or commercial press to take a chance on publishing this small specialized periodical. Also he had recently undertaken the private publication of another noncommercial work, *Language Origins*, which had an emphasis on sign languages and was also not economically attractive to the usual publishers of special materials.

The acceptance in the profession of *Language Origins* helped convince the editor of *Sign Language Studies* to publish the journal quarterly as a private enterprise. It has been appearing as a quarterly from Linstok Press ever since. The name Linstok, with "linguistics" and "Stokoe" as roots, was chosen in part because linstock (also lintstock or linstok) was used to carry a spark to a loaded cannon that could set off a considerable explosion. Linstok Press was incorporated in the State of Maryland in 1977, with William C. Stokoe, editor, and Ruth Stokoe, manager, as sole stockholders.

VOLUME/ISSUE NUMBERING

Because *SLS* began as a semiannual journal and became a quarterly, its volume and issue numbering system is unusual. A volume is identified by year, not by a volume number, but each issue is numbered serially and has page numbers running consecutively through the volume beginning with the first page in the spring issue through the last in the winter issue.

READERSHIP AND CIRCULATION

Sign Language Studies is designed to serve a broad spectrum of persons interested in the language of deaf populations, especially anthropologists, audiologists, linguists, psychologists, and sociologists. It also attracts others with an interest in sign languages and all their implications, including the issue of the education of deaf persons and the policies for treatment of minorities and minority languages. The nonscientist readers include administrators and teachers in special schools, deaf persons and parents of deaf children, and all who address language problems in children and adults.

Sign Language Studies goes to many of the major university and research libraries of the world. Circulation is approximately 450, with about half going to libraries and United States institutions, more than one-fourth to Canadian and overseas institutions and individuals, and the rest to individual subscribers. Subscriptions are increasing to community colleges with programs for deaf students, interpreter training, and other services. *See* EDUCATIONAL PROGRAMS: Community Colleges.

Another way to characterize the *SLS* audience is by area of interest: the acquisition of language by children both deaf and hearing; language development in usual and unusual circumstances; the grammars of sign languages; the culture and social characteristics of sign language communities; parallels and differences between signed and spoken languages; language and its relation to brain, nervous system, and musculature; descriptions of sign languages of deaf populations, urban and remote; language and cognitive development (when speech and hearing are not in the picture); language origins; and so on.

FUNCTION

Sign Language Studies serves to disseminate vital information—namely, that language is more than and different from speech and hearing, that human language has developed with gestural as well as with vocal expressive systems, that users of signed languages are as capable cognitively and are as fully human as are users of the more familiar spoken languages. *SLS* also serves to link across the world a body of scholars whose curiosity and diligence have led to research results that formerly could not find space in more conservative specialized journals.

EDITORIAL BOARD

A distinguished company of assistant editors has helped to define and broaden the journal's function. On the first board were Ursula Bellugi, George Detmold, William Nemser, Jerome Schein, and Frederick Schreiber. Gordon Hewes joined the board in 1973. From 1976 to 1979 H. Russell Bernard served as associate editor of *SLS*, then continued on the board as assistant editor. In 1978 John Bonvillian, Harry Hoemann, Kathryn Meadow, Terrence O'Rourke, and James Woodward became assistant editors. More recently, Charlotte Baker-Shenk, Dennis Cokely, and Betty Colonomos accepted the responsibility. The broad interests and penetrating scholarship of these persons have led readers into new areas and shown them unsuspected connec-

tions between several bodies of knowledge. *See* SCHREIBER, FREDERICK CARL.

SUPPLEMENTS

In 1980 a selection of 17 articles that had appeared in *SLS* was published as *Sign & Culture: A Reader for Students of American Sign Language*. This group of articles from the journal has become a standard resource for teachers and students of the language. Many programs, however, which go more deeply into the language than a course or two keep the entire run of *Sign Language Studies* at hand as supplementary reading. In 1985, with Virginia Volterra of the Institute of Psychology in Rome, Stokoe edited, in *SLS* format, the proceedings of the 1981 Third International Symposium on Sign Language Research. Entiled *SLR '83* and published jointly by that institute and Linstok Press, the volume both extends the coverage of *SLS* to national sign languages not well known and attests to the wide influence of the journal.

MANUSCRIPTS FROM CONTRIBUTORS

Contributed articles are welcomed from subscribers and members of subscribing institutions. The manuscripts may be research articles, brief research reports, case histories, and reports on field studies. The scope is flexible, and the volunteer reviewers, assistant editors, and editor are willing to consider the unusual. Length is also flexible; published articles may range from brief reports of a few pages to monographs that fill a whole issue (30,000 words or more, but publication entails preliminary negotiation). Authors of published articles receive 25 offprints, pay no page costs, and are not asked to read proofs. Authors are urged to avoid "scientese," to state clearly the problem they addressed, the steps they took, and the results they achieved, using first person, without tortuous passive voice constructions.

William C. Stokoe

SIGN LANGUAGE TEACHING

Sign language teaching in the United States has moved from the basements of houses of worship and the homes of deaf people into colleges and universities across the country. It is developing into a discipline of its own, complete with theories of teaching methods, publication of texts, and emerging careers in sign language–related professions. Though the instruction of sign language is now a legitimate profession, it is not free from controversy and concerns. A near-century of pejorative attitudes and misinformation about the nature of sign language and its status as a language has profoundly affected the way sign language has been taught. More recently, changing attitudes based on more accurate information are leading to a more humanistic respect for the language of the American deaf community, American Sign Language (ASL). These attitudinal changes are now often fostered by sign language teachers. *See* SIGN LANGUAGES: American.

LEARNERS

The majority of sign language learners in the United States are hearing persons choosing to learn how to communicate with deaf Americans. The irony of this phenomenon is that relatively few deaf people are taught sign language in schools; most often they acquire their sign language skills from peers, mostly children, and in rarer instances from their parents. Deaf persons sometimes acquire their sign skills as adults by interacting with other members of the deaf community; this is especially true of deaf children mainstreamed in public school programs. The public school environment is not conduciced to planned sign language learning, and in many cases such learning is discouraged. However, despite major obstacles to acquiring ASL, historically a majority of deaf people have achieved competence in the language by adulthood.

Hearing people desire to learn sign langauge for many reasons, ranging from a personal interest in communicating with deaf people to job requirements for meeting professional obligations, as is the case with community service providers, vocational rehabilitation counselors, and teachers. The popularity of sign language learning in part has to do with state and federal laws, regulations, and mandates requiring equal access to human services afforded all citizens by local, state, and federal governments. Media attention also has created an awareness and resulting interest to learn sign language.

People can pursue an associate or bachelor's degree in sign language. It is not uncommon for students to continue their sign language studies in areas such as interpreting, sign language linguistics, deaf education, vocational rehabilitation, and any number of human service program electives. The combining of sign language courses with other major or minor areas of study in educational programs is a frequent choice of sign language learners.

TEACHERS

Teachers of sign language possess a diverse range of experiences, skills, qualifications, and attitudes. For many years they were mainly individuals interested in teaching hearing people sign language so that they in turn could assist deaf people in understanding religious concepts. Sign language teachers in the 1960s and the 1970s had other ca-

reers in deaf education, interpreting, and vocational rehabilitation. Eventually it was recognized that deaf people could also instruct sign language, and thus active recruitment of deaf instructors began. However, a major problem was that there were no training programs for sign language teachers. There still are relatively few opportunities for a person to acquire sign language teaching skills and knowledge on an ongoing basis. Most teachers learn their craft from other teachers and by modeling the methods of master teachers or the techniques of second-language teaching texts or programs that are derived from spoken-language resources.

The hiring and employment of sign language teachers is frequently an unstructured and random process. This may not always be the case in university or college settings, but a significant number of ill-trained, incompetent, underprepared, but well-meaning sign language teachers are found in continuing education and adult education courses, many religious programs, and last-minute courses offered by community service agencies. The hiring of novice sign language communicators with below-average skills in sign language points out that interviewers frequently do not know what to look for or ask when dealing with applicants. The learning of sign language is viewed by such hiring authorities as a novel, fun, or popular thing to do—rather than as the learning of the language of a distinct cultural group.

METHODS

Misuse of the term sign language has resulted in its being used to describe courses in manual codes for English as well as courses in the sign language of the deaf community, ASL. Thus, sign language learners often enroll in courses without knowing the type of signing to be taught or the method to be used by the instructor. This has a far-reaching effect on the learner's intentions to continue in any type of sign language program or course sequence. A sign language teacher's goal and method of instruction very often will determine the success or failure of interactions between deaf and hearing individuals. *See* MANUALLY CODED ENGLISH.

For many years it was thought that communicative competence in sign langauge could be achieved at the vocabulary level alone. The problem with instructing new learners only in vocabulary is the very natural tendency for learners to place signs into the word order of English, not ASL. Teachers did not teach ASL, but only taught those signs that were thought to have a close correspondence to English words. Major portions of the vocabulary of ASL (especially vocabulary involving classifier handshapes) were rarely, if ever, shown to the students. As a result, many hearing people began signing in an English-like manner.

Through research, however, there emerged evidence of phonological and grammatical levels of American Sign Language. Because of these findings, it was possible to redesign teaching methods and incorporate grammatical patterns and drills using second language teaching approaches and methods.

Historically, sign language teaching can be categorized by the following general methods:

1. Vocabulary approach. Vocabulary is emphasized and taught with the use of word-sign lists and word-sign pairs. Textbooks are often illustrations of sign and focus on word-sign correspondences. This method does not teach vocabulary items in context, and so the student does not learn the correct semantic and syntactic uses of each sign.

2. Grammar-translation approach. This includes discussion of ASL linguistic principles and ASL-English comparisons, providing a more strongly theoretical rather than practical knowledge. Much class time focuses on talking about ASL rather than seeing and using it. Linguistic rules are frequently memorized, and there is emphasis on English-to-ASL drills or ASL-to-English exercises.

3. Audiolingual approach. This relies on sign dialogues and a heavy use of drills constructed to illustrate particular syntactic patterns or vocabulary items. Rote memory is a major tool for learning. The emphasis is on learning to produce the vocabulary and grammar of ASL correctly, rather than on using ASL to communicate effectively.

4. Direct method. The direct method, or its recent expansion called the interactive approach, does not explain the language as in the grammar-translation method, but rather focuses on developing conversational competence in ASL. Sign vocabulary and grammar are taught by using ASL only; any use of English is discouraged. Vocabulary is often presented by using objects available in the classroom; the use of slides, pictures, overheads, and actions is emphasized. Dialogues and some drills may be used to augment classroom activities. However, the focus is always on function rather than form, effective communication rather than perfect production.

There are many other second-language teaching methods. Generally speaking, most sign language classes and programs may use any one or a combination of the above methods, in addition to the creative approaches used by individual teachers.

SUPPORT SYSTEMS

Because there exists no centralized source of sign language teacher training, there is no ongoing consistent flow of information and knowledge. The Sign Instructors Guidance Network (SIGN), a section of the National Association of the Deaf (NAD), at one time was recognized as such a source, but has come to experience a lack of support by its members. There is a very low priority for the SIGN organization within the overall structure of NAD. Because of this attitude, there is frustration and a lack of shared information among sign language teachers that does not promote and encourage professional growth. This may be why many sign language teachers choose to acquire their skills through other means, by enrolling in undergraduate and graduate programs in education, curriculum development, testing, linguistics, second-language teaching, and related areas of study. *See* NATIONAL ASSOCIATION OF THE DEAF.

Attitudes toward deaf people, however, are the single most prevalent concern expressed by deaf people. Frequently it is said that average communicators of sign language with good attitudes often are seen as more sincere than skilled signers with poor attitudes. This phenomenon is a recurring one and can often be traced back to the teacher. It is often expressed that the single most appreciated characteristic of a sign language user is one in which there is an obvious respect and encouragement for the use of sign language and its users, deaf people. The fostering of such attitudes can only come from competent teachers.

Another source of information was the National Symposium on Sign Language Research and Training which was held in 1977 (Chicago, Illinois), 1978 (San Diego, California), and 1980 (Boston, Massachusetts). This event was sponsored by the NAD and a network of colleges and universities. At the 1980 symposium, which attracted approximately 650 people, there was evidence that sign language teachers were in great need of information.

For information about sign language teaching, teachers often will consult with their peers within sign language programs, or they will, if budget permits, purchase textbooks, videotapes, and other materials. They may also seek out other sign language teachers who are recognized authorities in the hope of acquiring new leads on teaching methods or ways to solve particular problems.

TEXTBOOKS

For many years sign language texts carried illustrations or pictures of individual sign vocabulary on each page. Sometimes these books had explanations of why a sign was made the way it was, or had comments as to its origin. Such textbooks include *The Joy of Signing* and *Talk to the Deaf* by Lottie Riekehof, and *Talk with Your Hands* by David Watson. These texts did not provide any information about the structure or history of sign language. *A Basic Course in Manual Communication* by T. J. O'Rourke was the most popular text during the late 1960s and early 1070s. Lou Fant's text, *AMESLAN: An Introduction to American Sign Language*, which was one of the first texts with information about the structure of ASL, was often used as a supplement to O'Rourke's text. There was no text that had a comprehensive grammatical focus and addressed the needs of sign language teachers until Charlotte Baker-Shenk and Dennis Cokely authored a series of texts that included the following: *American Sign Language: A Student Text, Units 1-9, 10-18 and 19-27, American Sign Language: A Teacher's Resource Text on Curriculum, Methods and Evaluation*, and *American Sign Language: A Teacher's Resource Text on Grammar and Culture*. See SIGN LANGUAGE TEXTBOOKS.

Since the publication of this series, additional texts have been published by other authors, finally providing sign language teachers with resources to carry out their classroom lessons and objectives. Increasingly, there are more videotapes, films, games, activities, and other sign language resources that teachers can modify to augment their teaching effectiveness.

ISSUES

Probably two of the issues mentioned most frequently by sign language teachers relate to the development of positive attitudes on the part of the learner toward deaf individuals and their culturally distinct community; and the type of signing taught (ASL, Pidgin Sign English, or Signed English).

It appears that learners who have internalized healthy, positive, accepting attitudes toward deaf people will be likely to project such attitudes to most people they communicate with, despite human differences. As previously stated, learners who acquire excellent skills with sign language may not always possess communicatively healthy attitudes toward people in general, and toward deaf people in particular.

The type of signing taught concerns the philosophical differences reflected in various programs. These differences may conflict and cause anxiety for sign language learners as they meet peers from other programs and begin to see a disparity in instructional and attitudinal approaches to their learning environment.

Today's increased interest in sign language is due to public awareness and state and federal laws that affect deaf people. There are almost 300 postsecondary programs that offer sign language courses for credit, as compared with the few ASL courses being offered to deaf children in day and residential programs. Typical teachers of sign language in churches, adult education programs, and colleges are hearing people with minimal ASL skills that may not be sufficient for normal, spontaneous, and successful communication. Very few sign language teachers are certified by the only organization in the United States that certifies sign language teach-

ers. The certification involves testing a person's qualifications in teaching sign language, including knowledge of teaching methods, curricula, student evaluation, the grammatical structure of ASL, and information about deaf culture.

Bibliography

Baker, C., and D. Cokely: *American Sign Language: A Teacher's Resource Text on Curriculum, Methods, and Evaluation*, 1980.

————: *American Sign Language: A Teacher's Resource Text on Grammar and Culture*, 1980.

Caccamise, F., M. Garretson, and U. Bellugi (eds.): *Teaching American Sign Language as a Second/Foreign Language*, Proceedings of the 3d National Symposium on Sign Language Research and Teaching, National Association of the Deaf, 1981.

Cokely, D. (ed.): "College Level Sign Language Programs: A Resource List," *Reflector*, vol. 8, Winter 1984.

————: "Sign Language Teaching, Interpreting, and Educational Policy," in C. Baker and R. Battison (eds.), *Sign Language and the Deaf Community*, 1980.

Gannon, J. R.: *Deaf Heritage: A Narrative History of Deaf America*, 1981.

Hammerly, H.: *Synthesis in Second Language Teaching: An Introduction to Linguistics*, 1982.

Dennis Berrigan; Kenneth O. Rust

SIGN LANGUAGE TEXTBOOKS

In many ways, the history of sign language textbooks in the United States reflects the social history of American Sign Language (ASL). Early texts are explicit about the reverence in which ASL was held by American deaf people. At the same time, their authors were unsure about the status of ASL as a language. Thus, the early references to the nature of ASL are often difficult to accept, given the linguistic viewpoint now held as to its status. The modern reader may, for instance, look to early authors for evidence of what is now known—that ASL is in fact a language. Such premature intellectual attitudes are hard to find; yet, in terms of its social, psychological, and educational significance, the early authors, and the National Association of the Deaf's filmed signers as well, agreed on the irrevocable value of ASL. If they had presented their case successfully, the history of American deaf education might be different. See SIGN LANGUAGES: American.

SIGN LANGUAGE INSTRUCTION

That ASL proponents (and by extension, deaf children) were unable to fend off the immediate impact of oralism is well known, and is reflected by the paucity of sign language texts written from the 1930s through the 1950s. This is not to say there were none; rather, they were extraordinarily restricted. No longer were schools for deaf children concerned with educating their instructional staff in manual communication. Any concerns for educating hearing people in the language of signs were restricted to certain religious establishments, and to a limited degree, to Gallaudet College, which continued to be the refuge of sign language masters. *See* GALLAUDET COLLEGE; LANGUAGE: SIGN LANGUAGE TEACHING.

A resurgence of interest in signing and instruction in sign language skills preceded the trend in American deaf education now known as total communication. New books started appearing in the early 1960s, before total communication became a solid force for change in the classroom. Similarly, the trend in sign language classes, which began in this period, was shifting away from instruction primarily for church and religious workers and instructors of deaf children. Classes now began to appeal to all who had an interest in deaf people and their experience, including the general public. The publishing history of sign language textbooks reflects this shift in emphasis. *See* HISTORY: Sign Language Controversy; SOCIOLINGUISTICS: Total Communication.

EARLY TEXTS

This article discusses textbooks representative of major trends in sign language and changes in attitude toward it. Texts that do not purport to show the reader or the student how deaf people communicate have been excluded. For example, texts on codes for English, which are more concerned with pedagogical issues for young deaf children, are not included.

Sign language texts have been written and published in the United States since early in the twentieth century. Examples include Schuyler Long's *The Sign Language: A Manual of Signs* (published 1918), and J. W. Michaels's *Handbook of the Sign Language of the Deaf* (1923). Like French texts before them, such as Abbé Sicard's *Théories des Signes, ou Introduction a l'Etude des Langues* (1808) and P. Pélissier's *L'enseignement primaire des sourdes-muets à la portée de tout le monde, avec un iconographie des signes* (1856), early American books on sign language were designed for teachers of deaf children or for religious and clerical personnel interested in working with deaf children and adults. Pélissier's book is especially important because he recorded signs as deaf people were using them, not as hearing people thought they should be used. *See* SICARD, ABBÉ ROCH AMBROISE CUCURRON.

In the early days of American deaf education, hearing teachers at the American School for the Deaf in Hartford, Connecticut, paid Laurent Clerc to teach them to sign. One can assume that similar classes and teaching arrangements were common practice in various schools around the nation. What provisions were made for parents, if any, is unknown. *See* AMERICAN SCHOOL FOR THE DEAF; CLERC, LAURENT; EDUCATION: History.

The books by Long and Michaels typify those written for the next 50 to 60 years. They are not language textbooks analogous to a French or Spanish text, but are lexicons, arranged by English word entries. Sometimes they are additionally organized by semantic field, as Long's book is. Photos were used sparingly, and drawings were apparently not considered a practicable solution. Instead, signs are described in English prose. For example, Long's description of the sign SLEEP reads as follows: "Draw the right '5' hand down across the length of the face, touching the palm against it," and Michaels as: "(1) Draw the right palm down before your face and as you do so, close the fingers around the thumb. (2) Close the eyes. (3) Breathe easily."

The description of signs in both of these early books reflect the view of ASL as an iconographic "picture" language, focusing on the more iconic features of signs. Yet, in their more general reflections on the language of signs, both authors demonstrate the deepest regard and love for the language. Long, for example, wrote, "It is impossible for those who do not understand [the sign language] to comprehend its possibilities with the deaf . . . its wonderful power of carrying thought to intellects which would otherwise be in perpetual darkness." And Michaels said, "The single . . . thought in all signing should be *to make your meaning clear* . . . Remember . . . this is the language of the deaf. Be a conformist, not a reformer, in the use of this language."

MODERN TEXTS

In the early to mid 1960s, a surge of publications appeared. David O. Watson's *Talk with Your Hands* (1964), Lottie Riekehof's *Talk to the Deaf* (1964), Lou Fant's *Say It with Hands* (1964), and Roger Falberg's *The Language of Silence* (1963) were published. Watson's and Riekehof's books became quite popular for use in the relatively new kind of class aimed neither at teachers nor at religious groups. In the late 1960s and early 1970s, sign language classes began to burgeon under the aegis of the National Association of the Deaf. These classes, while obviously of value to the same populations previously served, now were aimed at the needs of parents and would-be interpreters, and increasingly attracted the attention of the general public. *See* NATIONAL ASSOCIATION OF THE DEAF.

These books were the first to use extensive drawings of signs. Fant's book was also the first text to attempt to present signs according to their own "alphabetical" order. That is, Fant, influenced by the seminal linguistic research of William Stokoe, organized the signs according to handshapes, rather than English gloss or definitions. Lesson 8, for example, includes only signs made with an A handshape, such as MEMORIZE, DAILY, and TOMORROW.

Falberg was unique in his attempt to present American Sign Language as a language. Other authors had used vague terms and doubtless had full respect both for the language and for the deaf users in the community. Nonetheless, Falberg's attempt was a first, despite the fact that he was working purely from instinct. Since it was 1963, serious research on ASL had barely begun, and little of it was available to the general reader. Still, Falberg's book is notable because of his viewpoint. For example, Falberg argues that signs are not representations of words but symbols of things and events, equivalent to words, not mere substitutes for them.

Another important work published in the mid-1960s was not a sign language text in the sense of the others. Because of its symbolic importance, however, it is significant. A true dictionary of ASL by William Stokoe, Dorothy Casterline, and Carl Croneberg was published in 1965, and this eventually led to the serious academic interest in ASL which began to take hold in the 1970s and 1980s. While not intended as a textbook, the *Dictionary of American Sign Language* presented, for the first time, in-depth technical and linguistic information of a serious nature about ASL (building on the ideas first published in Stokoe's 1960 monograph *Sign Language Structure*). For example, the dictionary uses an invented symbol system to "write" signs and treats ASL as a foreign language. That is, it defines signs by English definitions and expects the reader to learn to use the writing system in order to make use of the book.

Three major developments characterize the sign texts published in the 1970s, including such books as Fant's *Ameslan: An Introduction to American Sign Language* (1972), Willard Madsen's *Conversational Sign Language II: An Intermediate-Advanced Manual* (1972), and Harry Hoemann's *American Sign Language* (1975). First, authors began to make efforts to produce real language texts. That is, books began to appear with dialogues and notes on grammar as well as vocabulary. Authors made serious attempts to present sentences and whole discourses according to the way deaf people used the language. For example, Hoemann includes grammatical notes at the end of each chapter, in which he explains usage, semantic differentiation of certain signs, and "pronunciation." This represents a great step away from the lexical approach still apparent in works such as Terrence J. O'Rourke's *A Basic Course in Manual Communication* (1973).

Second, the content of the dialogues reflected the experience of deaf people. This also is a distinct change from the more English-oriented texts. For instance, Fant's Lesson 14 is a monologue that includes the (English) sentence, "My light was broken, so I went to the door, because I thought someone might be knocking." To the naive hearing student, such a sentence is virtually impossible to decode. Thus Fant introduced not only grammatical issues and vocabulary, but cultural information as well.

Finally, after decades of church- or school-published books, three publishers came to dominate the field. Two of these, Gallaudet College and the National Association of the Deaf, are long-standing institutions in the deaf community and have a reasonable and abiding interest in the maintenance and increase of sign classes and in the way that the deaf experience is presented to the public.

More remarkable was the entrance of private enterprise into the field of sign language teaching and materials. Joyce Media, Inc., became affiliated with Fant shortly after the publication of his groundbreaking book, *Ameslan*, in 1972. Joyce Media, with Fant, produced supplementary educational materials—films of conversations and dialogues in ASL and of historical and biblical accounts intended for sign language students and for use in the deaf community. Later, the company T. J. Publishers entered the field and restricted itself to sign language materials and information on deafness, including such volumes as James Woodward's *Signs of Sexual Behavior* (1979). Other companies from the mainstream of American publishing have also entered the field. For example, Fant's *The American Sign Language Phrase Book* (1984) was published by Contemporary Books, and Elaine Costello's *Signing: How to Speak with Your Hands* (1983) was published by Bantam. Neither of these companies specializes in language texts or in deafness-related information.

At the same time that sign language classes were spreading and these other changes were taking place, the notion that ASL was a true language was also beginning to take hold. Scientists who study language were beginning to recognize the significance of such claims, and more and more linguists started applying their energies to understanding how a language could be structured without sound. Sign language teachers began to realize how little they knew about the language they were teaching, and realized that teaching a language is different from just teaching signs. Thus, a demand rose for a different kind of sign language textbook.

The more recently published texts reflect these two currents in sign language instruction: the increased interest in ASL among the general public and the more scholarly approach to teaching ASL. The former had led to a market for trade books aimed at the curious public, which is being met by books such as those by Fant (1984), Costello (1983), and Lottie Riekehof's *The Joy of Signing* (1978). Such texts represent the modern versions of the lexicon-type of book. They are generally organized around semantic groupings and reflect changes in the academic view of ASL only in a limited way.

Academic classes, on the other hand, are using books such as *A Basic Course in American Sign Language* (1980) by Tom Humphries et al., *American Sign Language: A Student Text* (1980) by Dennis Cokely and Charlotte Baker, and *American Sign Language* (1984) by Catherine Kettrick. These are all significant in that their authors have linguistic training, and they try to incorporate linguistic information and principles of second language learning skills into their format.

SUMMARY

Sign language texts in the United States demonstrate the current status of the language in the educational setting. In the latter part of the twentieth century, there has been acute academic interest and activity in the area of ASL; textbooks appropriate for use in the college setting are now available to meet that interest and activity. Similarly, general public interest and support for sign language has generated increased numbers of texts. General trade book publishers, as well as special publishing companies, have taken note of these developments. Because of the increased general interest in sign language and in the deaf community, and because of more sophistication in understanding the language and lives of deaf people, sign language texts have likely changed their nature forever.

Bibliography

Babbini, Barbara: *Manual Communication*, 1974.

Cokely, Dennis R., and Charlotte Baker: *American Sign Language: A Student Text*, Units 1–9, 10–18, 19–27, 3 vols., 1980–1981.

Costello, Elaine: *Signing: How to Speak with Your Hands*, 1983.

Falberg, Roger: *The Language of Silence*, 1963.

Fant, Lou: *The American Sign Language Phrase Book*, 1984.

———: *Say It with Hands*, 1964.

———: *Ameslan: An Introduction to American Sign Language*, 1972.

Hoemann, Harry: *American Sign Language*, 1975.

Hotchkiss, J. C.: *Memories of Old Hartford*, film produced by the National Association of the Deaf, 1913.

Humphries, Tom, Terrence J. O'Rourke, and Carol Padden: *A Basic Course in American Sign Language*, 1980.

Kettrick, Catherine: *American Sign Language*, 1984.

Long, J. Schuyler: *The Sign Language: A Manual of Signs*, 1918.

Madsen, Willard: *Conversational Sign Language II: An Intermediate-Advanced Manual*, 1972.

———: *Intermediate Conversational Sign Language*, no date.

Michaels, J. W.: *Handbook of the Sign Language of the Deaf*, 1923.

O'Rourke, Terrence J.: *A Basic Course in Manual Communication*, 1973.

Riekehof, Lottie: *The Joy of Signing*, 1978.

———: *Talk to the Deaf*, 1964.

Sicard, l'Abbé: *Théorie des Signes, ou Introduction a l'Etude des Langues*, 1808.

Stokoe, William C., Jr., Dorothy Casterline, and Carl G. Croneberg: *A Dictionary of American Sign Language*, 1965.

Watson, David O: *Talk with Your Hands*, 3 vols., 1964.

Woodward, James: *Signs of Sexual Behavior*, 1979.

Marina McIntire

Illustration

Sign language illustration is the act of making graphic images that record signs and clearly depict their parts: handshape, movement, location, palm orientation, and sometimes facial expression, head movement, and eye gaze. Such images can be created in the form of a drawing or a photograph. The publishing field accounts for most current sign language illustrations done in deafness-related textbooks and dictionaries. Other markets include schools developing curriculum materials and facilities for sign language research.

Sign language depiction is unique among language recording methods because of the visual-gestural nature of sign language. The full range of methods includes word descriptions in another language, sign notation systems, sign illustrations, sign photographs, film and video recording, and computer programs. Throughout the history of sign language publications, drawings and photographs have been chosen most often. The obvious reason is that these representations do not require large amounts of time to decipher or the learning of a new set of complex symbols as in notational systems. *See* SIGN WRITING SYSTEMS.

Sign language illustrations, when used properly in conjunction with the direct experience method of teaching, are utilized as a memory device. A student's first exposure to new signs should be from a live teacher supplemented with films and video recordings. Imagine a person trying to learn spoken French just by studying French words in a language textbook. A student of sign language would have the same difficulty by studying illustrations alone. Problems would arise in learning appropriate usage, shades of meaning, and proper articulations of signs, regardless of how well the depictions are presented.

SIGN ILLUSTRATOR

The sign language illustrator of today is a highly specialized technician involved in guiding trends within the field of deafness-related publications. Along with the basic ability to render the human figure, the sign language illustrator must have good signing skills, knowledge and experience of deaf culture, and a solid background in sign language linguistics. Other responsibilities include the choosing and scheduling of sign models, studio space, and specialized equipment appropriate for the method of depiction chosen for a particular text. Whether creating a small set of drawings for a language article or thousands for a sign dictionary, consistency and standardized movement conventions are crucial. At present, only a small number of artists are involved with this newly developing profession.

EVOLUTION OF CRAFT

The need for sign language illustrations was first established in religious and educational institutions as early as the sixteenth century. Illustration and publication techniques of the time were primitive. Artists were limited to working in woodcut and metal engraving techniques that lent themselves only to static depictions of human forms and movement. Artists either could not, or simply did not, develop any means for more sophisticated representations of signs and signed languages.

During the nineteenth century the development of new phototransfer processes and printing techniques revolutionized the field of publication. Books could be produced with new approaches to capturing the illusive nature of sign language movements. For example, J. S. Long (1918) was the first author to use a combination of photographic and illustrative techniques. The end products were photographs retouched with arrows. These representations, however, contained less grammatical information than is recognized and included today.

Starting in the 1960s, two major developments within deafness had a dramatic impact on the quality, accuracy, and demand for sign language depiction. The first of these developments was the shift in education of deaf children away from oralism and toward total communication. This shift caused a need for new printed materials that included sign images for instructors of sign language, as well as for curricular needs in the education of deaf children. The second development arose out of a surge of interest in research into the nature of signed languages. Researchers' needs for publishable representations of their observations in this area prompted accurate depictions beyond what had ever been required in the past. This more comprehensive approach fed back onto the needs and requirements of sign language educators; most sign language textbooks now reflect these new standards.

TECHNIQUES

Sign depiction techniques generally fall within two categories: line art and photographs. The advantages and disadvantages of each method have been broadly debated by consumers and researchers. The obvious advantages of line drawings are that the illustrator can select and focus attention on single or multiple aspects of each sign unit. A second advantage is the lower cost of line-art production, layout, and printing. Financial expenditures for making photo collages from black and white photographs can be high, and there are additional costs of screening and printing these as halftones in a textbook.

Hand-drawn illustrations can take many forms. They can be as minimal as a simple outline without shading and as fully developed as a completely shaded drawing. The contents of the picture can contain just a closeup of the hands or a full view of the signer from the waist to the head. The style can be cartoon, semirealistic, or nearly photographic in its realism. Six ways of creating hand-drawn illustrations have been used over the years: drawing from memory, drawing while referring to a mirrored self-image (self-model), drawing from a live sign model (live model), drawing from a projected slide or photograph (projection trace), drawing from a photograph print (overlay trace), and drawing from a video screen (video trace).

Photographic depiction of signs can be as simple as a single photograph or as complex as a photo collage of cut and pasted photographs. These images can have additional retouching to include arrows and other information. A more unusual method captures signs in motion that are lighted only by a flashing strobe light, while another technique uses an extended time exposure under normal studio lighting. These last two methods, although visually fascinating, are used mostly for research or artistic endeavors. Other variables during photo sessions include contrasting backgrounds and clothing that can enhance the reader's ability to focus on the desired information.

One of the most important issues in either format is the selection and use of deaf models whose native language is American Sign Language (ASL). This assures that the correct linguistic information is obtained for the final depiction. The sign models are in this way acting as additional language consultants and must have special skills beyond their language abilities. One of these is the talent to "freeze" their manual and nonmanual movements midsign for the camera. More importantly perhaps, sign models must be able to introspect at some depth about the characteristics and forms of signs in order to help record crucial linguistic elements.

MOVEMENT CONVENTIONS

When looking at depictions of sign language, how do readers know what movements are taking place? The answer lies heavily with the readers' visual intuitions and past experience viewing scientific diagrams and cartoon art. Another factor is their ability to learn sign depiction conventions. These are ways in which the illustrator establishes visual cues, intuitive or arbitrary, for certain types of movement.

One of the most common ways of capturing sign language movements is with the multiple-position image. The most important hand positions in the sign are selected, usually the first and the last, and depicted in a way that most clearly shows the handshapes, locations, and hand orientations. If only the right hand moves, as in the sign DAY, then the first and last positions of the right hand will appear and the left hand will be shown in a single stationary position. When both hands move, as in the sign MAYBE, then both first and last positions of both hands will appear. Similarly, facial expressions and head positions that change during a sign can be represented by depicting their initial and end configurations.

Arrows are added to sign images to complete the set of articulation cues with movement and to make two-dimensional representations appear more three-dimensional. Arrows can be rendered with solid or dotted lines or in a more dimensional way involving ribbon arrows. These arrows show the sign movement path whether straight, curved, circular, back and forth, up and down, zigzag, or spiral. In signs where a similar movement is repeated in the same space, as in the sign FRIEND, a two-stage drawing may be needed to show clearly each segment. If a sign is shown where location and directionality are essential, then added diagramming can be used as in JOHN-GIVE-TO-MARY. In some multisegmented signs the arrows may be accompanied by numbers to clarify proper sequencing as in the example ASK-TO-EACH-OF-THEM.

The viewing angle of a sign, whether for a drawing or a photograph, is also a highly important consideration. Artists have depicted signs from almost every angle possible, including from over the shoulder as in the example by the illustrator—author D. O. Watson. From a full-front view, sign movements that are parallel to the flat printed page are easy to represent with an arrow as in the example sign DAY. This angle is not as appropriate for signs with movements on an axis perpendicular to the point of view such as the sign I-GIVE-YOU. A three-quarters view works better in this situation. An exception to this rule is when a full-sign phrase or sentence is being shown and the viewing angle must be kept constant throughout each drawing frame to enhance other elements such as body turns or twists.

Movement path has never been too difficult to show in sign language illustrations, but movement quality has. In an effort to show motions that are fast, slow, soft, constrained, or stressed, other conventions are required. One way to include this information is to vary the style of the arrow: narrow = fast and wide = slow, or solid = fast and dotted = slow. Another method incorporates classic comic book and cartoon lines called swoosh and pow marks. When all else fails, the insertion of time lines beneath the sign image will solve the problem.

Until recently the depiction of nonmanual cues was frequently neglected. However, as an integral part of sign communication, they lend important information such as intonation and the marking of grammatical devices (as in topicalization and embedded clauses). During signing the body may turn, bend, and lean. The head can nod (affirmation), shake (negation), tilt, raise, and lower. The face can change positions of a vast assortment of facial muscles affecting eye gaze, eyelids and brows, mouth, and so on. These more subtle movements are depicted in almost every way possible, including repeated images, arrows and swoosh marks, and facial lines and creases. See SIGN LANGUAGES: Facial Expressions.

Bibliography

Cokely, Dennis R., and Charlotte Baker: *American Sign Language, A Student Text: Units 1–9*, T. J. Publishers, Silver Spring, Maryland, 1980.

Czech, Franz Hermann: *Versinnlichte Denk und Sprachlehre*, Wien, 1836.

Humphries, Tom, Terrence J. O'Rourke, and Carol Padden: *A Basic Course in American Sign Language*, T. J. Publishers, Silver Spring, Maryland, 1980.

Long, J. Schuyler: *The Sign Language: A Manual of Signs*, Omaha, Nebraska, 1918.

Newell, Bill: *Basic Sign Communication*, National Association of the Deaf, Silver Spring, Maryland, 1983.

Stokoe, William C., Dorothy C. Casterline, and Carl G. Croneberg: *A Dictionary of American Sign Language*, Linstock Press, Washington, D.C., 1965.

Sullivan, Mary Beth, and Linda Bourke: *A Show of Hands*, Addison-Wesley, Reading, Massachusetts, 1980.

Watson, David O.: *Talk with Your Hands*, 1964.

Frank Allen Paul

SIGN LANGUAGES

Sign languages are gestural systems, although gestural systems are not necessarily sign languages. A gestural system may simply pair gestures with meanings. If the gestural system also includes a system for making all kinds of sentences out of its signs (words), then it is a sign language. To form sentences, the system imposes order on the words or requires changes in the form of words, or both. This is exactly true of the sentence-forming system of sign languages. The change in sign forms when the signs are used in sentences is one feature that makes possible distinguishing sign languages from sign code systems.

Code systems using gesturally produced "signs" actually use their signs, not as words of a sign language, but to stand for the words of a particular spoken or written language. Systems known as manually coded English (MCE), signed Swedish, and so on, or by the copyrighted names "Seeing Essential English" and "Signing Exact English," both abbreviated SEE, differ from sign languages because they do not use sign language systems to make sentences. Their sentences are made according to the system in the language they encode, that is, English, Swedish, and so on. Because the signs of sign codes represent words of a spoken language, they generally do not change form. However, if the represented language requires a change of word form (for example, "go" to "going"), many of these sign code systems use two signs, one sign for the base word and a second sign for the ending. *See* Manually coded English.

Two Kinds of Sign Language

Anthropologist A. Kendon has suggested the terms primary sign languages and alternate sign languages to distinguish two kinds of sign languages. The former are sign languages used as the first, main, or only language by members of a social group. The latter are sign languages used by persons who have a spoken language but do not or cannot use it for some reason.

Alternate sign languages are extremely interesting systems from which there is much to learn about the relations of language to culture and of language to language (especially signed to spoken). Kendon has made the most extensive study of an alternate sign language—that used by the Warlpiri tribe in Australia. Similarly, M. Skelly in the 1970s and G. Mallery in the nineteenth century studied the alternate sign languages used by Native Americans.

Primary Sign Languages
and Spoken Languages

In a primary sign language, the signs (words) only occasionally correspond closely with the words or signs of some other language; these signs change form according to the rules of their sign language's sentence-forming system. It is important to note a subtle sameness and difference here: Because primary sign languages are languages, each one has a word-forming system, a sentence-forming system, and an overall controlling system. In this respect they are exactly like any other language, whether spoken or signed. However, because the word-forming material is gestural in the one case and vocal in the other, the word-forming system of a sign language and the word-forming system of a spoken language must be (must sound or look) quite different. (Sign languages are soundless; spoken languages, invisible.) Despite the differences, these word-forming systems as systems are alike, and both, as R. Battison has demonstrated, can be called phonological (and morphological) systems.

The systems for putting words together to make sentences, also known as syntax, likewise show both similarity and difference when the vocal and the gestural modes of production are considered. To the user of any language, the processes of understanding and being understood are of first importance, and so not only word meanings but also sentence meanings must be made clear. Besides the ordering of words and form changes of words already mentioned, spoken languages use vocal material to make sentences. Changes in tone of voice, pitch, stress, and timing can be signals that mean, for instance, "I am asking a question that needs yes or no as an answer" or "This sounds like a question but I don't really expect you to answer." In such cases and many others, the voice is producing sound signals that do not make words but do tell a listener what kind of sentence message is being expressed.

Sign languages similarly use gestural materials for more than making their words (signs). Signers' eyes, faces, heads, as well as their hands and arms are used to produce signals that similarly indicate questions and what kind, or that say, for instance, "This is what I'll be talking about; I'll explain immediately." Question signals and topic markers like these have been explored by several linguists since the mid-1970s, especially C. Baker-Shenk, S. Liddell, and C. Padden. Knowledge about sign language syntax is thus not very old, but to all indications, sign language syntax and spoken language syntax are fundamentally the same thing, a function of the human brain, not peculiar to either the human vocal auditory or the human gestural-visual systems, used for making meaning-bearing units longer than words.

What Primary Sign Languages Look Like

Most of the systems that have been called sign languages make more or less use of actions of the arms and hands. Primary sign languages, however, use these in combination with nonmanual activity (movements of the face, head, eyes, and torso), both to form the words of the particular language and to make the signals needed for the sentence-forming system to work.

Those unfamiliar with primary sign languages are often skeptical, questioning how gestures can make enough contrasts to operate a genuine language system. Surprisingly, the potential for significant contrasts in body actions is much greater than the potential in human voices. Part of the reason for this is the nature of vision itself: people can see heads, eyes, faces, arms, hands, and bodies all at once and comprehend a whole array of large or subtle differences. The other reason that sign language signals are so rich in possible contrasting elements is the complexity of the human facial, skeletal, and muscular systems whose parts can act simultaneously. Hands and arms can be in one of thousands of possible configurations while the face is showing one or more of the thousands of possible combinations of its actions.

APART FROM THE HANDS

Fortunately for the observer of sign languages, no sign language uses even a large part of this potential. What a language like American Sign Language (ASL) does with them can be considered typical. First, eyes are not only the receptors for sign language, but (unlike ears) are a major part of the expression as well. Eye gaze direction is used to control interaction, to manage turn-taking, and to indicate dislike of or inattention to what another signer is saying. Eye gaze is also used in the pronominal and sentence-forming system; for example, a momentary gaze down or to the side can mark, with or without other signals, a major juncture such as the joining of a dependent and an independent clause. The facial actions that include eyebrow raising, pulling the brows together, and raising the upper lids signal such important indications as "question being asked that requires a yes or no answer," "question that asks for new information," "question form that does not really expect an answer," or "this is the topic I'll be telling you about." Similar phenomena are being found in Norwegian, Swedish, Danish, British, and other sign languages.

ARMS AND HANDS

The actions of arms and hands in sign languages have been the object of much attention since the eighteenth century, and some notice of hand signs (for words, letters, or numbers) has been taken since ancient times. Treating these actions as parts of a primary language system, however, is of recent date. There are so many ways of displaying a hand that few if any descriptions are complete, but since the 1960s linguists, from one direction, and choreographers interested in accurate dance notation, from another, have provided promising outlines.

If the hand from wrist to tips of the fingers is considered apart from the thumb, it may be "closed" (curled in) as linguists say, or "flexed" as kinesiologists put it. The hand may be flexed at the knuckle joints but extended at the two sets of distal joints; or this may be reversed—the outer joints flexed (hooked) but the knuckle joints held straight. Finally the hand may be "open" (linguistics) or "extended" (anatomy). This describes four states of the hand (disregarding for now the thumb), but the conditions "tense" and "lax" (from the phonetics of spoken languages) also give intermediate states. For example, a tense open hand is stiff or even recurved; and lax, it is a little concave; a lax hooked hand makes a curve at the end instead of a sharp-angled hook. Thus there are at least eight states, but the fingers may act independently the same way. One finger may assume these states of flexion-extension, and there are four fingers ($4 \times 8 = 32$). Any two fingers may act in unison ($6 \times 8 = 48$); three fingers ($5 \times 8 = 40$) also. Thus, there are, not counting the thumb, 88 states or configurations, in theory at least—actually more because the independent digits may do one thing while the rest of the hand is in any other of its eight positions. Moreover, when two fingers are separated by their action from the rest, it is not necessary that both of them have the same degree of flexion.

In multiplying eight by eight by eight, the number of possible hand configurations becomes large very quickly, but the number of handshapes that do occur as structure points in a sign language's word-forming system are far fewer—first because some of the configurations are possible only with long painful practice, and second because there are so many other ways to make the needed contrasts.

One such way is the thumb position. Because of its joint structure the thumb not only can flex in two ways and extend, but also can oppose the hand or finger or fingers, and furthermore can make or not make contact with other hand parts. This variation, of course, multiplies potential hand configurations by several times.

Next, even all these different hand configurations need not make all the necessary contrasts, simply because the hand is at the end of the whole upper limb. Changes at the shoulder, elbow, and wrist directly change the hand's position. For example, the active (usually right) hand in open configurations may be struck into the palm of the other hand in many ways. Three ways, which clearly contrast, make the contact palm to palm (as in applauding), little finger (ulnar) edge to palm, or back to palm. The contrast of these three pairs (a/b, a/c, b/c) was taken at one time to be a separate parameter of signs, and has been called, variously, the hand's orientation, point of contact, or grounding. Anatomically considered, however, the hand's posture is the inescapable result of states of the arm-hand system. The contrasts in this example are caused by pronation, neutral rotation, and supination of the active forearm. Changing nothing else, if the elbow is flexed sharply, the hand must appear in front of its maker's face. Now the same three forearm states (prone, neutral, supine) present the (flat or open) hand: palm away, thumb (radial) edge toward signer, and palm in.

As the example shows, forearm rotation and elbow flexion provide many more possibilities for contrasting one stationary arm-hand configuration with another. But the wrist can bend and straighten or even bend back, and the wrist can also adduct and abduct, that is, make an angle with the ulnar or radial edge of the forearm. Even more changes in the system can come from the shoulder because of the structure of this joint: the upper arm may be at the side, lifted out to the side (abducted), or pulled in and a little way across the trunk (adducted). The upper arm may also flex (move forward) or extend (move back); and in addition, it can rotate in its socket: medially (to swing the horizontal forearm across the body) or laterally (to swing the horizontal forearm out to the side in the frontal plane), and remain between these two (so the horizontal forearm points forward).

When the number of potential handshapes, calculated at well over one thousand, is multiplied by the number of other states that the arm system can assume, far more possibilities for contrast exist than any language could make use of. Some of these states (for example, pronation, supination, and no rotation of forearm) are used in many primary sign languages to make major contrasts, the kind of contrast that separates one word from another word. Others of these states are entailed; that is, they are changes that go along with other, major changes but do not themselves produce word-changing differences.

But this description has not yet touched what some consider the most salient feature of a sign language watched by a nonsigning observer. So far only some of the contrasts of the facial system and those of the stationary arm-hand have been looked at. Manual signs, however, are made of both stationary (hold) segments and active (move) segments.

The muscles acting on the joints that produce the so-called manual movements are the same muscles that produce the states of the stationary arm-hand(s). Various ways of describing these movements have been used. In the first linguistic treatment and the first dictionary to list signs of ASL other than as word translations, the actions were considered as abstract spatial changes (up, down; forward, back; sideways; circular) and as interactions (touching, approaching, linking, and so on). Subsequent essays in sign phonetics have distinguished path movement from nonpath and have specified source and goal, while noting for circular movements which of three planes (horizontal, frontal, sagittal) is involved. In these descriptive projects, the interaction, point, and nature

of contact are described in specifications of the active hand.

The preceding introduction to the types of body part configurations and movements that make up primary sign languages reveals both their complexity and the scientist's difficulty in describing them. The task is compounded by the fact that signers form these hand and arm, facial, head, and eye configurations and movements quite rapidly and, frequently, simultaneously.

SIGN LANGUAGES AND CULTURE

When attention is turned from how sign languages construct their words (signs) and their sentences to the role of sign languages, the focus changes from the structure of language to questions related to the use of sign language.

The typical users of a primary sign language are deaf people. People who cannot hear the sounds of language—or, if they have some ability to hear, cannot make the myriads of distinctions between different incoming language sounds—quite naturally acquire a primary sign language.

Hearing children of deaf signing parents, especially the oldest siblings, also use primary sign languages for interaction with their parents and parents' friends. They may choose to maintain their relationships with members of the deaf community as they get older, and continue to use sign language. Some hearing people learn and use a primary sign language as adults because their profession involves work with deaf people.

However, not all deaf people use primary sign language. And many "deaf" users of sign language are not functionally deaf; they may even have sufficient hearing to use the telephone. Instead, the primary users of primary sign languages are what is called Deaf—where the capital denotes participation in Deaf culture, not degree of hearing loss. Thus, the primary users of these sign languages are people with a hearing loss who are members of Deaf culture, sharing in its values, norms, tools, and language.

But this immediately poses another question. When 90 to 95 percent of persons born deaf do not have deaf, sign language–using parents, how do they acquire a sign language, as primary or whatever? It seems possible to say that for congenitally deaf children to use gestures in interacting and communicating is innate; they do it naturally. But of course it is also natural for hearing children to use body, facial, and arm-hand gestures themselves and to respond to such gestures of others as means of communication—and all this before they learn to concentrate their communicative signals in the vocal mode. Deaf children limited to interaction in hearing families develop a communicative system that works fairly well at home; the system is called home signs by users of ASL. It is also true that users of home signs, when they begin to interact with less sheltered deaf people, drop home signs and almost immediately learn a primary sign language with wider currency. More research is needed to determine whether a true syntax, a sentence-forming system using gestural signs, can develop in a deaf child who has no contact with users of a primary sign language. Sentences that invariably reflect use of an established sentence-forming system may be necessary in a child's environment if the child is to acquire the language system of that environment. *See* SIGNS: Home Signs.

In this matter one of the key issues of linguistics is central. Is a human born with syntax; that is, is the knowledge of how to make and use sentence-forming systems born into each person? Or, is making words out of material at hand all that is innate? Is trying to communicate an inborn imperative? And is the natural outcome just the ad hoc coupling of words until one learns from others how it is done? The study of sign languages and their acquisition by deaf and hearing children is adding invaluable information to the continuing search for answers to these questions.

However genetic programming and social experience combine in the acquisition of language, it is clear that one of the chief functions of language is to mediate social interaction, to communicate. Another is to signify, that is, to enable an individual to formulate, consider, modify, and otherwise deal, in isolation from others, with personal thoughts, ideas, feelings, and the like. A third function of any language reaches beyond the individual and any social, communicating group. Because the individual learns the meanings of words and the meanings of sentences from others, the shared language is more than an individual accomplishment or possession (though much research focuses only on individual subjects and their language performance). The child being socialized through language into the group learns part of what others know, but the child's experiences are not identical with the experiences of associates. Thus what their language is about is the experiences of the group, but, more than that, it is about the experiences of all other users of the language living and dead. In brief, it is about the culture of its users, when culture is taken to mean the experiences and joint knowledge, values, judgments, and beliefs of all of the users of the language. Since languages pass from generation to generation, culture unites not just the living but also the deceased who used the language in their time. As such, primary sign languages reflect the culture of deaf communities and unite deaf signers with their heritage.

Bibliography

Baker, Charlotte, and Dennis Cokely: *American Sign Language: A Teacher's Resource Text on Grammar and Culture*, T.J. Publishers, Silver Spring, Maryland, 1980.

Battison, Robbin: *Lexical Borrowing in American Sign Language*, Linstok Press, Silver Spring, Maryland, 1978.

Bonvillian, John, et al.: "Language, Cognitive and Cherological Development: The First Steps in Sign Language Acquisition," in W. Stokoe and V. Volterra (eds.), *SLR '83*, pp. 10–22, Linstok Press, Silver Spring, Maryland, 1985.

Goldin-Meadow, Susan, and Heidi Feldman: "The Creation of a Communication System," *Sign Language Studies*, 8:275–334, 1975.

Kendon, Adam: "Knowledge of Sign Language in an Australian Aboriginal Community," *Journal of Anthropological Research*, 40:556–576, 1984.

Liddell, Scott: *American Sign Language Syntax*, Mouton, The Hague, 1980.

Mallery, Garrick: *Sign Language Among the North American Indians*, 1881, reprint in Approaches to Semiotics Series, Smithsonian Institution, Washington, D.C.

Padden, Carol: "Some Arguments for Syntactic Patterning in American Sign Language," *Sign Language Studies*, 32:239–259, 1981.

Skelly, Madge: *Ameri-Indian Gestural Code Based on American Indian Hand Talk*, Elsevier, New York, 1979.

Stokoe, William: *Sign Language Structure: An Outline of the Communication Systems of the American Deaf*, O.P. 8, Studies in Linguistics, Buffalo, New York, 1960.

———, Dorothy Casterline, and Carl Croneberg (eds.), *A Dictionary of American Sign Language on Linguistic Principles*, Gallaudet College Press, Washington, D.C., 1965.

Volterra, Virginia, and Cristina Caselli: "From Gestures and Vocalizations to Signs and Words," in W. Stokoe and V. Volterra (eds.), *SLR '83*, pp. 1–8, Linstok Press, Silver Spring, Maryland, 1985.

William C. Stokoe, Jr.

Origins

The origins of sign languages cannot be later than the origins of the human species. Some hold that it is language that distinguishes true humans from prehuman fossil ancestors; others say that culture is the distinguishing feature. Because culture can be inferred from solid evidence and because spoken language before the invention of writing leaves no direct traces, culture may seem the stronger of the two. But such a belief and all other evidence of human culture imply just as strongly language and humanity as any one of these three implies the other two.

Whether the first languages were spoken, signed, or expressed by a combination of vocal and gestural signals may never be known, but there are several arguments for supposing the first languages to have been sign languages. First, evidence from careful studies of the earliest communication of infants, both hearing and deaf, shows that they do use body movements and voices to communicate.

They make these gestures and vocalizations as their care-givers interact with them, and later they turn them into actual symbols, respectively signs and words. (Signs and words are behaviors that refer symbolically, even if their referents are not present in the immediate context.) What is significant is that the fully symbolic use of gestures as signs occurs earlier than the fully symbolic use of vocalizations as words. This finding suggests that what is true for developing infants may also be true for the species, that is, symbolic behavior appeared first in signs, only later in words.

Another indication of priority comes from microanalysis of communicative behavior, which shows that the communicator's speech and gesticulation (that is, body movements accompanying speaking) work together synchronously to express a message. The significant point here is that an interruption serious enough for the speaking to stop often allows the gesticulatory behavior to go on uninterrupted.

It also happens that a gesture, for example, a head nod, smile, or eye movement, may actually "say" first what a speaker is going to express in words a split second later. Here, as with interruption, the implication is that the uttering of the information by gestural means is an older, earlier acquired method of signifying and communicating, mastered in the evolution of the species before the uttering of information by vocal means, and perhaps operating through neural circuits less subject to disruption than hearing and speaking.

BEGINNINGS OF CONNECTED LANGUAGE

Other arguments for thinking that sign languages as complete languages originated before spoken languages rest on syntax, or connected language, and not on the separate symbols as signs or words. Consider, for instance, an occurrence that must happen many times daily and be talked about in any imaginable culture: someone hands, gives, or offers something to someone else. In the language of school grammars the elements needed to express this occurrence are a subject, a verb, a direct object, and an indirect object. In other terms, an actor gives an object to a beneficiary. But however grammarians parse or explain it, whoever talks about it (in whatever language) has to make the relations of three things to the verb perfectly clear—who is doing the giving, what is being given, and who is the recipient. Spoken languages make these relations clear by using a particular order of the four elements, by varying their forms, or by a combination of both order and form. For example, in English, "she gave him that" shows both order (subject-verb-indirect or direct object) and form ("she" vs. "her" and "him" vs. "he"). But however differently spoken languages manage the matter,

they are all alike in having to utter the four elements one at a time and one after another—there is one dimension and direction in their syntax. Sign languages are not so limited; they have a very different syntactic dimensionality. The direction of movement in producing a sign language sign for "give," "tell," "offer," and so on makes clear who is giver and who is receiver. Often because a signer has two hands as well as a head and eyes, some part of the signer's person visibly represents at the same time one or more of the elements in this relationship.

Here, the argument for the origin of language in signs being earlier over language in words depends on how the acts of symbolization and reference are more likely to have evolved. A sign language puts the parts of a statement's structure into four-dimensional form: the visible changes of the person signing occupy different places in the three-dimensional space the signer can reach, and the changes occur over time. A spoken language can only vary the audible behavior of the person speaking over time, but the spoken language represents abstractly (by form, by order, or both) the relation of giving to what is given, the relation of that to the actor, and all of that to the receiver. It seems much more likely that the moving picture presented to the eyes and brain by sign language has evolved into the abstract relationships a speaker presents to the ears and brain. It is difficult to imagine how human communicators could have started with all the relationships of act to object to actor to recipient abstractly represented and arbitrarily symbolized in the stream of speech; it is even more difficult to imagine why at some later time all this highly abstract multilevel material would then be projected visually onto a moving spatial representation, as it is in a sign language.

It is true that many schemes for memorizing involve projecting lists of unrelated things onto a spatial scheme, for instance, an imagined house of many rooms. But this also argues that spatial relations are fundamental and even in imagination may provide a framework for relating things not otherwise associated. The relationship of an act of giving to its sign language expression is more fundamental: the real giver and receiver occupy different places, and the object given moves from one place to another; the signing used relates the event symbolically. What is signed "means" the event, even though the one signed to has not seen it, or even though the event is imagined. But the signing is also iconic; certain features of the spacial relations in the real or imagined event are preserved in the signed utterance. These features need not be precisely reproduced; but the signed representation will still contain movement and spatial relations characteristic of the class of actual events involving transfer of an object from one person to another. Thus, even with its iconic relation, the sign language expression works as a symbol, denoting not so much a specific event as a class of events.

Iconicity in the symbolism of the sign language expression is inevitable; gesturing persons and persons doing things such as giving are bound to look and move similarly at times. There is no need and usually little possibility for spoken expression to show representative features of what it relates. It is easier to suppose that over time human communicators using the iconic-symbolic mode evolved a symbolic mode without the iconicity that a visual transmission system imparts.

The strongest argument, then, for the priority of sign language depends on the existence of a full system—not just signs as separate symbols, but syntax as well—that can describe an act of giving and multitudes of more and less complex relationships. When signs and words only have been compared, the iconicity of signs and the almost completely arbitrary symbolism of words have led theorists since the time of Ferdinand de Saussure (1857–1913) to take the latter as linguistic, true language, and the former as something less. But when the expression of propositions (symbols with syntax) is examined, signed language not only takes on all the requisite symbolic functions of language but also appears as the likeliest precursor to spoken language.

GESTURES BEFORE HOMO SAPIENS

Chimpanzees, gorillas, and orangutans, the higher apes, have upper limb and facial structure that have caused observers from the earliest times to note how they resembled or caricatured human appearance and actions. It is possible to attribute to all of these species the use of gesture, that is, movements meant to communicate. Whether they progress to symbolic use, to signs, may be debated, but accounts of diverse experiments tend to support the conclusion that they may indeed use gestures, plastic chips, chalk lines, computer keys, and so on symbolically. What is far from clear is whether any of these animals has control of connected sign language with regular syntax. *See* GESTURES: Nonhuman Signing.

Whatever the resolution of this question, it is clear that if signs begin as gestures, as movements of the body intended to communicate, the origin of the elements of a sign language go far back indeed. Elements very similar in appearance to those of human sign languages originated with primates capable of occasionally using their forelimbs as hands and their arms to gesture. Fully symbolic use of gestures is difficult to find reliably in species other than humans, and connected language, the building of propositional structures with complex

relations and their unequivocal expression, would seem to have occurred, along with full bipedalism, with a new social structure based in improved communication, and with the shared, stored, accumulated knowledge—in short, culture—which resulted from all this. Sign language may not be a lot older than spoken language, but it can hardly be younger than either spoken language or the human species.

Bibliography

Hockett, C. F.: "In Search of Jove's Brow," *American Speech*, vol. 53, no. 4, Spring 1978.

Kendon, A.: "Gesticulation, Speech, and Gesture Theory of Language Origins," *Sign Language Studies*, 9:349–373, 1975.

Volterra, V.: "Gestures, Signs, and Words at Two Years: When Does Communication Become Language?", *Sign Language Studies*, 33:363–376, 1981.

Wescott, R. W., G. W. Hewes, and W. C. Stokoe (eds.): *Language Origins*, 1974.

William C. Stokoe

Facial Expressions

Hearing people who observe deaf people signing often comment that the signers seem to use "a lot of facial expression." This difference in deaf signers' faces has been noted by various writers for well over 300 years. Some writers have reacted negatively, decrying the use of such "extreme grimaces" and "uncouth, distorted expressions," while others have taken a more positive, inquisitive approach, wondering what causes deaf signers' faces to show such "intense animation."

Until the late 1970s, most people thought that all these facial expressions were showing the emotions of the signer. Then careful studies of signers' facial behaviors began to reveal that, while deaf people do express their emotions with their faces, they also use their faces as part of their language.

Unlike spoken languages that are built from only one "material," that is, sound, the signed languages of deaf communities are built with movements of several different parts of the body—the hands and arms, head, torso, eyes, and face. Whereas sounds must occur one at a time to form words and sentences, the different parts of the body can move at the same time to form signs and sentences.

The face is one of these moving parts that has several important roles in the language. Some facial expressions, often in combination with head movements, are themselves signs. For example, the sign YEAH-I-KNOW-THAT in American Sign Language (ASL) is made by twitching one side of the nose. The sign DON'T-KNOW in Swedish Sign Language is made by puffing out one cheek and letting the air pop out. In Providence Island Sign Language (PROVISL), the sign TO-LIKE-SOMETHING is made by raising the eyebrows, pursing the lips, and sucking in air. Although many signed languages have signs that are made with facial expressions (without hand movements), the number of these signs is usually very small.

Much more often, facial expressions will occur at the same time as signs are made with the hands and arms. Sometimes these facial expressions are a part of the sign. For example, the signs SMALL-PIG, CAT, and DOG in Providence Island Sign Language are all made with identical hand movements, but have different facial expressions. Most

often, however, these facial expressions are either modifiers or grammatical signals.

MODIFIERS

There appear to be at least 20 facial expressions in ASL that are modifiers. These facial expressions, like adverbs and adjectives, modify or add to the meaning of something else. For example, one of the modifiers adds the meaning "very close to the present time" or "very close to a particular place." If this facial expression appears while the signer makes the manual (with the hands) sign NOW, it

Examples of signs without and with facial modifiers. The movement of the hands also changes somewhat to reflect the modified meaning. (After C. Baker and D. Cokely,

American Sign Language: A Teacher's Resource Text on Grammar and Culture, **T. J. Publishers, Silver Spring, Maryland, 1980)**

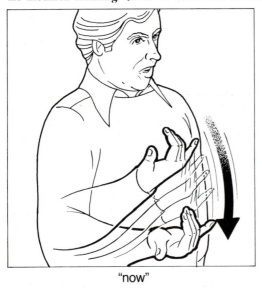

"now"

"right now"

"arrived"

"just arrived"

"without paying attention"
"carelessly"

Examples of facial expressions that are modifiers. (From C. Baker and D. Cokely, *American Sign Language: A*

"normally"
"regularly"

Teacher's Resource Text on Grammar and Culture, **T. J. Publishers, Silver Spring, Maryland, 1980)**

adds the meaning "very close to now" or "right now." If the facial expression appears while the signer is indicating that someone has "arrived," it means the person has "arrived very close to now" or "just arrived."

Another modifier in ASL means "without paying attention" or "carelessly." If this facial expression appears with a sign like WRITE, it means "write carelessly." Another modifier means "normally" or "regularly." If that modifier appears with a sign like WRITE, it means "write at a regular/expected pace." These kinds of modifiers appear frequently in signed languages. However, linguistic researchers are just beginning to study them to find out what they look like and what they mean.

How much do these modifiers differ from one language to another? Some modifiers seem to occur in several signed languages. For example, the "puffed cheeks" expression which generally means "large, a lot, of great magnitude" has been observed in the signing of Thai, Swedish, Roman, and American signers. However, some of the other modifiers which appear in ASL do not seem to be a part of other signed languages.

GRAMMATICAL SIGNALS

Facial expressions have another very important role in signed languages. They help tell the receiver (the person watching) what kind of sentence he or she is seeing. Is it a question? If so, what kind of question? Is it a statement? A negative statement? A conditional statement? The parts of a language that provide this kind of information are called grammatical signals.

Research has found that signers use specific facial expressions and head movements to distinguish at least 13 different kinds of sentences in ASL. For example, there are at least three kinds of questions in ASL, and each appears with a different grammatical signal. If the question is a *yes-no question* like "Is it you?", the signer will have a facial expression with raised eyebrows and raised upper eyelids and head movement that tilts forward/downward.

If the signer wants to ask a *wh question* like "Who went to the meeting?", the signer will use a different facial expression. In this expression, the eyebrows are lowered and drawn together. If the signer wants to ask a *rhetorical question* like "Who went to the meeting? Nobody!", the facial expression and head movement will again be different from that of the first two types of questions.

People who try to "write" ASL sentences for the purpose of teaching often draw a line above the glosses (approximate English translations) for the signs in a sentence to show that a grammatical signal appears while those signs are being made. The letters above the line are a way of identifying which signal it is. For example, "q" means "yes-no question"; "wh-q" means "wh question"; and "rhet.q" means "rhetorical question." Thus, a signer can remake the sign WHO with two different grammatical signals—"wh-q" and "rhet.q."

Sometimes more than one grammatical signal will occur at the same time. For example, in ASL there is a signal for "negation" that involves shaking the head and often appears with a brow "squint" and mouth "frown." One type of negative facial

"you"

Sign without and with facial yes-no question signal. (After C. Baker and D. Cokely, *American Sign Language: A*

"you"

Teacher's Resource Text on Grammar and Culture, T. J. Publishers, Silver Spring, Maryland, 1980)

Facial expressions which are grammatical signals marking wh questions and rhetorical questions. (From C. Baker and D. Cokely, *American Sign Language: A Teacher's Re-* *source Text on Grammar and Culture*, T. J. Publishers, Silver Spring, Maryland, 1980)

(wh-q)
WHO

Example: "Who went to the meeting?"

(rhet.q)
WHO

Example: "Who went to the meeting? Nobody!"

expression is pictured here; "neg" stand for "negation" and mean that the signer's head is shaking side to side. If the signer asks a question like "Aren't you going?", both the "neg" and the "q" signals will appear. Notice how the signer's facial expression and head movement in this photograph differ from the yes-no question signal with "you."

Sometimes a facial modifier and a grammatical signal will occur at the same time. For example, if the signer is describing a meeting and comments that "many people were there," the signer might use the "puffed cheecks" modifier mentioned previously. But suppose the receiver is surprised to hear that so many people were in attendance and asks, "*Many* people were there?" This question might appear with both the "puffed cheeks" modifier and the "q" signal.

Facial expression can also show the signer's emotion at the same time that it acts as part of the language (for example, as modifiers and grammatical signals). For example, if a signer's eyebrows and upper eyelids are raised higher than is normal for yes-no questions, it shows that the signer is also "surprised." So in this example, the signer's face can be showing three things at the same time:

(1) that she is "surprised," (2) that she is asking a yes-no question, and (3) that she is focusing on the idea of "many."

Signers are able to express a lot of information on the face because the facial muscles are complex. Alone, these muscles can make over 1000 different expressions. Another reason why signers can express so much information on their faces is because the receiver normally looks directly at the signer's face (not hands) and thus sees this area of the signer's body most clearly.

DIRECT ADDRESS

Another way that signers use their faces is when they are quoting what someone said. This is called direct address. For example, by turning the body from facing forward (which is the normal position) to facing left or right, the signer can "become" another person. Then the signer will try to look and act like that person while showing what the person said. To show a dialogue between two people, the signer can shift back and forth between two positions, each time changing facial expression to show both the feelings of that particular person and what that person said.

Facial expressions which are grammatical signals marking negation and yes-no questioning. (From C. Baker and D. Cokely, *American Sign Language: A Teacher's Resource*

Text on Grammar and Culture, **T. J. Publishers, Silver Spring, Maryland, 1980)**

(neg)
NOT

Example: "I'm not going."

(neg + q)
NOT

Example: "Aren't you going?"

Example: "Many were there."
Facial modifier without and with yes-no question signal. (From C. Baker and D. Cokely, *American Sign Language:*

Example: "*Many* were there?"
A Teacher's Resource Text on Grammar and Culture, **T. J. Publishers, Silver Spring, Maryland, 1980)**

FACIAL EXPRESSION IN DIFFERENT SIGN COMMUNICATION SITUATIONS

As shown above, the ways that signers use facial expression while communicating in a signed language like ASL is very complex. Some facial expressions are part of the vocabulary and grammar of the language, while others show the signer's feelings.

However, when signers are communicating in a pidgin sign language or a manual code for a spoken language like English, they generally do not use their faces in these ways—especially if they are speaking while they are signing. People who use less of the grammar of ASL and whose signing is more like English use less facial expression. When people are communicating in manual codes for English like SEE II or Signed English, facial expression is often not used at all, except to show the signer's feelings. *See* MANUALLY CODED ENGLISH; SOCIOLINGUISTICS: Sign Language Continuum.

Hearing signers tend to show less facial expression than deaf signers. This is because hearing signers generally do not know the signed language very well and because they are more influenced by their spoken language. Therefore, deaf people sometimes joke that a hearing person's signing is "monotonous" or "boring."

People sometimes wonder if deaf persons are more sensitive to "seeing" facial expressions than hearing people. Clinical tests of how well deaf and hearing people recognize expressions that show emotions have not found any real differences between the two groups. However, if these tests were to focus on recognizing facial expressions used in sign languages like ASL, the results would probably be different. It is likely that deaf signers who use ASL would be better able to recognize quickly these expressions because they need to be able to do so to communicate in ASL.

Hearing people sometimes wonder if deaf people facially express their emotions in the same way as hearing people. Research on hearing people all over the world has shown that they will spontaneously express their emotions with their faces in the same ways. However, a person's culture may have rules that dictate what emotions can be shown in public. For example, middle-class white adult urban males in the United States are not supposed to show sadness or fear in most public places. Their female counterparts are not supposed to show anger, and so when these women are angry they often try to smile (while gritting their teeth!).

The culture of deaf people also affects the way they use their faces. Part of a deaf person's culture is sign language. As shown above, the language has rules that determine what kind of facial expression the signer should have at certain times. So, if the signer is feeling a particular emotion while signing, it is possible that because of the language rules the emotion will not be shown in the usual way. For example, people who are angry usually lower their eyebrows and draw them together into a squint. But suppose a deaf person while angry asks a yes-no question in ASL (which is signaled by raising the eyebrows). What will happen on the signer's face? Often the outcome is that the signer both raises and draws the eyebrows together. (This eyebrow position looks like the one in the previous photograph: "neg + q.") So, in this case the language rule will change the signer's expression from the expected brow squint into a raised brow squint.

Sometimes hearing people get confused because of these kinds of changes in deaf people's facial expression. They may think the deaf person is angry when the individual is simply asking a wh question or a negated yes-no question.

Although hearing people sometimes misunderstand deaf people's facial expressions, deaf people who use different signed languages seem to be able to understand each other's face fairly well. For example, if deaf people from Sweden, England, and the United States get together, they probably will not know most of each other's signs, but they probably will know when the other person is asking a question or describing something that is "really big." This is because the signed languages in each of these countries use facial expression in some similar ways. Comprehensive research has not yet been done to find out how alike are signed languages of the world in their use of facial expression, but many similarities have already been observed.

Bibliography

Baker, C.: "Sentences in American Sign Language," in C. Baker and R. Battison (eds.), *Sign Language and the Deaf Community: Essays in Honor of William C. Stokoe*, pp. 75–86, National Association of the Deaf, Silver Spring, Maryland, 1980.

———— and D. Cokely: *American Sign Language: A Teacher's Resource Text on Grammar and Culture*, pp. 12–25, 121–164, T. J. Publishers, Silver Spring, Maryland, 1980.

Ekman, P.: "Universals and Cultural Differences in Facial Expressions of Emotion," in J. Cole (ed.), *Nebraska Symposium on Motivation*, pp. 207–283, University of Nebraska Press, Lincoln, 1972.

Lawson, L.: "Multi-channel signs [in British Sign Language]," in J. Kyle and B. Woll (eds.), *Language in Sign: An International Perspective on Sign Language*, pp. 97–105, Croom Helm, London, 1983.

Vogt-Svendson, M.: "Mouth Position and Mouth Movement in Norwegian Sign Language," *Sign Language Studies*, 33:363–376, 1981.

Washabaugh, W., J. Woodward, and S. DeSantis: "Providence Island Sign Language: A Context-Dependent Language," *Anthropological Linguistics*, pp. 99–105, March 1978.

Charlotte Baker-Shenk

American

American Sign Language (ASL, Ameslan, Sign) is a visual-gestural language that is used as a primary means of communication by a population of signers in the United States and Canada. Although people who use ASL live within predominantly English-speaking communities, ASL is unrelated to spoken English. ASL is transmitted from one generation of signers to the next. Children whose parents use ASL learn it as a first language. Other children learn ASL in schools from friends and deaf adults.

Formerly there was no distinct name for ASL other than simply "sign language." For most of its long history, many people believed that ASL developed from and was based on English. They described the sign language used by deaf people by comparing it to English. Sign language was either "grammatical and in proper English word order" or "ungrammatical and shortcut English." At that time, there was not yet a way to understand and analyze the structure of the sign communication used by the deaf population.

Largely as a result of a revolution of ideas about language and thought during the early 1960s, several linguists and psychologists began to view the sign language of deaf people in a different light. Like many of their contemporaries, they believed that all human beings are born with an innate language capacity. They wanted to study sign language to see whether language could develop in a form other than speech. At first, many linguists were skeptical that sign language would demonstrate features comparable to spoken language. They thought that the fact that sign language relies on gestures would limit the capacity of the language to express the full range of complex ideas available in spoken language.

Using tools and techniques developed from the study of spoken languages during the 1960s, the linguists who first studied the structure of sign language found that there were two major distinct varieties of signing used by deaf people. The earlier impression that there was one general sign language used by deaf people was incorrect. Deaf signers use a different variety of signing, depending on the setting of the conversation, the persons participating in the conversation, and the topic of the conversation itself.

When deaf people are among themselves in settings which are familiar to them and controlled by them, such as within deaf families or sports events and club parties organized by deaf people, they tend to use more ASL. In situations that involve contact with hearing, English-speaking individuals, such as educational situations or large public affairs of mixed groups of hearing and deaf people, deaf signers tend to change to a variety of signing that incorporates more features of English; this variety of signing is called Sign English.

The distinction between Sign English and ASL enabled linguists to examine the structure of ASL more clearly. They found that, contrary to previous ideas, ASL was not "ungrammatical" signing. They discovered many regular rules which demonstrated that it had a complex grammar, similar to those found in spoken languages.

ASL Users

ASL is the primary language of communication for large numbers of individuals living in the United States and Canada. However, not all signers in Canada are users of ASL; independent sign languages have been described for individuals in certain French-speaking areas of Canada, in Nova Scotia, and near the Arctic Circle (Eskimo populations). No accurate census of users of ASL is available, but estimates of primary users vary from 100,000 to 500,000. Primary users include several groups of signers: native signers, who have learned ASL as a first language from deaf parents; fluent signers, from hearing families, who learned ASL from other deaf individuals; and hearing children of deaf parents, who have learned the language from childhood and continue to use it fluently with deaf people. *See* DEAF POPULATION: Deaf Community.

In addition to the population of primary users, there is a growing population of individuals who have learned ASL as a second language. Due to larger public exposure to deaf people and ASL and better appreciation of signed languages, there has been increasing demand on the part of the hearing public for instruction in ASL. Another population of second-language learners in ASL are deaf immigrants, including deaf people from Mexico and Southeast Asia.

Major Varieties

Until the 1960s almost all black deaf students in the south were segregated in separate schools for deaf children. As a result of imposed isolation from white deaf people, a different variety of ASL developed among black deaf people in the United States. While there was a large influx of the white variety of ASL into black deaf schools from white teachers and other white individuals, black deaf signing contains much sign vocabulary not found in the white variety of ASL, as well as some different grammatical structure. Due to a relaxation of segregation policies, many black deaf signers, especially younger signers, are knowledgeable in the white variety of ASL, but very few white signers are skilled in the use of the black variety. With the exception of a very small body of research on black signing, research on ASL has largely concentrated on the vocabulary and structure of the white variety. *See* SOCIOLINGUISTICS: Sign Language Dialects.

Current Status

Deaf people have always demonstrated intense pride in their sign language, but there has also been a great deal of confusion and shame about ASL. Although deaf people used ASL among themselves in familiar circles of friends and relatives, they were very aware that use of ASL was less tolerated in the outside hearing society. In American society, knowledge in the use of English is a highly valued skill. Because sign language had always been described in terms of English, ASL, the variety of sign language which was least like English, was easily dismissed as "broken English." Higher status and intelligence were attributed to those individuals who used a variety of signing more like English, and low status to those who did not.

From the time of publication of *A Dictionary of American Sign Language* (1965), important advances have been made in the understanding of the structure and use of ASL. Addressing questions raised by linguists and psychologists about the nature of human languages, this research has demonstrated that ASL is not derived from, nor is it a reduced form of, spoken English; it is an independent language which developed in a different modality. While the grammar of ASL differs from English in many respects, these grammatical features are not unusual to ASL, but can be found in other spoken languages of the world. Furthermore, these studies presented an analysis of ASL as a highly structured and complex language with a range of expressive powers comparable to other human languages.

A new awareness of the possibilities of ASL have instilled a sense of pride in deaf signers regarding ASL. Whereas deaf signers previously used ASL rarely in a public setting, many now choose to use it for lectures before large groups of deaf and hearing people. A new art tradition based on ASL has begun to flourish. Dramatic presentations have been staged in ASL, including original plays written by deaf writers. New styles of poetry have emerged which experiment with rhyming devices special to the form of ASL. Storytelling in ASL previously exchanged only among deaf people is now presented at public conferences. *See* FOLKLORE; PERFORMING ARTS; SIGNS: Artistic; THEATER.

Increased awareness about ASL on the part of sign language teachers has led to changes in sign language instruction. Previously, except for hearing children of deaf parents, few hearing individuals learned ASL. Sign language teachers were reluctant to teach ASL because they believed students would resist instruction in a form of signing unlike English. Whereas in the past ASL was thought to be unworthy of academic interest, many educational institutions now provide classes in ASL as well as advanced courses on linguistic analysis of ASL. In some colleges and universities, hearing students can specifically request classes in ASL to satisfy a foreign language requirement.

Changing attitudes toward ASL have also influenced the field of sign language interpreting. More interpreter training programs require extensive instruction both in ASL and about ASL. Interpreters have become more aware that there are differences in ASL and Sign English interpreting and that differences in meaning are possible, depending on their choices of sign vocabulary and structure. New models of interpreting in ASL are being tested which draw from existing models used for foreign language translation between spoken languages. *See* INTERPRETING.

While there have been many significant changes in attitudes about ASL, there is still resistance to use of the language in some arenas. Although schools and educational programs for deaf children acknowledge that ASL is used by some deaf teachers as a teaching tool, by and large, schools do not officially recognize ASL as a language of instruction for deaf children. Arising out of a new understanding about the linguistic status of ASL, there has been strong encouragement from members of the deaf community that schools actively explore ways to include more instruction in ASL. Pointing to the example of bilingual instruction in Spanish and English for Spanish-speaking children in the United States, supporters of the bilingual approach say that teaching deaf children in ASL will have many benefits. But school administrators have mixed feelings about increased use of ASL in their schools; they fear that teaching deaf children in ASL will discourage development of their English language abilities. Supporters of bilingual education for deaf children say that evidence from research in other bilingual settings shows that instruction in a first or familiar language may actually help learning a new language. However, beyond some academic interest, proposals for bilingual instruction in ASL and English have received little support from educators of deaf children. *See* EDUCATION: Communication.

After a long history of oppression of ASL, there still remains disagreement among deaf people themselves about the status of ASL. While many have developed new appreciation for the language, others still have ambivalent feelings about its use by deaf people. Some feel strongly that it indicates negative status and refuse to use it. Others feel that ASL is appropriate for use among deaf people themselves, but are reluctant to expand its use outside of these traditional settings. There are many strong social forces that operate to restrict more widespread changes in attitudes toward ASL and its use, among them a strong bias toward use of

the English language in American society. Since deaf people work and live within American society, they are well aware of America's views of language use. But as America becomes increasingly pluralistic, and growing populations of its citizens speak a language other than English, America may become more willing to accept multilingualism within its boundaries. *See* SOCIOLINGUISTICS: Language Attitudes.

STRUCTURE

Language is largely an unconscious activity. Speakers as well as signers of a language are not necessarily aware of why they use their language the way they do. They know how to use the language; they know which sentences are good or bad, but they do not necessarily know why they are good or bad. The job of the linguist is to break down a speaker's or signer's knowledge of the language and write a "grammar" or a set of rules which describes that knowledge. The linguist must describe the language as it is actually used, not how it should be used.

Linguists study languages at several levels. The most basic level is call the phonological level, or the level of analysis of the signal itself. This is the level at which the sounds of the spoken word or the parameters of the sign are put together to form a unit. The next level is called the morphological level. Here the basic unit is called the morpheme. Morphemes include root words and affixes (including prefixes and suffixes). The level of studying the structure of the whole sentence is called the syntactic level. Examples of ASL structure at each of these levels are given in the following sections.

Phonology The word "phonology" means the study of sound. A spoken word is made up of distinctive sounds, or phonemes. The spoken word "mat" is composed of a sequence of three phonemes, /m/, /ae/, and /t/. The word "bat" has almost the same sequence of sounds except for the first sound in the word, /b/ instead of /m/. A phonology of a spoken language contains a list of the different sounds that make up the words of the language. It may seem incorrect to apply the word "phonology" to the study of the parts that make up a sign, but the same principles that are applied in the study of the spoken word have been found to hold true for a sign as well.

In *A Dictionary of American Sign Language*, W. C. Stokoe analyzed signs in very different ways from previous dictionaries. He broke down signs into three smaller units: the handshape of the sign, its movement, and the location of the sign on or near the body. Later, other investigators added a fourth unit: the orientation of the palm. The four

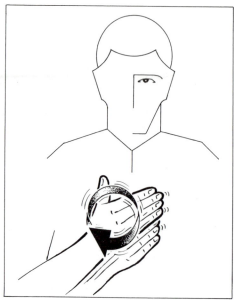

Please

units are called the parameters of a sign. For example, in the sign PLEASE, the handshape is a closed 5, movement is circular, the location is the chest, and the palm is oriented toward the signer. Another example of a handshape parameter is the index finger in the sign DEAF. In this sign, the palm is oriented outward from the signer, and it has double contact. Its location is on the side of the head. Another sign, INDIAN, has almost the same set of parameters as the sign DEAF, with the exception of one: the handshape of INDIAN is different, with the thumb and index finger formed in a circle. A distinctive change in one parameter, such as a difference in handshape, is sufficient to indicate two different signs with different meanings.

While differences in handshapes are important for meaning, there is no difference between the same sign articulated with the left or right hand.

A signer who is right-handed uses the right hand predominantly for articulation of signs, and a left-handed person uses the left hand. There is no loss of comprehension, and in fact, signers are often not aware of each other's dominant hand.

In spoken languages, the inventory of phonemes in one language is not identical in another language. For example, the gutteral /r/ sound in German is not found in English. Likewise, the /w/ sound in the English word "window" is absent from German. Each language has its own set of possible phonemes. When people try to speak an unfamiliar language, their speech will be heavily accented, for they are not skilled in the production of sounds unfamiliar to them.

Similarly, in ASL the set of possible parameters is different from the set of possible parameters in another sign language. The set of possible hand-

extended ring finger handshape

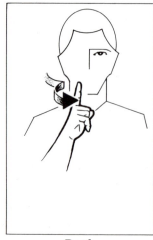

Deaf

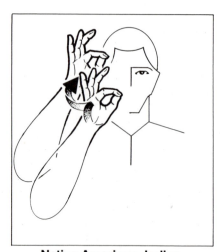

Native American, Indian

shapes in Chinese Sign Language, for instance, includes the extended ring finger. Chinese signers use this handshape for the sign YOUNGER-BROTHER, but this handshape is not contained in the inventory of possible handshapes in ASL. ASL signers learning Chinese Sign Language need to learn new handshapes or movements which are not found in ASL. Thus, in the same way that an English speaker speaks heavily accented German, the ASL signer's Chinese signs will also be heavily accented.

In addition to an inventory of phonemes, each spoken language has rules for the combination or ordering of phonemes. For example, in English a word may begin with a sequence of consonants such as /st/ or /pl/, but no word in English may begin with */tp/ (an asterisk is used here to indicate that the sequence never occurs naturally). The phoneme /ŋ/ (the final consonant sound in the English word "sing") can appear at the end of an English word, but not at the beginning. These rules vary from one language to another. In some African languages, /ŋ/ is possible at the beginning of a word. *See* LANGUAGE.

ASL also has rules for combining the units of a sign. There are specific rules for how handshapes and movements are combined in two-handed signs in ASL. Two-handed signs are signs that use both hands as opposed to those that use only one, as in DEAF and INDIAN. In those two-handed signs that have different handshapes, such as SOMETIMES, CHARGE, WORM, APPROVE, PUT-DOWN, and ENOUGH, the dominant hand (for right-handers, the right hand; for left-handers, the left hand) moves, but the nondominant hand does not. For those two-handed signs in which both hands move, both hands will have the same handshape, as in GO, PROCESS, ENCOURAGE, ARGUE, DISAGREE, and WALK.

There are other ways in which signed and spoken languages share similar phonological principles. In both the spoken word and the sign, units are arranged in a sequence. In a spoken word, the phonemes are arranged in sequential order, one phoneme after another. In a sign, there is also sequential order within a sign. For example, DEAF contains a sequence in which the hand makes contact with the face at one point and then moves to another contact point. Other signs involve a sequence of handshapes which must be followed in order. As the current understanding of sign phonology improves, more fruitful parallels between the sign and the spoken word can be made.

Morphology Morphology is the next higher level of analysis; at this level, the focus of attention is the unit of the word, or the sign. A word or sign is a bounded symbol; it is the minimal linguistic unit which has a meaning or grammatical function.

Words are composed of morphemes, the basic units of meaning. Each word has at least one morpheme, and some have more than one. For example, the English word "cat" is composed of only one morpheme, but the plural "cats" has an additional morpheme, the plural morpheme indicated with the "-s" ending. English words are made up of root morphemes, such as "cat," and affixes. Affixes include prefixes, such as "re-" in "reexamine," and suffixes like the plural ending "-s" and tense endings like "-ed" as in "walk<u>ed</u>."

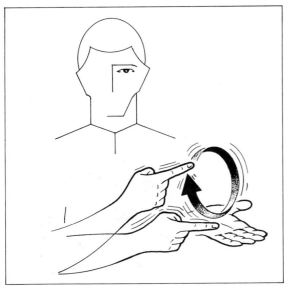

**Sometimes,
occasionally**

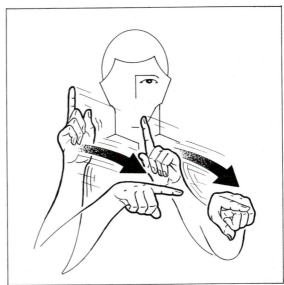

Go

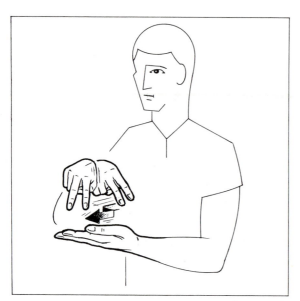
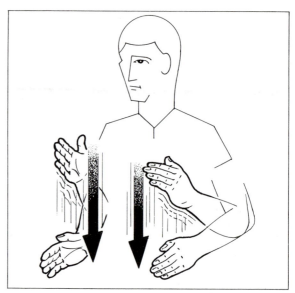

Dancer (dance + agent)

Morphemes which give additional grammatical information like the plural and tense suffixes in English are called inflectional morphemes. Other inflectional morphemes in English are the progressive morpheme "-ing," as in "he is walking," and the third person (he/she/it) singular morpheme "-s," as in "he or she walks."

ASL signs also can be analyzed into morphemes. Some signs are composed of a single morpheme, as in the sign DANCE, and others are composed of more than one morpheme. For example, the sign DANCE + Agent ("dancer") is made up of two morphemes: DANCE followed by a suffix meaning "person."

Some ASL signs contain inflectional morphemes; one large category of inflectional morphemes in ASL are those which mark adjectives and verbs for aspect. Aspect indicates how states or actions are distributed over time—for example, frequently or occasionally, continually or repeatedly. Unlike English, aspect inflectional morphemes in ASL are not suffixes; they are movement units that are added to the basic sign, and the movement of the basic sign changes. For example, the basic sign GO has a single movement. But the sign GO with an aspect morpheme meaning "repeatedly" has a different movement: the movement is not single, but repeated with a particular tempo. Other aspect morphemes in ASL have distinct movement units which are added to the basic sign.

In addition to verbs, some adjectives in ASL add aspect morphemes. The basic sign BE-SICK involves a single short movement, but the sign SICK with an aspect morpheme meaning "for a long time" has a large elliptical circular movement. Compared to English, ASL has many more aspect morphemes,

each indicating different distributions of time. English does not inflect words for "continually" or "for a long time," as does ASL, but must use separate words to indicate these time concepts. On the other hand, English also has inflectional morphemes which indicate points of time, or tense (past and present), but ASL does not inflect for tense. ASL indicates the notions of past, present, future through separate time signs such as TOMORROW, YESTERDAY, LAST-YEAR.

In addition to inflectional morphemes, another type of morpheme is called a derivational morpheme. Inflectional morphemes add grammatical information, but derivational morphemes change

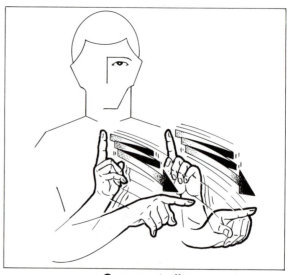

Go repeatedly

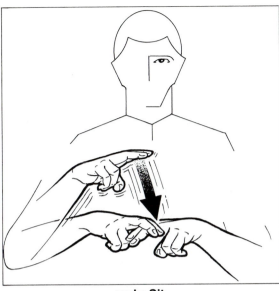

verb: Sit

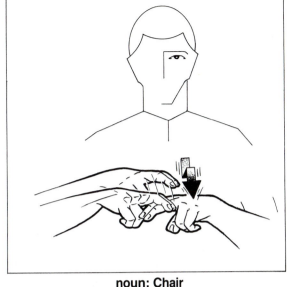

noun: Chair

the meaning of a word or sign. Derivational morphemes also change the part of speech or grammatical category of a word or sign. In English, "act" is a verb, but then the "-ion" suffix is added, as in "action," the word is not a verb but a noun.

As in inflectional morphemes, derivational morphemes in ASL are not separate signs added to the beginning or end of a sign but are movements added within the basic sign. For example, the verb SIT has a single movement. A noun can be derived by changing the movement of the verb to a short repeated movement, and the sign is no longer the verb SIT but the noun CHAIR. Other examples of verb-noun pairs are: FLY–AIRPLANE; OPEN-

DOOR–DOOR; GIVE-TICKET–TICKET. Other derivational morphemes in ASL change nouns to adjectives and verbs to noun activity signs.

Another class of signs in ASL called "classifiers" are combinations of two or more root morphemes. For example, the sign VEHICLE-HERE ("a vehicle located here") has two root morphemes. One root morpheme, the handshape, indicates the class of nouns which the sign represents (all surface vehicles such as cars, bicycles, boats, trucks, and motorized wheelchairs), anda the second root morpheme is the short movement which indicates location. Other combinations of root morphemes are used to represent different types of movement such as "vehicle on a straight path," "vehicle on a winding path," or combinations of two classifiers with two hands for "one vehicle passing another." Classifiers, but not other signs, can have these root combinations. Because classifiers have many possibilities for combining root morphemes in different ways, they are often used in creative signing such as poetry and fantasy storytelling. While English does not have classifiers, classifiers are not limited to ASL; many languages such as Japanese and Chinese have classifiers also.

Vocabulary Processes. ASL vocabulary is constantly expanding to meet new needs. As new technologies and ideas appear, new vocabulary must be devised to talk about them. ASL has several resources for development of new vocabulary.

One productive resource in ASL combines two independent signs into a single unit. The English word "spaceship" was invented to describe a metal object that is rocketed into space. It was formed by combining the word "space" and the word formerly used for vessels in water, "ship." Another

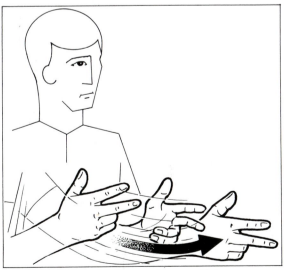

One vehicle passing another

example of a combination in English is the word "smog" which for formed from parts of two words: "smoke" and "fog." ASL has many signs that are formed by combining two other signs. For example, the sign DECODER, used to describe a new device that decodes a broadcast signal into captions on the television screen, is a combination of two other signs: TELEVISION and CAPTION.

Derivational morphology in ASL provides another resource for developing new vocabulary. Nouns are derived from verbs by adding derivational morphology. For example, the noun BLOW-DRYER is derived from the verb BLOW-DRY-HAIR by changing the movement of the verb to a short repeated movement.

Classifier morphology is useful not only for poetry and storytelling but as a source for new signs. By constructing combinations of classifier morphemes in particular ways, signers devise new signs for new objects. A new sport called "hang gliding," in which a person suspended from a harness and attached to a large kite rides wind currents, has led to the invention of a new sign. The sign is formed from combining the classifier for "two-legged person" and the classifier for "large flat object" (the kite), to represent the glider.

Borrowed Vocabulary. Creating new vocabulary by borrowing from other languages is a common practice in English and other languages. Much of the vocabulary in English is borrowed: patio, macho from Spanish; boutique, detente from French; kindergarten from German; parka and moose from American Indian languages. There are many reasons why languages borrow vocabulary from each other. Because many speakers of English associate French with high status, a small shop called a "boutique" rather than a "shop" is more likely to attract a richer clientele. Convenience is another motivation, as in the borrowing of animal and plant names from indigenous languages, such as koala and kangaroo from Native Australian languages.

Likewise, convenience and prestige are among some reasons why ASL borrows from English vocabulary. Additionally, because ASL is a minority language in English-speaking countries, there is strong pressure to replace ASL vocabulary with English-based signs. In spite of these efforts, ASL is surprisingly resistant to a large-scale influx of English vocabulary.

One primary means of borrowing from English is by way of fingerspelling. Fingerspelling contains distinct manual representations for each letter of the English alphabet. Fingerspelling is used primarily for representation of English names or terms, such as names of individuals, place names, and technical terms in English which must be represented in their original form, such as "*Homo sapiens.*"

When a fingerspelled word is borrowed into ASL, it undergoes changes to make it more like a sign in ASL. The borrowed word has become a "fingerspelled sign." For example, the fingerspelled sign #JOB (the pound sign "#" is used as a convention for indicating fingerspelled signs) has two different handshapes instead of three in the fingerspelled word, and the sign is made with a single twisting movement. In the process of borrowing, the fingerspelled word has changed not only in form but also in meaning. The word "job" in English is used to mean "occupation," "livelihood," or "responsibility" (as in "it is her job to make sure everything goes smoothly"), but in ASL the fingerspelled sign #JOB has only the meaning of "occupation" or "livelihood," and not of "responsibility."

Another means of borrowing from English is initialization of signs. Most ASL signs are not initialized. In noninitialized signs, there is no relationship between the handshape of the sign and the first letter of the English translation for the sign. For example, the handshape in the sign DOLL is the same as the letter "X" in the fingerspelled alphabet. But in initialized signs, the handshape is purposely chosen to represent the first letter of the English translation. Examples of initialized signs are B̲LUE, W̲ATER, P̲ERSON, F̲AMILY, G̲ROUP, M̲ATHEMATICS. In contrast to these examples, there are other initialized signs invented for pedagogical purposes which are not accepted for use by ASL signers.

Syntax: Grammatical Categories   Morphology focuses on the structure of morphemic units within a word or sign; syntax is the study of the function of words and signs within the sentence. Each word has a particular grammatical function in a sentence, for example, noun, verb, or adjective. Mem-

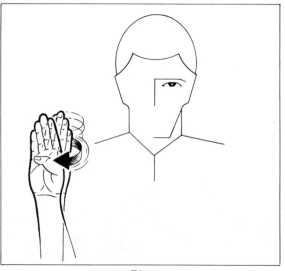

Blue

bers of each category have different grammatical properties. In English, only nouns can take plural suffixes, and only verbs can add tense and aspect suffixes.

ASL signs likewise have categorical distinctions. Nouns in ASL, for example, can be preceded by a number, but verbs or adjectives cannot. The phrase TWO GIRL ("two girls") is acceptable, but not *TWO WALK or *TWO SICK. This fact about nouns can be used to demonstrate the difference between the verb and the noun in a verb-noun pair. The noun CHAIR and the verb SIT have almost identical forms, except that the noun contains a short repeated movement and the verb has only a single movement; but this difference in movement is sufficient to show they are grammatically distinct. The phrase TWO CHAIR ("two chairs") is possible, but not *TWO SIT, because numbers only precede nouns, not verbs.

Adjectives in ASL can add an inflectional morpheme to indicate "intensive" aspect ("increased intensity of"). Like other aspect morphemes in ASL, the intensive aspect morpheme is not a separate sign which is added at the beginning or end of the adjective, but a long, tense movement which is added within the sign itself. For example, the ASL adjective SICK has a short, repeated movement. But when the intensive aspect morpheme is added to the basic sign, the shape of the sign changes to a single long, tense movement. This sign no longer means "sick," but now means "very sick." Only adjectives in ASL can add this morpheme with this additional meaning; nouns and verbs cannot.

Facial expression is very important in ASL. Not only does it convey emotions of the signer such as surprise, sadness, or joy, but certain facial expressions are grammatical signals as well. Facial adverbs are one example of facial expressions with grammatical meaning in ASL. Facial adverbs in ASL appear with verbs and adjectives but not nouns. For example, the facial adverb that is written this way: __ th __ is a specific configuration of the mouth and tongue which means "without attention." It can only appear simultaneously with a manual verb or adjective, and not with a noun. Just as it would be ungrammatical to say in English, "I saw a slowly chair," it is ungrammatical in ASL to use the __ th __ facial adverb with the manual sign CHAIR. But different facial adverbs can be used simultaneously with adverbs such as WALK to mean "walk carelessly," or with adjectives such as SICK to mean "become sick inadvertently."

The previous example demonstrates that facial expression is as important as the manual sign in ASL. Those facial expressions which are a part of the grammar of ASL, for example facial adverbs, are not randomly used, but follow strict limitations. The fact that a facial adverb cannot be used with a noun shows that there are rules for use of these facial expressions. While the particular form of the adverb in ASL is different than in English, adverbs in both ASL and English have the same grammatical properties: they can be used with verbs and adjectives but not nouns.

Syntax: Sentence Structure There has been much confusion about the nature of sentence structure in ASL. For a long time, people believed that ASL lacked sentences, and signs were only ordered together depending on the preferences of the individual signer. Now, after several years of research on ASL sentence structure, a clearer picture of ASL sentence structure is beginning to emerge. There are rules for combining signs into a sentence; these rules form the basis for signers' grammaticality judgments about what makes up "good" and "bad" sentences in ASL.

The structure of sentences in spoken languages is traditionally described in terms of grammatical relations, the most central of which are subject, direct object, and indirect object. In the English sentence, "The girl threw the ball to the boy," "girl" is the subject of the sentence; "ball" is the direct object, or the object which receives the action of the verb; and the indirect object, or the goal of the action, is "boy."

Grammatical relations are realized in different ways in spoken languages. English, like other Indo-European languages, such as French and Spanish, is a "subject-verb-object" (S-V-O) language; grammatical relations are expressed through word order. The subject of the sentence precedes the main verb, and the objects of the sentence appear after the verb. Other languages have different word orders; for example, in Turkish and Navajo, both the subject and object appear before the main verb.

In other languages, like Russian and certain American Indian languages like Southern Tiwa, grammatical relations are expressed by inflectional morphology on verbs. In these languages, the subject or the object of the sentence is indicated by affixes on the verb. In Russian, the subject of the sentence is indicated by a suffix placed after the verb stem. The verb stem meaning "to read" is citaj-. The word citaju means "I read," but citajut, "they read." The suffix contains information about the person (I, you, and so on) and number of the subject (I or we, you or you all, he/she/it or they).

In ASL there are three major verb classes. One class of verbs contains inflectional morphology for the subject and object of the sentence. Examples of these verbs are GIVE, SHOW, SEND, ASK, INFORM, BAWL-OUT, HATE, PAY. These verbs change in form to show the person and number of the subject and object. For example, I-GIVE-YOU ("I give to you") has a movement away from the signer toward the other person (the addressee), but in I-

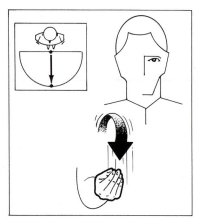
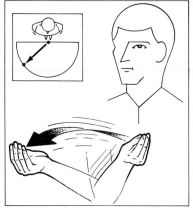
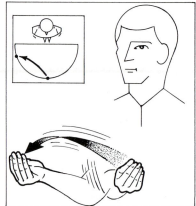

| **I give you** | **I give him** | **You give him** |

GIVE-HIM/HER/IT ("I give to him, her, or it"), the direction of the movement is to the side, from the position of the signer to the "third person" (he/she/it). When the subject of the sentence is "you," the verb moves from the direction of the addressee to the third-person location, YOU-GIVE-HIM/HER/IT.

The subject of the sentence and the verb inflection must agree. If the subject of the sentence is "I," but the verb contains a subject inflection for "he," the sentence is ungrammatical for ASL: *I HE-GIVE-YOU. This sentence is as ungrammatical in ASL as is the English "I gives to you."

Another class of verbs does not contain inflectional morphology; these are verbs such as KNOW, ACCEPT, DOUBT, HIDE, INTERPRET, LIVE, WALK, EXERCISE, FORGET. These verbs do not change in form even if the person and number of the subject and object change. For example, in the sentences I KNOW YOU ("I know you") and YOU KNOW ME ("you know me"), the form of the verb stays the same. In sentences with these verbs, the subject and object are indicated by sign order, which is subject-verb-object.

The third class of verbs contain a set of verbs discussed in the previous section on morphology: classifier verbs. These verbs do not contain inflectional morphology for person and number, but they can add other morphology for manner, direction, and location. Sentences containing this particular class of verbs are least understood. Some studies suggest that sign order for sentences with classifier verbs is object-subject-verb, but a recent study proposes that subject-verb-object may be the correct order for these sentences. As more work is completed on syntactic structures in ASL, the structure of these as well as other sentences in ASL will become better defined.

The fact that both ASL and English have subject-verb-object orders does not necessarily suggest that ASL is influenced by English. There are spoken languages in the world that have subject-verb-object word orders but are unrelated to English—for example, Swahili, a language spoken in Africa. Furthermore, there are many aspects of ASL syntactic structure which are unlike English—for example, the three different verb classes described for ASL do not exist in English. English verbs do not inflect for person and number of both the subject and object of the sentence. Nor are there English verbs which have the same morphological characteristics as classifier verbs in ASL.

FACIAL EXPRESSIONS IN ASL

Facial expressions play an important role in ASL sentences. Different types of expressions indicate the topic or focus of a sentence, mark negatives, and indicate relationships between different clauses within the sentence. For example, specific facial expressions mark relative clauses and conditional ("if. . .then. . .") clauses. In ASL sentences with relative clauses, there is no relative pronoun such as the English words "that" or "who," but the relative clause is accompanied by a specific facial expression which is absent during the main clause. For example, in the ASL sentence

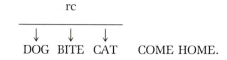

rc
↓   ↓   ↓
DOG BITE CAT　COME HOME.

("The dog that bit the cat came home.")

the relative clause (rc) facial expression appears only during the manual segment: DOG BITE CAT. Changes in the facial expression mark the distinction between the relative and main clauses in the sentence.

Different types of facial expressions also distinguish different types of questions in ASL. Yes-No questions in ASL, or questions that ask for an affirmative or negative response, are marked with raised eyebrows. But WH-type questions in ASL, or questions that ask for specific information ("who, what, where, when, which, how," and so on) are marked by eyebrows which are squeezed together. WH-type questions that are "rhetorical," meaning the speaker only raises them to make a point and does not expect a response from the addressee, have not squeezed, but raised eyebrows. These examples demonstrate that while the role of the face in English is primarily to convey nonverbal information, facial expression in ASL is an essential part of its grammar.

Bibliography

Baker, Charlotte, and Dennis Cokely: *American Sign Languages: A Teacher's Resource Text on Grammar and Culture*, T. J. Publishers, Silver Spring, Maryland, 1980.

Battison, Robin: *Lexical Borrowing in American Sign Language*, Linstok Press, Silver Spring, Maryland, 1978.

Klima, Edward, and Ursula Bellugi: *Signs of Language*, Harvard University Press, Cambridge, Massachusetts, 1979.

Lidell, Scott: *American Sign Language Syntax*, Mouton, The Hague, 1980.

————: "An Investigation into the Syntactic Structure of American Sign Language," 1984.

Padden, Carol: "Interaction of Morphology and Syntax in American Sign Language," unpublished doctoral dissertation, University of California, San Diego, 1983.

Stokoe, William: *A Dictionary of American Sign Language*, 2d ed., Linstok Press, Silver Spring, Maryland, 1976.

Supalla, Ted: "Acquisition of Verbs of Motion and Location in American Sign Language," unpublished doctoral dissertation, University of California, San Diego, 1982.

Woodward, James: "Black Southern Signing," *Language in Society*, 5(1):211–218.

Carol A. Padden

HISTORY

Although something is known of the historical events that have impinged on American Sign Language (ASL) and its predecessors, very little is known of the history of the language itself and the changes in vocabulary and structure it has undergone.

The history of ASL reaches back to the French Enlightenment, if not earlier. The first pertinent document is probably the book published in 1779 by Pierre Desloges, a Parisian bookbinder who was deafened by disease at the age of seven. According to the preface, it is the first book ever to come from a deaf author, and was written to defend sign language against false imputations published by the Abbé Deschamps, a disciple of the "master de-mutizer" Jacob Pereire. Deschamps advocated oral instruction of deaf people and the exclusion of sign, which he denigrated as limited and ambiguous. *See* DESLOGES, PIERRE.

Era of the Abbé de l'Epée Although Charles Michel de l'Epée (1712–1789), who founded the education of deaf people as a social class in the late 1760s, is

sometimes said to have played a critical role in establishing French Sign Language (FSL), Desloges implies that deaf Parisians had a common manual language earlier in the Enlightenment. Desloges wrote that the Abbé de l'Epée learned FSL from deaf persons. Further evicence that FSL predated Epée comes from the testimony of a delegate to the National Convention at the time of the Revolution, who indicated that before the Abbé de l'Epée deaf people communicated among themselves and with others close to them by using their own sign language grammar. It is reasonable speculation that the two deaf sisters in Paris who, according to Epée, launched him on his career of educating deaf students, were members of this sign language community. *See* L'EPÉE, ABBÉ CHARLES MICHEL DE.

Epée was misled, as many scholars have been since, by the great differences between the structure of his own language and the manual language of the deaf community. Because French grammar relies heavily on word endings and word order while sign language does not—it conveys many similar ideas by systematically modifying the movements of the signs themselves—Epée thought that FSL lacked rules. Thus, with the aid of his pupils, he undertook to choose or invent a sign for all the word endings in French, for all the articles, prepositions, auxiliary verbs, and so on, until virtually every French sentence had its counterpart in this manual French, could be transcribed into it, and recovered from it. Whereas the oralists sought to replace sign language with spoken French, Epée sought to convert it into a manual version of the national language.

The two sisters to whom Epée presumably taught this manual French in daily lessons at his home were soon joined by other pupils. In the late 1760s the class had 6 students; a decade later, there were 30; by the time of the Abbé's death in 1789 there were over 60. Perhaps the language these pupils used among themselves was that to which Desloges referred, which will be referred to here as Old French Sign Language (OFSL). Epée's handwritten notebooks contain the first act of a little play to be performed by his pupils at one of his public exercises. On one side of the page is the text in French. On the other side, in a different order, appears not a translation into OFSL but the basic signs (as French glosses) that would allow Epée to explain the meaning of the French sentences to his pupils. From this limited evidence, it appears that Epée may have learned some of the vocabulary and sentence structure of OFSL. During his lifetime, his disiples returned from Paris to their native lands and founded a dozen residential schools for deaf children throughout Europe—from Rome to Amsterdam, from Madrid to Vienna. It is not known to what extent the manual French and, possibly, OFSL they learned in Paris influenced the manual language used by their disciples and pupils, who went on to found yet other schools.

Paris School On Epée's death, his disciple, the Abbé Sicard, who had studied with the master for a year and had then returned to Bordeaux to found his own school, took the reins of the newly nationalized Paris school. In speaking of his prime pupil in Bordeaux, Jean Massieu, Sicard said that they taught each other the signs of their respective languages. However, it is known on the authority of a leading pupil of the Paris school, Ferdinand Berthier, later dean of the deaf faculty there, that "Sicard never used the language of his pupils, only chalk, fingerspelling, or, occasionally, manual French." *See* BERTHIER, JEAN FERDINAND; MASSIEU, JEAN; SICARD, ABBÉ ROCH AMBROISE CUCURRON.

Jean Massieu, born deaf, as were his five brothers and sisters, was appointed head teaching-assistant at the Paris school; his autobiography implies that his family used their own "home signs." What language Massieu used with his pupils in Paris is not known—presumably manual French in class and OFSL outside class. By the time of Sicard's death in 1822, the Paris school housed some 150 pupils who used a common sign language, presumably OFSL, which was mastered and described by his godson and the later head of studies, R. A. Bébian, in 1817 (later described by Rémi-Valade, in 1854). Sicard's disciples carried manual French and possibly OFSL back to their native cities as they founded most of the 21 schools in France and some 60 in all throughout Europe that flourished in Sicard's lifetime. The pupils, too, disseminated their sign language: from the Paris school alone came mathematicians, chemists, painters, sculptors, poets, sailors and soldiers, men of letters, and deaf teachers of deaf students, who traveled throughout France and Europe. Several of the teachers, such as Claudius Forestier, founded schools of their own for deaf children.

Influence of Laurent Clerc Seven years before Sicard's death, Thomas Gallaudet, a Protestant minister from Hartford, Connecticut, was sent by philanthropists to London to acquire the art of instructing deaf people. Refused entry to British schools for deaf children, which were monopolized by the family of famed oralist Thomas Braidwood, Gallaudet had recourse to the Abbé Sicard who, as it happened, was giving public demonstrations of his methods in London, aided by two of his most outstanding pupils, Jean Massieu and Laurent Clerc. At Sicard's invitation, Gallaudet soon joined them in Paris and spent a few months studying Sicard's methods, receiving lessons in manual French from Massieu and Clerc, and attending their classes. The Library of Congress has on file a paper tablecloth on which the first of these lessons took place in a Paris cafe; it records Clerc's explanation of the signs in manual French corresponding to various verb tenses. Gallaudet apparently improvised a notation to help him remember them, and in the end, he asked Clerc to return to Hartford with him. *See* BRAIDWOOD, THOMAS; CLERC, LAURENT; GALLAUDET, THOMAS HOPKINS.

Shortly after arriving in Hartford in August 1816, Clerc and Gallaudet began a five-month fund-raising tour in the northeast, where they met many deaf people. Clerc apparently had little difficulty in communicating with them, but it is unclear what this indicated about his sign language and theirs. In April 1817 the "Connecticut Asylum" opened its doors to seven deaf pupils from various New England cities, several from families with other deaf members. The language of the classroom was apparently Clerc's manual French adapted to English, which will be referred to here as manual English. Clerc taught the system to the early hearing teachers, who were also in constant contact with the pupils. Soon Clerc was giving private lessons in "his language" (manual English?) to nearly a dozen hearing teachers from as many eastern cities. The teachers went back to several states to found their own schools in turn. By the end of the first year at Hartford school there were 31 pupils from 10 different states. Among the possible sources for the language they used among themselves in the dormitories and at play, if not in the classroom, should be listed Clerc's manual English, his OFSL, the "home signs" brought by children from their families, pantomime, and new signs generated in the setting of the school. In any case, the pupils' language was not manual English. There is only speculation concerning how this manual language was amalgamated. *See* AMERICAN SCHOOL FOR THE DEAF.

In 1821 Clerc spent six months in Philadelphia organizing the curriculum of the Pennsylvania Institution, and in 1830 a hearing professor, Léon Vaïsse, came from the Paris school to do the same at the New York Institution. By the 1830s Bébian was successful in his campaign to "tear down the scaffolding on the sign language erected by Epée and Sicard." F. A. P. Barnard wrote that Hartford discarded the "unwieldy and cumbersome machine" (for example, the grammatical signs and oral-language word order). Instead, he explained that to say in the pupils' sign language "A man kicks a dog," "I must first make the sign of a dog and assign it to a location. I must then make the sign of a man, giving it also a suitable location, and finally represent the action as passing in the proper direction between the two." J. R. Keep, among others, illustrated some of the syntax of the pupils' language by translating signed short stories word for word into English and then comparing them with fluent English versions. There, little evidence is found of manual English and much evidence of the principles at work in modern ASL.

Other Influences Comparing dictionaries of contemporary FSL and ASL, it has been reported that there are 58 percent cognates for a sample of 872 signs. Such a high degree of overlap, in the absence of any significant contact between the two deaf communities other than Clerc (and possibly Vaïsse), suggests that, located at the hub of American deaf education, Clerc exercised an influence that must have been very great indeed. On the other hand, it is argued that the considerable divergence of the two vocabularies could not have been achieved in merely a century and a half without an external force operating on one or both languages, from which it has been concluded that the ASL that came to be used in the schools must have been heavily influenced by, even creolized with, the signing systems brought to the schools by the deaf children. Of the first 100 pupils at the Hartford school, 80 were prelingually deaf and 28 came from 23 families in which there were 40 other deaf children. Indigenous signing systems were to be found not only in deaf families but also in a few deaf communities such as those on the island of Martha's Vineyard, Massachusetts, and at Henniker, New Hampshire. *See* HISTORY: Martha's Vineyard.

On the other hand, there is the large and growing portion of successive generations of deaf people, right down to the present, who come from hearing homes and who learn ASL relatively late in life, often on arriving at school, often after learning English. Thus the signing community is unlike other language minorities, in that a preponderance of its members do not acquire the language natively. This force must also shape the language transmitted from generation to generation.

Yet another historical force at work on ASL is a tendency for signs to lose their mimetic origins as they become encoded. That is, they conform to the rules of sign formation, which are presumably motivated in turn by natural phonetic processes, such as ease of articulation and ease of perception. As early as 1827 De Gérando discussed at length the contrast between the elaborate mimetic signs prescribed by Epée and Sicard and the "reduced" counterparts actually used by deaf signers. A decade later Harvey Peet made the same distinction and added that as new signs were introduced into the residential schools by the pupils they rapidly underwent this type of "abridgment." The resulting signs were simpler, were more arbitrary, and allowed a much wider range of conversation than their mimetic precursors. Comparing shared entries in dictionaries of OFSL and ASL across the ages, beginning with Pélissier's in 1856, N. Frishberg concluded that over time, signs tend to become more symmetrical, more centrally located in

the signing space, and more "fluid" in execution. Such trends, however, may be confounded by errors of sampling: some dictionaries were compiled by hearing people who knew no sign, others by deaf people who did. Some compilers were at pains to emphasize the representational properties of signs, some were not. Some informants may have provided citation forms of signs while (possibly later) informants gave more conversational versions—that alone could give the appearance of some of Frishberg's trend.

Disseminating ASL In America, as in France, the mother school soon sent its teachers and deaf graduates throughout the country to teach in various deaf schools and to found new ones. As early as 1834 a single sign dialect was recognized in the schools for deaf and dumb students. By the time of Clerc's death in 1869, over 1500 pupils had graduated from the Hartford school, and there were some 30 residential schools in the United States with 3246 pupils and 187 teachers, 42 percent of them deaf. Most such pupils and teachers married other deaf persons and had children, and this, too, helped to disseminate ASL.

The latter half of the nineteenth century saw increasing emphasis on oral rehabilitation and oral instruction of deaf people. The American Association to Promote the Teaching of Speech to the Deaf (now the Alexander Graham Bell Association) was formed in 1890 and, also with Bell's impetus, large numbers of oral day schools began to open, attracting many deaf children of hearing families who otherwise would have entered the signing residential schools Soon ASL left these latter classrooms as well: in 1867 there were 26 American institutions for the education of deaf children, and all taught in ASL; by 1907 there were 139, and none did. (A few manually taught classes for the "oral failures" survived, however, in some schools.) The fraction of the teachers who were deaf themselves and who, for the most part, would be expected to communicate with the pupils in ASL, fell equally precipitously, from 42 to 17 percent—and most of the latter taught manual trades. One effect of this resurgence of oralism was that many users of ASL became more fluent in English and the one language had more opportunity to shape the other. Possible consequences for ASL include more fingerspelled words, more initialized signs, more sign formations based on fingerspelling, and a tendency for a characteristic ASL sentence order, subject-object-verb, to be replaced by the English subject-verb-object. The National Association of the Deaf defended vigorously but unsuccessfully the role of ASL and deaf teachers in the schools. In 1911 it feared the extinction of the language and completed a valuable film project that recorded the language of great deaf orators. National and international congresses of the deaf in Europe proved equally unable to stem the tide of replacement, and the languages of their deaf communities, many of them "sister languages" of ASL, were banished from their schools. *See* ALEXANDER GRAHAM BELL ASSOCIATION FOR THE DEAF; BELL, ALEXANDER GRAHAM; HISTORY: Sign Language Controversy; NATIONAL ASSOCIATION OF THE DEAF.

Sign language could not be banished from the lives of deaf people, however; most of them continued to take deaf spouses and to use their manual language at home, with their children, and at social gatherings. After nearly a century with English as the language of instruction in American schools for deaf children, many professionals have called attention to the spontaneous development of an ASL-English pidgin, dubbed Pidgin Sign English (PSE), which uses ASL signs in English word order and many English grammatical devices, while largely dispensing with the rich morphology of ASL. It may have been encouraged by the growing tendency since the early 1960s for teachers of deaf children to accompany their speech with signs, a practice called simultaneous communication (or sometimes, erroneously, total communication).

The ostracism of sign language from the schools continues largely unabated to the present, although certain developments in linguistics and allied disciplines may lead to change. The manual communication of deaf adults in America came under the scrutiny of language scientists beginning in the 1960s with analysis of the structure of signs, and continuing in the 1970s with analysis of the structure of signed utterances. It quickly came to be known among scholars that ASL possessed these two levels of patterning characteristic of natural languages and that it therefore invited the same kinds of scientific investigation as oral languages do. There followed studies of children learning ASL as a native language, of the dialects of ASL and its social registers, of its historical evolution, of its similarities and differences with other sign languages, of its mechanisms for borrowing from oral language, of its stylistics and poetics, and of its neurological organization and functioning in the perception, memory, and recall of messages.

These developments, abetted no doubt by an increasing American tolerance for cultural pluralism, have inspired a regrowth of ASL prestige, instruction, and use. Deaf teachers are once again in demand, although they serve more the astonishing numbers of hearing adults who wish to learn ASL than they do deaf children in the schools. Congresses, workshops, books, and journals about ASL are appearing at a high and growing rate. There is an increasing interest in the culture and art forms, such as the theater and poetry, of the signing community. Some schools for deaf children have re-introduced manual language in the classroom. It seems the United States is on the threshold of an era in which manual communication will again flourish.

Bibliography

Lane, H: *When the Mind Hears*, Random House, New York, 1984.

———— and F. Grosjean: *Recent Perspectives on American Sign Language*, Lawrence Erlbaum Associates, Hillsdale, New Jersey, 1980.

Harlan Lane

Australian

There are no government census figures showing the numbers of deaf people in Australia who use sign language. However, in each state of Australia there is a large, long-established social welfare, counseling, recreation, and community education agency for deaf and hearing-impaired people. Most deaf people who use sign language have a connection with those agencies and are thus on address lists. A count of one such list, the address list, shows about 2300 deaf persons in the state of Victoria. This is 0.0564 percent of the Australian Bureau of Statistics count of the 1985 total population of Victoria (4,075,900 persons). Therefore, by applying that 0.0564 percent to the Australian population and adding an estimate of deaf children using sign language in schools, a conservative number of deaf people in Australia who used sign language in 1985 is from 9000 to 9500.

HISTORY

The deaf sign language in common use in Australia includes the British two-handed system. There is some minor use of the Irish one-handed alphabet, and since 1970 or so, some introduction of the American one-handed fingerspelling and sign language. The latter was hastened by the visit of the American National Theatre of the Deaf in 1974.

The British two-handed system was brought to Australia in 1860 when the first two schools for deaf children were established, the first in Sydney, and three weeks later the second in the state of Victoria, in the capital city of Melbourne. According to records, it was a Mr. Pattison, a deaf man educated at the Edinburgh Deaf and Dumb Institution, who began the Sydney school. Another deaf man, F. J. Rose, who was educated at the Old Kent School in London, started the Melbourne School.

The records show that some of the teachers from these two early schools moved to Adelaide in South Australia to establish a school there in 1874. Over the years there has been a limited interchange of teachers from school to school and also some directly from the United Kingdom. Thus, the two-handed system spread.

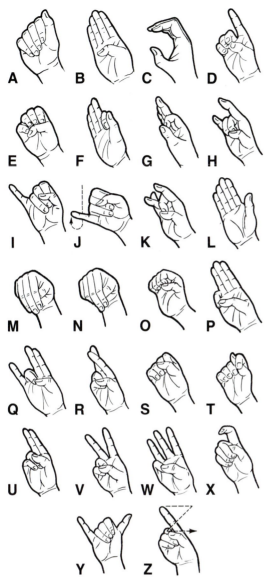

One-handed manual alphabet for fingerspelling to sighted deaf persons in Australia. It differs in six places (letters G, H, K, L, P, Q) from the American system.

Irish one-handed fingerspelling is in the letters F, G, H, K, L, P, and Q.

CURRENT STATUS

English is the national language of Australia. Sign language, as with other community languages (for example, Italian, Greek, and Vietnamese), has no special legal status. However, it is widely acknowledged as the language that many deaf people use. Evidence of this is its actual visible use by deaf people and the extensive provision made for deaf sign language interpreting services in legal, medical, social work, and recreation and cultural areas.

Two-handed manual alphabet for fingerspelling in Australia. Note that each symbol forms, or at least suggests, the letter it represents.

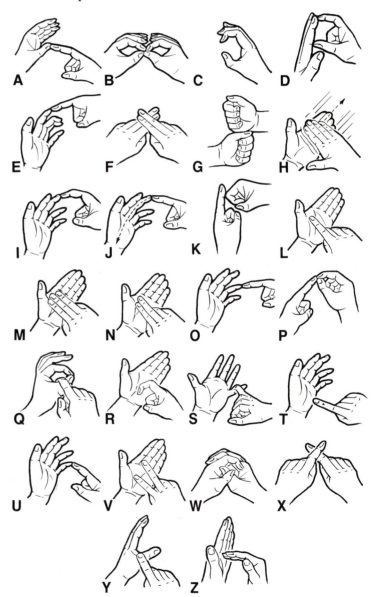

In 1875 Sister Mary Gabrielle Hogan came from Cabra, Dublin, in Ireland, to found the Rosary Convent in Waratah, New South Wales. She brought with her the Irish one-handed alphabet. The Christian Brothers founded St. Gabriels at Castle Hill, an outer suburb of Sydney, New South Wales, in 1922. Like the Sisters, they came from Cabra. From both these residential Catholic institutions, the first for girls and the second for boys, the one-handed Irish fingerspelling system spread throughout Australia. However, the use of this system is not so widespread among the present-day younger pupils from those schools because the emphasis in Catholic schools is now on oral methods with cued speech as a support. The difference between American and

The use of sign language in Australia has had its critics. Those who question its use feel it prevents the acquisition of speech and of correct English. Today, however, there is almost widespread acceptance of sign as a language in its own right; a language that is not to be confused with English structures.

STRUCTURE

To date there has been no formal study of the structure of sign language used in Australia. However, observations of the language suggests that the findings of British Sign Language research may equally apply to Australian Sign Language. The *Dictionary of Australasian Signs* was published in 1982. It records those signs selected for educational use in Australia. The signs in the book are used in English word order.

However, in its purest and most natural form, sign language does not follow English word order. For example, FOOD—YOU WANT MORE, with a questioning look on the face, is Australian Sign Language format. This translates in English to "Do you want more food?" At times fingerspelling is also interwoven into the fabric of the conversation. Sign language is rich in concepts, and the most complex ideas can be conveyed through it. *See* AUSTRALIA.

Bibliography

Dominican Nuns and Christian Brothers: *How to Converse with the Deaf in Sign Language*, Bishop of Maitland, Newcastle, New South Wales, 1942.

Flynn, John W.: *No Longer by Gaslight: The First Hundred Years of the Adult Deaf Society of Victoria*, Adult Deaf Society of Victoria (now Victorian Deaf Society), Melbourne, 1985.

Jeanes, Raymond C., and Brian E. Reynolds: *Dictionary of Australasian Signs*, Victorian School for Deaf Children, Melbourne, 1982.

J. W. Flynn

Australian Aboriginal

Complex gesture systems or sign languages are traditional alternatives to speech in some Australian Aboriginal societies. They are used by deaf persons in the southern, central, and western desert regions of Australia; coastal Arnhem Land; some of the islands of the north coast; the western side of the Cape York peninsula; and the islands of the Torres Strait. Use of sign language has never been reported from the coastal regions east of the Great Dividing Range or from southeast Australia.

The most complex of these sign languages are those used in the central desert regions. Among such groups as the Aranda, Warlpiri, or Warumungu, sign language has been most highly developed by women who do not speak when in mourning. A woman bereaved of her spouse, child,

or daughter's husband may remain silent for a year or more. Her immediate sisters and certain other female relatives of the deceased may also observe a period of silence, although not for as long a time. During such periods, sign language is used, sometimes accompanied by a sort of grunting.

Sign language may also be used in normal daily life, such as for conversation at a distance or in situations where the use of speech is difficult, for example, between the front seat and payload passengers in a truck. It is also commonly used as an accompaniment to speech.

In some groups, sign language is also used extensively by men. Among the Mudbura and Djingili of north-central Australia, sign language was, until recently, required of young men during male initiation ceremonies. It is also reported that, among the Djingili, men without gray hair observe a period of silence when in mourning, just as the women do. The use of manual signs by men during hunting has often been reported from many different places. Such signs may also serve as a means of communication between speakers of different languages, but this is not well attested.

Study of the sign languages in use by the women of central desert groups shows that large vocabularies have been developed. In Warlpiri sign language, according to one analysis, 40 different handshapes are employed, 19 articulation locations, and 22 distinct movements. Three-quarters of the signs require only one hand. Only two signs have been recorded that involve the use of facial action. Contrary to the findings on sign languages in most deaf communities, facial action appears not to have any grammatical functions in Warlpiri sign language. Signs match words in the spoken language, and many signs parallel the structure of the words they match. For example, in Warlpiri there are a number of words that, although different in meaning, differ in form only because one adds a repetition, as in *wanta*, "sun," and *wantawanta*, "red ant." The sign for "red ant" adds a repetition of the sign for "sun." Similarly, many verbs in Warlpiri are compounds, and likewise, the signed equivalents of these verbs are compounds.

Sophisticated signers can also use signs to render several of the case and derivational endings of the spoken language. However, tense is not expressed in sign, nor are there signed equivalents for the endings by which the grammatical relations of subject and object are indicated. Modulation of manner of sign movement and of variation in direction of movement is used in this sign language to express different meanings to a limited extent. The use of spatial location for pronominal reference in discourse has also been observed.

Comparative study of sign languages in several central desert groups shows that there is considerable variation in vocabulary from one community to another. Although as much as 60 percent of the sign vocabulary may be held in common by adjacent communities, groups more widely separated may share less than one-quarter of their signs. The proportion of signs shared between different language communities, however, is always higher than the proportion of shared spoken words.

As far as can be determined, these Australian Aboriginal sign languages differ from primary (deaf) sign languages in ways that suggest that they have evolved in the direction of becoming a signed version of the associated spoken language. Those signers who are the most fluent in the use of sign language and who command the largest vocabularies are also the ones who come closest to a detailed rendition of the spoken language in manual form. In this respect they differ markedly from deaf and hearing users of signed versions of spoken language (such as Signed English), who tend to abandon the structures of the spoken language in their signing as they become more fluent.

Bibliography

Kendon, A.: "Iconicity in Warlpiri Sign Language," in R. Posner, M. Herzfeld, and P. Bouissac (eds.), *Iconicity: Essays on the Nature of Culture*, Stauffenberg Verlag, Tübingen, 1985.

————: "Knowledge of Sign Language in an Australian Aboriginal Community," *Journal of Anthropological Research*, 40:556–576, 1984.

————: "Sign Language of the Women of Yuendumu: A Preliminary Report on the Structure of Warlpiri Sign Language," *Sign Language Studies*, 27: 101–112, 1980.

Umiker-Sebeok, D. J., and T. A. Sebeok (eds.): *Aboriginal Sign Languages of the Americas and Australia*, vol. 2, *The Americas and Australia*, Plenum Press, New York, 1978.

Wright, C.: *Warlpiri Hand Talk*, Northern Territory Department of Education, Darwin, 1980.

Adam Kendon

Belgian

Although research in Belgian Sign Language has only begun, it appears that Belgian Sign Language has many of the same characteristics found in other sign languages, such as the use of space for syntactic purposes and movement for morphological marking. Belgian Sign Language should be considered as a general term for a variety of dialects used by deaf people in Belgium. Its roots are mainly in the sign language used in deaf schools. The first schools for deaf people adopted signs from the (Old) French Sign Language either directly or indirectly. It is not possible to cite a date for the introduction of sign language in Belgium, although contacts with

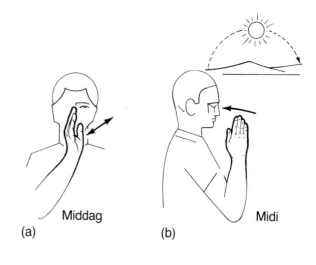

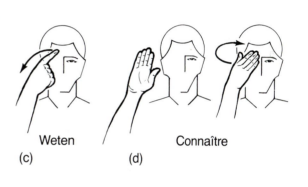

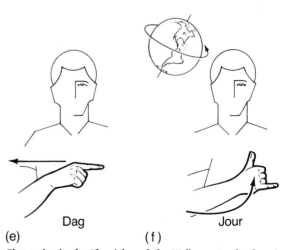

Sign pairs in the Flemish and the Walloon standard variation. (a, b) Identical signs, meaning "noon" (Flemish, MIDDAG; Walloon, MIDI). (c, d) Similar signs, meaning "know" (Flemish, WETEN; Walloon, CONNAITRE). (e, f) Different signs, meaning "day" (Flemish, DAG; Walloon, JOUR). (After Federatie van Nederlandstalige Dovenverenigingen, *Woord en Gebaar*, 1983)

the Paris National Institute in the period 1820–1830 can be considered crucial.

A special kind of Signed Dutch, the system Van Beek, which was designed in Sint-Michielsgestel, Holland, to represent Dutch in a manual way (including invented signs for prefixes, plural endings, and so on) has also had a limited influence on Belgian Sign Language. This artificial sign code was supposed to facilitate the learning of Dutch by deaf students. However, its use has remained restricted to the northeast Flemish region of Belgium.

Admitting the existence of significant regional variants, it still seems legitimate to speak of one Belgian Sign Language. Despite the fact that two languages are spoken in Belgium (Dutch in the North and French in the South), the sign language dialects used in the North and South are surprisingly similar. In one study, conducted in 1984, the Flemish-Walloon correlation appeared to be among the highest, much higher than the Flemish-Dutch (from the Netherlands) correlation. One of the reasons for this similarity of sign language dialects across Belgium is that in Brussels three schools for deaf pupils (possibly accounting for one-third of the Belgian deaf youth in the past) have been open for deaf children from the Flemish as well as from the French part of the country. Also the fact that these schools were led by Catholic sisters and brothers who ruled schools in Flanders gives evidence for the existence of Belgian Sign Language. Belgium's very small size and dense population are also important factors that favor one sign language.

Exact figures about Flemish and Walloon sign variation are only partially available.

Since the 1970s, two independent phenomena in Belgium seem to have influenced sign language development. On the one hand, the Belgian political structure is tending toward a relative federalization into a Dutch-speaking northern area and a French-speaking southern area. This encourages deaf clubs to associate separately according to the Flemish-Walloon distinction (for example, in order to get funds). It also makes contacts and collaboration between the Flemish schools and the French schools more difficult.

A second development is related to a new appreciation of sign and sign language since the later 1970s. This has encouraged deaf people to defend their use of signs in a country with a strong oralist tradition. While the deaf people prefer to use Belgian Sign Language among themselves, they support the development of Signed Dutch/Signed French (Nederlands met Gebaren/le Français Signé) as an interface communication system between hearing and deaf people. They think these manual codes are easier for parents, teachers of deaf students, consultants, and so on, to learn. The training of interpreters that started in 1981 was originally centered on providing fluency in Signed Dutch/Signed French, but the demand for knowledge of regional sign variants and pure sign language mechanisms has become an added objective of the training programs.

Another factor influencing the development of Belgian Sign Language has been the publication of sign vocabularies that are the proposed standard lexicons for the Walloon and the Flemish regions. These books were edited by two deaf language planning committees, the Federatie van Nederlandstalige Dovenverenigingen (for Flanders) and the Commission Francophone du Langage des Sourds (for Wallonia).

Belgian Sign Language research has been highly influenced by research on American Sign Language and has mainly focused on identification of sign variants, phonological aspects, and developmental studies of deaf children acquiring signs together with other communication codes. Future research is expected to elaborate on these topics and start to focus on syntactic structures and mechanisms. *See* BELGIUM.

Bibliography

Bunkens, M., K. Ceustermans, and V. Van Wassenhove: "Een exploratief onderzoek naar het voorkomen van dialectzones van Gebaartekens in Vlaanderen," unpublished dissertation, Antwerp, KVH, 1984.

Claeys, O.: "De eerste decennia van doovenonderwijs in schoolverband in Belgie," in *Liber Amicorum Prof. Dr. V. D'Espallier*, Universitaire Pers, Leuven, pp. 187–209, 1976.

Commission Francophone du Langage des Sourds: *Dictionnaire du Langage des Signes*, Liege, 1983.

Federatie van Nederlandstalige Dovenverenigingen: *Woord en Gebaar*, Gent-Gentbrugge, 1983.

Woll, B.: "The Comparative Study of Different Sign Languages: Preliminary Analyses," in F. Loncke, P. Boyes-Braem, and Y. Lebrun (eds.): *Recent Research in European Sign Languages*, Lisse, Swets, and Zeitlinger, pp. 79–91, 1984.

Filip Loncke

Brazilian

The sign language of Brazil is remarkably homogeneous for so large a country. Although there are different dialects, they appear to pose no barrier to communication among members of the deaf community throughout most of the country. The northern states, however, are separated from the main portion of Brazil by the Amazon River. Their sign language has not yet been studied, but it likely differs more from the dialects of the central and southern states than these latter dialects differ from each other.

A major exception to the relative homogeneity of Brazilian Sign Language may be found among isolated tribes of South American Indians. When a sufficient number of deaf persons live in a tribal area to develop a sign language, it usually is not the same as the sign language of the larger deaf community.

The homogeneity found in the sign language of Brazil is probably a result of the unifying influence of the first school for deaf people in Brazil, founded in Rio de Janeiro in 1857 by Ernesto Huet, a French deaf teacher. The school is attended by deaf children from all over Brazil. Following the Milan conference in 1880, Brazilian schools for deaf children adopted exclusively oral educational approaches. Recently, however, there has been an increased interest in Brazilian Sign Language both by linguists and by educators. At least one school, Escola Especial Concordia in Porto Alegre, has officially adopted total communication as its philosophy. *See* EDUCATION: Communication; HISTORY: Congress of Milan.

There is internal evidence of a connection between Brazilian Sign Language and the sign languages of Europe and North America. Brazil's one-handed alphabet is very similar to the alphabet published by J. Pablo Bonet and used by Abbé de l'Epée and Sicard. Since the alphabet corresponds to written Portuguese, it includes a "c" cedilla and four accents. Fingerspelling is used in Brazilian Sign Language for proper names, such as INSTITUTO EDUCATIONAL DE SÃO PAULO (São Paulo Institute); for abbreviations of proper names, such as C.E.E.E. (the public utility); for fingerspelled signs, such as SIM (yes), OU (or), AZUL (blue); for technical terms, such as LITOGRAFIA (lithography); and for emphasis, such as NUNCA (never). The manual alphabet also is used to make initialized signs, such as FUTURO (future) signed with the "F" hand and VINHO (wine) signed with the "V" hand. *See* PABLO BONET, JUAN.

Brazilian Sign Language appears to have a completely adequate vocabulary for ordinary social purposes within the deaf community. Signers are able to convey a variety of nuances not only by their choice of vocabulary but also by means of a variety of grammatical inflections and other changes in the way in which signs are executed. Head movements and facial expression have important grammatical functions, including showing that a sentence is a command or a question. Signers use visual cues, especially changes in the direction of their eye gaze, to control the flow of conversations. The ends of sentences or phrases are indicated with pauses, changes in eye gaze or body orientation, and changes in the rhythm of signing.

Classifiers (handshapes that represent or describe certain types or "classes" of objects) are used extensively as a means of pronominal reference. Upright index fingers brought together in neutral space may represent two persons meeting. The vertical left index finger may represent a post as the right hand, palm down, represents a car skidding on a curve and striking it.

The space around the signer's body also has important grammatical uses in Brazilian sign discourse, affording a frame of reference for directional verbs, for indexing real or imagined referents, and for spatial agreement between verbs and their subjects and objects. Space may also be used for graphic descriptions, such as proposed improvements for the Porto Alegre deaf club, including a barbecue, a fence, a paved driveway to the street, and lights on both sides of the driveway. *See* BRAZIL.

Bibliography

Brito, L. F.: "Similarities and Differences in Two Brazilian Sign Languages," *Sign Language Studies*, vol. 42, Spring 1984.

Hoemann, H. W., E. Oates, and S. A. Hoemann (eds.): *Linguagem de Sinais do Brasil*, Centro Educacional para Deficientes Auditivos, Porto Alegre, 1983.

Oates, E.: *Linguagem das mãos*, Gráfica Editora Livro, Rio de Janeiro, 1969.

Harry W. Hoeman

British

British Sign Language (BSL) is the language of the deaf community of the United Kingdom (including Northern Ireland). It is a rich and highly complex language of the hands, face, and eyes that uses space, movements, and time to create its meanings. Though British sign language was ignored for almost 100 years, its study now helps to provide more knowledge about the nature of language in general.

The deaf community in the United Kingdom consists of those whose attitude toward their own deafness and desire to communicate bring them

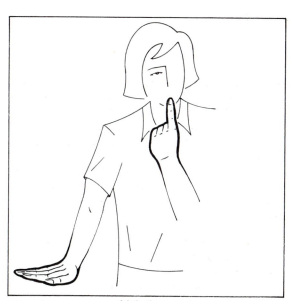

Little/boy

Simultaneity: LITTLE/BOY.

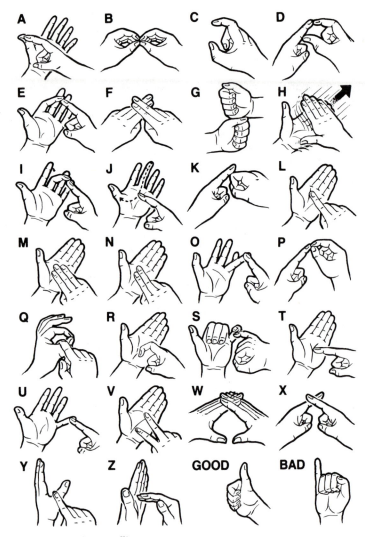

Two-handed fingerspelling.

when they do, they marry other deaf people (92 percent). The deaf population is closely knit with well-structured regional and national organizations. The cohesiveness of the deaf community enables deaf signers to communicate comfortably with each other despite all the regional differences in BSL vocabulary and dialect. Increasing television exposure of BSL (as distinct from manually coded English) is also decreasing the amount of regional variations as well as elevating the status of BSL and promoting its acceptance.

Records of BSL can be traced back to J. Bulwer's *Chirologia* (1644) and *Philocophus* (1648) which, unlike other works of the time, were actually based on knowledge of deaf people communicating. The two-handed fingerspelling used throughout the United Kingdom and in the Commonwealth first appeared in an anonymous pamphlet, *Digiti Lingua* (1680). However, BSL became more commonly recognized when deaf schools were established in the late eighteenth century; some form of BSL was in use at Braidwood's first school. By the mid-nineteenth century, the British combined method of education, which relied on both signs and English, was recognizable as distinct from the German and French methods. Even the writings of Charles Dickens mentioned this use of signs in the schools. Understanding of BSL reached its peak with the writings of E. Tylor (1874) and W. Scott (1870). This knowledge was subsequently lost in the race for oralism and has only begun to be relearned as the total oral approach has come under serious questioning. BSL is now the domain of educators, linguists, psychologists, and an increasing corps of deaf researchers and tutors. *See* BRAIDWOOD, THOMAS; EDUCATION: Communication.

There is as yet no official recognition of BSL (and legislative intervention of this sort would be unusual in the United Kingdom), but there is increasingly widespread acceptance of BSL through research efforts and deaf people's higher profile. As is the case in most countries where the progress of signing has been examined, attitudes to BSL are confounded by manually coded English forms of signing. The pattern at individual, institutional, and national levels shows a shift from oral-only communication, to manually coded forms of speech, and then to the natural sign language. However, this natural form of BSL, perhaps because of its suppression in schools, has been little influenced by educational borrowings from English. Like other natural sign languages, BSL appears to have a topic-comment structure, but description of its elements is still at an early stage. Complex use of classifiers and the appearance of simultaneity, where two meaningful sign units appear together in time, increase the task of accurate description of BSL. Similarly, the rich inflection system of BSL, in which

into regular interaction with each other. The community goes beyond the confines of deaf social clubs and incorporates those from different educational backgrounds. The common language of this community is BSL. There is no adequate figure for the number of users of BSL because of the attitudinal aspect of use, but up to 30,000 deaf people in the United Kingdom have profound hearing losses and have had educational provision in BSL because of their deafness.

Deaf parents have hearing children about 90 percent of the time, and deaf children are mostly born to hearing parents (only 5–6 percent are born to two deaf parents). In the home, the language used is predominantly English, so deaf people have to marry into the deaf community in order to use BSL at home. Deaf people are less likely to marry (65 percent) than are hearing people (75 percent), but

Book

Books

Plurals with repetition of movement: BOOK and BOOKS.

Bibliography
Brennan, M., et al.: *Words in Hand*, Moray House College, Edinburgh, 1984.

Deuchar, M.: *British Sign Language*, Hutchinson, London, 1984.

Kyle, J. G., and B. Woll: *Sign Language: The Study of Deaf People and Their Language*, Cambridge University Press, 1985.

Scott, W. R.: *The Deaf and Dumb*, Bell and Daldy, London, 1870.

Tylor, E. B.: *Researchers into the Early History of Mankind*, Murray, London, 1874.

J. G. Kyle

Canadian

Canada has 10 provinces: Newfoundland, Nova Scotia, New Brunswick, Prince Edward Island, Québec, Ontario, Manitoba, Saskatchewan, Alberta, and British Columbia—and the Yukon and Northwest Territories. Its population is nearly 22,000,000, of whom more than 40 percent are of British descent and approximately 30 percent are of French descent.

Canada has two official languages, English and French, with both accorded equal status by the Canadian constitution. Deaf culture and sign languages in Canada have also evolved along bilingual lines. At least two wholly distinct, indigenous sign languages are known to exist: Canadian Sign Language (CSL) and Langue des Signes Québécoise (LSQ). The former is used primarily by deaf persons with close cultural ties to the English community, while the latter is used primarily among French deaf persons throughout Canada (with the largest concentration of users residing in Québec). Anecdotal evidence suggests the existence of two other distinct sign languages, one used by Eskimos in the northern regions and one, called Maritime Sign Langue, that was used by the deaf community in Nova Scotia (but now is remembered only by older deaf people). However, neither of these has been investigated formally.

HISTORY

Although CSL and LSQ are structurally and grammatically distinct sign languages, used by distinct cultural groups, many questions remain concerning their relationship to other sign languages. Some signers report that CSL shares structural properties with the sign language that is used by deaf persons in England, British Sign Language (BSL). Others report that LSQ shares certain properties with the sign language used among deaf persons in France, Langue des Signes Française (LSF). Further, the extent to which either CSL or LSQ shares important

the way signs move changes to show person or number and in which verbs can also give information about time and aspect, makes for a mammoth linguistic task, to complete its description.

As seen by a comparison of their grammatical structures, BSL and English are quite separate languages; their main connection is through the distinctive two-handed manual alphabet which is based on the English alphabet. BSL is a developing language, and as it gains greater acceptance among the hearing community, both its use and the understanding of it will increase. *See* UNITED KINGDOM.

structural properties with the sign language used in the neighboring United States, American Sign Language (ASL), is not fully understood; preliminary evidence, however, does point to a strong overlap between ASL and CSL, but not ASL and LSQ.

There are at least two reasons for the minimal structural overlap between ASL and LSQ. First, the differences between the two sign languages reflect their natural evolution within two distinct cultures. Second, the population who are French, are deaf, and communicate primarily in LSQ represent a small, isolated minority. In northern Québec, for example, there are still pockets of signing French deaf people who for generations have had little contact with the outside world. As recently as the early 1970s, French deaf children were educated in religious environments that were strictly segregated on the basis of sex: males went to residential schools run by priests who were largely educated in France and provided an LSF-LSQ environment, while females went to residential schools that were run by nuns who were influenced by schools in the United States and provided an ASL-LSQ environment. This has resulted in lexical (but not syntactic) variation between French deaf males and females.

Those deaf children in the English community who attend schools working within a total communication philosophy are often exposed to some form of manually coded English (such as Signed English, as well as Pidgin Sign English). Similarly, deaf children from the French community are frequently exposed to some form of manually coded French (such as Signed French, as well as Pidgin Sign French). It is extremely rare for a deaf child to receive formal bilingual instruction in both LSQ and CSL. Although some adults do achieve a working knowledge of the sign language to which they were not formally exposed, most do not.

Finally, preliminary research has revealed that both CSL and LSQ have grammatical properties that are largely independent of the majority, spoken languages in Canada (English and French, respectively).

CURRENT STATUS

Although Canada's institutions traditionally have supported an oral rather than sign-based educational philosophy for deaf individuals, the current approach supports the total communication philosophy of education. Additionally, serious interest in deafness and especially in sign language research has emerged both nationally and regionally. Nationally, the need for research in sign language was acknowledged in the 1981 report of the Special Parliamentary Committee on the Disabled and the Handicapped. The report urged the federal govern-

ment, working through the Canadian Council of Deafness and its affiliates, to encourage the establishment of sign language departments at an English-speaking university and at a French-speaking university. These departments would recognize sign language as a distinct language, developing curricula and standards similar to those of other language courses, and they would train sign language interpreters to permit deaf students to follow regular courses. Moreover, the federal government, acknowledging sign languages as real languages, has given them equal status to other languages in its Translation Bureau of the office of the Secretary of State.

Four university-based research progams for the study of deafness have emerged: McGill University, the University of British Columbia, Université de Moncton (New Brunswick), and the University of Alberta. Other programs in residential schools and community colleges throughout Canada provide training for teachers of deaf children. Further, programs designed for the training of skilled sign language interpreters have been established, including those at the University of Toronto and the University of New Brunswick.

Serious interest in sign language research exists on the regional level as well. The Canadian Coordinating Council on Deafness is sponsoring research on and development of a standard dictionary of CSL. Researchers at the University of Alberta have begun analyses of the dialectal variations of CSL in three Prairie provinces—Alberta, Saskatchewan, and Manitoba—and they are also preparing a dictionary of these regional variations. Research on the structure and grammar of LSQ has begun at the Institut Raymond-Dewar in Montréal. These researchers have completed a standard dictionary of LSQ. Finally, research on the acquisition of LSQ and CSL, the linguistic structure of LSQ and CSL, as well as on the psycholinguistic processing of sign languages, has begun by researchers in McGill University's psychology department.

STRUCTURE

Research on the structure and grammar of Canadian sign languages is still in its infant stage. Except for compilations of the lexicon into dictionaries, almost nothing is known about the precise linguistic structures and grammatical processes associated with either LSQ or CSL at this time. Preliminary linguistic analyses by researchers in McGill University's psychology department have revealed that certain structural properties of sign language appear to be universal and modality-specific. As has been observed in ASL (and other sign languages), systematic changes in movement, space, and facial expressions are the primary linguistic devices for signaling changes in meaning in both

LSQ and CSL. For example, patterned contours of movement can be added to specific classes of signs to change their meanings in regular ways. Signs are established at abstract spatial indices in front of the signer's body in both CSL and LSQ; these spatial indices play a central role in pronominal and anaphoric referencing. Certain classes of verbs move between spatial indices, thereby marking grammatical subject and object and forming the nucleus of the verb agreement system in the two sign languages. Furthermore, specific facial expressions modify certain grammatical classes of signs and serve important syntactic functions in both sign languages.

While there appears to be some overlap in the phonemic inventories of LSQ and CSL (and ASL), many formational features in LSQ mark phonemic distinctions that are simply absent from CSL or ASL, appearing instead to be unique to the phonological system of LSQ. Although the global contours of CSL and LSQ have been mapped out, the precise inventory of linguistic units (on both the phonological and morphological levels) and the rules for combining them await discovery; an understanding of these issues is currently the focus of intensive research. *See* CANADA.

Bibliography

Bourcier, P., and J. Roy: *La Langue des Signes (LSQ)*, Publication Bourcier & Roy, Québec, 1985.

MacDougall, J. C.: "Education of the Deaf in Canada: An Update," *Canadian Psychological Review*, 1:53–58, 1979.

Mayberry, R.: "French Canadian Sign Language: A Study of Inter-Sign Language Comprehension," in P. Siple, *Understanding Language Through Sign Language Research*, pp. 349–372, Academic Press, New York, 1978.

Nickerson, Forrest: *Deaf Heritage in Canada*.

Petitto, L. A.: " 'Language' in the Pre-linguistic child," in Kessel (ed.), *The Development of Language and Language Researchers*, LEA, Hillsdale, New York, 1986.

Laura Petitto

Chinese

Chinese Sign Language (CSL) is the standard gestural medium of communication among deaf people in Mainland China. It was proposed by the Sign Language Reform Committee in the late 1950s, and in 1961 the Ministry of Internal Affairs and the Ministry of Education jointly published a book containing some 2000 signs (*An Initial Version of Standard Signs for the Deaf*). Another 1000 signs were added in its 1979 and 1981 editions. The lexicon in this book comprises dialectal signs common to most regions, and newly invented ones intended to fill lexical gaps in topics such as farming, cottage industry, kinship ties, and politics. A total of 41 recurrent handshapes (not counting the neutral, relaxed handshape) appear in this lexicon.

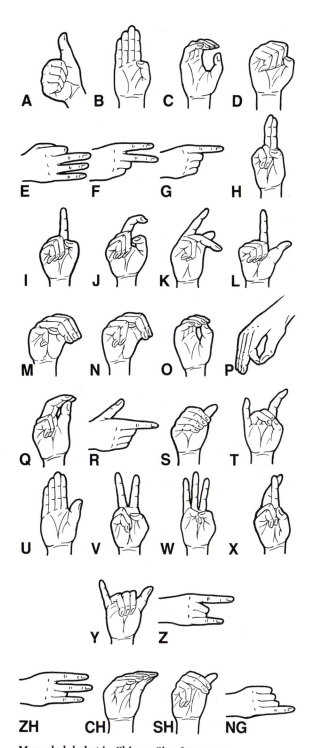

Manual alphabet in Chinese Sign Language.

The ultimate goal of the Reform Committee was to provide the deaf population with a full-scale standard sign lexicon while continuing to tolerate dialectal signs, the most influential of which are those of the Shanghai dialect. As for syntax, the authorities concerned merely pointed out that sign ordering in gestural sequences, as performed by Chinese deaf people, basically has the verb in the final position and the modified followed by the modifier, for example: CAT MOUSE CATCH; BOY CHAIR SIT; EAT NOT; GIRL BEAUTIFUL THREE. Officials had hoped that this sign order would fall into line with the Chinese subject-verb-object type of word order through increasing exposure of deaf persons to Chinese written language.

MANUAL ALPHABET

Apart from a list of standard signs for names of foreign countries, such as the Soviet Union, Sweden, and the United States, there are very few signs in CSL or in the dialects that can be suspected to be of foreign origin. Even though the first school for deaf Chinese was set up in 1887 by the American missionary C. R. Mills and his wife, ASL did not make any impact on the Chinese signs. The Mills couple, however, should be given credit for initiating a manual alphabet, albeit shortlived, in the Chinese sign system. The present manual alphabet (26 letters and 4 digraphic consonants) was designed in 1958 and officially adopted in 1963.

The manual alphabet is meant to fingerspell words and is mainly used as a pedagogical vehicle in schools. Deaf signers seldom use it among themselves. When they want to refer to the graphic form of a character, deaf people tend to write it on the palm or in the air. Nevertheless, the manual alphabet marks its presence in CSL's neologisms. For example, functional words in spoken Chinese are rendered as abbreviation signs (*yin-wei*, "because" = Y + W) or as initialized signs (*jiu*, "then, soon" = put the hooked index finger of the J-hand on the other palm, and draw the J-hand inward).

CHARACTER SIGNS

Characters (or ideograms) are still the current form of writing for the Chinese. Twenty-two of them are found in CSL. The campaign to simplify ideograms encouraged the creation of more such signs. Many of these character signs are well integrated into the sign system in that they are capable of incorporating other morphemic elements. For example, the character sign MAN (both index fingers pointing up obliquely, the tip of one against the second joint of the other), when made with a horizontal circular movement, signifies "there are people all around"; if an oriented movement is given to the sign INTRODUCE (L-hand pointing obliquely downward, its inner arc, formed by the thumb and index finger, resting on the fingertips of a V-hand pointing obliquely upward), it can specify who is introducing (someone or something) to whom; PUBLIC (one hand with its thumb and index circle forming a circle inside the arc of an L-hand, palm downward) can take a derived meaning of "for-

The sign INTRODUCE.

The sign PUBLIC.

feited to the public weal, confiscated" if the hand with the small circle pivots downward.

TABOOS

In the 1960s, the proposed CSL was criticized by people who insisted that certain vernacular signs retained by it should be dropped because of their association with the "corrupt" life of the past. For example, the signs GOLD and FEMALE were considered to be ideologically and politically unsuitable because they reminded people of the custom of wearing gold rings and earrings. The signs PEKING and CAT also lost favor because the former suggests a mayor wearing a sash and the latter reflects the way in which "bourgeois" people caress their pets. Still, the vernacular forms of these items continue to appear in the lexicon of CSL.

Certain signs, also considered to be taboo, were eliminated from CSL publications, two noteworthy examples being JAPAN and MAO ZEDONG. JAPAN, before the Sino-Japanese War (1937–1945), was signed by putting a fist (the sun) on the other palm (the horizon)—a reference to the etymology of "Japan" as read in Kanji or Chinese. But, since the war, Chinese signers have expressed their sentiments by reversing the action into the insulting gesture of hitting the thumb side of a fist with the other palm. With improved relations between the two countries, this pejorative sign has had to be replaced by yet another one. The sign for MAO (tip of index finger touching corner of chin—a reference to Mao's prominent mole) is considered to show a lack of respect for the great leader and has been officially replaced by M + PRESIDENT or M + AUTHORITY. Despite official prescription, deaf people may not be so prompt to change their linguistic habits.

USERS

Officially there are 3 million deaf people in China. The number of these people using CSL is still a matter of conjecture. Schools for deaf people and workshops or farms exclusively for deaf adults are the two principal channels for the propagation of CSL. Those who have no exposure to these channels—probably a great many, if not the majority of China's deaf population—continue using their own dialectal signs or home signs (this is especially true of people living in the remote countryside). With a total of 3000 lexical items available in CSL, it is certain that even those who have mastered CSL often continue to use portions of their own dialects as well. *See* CHINA, PEOPLE'S REPUBLIC OF.

Bibliography

Yau, Shun-chiu: *The Chinese Signs: Lexicon of the Standard Sign Language for the Deaf in China*, Langages Croisés, Paris-Hongkong, 1977.

———: "Ombres Linguistiques Chinoises," *Coup d'Oeil*, no. 39, Ecole des Hautes Etudes en Sciences Sociales, Paris, 1984.

Zhou, Youguang: "The Chinese Finger Alphabet and the Chinese Finger Syllabary," *Sign Language Studies*, 28: 209–216, 1980.

Shun-chiu Yau

Danish

In Denmark deaf people consider themselves a linguistic minority with Danish Sign Language (DSL) as their primary language. Approximately 3500 people are deaf. The five schools for deaf students

are all manual, and most of the mainstream programs, which integrate deaf children into hearing schools, accept manual communication.

HISTORY

The first school for deaf pupils was established in 1807 with teaching methods based on sign language. Its founder, P. A. Castberg, had adopted these methods from the Abbé de l'Epée in France. Castberg described how his students were already using sign language, and how he developed teaching methods and materials on the basis of this language. When there was not a sign for a certain concept, he borrowed a French sign. This early influence from French Sign Language can still be recognized in the DSL vocabulary.

The first oral school was established 1881, but DSL was never totally banned from the school system. Danish Sign Language kept developing because the small size and the flat geography of Denmark allows easy social interaction among deaf people. *See* DENMARK.

CURRENT STATUS

Spoken Danish's influence on DSL is limited primarily to vocabulary borrowing. When DSL signs are combined with spoken language, it is not really DSL. It is called Signed Danish or, as deaf people label it, "hearing people's sign language." This type of signing is used mostly in communication between deaf and hearing persons and in interpreting. Traditionally this has been considered "good language," whereas DSL was "poor" language.

A radical change, however, has occurred since the 1970s, and the status of DSL has grown both within and outside the deaf community. In 1979 the Danish Association of the Deaf (LF) passed a resolution on DSL, which claimed the rights of deaf people to have their own language and bilingual education with DSL as their first language. This resolution has been supported by the parents' associations. In 1982 two schools started bilingual programs with DSL as the first language. All teachers of deaf pupils are taught DSL or Signed Danish, and parents are encouraged to attend courses in total communication and DSL. Danish Sign Language is used on television and video productions for deaf children and adults, whereas combined signing and speech dominated in the past. Deaf people are entitled to full interpreting services in continuing education courses (after eight years of school). Deaf teachers and teachers' assistants are employed by deaf schools.

Still, DSL is not officially recognized as a language for several reasons: it cannot be studied at universities or colleges; no formal education for in-

[1] **IT-IS** (index left) [2] **RECENTLY** (just) [3] **TALK-ABOUT** [4] **I** [5] **HAVE-BOUGHT** [6] **CAR.** Translation: It's her over there, I've just talked about, who has bought a car.

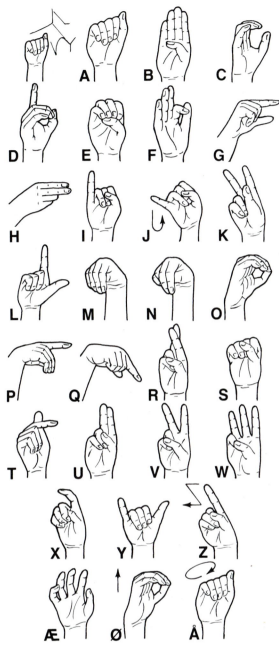

The International Hand Alphabet plus three Danish signs.

Danish Sign Language features that have been described are: simultaneity, spatialization, word order, sentence markers, time and aspect, verb modulations, lexical borrowing, noun-verb pairs, pronominalization, and proforms.

In the example shown in the illustration, the simultaneous use of hands, mouth, eyes, head, and facial expressions occurs all through the sentence. In the sign IT-IS, for example, the mouth movement is as necessary a part of the sign as the four manual aspects—hand configuration, movement, placement, and orientation—whereas the shift in eye gaze helps to define whom the signer is talking about and whom the signer is talking to. The head tilt and the tense facial expression accompanying the next four signs define this part of the whole sentence as a subordinate clause. In the sign RECENTLY, the mouth movement modulates the sign to mean "just recently." HAVE-BOUGHT is a modulation of BUY, where the original repeated movement of the sign is changed to a single, abrupt movement. Furthermore, the signs RECENTLY, TALK-ABOUT, and I are produced while simultaneously holding the IT-IS sign.

Spatialization in this example refers to the third person. Referring is done through the use of eye gaze and indexing. Based upon their relation to spatialization, DSL verbs are divided into three categories: directionalized, position placeable, and stationary verbs. The sign TALK-ABOUT is a stationary verb, and BUY is a position placeable verb.

The first DSL dictionary was published in 1872, and the 1979 dictionary included approximately 6000 Danish words and equivalent signs. The vocabulary of DSL is in the process of expanding as signing is used more extensively in media and educational programs, particularly when technical terms are included.

Mouth-Hand System (MHS) and fingerspelling have become integrated parts of DSL. Several signs are rooted in MHS and fingerspelling; MHS is used more extensively than fingerspelling. The International Hand Alphabet was introduced in 1975 by the World Federation of the Deaf for use in international conferences, and is now used with the old hand alphabet in Norway, Denmark, and Finland. *See* MOUTH-HAND SYSTEMS; WORLD FEDERATION OF THE DEAF.

Bibliography

Engberg-Pedersen, E., B. Hansen, and R. Kjær Sørensen: *Døves Tegnsprog: Træk of dansk tegnsprogs grammatik*, Arkona, 1981.

Hansen, B.: *Aspects of Deafness and Total Communication in Denmark*, Døves Center for Total Kommunikation, 1980.

Jørgensen, Johs: *Tegnsproget: Dets Væsen og dets Grammatik*, Jul. Gjellerup, 1910.

Britta Hansen

terpreters exists; and the main research and teaching in DSL is done by a private institution, the Center for Total Communication, with no public financial support.

STRUCTURE

The first description of DSL was published in 1910 by a minister, Johannes Jørgensen. Linguistic research on the grammar of DSL started in 1974, and the first "comprehensive" book on salient grammatical features was published in 1981.

Dutch

Of the Netherlands' 14,400,000 inhabitants, 3.4 percent (approximately 400,000 people) are hearing-impaired to the extent that understanding speech in a quiet environment is difficult; approximately 28,000 have no functional hearing at all. Each year about 175 children up to three years of age are diagnosed as deaf by sociomedical services and are enrolled in home training programs. There are about 20,000 deaf adults who use sign language.

It has been proposed that Dutch Sign Language be officially called Sign Language of the Netherlands (SLN). At least five varieties of SLN have been identified, each related to one of the five schools for deaf students. These schools have an enrollment of about 1500 pupils. The schools range from strictly oral (St. Michielsgestel) to moderately oral (Amsterdam, The Hague, Rotterdam), and one uses total communication (Groningen). *See* EDUCATION: Communication.

HISTORY

Henri Daniel Guyot, a Protestant minister in Groningen and descendant of a Huguenot refugee from France, came across the work of Charles Michel de l'Epée by accident while visiting Paris in 1784. Guyot stayed as Epée's guest for 10 months to study his method. When he returned home, he started to teach a deaf boy and girl by that method. In 1790 the first Dutch school for deaf children, based upon Epée's principles, was founded in Groningen. Guyot and later his two sons were its first directors. Sign language was the medium of communication, but some speech and speechreading were taught.

The school at St. Michielsgestel was founded in 1840; it used a variety of Signed Dutch (SLN augmented by signs invented for Dutch grammatical morphemes) artificially conceived by Martinus van Beek around 1827. This school did not give up its signing system in favor of speech until 1907. The three other schools, in Rotterdam (founded 1853), Leiden (1891; moved to Voorburg near The Hague in 1926), and Amsterdam (1911), were orally oriented from the beginning. Their pupils and alumni, however, have developed their own signs, some of which show the influence of the Groningen school—and so, indirectly, of Paris; other signs appear to be of local origin. The Van Beek signs have had little influence beyond the pupils and alumni of St. Michielsgestel, but can still be found among them. *See* L'EPÉE, ABBÉ CHARLES MICHEL DE; NETHERLANDS.

CURRENT STATUS

The current status of SLN is best characterized as transitional. In accordance with oral tradition, a few decades ago signing was considered primitive, interfering with abstract thinking, damaging speech, preventing integration, and so forth. The two main factors responsible for a rapid change toward a more positive attitude are new research findings and a stronger awareness among deaf adults of their own identity and rights. This awareness has been developed by the Dutch National Council of the Deaf (founded 1977), which is run by deaf persons themselves and includes all other deaf organizations in the Netherlands. The council presented itself quite successfully to the public at large through well-publicized national congresses in 1979 and 1983. There is close cooperation between the council officers and those engaged in sign language research. Their joint influence upon educational institutions, parents' organizations, government officials, and the public is clearly growing.

STRUCTURE

Before research started to prove otherwise, the communication of deaf individuals among themselves in the Netherlands was believed to be carried out in different varieties of Signed Dutch, with both signs and speech and, occasionally, some simplifications in grammar. The last were supposedly related to characteristic features of visual communication, such as leaving out function words and inflections. It has become evident, however, that this variety of Signed Dutch is a code used mostly in contexts where the influence of spoken Dutch is strong—for example, at official events or at meetings where hearing people are also present. In spontaneous conversations among deaf people, they appear to use a true sign language. When compared with other sign languages that have been studied for a longer period of time, the Dutch varieties show both specific and universal features. In other words, the grammar of SLN has its own specific rules, but features which are found in other sign languages, such as the American and British varieties, appear also in SLN. Some of the grammatical aspects, such as facial features to mark negations and questions, the use of directionality in verbs, and the use of classifiers, are clearly different from Dutch grammar but generically related to other sign languages. Classifiers that seem to occur most in SLN are the one-handshape to indicate persons or tall, thin objects, the B ↓ handshape to indicate cars and ships, and the V ↓ handshape to refer to animals or persons that are standing. The classifier used in American Sign Language to refer to cars is not found in SLN. The conclusion that the Dutch deaf population uses a true sign language seems warranted. *See* SOCIOLINGUISTICS: Sign Language Continuum.

Dutch finger alphabet. (From *Vingerspelling*, Stichting Nederlandse Dovenraad)

Bibliography

Ligtenberg, C. L. van, and H. Holboom: *Over horen en slecht horen* (*On Hearing and Impaired Hearing*), Stafleu, Alphen aan de Rijn, 1982.

Schermer, Trude: "Analysis of Natural Discourse Amongst Deaf Adults in The Netherlands," *Proceedings of the III International Symposium on Sign Language Research*, Rome, June 22–26, 1983.

Tervoort, Bernard T. (ed.): *Hand over Hand: Nieuwe inzichten in de communicatie van doven* (*Hand over Hand:*

New Insights in the Communication of the Deaf), Coutinho, Muiderberg, 1983.

Bernard T. Tervoort

Finnish

Finland is a northern European nation of 129,615 square miles (337,000 square kilometers) and approximately 5 million people. Its official languages are Finnish, Swedish, and Lappish (spoken in some parts of Lapland).

There are some 8000 deaf persons, of whom about 5000 use sign language as their primary means of communication. There are also many hearing people who can sign. The official name of the sign language is Finnish Sign Language (FinnSL); the national name is *viittomakieli*.

There are two major dialects of FinnSL, one used by those deaf persons who belong to the Finnish-speaking majority and the other used by the Swedish-speaking minority. The Swedish minority has 1 school compared with the 17 schools of the Finnish majority. Signing is accepted as a supportive device in the Finnish schools for deaf pupils. However, most teachers use Signed Finnish, not FinnSL; there are no deaf teachers for deaf children in Finland.

HISTORY

Throughout the history of FinnSL, there have been deaf individuals who have actively advanced the right of deaf people to have their own language. C. O. Malm, the founder of the first school for deaf individuals in the 1850s, was deaf himself. He had been studying in the Manilla School for the Deaf in Sweden, and he brought the Manilla dialect as well as the Swedish Manual Alphabet to Finland (The International Manual Alphabet has since replaced the Swedish Manual Alphabet). The Manilla dialect began to change very quickly as it merged with the indigenous dialects of the local population. The first dictionary of FinnSL (1910) was compiled by D. F. Hirn, one of Malm's first students.

After the Congress of Milan (1880) the oral method became prevalent, and FinnSL was no longer used in the education of deaf children until the beginning of the 1970s. The deaf community founded their own association in 1905 to defend their rights (the Finnish Association of the Deaf). This association has been very active in raising public awareness and respect for sign language. See HISTORY: Congress of Milan.

CURRENT STATUS

There are no sociolinguistic studies concerning the status of FinnSL or the prevailing attitudes of deaf

The 37 handshapes used in Finnish Sign Language.

and hearing people toward FinnSL. Younger deaf persons usually have a positive attitude toward FinnSL. However, deaf individuals disagree among themselves about which system of signing should be used in educating deaf children. The two competing systems are FinnSL and a pidgin-type of signing called Signed Finnish. Signed Finnish is a combination of the syntax of Finnish and the vocabulary of FinnSL. It is used by those signers for whom both channels of communication (hearing and sight) have been available, that is, hearing and hard-of-hearing persons and those who lost their hearing later in life. Deaf people who have learned Finnish can understand and produce Signed Finnish, but they do not use it among themselves.

Although the teachers of deaf students use Signed Finnish, the attitudes of most other hearing people toward FinnSL are positive. Most parents of deaf and hard-of-hearing children accept and use signing. Parents are offered government-paid courses on FinnSL. Many persons who meet deaf people in their occupations (social workers, nurses, kinder-garten teachers, deaconesses, and so on) are willing to study FinnSL.

The mass media are also interested in the sign language. There are some signed television programs (10 to 15 minutes a month). The Ministry of Education is supporting a major video project in which all deaf people are offered a video recorder, and are sent signed programs produced by the Finnish Association of the Deaf every month. The ministry also funds the sign language research projects housed at the Research Center for Domestic Languages.

FinnSL is used in practically all situations during the life of deaf persons. The government pays for interpreters who accompany deaf individuals to the hospital, college, church, festivals, meetings, and so on. The major problem is the shortage of interpreters.

STRUCTURE

Research on FinnSL began in the Department of General Linguistics at the University of Helsinki in

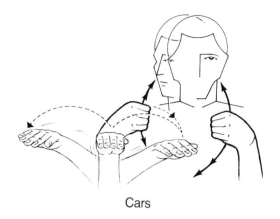

Cars

June 1982. Some structural features of FinnSL revealed by this research are presented below.

All signs have a substructure; a so-called cherematic or phonologic structure which consists of handshapes, places of articulation, and movements. There are 37 different handshapes in FinnSL; 31 of these are distinctive and the rest are variants. Six of the 31 handshapes are very rare, and they are not an integrated part of the core system of handshapes. There are 12 places (locations of signs) and 24 movements.

Handshapes have been classified into three main groups on the basis of the selected fingers. These groups are the none-finger (fist), one-finger, and multifinger handshapes. Two restrictions have been found in forming the handshapes: every multifinger handshape must include at least one finger which appears in a one-finger handshape; and the fingers

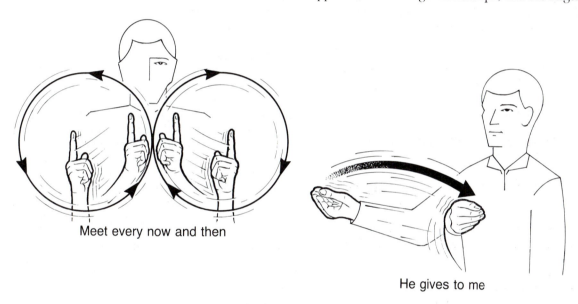

Meet every now and then

He gives to me

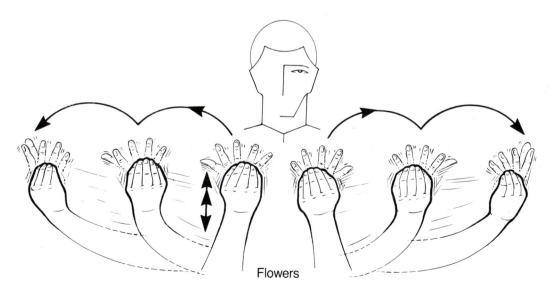

Flowers

that appear in a multifinger handshape must be either those beside each other or those farthest from each other.

Handshapes, places, and movements are central in the grammatical structure of FinnSL as well. The following grammatical processes have been observed: affixation (which uses handshape classifiers) and modification, which can be subdivided into aspectual modulations (involving changes in movement) and changes in orientation (involving specified places). Examples of these are AUTO+B+B+B "cars," TAVATA+freq "meet every now and then," and ANTAA2-1 "He gives to me." These grammatical processes have been observed in other sign languages as well. A third major grammatical process is reduplication, by which is meant repetition of a single movement root. Reduplication is a means of expressing number or plurality. Different signs are reduplicated in existential and agentive structures:

TUOLLA KUKKA-KUKKA-KUKKA-KUKKA
[KUKKA = flower]
Tuolla (on) kukkia.
"There (are) flowers there"

TYTTÖ KUKKA POIMIA-POIMIA-POIMIA
[POIMIA = pick]
Tyttö poimii kukat.
"The girl is picking up those flowers"

In existential structures, the nominal sign is reduplicated. When an agent is introduced into this kind of structure, the nominal sign remains in its basic form and, instead, the verb is repeated. This kind of reduplication is similar to the reduplication that occurs in aspectual modulations.

Terhi Rissanen

French

French Sign Language (Langue des Signes Française, or LSF) is the primary means of communication in the deaf community of France. LSF was the first sign language, at least in the Western world, to gain recognition as a language in itself. Because of the work of the Abbé de l'Epée and his disciples, LSF became in the nineteenth century the most influential sign language in the world.

HISTORY

A sign language was used in France as early as the sixteenth century and probably well before. The sixteenth-century essayist Michel Montaigne mentioned in 1580 that the signs used by deaf people must have a "gestural grammar." The observations of Pierre Desloges prove that the LSF of the eighteenth century was a fully formed and codified language. *See* DESLOGES, PIERRE.

At the end of the eighteenth and the beginning of the nineteenth centuries, the Abbé de l'Epée and the Abbé Sicard took certain signs from LSF, added some signs of their own invention to represent the grammatical structures of French, and created their famous "methodical signs" (the first attempt to make a sign language conform to the structures of a spoken language). *See* SICARD, ABBÉ ROCH AMBROISE CUCURRON.

The nineteenth century was marked by much publicized debates in the field of education between signers or followers of the French method, and oralists, those who believed in the German method supported by Samuel Heinicke. The publicity attracted the attention of large audiences of intellectuals and people in power from numerous countries. Disciples of the French method were sent all over the world, to Scandinavia, Austria, Italy, Spain, Russia, America. As a result, French signs were exported to many countries, with the most successful transplanting of French signs being in the United States. *See* HEINICKE, SAMUEL.

Some researchers have argued that 60 percent of modern American Sign Language (ASL) is derived from French signs. In France, when the failure of the artificial methodical signs became evident in the 1820s, Auguste Bébian (a hearing godson of Sicard) and his student Ferdinand Berthier argued that LSF, the "natural language of signs," should be recognized as the primary language of instruction for deaf students. The first deaf movement was thus born in France with the demand for recognition of those who were deaf as a people with their own language and the same rights as hearing people. *See* BERTHIER, JEAN-FERDINAND.

For a half century (1830–1880), LSF was taught in many of the classrooms of the large residential schools by deaf and hearing teachers. Bébian and Berthier began working on a system of notation for LSF, and in 1854 Y.-L. Rémi-Valade published his *Lexical and Grammatical Studies of Natural Sign Language*. Rémi-Valade, though he mistakenly insisted that sign language was universal and that it painted meanings in the air without the conventions of spoken languages, nevertheless did present some of the fundamental conventions, or grammatical rules, of LSF.

The battle between oralists and signers culminated in the Congress of Milan in 1880, after which signs were banned in French schools by ministerial decree. LSF again became a language learned and transmitted exclusively inside the deaf community. *See* HISTORY: Congress of Milan.

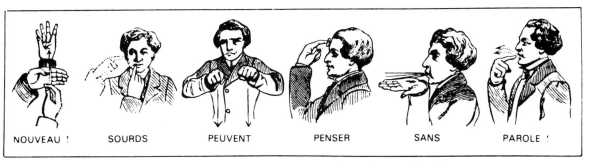

NOUVEAU ! SOURDS PEUVENT PENSER SANS PAROLE !

Some of the old French signs that were adopted into the ASL vocabulary (after P. Pélissier).

CURRENT STATUS

A second movement for the recognition of LSF appeared in the late 1970s because of dissatisfaction with the results of the educational system for deaf students in France and because of extensive contacts between French and Americans in the 1971 and 1975 congresses of the World Federation of the Deaf in Paris and in Washington. *See* WORLD FEDERATION OF THE DEAF.

Today, most of the classes in LSF are taught by deaf people outside established, deaf-related institutions. Classes are sponsored by private nonprofit associations that are trying to promote awareness of the deaf culture. Teachers with five or more years of experience are often called upon to train other deaf people to set up classes in other areas.

Schools for deaf students have been slow to accept signing in the classroom, and thus artificial versions of manual French have not been widely used. Simultaneous communication is tolerated in vocational training programs and for use with multiply handicapped people. LSF is practiced in only a few select experimental bilingual classes.

The French deaf movement is still far behind the American movement, and there is still very little linguistic research on LSF.

USE

LSF is the principal mode of communication for 50,000 to 100,000 signers in France (there is no census of the deaf population, and estimates vary widely). Primary users of LSF include native deaf signers, fluent deaf signers from hearing families who learned LSF early from their peers in residential schools, the few hearing children of deaf parents who learned LSF as children and who continue to use it in the deaf community, and deaf persons who were sent to school in France from former French colonies or possessions and remained there.

Since the late 1970s a growing number of hearing people who either have deaf children or teach in schools for deaf students are learning LSF as a second language, as are some hearing people who have heard some publicity about the deaf movement and are simply curious. Some hard-of-hear-

ing people have begun to enroll in LSF classes as the stigma attached to deafness lessens with such publicity. Immigrant adult deaf people from Arab countries in North Africa, from eastern Europe, and from Italy and Spain informally pick up some LSF upon arrival in France.

MAJOR VARIETIES

Like ASL signers, LSF signers use several varieties of signing, depending on the situation in which they find themselves: LSF and signed French, formal and informal levels of LSF, and regional variations in vocabulary. Differences in signs from one large residential school to another are greater than regional variations in the United States, probably because France never had the kind of continuous unifying standard that Gallaudet College has provided for American signing communities.

Variations between male and female users of LSF have declined greatly since boys and girls were allowed to attend classes together beginning in the 1960s. In spite of regional differences that some have considered very great (one can find as many as 10 different signs for a concept as basic as "mother"), fluent signers of either sex and from any area of France are able to understand each other without difficulty.

STRUCTURE

A preliminary survey of some basic grammatical structures of LSF published in 1983 indicates that LSF functions much as ASL does. On the phonological level, the handshapes used in French signs are pretty much the same as those in ASL, with the exception of the French "T" handshape. (There are

T

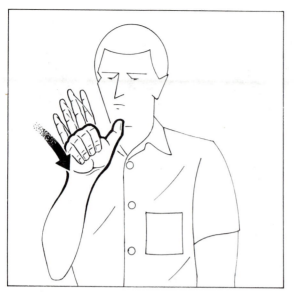

Example of the use of facial expression with hand parameters for signing: IMPOSSIBLE and HATE.

several other minor differences between the American and French manual alphabets.) In France, facial expression is generally accepted as the fifth parameter of sign formation in order to differentiate minimal sign pairs made with the same handshape, orientation, location, and movement, such as IMPOSSIBLE and HATE. Rules for combining the sign parameters seem to be the same in both languages, though there may be differences in where points of contact are allowed on certain handshapes.

The same processes for building new vocabulary that exist in ASL are present in LSF: combination of existing signs, initialization of signs (as yet in-frequent), fingerspelled loan words that are modified into signs, and so on. Signs are inflected for temporal aspect similarly to ASL.

Certain nouns and verbs are differentiated in the same manner as they are in ASL, though the difference in muscular tension between nouns and verbs in noun/verb pairs seems to be more important in LSF.

Use of classifiers is strikingly similar to that of ASL, though the familiar surface vehicle classifier ("3" handshape) in ASL is not used in LSF: LSF users make a vehicle with the flat hand palm down.

LSF verbs, like those of ASL, fall into three categories: verbs that change direction to incorporate

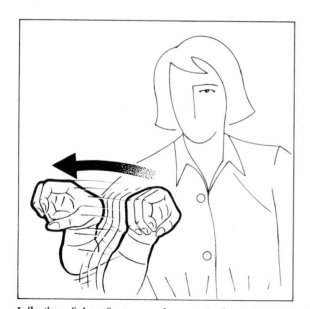

Inflection of signs for temporal aspect similar to ASL: PERSON GOES and PERSON-GOES-REPEATEDLY.

personal pronouns (I-GIVE-YOU, YOU-GIVE-ME); verbs that do not incorporate personal pronouns (KNOW, DO); and classifier verbs.

The facial expressions used in ASL to indicate the topic and to signal negative sentences, questions, and conditional and relative clauses are also found in LSF.

More serious linguistic research on LSF carried out by qualified linguists working with native LSF users will have to verify these hypotheses and point out more structural differences between these two sign languages, but the strong historical relationship between ASL and LSF and the similarities in their structures show clearly that they belong to the same language family.

Bibliography

Moody, W., et al.: *La Langue des Signes: Entre les Mains des Sourds*, International Visual Theater, Paris, 1983.

Pélissier, Pierre: *L'Enseignement primaire des sourds-muets mis à la portée de tout le monde, avec une iconographie des signes*, P. Dupont, Paris, 1856.

Rémi-Valade, Y.-L.: *Études sur la Lexicologie et la Grammaire du Langage Naturel des Signes*, Paris, 1854.

William Moody

German

In the Federal Republic of Germany (West Germany), the sign language of the deaf population is commonly called *Deutsche Gebärdensprache* (DGS). Its relationship to the sign languages in other German-speaking countries (German Democratic Republic, Austria, Switzerland) has not yet been investigated. DGS is used by almost all the prelingually profoundly deaf people in West Germany, whose number is estimated at 50,000, of which approximately 22,000 are members of the organization Deutscher Gehörlosenbund (German Deaf Association). While the term *Gebärdensprache* (sign language) is employed by both deaf and hearing people, many deaf persons also use the verb *plaudern* (to chat). The feeling is growing, however, that it has pejorative connotations and should be replaced by *gebärden*. There is considerable regional variation in DGS on the lexical level, but the dialects—which appear to be tied to the schools for deaf children—are easily mutually intelligible.

Use

Very little is known about the history of DGS. Similarities that have been noted by native signers suggest that it is related to French Sign Language and other sign languages of continental Europe, but to date the evidence is only anecdotal. The lack of information about DGS is largely due to the strong tradition of oralism in Germany. If signs were not banned entirely from the classroom, they were treated only as a means of improving the acquisition of spoken German, and even today, schools for

deaf students do not employ deaf teachers. Only a few educators, such as Otto Kruse (1801–1880, himself deaf), Johann Heidsieck (1855–1942), and Matthias Schneider (1869–1949) advocated the use of signs, but they had in mind some kind of Signed German rather than DGS.

DGS has no official status in West Germany and is not treated on a par with other minority languages. Ministerial guidelines for the schools for deaf people do not recognize DGS as a language in its own right, and mention signs, at the most, as one of the manual aids that may be used to further the mastery of speech and as a means of teaching multiply handicapped deaf children. Even among deaf individuals themselves, an awareness of DGS as a separate language is beginning to develop only gradually. Although DGS is the normal medium of in-group communication within the deaf community, Signed German still enjoys great prestige. On television, there is a weekly half-hour program for deaf viewers that presents Signed German, but not DGS. Signed German also tends to be what is taught in evening classes in *Gebärdensprache*, although some interpreters are now being trained in DGS as well. An important step toward the promotion of DGS was taken in 1984, when the research unit Forschungsstelle Deutsche Gebärdensprache (headed by Siegmund Prillwitz) was founded at the University of Hamburg, which also offers courses in DGS given by deaf teachers.

Characteristics

Research on the structure of DGS is still in its initial stages. It seems to share some of the typical properties of American Sign Language (ASL), but like other European sign languages it makes greater use of lip movements. The syntax does not follow that of German, however, and the lip movements ac-

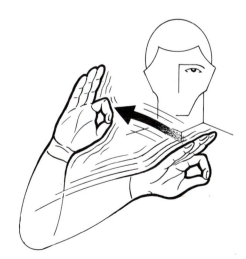

REGULARLY in DGS.

T in the German alphabet and in the American manual alphabet.

companying signs need not represent spoken German words. For example, "every Saturday" is expressed by the sign SAMSTAG (Saturday) repeated twice and the simultaneous lip movement for /zazaza/; for "hospital," the word *Krankenhaus* (hospital) is mouthed, but the manual sign that goes with it is LIEFERN (to deliver); the sign for "regularly" consists of a hand movement plus a nonmanual component, a slow release of air from the puffed cheek.

Fingerspelling plays a minor role. Many signers (especially older ones) do not know the manual alphabet, which is based on the American one—except that the symbol for "T" was replaced by a visual representation of the letter because the "fig hand" is an obscene gesture in Europe. Special manual symbols for the letters ä, ö, ü, and β have also been suggested, but they are not generally accepted.

More influential than fingerspelling is PMS (*Phonembestimmtes Manualsystem*), a manual system that represents phonemes (sounds) rather than letters and is used to teach articulation in many schools for deaf children. Some DGS signs incorporate the PMS symbol for the initial or final sound of the corresponding spoken German word. For instance, NUR (only) and WENN (if) are signed with the index finger touching the nose, which indicates the nasal articulation of the *n*. *See* GERMANY, FEDERAL REPUBLIC OF.

Bibliography

Prillwitz, Siegmund: *Zum Zusammenhang von Kognition, Kommunikation und Sprache mit Bezug auf die Gehörlosenproblematik* (research report on the communication of the deaf), Kohlhammer, Stuttgart, 1982.

Starcke, Hellmuth, and Günter Maisch: *Die Gebärden der Gehörlosen: Ein Hand-, Lehr- und Übungsbuch* (sign dictionary aimed at hearing users that attempts to standardize signs largely in accordance with GESTUNO), Deutsche Gesellschaft zur Förderung der Hör-Sprach-Geschädigten, Hamburg, 1977.

Regina Leven; Joachim Mugdan

Ghanaian

Two distinct sign languages are used in Ghana by deaf people: one, related to American Sign Language (ASL), can be called Ghanaian Sign Language; and the second, unrelated to any other known sign language, can be called Adamorobe Sign Language (AdaSL). In addition, an unknown number of home sign systems may be in use.

Ghana is an independent nation of West Africa. Prior to 1957 it was a colony of England called the Gold Coast; thus, English remains the national language. Among the indigenous spoken languages, six are used by a majority of the Ghanaian people: Ashanti, Fante, Ewe, Twi, Hausa, and Ga. The number of deaf people has not been accurately counted, but there are at least nine school sites where education is offered to deaf children and adolescents.

The first school for deaf students was founded in Ghana by Andrew Foster, an American missionary, who introduced ASL along with educational methodology. Students recruited from around the country to the main school at Mampong-Akwapim graduate with language instruction in the Ghanaian adaptation of ASL, and at least one spoken language. The result often is that they are able to find work in developing industries (such as manufacturing), but may be unfamiliar with the language of their families' local region. Several deaf Ghanaians attended Gallaudet College, and resettled in the United States or returned to work in education in Ghana. *See* FOSTER, ANDREW JACKSON; GALLAUDET COLLEGE.

Brief investigation suggests that Ghanaian Sign Language differs from ASL in lexical inventory. New, local signs may substitute for standard ASL forms, or augment the lexicon, and some ASL forms have changed in the Ghanaian setting—for example, DAY is signed without a base hand; GOD, with index finger extended rather than a flat hand. The brevity of field research does not indicate whether these changes are systematic or sporadic, and does not give an understanding of the interplay between English, other spoken languages, and Ghanaian Sign Language in relation to syntactic or structural relations in the sign language.

Adamorobe is a village in the eastern region of Ghana. It has one of the highest deaf populations any place in the world: 15 percent of the population are reported to be deaf, as a result of a genetic recessive autosome. The deaf people are fairly evenly distributed throughout the age range of the population, and are considered full citizens for the purposes of communal labor, taxes, and other responsibilities of adult life. The villagers make their living through farming; sale of firewood and produce, both at market and to the army; and seeking wage employment in the district capital, Aburi, as shopworkers, caretakers in the Botanical Gardens, and the like. No deaf persons are employed out of the village. *See* HEARING LOSS: Genetic Causes, Incidence and Prevalence.

The hereditary chief, Nana Kwaakwa Asiampong II, and other elders of the village indicate that Adamorobe may have been settled for 200 years. Deaf people have been there for as long as anyone remembers. Most of the deaf people in Adamorobe have had no contact with ASL as adapted in the state schools in Ghana, since the previous chief did not permit school attendance out of the village. Adamorobe Sign Language is thus a traditional deaf sign language, possibly with as long a history as French Sign Language or ASL. Hearing people with deaf relatives, those with religious or ritual offices within the village, and those with deaf neighbors are more likely to know, understand, and use AdaSL than those who work outside of the village, who have no deaf relatives, and so on.

The sign language uses both one- and two-handed signs, with rhythmic variations and facial expressions as important additional dynamics. Handshapes which have been proposed on the basis of ASL to be more "basic" and universal do indeed appear. Several other handshapes occur which are unknown from ASL, as in WAISTBEADS or WEDNESDAY. In addition, signs have been found that use the elbow contacting the trunk (with no specific handshape) as the major articulator (such as CHASE, DON'T-WANT). Like other deaf sign languages, AdaSL uses spatial relationships to convey many syntactic structures. Signs change direction and orientation to show agent and object relations (for example, I-ABUSE-YOU versus YOU-ABUSE-ME). Eye gaze and directionality interact crucially: the difference between the senses SEE-x and SHOW-x is conveyed by changes in eye gaze and angle of hand movement. AdaSL has traditional greetings, ritual insults, and the capacity to function in every context where one might need to communicate. The signing abilities of different individuals do not differ markedly; for the most part, all of the deaf people are fluent, productive, and communicative.

The syntactic mechanism known from ASL, where the nondominant hand serves as the reference index for ordering items in the discourse, is not familiar to AdaSL users, nor is it intelligible to them. For example, the English utterance "I have five children; the first, a boy, is hearing; the next three are girls, all hearing; and the baby boy is deaf" would be most efficiently expressed in ASL by using the nondominant hand as reference indices for the five children, thumb for oldest, smallest finger for youngest. Investigations do not indicate what alternative forms of complex grammatical expression are available to signers using AdaSL. It is, however, precisely in such intricacies of grammar

where divergent development in sign languages of unrelated traditions may be expected.

An open question of some interest is the possible relationship between AdaSL and the gestural trade jargon used in markets throughout West Africa. Providence Island Sign Language has been shown to borrow from the gestural repertoire of the hearing islanders. Further investigation will have to determine whether or how much AdaSL has borrowed from a gestural trade language of market women in Ghana.

Bibliography
David, J. B., et al.: "Adamarobe—A 'Deaf' Village," *Sound*, 5:70–72, 1971.

Nancy Frishberg

Indian

Sign language is an integral part of the deaf communities in India. It is estimated that Indian Sign Language (ISL) is used by over 1,000,000 deaf adults and by approximately 500,000 deaf children, less than 5 percent of whom attend special schools for deaf students. While there are 15 official languages in India and over 200 different dialects among them, there is only one Indian Sign Language. Over 75 percent of signs from all regions are cognates (having a common root). There are four major regional dialects centered in major urban areas: Delhi (North), Calcutta (East), Bangalore-Madras (South), Bombay (West). These dialects are not tied to schools for the deaf, since ISL is not used for "academic" instructional purposes. For political reasons, the Delhi variety of ISL has the largest sphere of influence. For example, in Jameshedpur, a city about 1000 miles (600 kilometers) away from Delhi but within 200 miles (120 kilometers) of Calcutta, signing resembles the Delhi variety much more than the Calcutta variety.

HISTORY

Formal linguistic research on ISL, begun in 1977, shows that it is not related to the French Sign Language group, which includes French, Spanish, and American Sign Language, among others. While there is some influence from British Sign Language in the fingerspelling system used with ISL and in a few of the individual signs, such as "good" and "bad" in Delhi, the vast majority of Indian signs are not related to European sign languages.

Indian Sign Language apparently developed indigenously in India. Contrary to popular opinion among hearing people, ISL has no relationship to hand gestures used in classical Indian dance forms. The use of ISL extends into some parts of Pakistan and Bangladesh, and might extend into other areas as well.

STATUS

Indian Sign Language is autonomous from oral languages in India and is used primarily by deaf people to converse with other deaf people. Deaf people with good oral skills sometimes may approach oral language structures in their signing, but the majority of deaf people use ISL in its pure forms. There is no diglottic situation between ISL and any other signed varieties in India, since ISL is not used in academic education and since very few hearing people in India can sign.

Hearing people seem to view ISL quite negatively. Hearing people often say that ISL does not have a grammar and is merely a collection of gestures. Furthermore, some Americans have tried to impose their signing systems on Indian deaf people, believing that there was no indigenous Indian Sign Language.

These outside influences have resulted in some sociolinguistic problems for the Indian deaf community. For example, the deaf community in Bombay is becoming polarized between two groups: a majority who want to use ISL and see it used in academic environments, and a small but influential group who value American Manual English and who have tried to adopt it. However, the manual English used by these Indians in Bombay has undergone so many changes that American signers cannot understand it very well. *See* MANUALLY CODED ENGLISH.

Indian deaf students suffer from sign language discrimination. Unlike hearing children, deaf children in India usually are exposed to oral English alone. Some schools use a smattering of artificial American Manual English signs along with oral instruction, and at least one school in the South uses a mixture of Indian signs, American signs, and American Manual English signs along with oral English instruction. However, most teachers are not fluent in any form of signing. Most Indian schools do not have teachers skilled in ISL, and few schools have any deaf staff members. Those staff members who are deaf are either dormitory staff or vocational teachers; none teaches in academic programs.

Instruction in vocational programs, in contrast to academic programs, often is given in ISL. This could be attributed to the presence of deaf teachers in these programs.

PHONOLOGY

Indian Sign Language has all of the simple handshapes that are found in all other researched sign languages. These handshapes are B, 5, G, A, S, C, bO, O, and F. Indian Sign Language also has some more complex handshapes (which are also found in some other sign languages): H, V, Y, I, 3, X, and 8. It does not have certain other complex hand-shapes that are found in only a few sign languages. For example, ISL does not have K, R, T, E, 7, D, M, and N handshapes.

The analysis of locations in ISL is not complete, but ISL has signs made in the lower- and upper-arm areas; high, center, and low trunk and shoulder areas; forehead, eyes, nose, mouth, chin, throat, cheek, and ear areas; and hand and zero areas.

Movements and orientations in Indian Sign Language have not yet been systematically analyzed.

FINGERSPELLING

Indian deaf people use the British two-handed alphabet to spell English words and Indian languages according to the traditional Indian romanization principles. In Bombay, deaf people use the British two-handed system for consonants and a one-handed system for vowels. Some hearing people have attempted to develop fingerspelling systems that look like the printed characters; however, these systems have been unwieldy and have not been adopted by the deaf community. There are very few initialized signs in Indian Sign Language. *See* SIGNS: Fingerspelling.

SYNTAX

Data on ISL syntax were collected on film in both structured and unstructured settings. A preliminary analysis of ISL syntax indicates that its grammar is highly complex. Some of the basic findings are summarized below.

These few examples illustrate a definite set of grammatical rules in ISL. ISL syntax does not parallel the syntax of the spoken languages with which various deaf communities have contact.

1. Whenever there is a sentence containing a subject and a verb, the subject always precedes the verb.

MAN CRY

The man cried.

2. For sentences containing a subject, verb, and object, 95 percent of the sentences have a subject-object-verb word order.

WOMAN PRONOUN (right) MAN PRONOUN (left) LOOK (directional from woman to man)

The woman looked at the man.

3. Negatives are placed after the verb.

MAN CRY NOT

The man did not cry.

4. Past tense in ISL is expressed by a past marker at the end of the sentence.

MAN CRY PAST

The man cried.

5. Most adjectives occur after nouns. However, color adjectives often precede the noun.

MAN GOOD WOMAN LOOK

The good man looked at the woman.

MAN WHITE BALL LOOK

The man looked at the white ball.

Bibliography

Vasishta, Madan: "Pilot Project for a Comprehensive Study of Sign Languages of India," Gallaudet College, Washington, D.C., 1975.

————, James Woodward, and Susan De Santis: *An Introduction to Indian Sign Language: Focus on Delhi*, All India Federation of the Deaf, New Delhi, 1981.

————, ————, and Kirk Wilson: "Sign Languages of India: Regional Variations Within the Deaf Populations," *Indian Journal of Applied Linguistics*, vol. 4, no. 3, June 1979.

Madan Vasishta; James Woodward;
Susan De Santis

International Gestures

International gestures comprise a highly flexible and practically uncoded form of gestural communication between signers who do not share a common sign language but want or need to communicate without an interpreter. Based on a kind of nonverbal communication (or, more precisely, gestural-visual communication), international gestures can vary enormously depending on the origins and the creativity of the persons who are signing. They are most frequently used between deaf persons who make international voyages, either for tourism or for international meetings.

HISTORY

Over the years, from at least as far back as the eighteenth century and probably well before, international gestures evolved from a real need among deaf people to share their experiences and ideas with a gestural-visual mode of communication which suited their condition but set them apart from the hearing communities in which they lived. In Europe, whence come most of the historical records on this subject, many different cultures lived in close proximity and international exchanges were frequent.

In the days before the Abbé de l'Epée when signs were deemed unacceptable by hearing people and before large deaf schools began to serve as rallying points for deaf communities, deaf individuals actively searched out their "brethren" both in their own country and in neighboring countries. In the nineteenth century when signs were gaining some acceptance by hearing people in France and the United States, international gestures were often lauded as the universal language sought for so long by various philosophers.

In fact, international gestures do not constitute a true language at all. They are not used for everyday communication among a group of people who live together constantly, and a linguist would say that they do not fulfill the requirement of economy for a language (it takes more time to create or invent a way to gesture an idea than it does to sign it in a conventional sign language).

Nor are international gestures really universal. In a group of signers from France, Spain, and the United States, whose sign languages belong to the same family of languages, the international gestures that appear in the group will be very different from those developed in a group composed of, say, Asians and Scandinavians.

In the Western world, international gestures have been mostly influenced by the French-American family of sign languages because of the grand publicity given to French signs by the Abbé de l'Epée and his disciples and because of the leading role played by French and American persons in international deaf organizations since the nineteenth century. See L'EPÉE, ABBÉ CHARLES MICHEL DE.

GESTUNO

The Commission on Unification of Signs of the World Federation of the Deaf has attempted to standardize international gestures with the book *Gestuno*. A collection of almost 1500 signs chosen or invented by the commission as a basic international vocabulary, Gestuno will undoubtedly have an influence on the evolution of international gestures. But like Esperanto (the international spoken-written code), Gestuno has faced several problems: only a few people are willing to learn the new vocabulary, the resulting communication is often too limited or inefficient, and the situations in which it is used are infrequent. Moreover, in international meetings, delegates from countries with highly developed interpreting services invariably prefer interpreting in their own sign language (and even when international gestures are used, precise minutes are generally distributed in a written language and translated). For these reasons, interpreters are rarely trained in international gestures, and delegates who do not bring their own interpreters are left to fend for themselves. See WORLD FEDERATION OF THE DEAF.

Gestuno is the first attempt at standardizing a type of communication that seems to defy standardization. To be sure, a common vocabulary is useful, but the natural evolution of international gesturing over the years seems to have been more related to a sensitivity to the structure of gesturing—how the gestures are put together—rather than to the question of which gestures should be chosen as standard.

DEVELOPMENT

Since the vocabularies of different sign languages are different—and sometimes radically so—a particular group of signers from different countries will have to establish "their" vocabulary of gestures based on common experiences.

The process of vocabulary building is relatively simple and rapid. If the concept is something concrete, it is described in its visual aspects, and a gesture is agreed upon so that further reference can be made to it without the description process (the agreement is usually accomplished in a split second: "This gesture OK?", "OK."). The gesture agreed upon may be a gesture incorporating a visual aspect of the thing described, or it may be a fairly arbitrary gesture borrowed, say, from the sign language of either the speaker or the viewer.

If the concept is more abstract, the idea is symbolized by a gesture readily recognizable ("love" by a heart with an appropriate facial expression, and so on). Once a new gesture is understood (either by explanation or simply by the context), it is considered automatically established for use in the group and becomes part of the group's lexicon. Often explanations of new vocabulary include a liberal use of the gestures for "same" and "different": it is "same" (or like) such-and-such, or it is "different" (or not quite the same) from so-and-so. This whole process, of course, occurs in an atmosphere of doing whatever is necessary to be understood; the process is a natural one arising from the need to communicate and a willingness to try various ways to get one's message across.

Most linguists would agree that in foreign-language learning the acquisition of vocabulary is something that happens naturally in practicing one's new language: as one has need of a certain word, it is learned. More important is the acquisition of the sentence structures which lie behind the vocabulary. The same could be said of international gesturing: as a gesture is needed, a speaker will find it (or a viewer will help to find it). As to the putting together of the gestures, native signers in all sign languages are especially sensitive to facial and manual cues that sign languages seem to have in common: localization in space of persons and things whether they are present or not; incorporation of subjects and objects by modifying the direction of the gesture; subtle changes in body posture to clarify who is doing what or who is speaking to whom; nuances in the speed, size, and intensity of movements that, when exaggerated, contribute to a theatrical "acting out" of what one is saying; facial expressions and head movements which transform sentences into questions or commands. In addition, signers are attuned to a mode of communication in which eye contact is especially important, and, in fact, in international gesturing there is a kind of continual eye dialogue saying, "You understand? Good. Not clear? How about this?"

Linguists who studied sign languages in the 1960s and 1970s often minimized the pantomimic elements in their studies to concentrate on the "arbitrary," but sign languages do include much more imitation of actions than spoken languages include imitations of sounds (onomatopoeia). And this fa-

cility of signers to visualize and to imitate, to "act out" what they mean, has contributed to the spontaneous evolution and success of international gestures.

IMPORTANCE

International gestures are important for several reasons. They evolved naturally among deaf persons without the arbitrary invention of a pseudo-language like Esperanto. If they depend more on creativity (in the use of symbols and metaphors they often attain the level of poetry) than on a set vocabulary and a strict syntax, and if they are not as efficient as a conventional language, they *are* the basis for persons from different cultures to search together for a common ground of understanding without interpreters and intermediaries.

Bibliography
Gestuno: International Sign Language of the Deaf, British Deaf Association, Carlisle, 1975.

Bill Moody

Irish

Historically, deaf education in the Republic of Ireland has been centered in the city of Dublin, which now has a deaf population of approximately 800. The largest schools there, referred to as the Cabra schools (in Cabra, Dublin), are St. Joseph's School for Deaf Boys, with approximately 300 students, and St. Mary's School for Hearing-Impaired Girls (formerly St. Mary's School for Deaf Girls), with approximately 350 students.

The sign systems used at these schools are historically related to a French sign system that was used in the 1800s at a school in Caen, Hormandy, called Le Bon Saveur. This manual code for French was devised by Abbé Jamet of Caen, a disciple of Abbé Sicard.

Two Dominican Sisters, Sr. Mary Magdalen O'Farrell and Sr. Mary Vincent Martin, and two deaf girls studied the teaching techniques at the Caen school in 1846 and brought it to St. Mary's, where at least two changes were imposed on the borrowed French signs. An Irish Vincentian priest, Father John Burke, C.M., modified the French sign system so that it could be used to express English grammar instead of French grammar. The signs were also modified to make them more "soft and feminine" for the girls at St. Mary's and more "bold and masculine" for the boys at St. Joseph's, a school started by the Christian Brothers in 1856. Thus gender-specific vocabularies were developed, which today are said to diverge by 30 percent.

No record is available concerning the origin of the sign changes in the manual alphabet from the original French system. However, it appears from an engraving of Abbé Jamet, which was published

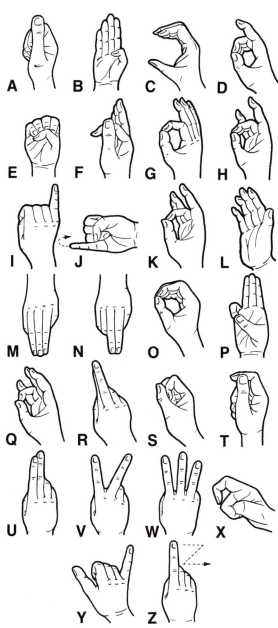

The Manual Alphabet was originally published by Abbé Jamet in 1847; the letter "T" was modified toward the end of the 1800s at St. Joseph's and used in the Catholic Institution for the Deaf and Dumb, in Cabra, Dublin.

in the first report of the Catholic Institution for the Deaf and Dumb in 1847, that he had a role in the changes, which became distinct to Ireland. Toward the end of the 1800s, the handshape for "T" was modified at St. Joseph's. However, the older form for "T" as well as the older form for "X," which involved use of both hands, were retained at St. Mary's.

Today there are at least three types of sign systems used in the Dublin deaf community—the old, the new, and the informal. Most deaf people and hearing educators acknowledge only the old and new forms as legitimate, since both are manual codes for English, and are said to be grammatical systems. The informal system, unofficially called Deaf Sign Language, is used by deaf people in informal settings. This informal type of signing is said to be an abbreviated form of the old Cabra school signs because it shares the same vocabulary and does not follow English grammar. Initial observations suggest that this informal variety does have a grammar with structural features, such as directional verbs, like that of other indigenous sign languages.

Both the informal system and the old system use gender-distinct vocabularies. Preliminary research indicates that differences exist in basic areas, such as religious, color, and family terms, as well as with other nouns, verbs, and adjectives. However, deaf males and females do not seem to have problems understanding each other. Women report that they learn the men's signs once they start dating, and use them with their husbands after marriage. However, it also appears that the women do not stop using female signs after marriage, but continue to use them with women and girls and for discussing so-called women's topics, such as certain aspects of childrearing.

The new or unified sign system, which many call Irish Sign Language, is a manual code for English that has only one vocabulary for both males and females. This system was introduced in the late 1970s, largely in response to the absence of instruction in the old signs at the Cabra schools. Since the implementation of oralism at St. Mary's in the late 1940s and at St. Joseph's in the late 1950s or early 1960s, signing has not been taught at Cabra, with the exception of the manual sections. The manual sections are reserved for multiply handicapped children and some profoundly deaf children without multiple handicaps who have been unable to succeed through the use of the oral method alone.

The new sign system is the product of the Unified Sign Language Committee, which consisted of deaf people and hearing people interested in at least four primary goals. First, they wanted to produce a dictionary of Irish signs that could be used by professionals who work with deaf people (a dictionary of new signs entitled *The Irish Sign Language* was published by the National Association of the Deaf in 1979). Second, the committee wanted to make sure that the sign system had all of the signs needed to express every grammatical unit of English. The committee invented new signs where there were apparently no signs available in the old Cabra system for particular English words or grammatical units. Third, the committee wanted to standardize the vocabulary for use by both men and women. The committee decided which of two signs for a given concept would be maintained, either the female sign or the male sign. The majority of signs chosen for this unified system were the male signs. Fourth, the committee perceived a need for a written record of grammatical signing (that is, Manual English) for deaf people's reference. Since educators no longer teach signing in the Cabra schools (except in the manual sections), some people have become concerned that deaf people will forget their grammatical signing or that young people will never learn how to sign properly.

The majority of signs in the new system are based on the initial letter of the corresponding English word and are usually grouped into classes of related ideas. For example, the signs for the words "busy," "do," "exercise," "practice," "serve," and "work" are identical except for their different handshapes. Despite goodwill from the adult deaf community toward the projects, this reformed language has not been absorbed by the community; many deaf people are said to prefer the older signs. However, it is used in the manual departments of both Cabra schools and in some sign language classes throughout the country.

Irish Signs in Other Countries   Irish signs were imported to several schools in other countries: the Dominican School for Deaf Children at the Cape of Good Hope, South Africa, which was founded by six nuns from Cabra in 1863; the Waratah School for Deaf Children in New South Wales, Australia, founded by a deaf nun from Cabra, Sr. Gabriel Hogan, in 1875; and St. Gabriel's School for Deaf Boys at Castle Hill, New South Wales, Australia, founded by two Brothers from Cabra in 1922. For several decades, Irish signs were also used at St. Vincent's School in Toolcross, Scotland, before being dropped in favor of native British signs.

Current Status   In the past, protagonists of oralism disapproved of using sign language in public and on television (often preventing its usage), but today sign language is more accepted. The adult deaf community increasingly has asserted its rights. Sign classes now are offered throughout the country, with the new manual code for English the form of signing being recognized and accepted. *See* IRELAND, REPUBLIC OF.

Bibliography
   Burke, J.: *Manuscripts*, St. Mary's School for Hearing-Impaired Girls, Cabra, Dublin.
   Forde, J. C.: *Centenary Record*, St. Joseph's School for Deaf Boys, Cabra, Dublin.

Barbara LeMaster; Stanislaus Foran

Israeli

Israeli Sign Language (ISL) is used, with minor dialectical variations, by deaf people in the State of Israel. In that nation there are an estimated 4500 people with a hearing loss of 75 dB or more. Deaf immigrants from Germany in the 1930s brought with them their sign language, and this gradually merged with the local sign language. Large-scale immigration into Israel after the country gained independence in 1948 brought a new influx of signs from European, North African, and Middle Eastern countries, which also affected ISL. No significant attempts have been made by hearing people to introduce changes into ISL; the educational system was completely oral until quite recently, and systematic efforts to enrich the vocabulary of ISL started only in the mid-1970s (by a committee appointed by the Association of the Deaf in Israel). Thus, in its present state, ISL has a very short history and has been left relatively uncontaminated by external intervention. This makes for a unique opportunity to study the origins of manual languages and the laws of their development. *See* ISRAEL.

The number of people using ISL is estimated at 5000, which includes deaf people themselves, parents of deaf children, and other hearing persons who work with deaf students or clients (teachers, social workers). Not all deaf people use ISL, however; those who have attained a good command of Hebrew often use it even when communicating among themselves, and may not even know ISL.

The first school for deaf students in Israel was founded in Jerusalem in 1934 by a teacher from Germany, who had introduced the oral method prevalent in that country. The Jerusalem school and other deaf schools in Israel were once completely oral, but teachers have been increasingly using signs to supplement oral teaching. Some teachers are taking courses in ISL offered at the Association of the Deaf in Israel, in Tel-Aviv. The association's courses in ISL are also attended by social workers who work with deaf people and by other interested persons. The association also offers a training course for prospective teachers of ISL. Courses in ISL for students training for work with deaf persons (teachers, social workers) are also offered at Tel-Aviv University.

Deaf people appearing before law courts or the rabbinical courts or those who come into contact with the police are provided with ISL translators as a service by these agencies. The Association of the Deaf in Israel now offers a course for translators, with counseling from Gallaudet College. Simultaneous translating into ISL is also occasionally provided by the public television network. *See* GALLAUDET COLLEGE.

A fingerspelling system for Hebrew was designed in 1976 by a committee of the Association of the Deaf in Israel. Sixteen handshapes for Hebrew letters were taken over from the American manual alphabet, and those for others were newly devised.

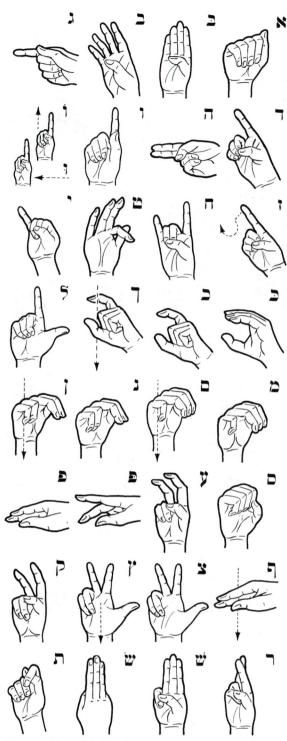

Fingerspelling alphabet for Hebrew. (Courtesy of the Association of the Deaf in Israel)

This fingerspelling is being used in some schools.

Due to the short history of ISL, the meaning of most signs is still transparent. There has been little time for the process of "leveling" and simplification to take its toll on the iconicity of signs (as has been the case, for instance, with the American Sign Language). Further, the order of signs in ISL is still very flexible. The influence of Hebrew vernacular is seen only in the signing of those with a good command of Hebrew. Even here, there is only a statistical tendency to prefer word order of Hebrew (which is predominantly subject-verb-object), and this order is not mandatory. Only two ordering rules seem to be strictly adhered to: (1) noun + adjective, or more precisely, the modifying sign follows the sign for the thing it modifies (for example, ELECTIONS NEW, CLOCK ROUND); and (2) quantifiers precede the sign for the entity quantified (TWO CARS, MUCH MONEY), or both precede and follow it (ALL NUMBER ALL, FIVE-MONTH, (single sign) FIVE).

The major structural characteristics of other sign languages—positioning of the *dramatis personae* in the space surrounding the signer, simultaneity of signs, and so on—have also been found in ISL, which was one of the first sign languages for which these characteristics were described.

Bibliography

Cohen, E., L. Namir, and I. M. Schlesinger: *A New Dictionary of Sign Language*, Mouton, The Hague, 1977.

Namir, L., and I. M. Schlesinger: "The Grammar of Sign Language," in I. M. Schlesinger and L. Namir (eds.): *Sign Language of the Deaf: Psychological, Linguistic, and Sociological Perspectives*, Academic Press, New York, 1978.

Shanary, J.: "Social Background of the Israeli Sign Language," Working Paper no. 9, April 1969, Department of Psychology, Hebrew University of Jerusalem and Association of the Deaf in Israel.

I. M. Schlesinger

Italian

Visual-manual signs are the prevailing means of communication among deaf people throughout Italy. Unfortunately, appropriate information on the signing community is lacking, and the number of signers cannot even be estimated.

STATUS

Within Italian society, signs are known simply as "gestures." The assignation Lingua Italiana dei Segni (LIS), still rarely used, is now officially applied to Italian signs, as research findings show that they constitute an autonomous language. Although most research on LIS has been conducted in Rome, the results appear largely applicable to other areas, such as Sicily, and although signers of different regions seem to communicate fluently among themselves, differences in the signs used throughout Italy exist. It is still not known whether such differences reflect major or minor linguistic variations, or whether they are related to specific contexts, such as schools for deaf children (all oral), or to particular geo-

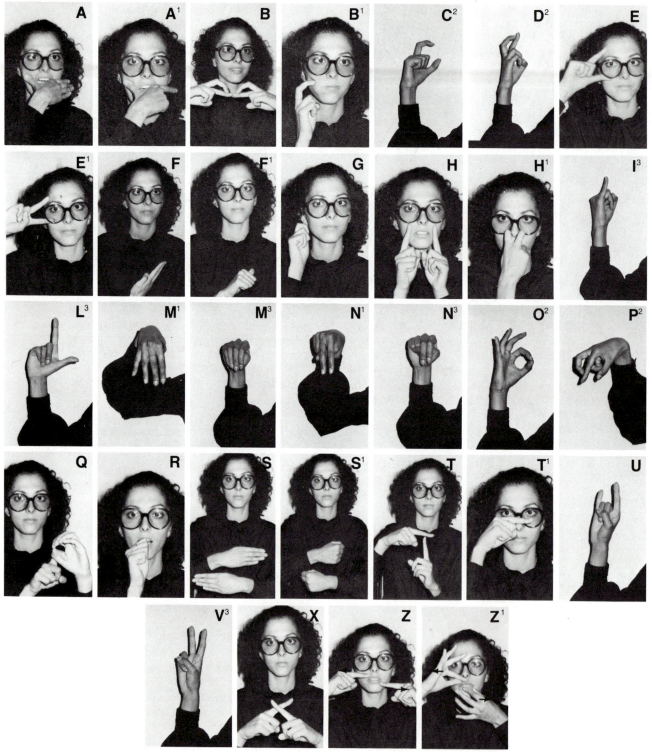

Old Italian manual alphabet which is used to some extent by old deaf people. Letter configurations are marked as follows: "1" are variants; "2" are frequently used along with, or in place of, the configurations for the same letters of the new alphabet; "3" have been retained unchanged in the new alphabet.

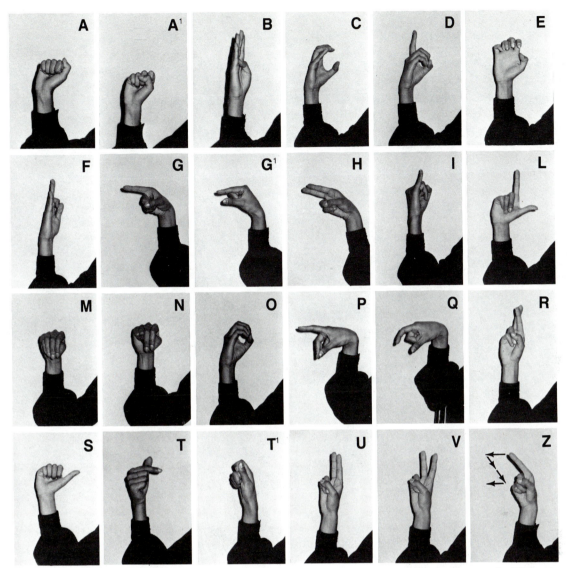

New Italian manual alphabet which is used especially by young deaf people. Letter configurations marked "1" are variants.

graphic areas. In the nineteenth century, signs were used for educational purposes. However, the establishment of a strong oralist tradition, beginning in 1880, prevented any further development of signs within educational contexts. *See* HISTORY: Congress of Milan.

LIS is a minority language, subordinate to both standard Italian and the numerous Italian dialects. In fact, among hearing people the prevailing view is that signs are gestures, with none of the linguistic features common to all spoken languages. Partly accepted within the deaf community, this view has interfered negatively with the awareness that LIS is a language and not simply a rich communicative system, as many signers currently appear to per-

ceive it. The sociolinguistic isolation of signers has contributed to this situation: LIS is used only within deaf families, deaf clubs, and schools outside the classroom. It is never officially used in educational contexts and is rarely used in communication between deaf and hearing people, where deaf persons resort to speechreading and speech. Since deaf people's oral language skills are generally limited to standard Italian, communication between signers and dialect speakers is often very difficult. *See* SPEECHREADING.

CHARACTERISTICS
Contrary to the view that Italian signs are gestures, research has shown that they constitute a lan-

Queen

Army General

(a)

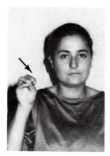
To call

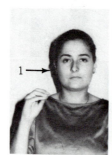
He calls

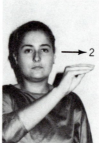
Him

To wait

To wait for
a long time

(b)

Woman

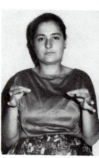
Thread

Cuts thread

Book

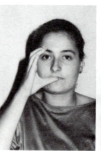
Glass

Glass-on-book

(c)

(d)

Examples of Italian Sign Language. The words below each picture are English glosses of the LIS signs. (a) Signs with the "4" handshape. (b) Morphological processes. (c, d)

Syntactic pattern: (c) "The woman cuts the thread." (d) "The glass is on the book."

guage, LIS, with proper phonological, morphosyntactic, and semantic structures. A limited number of distinctive phonological components (locations, handshapes, movements, and orientations), which combine regularly to generate all the signs of LIS, have been identified. Relevant linguistic differences between these components and those of other sign languages have been noted. For example, the "4" handshape is distinctive and very frequent in LIS but not in American or British Sign Languages. The

morphological and syntactic processes of LIS exhibit some structural features that are not found in most spoken languages, and appear to be distinctive of the visual-spatial modality. For example, different morphological distinctions can be specified within a sign, as morphemes are simultaneously superimposed upon the sign itself, to change its syntactic function or meaning. It is also possible to produce two different signs at once, using both hands as articulators, and to arrange these in space, with their morphological modifications, thereby expressing syntactic relations simultaneously rather than sequentially.

The structural features of LIS render it significantly different and autonomous from other languages, including Italian. However, standard Italian influences LIS through a particular channel which seems to play the same function in LIS that fingerspelling plays in other sign languages, namely, in the frequent use of speechreading and voiceless articulation, especially for clarifying signs that are formationally similar or vary across signing communities. Fingerspelling, by contrast, is scarcely employed, but both a new and, in part, an old manual alphabet are used.

Some features of LIS partly resemble those that have been found in other sign languages. However, the particular grammatical distinctions that are marked in LIS, as its lexicon and semantic structures, appear to be language-specific. *See* ITALY.

Bibliography

Carmel, S. J.: *International Hand Alphabet Charts*, 1975.

Facchini, G. M.: "Riflessioni Storiche sul Metodo Orale e il Linguaggio dei Segni in Italia," in V. Volterra (ed.), *I Segni come Parole*, 1981.

Volterra, V. (ed.): *La Lingua Italiana dei Segni: LIS*, Technical Report, Instituto di Psicologia del Consiglio Nazionale delle Ricerche, Roma, 1983.

———— et al.: "Order of Elements in the Sentence in Italian Sign Language," in F. Loncke, P. Boynes-Braem, and Y. Lebrun (eds.), *Recent Research in European Sign Language*, 1983.

Elena Pizzuto

Japanese

Japan has a population of about 120 million, 70 percent of whom live on the coastal plains of the Pacific Ocean and Seto Island Sea. In 1980 the hearing-impaired population numbered 317,000. The exact number of deaf signers is unknown, but more than 95 percent of deaf Japanese are presumed to understand sign language and 80 percent of them, fingerspelling.

NAMES

Shuwa, literally "hand talk," is now the official name of the Japanese Sign Language. Most of the Japanese nation has come to an awareness of its meaning during the 1980s. Before World War II, sign language was called *Temane*, literally "hand imitation." Its use, however, was prohibited in schools for deaf children.

EDUCATION

There are 107 schools for deaf students in Japan, all of which are officially oral except the Tochigi School, which uses the simultaneous method. Still, sign language has been preserved among students in each school. Teachers today sometimes learn it from their students and use it in class, especially in middle and high schools. Each school has its own sign vocabulary. Often graduates from different schools find it hard to communicate with each other through signs and will add lipreading to aid their communication.

The first school for deaf and blind children in Japan was established in Kyoto, the former capital city, on May 24, 1878, by Tashiro Furukawa, with 20 blind and 29 deaf pupils. He used the manual method, and invented manual alphabets (though none was to prevail), many signs, and other ways of communication, such as writing letters on the back of the deaf person and dictation with signs.

CURRENT STATUS

In 1968 Takashi Tanokimi and his colleagues in the Tochigi School began using the simultaneous method, in which a kind of Signed Japanese (or Manually Coded Japanese, MCJ) is used as one of the channels to produce and receive spoken Japanese. Their sign language is called Simultaneous Methodic Signs, which strictly represents postpositions and suffixes by fingerspelling, in contrast to Traditional Signs or Japanese Sign Language (JSL). Their terminology has prevailed in deaf education and among deaf communities, but some people still call Signed Japanese grammatical signs and JSL natural signs. Except in the Tochigi area, Simultaneous Methodic Signs are not accepted by the deaf communities and interpreters. On many occasions, deaf people and interpreters use Pidgin Sign Japanese (PSJ, or in Tochigi's terminology, Middle Type Signs). Signed Japanese, PSJ, and JSL constitute sign diglossia. PSJ is often used in formal situations, especially in television programs, lectures, speeches, and so on.

STRUCTURE

The structure of JSL is not yet well understood. Research on its phonological structure and notational system, however, has shown that there are several hand configurations, locations, and movements that are different from those in American Sign Language. The Japanese Association of Sign Language Studies was founded in 1974, and many papers concerning JSL have been presented. Most of them have been on phonology and other fields, with few on morphology, syntax, and semantics. *See* JAPAN.

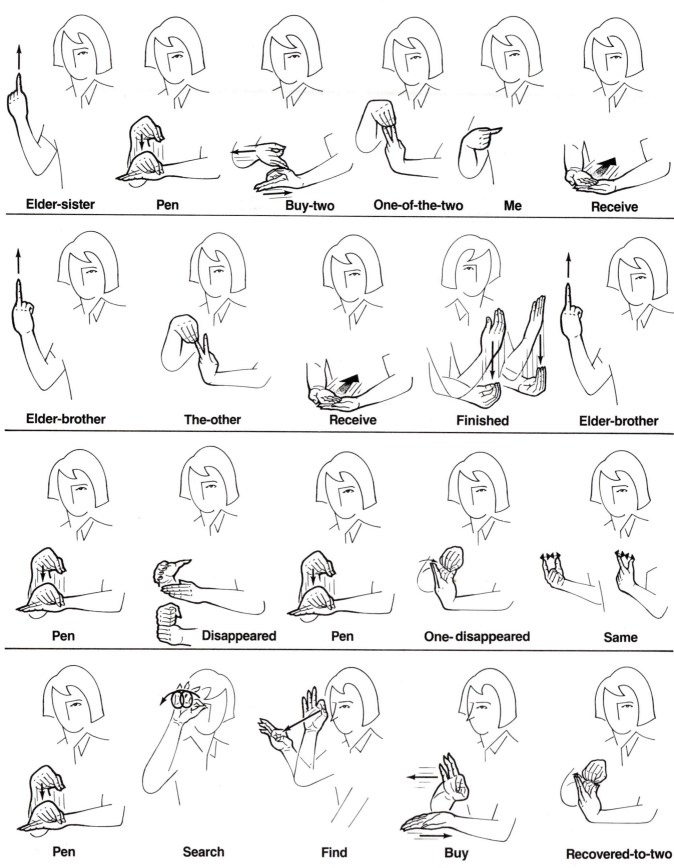

Elder-sister	Pen	Buy-two	One-of-the-two	Me	Receive

Elder-brother	The-other	Receive	Finished	Elder-brother

Pen	Disappeared	Pen	One-disappeared	Same

Pen	Search	Find	Buy	Recovered-to-two

Comparison of translations into Japanese Sign Language (left page) and manually coded Japanese (right page) with English lexical translations. English: "My elder sister bought one pen each for my elder brother and me. He lost it and bought the same one himself." Japanese: "Ane ga watashi to ani ni ippon zutsu kattekureta pen wo, ani wa naku-shite shimatta node, jibun de onaji pen wo mitsukete katta." [After Takashi Tanokami, *Shuwa No Sekai* (The World of Sign Language)]

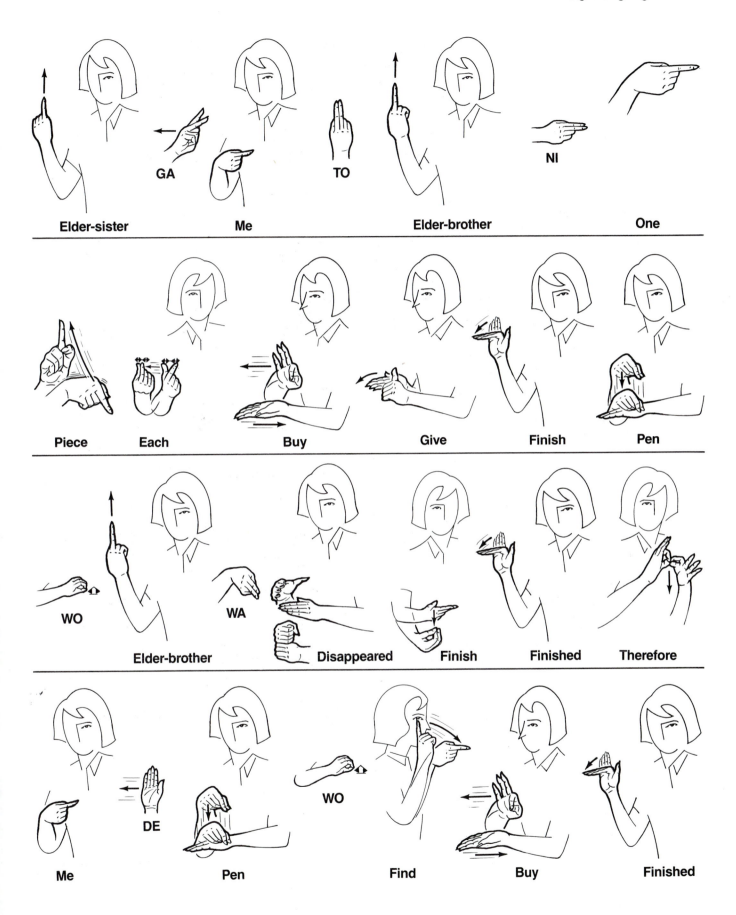

Elder-sister   Me   Elder-brother   One

Piece   Each   Buy   Give   Finish   Pen

Elder-brother   Disappeared   Finish   Finished   Therefore

Me   DE   Pen   WO   Find   Buy   Finished

GA   TO   NI   WO   WA   WO   DE

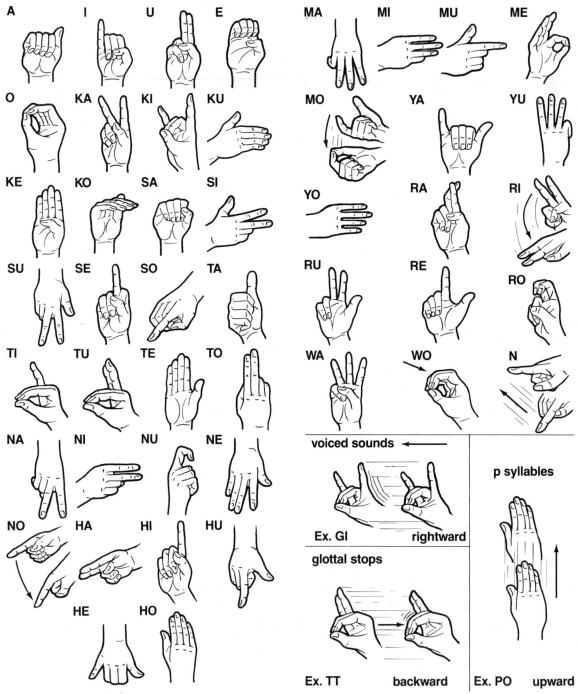

Japanese manual alphabet.

Bibliography

Honna, Nobuyuki, et al.: "Toward a Notation of Japanese Sign Language," in *Proceedings of Japanese Association of Sign Language Studies*," JASLS, 1985.

Japanese Federation of the Deaf: *Our Signs*, vols. 1–9, JFD, Tokyo, 1984.

Japanese Society for Rehabilitation of the Disabled, Inc.: *Rehabilitation Services for the Disabled in Japan*, JSRD, Tokyo, 1975.

Kanda, Kazuyuki: *A Study of Manual Alphabets*, Koseikan, Tokyo, 1985.

Nakano, Yoshitatsu: "Communication for Hearing-Handicapped People in Japan," in Herbert J. Oyer (ed.), *Communication for the Hearing Handicapped*, University Park Press, 1976.

Kazuyuki Kanda

Malaysian

The Federation of Malaysia is a Southeast Asian nation of about 130,000 square miles (325,000 square kilometers). People of Malay, Chinese, and Indian origin together constitute approximately 85 percent of its total population of 14 million, the balance being indigenous peoples and others of diverse origin. About 31,000 deaf persons were recorded in 1980. Three systems of manual communication have been called sign languages in Malaysia. These will be referred to as Penang Sign Language (PSL), Kuala Lumpur Sign Language (KLSL), and Bahasa Malaysia Kod Tangan (BMKT) or manually coded Bahasa Malaysia. No figures are available on the users of these three systems, but 20 percent of the deaf population would be a generous estimate. It is assumed that home signs are used by the remaining deaf persons in the country.

PENANG SIGN LANGUAGE

The first school for deaf students in Malaysia was established in Penang in 1954. With the expansion of this school into a residential institution, the Federation School for the Deaf, the first Malaysian deaf community was created. Despite the fact that the school practiced strict oralism, a gestural form of communication soon evolved surreptitiously among the students. Its use was limited, though, because most of those who left the school usually returned to the isolation of their own homes. The use of PSL appears to have declined sharply since the late 1970s due to the spread of other sign systems. Unfortunately no serious attempt to study PSL was ever made locally. However, some videotaped samples may be available at Gallaudet College.

KUALA LUMPUR SIGN LANGUAGE

During the late 1960s, American signs were introduced by Tan Yap for use by members of a club for deaf adults organized under the auspices of the YMCA in Kuala Lumpur, the capital of Malaysia, and also for instructional purposes at the Selangor School for the Deaf. These signs are used in a word order which is neither exclusively English nor Malay.

Because of frequent visits by its members to their own home towns and villages, the YMCA deaf club has exerted considerable influence over the type of manual communication used by deaf people in Malaysia since the mid-1970s. Many former users of PSL now use KLSL. Several thousand copies of T. O'Rourke's *A Basic Course in Manual Communication*, which describes signs used in the United States, have been distributed since 1978 on a free-of-charge basis to deaf individuals and other interested persons throughout the country by the Society for the Deaf in Selangor and the Federal Territory.

Thus, the use of predominantly American signs in a mixture of English and Malay word order is the main manual communication system used in Malaysia. This system adapts very readily to the manually coded form of Bahasa Malaysia, known as Bahasa Malaysia Kod Tangan, which has been under development by the Ministry of Education since 1978, and is increasingly used in government educational programs for deaf people.

BAHASA MALAYSIA KOD TANGAN

In 1978, following its acceptance of total communication philosophy, the Ministry of Education appointed a Total Communication Working Committee to develop a suitable manual communication system for the country. Examination of Swedish and American attempts at manually coding their respective national languages revealed the fact that many of the problems which were encountered would not arise in Malaysia because of the comparatively noninflected nature of the Malay language. While Bahasa Malaysia does have some affixes, chiefly to indicate semantic changes, it is not inflected for case, number, gender, or tense. Development of a manual code for the Malay language appears relatively easy. See SOCIOLINGUISTICS: Total Communication.

In order to ensure that full consideration would be given to local signs, the Total Communication Working Committee assigned the initial task of selecting signs as well as devising new ones to a team of teachers at the Federation School. Included in the team were individuals who could advise on local signs (other than the Penang ones) and on American signs and their structure. A schedule of slightly over 900 signs was prepared by this team before the end of 1978.

The initial list of 900 signs has since been revised and expanded to 1600. This number must, however, be regarded merely as the lower limit of a vocabulary which can be expanded very considerably through the use of affixes. For example, the Malay word "ajar" means "teach," but it can be combined with suitable affixes to form words which vary widely in semantic content:

BAHASA MALAYSIA	ENGLISH
ajar	teach
ber-ajar	courteous
bel-ajar	learn
pel-ajar	student
ter-pel-ajar	scholarly, learned
ajar-an	teaching, doctrine
pel-ajar-an	lesson, education
mem-pel-ajar-i	study, examine carefully

In addition, the language is exceedingly rich in idiomatic two-word expressions. The following are a few examples from among more than three dozen common combinations which use the word *mata*:

BAHASA MALAYSIA (LITERAL MEANING)	IDIOMATIC MEANING
mata mata (eye eye)	policeman
mata gelap (eye dark)	detective
mata air (eye water)	sweetheart, spring
air mata (water eye)	tear
mata ikan (eye fish)	wart
mata buku (eye joint)	knuckle

Despite such parsimony of word usage in Bahasa Malaysia, and despite almost excessive use of initialization in the creation of new signs, teachers report an urgent need for a very large number of additional signs to meet the requirements of secondary school education. Meanwhile, all words which have no equivalent signs as yet are fingerspelled. The international version of the American manual alphabet with a modified "t" is used for this purpose.

Malay is an extremely flexible language. In Malaysia it exists in three commonly used forms. First, the form in which it is often used in the *pasar* or market place (mainly among non-Malays) makes minimal use of grammatical affixes. This is the language form which the signing of deaf Malaysians approximates at present. This form of signing would be fairly intelligible to American signers since it uses a great preponderance of American signs. It does not use a copula, and even places the qualifier after the noun, as in American Sign Language. Second, the colloquial form used among native Malay speakers generally includes somewhat more grammatical and semantic affixes than the "pasar" form, both in the types of affixes used and in the frequency of their use, although this frequency also tends to vary considerably with dialect. Finally, at the extreme end of the scale, is Bahasa Malaysia which is formal Malay. It is also the form in which the Malay language is written. In this case the occurrence of affixes can, in exceptional instances, be as high as one every three words. This is the form of Malay which is manually coded as BMKT.

It should be borne in mind that BMKT merely makes it possible for deaf signers to use "pasar" Malay, colloquial Malay, or Bahasa Malaysia, in much the same way as a native speaker of the Malay language would, depending upon the formality of the occasion. This is not analogous to code switching from, for example, American Sign Language to any form of manual English. Because Bahasa Malaysia is also the written form of the language, educators expect that BMKT will be of direct help to deaf people in developing high levels of reading and writing skills.

Bibliography
Bahasa Isyrat, vols. 1–3, Ministry of Education, Malaysia, 1978.
Bahasa Malaysia Kod Tangan, Ministry of Education, Malaysia, 1984.

Tan Chin Guan

Mexican

There are an estimated 1,300,000 deaf people in Mexico. They commonly refer to themselves as *Los Silentes*. Their signs have mainly been referred to as *la mimica* or *hablar con manos* (to speak with hands). As it gains recognition, Mexican sign is becoming known as LSM, or *Lenguaje de Señas Mexicanas* (Mexican Sign Language). *See* MEXICO.

LSM is widely used throughout Mexico, although in the east from Oaxaca to Yucatán the high Indian population may account for the significant variations in some signs. Most schools for deaf children are oral. Those schools that do use signs frequently invent their own. Leaders in the deaf community are working with the government to improve teacher training and include LSM in the schools. They are also working to develop social programs to educate the public about LSM.

Eduardo Huet was a deaf Frenchman who came to Mexico in 1866. In 1867, due to his persistence, the first training institute for teachers of deaf students in Latin America opened in Mexico City. Huet was a staunch advocate of the use of sign language in deaf schools, and he was probably a major influence in the development of LSM.

Among deaf people themselves, LSM is the preferred method of communication. At one time, the government did not recognize LSM as a language at all. There are no classes or information available to the public about LSM. There is no body of professional interpreters. There are no laws or funds to provide or train interpreters. There is a five-minute segment of national news presented in LSM on television daily.

LSM does not follow Spanish grammar rules. The placement of words signed will depend on context and content. Variations in speed, size, and duration of the sign can be used to alter its meaning. There are no alternative codes that follow spoken Spanish structure, such as the Signing Exact English (SEE) system in the United States.

In spoken Spanish, a single root verb will change endings to indicate tense and person to whom the action refers. In LSM, as in ASL, there are no correlating signs to specify verb ending changes in themselves. Instead, changes in the movement (duration, speed, frequency, and placement) of the root sign provide this information. Plurals may be expressed by adding the sign MUCHOS after the noun, as opposed to fingerspelling an "s."

In nouns referring to persons of male or female gender, like grandpa/grandma or uncle/aunt, the word will be signed in its masculine form with a special female qualifier sign added after it. This only applies when the personal noun in Spanish follows the same pattern—for example, *tio/tia* (uncle/aunt) or *abuelo/abuela* (grandpa/grandma).

Similar to written Spanish, the sign indicating a question is made at the beginning of the LSM sentence. The sign literally translates as *pregunta* (question) rather than as a punctuation mark.

Negatives may be expressed by a shake of the head or the inclusion of the sign NO/NOT before or after the verb. Some signs, however, specifically express the negative within the sign itself. LSM is a beautiful and articulate language whose potential is only just now beginning to be recognized by the people of Mexico.

Bibliography

Gomez Palacio, M., et. al.: "Dirreccion General de Educacion Especial," *Mis Primeras Señas: Una Introduccion al Lenguaje Manual*, Mexico D.F., 1983.

Parra, A. K.: "Other Deaf Americans: Problems and Pride of Deaf Mexicans," *Deaf American*, vol. 36, no. 7, 1984.

Parra, Carlos A., and A. K. Parra: *LSM/ASL: A Dual-Mode Dictionary of Lenguaje de Señas Mexicanas and American Sign Language*, 1986.

Alison Parra; Carlos Parra

Norwegian

Norwegian Sign Language (NSL) is primarily used by about 4000 deaf people, a number almost equal to the deaf population in Norway. Some hearing children of deaf parents learn NSL as their first language, and a few hearing parents, teachers, and other people associated with the deaf community are also competent users of the language.

In 1981 the Norwegian Association of the Deaf decided that the official name of both NSL and the constructed code Signed Norwegian would be Sign Language. However, in order not to confuse NSL with Signed Norwegian and vice versa, the two different forms of signing are often labeled with different names by the users.

The major sign dialects seem to be primarily associated with the three schools for deaf students located in Holmestrand, Oslo, and Trondheim. Today the schools are all manual in the sense that the teachers use Signed Norwegian for educational purposes and also in communication with the pupils. Both teachers and pupils use voice (speech) in addition to signs when communicating with each other. Among themselves, pupils use NSL during their lessons as well as outside of school.

HISTORY

NSL developed rapidly in the nineteenth century. The first school for deaf students was founded in 1825 in Trondheim. The headmaster, Andreas Møller, was deaf, and had received his education in the school for deaf students in Denmark. Around 1878, the first deaf club was founded.

Official Norwegian manual alphabet.

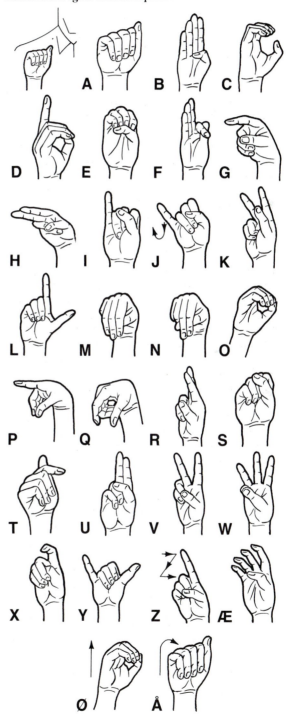

Despite the fact that historically the use of NSL has often been prohibited in the schools, it was, and still is, in the schools that NSL is passed on from one generation to the next. The pupils have always—clandestinely or openly—used NSL when communicating with each other.

The first known description of NSL was written by Sigvald Skavlan, a school headmaster, in 1875. Skavlan's contribution is a short but interesting description of NSL signs, as well as of the structure and grammar of the language.

In the nineteenth century, other sign languages may have influenced NSL, as some teachers of deaf students went abroad to get their education. For example, it is presumed that Møller brought home from Denmark the Danish manual alphabet, which is one-handed. At the same time, a two-handed manual alphabet (whose origin is unknown) was being used at some other schools.

Since 1970 the International Hand Alphabet system has been the official one in Norway; the two-handed system is today officially labeled the manual alphabet for deaf-blind people. However, handshapes from the earlier (before 1970) Norwegian one- and two-handed alphabets are still in use.

RESEARCH

Linguistic research on NSL started around 1980. Two research projects were launched: one by a deaf research scholar, Odd-Inge Schröder, who started his project at the University of Oslo in 1981, and one by Marit Vogt-Svendsen at the Norwegian Postgraduate College of Special Education near Oslo in 1979. In 1983, in the Department of Linguistics at the University of Trondheim, Sign Language was taught for the first time as a university subject. Sign language research in two other Scandinavian countries, Denmark and Sweden, begun about 10 years before the research in Norway, has been of tremendous importance for the development of sign language research in Norway. *See* DENMARK; SWEDEN.

CURRENT STATUS

Since the late 1970s there has been a positive change in attitude toward NSL among deaf people as well as among hearing people. There is a growing demand that NSL should be officially recognized as a language and used systematically in deaf education. This change is also reflected in television programs and courses about deafness and communication where Signed Norwegian was formerly the only code accepted. Another example of the growing acceptance of NSL is reflected in the sign language interpreter training courses that the Norwegian Ministry of Education has organized since 1976.

STRUCTURE

NSL is as richly structured syntactically, morphologically, and phonologically as other sign languages whose grammar has been studied. Few major grammatical differences between sign languages have been observed, whereas quite a few similarities have been pointed out. For example, exactly the same syntactic devices are used in NSL as in American Sign Language for questions answerable by either yes or no. The eyebrows are raised while the manual signs are being produced, the eyes are widened, the head is tilted forward (or downward), and the signer looks at the addressee. It is not the order of signs that distinguishes this type of question from statements, but the use of non-manual (face, head, eye gaze) behaviors.

In contrast to the lexicons (vocabulary) of American and Swedish sign languages the NSL lexicon contains almost no fingerspelled signs—signs that "borrow" from the spoken language by fingerspelling a word in a specially stylized manner. Many signs of this type have been reported for both American and Swedish sign languages.

Although the manual alphabet is used infrequently in NSL, another borrowed element is probably more widely used in NSL than in either American or Swedish sign languages, that is, lip movements borrowed from spoken words. Such lip movements can be seen at particular places in almost every NSL sentence.

Bibliography

Schröder, O.-I.: "Fonologien i Norsk Tegnspråk," in J. M. Tellevik, M. Vogt-Svendsen, O.-I. Schröder (eds.), *Tegnspråk og undervisning av døve barn*, 1983.

Skavlan, S.: *Trondhjems Døvstumme-Institut: Program udgivet i Anledning af Institutets 50-aarige Bestaaen*, 1875.

Vogt-Svendsen, M.: "Lip Movements in Norwegian Sign Language," in J. Kyle and B. Woll (eds.), *Language in Sign*, 1983.

———: "Mouth Position and Mouth Movement in Norwegian Sign Language," *Sign Language Studies*, 33:363-376.

Marit Vogt-Svendsen

Philippine

The Republic of the Philippines has nearly 7100 islands located south of Taiwan and east of China. The population is 52 million, with an estimated 100,000 deaf people. The Philippine School for the Deaf (PSD) teaches the official languages, Filipino and English. Teachers use total communication to speak and sign at the same time. The major spoken dialects are Tagalog, Ilocano, Ilonggo, Cebuano, and Bicolano.

Philippine Sign Language (PSL) is part of the culture of deaf people in the Philippines. However,

PSL signs are now called local signs since American Sign Language (ASL) has become so predominant. ASL was introduced by Delight Rice, whose parents were deaf. She was the organizer and first president (1907–1923) of PSD. Her successor (1923–1936), Julia Hayes, was a sign language specialist who encouraged speechreading and lipreading. In 1962 signs were taught regularly at PSD's high school, the Philippine Association for the Deaf (PAD), Vocational Rehabilitation for the Deaf, and various Bible institutes by the Reverend S. W. Shaneyfelt. His goal was to help increase the vocabulary of signs, to "upgrade" and standardize them. He also encouraged a more "structured" language and the use of initialized signs. In 1974 the teachers of PSD were instructed to attend a course on sign communication taught by Shaneyfelt and his associates.

The Philippine Association for the Deaf (which also uses total communication in its school), the Philippine School for the Deaf, and the Southeast Asian Institute for the Deaf (SAID) have each sponsored and hosted a number of workshops and seminars that included sign communication topics. They have also worked in cooperation with the Ministry of Education and Culture Special Education Unit along with other agencies and institutions that serve the needs of deaf people.

Frances Parsons, a Peace Corps consultant from Gallaudet College in Washington, D.C., who is deaf herself, held several seminars on total communication. She was instrumental in getting deaf Peace Corps volunteers to go to the Philippines and spearhead the concept of speaking and signing simultaneously. It was deaf Peace Corps volunteers who helped SAID produce the first sign vocabulary book in the Philippines. From its beginning SAID has provided instruction in sign vocabulary for interested parties both deaf or hearing. It has always been a total communication school.

The Philippine Registry of Interpreters for the Deaf (PRID) was organized in 1977 by the then existing agencies serving deaf people. PRID began to conduct sign classes and to train professional interpreters, which helped standardize signs.

Professional interpreters are found in schools with mainstreaming programs, on television programs, in vocational education, in the courts, in colleges, and in churches. Some church services are completely sign-oriented for deaf people.

The sign vocabulary book, *Love Signs*, published in 1979, includes drawings of signs in PSL and ASL. The sign names are in Filipino and English. Children's story books showing drawings of signs were produced shortly after by the same author. The Peace Corps volunteers assisted in establishing the books, taking them wherever they went teaching

The **T** and **G** of the Philippine Sign Language. For **G**, the traditional position is at the left; the latest position is at the right.

deaf people and promoting total communication throughout the Philippines.

The T of the PSL alphabet is the only letter officially different from the other letters of the American alphabet. The agencies of PRID decided to modify the T to make it more socially acceptable in the Philippines. The G also creates some question among deaf people. There are two G hand positions now in use in the Philippines. The latest G position can be easily confused with the Q hand position if the signer is not careful. Therefore, the traditional G is still used by many individuals. To date, there has been little linguistic research on the structure of indigenous PSL.

Bibliography

History of the School for the Deaf and Blind: Philippines (1907–1963), Ministry of Education and Culture, Special Education Section—Emilio H. Severino, Special Subjects and Services Division, in charge.

Shaneyfelt, S. W.: *Love Signs*, 1979.

S. Wayne Shaneyfelt

Plains Indian

The Indians of North America developed to a high degree of sophistication both the use of a sign language in direct-contact situations and the use of pictography (picture writing) to record events and to send messages. It is tempting to assume that the relationship between these two visual communication systems is comparable to the written versus spoken forms of a single language, but this analogy is inappropriate. Frequently, pictographs depict signs, indicating an influence of one system upon the other; however, grammatically they share little in common. They are thought of in tandem because they served the needs of one of the most interesting linguistic communities in the history of North America—the Plains Indians.

Origins

Plains Indian Sign Language (PSL) arose as a consequence of the introduction of horses by the Spanish from the south and guns by the French from the east. By the mid-eighteenth century, the combination of the gun and the horse allowed the tribes in the Plains to become more mobile and efficient hunters with a nomadic way of life and widely expanded and often overlapping hunting grounds. This led to a great admixture of languages and dialects. PSL arose as a trade jargon, or interlanguage, between these linguistically diverse groups.

The Plains are bounded by the Great Lakes and the Mississippi River to the east, the Rocky Mountains to the west, central Texas to the south, and the Saskatchewan River Basin to the north. The Plains Indians were actually several distinct subcultures, speaking a multitude of mutually unintelligible languages and dialects at the time of the Europeans' arrival in the sixteenth century. Those in the eastern part of the Plains were semiagricultural tribes that had migrated from the Woodlands up the Mississippi and Missouri rivers. They left their villages only periodically to make war excursions or to hunt buffalo on the Plains like the nonagricultural tribes further west. Even in the eighteenth century, when interaction between these groups was at its height, these subcultures remained distinct. They were united by shared hunting grounds, trading relations with each other and with white people, and by the use of PSL.

The buffalo-based economy of the Plains and the signing trade jargon it gave rise to was a relatively late and short-lived phenomenon. At its height, PSL was a communication system used not only in trade but at every level of social interaction. In the late nineteenth century, the lifestyle that gave rise to the need for PSL once again changed, with the depletion of the buffalo herds and the restriction of Indians to government-established reservations. PSL owes both its birth and its virtual death to the intrusion of white culture into Indian life.

USE

PSL has not totally disappeared. Unlike traditional trade jargons that have been restricted to use between groups with mutually unintelligible languages, PSL appears to have shifted toward use within tribes sharing a common spoken language. Today, although its use is greatly reduced, it is no longer restricted only to male hunters. It is seen most productively in storytelling, but vestiges of it remain frozen into rituals, legends, and prayers. Josephine White Eagle, a Winnebago, was exposed to PSL while living among the Cheyenne and Arapahoe of the Clinton, Watonga, and Kingfisher areas of Oklahoma in 1935. Several tribes lived in that area, and people of all ages and genders were seen to use some form of PSL. It was still used intertribally to some extent, and it was also used daily in the homes, at various social gatherings, and frequently at prayer meetings. White Eagle also observed a deaf Cheyenne who lived in Kingfisher regularly communicate completely in PSL with his

hearing grandson. The conversations would be lengthy and the signing more fluid and quick than that of hearing users of the language, but this deaf signer seemed to be understood by all of the people with whom he came in contact. Although never becoming a fluent signer of PSL, close examination of the signs that White Eagle can still remember reveals that they clearly come from PSL and have very little in common with the American Sign Language (ASL) signs used by the majority of the deaf population in the United States.

It is difficult to reach definite conclusions concerning the structural properties of PSL. Extensive documentation of signs and sign texts is available owing to the diligent efforts of anthropologists and military research personnel, but any detailed formal analysis of PSL and comparison with co-occurring spoken languages remains to be done.

CHARACTERISTICS

Although there is little substantive evidence, it has been assumed that PSL, like other manual interlanguages, is dependent upon the spoken language of the signer. In a 1938 study of PSL, John P. Harrington of the Smithsonian Institution offered the following evidence of PSL's spoken language dependency based upon the comparison of PSL signers whose differing spoken languages compounded words in opposite orders. For example, in Kiowa, the word for God is a compound of *daa'k'ia* (medicine) and *'eidl* (big); whereas in Ojibway it is a compound of *kihtci* (big) followed by *manitoo* (spirit). In PSL, the sign for God is also a compound made up of one sign meaning "medicine," "mystery," or "spirit" and another meaning "big." The order of the compounded signs varies, however, depending upon the spoken language background of the signer. The Kiowa signer signs MEDICINE/SPIRIT + BIG and the Ojibway signer does the opposite, BIG + MEDICINE/SPIRIT. Other support for the spoken language dependency of PSL comes from the fact that idioms in PSL are frequently word-for-word translations of spoken language idioms; signing is often accompanied by speech (argued by some to be a modernism); and it lacks any language-particular facial expressions—a common characteristic of spoken language–dependent codes (like Signed English, for example).

A few linguistic characteristics of PSL can be considered, keeping in mind the possibility that certain word order and word formation properties may have varied as a result of the spoken language of the signer. One of the most concise sources of such information is a grammatical sketch written by A. L. Kroeber in 1958. Formationally, the signing space for PSL is significantly larger than that of ASL. This may be related to the conditions under

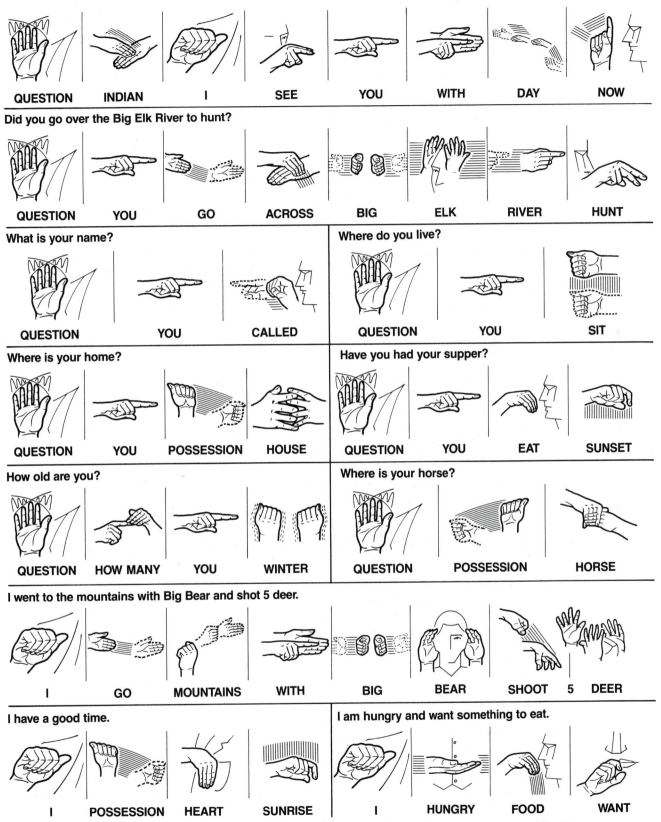

Who was that Indian I saw you with today?

QUESTION — INDIAN — I — SEE — YOU — WITH — DAY — NOW

Did you go over the Big Elk River to hunt?

QUESTION — YOU — GO — ACROSS — BIG — ELK — RIVER — HUNT

What is your name?

QUESTION — YOU — CALLED

Where do you live?

QUESTION — YOU — SIT

Where is your home?

QUESTION — YOU — POSSESSION — HOUSE

Have you had your supper?

QUESTION — YOU — EAT — SUNSET

How old are you?

QUESTION — HOW MANY — YOU — WINTER

Where is your horse?

QUESTION — POSSESSION — HORSE

I went to the mountains with Big Bear and shot 5 deer.

I — GO — MOUNTAINS — WITH — BIG — BEAR — SHOOT — 5 — DEER

I have a good time.

I — POSSESSION — HEART — SUNRISE

I am hungry and want something to eat.

I — HUNGRY — FOOD — WANT

Examples of sentences from Plains Indian Sign Language. (After W. J. Tomkins, *Indian Sign Language*, Dover Publications, New York, 1978)

which signing most frequently occurred rather than to any language difference. PSL was more frequently signed at distance and was also generally observed in formal or ceremonial situations. A counting system was used that differs considerably from that of ASL, and there was no form of fingerspelling. There are both one- and two-handed signs, involving a range of symmetrical and asymmetrical movement relations comparable to those found in ASL. Body parts are frequently used as locations for signs, often indicating a semantic grouping of signs (forehead = cognition, eyes = vision, mouth = locution, and so on). There are no reports of nonmanual body parts alone being used as signs. Even the sign for "yes," which supposedly indicates nodding the head, involves a raised index finger that bends forward.

Signs could be morphologically modified. For example, two-handed or doubly articulated signs often indicate plurality or iteration. Directionality was used to indicate source-goal or active-passive distinctions. The sign meaning "to charge others" is made by having both fists near the right shoulder move sharply down and leftward while the fingers snap open. The signs for "to charge against us" is made by reversing this action, starting with the fists well out in front of the body and snapping them open toward the signer's own face. Similar alternations are found between the signs for "give you" and "give me," or "pity you" and "pity me."

Pronouns are indicated by pointing to the referent. There are no grammatical differences for subject-versus-object pronouns. Plurality can be indicated by suffixing the sign for "all" to nouns or pronouns. Possession is indicated by adding a possessive marker to the pronoun. Grammatical markers generally follow the sign to which they are associated, but elements like the possessive pronoun generally precede the noun, such as YOU + POSSESSIVE HOUSE = "your house."

Compounding of two or more signs appears to have been an extremely productive means of expanding the PSL lexicon: alike = FACE + SAME; bury = BLANKET + WRAP + DIG; angry = BRAIN + TWISTED; elope = STEAL + WOMAN; government agent = WHITE + CHIEF + GIVE + FOOD. Two types of elements are always compound-final, negatives (absent = SIT + NOT, soft = STONE + NOT) and locatives (bridge = LEVEL + RIVER + ACROSS, help = WORK + WITH). Negatives are also sentence-final in PSL, and locatives, in the spoken languages of the Plains area, tend to be suffixes.

PSL shares with ASL the fact that it is a discourse-oriented language, meaning that it orders utterances in terms of old information followed by new information. As in many such languages, sentences in PSL can be rather lengthy and complex, but they do not overtly express sign counterparts of conjunctions (and, but, or), determiners (a, an, the), complementizers (which, that), an infinitive marker (to), or forms of the verb "to be." Verbs are not separately marked for past, present, or future, but tense marking is established in a separate sentence or by a separate time sign.

Unlike ASL, where question signs either occur at the beginning and end of the sentence or occur only sentence-final, question signs in PSL are invariably in initial position. The question sign itself, however, shares much in common with the question marker sign in ASL. In both instances there is one question sign that can mark both "yes/no questions" and "who, what, where, and how questions." The interpretation of the question sign depends upon the context in which it occurs.

Since the mid-1950s, although the fields of linguistics and anthropology have grown by leaps and bounds, PSL has been virtually ignored. As a result, little is known concerning the current status of this language or its future prospects. Considering the advancements made in the field of sign language research since its beginnings in the early 1960s, the extensive body of data on PSL, both in note form and on film, deserves a second look. It is an untapped resource of invaluable information.

Bibliography

Kegl, J. A., and G. Nigrosh: "Sign Language and Pictographs: A Comparison of the Signs and Picture Writing of the North American Plains Indians," unpublished manuscript, Brown University, Providence, Rhode Island, 1975.

Mallery, Garrick: *Sign Language Among the North American Indians Compared with That Among Other Peoples and Deaf-Mutes*, Mouton, The Hague, 1972 (original in U.S. Bureau of Ethnology Annual Report, vol. 1, 1881).

Tomkins, W. J.: *Indian Sign Language*, Dover Publications, New York, 1969.

Umiker-Sebeok, D. J., and T. A. Sebeok (eds.): *Aboriginal Sign Languages of the Americas and Australia*, vols. 1 and 2, Plenum Press, New York, 1978.

West, La Mont: *The Sign Language, An Analysis*, unpublished doctoral dissertation, Indiana University, Bloomington, 1960.

Judy Anne Kegl; Josephine White Eagle

Polish

Poland is a Middle European country with 37 million inhabitants. There are about 700,000 people with hearing impairments, of whom about 50,000 are deaf. The only all-nation social organization is the Polish Association of the Deaf (Polaki Zwiazek Gzuchyeh, or PZG) with 25,000 members.

HISTORY

The development and spread of the sign language in the environment of deaf people is closely related with the development of specialized deaf education; hence, its name, the school sign language.

The Institute of the Deaf and Dumb, established on October 23, 1817, by Father Jakub Falkowski, was the first specialized school in Polish territory. Father Falkowski had introduced the mime (manual) method together with a manual alphabet based on the French model, with special signs for letters peculiar to the Polish language. This school sign language was used by priests and preachers of various faiths to teach religion. However, other schools established after Falkowski's death were in principle based on the oral method.

In 1879 Father J. Hollak and Father T. Jagodzinski, religion teachers in the Institute of the Deaf and Dumb, developed and edited the first Polish descriptive dictionary of the sign language, with about 12,000 entries on 535 printed pages. This was also an attempt to unify Polish Sign Language, since various regional dialects existed in the Polish special schools for deaf children.

In the period between the world wars, only 12 percent of deaf children attended schools in Poland; the other 88 percent remained illiterate, exempted from compulsory school attendance due to lack of adequate specialized schools.

Official statistics in 1924 recorded nine establishments for deaf students with 693 wardees. By 1938 there were 16 establishments with 1311 wardees. The oral method was used in all of the schools, while the school sign language was condemned and banished by the educational authorities.

The situation changed after World War II. Nine establishments existed in 1947 and 857 children attended. By the 1982-1983 school year, Poland had 10 kindergartens and kindergarten groups, 23 primary schools for deaf children, 5 schools for hard-of-hearing children, 13 basic vocational schools, and 2 secondary vocational technical schools and vocational grammar schools, enrolling altogether 5000 deaf and hard-of-hearing children. Another 1000 children attended various types of general-purpose schools together with hearing children.

The oral method was used in all of the schools, although the manual alphabet was tolerated in some. However, the quantitative increase in special schools for deaf children but inadequate results of the education achieved by the pupils, particularly in mastering the Polish language, induced the Polish Association of the Deaf to organize efforts to promote the proper use of the school sign language and the Polish manual alphabet. This was to take place not only in special schools, but also within the framework of the widening statutory activities of the association and in the everyday life of deaf people.

CURRENT STATUS

The most important activities of the Polish Association of the Deaf pertaining to the school sign language have been as follows. In 1949–1952 the association organized about 500 primary education courses for 4100 illiterate deaf people within the framework of an all-Poland campaign to liquidate illiteracy. The unified Polish manual alphabet was introduced into the first Polish primer for adult illiterates, entitled *Our Book* (1950) by J. Landy-Brsezinska and W. Tuzodziecki.

Next, the Polish Association of the Deaf undertook a major project to unify the school sign language; to develop teaching curricula, methods, textbooks, and other teaching materials; to educate sign language interpreters to meet the needs of deaf people, of the special education system, and of work enterprises; and to continue its publishing program.

The Polish Association of the Deaf is the first social organization of deaf people in Europe to have a scientific council, existing since 1949 under various names. This council initiated the Polish way of rehabilitating the deaf child of kindergarten age, described in the Fifth Congress of the World Federation of the Deaf (Warsaw, 1967). Results of scientific investigations into the problems of deafness enabled the establishment in 1959 of the Clinic for Rehabilitation of Children and Youths with Hearing Defects, which uses total communication.

The Polish Association of the Deaf also operates the special Committee for Unification of the Sign Language, which has developed and edited several specialist publications. The Polish television since 1982 has regularly broadcast programs for deaf viewers entitled *In the World of Silence*, along with other programs based on the unified sign language. Results of the all-Poland campaign to educate sign language interpreters, carried out by the association since 1965, have made possible the use of interpreters at special events organized for deaf people as well as in vocational education courses, in medical clinics, in courts, in social service agencies, in enterprises employing a number of deaf workers, and in some of the special schools.

STRUCTURE

Teachers of deaf people criticize the school sign language as being primitive, not having the inflection typical for Slavic languages, and being grammatically different from the Polish language. They say that to use the school sign language properly and in accordance with Polish language grammar, the Polish manual alphabet must be used to spell the word endings that indicate grammatical form. This supposedly overcomes the grammatical differences between the school sign language and the Polish language.

Two principal methods of using the sign language in Poland are known. The school sign language (Polish Sign Language) is the most common one; American Sign Language and French Sign Language are its analogs. The second is that introduced by the Polish Association of the Deaf under the Polish name *migany jezyk polski* (Polish finger language). It is used for certain educational purposes and has two forms: (1) simplified—Seeing Essential Polish (Seeing Essential English is its analog); and (2) full—Signing Exact Polish (Signing Exact English is its analog).

It is now apparent that the deaf child in Poland is in principle a two-language child. The school sign language is the mother language; the Polish language remains practically a foreign language and is mastered with much greater difficulty.

Bibliography

Hendzel, J. K.: *Turystyczny szownik jezyke migowege*, PTTK, W-wa, Krakow, 1981.

Szczepankowski, B.: *Ideografia*, PZG, W-wa, 1978.

————: *Jezyk migowy*, cz.I. Wprowadzenie, W-wa, 1974.

————: *Jezyk migowy*, cz.II. Daktylogretia, W-wa, 1974.

Stanislaw Sila-Nowicki

Portuguese

Portuguese Sign Language (PSL) is the native language of a considerable part of an estimated population of 8000 deaf people in Portugal.

It is called *Lingua* (or earlier, *Linguagem*) *Gestual Portuguesa*. PSL is not derived from Portuguese, which influenced it in only a rather limited way due to some particular conditions in the coexistence of the languages.

Two different sign dialects are usually reported by deaf people as existing in Lisbon and Oporto, the cities where the oldest and most outstanding schools are located. However, lexical variation is also found in these regions, and different signs are easily identified as belonging to a certain school.

HISTORY

The history of PSL is strongly related to the education of deaf people and may be traced back to 1823 when Per Aron Borg, who is regarded as the founder of the teaching of deaf people in Sweden, established in Lisbon the first Portuguese school for deaf children. The school started with eight students under the protection of the king of Portugal and with state support. The method used was called mimic, in the terminology of the early twentieth century. *See* SWEDEN.

If Borg put into practice his ideas about using the natural language his pupils already had, then one can assume that the foundations for PSL were taken from Borg's Portuguese deaf students. Considering, however, that their knowledge increased with education and that new signs would be needed to express newly acquired concepts, at least some signs taken from Swedish deaf people might well have been introduced by Borg.

The manual alphabet, taken as an artificial instrument to help in teaching, is a different matter. The same reasons that led Borg to create and introduce it in Sweden were also valid in Portugal. The spread of Borg's manual alphabet to Portugal is apparent from a chart, published in 1913, of the alphabets of Sweden, Portugal, and Finland. More similarities still exist between the Portuguese and Swedish alphabets than between the Portuguese and any other. The resemblances are even greater if the comparison is made with older versions of the Portuguese alphabet.

The first attempts to introduce the oral method occurred about 1890, but only in the beginning of the twentieth century was it generally adopted. No official resolution was ever passed in Portugal to recommend any communication method in the educational system. However, supporters of the oral method have tried to defend their views by referring to a 1906 decree in which the government raised the funding assigned to the recently reorganized school and pointed out "the convenience to establish the pure oral method."

CURRENT STATUS

After 1975 there was a great increase in the number of deaf students who attended secondary schools. Deaf students were grouped in the newly created special classes. Some educators started to doubt the value of the oral approach and to show an increasing interest in learning to sign.

As a result, the language of this new generation of signers is quite different from the older one. It shows more and more influence of the coexisting oral language. For instance, Portuguese word order is followed with more exactitude; in an increasing number of situations, manual signs are accompanied by the mouthing of Portuguese words; new concepts for which there is no sign might be transmitted either as a fingerspelled word or by the mouthing of the Portuguese word sometimes accompanied by a manual sign which usually is just the hand configuration for the first letter of the word articulated orally. Initialized signs, once created, may be adopted or substituted by others more compatible with established sign conventions.

Bibliography

Bergman, B.: *Signed Swedish*, National Swedish Board of Education, Stockholm, 1979.

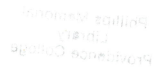

Mora, D.: *O Censo da População Deficiente*, working paper, Lisbon, 1985.

Santos, A.: *O Ensino dos Surdos-Mudos em Portugal*, Lisbon, 1918.

——: *Situação do Analfabetismo nos Distritos do Continente em 1981*, Publicação da Divisão de Estudos da D.G.E.A., Lisbon, 1984.

Maria Isabel Prata

Providence Island

Providence Island is an isolated Caribbean island. Although it is governed by Spanish-speaking Colombia, the first language of hearing islanders is an English creole. At least 19 of the island's 2500–3000 people were born deaf. Most people on the island know and use Providence Island Sign Language (PROVISL), although signers in the eastern part of the island sign differently from signers in the western part. There is also some sign variation between villages within each of these two general areas.

HISTORY

Research to date shows no relationship between PROVISL and any European or South American sign language. PROVISL developed indigenously and appears to be about 100 years old.

The first permanent settlement of Providence occurred around 1787 by 10 English-speaking whites and 12 blacks. By 1835 there were 342 English-speaking inhabitants. The population of Providence did not greatly expand until around 1900. Caesar Newball (born circa 1880) probably was the first deaf person to live on Providence and the first fluent user of PROVISL. Since Newball's time, PROVISL has expanded in use so that the great majority of both deaf and hearing people on Providence are competent in PROVISL. *See* HISTORY: Martha's Vineyard.

STATUS

PROVISL is autonomous from oral languages on Providence Island; its dialect variation is not related to that of oral languages. PROVISL is used for all everyday activities between deaf and deaf and between deaf and hearing islanders. It is not used in education, however, since education is controlled by nonislanders. Hearing people sometimes employ a word order similar to English when they sign, but there is no formal sign continuum for hearing people. Deaf people do not approach English word order when they sign. There is also no diglossic situation between PROVISL and any other signed varieties, since there is no separate deaf community on Providence Island. *See* SOCIO-LINGUISTICS: Sign Language Continuum.

Most of the hearing people on Providence have very positive attitudes toward deaf people and PROVISL. Studies indicate that 70 percent of the hearing population believe that the union of two hearing persons is more likely to cause deafness on Providence than the union of a deaf person with a hearing person or with another deaf person. Deaf people are viewed as equally or more intelligent, equally mature, and less likely to have mental problems, or at least no more likely to have mental problems, than hearing people. Finally, while the introduction of a cash economy on Providence Island is creating specialization of jobs and resulting in some discrimination against deaf people, deaf workers still receive the same pay as hearing workers for the same jobs.

PHONOLOGY

PROVISL has a relatively small set of handshapes—in fact, one of the smallest in the world. This offers a unique insight into the minimum number of handshapes necessary for a sign language. PROVISL has the following distinctive handshapes: 1, 5, S, O, F, bO, C 2. (The handshapes X, Y, I occur very rarely at the phonetic level in PROVISL; however, it is possible to derive all X and I handshapes from an underlying 1 handshape. Y handshape occurs only in one morpheme of the language, BOAT-MAST.)

PROVISL has the expected gross locations of arm, trunk, face, hand, and zero tabs. However, it also has leg and any-tab signs. These last two locations are not commonly found in sign languages. Leg tabs are either upper or lower leg (including foot). Arm tabs are either upper or lower arm. Trunk tabs include shoulder, high, mid, low, ipsi (same), and low center. Face tabs include entire face, high, mid, low, side of face, ear, and neck.

Orientation is not distinctive in PROVISL for leg, arm, trunk, or any-tab signs. It is distinctive for face, hand, and zero tabs. No systematic analysis of movements in PROVISL has occurred.

From the evidence to date, PROVISL has one of the most extensive systems of distinctive nonmanual markers at the phonological level. One study reports that 25 percent of a list of citation forms of signs had some kind of nonmanual movement associated with the sign. Most of this movement was mouth (not speech-related) movement, followed by eye movement. Also fairly commonly found were shoulder, trunk, nose, and leg movement. Signs such as PUSS (CAT), DOG, SMALL-PIG; MAN and FATHER; WOMAN and MOTHER; HOW, ASK, DON'T KNOW as well as many other signs are distinguished only by nonmanual markers.

SYNTAX

There is little systematic research on the syntax of PROVISL. However, the following principles are of interest. In terms of word order, PROVISL has: (1) preferred subject-verb word order in intransitive sentences; (2) preferred subject-object-verb word order for transitive sentences; (3) preferred noun-adjective-numeral-determiner word order for noun phrases; (4) preferred verb-negative word order; and (5) same word order for statements and questions.

Like most subject-object-verb languages, PROVISL allows variation in this word order. Also, like most noun-adjective languages, PROVISL allows variation in this word order.

Time is represented syntactically (by a separate sign), not morphologically (as part of the verb sign). Some sections of the island distinguish present (not signed), PAST (with the outward ipsi movement), and FUTURE (with inward movement). Other parts of the island distinguish present (not signed) and NONPRESENT (with outward ipsi movement).

Modal verbs like CAN are incorporated nonmanually into the verb sign.

SUMMARY

PROVISL provides important insights into the nature of language. The sociolinguistic interaction of deaf and hearing people on Providence Island demonstrates that it is possible for deaf people to be integrated into hearing society, if hearing people adapt to the needs of deaf individuals. Furthermore, PROVISL, with its small number of distinctive handshapes, yet its extensive use of nonmanual expression, illustrates important constraints on sign language phonology. Finally, the use of constructions such as subject-object-verb word order and present/nonpresent time clearly shows that PROVISL has an autonomous grammar from the oral languages used on the island.

Bibliography

Washabaugh, W., J. Woodward, and S. De Santis: "Providence Island Sign Language: A Context-Dependent Language," *Anthropological Linguistics*, pp. 95–109, March 1978.

Woodward, J.: "Beliefs About and Attitudes Towards Deaf People and Sign Language on Providence Island," in J. Woodward, *How You Gonna Get to Heaven If You Can't Talk with Jesus: On Depathologizing Deafness*, pp. 51–74. T. J. Publishers, Silver Spring, Maryland, 1982.

James Woodward

Puerto Rican

Puerto Rican Sign Language (PRSL) is related to, but distinct from, the sign language used in the mainland United States.

POPULATION CHARACTERISTICS

Puerto Rico is an island in the Caribbean, approximately 100 by 30 miles (160 × 48 kilometers), politically designated a commonwealth of the United States. The people are thus United States citizens and English is one of their spoken languages. Since, however, the island was a colony of Spain for many years, much Spanish influence is still evident, and Spanish is the first spoken language for most of the island's inhabitants.

The deaf population is estimated at from 8000 to 40,000 individuals by rehabilitation and educational agencies, although Puerto Rico was not part of the deaf census conducted by the National Association of the Deaf in 1974. Several reasons can be given for supposing that even the larger figure may be an underestimate. Deaf children on the island may be educated either at the San Gabriel School for the Deaf in Puerto Nuevo (within the San Juan metropolitan area) or in any of nearly 30 special classrooms operated by the Department of Instruction around the island. However, there are no educational facilities for deaf students beyond primary level, and therefore some families move to New York, Florida, Illinois, or other parts of the United States while their deaf children are in school. Some of these deaf individuals may choose to return to Puerto Rico upon reaching adulthood and may have no contact with the rehabilitation system after that. In farming or fishing communities in outlying areas of the island, deaf individuals may live within their family units throughout their whole lives, never becoming part of the educational system and never receiving rehabilitation services. These people would probably not be included in the estimate above.

ORIGINS

The history of PRSL is related to the history of public education for deaf children. In 1907 an American order of nuns, the Dominicans, came to San Juan and founded the San Gabriel School for the Deaf. They introduced the sign language used in the United States at that time, namely American Sign Language (ASL), to the instructional setting in Puerto Rico as part of the combined method of instruction. The location of the school changed at least twice within the San Juan area, and in the 1950s the administration of the school also changed. A Spanish teaching order, the Benedictines, introduced the oral method at this time and forbade the use of signing in the school. The spoken language that was emphasized during the tenure of the original order was English, but Spanish became the language of instruction in both deaf and hearing schools. In the 1970s a Lutheran group from Canada founded a school in the Luquillo area, which uses English and Signed English as the mediums of instruction. Also in the 1970s instructors from the New York University Deafness Research and Training Center gave special training courses in Signed Spanish for rehabilitation workers including counselors, instructors at the vocational training center, and interpreters. At least four persons were also given training in interpreting for deaf people in New York and California in the early 1970s. *See* EDUCATION: Communication.

At least four varieties of sign language are used on the island. In addition, an undetermined number of home sign systems exist within particular households. Signed Spanish is a pidgin language used by deaf persons in contact with Spanish-speaking hearing persons: it uses many features of Spanish word order, uses some initialized signs (where the hand configuration of the sign matches the manual alphabet shape of the first letter of the Spanish word it represents), and may incorporate fingerspelling and special signs intended to convey Spanish grammatical function words (*es, que,* and so on). Signed English is a pidgin language used by deaf persons who may have been educated largely in the United States and who come in contact with English-speaking hearing people: it follows the word order of English, incorporates initialized signs, may incorporate fingerspelling and, like the Signed Spanish, uses some special signs for English grammatical forms (*is, -ing,* and so on). Each of the pidgins includes mouth movements that more or less match the spoken language forms of words. Signed Spanish is the most common form of language used by hearing persons in communication to deaf persons, including on the nightly television news, in interpreting, and in rehabilitation settings. *See* MANUALLY CODED ENGLISH; SIGNS: Home Signs.

CHARACTERISTICS

Puerto Rican Sign Language is a gestural-visual language which is thought to have stemmed from American Sign Language around 1910. The separation between these two language communities has never been total, although some individuals only use PRSL. The most obvious differences between PRSL and ASL are (1) the absence of fingerspelling or fingerspelled loans as a method of borrowing from spoken language in PRSL; (2) signs that are related but systematically different; and (3) signs that are unrelated between athe two languages. At the present time, too little is known to determine in what ways the grammars (morphology, syntax) have diverged from one another.

Fingerspelling is known to PRSL users, but only as a way of representing written words, by slowly indicating each letter. There is no rhythm or flow toward fluent fingerspelling, and the whole body of forms which ASL has borrowed from English through restructuring fingerspelling does not exist. Given that Spanish is the spoken and written language used most, it might be expected that Spanish forms would undergo restructuring, but these have not been observed. In fact, where ASL has restructured fingerspelled words into signs, PRSL has dis-

tinctive signed forms. PRSL and Signed Spanish both use initialized forms for the days of the week which correspond to Spanish spelling (ASL: MONDAY; PRSL: LUNES). Name signs for people and some place names in Puerto Rico do use initial letter handshapes, for example, SAN-JUAN, PONCE, MAYAGUEZ, but this process does not seem to be productive in other semantic fields. *See* SIGNS: Fingerspelling.

American Sign Language is used by some deaf Puerto Ricans who have gone to school or worked in the United States. A small but visible number of individuals have chosen to migrate to Puerto Rico, because of health, family, or business reasons, and they then may use ASL either with one another or as their preferred active language.

Structural aspects of PRSL that mark it as a natural sign language include the structured use of space to mark relations between objects or ideas, the use of classifiers and size and shape specifiers, the productive use of compound signs to name novel objects or ideas, and the variation in the movement dynamics of signs to signal consistent variations in temporal and distributional aspect.

Of some interest is the relationship between the sign language varieties in the New York City area and in Puerto Rico, as both of these differ from standard ASL. In a few cases the same sign is shared by the two varieties, but not elsewhere in the United States. Examples are LECHE/MILK (as a noun), two hands in fists with thumbs extended, brushing up and down against each other along the midline; AYER/YESTERDAY, Y-HAND (though presumably not an initialized shape) contacts lower cheek, then midchest. Both of these cases show relationship to standard ASL forms, but the variants are consistent and distinct from the expected ASL signs.

Attitudes of hearing people in Puerto Rico are in general positive and open toward gestural communication. Perhaps because there is less literacy, or perhaps because the population is smaller and more homogeneous than in the United States at large, hearing people appear to be willing to enter into gestural interaction with deaf individuals in ordinary public settings (in restaurants, shops, and so on).

Nancy Frishberg

Rennellese

The Rennellese Sign Language was developed at the beginning of the twentieth century on Rennell Island, a raised atoll in the Solomon Islands. Though situated in Melanesia, the Rennellese are Polynesians who arrived on the island 24 generations ago. Because of the island's small size (250 square miles or 640 square kilometers), its isolated geographical position, and its bad anchorage, the islanders lived almost entirely without outside contact until 1938.

According to oral traditions, there was never a deaf person on the island before the birth of the boy Kagobai about 1915. For that reason no sign language existed on the island. The vocal language, one of the most copious Polynesian languages, thus had no terms for "deaf" or "mute." There existed only a term for being "hard of hearing," referring to the impaired hearing of old people. In order to transcend the world of communicative isolation, Kagobai developed a communicative device. It consisted of a number of signs which can be combined into sentences by way of a very simple grammar. A systematic analysis of the syntactical rules has not yet been conducted.

Structurally one can distinguish between three sign categories: indicative signs, imitative signs, and symbolical signs. The indicative signs vary with their degree of proximity to the signer's own body. The signer can touch a body part, point to phenomena within sight, or point with sweeping movements to far-away objects of mainly geographical or astronomical art. The imitative signs are concerned with all parts of everyday life and constitute the largest part of the sign vocabulary. A coconut crab, for example, is signed by its characteristic movements. It is within the group of symbolic signs that one finds the greatest creativity. In most of these signs basic cultural values are encoded, for example, the sign for "brother-sister." This sign consists of two extended index fingers facing each other with their dorsal sides, thus signifying the socially determined brother-sister avoidance tabu.

Several signs consist of two or more constituents, such as the sign for "past," which is based on an arm movement toward the horizon, indicating

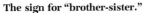

The sign for "brother-sister."

something far away, and a hand movement to the neck, indicating "killing." The past thus means that something is as far away (in time) as when the Rennellese still killed each other. For many of the signs there is a close relationship to the cultural values of the society.

On the decoding side one finds that some of the signs are interculturally understandable, such as the sign "to drink" or "to copulate." Some signs are not interculturally understandable, as the sign for "brother-sister." Other signs are not immediately decipherable. These are idiocyncratic signs, the meaning of which is not accessible without further explanation. Such a sign is used for "father," in which the signer points to the position of the tattoo on the buttock. The sign creator's own father had such a tattoo.

Whether or not the Rennellese signs constitute a language (which only a syntactical analysis can determine), the creation of this communicative vehicle required intellectual effort and a deep-rooted desire to penetrate the barrier of silence.

Bibliography

Kuschel, R.: *A Lexicon of Signs from a Polynesian Outlier Island: A Description of 217 Signs as Developed and Used by Kagobai, the Only Deaf-Mute of Rennell Island*, Akademisk Forlag, Copenhagen, 1974.

———: "The Silent Inventor: The Creation of a Sign Language by the Only Deaf-Mute on a Polynesian Island," *Sign Language Studies*, 3:1–27, 1974.

Rolf Kuschel

South African

The Republic of South Africa, located at the southernmost tip of Africa, comprises four provinces: Cape Province, Natal, Transvaal, and the Orange Free State. South West Africa–Namibia, which borders the republic on the northwest, was mandated to South Africa by the United Nations after World War II to govern at its own expense. The Republic of South Africa includes legislated "homelands" occupied by indigent black people of various cultures and ethnic origin.

Historically, South Africa was the meeting point of many nations from Africa, Asia, and Europe, resulting in a mosaic of nations, colors, religions, educations, language traditions, and development levels. Vast cultural differences still exist among the more than 27 million people of South Africa. Certain tribes such as the Khoisan still live as their forefathers did centuries ago, while members of other tribes and ethnic groups have advanced to the highest levels of technological development. The population embraces nine major language groups, each group being proud of its heritage. This pride in the past, combined with traditional political structures, has greatly influenced the educational policy and structure.

HISTORICAL OVERVIEW

Approximately 120 years ago, the Dominican Sisters of the Catholic Church of Ireland established the first school for deaf children of English families. The North British system of communication was introduced in this school in those early years.

During 1881 W. Murray of the Dutch Reformed Church established a school for deaf children from Afrikaans-speaking homes. Allegedly the British Sign Language system was introduced in this school. By the turn of the century three schools were in existence. Controversy concerning the communication medium had already started during this period and continued for more than 80 years. This history of deaf education has had a significant influence on the communication systems of adult deaf people today.

EDUCATION POLICY

The current policy of deaf education in South Africa can be divided into three major categories, that is, black school children, white school children, and colored (mixed racial) and Indian (Asian) school children. There are 29 schools for deaf pupils with a total of 4000 children.

Schools for black children are governed by various private groups such as churches and welfare organizations. They receive state aid and therefore are subject to the policy of the Department of Education and Training. This department introduced a manual code based on the Paget-Gorman system in the schools under its jurisdiction around the early 1950s. The manual *Talking to the Deaf* replaced the Paget-Gorman system during 1980 and now forms the model for signing in these schools. This form of signing follows the grammatical rules of the spoken language and is used to facilitate acquisition of that spoken language. The rationale for this communication method is to teach deaf children to communicate not only with deaf peers but also with hearing persons so that they can become part of both communities. *See* GORMAN, PIERRE PATRICK.

As is the case with schools for black deaf children, the schools for white deaf children are state-aided and governed by churches. These schools are subject to the policy of the Department of Education, which aims to "socialize" deaf people and integrate them into the hearing communities.

Formerly, no school was permitted to use any signing system for formal education. The policy now adopted does not exclude any method to teach children under its jurisdiction on any grounds as long as the method helps children to learn. Two schools have already introduced Coded Afrikaans in signs contained in *Talking to the Deaf*, as well as in other manuals. This method is used in a limited way, as the emphasis is still on the oral method.

The two departments responsible for colored and Indian deaf children have followed the lead of the Department of Education for white children.

DEAF ADULTS

Communication between deaf adults is usually by way of sign language and fingerspelling. There are a number of dialects that have developed unofficially at each particular residential school and have been passed on from one generation to the next. Variations from school to school are said to cause considerable confusion among adult deaf people, as signs used in one locality are not necessarily used in another. Very few hearing people can conduct a conversation with deaf people in the deaf sign vernacular. Speech augmented by signs and fingerspelling is a normal method of communication between hearing and deaf people.

Nine different sign language systems exist in South Africa. The deaf population is divided into four sign language groups: black deaf (approximately 6000), English-speaking white (2000), and Indian deaf (900), colored deaf (1200), and the Afrikaans-speaking white deaf (2000).

Today all deaf people possess some knowledge of English, Afrikaans, or other indigenous, spoken language. Most deaf people use the sign language of their particular region, which has been passed on from generation to generation. Only a few hearing signers who have deaf parents or other relatives can use sign language. The "deaf" language, understood to some degree by most deaf people in South Africa, differs entirely from "hearing" language. Signs often correspond to concepts, not spoken words, and do not necessarily have a word equivalent.

RESEARCH

Norman Nieder-Heitmann, formerly vice-chairperson of the South African National Council for the Deaf, was appointed during 1974 to a one-man committee to research the various sign language systems in South Africa and to investigate the possibility of standardizing the signs. This was the first step to codify the signs used in South Africa to aid schools, employers, hospitals, social workers, ministers of religion, and interpreters of all language groups. In 1978 the Department of Education and Training took over the project by appointing Nieder-Heitmann as a full-time research officer.

Nieder-Heitmann decided from the onset that it would be expedient to conduct a preliminary survey before undertaking this vast project. This enabled him to determine the amount of uniformity in the signs used throughout South Africa, whether these signs were adaptable, and what the roots of such signs were.

During the initial stages of the research project

it was found that 60 percent of the signs were of British (or Australian) origin. Few signs of American origin were being used, and no Paget signs could be identified, despite the fact that the Paget-Gorman system had been taught in many schools for 15 years.

Seven years after the appointment of the one-man committee, the first dictionary on signs in South Africa was published under the title *Talking to the Deaf.* It contained some 1500 words and signs, overlapping the four major language groups. Since the need existed to continue the research, the South African National Council for the Deaf reappointed a research committee. The committee tested the validity of the signs contained in the manual by questioning seven deaf leader groups from various regions in South Africa. From the research it was found that almost 95 percent of the signs in the manual were recognized by these groups, although not necessarily used by all of them. The deaf groups also said that they would be prepared to accept these signs if no alternative was available. Of the signs in the manual, 60 percent correspond with American Sign Language and 35 percent with Gestuno.

The one-handed manual alphabet is now recognized as the official fingerspelling method. The two-handed manual alphabet, which was used in the past by older deaf people, especially those who attended Afrikaans schools, will be phased out over a period of time. The committee has not as yet finalized its work.

INTERPRETERS
No formal training programs for sign language interpreters exist in South Africa. Hearing children of deaf parents, teachers, ministers of religion, and social workers act as interpreters in courts of law, at meetings, and at church services. Some of the interpreters in courts of law are officially appointed by the Department of Justice. No specific qualification is required for this appointment, and each interpreter uses signs almost at random, according to personal taste and the particular needs of the deaf person. Interpreters are not used at postschool training institutions for practical reasons. *See* SOUTH AFRICA, REPUBLIC OF.

Bibliography
Gouws, M.: *Onderwys en Skoolvoorligting vir Dowe Leerlinge,* HSRC Report 0-37, Pretoria, 1957.

Hamilton, J. H.: "Vocational Training and Career Guidance for the Deaf," *Education News,* September 1983.

Nieder-Heitmann, N.: "A Survey of Modern History of Deaf Education," *Silent Messenger,* SANCD, March 1973.

———: *Talking to the Deaf,* Government Printer, 1980.

Rhoodie, E.: *Third Africa,* 1969.

South African National Council for the Deaf: *Jubileum Publication of the South African National Council for the Deaf,* 1979.

Viljoen, S. W.: "Uniform Sign Language for South Africa," *Silent Messenger,* vol. 5, no. 3, SANCD, July/August 1982.

Johan M. Herbst

Spanish
The origins of sign language in Spain are unknown. While Friar Pedro Ponce de Leon (1512?–1584), a Spanish Benedictine monk, is considered to be the person who invented a communication system to teach deaf people, it seems that he did so through the oral method, not with sign language. In several extant portraits he is ostensibly shown with his hand in a closed fist, as if to indicate that he used the fingerspelling system; however, there is no proof indicating that he did so. *See* PONCE DE LEON, PEDRO.

USAGE
Gestural language is generally used by all deaf Spaniards. Fingerspelling is used rarely and almost exclusively for proper names (or persons or cities, for example) or when an appropriate gestural sign is lacking. Spanish Sign is extensive, energetic, and very expressive.

The small differences in gestures throughout Spain do not impede comprehension in any way. The only exception is Catalonia, where there is a quite differentiated and "native" sign language, even though the common gestures of Spanish Sign predominate. This general comprehension was not always the case, however, for in the past each city and each school for deaf children would alter the Spanish Sign Language. Moreover, school teachers are not required to know Spanish Sign.

The Spanish National Confederation of the Deaf has made various attempts to avoid differences in sign usage and the ensuing confusion they create. The most ambitious is the publication of the *Dictionary of Spanish Sign (Diccionario Mimico Español)* which, with 584 pages, 3258 words, and nearly 5000 photographs, should serve to unite Spanish Sign.

CHARACTERISTICS
Spanish Sign structure is poorly understood and perhaps quite irregular. The subject, verb, and object or predicate of a sentence, for example, do not seem to have a well-defined order. Thus, it is a common occurrence for a deaf person to sign "Book a read I," "I a read book," or "I read a book." As new generations of deaf students acquire better education, the structure of Spanish Sign will become more standardized. Similarly, prepositions and conjunctions are seldom used, though with the new tendency toward total communication their usage

is increasing. *See* SOCIOLINGUISTICS: Total Communication.

Verbs are usually made with one gesture (corresponding to the infinitive) to which are added, at the beginning or at the end, prefixes or suffixes. These correspond to the signs NOW, BEFORE (much before, little before), and AFTER (much after, little after). The masculine and feminine gender, when required for persons or animals, are also indicated by placing the signs corresponding to MAN (male) or WOMAN (female) before the noun.

Proper names are normally indicated by a gesture characteristic of the person referred to. The gesture generally mimics a physical peculiarity of the person.

THE FUTURE

Spanish Sign Language suffers from the seemingly unending argument in Spain between defenders and enemies of sign language usage by the deaf population. This conflict is reflected, for example, in the lack of unity in communication methods in schools for deaf children: some schools allow the use of signs while others forbid it. There is also debate over the proposed Law of School Integration, which calls for the education of deaf children in hearing schools, even though the Spanish Ministry of Education has stated that its passage will not harm the existing schools for deaf children.

The Spanish National Confederation of the Deaf is an avowed defender of sign language, not as an end in itself but as a way to achieve better mastery of oral language, better understanding of educational and cultural materials, and greater agility and speed in communication among deaf individuals. For that reason, the confederation offers courses in sign (in its meeting hall and through the various Spanish deaf associations) for hearing people, and lobbies the Spanish government for the creation of a group of recognized official interpreters. *See* SPAIN.

Bibliography

Pinedo Peydró, Felix-Jesús: *Diccionario Mímico Español*.

————: *El Sordo y Su Mundo*.

Felix-Jesús Pinedo Peydró

Swedish

Sign language in Sweden is the primary language of approximately 8000 deaf people and the first language of an unknown number of hearing children of deaf parents. It is used as a second language by an increasing number of parents, teachers, and others.

HISTORY

Swedish Sign Language was first used pedagogically in the Manilla School in Stockholm, which was founded as a school for deaf children in 1809 by Per Aron Borg. Borg was inspired to begin deaf education after seeing a play by the French author Bouilly about the work of Abbé de l'Epée. Borg did not visit the deaf school in Paris, but he read and translated literature on deaf education and spent some years in Portugal, starting deaf education there. Borg did not create any "grammatical signs" (signs that would translate Swedish words or affixes), but designed a manual alphabet that is still used in Sweden. *See* L'EPÉE, ABBÉ CHARLES MICHEL DE.

Swedish Sign Language has no known genetic relationship with other sign languages. In other words, Swedish Sign Language is not based on, or derived from, any other sign language. However, it might have influenced the sign language in Finland when the first deaf school there was started by a former deaf pupil of the Manilla School, Oskar Malm. Malm at least introduced the Swedish manual alphabet, which was used in Finland until the international alphabet was adopted in 1965.

The first attempt to describe Swedish Sign Language was made by Oskar Österberg, a deaf man. He published a book in 1916 describing approximately 1200 signs, using 374 illustrations.

CURRENT STATUS

Sweden's attitude toward the deaf minority and sign language has changed drastically since 1970. Deaf people today are regarded as a bilingual minority, with their own cultural traits within Swedish culture. Officially this is most clearly expressed through the 1983 curriculum for the five schools for deaf students in Sweden: it proclaims sign language as the language of instruction in all subjects, and establishes sign language as a separate subject. Deaf people are encouraged to become teachers. Sign language is taught at the University of Stockholm to deaf students to provide academically trained sign language teachers. Hearing teachers are offered education in sign language.

Most parents start to learn Swedish Sign Language (or Signed Swedish) soon after the discovery of deafness in their child. The National Association for Deaf and Hearing Impaired Children, a parents association that works in close cooperation with the Swedish National Association of the Deaf and with local deaf clubs, advocates sign language in the family as well as in schools and preschools for deaf children.

The heightened status of sign language is also indicated in the right of deaf persons to obtain the service of sign language interpreters, free of charge (paid for by the government), whether in official or private situations. *See* SWEDEN.

STRUCTURE

Sign language research started at the University of Stockholm in 1972 with Brita Bergman's investi-

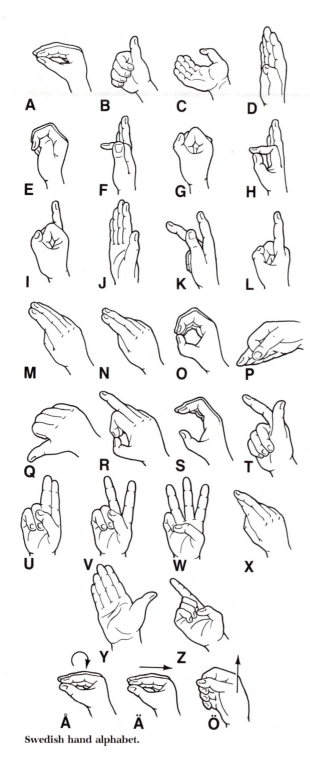

Swedish hand alphabet.

their primary language did not acquire it before they started school at seven years of age. Swedish research focuses on the sign language of this majority of the deaf population rather than on the language of the small minority who have deaf parents and acquired it as a first language. Studies of sign language acquisition also focus on children of hearing parents.

In contrast with the past, today deaf children usually acquire sign language before the age of three or four, since most parents now use it to varying degrees when the children are small. The role of signing hearing parents and deaf peers for early sign language acquisition continues to be the prime object of study.

As in all other sign languages being investigated, Swedish Sign Language has a complex structure on all levels that is just being revealed. The dominant features of spatial arrangement and simultaneity govern the structure of individual signs as well as the structure of clauses and sentences. Signs are not only produced manually; eyes, lips, face, and head and body posture are also used as parts of individual signs and for grammatical markings of clause types and sentence types.

Signs can be modulated in regular ways for regular changes of meaning. Especially for verb signs, there is a rich system of modulation. New signs are created either within the language or by borrowing. Within the language, signs are created on the basis of iconicity, by compounding, or by modulating existing signs. Borrowing can be from other sign languages, which is rare, or from Swedish through fingerspelled signs or loan translation compounds.

All these features of Swedish Sign Language are very similar to findings from other sign languages, which suggest that sign languages may be more similar to each other than spoken languages are. At the present level of knowledge, however, it would be premature to form an opinion on the degree of similarity. Sign language research is still very young, and there are still only a few native signers involved in it. When analyses of sign languages become more refined, structural differences perhaps will be more apparent.

Swedish Sign Language differs from other sign languages because of the set of handshapes used in the manual alphabet and because lip movements from spoken Swedish may be used with signs, especially those for concrete nouns, and are always used with fingerspelling. In fact, those letters that can be easily lipread (for example, vowels) are sometimes not fingerspelled. There are no available data on how spoken Swedish might influence sign language at higher levels of grammar, such as the order of signs in sentences.

gation of Signed Swedish, but it soon changed into work on the structure of Swedish Sign Language and the acquisition of sign language in small children. One important fact about sign language in Sweden is that a majority of those who use it as

Bibliography
Bergman, B.: *Studies in Swedish Sign Language*, 1982.
Österberg, O.: *Teckenspråket*, 1916.
Wallin, L: "Compounds in Swedish Sign Language in Historical Perspective," in J. Kyle and B. Woll (eds.), *Language in Sign*, 1983.

Inger Ahlgren

Swiss

There are no official national statistics on the number of deaf persons in Switzerland. Unofficial estimates place the number at approximately 7200, a figure that does not include hard-of-hearing individuals, but may include persons deafened by old age. Approximately 6000 of these deaf people live in the German-speaking part of Switzerland, about 1000 in the French-speaking part, and approximately 200 in the Italian-speaking area.

Manual communication used by deaf people is commonly referred to in the German area as *natürliche Gebärde* (natural gestures), and in the French area as *langage gestuelle* (gestural language). Persons who regard this manual communication as a real language are tending to use the more specific terms, *Gebärdensprache* (sign language) and *la langue des signes* (sign language). In both the French and German areas, there are regional lexical variations of signs which seem to be tied to the schools for deaf people. That is, students at one school would learn some signs that were not used at another school, and vice versa.

In the German area, alla the regional public and private schools for deaf children use purely oral teaching methods, with two exceptions: the school for multiply handicapped deaf students in Wabern and the Zürich cantonal school. The Wabern school uses gestures in the classroom, while the Zürich cantonal school uses a system of signed German together with spoken German in the classroom.

In the French area, the school for deaf students in Geneva (Centre de Montbrillant) has adopted a bilingual method in which both the local sign language and oral French are used in the classroom. In Lausanne, a kindergarten class reported using "total communication." All the other regional schools for deaf pupils in the French area report using "oral methods with the support of gestures."

In the Italian area of Switzerland, the school for deaf children in Locarno reports using a "purely oral" method.

History

In 1777 Heinrich Keller, a minister in Schlieren near Zürich, began the first classes for deaf people in Switzerland when he undertook the education of two young deaf boys. His method, which he developed before he had read the Abbé de l'Epée's work, was aimed at teaching his pupils the spoken language but involved using signs in the beginning classes. A young teacher who worked with Keller, Johann Conrad Ulrich, spent the year 1782–1783 in Paris observing Epée's methods. His firsthand reports on these methods were not available in 1783 when the teachers of the Akademisches Gymnasium in Zürich assembled to weigh the relative merits of Epée's and Samuel Heinicke's methods of teaching deaf students. There is evidence that the Zürich academics were not thoroughly familiar with the basic difference between Epée's use of signs throughout his school and Keller's use of signs only in the beginning classes. It has been suggested that the Zürich academics substituted the familiar methods of Keller for those of Epée, which they knew only through third-hand reports. *See* L'EPÉE, ABBÉ CHARLES MICHEL DE; HEINICKE, SAMUEL.

Upon his return to Switzerland, Ulrich began using some of Epée's methods, including, no doubt, many of the signs used in the Paris school. There is evidence that before his trip to Paris Ulrich was already familiar with the signs of the local deaf Swiss Germans attending the school in Schlieren. One could therefore postulate that the students and teachers working with Ulrich were subsequently exposed to a mixture of local Swiss and imported Paris signs. A teacher trained by Ulrich went on to open a school in the French part of Switzerland, and one of his teachers later opened a school in Bern.

In Zurich (and the rest of German Switzerland) the influence of Epée's methods and signs soon came to an end. The school for deaf children in Zürich opened in 1827 under a director from Germany and continued to have German directors, educated in the oral methods of Germany, for the following 91 years. Most of the teachers in schools for deaf people during this period were also trained in Germany.

Current Status

After more than 100 years of oral tradition in both the French and German areas of Switzerland, the status of signed communication today remains very low for the large part of the hearing and deaf population. Signing is commonly regarded, by both hearing and deaf people, as a primitive gestural system, incapable of expressing abstract ideas, useful only as a kind of support to the more superior spoken language.

Beginning about 1974, however, this low opinion of sign language began to change in some circles. This ongoing change in the status of sign language has reached different stages in the French and in the German areas.

In French Switzerland, a committee to study deaf

sign language was set up in 1975 by the Association suisse pour les sourds démutisés cantons romands (ASASM), an umbrella organization of groups concerned with deafness in the French area. The work of this committee led in 1978 to the establishment of sign language courses in several cities in the French area. In 1983 the sign language teachers, all of whom are deaf, formed their own professional association, Association suisse romande des enseignants de la langue des signes (ASRELS).

In 1981 the school for deaf pupils in Geneva began using the sign language used by the local deaf community in its new bilingual program. Both newspapers for the deaf community (*Le Messager* in Lausanne and *Les Mains de CRAL* in Geneva), as well as the Geneva chapter of the French organization Deux langues pour une éducation provide support for and information about sign language. Sign language is also used in the monthly, half-hour television program for hearing-impaired individuals in French Switzerland.

There are few trained interpreters who use sign language in Switzerland. The first training program for interpreters was set up in Lausanne in 1983 with the first class of students (who come from different cities in the French area and use different sign dialects) completing the three-year, part-time training program in 1986.

The French area, in general, benefited from its common spoken language with France, and hence its early and continued access to the information on sign language and sign language research which has been published in France. *See* FRANCE.

In the German part of Switzerland, there is a great lack of information in German on sign language research. This factor, combined with the continuing strong oral tradition in most schools, has worked to inhibit changes in attitudes toward signed communication. Nevertheless, more positive attitudes have begun to be expressed in some circles. Significantly, much of the impetus for this change of opinion about sign language has come from deaf persons themselves.

In 1983 the national deaf association (Schweizerischer Gehörlosenbund) drew up "10 Theses Concerning the Spoken Language and Signs," which have subsequently been the theme of several deaf conferences, articles in the local deaf newspaper (*Gehörlosenzeitung*), and presentations on the monthly, half-hour television program for hearing-impaired people in German Switzerland. These "10 Theses" take the stand that signing should be recognized as a natural and important part of the deaf community, that the schools have the responsibility of educating deaf people for their future lives in the deaf as well as in the hearing community, and that signs should be used in the schools, although always accompanying spoken German. The na-

tional deaf association also set up a committee in 1984 to begin collecting and standardizing regional signs in German Switzerland and to plan sign language courses. (The first course using the sign language of German Switzerland was offered in spring 1984 by the Zürich deaf association.) Deaf people also asked an umbrella organization of groups concerned with deafness in the non-French areas (Schweizerische Verband für das Gehörlosenwesen) to begin plans for the introduction of an interpreter training program for German Switzerland.

In 1982 the Forschungszentrum für Gebärdensprache (Center for Sign Language Research) was established in Basel. An association with members from all over German Switzerland was formed in 1983 to support this research center and especially to support the dissemination of information written in German about the sign languages used in Switzerland and the sign languages of other countries.

FORMS AND THEIR USE

The forms of signing used in both the French and German areas seem to range all along the continuum, from those forms that use predominantly sign language morphology and syntax to pidgin forms with varying mixtures of sign language and spoken language morphology and syntax. The question of who uses these different forms and in which situations remains to be investigated. Informal observation indicates that older deaf persons in both French and German areas tend to use a more spoken language–influenced pidgin form. The deaf people in the German area generally seem to consider their form of signing more dependent on spoken German forms (and deaf individuals in the French area seem to hold the same opinion of the form of signing most generally used in German Switzerland).

Sign languages or pidgin forms of signing are used for most activities in all deaf communities. In the schools, with the exceptions noted earlier, signing is not used in the classroom. However, the deaf pupils in many of these schools have been observed to use signs when communicating with each other outside of the classroom. Since the deaf children in many of these schools in Switzerland have little or no contact with deaf adults (there are no deaf people trained as teachers in Switzerland), the signs used by the children on the school playgrounds often differ from the signs used by the local adult deaf community.

In formal meetings, Swiss deaf adults seem to use a pidgin form of signing more influenced by their spoken language. This is particularly true of national meetings where, in typical Swiss fashion, two if not three languages are used. Interpretation at these kinds of national meetings of deaf people usually means interpretation between spoken French, German, and Italian, with the occasional support of signs.

Due to the lack of trained, or even untrained, sign language interpreters, there is little or no sign language used at institutions of higher learning or in professions in Switzerland. Some social workers and ministers who know signs may use them to varying degrees with their deaf clients. The insufficient number of sign language courses has meant that very few hearing people have learned the local sign languages. Due to the low status of sign language, even hearing children of deaf parents were rarely encouraged to learn this langauge. Many of the local associations of parents of deaf children still actively discourage their members from learning sign language.

LINGUISTIC STRUCTURE

There have been no systematic linguistic studies completed on Swiss sign languages. There are no published dictionaries of regional signs. The following comments on the linguistic structure of Swiss sign languages are therefore based on research in progress and on observations.

Phonology In both the French and German areas, there is no manual alphabet in common, everyday use by deaf people. An attempt has been made to introduce in the German area a German version of the international manual alphabet and, in the French area, the French manual alphabet. It will probably take some years before the majority of the Swiss deaf population incorporate fingerspelling into their everyday signing.

One consequence of this lack of a finger alphabet is a more restricted set of handshapes within the phonological systems of the languages. The more marked handshapes, which in languages such as American Sign Language are often found only in initialized signs (such as D, E, K, M, R, T, W), are lacking in most Swiss sign languages. Conversely, some handshapes which are not common in other sign languages are more frequent in the Swiss language.

Another consequence of this lack of a finger alphabet is the increased reliance on mouthing an equivalent word in the spoken language for concepts having no sign, especially many proper names. Sometimes the mouthed form, or "word picture," reflects only part of the spoken word. In some Swiss German dialects, the signs for "brother" and "sister" have the same manual component (a sign meaning "same") and it is only the accompanying word picture that differentiates the two forms.

Swiss signers also frequently mouth words to provide additional information in situations in which deaf individuals from two different dialect areas are conversing and are using different signs for the same concepts. Since there is such a small number of deaf persons living in any geographical area in Switzerland, it often happens that different dialect users converse together. Any linguistic report on the phonological components of Swiss French or Swiss German sign language will have to take into account, in addition to the normal manual and nonmanual parameters, this "word picture" component.

Informal observation of the morphology and syntax of the sign languages used in the German and French areas indicates the use of many of the same morphological and syntactic processes that have been found in other sign languages. These include the use of particular facial expressions, head tilt, eye gaze and body posture to mark different sentence types and role within the discourse, special handshapes used as classifiers, modification of the verb to show temporal and distributional aspect, and modification of location, orientation, and movement of some verbs to show agent/patient/beneficiary relationships. In both French and German area sign languages, the order of signs in certain types of signed sentences differs from the word order of the corresponding sentence of the spoken language. All of these observations remain to be systematically researched.

Bibliography

Boyes Braem, P.: "Zur Erforschung der Dialekte der Gebärdensprache in der deutschsprachigen Schweiz," *1. Bericht des Forschungszentrums für Gebärdensprache*, Basel, 1983. (A version of this report can be found in English in the Proceedings of the 3d International Symposium on Sign Language Research, Rome, 1983.)

Kolb, E.: Pfarrer Heinrich Keller in Schlieren," *Taubstummengemeinde Festschrift*, Zürich, 1961.

Sutermeister, E.: *Quellenbuch zur Geschichte des Schweizerischen Taubstummenwesens*, (2 vols.), Bern, 1929.

Penelope Boyes Braem

Taiwanese

Taiwan Sign Language (TSL) is used by an estimated 30,000 deaf people living in Taiwan, a province of the Republic of China. It is commonly referred to as *ziran shouyu* (natural sign language) both by deaf people themselves and by those hearing people familiar with the distinction between it and the so-called *wenfa shouyu* (grammatical sign language) or signed Mandarin system used in the schools for deaf children.

TSL can be divided into two major dialects: the Taipei dialect, associated with the Taipei Municipal School for the Deaf, and the Tainan dialect, which is used in the two provincial schools for deaf pupils, located in Tainan and Taichung.

TSL stems from three principal sources. The first is the form of the language that was used in Taiwan before 1895. In 1895 Japan began its 50-year occupation of Taiwan, and the second major influence began. After the founding of education for deaf people in Tainan in 1915 and in Taipei in 1917, teachers were sent from Tokyo and Osaka to the Taipei and Tainan schools respectively, and they used Japanese Sign Language in their classrooms. This sign language continued to be used in the schools of postoccupation Taiwan by students and by Taiwan's first deaf principal and former teacher at the Taipei school, Lin Wen-sheng. The third influence on TSL is that of Mainland Chinese Sign Language (MCSL) which was brought to Taiwan by a fairly large number of deaf refugees and former teachers of deaf students from the Chinese mainland in the wake of its communist takeover. It has also been introduced by students from Hong Kong who come to study at the schools for deaf students in Taiwan, and via graduates of an elementary school for deaf children in Kaohsiung which employs a form of MCSL.

TSL is a member of the Japanese Sign Language

Examples of character signs.

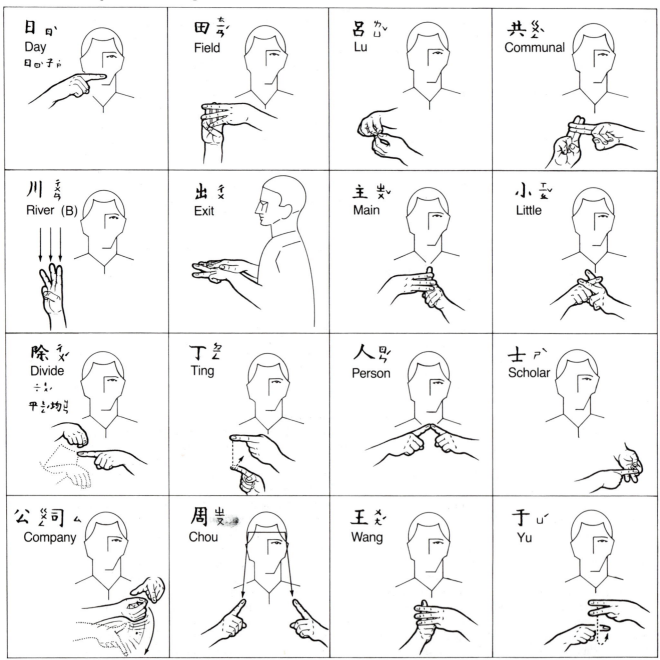

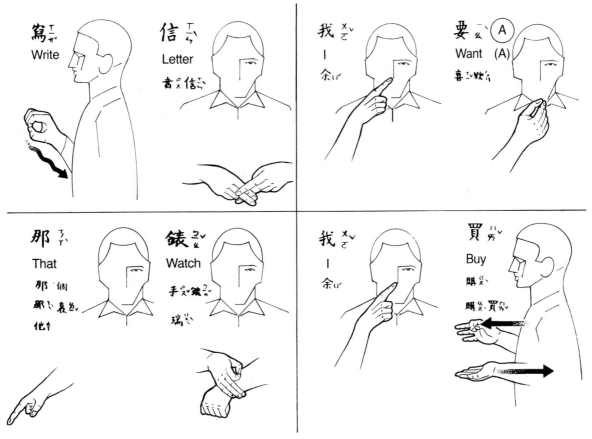

Examples of topicalizations.

(JSL) family, which also includes the sign languages of Japan and Korea. Among other similarities, approximately half of the vocabulary of TSL is either the same or very similar to that of JSL. However, TSL appears quite different from MCSL—only a small number of their signs are the same or similar, most of which are recent borrowings.

TSL is not related to any of the spoken languages of Taiwan, though it has borrowed a fair amount of vocabulary from Mandarin via palmwriting (the drawing of Chinese characters on the palm of the opposite hand) and character signs (signs that look like Chinese characters). Most hearing people regard TSL and any other forms of sign language as mere gesturing, and only a few deaf people are really able to appreciate the difference between their own native language, TSL, and invented versions of sign such as signed Mandarin.

TSL is the regular language of communication between adult deaf people and between deaf students at the three public schools in Taiwan. The teachers at the schools are officially required to use a form of signed Mandarin.

Syntactically, TSL appears to be an underlying subject-verb-object (SVO) language, though this order is frequently altered in order to topicalize some element of the sentence and in situations when other grammatical features of the verb influence the way in which the signs are ordered. Topicalizations often result, for example, in SVO sentences such as: HE WATCH, I 1-BUY-3 ("I bought his watch," or literally "His watch, I bought it"). Another example is WRITE LETTER, I WANT ("I want to write a letter," or literally, "As for writing letters, I want to do it"). The normal position for question words in TSL is at the end of the sentence, and negatives generally come after the verbs: HE LEAVE NOT, WHY ("Why didn't he leave?").

Some verbs in TSL can change their form to indicate subject and object relationships. For example, 1-TELL-3 means "I tell him/her," whereas 3-TELL-2 means "She/he tells you." Compounds in TSL are made up of two independent signs which have become fused into a single lexical item which has a meaning generally unpredictable from that of the two parent signs. When the signs BLACK and POUR, for example, are fused, the result is a compound meaning SOY SAUCE.

TSL phonology appears to be sequentially structured in terms of movements and holds. Making up the articulatory features of each of these move or hold segments are a variety of different hand

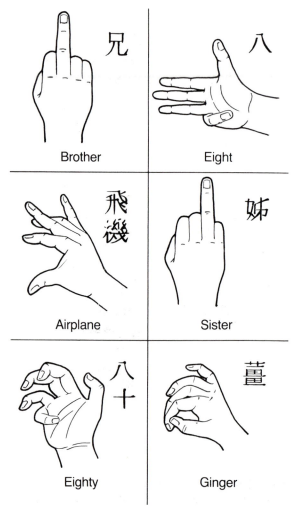

兄   Brother

八   Eight

飛
機   Airplane

姊   Sister

八
十   Eighty

薑   Ginger

Hand configurations unique to TSL.

configurations (well over 50), a large number of spatial and body locations, and various features to indicate point of contact and the orientation of the hands. Among the hand configurations which appear in TSL are several not commonly found in the sign languages of the world, including the handshapes used in the signs BROTHER, SISTER, AIRPLANE, GINGER, EIGHT, and EIGHTY.

An interesting characteristic of TSL is its lack of any form of fingerspelling. When a user of TSL wishes to convey a particular name, technical term, or specific item of vocabulary drawn from Mandarin, palmwriting is used. A form of the American fingerspelling alphabet does exist, but it is used primarily only in English classes at the schools for deaf children. *See* CHINA, REPUBLIC OF.

Bibliography

Chen, Julia Li-mei: "Taiwan shouyu yuyin jiegou zhi fenxi" (An analysis of the phonological structure of Taiwan Sign Language), unpublished manuscript in Chinese, 1984.

Smith, Wayne H.: "The Morphological Characteristics of Verbs in Taiwan Sign Language (tentative title), unpublished doctoral dissertation, Indiana Uiversity, in preparation.

———, Li-fen, and Ting (eds.): *Shou neng sheng chyau* (Your hands can become a bridge), vols. I and II (TSL textbook, in Chinese; an English translation of the text portions of vol. I is available), Deaf Sign Language Research Association of the Republic of China, Taipei, 1979.

Wayne H. Smith

Yugoslavian

Yugoslavia is a federative state comprising six republics (Bosnia and Herzegovina, Croatia, Macedonia, Montenegro, Serbia, and Slovenia), and two autonomous provinces (Kosovo and Voivodina). It has a population of 22 million speaking several languages. The number of deaf persons is about 60,000; it is estimated that about 30,000 of them know sign language. There is not yet an official name for the sign language used by deaf people in Yugoslavia.

The first users of conventional sign language were rare individuals from northern regions of Yugoslavia, once a part of the Austro-Hungarian monarchy, who from the beginning of the nineteenth century were sent to schools for deaf children in Austria or Hungary. The first school for deaf pupils opened in 1840 in Slovenia and used sign language together with speech for teaching. The second school, opened in 1885 at Zagreb, Croatia, by a deaf man, Adalbert Lampe, was a nonoral school, using sign language and writing only. Very soon, however, these two schools, as well as all other newly opened schools, became strictly oral. Sign language remained the means for communication among deaf individuals outside the classroom.

By 1945 Yugoslavia still had only a few schools for deaf persons, and less than a thousand of them were educated and could use sign language. All other deaf people were isolated and illiterate in small towns and villages, using perhaps some signs individually devised. It is possible even now to find in some villages small groups of illiterate deaf persons who evolved a kind of rudimentary sign language for their use.

During the first two decades of the new Yugoslavia (1945–1965), a number of schools and classes for deaf people were opened, and many thousands of deaf children had the opportunity to learn a common sign language. In the same period, several hundreds of illiterate youths and adults were enrolled in short-term general education and vocational training courses, where sign language was used as an indispensable tool of communication.

The Federation of the Deaf of Yugoslavia, founded in 1945, strongly supported sign language, advocating its use in teaching deaf children. Sign language still is not used in schools, however, except on a very limited scale. The total communication movement has had a positive influence, and although schools for deaf children remain oral, with most teachers not knowing sign language, opposition to signing is less rigid, except in schools using the strictly oral Verbo-tonal Method.

The use of sign language is still restricted mainly to communication among deaf persons. The number of hearing persons who can use it is limited to children of deaf parents and some workers employed by deaf organizations. These persons offer interpreting service in the courtroom, and when necessary assist in various public service areas. Sign language is used in monthly television broadcasts for deaf people.

The sign language in Yugoslavia, being primarily a means of everyday conversation within the deaf community, developed a limited vocabulary adequate to this purpose. However, its vocabulary is viewed as not sufficiently elaborate for the needs of higher education.

There are notable differences in the sign language used by distinct groups of deaf persons. Prelingually deaf individuals who attended special schools use a sign language whose structure and order of words are not similar to those of national spoken languages. It is characterized by pronounced facial expression and dynamic hand movements. While signing, deaf people in this group may utter or voicelessly articulate important words, or just their first syllables. This adds precision to their communication, because there are many signs bearing several meanings. There is, for example, only one sign—a fist on the breast—to denote a geographic region, Dalmatia, and all the towns of this region. If signers want to specify a town, they have to do so by lip movements. Prelingually deaf persons who did not attend school and cannot use speech employ a sign language with more pantomime and acting. For example, they specify a town either by describing the way to it or by describing some known building or other distinctive landmark. Postlingually deaf individuals use normal speech and signs simultaneously, while their facial and body movements are subdued. This type of sign language is adopted at conferences and in interpreting. In spite of these differences in sign language expression, deaf people in the three groups understand each other fairly well.

There are notable differences in vocabularies and signing styles among deaf people of various regions of Yugoslavia, although this does not create serious problems of comprehension. Most differences are tied to modes of signing in various schools for deaf pupils.

In 1979, the republic's organizations of deaf people started a project to standardize (unify) Yugoslavian Sign Language. By 1984 some 800 signs had

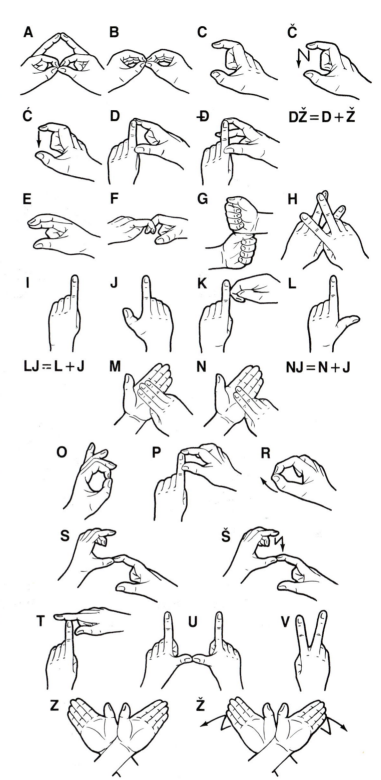

Two-handed alphabet of Yugoslavia.

been accepted to serve as a basis for an all-Yugoslavia normative sign language vocabulary. In the meantime, two republics (Serbia and Slovenia) prepared their own sign language vocabularies.

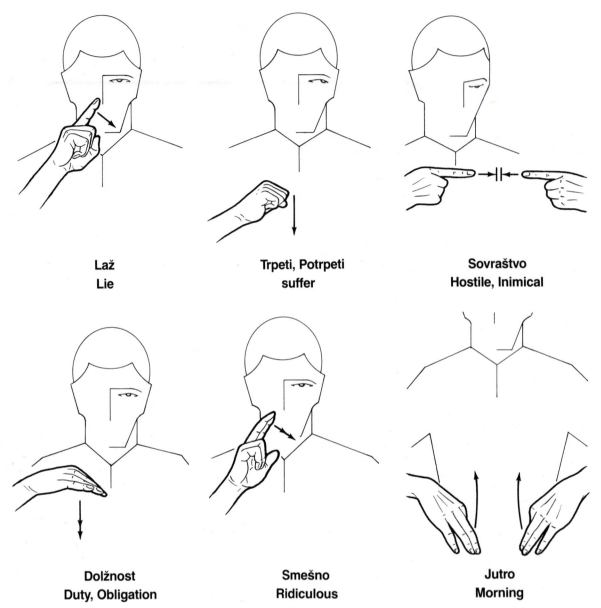

Laž
Lie

Trpeti, Potrpeti
suffer

Sovraštvo
Hostile, Inimical

Dolžnost
Duty, Obligation

Smešno
Ridiculous

Jutro
Morning

Six signs used in Slovenia as well as in other regions of Yugoslavia.

These are the first sign language books in Yugoslavia.

The manual alphabet is known by all literate deaf people in Yugoslavia, although they use it for communication only when around hearing persons. There is an officially accepted one-handed alphabet, based on the international alphabet of the World Federation of the Deaf, but in most republics and provinces of Yugoslavia a nonofficial two-handed alphabet is in use.

Andrija Zic

SIGN WRITING SYSTEMS

Discussion about writing sign language (sign language notation is a related but different matter) can be divided into theory about it and attempts at doing it. The attempts may seem unsuccessful in light of the theory, which suggests that signing cannot be written; but before the invention of alphabetic and ideographic scripts, the possibility of writing spoken language probably also appeared unlikely.

THEORETICAL CONSIDERATIONS

Signing is activity in real time, so that the Western convention of beginning on the left of a page and moving right to denote passage of time should be useful, given that a sign language utterance and a spoken language utterance are in many respects equivalent. Two facts make the simple writing line useless, however.

1. The left-to-right writing line is conventionally brought back across to the left, just below the line that has gone as far right as paper allows. Signing, being three-dimensional as well as temporal, requires the full two dimensions of a page. The written or printed page is really one-dimensional: it can still be read if cut into one-line strips and pasted into a single ribbon. One practical way out of the writing problem posed by language in three-dimensions-plus-time is to divide the page into smaller pages. The comic strip is an example and sign dictionaries often show one sign in two or more pictures, usually with the initial state of the signer (or signer's hands) in the leftmost position.

2. The sequences of two or more pictorial representations on a page for one sign already indicate the failure of the practice to perform what the nature of communication requires. The pictorial display represents only imperfectly, because two or three static instants in time are substituted for action that occurs in a continuous stretch of time, however brief. And if the picturing of single signs overtaxes the resources of the two dimensions of a page, then the writing of sign strings or sign language utterances or conversations is even less satisfactory. The problem for the writing of sign language is that the sign language sign is structured, it takes time, and in that time it may show motion or stay relatively motionless, or do both. Because there are often similar signs having different meanings, a number of characteristics must be made clear in any writing system. The graphic message on the page needs to represent all the features necessary to denote a specific sign and not one like it.

ATTEMPTS AT WRITING

Despite the magnitude of the problem, sign language writing has been tried; indeed, pictorial writing of certain signs is very ancient. Two main ways of reducing a sign utterance to graphic symbolization have been attempted. One begins with the pictorial representation and reduces and conventionalizes it, turning a series of drawings into something more like script calligraphy.

Some of these attempts have been relatively pure, that is, their devisers knew the language and singlemindedly pursued the goal of finding graphic signs that would indicate all the needed features and eliminate all those not needed. An early and excellent example of this is by R. A. Bébian (1825).

Dance Notation More widely known than attempts at the pictorial writing of sign are the attempts to use dance notation systems for sign language writing. Here the experimentation follows a different course—a system of highly developed dance notation is taken as a basis for depicting what a signer does while uttering a sign language sentence or taking a conversational "turn." Benesh, Rudolf Laban, Levy-Eshkol, and V. Sutton all have devised dance notation systems that have been applied to sign language notation.

Not yet clear is whether notational systems for recording all of what one or several dancers do with the whole body throughout a dance can be remade to record just what is significant in a signer's performance. One problem is scale: if the system can capture all possible changes occurring in a dance, can it capture the much more specialized changes occurring in the expression of a sign language? A second problem is purpose and function: one system records things as the things themselves, the movements of a dance; the other records things as "signs," movements that signify something else. This comes down to the question of whether a way of symbolizing physical action and a way of symbolizing language output are compatible or reducible to a single system.

Linguistic Analysis An entirely different approach to reducing individual signs to notation comes not from observing the physical actions of a signer or dancer, but from linguistic analysis. This approach is analogous to that of alphabetic writing, which of course did not start as analysis. Alphabets have a phonetic basis. For example, there are contrasted a sound created by quickly closing and opening the air passage by raising the tongue far back in the mouth, a sound created by a closing and opening made by the lips, and a sound created by a closing and opening made by the tongue tip behind the teeth. These sounds are known respectively as k, p, and t; but their real occurrence serves to distinguish *car / par/ tar* or *sick / sip / sit* and countless other triplets (and pairs made by contrast of any two). Single sounds, though, do not make a language or even its words. Real alphabetic writing began when what sounded like sequences of sounds were written as sequences of symbols for the sounds—letters. Words followed, then phrases, which led to writing as it is known today.

Sign language writing of an analytic kind, however, is still not at a position to take that step. W. C. Stokoe analyzed signs as simultaneous aspects of a single action rather than as sequences of elements. More recently S. Liddell has argued that manually produced signs do have temporal segments, HOLD and MOVE, as he terms them, which respectively display the hand or hands relatively motionless and clearly in motion. Stokoe's analysis is broader: a sign consists of what is acting and its action; signs expressed by facial actions are included along with those signs manually expressed. Liddell's analysis rests on the fact that human gestural actions are organized in time. Sign analysis must deal with this.

Until the temporal analysis can be reconciled with the aspectual, however, sign writing based on analysis and the analysts' notation cannot advance. More microanalysis is needed to relate time and space information in signing.

Aspectual analysis has a firm biological foundation. What the eyes see depends on the structure of the retinal cells. Some central cells are good at detail, while some peripheral cells are specially adapted to pick up motion. However, knowing exactly what is moving and knowing at the same time precise details about the movement also requires imagination or memory. For example, when people see a hand in rapid motion, they can report its direction, speed, and manner, but to report exactly how it is configured they have to see it, imagine it as not moving, or remember what it looks like in that sign.

Notation that is growing out of the HOLD-MOVE segmental analysis places the segments from left to right in order of occurrence, but specifies a number of simultaneous features down the page under each HOLD or MOVE. With abbreviated description of the features in the columns, a sign can be written on a half to a full page, but the list of features so abbreviated runs to several pages.

COMMON PRACTICE

For the reasons discussed above, there are many ways of sign language writing devised by many investigators for different purposes. One reason for writing sign language sentences is to provide the examples needed for discussion of sign language grammar, structure, or syntax. Most writers on these topics use words to stand for signs of similar meaning, but are not comfortable about doing so. The words, taken from the language of the writer, are used to represent signs—following the agreed-upon convention that word and sign share something of the same meaning, each in the respective language. These words, called glosses, are written from left to right, usually in capital letters. But besides giving only an approximate fit of word and sign meaning, such use of glosses makes a strange-looking sentence to a reader of the language that the words come from if the reader is unaware that the sentence is really representing a sign language sentence. Uninformed readers of such examples, in fact, have been known to quote such strings of cap-

italized words presumably to show that sign language has no grammar or is ungrammatical.

Even when used with understanding by investigators of sign language, the practice of writing sign sentences as strings of capitalized words does not convey the entire message. Therefore it has become common practice to use a convention like that of musical scores and to write various marks above and below the word-gloss line to stand for facial or head action, eye gaze changes, and so on. Once again, however, there is no standard system for using these indications of nonmanual activity; some use iconic marks to note what is done (for example, *carets* to show raised eyebrows); others label the syntactic category (for example, *topic, wh-question, yes-no question*).

LIGHT ON THE SUBJECT

Sign language writing is very difficult in theory and chaotic in practice. There is, however, some hope for preservation, archiving, and studying this language. The rapid advances in technology for storing and retrieving visual information on videotape, on videodisk, and in digitalized computers could make the search for a satisfactory form of sign language writing merely academic.

Bibliography

Bébian, M.: *Mimographie, ou essai d'écriture mimique, propre á regularise la langage des sourds-muets*, Paris, 1825.

Liddell, S.: "Think & Believe: Sequentiality in ASL Signs," *Language*, 60(2):372–399, 1984.

Stokoe, W.: *Sign Language Structure: An Outline of the Visual Communication Systems of the American Deaf,* SIL:O.P. 8, 1960.

William C. Stokoe

SIGNS

This article covers five specialized categories of signs: fingerspelling, artistic signs, name signs, home sign, and technical and invented signs.

Fingerspelling

Fingerspelling alphabets, or manual alphabets, have existed for many centuries and are found throughout the world, although not in all countries. The public often confuses fingerspelling with sign language, possibly because of the prevalence in the past of begging cards with the manual alphabet printed on them, and because deaf children often learn this alphabet, but fingerspelling differs in significant ways from sign language.

Manual alphabets are not naturally and spontaneously created by deaf people themselves, but are all the conscious inventions of hearing educators. They also differ from sign languages in that they are derivative of written language, being systems of handshapes and movements that represent alphabetic symbols. These symbols usually suggest the shapes of capital letters in printed or handwritten form. They are most directly comparable with other symbol systems derived from written languages such as Morse code and Braille. Both one-handed and two-handed alphabets are in use throughout the world. In many countries, variants have been developed for communication with persons who are deaf and blind. These variants consist of handshapes and movements articulated on the palm of the receiver of the message. *See* DEAF-BLINDNESS: Communication

Fingerspelling is used both as a self-contained means of communication and as an adjunct to sign language. The discussion here focuses on the history of manual alphabets, their forms, their use in education of deaf children, and their role in the communication of deaf adults.

HISTORY

Manual alphabets date back at least to the seventeenth century. The earliest manual alphabet may have been invented by Pedro Ponce de León (1520–1584), although it was first published by Juan Pablo Bonet in 1620 in a book entitled *Simplification of Sounds and the Art of Teaching the Dumb to Speak*. This one-handed alphabet is the ancestor of many of the manual alphabets in use today. It was taken to France by Jacob Rodriguez Pereire in the mid-eighteenth century and subsequently from France to the United States after 1816. Many of the original handshapes have changed in the past three and a half centuries, but the Bonet alphabet is still recognizable as the ancestor of the majority of one-handed manual alphabets, such as the modern American manual alphabet. In the Bonet alphabet, similarities with written forms are clearly visible in a number of letters, notably C, H, I, M, N, O, V, and Z. *See* PONCE DE LEÓN, PEDRO; PABLO BONET, JUAN.

The two-handed manual alphabet in use in Great Britain, in a number of nations in the British Commonwealth, and in several other countries is not related historically to the Bonet alphabet. The origin of this alphabet is less clear. John Bulwer, the first English writer on sign language, (*Chirologia*, 1644, and *Philocophus*, 1648), mentions "arthrologie," a system that apparently indicated the letters of the alphabet by pointing to the joints of the fingers. However, he gives no description of this manual alphabet. George Dalgarno, a Scottish educator and philosopher, in his book *Ars Signorum, Vulgo Character Universalis Philosophica et Lingua* (1661), provides what is probably the alphabet of Bulwer and the antecedent of the modern British two-handed alphabet. In Dalgarno's alphabet, the right index finger was used to point at vowels and the

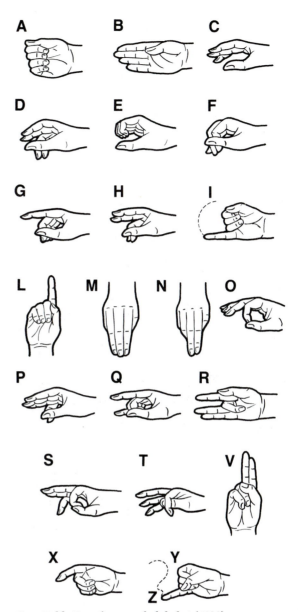

Juan Pablo Bonet's manual alphabet (1620).

right thumb at consonants. Dalgarno suggested that a glove printed with the locations of the letters would be a useful tool in learning the alphabet. Dalgarno's alphabet was never widely adopted, but a second alphabet, published anonymously in 1698 in a pamphlet entitled *Digitilingua*, is the direct ancestor of the modern British two-handed alphabet. This alphabet uses the Dalgarno principle of pointing to the tips of the fingers to indicate the vowels, although the remaining letters resemble the forms of printed letters, notably M, N, Q, R, T, X, Y, and Z.

This alphabet was widely adopted in a short time, and Daniel Defoe's book *Duncan Campbell*, published in 1732, includes a chart of this alphabet,

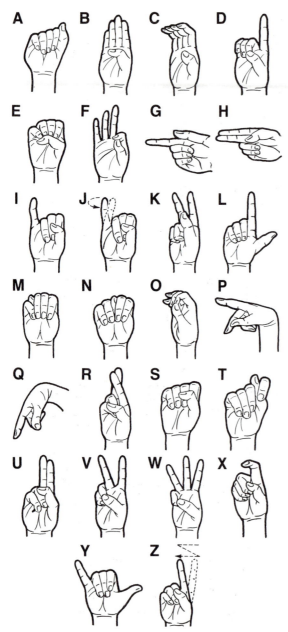

Modern American manual alphabet. (After J. Schein, *Speaking the Language of Sign*, **Doubleday, 1984)**

Most European and North and South American countries use fingerspelling derived from Bonet, even those countries where the written alphabet in use is not the Latin alphabet. In these countries, however, the relationship between the form of the manual alphabet and that of the written alphabet is less direct. For example, in the Hebrew manual alphabet, which has only recently been adopted, the handshapes of the Bonet alphabet have been used for letters with corresponding sounds in the Hebrew alphabet. The Hebrew letter *daleth* (pronounced /d/), for instance, is fingerspelled as the American *d*. In the Soviet Union, where the Cyrillic alphabet with 32 letters is used rather than the Latin alphabet, the manual alphabet was developed from the French version of the Bonet alphabet in the early nineteenth century. Some letters were adopted unchanged, where the written forms and pronunciation in French and Russian were both similar, as in the letters M and O. For other letters, a similarity in shape served as the basis for the use of a fingerspelled form. For example, the Russian letter Я looks much like a backward R and is fingerspelled with crossed index and middle fingers, as in the French and American *r*, although the pronunciation is /ya/. A third group of letters was created for some Russian written letters which did not resemble their French counterparts in either sound or shape. The Russian letter Л (pronounced /l/) is fingerspelled as an upside-down *v* which resembles the shape of the written letter. The manual alphabet adopted in Greece, another country where the Latin alphabet is not used, derives its forms in a similar way.

The Cyrillic, Latin, Greek, and Hebrew alphabets are all historically related and resemble each other in many ways. In those countries in which written alphabetic systems are not used, such as Japan and China, and in countries that use their own distinctive written alphabets, such as Thailand and Korea, other fingerspelling systems have been developed. In Japan, for instance, a syllabary, or writing system based on syllables instead of single sounds, is in use, and this forms the basis of fingerspelling. The Japanese system uses symbols from Bonet for syllables such as /ka/, /sa/, /ha/, and /ya/, which are fingerspelled as the American letters K, S, H, and Y respectively. Other syllables, such as /ki/, /ku/, /ne/, /ho/, use other configurations unrelated to Bonet. In China, an alphabet for writing Chinese has been developed and is used alongside the traditional Chinese writing system of characters, which is nonalphabetic. A manual alphabet has also been developed and is being introduced. Many deaf people, however, instead of fingerspelling, "draw" the outline of the Chinese characters, either on their palms or in the air. *See* SIGN LANGUAGES: Chinese, Japanese.

somewhat modified. *See* LITERATURE, FICTIONAL CHARACTERS IN.

A third alphabet was invented by Per Borg of Sweden, and was taken by him to Portugal where he established his first school for deaf students in Lisbon in the early nineteenth century. This is a one-handed alphabet, like Bonet's, but resembles it little in other respects, the only similar letters being E, F, I, M, N, O, U, and V, which resemble the shapes of printed letters. Both the modern Swedish and Portuguese manual alphabets are descended from Per Borg's.

In recent years, manual alphabets have been introduced in many countries for the first time, and the World Federation of the Deaf has adopted an International Manual Alphabet for use in international settings. *See* WORLD FEDERATION OF THE DEAF.

EDUCATION

Fingerspelling has had a role in deaf education since its earliest days. Bonet's 1620 book advocated teaching a one-handed manual alphabet as the first step in the education of deaf children. In this method, printed letters and the manual alphabet were learned simultaneously. The Abbé de l'Epée, in France, described in his book the use of fingerspelling as an initial means of teaching written language. This approach to deaf education has its more modern counterparts in the Rochester method of fingerspelling, speech, and lipreading, used in the United States, and in the neo-oralism of the Soviet Union. Interestingly, the Rochester method was initially supported by the oralist lobby. In Britain and Ireland, fingerspelling was the main educational medium until this century. All of these methods are based on using fingerspelling either on its own or in conjunction with speech as the main means of communication in the classroom, in the belief that fingerspelling provides the easiest input to the written language, and hence literacy, for the child. Most current programs for deaf students, involving manual and spoken communication, do not rely solely on fingerspelling, but use signs as well. *See* EDUCATION: Communication.

USE

The amount and function of fingerspelling used by signers is often related to factors such as age, sex, social context, and educational background. The most frequent role of fingerspelling is as an adjunct to signing, used for "foreign" words such as proper names, place names, and words not translated into sign. Among some signers it is also used for emphasis as in: How many meals did I eat yesterday? O-N-E (and I'm famished).

Although fingerspelling represents the words of written languages, even an utterance articulated entirely in fingerspelling, whether one-handed or two-handed, does not have uppercase letters, punctuation, or any break between words. The relatively slow articulation rate of fingerspelling when compared to speech (60 words per minute for fingerspelling, 100–150 for speech) is responsible. This speeding up and running together of handshapes results in production and perception of fingerspelling largely in terms of an "envelope" or global pattern, rather than as a series of individual letters. This was first described by Dalgarno in 1661: "it is as easy to represent a word as one composition with a confined action of the hand, though there

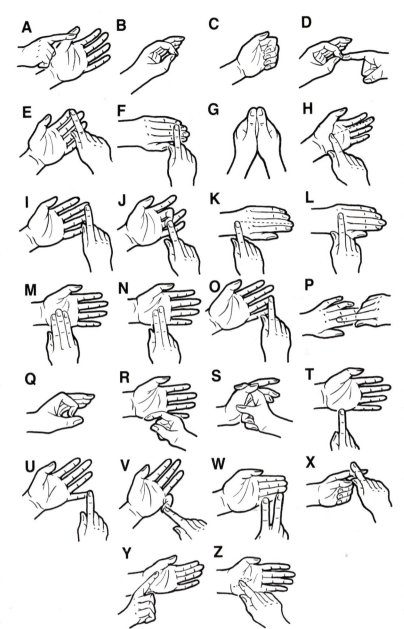

Digitilingua manual alphabet (1698).

be many distinct pointings as to make one word by an aggregate of many distinct letters."

The close proximity of fingerspelling and signing has led to mutual influences between these two separate modes. Sign-influenced fingerspelling is found in initialization, "loan" signs, and initial modification. Fingerspelling-influenced loan signs (indicated by the symbol #) are signs that derive from fingerspelled words, but that have been so altered, usually through changes in movement and orientation or through deletion or assimilation of handshape, that they are often not recognizable to deaf signers as having a fingerspelled origin. Ex-

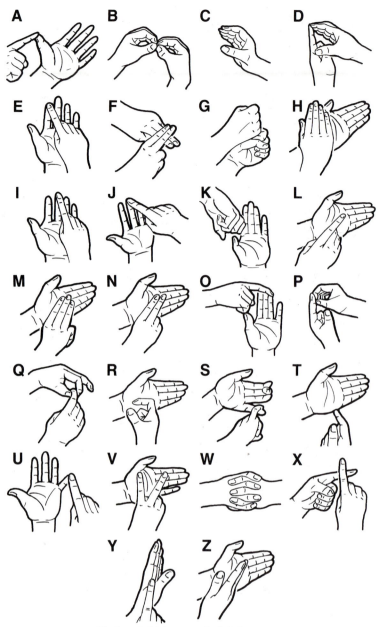

Modern British manual alphabet.

handshape. Some handshapes that occur in signs nearly always represent initialization because they rarely occur in natural (indigenous) sign languages. Most initializations occur as conscious inventions by hearing educators creating manual versions of sign languages.

Initial modification is found in languages such as British Sign Language, in signs where additional movements have been attached to fingerspelled letters. For example, in British Sign Language the sign GOLD was originally signed as a repeated G. In the modern sign, the movement is modified so that it resembles the movement of BRIGHT. These initial modifications might be considered to be loan signs, but there is no evidence of reduction from fully fingerspelled forms, and they differ from loan signs in certain other respects.

Artificially created forms using fingerspelling are often rejected by members of the deaf community. Their acceptability is influenced by sociolinguistic considerations, formal features such as the suitability of an initialized handshape in the context of a sign's movement, orientation, and location, and whether new lexical distinctions are provided. It is likely that fingerspelling and signing will continue to mutually influence each other.

Bibliography

Battison, R.: *Lexical Borrowing in American Sign Language*, Linstok Press, Silver Spring, Maryland, 1978.

(Pablo) Bonet, J.: *Simplification of Sounds and the Art of Teaching the Dumb to Speak*, 1620.

Bulwer, J.: *Chirologia: or the Natural Language of the Hand*, R. Whitaker, London, 1644.

———: *Philocophus: or the Deafe and Dumbe Man's Friend*, Humphrey Moseley, London, 1648.

Carmel, S.: *International Hand Alphabet Charts*, 1975.

Dalgarno, G.: *Ars Signorum, Vulgo Character Universalis Philosophica et Lingua*, J. Hayes, London, 1661.

l'Epée, Abbé de: *Instruction of Deaf and Dumb by Means of Methodical Signs: The True Manner of Instructing the Deaf and Dumb Confirmed by Long Experience*, Savage, Evans and Savage.

Quigley, S. P.: *The Influence of Fingerspelling on the Development of Language, Communication, and Educational Achievement in Deaf Children*, University of Illinois, Institute for Research on Exceptional Children, 1969.

Savage, R. D., L. Evans, and J. F. Savage: *Psychology and Communication in Deaf Children*, Grune and Stratton, Sydney, 1981.

Bencie Woll

Artistic

There are at least three types of artistic signing—creative play with handshapes, sign poetry, and storytelling. These artistic forms also have been referred to as art sign, creative uses of American Sign Language (ASL), poetic signing, and so on. In general, artistic forms of a language are different from everyday or standard forms of a language in several

amples in American Sign Language (ASL) include #BUT and #NO, in British Sign Language #ABOUT, and in French Sign Language #FIN (end).

In initialization, fingerspelling is incorporated into sign language by the process of changing the handshape of a sign to correspond (via the manual alphabet) to the first letter of the word that corresponds to the meaning of that sign. For example, in ASL the signs GROUP, FAMILY, and TEAM are distinguished by using the manual-alphabet handshapes G, F, and T respectively; in Chinese Sign Language, JIU (wine) is signed as DRINK with a J ways: (1) Artistic forms are derived from standard forms, but they "twist" or "break" linguistic rules of the standard form. (2) Artistic forms are used chiefly for the expression of values, feelings, and ideas, whether or not the addressee understands immediately; standard forms are used for communication to make sure the addressee understands. (3) The user of artistic forms is aware of the structure of the language and carefully selects particular words or signs to show language at play or the signer's thoughts, feelings, and attitudes.

Within the deaf community, there are at least two ways to evaluate artistic signing—by its linguistic structure and by its art. That is, the viewer may ask, "Is it in American Sign Language (ASL)?" and "Is it beautiful or meaningful?" In many cases, the answer is "yes" to both questions. However, sometimes artistic signing is not in ASL but still is considered beautiful or meaningful in some way. Thus the term artistic signing as used in this section includes not only poems, stories, and so on in ASL but also certain forms of signing that are influenced by the structure of English.

There are five known forms of creative play with handshapes. One traditional form is manual alphabet stories, or ABC stories. Here the handshapes of the manual alphabet are linked to various signs whose handshapes are the same or similar. These signs are then strung together in alphabetical order. For example, in one ABC story called "The Haunted House," the first sign means to knock on a door and has an A handshape; the second sign is made with a B handshape (on both hands) and means that a door is opening; the third sign has a C handshape and shows that someone is searching for something.

As the signs are strung together in alphabetical order, the signer also varies the rhythm of signing and uses role-shifting techniques to create as flowing or sensible a story as possible. For example, the haunted house story begins with slow signing ("I knocked on the door and then slowly opened it, peering into the room, looking . . ."). Suddenly, the pace changes to rapid, tense signing: ("Suddenly I hear"), E ("a scream—eeee!"), F ("My eyes dart to the right"), G ("in time to see something rush past and disappear"). When the signer makes the two-handed sign meaning to scream "eeee," the body is shifted to one side to show that the signer has changed roles and now is showing what someone or something else said or did. In this story, role shifting occurs several times, and the signer takes on the roles of a screamer, a man in a painting, a person who is hanged, and a person casting spells, in addition to the signer's own role. Throughout the story, the signer varies the speed and tension of the signs at various points to increase the excitement and suspense.

Number stories are structured in the same way as the ABC stories, but follow the order of cardinal numbers and use signs whose handshapes are similar to the number handshapes. The last number in these stories commonly varies from 10 to 25.

A third group of creative handshape play is called "Words/Names: one letter, one sign." This group is like the ABC and number stories but, instead of using signs in alphabetical or numerical order, the signs "spell out" the name of a city, person, brand name, or other particular word. One such handshape play spells out "San Francisco" as the signs weave a story about someone driving along S, seeing something ahead (A, referring to the city), and looking off at something else to the right of the city (N, referring to the bridge). As the handshapes of successive signs continue to spell out the name of the city, the story tells of looking up at the Golden Gate Bridge and imagining an earthquake collapsing the bridge and then, at the end, feeling relief to see the bridge still standing.

A fourth variety comprises stories told by using signs with the same or very similar handshape. For example, by using different variants of the 5 handshape, a long story is told about a man and woman marrying, the woman becoming pregnant and the womb swelling until finally she gives birth to a baby son. The parents are happy; the boy grows up, goes to school, grows up more, goes away to college, is superior in his studies, but then is called by the army to go away to war, and the story ends in tragedy. The entire story is created by using signs with very similar handshapes.

The last category consists of handshapes corresponding to letters from the manual alphabet that spell out an English word and, at the same time, create an image illustrating the meaning of that word. In one example, the left hand signs "tree" and the right hand spells out "falling leaf" as the handshapes gently fall from the tree, weaving in the wind. The last one (F) makes several final swirls before coming to rest on the ground.

Another example of this type spells out "reflection" with both hands contacting at the wrist. The effect is of one hand (the nondominant hand) mirroring or reflecting what the other hand is doing.

SIGN POETRY

In sign poetry, the artist consciously selects signs that share certain features. For example, the artist may create a poem with signs that have similar handshapes, movements, or locations on the body or in space. This is akin to rhyme or alliteration in spoken-language poems. The artist may select signs that can "flow" from the preceding sign into the following sign. The artist may select signs that have similar meanings, for example, signs referring to the people communicating, dialoguing, chatting, and relating to each other.

Other characteristics of sign poetry include the way the rhythm of signs, whole phrases, or the entire poem may be altered from the rhythm normally occurring in conversational signing. There also tends to be a conscious "balance" in the way the hands are used. That is, unlike conversational signing, in which one hand (called the dominant hand) tends to have a more active and continuous role, in sign poetry both hands tend to stay in action (in the signing space) or the hands alternate back and forth in the dominant role.

Three forms of sign poetry have been identified: poems that are translations from English or other languages into Sign, poems created in Sign and in English at the same time, and poems originally created in Sign and then perhaps later translated into English.

English-to-Sign poem translations are the most common form, yet in some ways the most difficult. The quality of such translations varies widely, and what is meant by "translation" spans the continuum from a simple sign-for-word coding (thereby maintaining the original English structure) to a complete restructuring into ASL.

There are two basic reasons why English-to-Sign translations have been the most common form of sign poetry. First, most people have been (and many still are) unaware or unable to accept that ASL is an independent, capable, and sophisticated language. So if they wanted to express a poem, they simply would choose an English poem that they liked and then would attach signs commonly associated with key English words in the poem. For poetic quality they might add a singsong rhythm and also alternate hand dominance to give more balance to the hands. Second, due to lack of awareness or a devaluation of ASL, people have generally felt that the language is not capable of creating original and complex poetry. When deaf poets create, they usually create in written English, and then translate their creation into ASL later.

However, as people have become more aware of ASL as a language and more knowledgeable about its structure and semantics, the two other forms of sign poetry have emerged: Sign and English poems that were created together in order to have impact in both languages, and original poems created in Sign and then perhaps translated later into English.

A poem created in Sign and English simultaneously can be appreciated separately (in either language) but is most effective when seen and heard together, or read and then seen in the same sitting. An example is the poem by Dorothy Miles entitled "Total Communication." The first part of the English version of the poem is: "You and I, can we see aye to aye/ Or must your I and I lock horns/ And struggle till we die?"

There is a play with the words "aye to aye" and "I and I" which sound like "eye to eye." To express the meaning "aye to aye" in Sign, the artist uses two hands simultaneously to show two heads nodding at each other in agreement. This clever use of two hands to represent the feelings and actions of the two people continues throughout the poem. For example, the two hands "lock horns" together and then, by acting simultaneously in the appropriate locations, express the dying of both "you" and "I."

An original Sign poem seems more free, because it does not have to conform to English structure and instead can fully exploit the capabilities of ASL, and is more profound in its expression of personal and cultural experiences. It can have more impact on deaf audiences. One example of an original ASL poem was created by Ella Mae Lentz and tells the experience of many deaf people: isolation, repressive oralism, sense of imprisonment, struggle for freedom. The rhythm of the poem punctuates the meaning of each segment. For example, a staccatolike repetition of signs in the beginning illustrates the violent, ceaseless, military march of the oralists who beat the deaf people into temporary submission. *See* Cultural programs: Poetry in American Sign Language.

STORYTELLING

The following describes the differences between artistic storytelling and everyday narratives in their extreme form, for the sake of clarity; however, in practice there are many gray areas between the extremes.

Physical Position. An everyday narrative is told informally while sitting or standing in a circle. In storytelling, the signer stands up and faces the audience which is seated in an arc. The storyteller "takes the floor."

Role of Audience. In any narrative, the addressee or audience generally is passive. However, in everyday narratives, the addressee does control aspects of the signer's behavior by expressing a desire for more information, lack of understanding, and so forth, which the signer then must respond to. In storytelling, the signer has the control and decides how much information and descriptive detail will be included according to that person's artistic intuitions. The audience responds with laughter, stillness, and so forth.

Eye Gaze. In everyday narratives, the signer gazes at the addressee's face at certain intervals to check for understanding or the need to clarify. In formal storytelling, the signer usually looks "above" the heads of the audience because the text is memorized and intended to be performed.

Signing Space. Everyday narratives use the same normal signing space as conversations, generally stretching from the head to the waist. In storytelling, the signing space extends to include the area above the signer's head and down to the knees.

Classifier Signs. In any good signed narrative, certain types of signs called classifiers are used extensively. These include body classifiers in which the signer "becomes" a character in the story and the signer's body, hands, and face perform actions that the character does in the story; body part SASSes (size-and-shape specifiers) in which the sign shows the action of a body part—like brows raising, dog ears half crooked, jaw drop, or Adam's apple moving up; and other classifiers in which the sign represents a noun and tells how that thing looks, moves, is handled, or where it is located in relation to other objects. However, in formal storytelling, these classifiers seem more exaggerated, crisp and clear, giving even more descriptive information and often giving the impression of pantomime. Perhaps this is similar to the way that spoken or written stories will add more descriptive information via greater use of adverbs and adjectives than normally occurs in everyday narratives.

There are three types of texts found in signed stories. Many stories are simply paraphrases of written stories, like "Goldilocks and the Three Bears." In other stories, the text is taken from a traditional source but adapted to make it more expressive of the deaf experience. For example, in one version of "The Three Little Pigs," the pigs are deaf and the world is hearing. In such stories, characters are often changed so that some are deaf and some are hearing, and the deaf characters win in the end.

The third type of text is still rare, but more deaf artists are now experimenting with it. These texts are original stories created by deaf people that express their culture and experience. For example, Ben Bahan has created an original story about a sparrow and the eagles. The eagles symbolize hearing parents and the hearing world; sparrows represent deaf people. By a freak accident, a sparrow egg gets into an eagle nest. So the sparrow grows up among eagles, attempting to be like them, and even has an operation on its beak to change it from being straight to being crooked. In the end, the sparrow realizes that deep in its heart it belongs to the sparrow family and is happiest there.

Bibliography

Freeman, D.: *Linguistics and Literary Style*, Holt, Rinehart, and Winston, New York, 1970.

Klima, E., and V. Bellugi: "The Heightened Use of Language," *The Signs of Language*, Harvard University Press, 1979.

Miles, D.: *Gestures: Poetry in Sign Language*, Joyce Motion Picture Co., Northridge, California, 1976.

National Theatre of the Deaf: "My Third Eye," performance videotape, Gallaudet College Library.

Ella Mae Lentz

Name Signs

Just as hearing people use spoken words, like Mary or John, that function as a name for a particular person, deaf people in the signing community use a sign (or fingerspelled word) to name a person. However, unlike the naming of hearing children who receive a first name, sometimes a middle name, and the parents' last name, this one "name sign" is the full name. For example, tapping a C handshape twice at the chin might mean Carol Lynn Smith.

In hearing communities, parents are usually the ones who assign names to their children. However, since less than 10 percent of deaf children have deaf parents (who naturally assign a name sign to their children, deaf or hearing), most deaf children do not receive their name sign from their parents. Instead, nearly half of the children are given a name sign by their signing peers after beginning school. Sometimes residential school counselors or teachers give a name sign to a deaf student who does not already have one.

One's name sign can change during different periods of one's life, or one can be known by one name sign among a particular group of people and by another name sign within another group. For example, an increase in status, like becoming school superintendent, might be reflected by a change in a particular feature of the name sign, or a person might change her or his name sign to reflect a new marital status.

A deaf researcher, Samuel Supalla, who has carefully examined how name signs are made, has discovered that there are two distinct types of name signs: descriptive and arbitrary. Descriptive name signs are iconic in that there is a reason for making the sign in a particular way, and the reason concerns some physical or psychological characteristic of the person. For example, a child with big eyes might have a name sign made near the eyes, or a shy child might have a name sign that moves up the face to reflect the child's blushing.

One study found that under 20 percent of these descriptive name signs referred to a positive attribute of the person, whereas 45 percent referred to a negative aspect of the person—like having poor vision (name sign referring to thick glasses), limping (name sign same as sign CRIPPLED), being overweight (name sign indicating fatness), or having a facial scar (name sign made at scar).

Deaf children, and occasionally adults, may use secret name signs for disliked teachers or other adults that are different from that person's regular name sign. For example, one person's public name sign might be a G on the shoulder, but secretly changed to a G facing the nose to show that person's big nose. Or another person's public name sign might be made with an R handshape at the forehead, but secretly changed so that the fingers bend repeatedly at the knuckles, like the sign that means "feeble-minded." Sometimes such hostile name signs become widely used.

Supalla's research finds that deaf and hearing children of deaf parents have name signs that are arbitrary rather than descriptive. Their name signs do not refer to any characteristic or behavior of the person named.

These arbitrary name signs seem to be composed of a very limited set of handshapes, locations, and movements—much more limited than the general set of signs in American Sign Language (ASL). For example, unlike regular ASL signs, almost none of the arbitrary name signs are made on the eyes, nose, mouth, ears, or hair. All of the handshapes are those that represent initials (like R or S, but not classifier handshapes like bent 5 or bent V). There are only four kinds of movement that are found in these arbitrary name signs, whereas many other kinds of movement are found in regular ASL signs.

All arbitrary name signs have alphabetically based handshapes derived from the initial of that person's written first, middle, or last name or nickname. For example, Marie Jean Philip might be signed with the handshapes M-P. Martina Joyce Bienvenu might be signed with the handshapes M-J. Ella Mae Lentz might be signed with an E handshape. Hugh Prickett might be signed with a P handshape.

Fingerspelling is another way to convey a name sign. Here the first name or nickname is spelled out, but in a contracted form.

The two systems that underlie the formation of descriptive and arbitrary name signs in the United States deaf community are both a part of ASL.

Bibliography

Meadow, Kathryn: "Name Signs as Identity Symbols in the Deaf Community," *Sign Language Studies*, 16:237–246, 1977.

Supalla, Samuel: "The Arbitrary Name Sign System in American Sign Language," *Sign Language Studies*, 1986.

Charlotte Baker-Shenk

Home Sign

Home sign is the generic term for the idiosyncratic sign languages or gestural behavior that is developed when deaf individuals are isolated from other deaf people and need to communicate with the hearing people around them. Often home sign is the first communication system of deaf children with hearing families, and so is sometimes called homemade sign language. Since only a few deaf persons may know and use a home sign language, such as the younger children in a school where sign language is not encouraged, home sign is also termed esoteric sign language, in contrast with standard sign language used in a larger community, termed exoteric.

Home sign differs from artificial sign languages, which are created to be a visual representation of a spoken language. Home sign also differs from these contrived or invented sign languages in that the latter are created by educators or communication theorists as whole systems, whereas home sign develops naturally, bit by bit.

SYSTEMS EVALUATION

Some scientists have been trying to discover if home sign systems are, in fact, languages. This question has been the subject of several case reports about isolated deaf signers. These reports find that certain important features, presumably present in all true languages, may be absent in such idiosyncratic, first-generation gestural systems. The terms conventional, traditional, shared, and standard often appear in such discussions.

Conventional Home sign systems may be considered conventional within themselves if the sign-to-meaning relationship is constant. That is, if the same sign has the same meaning from one occasion to the next, then the system is conventional. This is different from disordered language behavior where individuals may continually create new signs to represent a particular meaning on different occasions.

Traditional Home sign systems are called first-generation languages. In this respect they are like pidgin languages or contact languages. In the usual contact situation, each speaker knows a language, but not the language spoken by the other person. Home systems arise from contact between a signer who is deaf and knows only home signs, and speakers (hearing people) who know a spoken language but no conventional signed language. With even one more generation of use, it is assumed that a home sign system takes on more of the characteristics of a sign language. In this respect some sign languages share properties with Creole languages.

Shared Of course any two-way communication system by definition is shared if the users understand each other. But home sign systems are used by only a small number of participants. Moreover, the responsibility for the creation and maintenance of such a system lies primarily with the principal user, the isolated deaf person.

Standard A standard sign language is one which is acknowledged as generally the same over a community of users. Home sign cannot be standard since it has only one primary user.

DEVELOPMENT OF HOME SIGN SYSTEMS

Where does home sign come from? How is it created? Home sign arises from the daily contact of deaf persons with hearing persons, especially in the case where the deaf person has been isolated from contact with other deaf people. This circumstance might occur in two ways:

The parents of a deaf child might decide to educate the child by the oral method exclusively. The child will then have contact primarily with hearing people, family members, neighbors, teachers, tutors, and so forth. A very young deaf child does not have long contact with other deaf youngsters in an oral day program. Deaf adults who use communication methods other than oral are probably not employed at an oral school.

Alternatively, the hearing parent who does not have the financial means to support an oral education, or the orientation to education which would encourage this choice, might invent and exploit whatever gestural means of communication the child seemed to respond to. In the first case the parent will not be expected to participate in or even acknowledge the child's use of home signs, while in the second case the parent may be helping to develop the home signs along with the child.

HOME SIGN FROM ORAL HOUSEHOLDS

Studies of children who have created home sign systems are relatively few. S. Goldin-Meadow has studied videotapes of several children who were being educated orally. Without exposure to any traditional sign language, each deaf child developed his or her own gestural communication system. These home sign systems have several features which are like the normal features of any child's language: (1) The individual gestures were consistent, were segmentable from the stream of motor activity, and were separated into two types: deictic signs (pointing gestures to indicate objects) and characterizing signs (gestures indicating actions). Each of these types of signs has symbolic value. (2) Observers reliably assigned these signs to semantic categories, such as agent, action, and object, for utterances with more than one sign. The children used gestural order (first, second, third position in the utterance) consistently for different semantic categories. For example, the children more often signed the name of an object before signing the action attributed to that object: "truck roll" or "jar open" occurred more often than "roll truck" or "open jar." The object was named before the location more often than the reverse: "hat head" more often than "head hat." (3) The semantic categories did not all occur with equal frequency; rather, some were more likely to occur than others. (4) More than one proposition would occur in a single utterance. Such utterances then begin to look like complex syntactic constructions. The child-created gestural systems have many of the features found in hearing children's communication, but they have been developed without any overt linguistic model.

Of some importance is the observation that different children showed quite different amounts of gestural behavior. Some children were quite "talkative" and gestured a lot, while others were less expressive. Some children produced many whole sentences and a sizable proportion of complex sentences, while others did not.

What is the parent's influence on the child's gestural development? Does the parent's gesturing to the child, even though the parent does not know a sign language, encourage the child's gesturing? Analysis comparing mothers and children found that the mother seemed to be learning the home sign system from the child, not the child from the mother. In fact, (1) the mother did not consistently produce gestures for the same meanings as the child's signs; (2) the mother's sign combinations were less frequent than the child's combinations; (3) the mother's sign combinations did not occur in consistent orders or did not occur in the orders that the children used; (4) the mother's use of consistent orders followed by several weeks or months the child's consistent use of those orders. The child only rarely imitated the parent's gestures from an immediately preceding message; more often the child's gestures were spontaneous.

Goldin-Meadow and her colleagues have not investigated whether these children's home sign systems gradually begin to include mechanisms found in regular sign languages (directionality of movement of gesture, consistent assignment of location, use of rhythmic repetition of movement, and so forth). The observations which follow are more the result of anecdotal reports than of microanalysis of data.

CHARACTERISTICS

Six characteristics distinguish the production of home sign from the production of conventional, standardized, and traditional sign languages. These characteristics are also found to some extent in the communication between two deaf signers who do not share the same sign language (foreigner talk).

1. The signing space for home sign is larger, less well defined than for a traditional sign language. The person using home sign may feel more free to move upper torso, reposition the whole body, and reorient the body through involving the feet or through differences of height (such as bending the knees). In contrast, fluent users of a traditional sign language will generally make their movements within a well-defined space around the head and trunk. Movement of the feet (if standing) is likely to include no more than shifting of the weight. The

space in home sign and the way that movements occur within the space are perhaps more characteristic of pantomime in the lay sense.

2. Signs and sign sequences will be repeated in home sign. This use of repetition and of repetition with minor variations, including shortenings with each reiteration, might also be found in the communication between signers who do not share the same sign language. Thus, it may only be a characteristic of initial contact, and less noticeable among persons who have had extensive experience with one another. This characteristic implies that the exchange of information using home sign may be slower than communication using a shared system that has a high number of conventional signs and grammatical rules.

3. The number of distinct handshapes in home sign is fewer than in a traditional sign language. In home sign, the handshape of a sign may change from one occurrence to the next in seemingly unpredictable ways. Like traditional sign languages, home sign systems do not use many of the more marked handshapes; that is, those involving crossed fingers, insertion of thumb between fingers, extension of any fingers but the thumb or index, are all less likely to occur than those shapes which have been proposed as unmarked (fist, index extended, flat hand, spread hand, cupped hand, circle hand).

4. Eye gaze as a device within home sign does not function as would be expected from the understanding of traditional sign languages. In traditional sign languages, eye gaze regulates the interaction between signer and viewer. It also helps define grammatical locations of referents within the signing space. However, in home sign, insofar as the space is ill-defined, the use of eye gaze is similarly ill-defined or inconsistently applied. Eye gaze also does not reliably regulate signer-viewer interactions.

5. Unlike traditional sign languages, home sign systems seem to use more than the signer's hands and body. Objects from the environment may be used to represent themselves, other objects, or characteristics (for example, shape of the coconut hull, color of the tablecloth) in home sign.

6. Signs which are spontaneously invented are produced more slowly, awkwardly, and less fluently than those coined in a traditional sign language by systematically defined processes.

All of the above characteristics relate to two themes: First, the space in which language happens is not distinct from the space in which object manipulation occurs and in which the body moves (applies to 1, 3, 4, 5 above). Second, the signer of home sign is constantly checking and rechecking that the communication is being received, but is never secure in the communication flow (applies to 1, 2, 3, 4, 6).

However, these characteristics may describe the extreme case. Over time, continued contact with the signer in a community (family, work site, or the like) would probably make the home sign system less markedly distinct from a more traditional sign language.

RELATION TO HEARING GESTURES

One of the questions which has intrigued investigators is the extent to which deaf signs are related to or derived from hearing gestures. R. Kuschel collected examples of sign communication used by the only deaf person on the Polynesian island of Rennell. Kuschel categorized the signs into three groups according to how easily understandable they would be to different hearing audiences. Some signs would be understood by anyone. DRINK performed with a loosely held fist to the mouth, head tilted back, would be in this most transparent category. The second group would be understood by any member of that Polynesian culture—for example, BROTHER-SISTER RELATIONSHIP made with the index fingers of both hands vertically extended, wrists crossed so that the hands are back to back but separated by several inches. Within the Rennellese (and neighboring Bellona Island) culture, adult siblings of opposite sex avoid direct contact or interaction; the orientation of the hands in opposite directions symbolizes this culturally specific meaning. The third group of signs would be understood only by the one deaf signer and the people in regular communication with him or her. "Father" is made with the hand tracing the outline of the deaf person's own father's tatoo. This sign would be understood only by persons acquainted with the deaf person's specific situation. *See* Sign languages: Rennellese.

Washabaugh studied the hearing population on Providence Island (in the Caribbean) to find out if some of their commonly used gestures (called emblems) also occurred in the sign language used by a small group of deaf Providence Islanders. He found that all of these gestures of hearing people have meaning within the sign language of deaf people on Providence Island, although some of the meanings have changed in semantic function. Thus, hearing gestures can be seen as a resource from which parts of some sign languages may grow. *See* Sign languages: Providence Island.

So far, no one has looked carefully at the systematic ways in which members of a deaf community communicate with those who know only home sign. If signers who use a standard sign language can reliably participate in two-way communication with those who use only an idiosyncratic system, then there must be some aspects of idiosyncratic systems that are shared. And these characteristics must be part of the more general gestural systems which are available to all people, although not attended to or acknowledged or developed to any degree. The interplay of several channels of communication—for example, hands, space, eyes, mouth, angle of head tilt and bend coupled with the timing and rhythmic variations possible for each channel—allows for the potential of quite complex gestural communication in home sign as in traditional sign languages. The difference here is that for each home sign the whole set of conventions must be reinvented or rediscovered.

CRITICAL-AGE HYPOTHESIS

Of some interest for the theory of language and language acquisition is the question of a critical age for language learning. The deaf person who has only had experience with home sign until school age is in fact the statistically most frequent case: most deaf children have hearing parents who do not know or use a standard, traditional sign language. Sometimes an isolated individual in a hearing community who does not participate in formal education will reach adulthood before being exposed to a standard sign language. The critical-age hypothesis in simplified form says that the child is ready to acquire language from age 0 to 5 years, and that beyond puberty an individual who has not had exposure to any language will not be able to acquire one. Evidence from deaf children in orally oriented homes suggests that they will begin to create a languagelike gestural system on their own, even without stimulation or modeling from those in their environment. Equally intriguing, but even less well understood, is the question of what happens to those who finally do come in contact with a traditional sign language in adulthood. Can they acquire the full grammatical system of such a language late in life?

Bibliography

Goldin-Meadow, S., and H. Feldman: "The Creation of a Communication System in Deaf Children of Hearing Parents," in William Stokoe (ed.), *Sign and Culture*, pp. 362–375, 1980.

———— and ————: *Science*, 197:401, 1977.

———— and C. Mylander: "Gestural Communication in Deaf Children: Noneffect of Parental Input on Language Development," *Science*, 221:372–374, 1983.

Kuschel, R.: *A Lexicon of Signs from a Polynesian Outlier Island*, University of Copenhagen, 1974.

————: "The Silent Inventor: The Creation of a Sign Language by the Only Deaf-Mute on a Polynesian Island," *Sign Language Studies*, 3:1–27, 1973.

MacLeod, C.: "A Deaf Man's Sign Language," *Linguistics*.

Tervoort, Bernard: "Esoteric Symbolism in the Communication Behavior of Young Deaf Children," *American Annals of the Deaf*, 106:436–480, 1967.

Young, R.: "Sign Language Acquisition in a Deaf Adult: A Test of the Critical Period Hypothesis," Ph.D. dissertation (unpublished), University of Georgia, 1981.

Nancy Frishberg

Technical and Invented Signs

The decades since the 1960s have witnessed a need for rapid expansion of the sign vocabulary used in the United States. Two major contributing factors are increased use of signing in academic environments and increased opportunities in postsecondary education and career areas (especially technical areas) for deaf persons. The need for such a rapid expansion in sign vocabulary has led some people to invent signs (that is, to develop them artificially), while others have sought to develop signs in a more natural way. Both invented signs for general English vocabulary and invented and more naturally developed signs for technical vocabulary are discussed below.

INVENTED SIGNS

Sign invention has been based primarily on the desire by some people to provide teachers and students with a sign system that parallels spoken or written English on a one-to-one basis, that is, to have a sign for every English word and affix (prefixes and suffixes). The rationale for such a sign system or code is that if English is fully visible through signs to deaf children from an early age, development of English reading and writing skills will be facilitated. Also, sign invention has occurred for English technical vocabulary in an attempt to help meet the communication needs of teachers, students, and interpreters in secondary and postsecondary educational settings.

The three major invented sign systems or codes for English in the United States are Seeing Essential English (SEE 1), Signing Exact English (SEE 2), and the Gallaudet Preschool Signed English System. Each of these sign codes has based sign invention on English spelling, pronunciation, or meaning.

Seeing Essential English (SEE 1) SEE 1 invented signs are primarily based on the spelling of English syllables. For example, "window" is signed as WIND + OW, "always" as AL + WAY + S, "evaluate" as E + VAL + U + ATE, "typist" as TYP + IST, and "typical" as TYP + IC + AL.

Seeing Exact English (SEE 2) SEE 2 sign rules take into account three word types: base words which consist of a single free morpheme (for example, "right" and "book"; a morpheme is the smallest meaningful unit in a language); complex words which consist of a base word and an affix (for example, "books" and "walked"); and compound words which consist of two base words (for example, "underline" and "understand").

The SEE 2 rule for base words is the two-of-three rule based on English spelling, pronunciation, or meaning. If any two of these three are the same for two or more English words, all these words are signed the same. For example, "right" is signed the

**Sign-Word Examples for Signing Exact English (SEE 2) Based on the Two-of-Three Rule
(Spelling, Pronunciation, and Meaning)**

	Examples	Spelling	Pronunciation	Meaning	Signs
Homographs	wind, object*	same	different	different	different
Homonyms	right, run†	same	same	different	same
Homophemes	write/right, fair/fare‡	different	same	different	different

*The "wind" is strong and "wind" the clock. Put the "object" on the table and I "object" to that.
†That is the "right" answer, it is my "right" to vote, and turn "right." That was a long "run," she had a "run" in her stocking, and he will "run" the meeting.
‡Please "write" your answer and that is the "right" answer. My teacher is very "fair" and the "fare" costs too much.

same for "right answer" and "right to vote" since the spelling and pronunciation of these words are the same, though their meanings are different. "Right" and "write," however, would be signed differently since their spellings and meanings are different, though their pronunciation is the same.

The SEE 2 rule for complex words is to combine a base sign with a sign affix. For example, "books" is signed as the base word BOOK + the S handshape (regular, plural sign affix), and "walked" is signed as the base sign word WALK + the D handshape (regular, past-tense sign affix).

The SEE 2 rule for compound words is that if the meaning of the two base words separately is consistent with the two words together, then (and only then) the compound should be signed as a combination of the two base words. For example, "underline" is signed as UNDER + LINE, since the meanings of the two words separately are related to the compound formed when they are joined together, but "understand," having no relation to the meaning of the words "under" and "stand," would not be signed UNDER + STAND.

SEE 2 also uses letter initialization of American Sign Language (ASL) signs for sign invention. For example, the ASL sign MAKE has been modified from S to C handshapes to invent a sign for "create," and the ASL sign IMPORTANT has been modified from 9 to P handshapes to invent a sign for "precious."

Gallaudet Preschool Signed English System Invented signs in this system involve extensive use of letter initialization and compounding. For example, the ASL sign FOREST has been changed from a 5 handshape with a semicircular shaking movement in front of the signer to an F handshape with a stationary shaking movement in front of the signer; the ASL sign CAN has been changed from S handshapes to M handshapes on both hands to form the sign for "may"; and the ASL signs sometimes glossed as SIDE and WALK have been combined to form the sign SIDEWALK. *See* MANUALLY CODED ENGLISH.

SIGNS FOR TECHNICAL VOCABULARY

Sign materials for technical vocabulary include books, films, and videotapes. Among the content areas included in these technical sign materials are anthropology, art, business, computer, engineering, English, human sexuality, mathematics, medical, religious, television production, welding, and woodworking terminology. Major development of technical sign materials for academic environments has been undertaken at Los Angeles Pierce College in Woodland Hills, California, and at the National Technical Institute for the Deaf (NTID), Rochester Institute of Technology, in Rochester, New York; at Gallaudet College; and by the Silent Environment Educational Kamp in Ellensburg, Washington. *See* GALLAUDET COLLEGE; NATIONAL TECHNICAL INSTITUTE FOR THE DEAF.

Invented Signs In *Signs for Instructional Purposes,* the major publication on invented signs for technical vocabulary, the five guidelines followed in inventing signs are as follows.

1. An existing sign with a letter cue; for example, the sign invented for "plasma" was the ASL sign BLEED with a P handshape on the dominant hand. (The dominant hand refers to the hand with which a signer generally fingerspells and produces one-handed signs, and which is the moving hand in two-handed signs in which only one hand moves.)

2. A compound of two existing signs; for example, the sign invented for "differentiate" was formed by signing the ASL sign MAKE followed by the ASL sign DIFFERENT.

3. A compound of a letter and existing sign; for example, the sign invented for "plant" was formed by signing the ASL sign GROW followed by a shaking P handshape in front of the signer.

4. A completely new sign; for example, the invented sign for "radioactivity" was formed by having an R handshape on the dominant hand move sideways, away from an A handshape on the non-dominant hand.

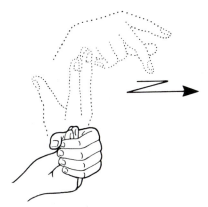

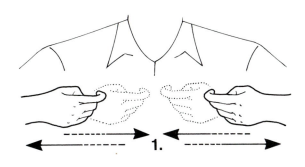

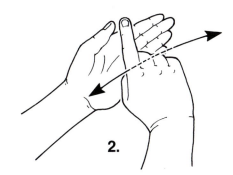

Sign invented for "plant," formed by producing the ASL sign for GROW followed by a P handshape with shaking movement. (After B. Kannapell, L. B. Hamilton, and H. Bornstein, *Signs for Instructional Purposes*, Gallaudet College Press, 1969)

5. A completely new sign with a letter cue; for example, the invented sign for "atom" was formed by having an A handshape on the dominant hand circle an A handshape on the nondominant hand.

Also, a few signs were created spontaneously, that is, without any construction guidelines.

More Naturally Developed Technical Signs The major projects on documenting more naturally developed technical signs have been coordinated at Los Angeles Pierce College and at NTID. The goal of both projects, respectively named the Techsign Project and the Technical Signs Project, is to produce and share materials that accurately depict signs currently used by skilled signers in academic and career environments. In both projects, emphasis is placed on natural sign development rather than sign invention. The main reason is that, as with the creation of spoken and written words, skilled

Sign developed for "ammeter," an instrument that measures electric current. (After L. Kushner, S. Diamond, and F. Casale, *Pierce College Techsign Project: Electronics*, Los Angeles Pierce College)

signers make use of natural means for developing and refining new signs and often resist using artificially invented signs. The most important part of this development process is the use of newly coined signs in everyday conversations and their subsequent modification, acceptance, or rejection by skilled signers. Whether a sign is modified, accepted, or rejected is largely determined by how well it facilitates communication and how well it matches the normal structure of ASL signs.

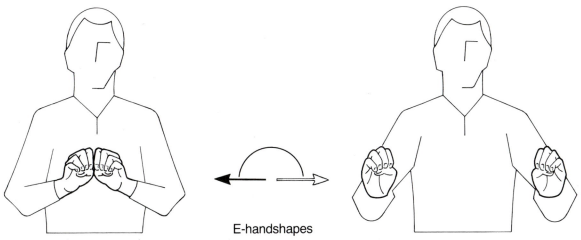

E-handshapes

Sign developed for "equation." (After F. Caccamise et al., *Technical Signs Project Manual 3: Mathematics*, Modern Talking Picture Service, 1982)

The following diagram illustrates the approach and the five general steps taken by the Techsign Project and Technical Signs Project. Similar to the

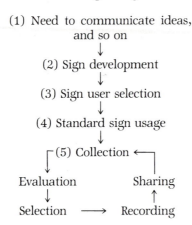

(1) Need to communicate ideas,
and so on
↓
(2) Sign development
↓
(3) Sign user selection
↓
(4) Standard sign usage
↓
(5) Collection ←
Evaluation   Sharing
↓   ↑
Selection ⟶ Recording

development of words in any modality, sign-word usage is part of a natural process that begins with a need to communicate ideas, concepts, and feelings. This leads to the development and selection by skilled sign communicators of agreed-upon signs for communicating them. At this point, the Techsign Project and Technical Signs Project procedures for sign collection, evaluation, selection, recording, and sharing begin. These procedures are ongoing in order to include both new signs and modifications that occur in signs through normal (sign) language use and development. These procedures, and the materials that result, are akin to the process used for producing dictionaries.

Sign materials produced by the Pierce College Techsign Project consist of matched books and videotapes in subjects such as advertising art, automotive, electronics, machine tools, real estate, and welding. Sign materials produced by the NTID Technical Signs Project include manuals and videotapes for signs in areas such as career education, communication (speech pathology and audiology), English, mathematics, photography, psychology, religion, science, and social work.

FUTURE SIGN DEVELOPMENT AND USE

The expansion of sign vocabulary used in the United States may be expected to continue as deaf persons' participation in academic and career environments and content areas increases. Regardless of how a sign develops (invented or natural development), its acceptance by skilled sign communicators will determine whether the sign will contribute to effective communication.

Bibliography

Anthony, David A., Wilmina G. Dekkers, and C. Bradley Erickson: *Seeing Essential English: Codebreaker*, Pruett Publishing, Boulder, Colorado, 1978.

Bellugi, Ursula, and Don Newkirk: "Formal Devices for Creating New Signs in American Sign Language," *Sign Language Studies*, 30:1–35, 1981.

Bornstein, Harry, Karen L. Saulnier, and Lillian B. Hamilton (eds.): *The Comprehensive Signed English Dictionary*, Gallaudet College Press, Washington, D.C., 1983.

Caccamise, Frank, et al: *Technical Signs Manual 1: Videotaped and Print Materials for Signs Used in Academic and Career Environments*, 2d ed., Modern Talking Picture Service, St. Petersburg, Florida, 1982.

——— et al.: *Technical Signs Manual 3: Mathematics*, Modern Talking Picture Service, St. Petersburg, Florida, 1982.

Frishberg, Nancy: "Arbitrariness and Iconicity: Historical Change in American Sign Language," *Language*, 51(3):696–719, 1975.

Garcia, W. Joseph (ed.): *Medical Sign Language*, Charles C. Thomas, Springfield, Illinois, 1983.

Gustason, Geri, Donna Pfetzing, and Esther Zawolkow: *Signing Exact English*, National Association of the Deaf, Silver Spring, Maryland, 1980.

Jamison, Steven L. (ed.): *Signs for Computing Terminology*, National Association of the Deaf, Silver Spring, Maryland, 1983.

Kannapell, Barbara, Lillian B. Hamilton, and Harry Bornstein: *Signs for Instructional Purposes*, Gallaudet College Press, Washington, D.C., 1969.

Kushner, Larry, Susan Diamond, and Francis Casale: Techsign Project sign manuals for *Advertising Art, Architecture, Automotive, Accounting*, and several other academic or career areas, Los Angeles Pierce College, Woodland Hills, California.

Frank Caccamise

SILENT NEWS

The *Silent News* is an independent national newspaper reporting on news relevant to deaf people and deafness. It was founded in 1969 by Julius Wiggins and was published monthly by the Silent Press, Inc., for four years. In 1973 the Silent News, Inc., a nonprofit corporation, was formed and has published the newspaper since that time. The majority of the staff of the *Silent News* is deaf, as are the reporters, correspondents, and photographers.

The *Silent News* serves both the general deaf public and those involved professionally in the field of deafness. Among deaf people, readers range from high school students to the elderly. Hearing parents and relatives of deaf people also read the *Silent News*. Included among its professional readership are teachers, social workers, and interpreters. In addition, many public and university libraries receive the *Silent News*.

The paid circulation of the *Silent News* is 7000 subscribers. Considering family ratios and the number of subscriptions going to organizations, agencies, schools, universities, and libraries, it has been estimated that over 30,000 people read the *Silent News* monthly.

The *Silent News* publishes news that is particularly relevant to deaf people and deafness. Standard daily newspapers do not publish news of this kind. Through a national network of reporters and contributors, the *Silent News* gathers together a vast amount of information.

Each month, the *Silent News* reports on the latest legislative, technological, medical, and sports developments. In addition to full coverage of major national events and conventions, there are feature columns targeting statewide news, TDD tips, travel, and entertainment. Personal profiles of unique deaf people are also included.

People interested in submitting articles to the *Silent News* are encouraged to do so. Topics should be relevant to deaf people and deafness.

Julius Wiggins

SMITH, ERASTUS
(1787–1837)

Erastus "Deaf" Smith is best known for his role in the Texas Revolution to gain independence from Mexico. He was the chief scout and spy for General Sam Houston, commander in chief of the Texan army, and became one of Texas's folk heroes. He was once asked if his hearing loss was a disadvantage, and he replied that he felt it had helped him to develop the ability to keep a sharp lookout and not to be annoyed by the whistling of bullets.

Smith was born on April 19, 1787, in Dutchess County, New York, the son of Chileab and Mary Smith. He was a frail child, prone to a number of ailments in addition to his hearing impairment, present since an illness in infancy. Even with three brothers and four sisters, he was a quiet child who preferred solitude. He received whatever schooling was available in the rural area near Poughkeepsie. In 1798, when he was 11, his family moved to Clairborne County, Mississippi.

Smith visited Texas for the first time in 1817, then returned to Mississippi to take care of family affairs, his father having died about two years earlier. After much thought, he moved to Texas permanently in 1821.

In that year Mexico won its independence from Spain. Then 34 years old, Smith had so far led an ordinary life. Though not totally deaf, he could not follow regular conversations within a group of people, but managed fairly well on a one-to-one basis. He earned the Spanish nickname of *el Sordo* ("the Deaf One") and later the name "Deaf" Smith. This was not to show him disrespect but rather to distinguish him from other Smiths.

Smith became thoroughly familiar with the San Antonio area through exploring and through hunting trips for business and pleasure. He trained his dog to warn him of danger by tugging on his clothes instead of barking.

In 1822 Smith married a Spanish widow, Guadalupe Ruiz Duran, of San Antonio. Between 1823 and 1828 she bore three girls and one boy. Smith became a Mexican citizen as a result of his marriage and gained proficiency in Spanish, a difficult accomplishment considering his hearing impairment.

Smith led a relatively quiet life at home from 1823 to 1835. To curb his restlessness, he hunted buffalo, traded, scouted, guided new settlers and prospectors, and even searched for silver at one time. He became acquainted with men like James Bowie, William Barrett Travis, Jr., and James W. Fannin, all of whom later died at the Alamo. Smith was a guide and scout for Travis and Fannin, who were involved in revolutionary and military affairs.

He built a home in the La Villita section of San Antonio and was a loyal Mexican citizen with Mexican friends. Uninterested in "Anglo-Saxon" ideals of liberty and independence, he had come to Texas to take his chances under Mexican rule. He did not expect Texas to join the United States. Circumstances, however, would soon change his outlook.

Between 1832 and 1835, friction developed between the United States settlers in Texas and the Mexican government. Antonio de Santa Anna had made himself dictator of Mexico in 1832, throwing out the governor and legislature of the joint state of Coahuila and Texas. The Texans eventually formed their own provisional government, and Stephen F. Austin became commander in chief of the Texan armed forces. The Mexican general Martin Perfecto de Cos attempted to quell this open rebellion, and the Mexican forces were driven back to San Antonio, marking the beginning of the Texas Revolution in 1835.

Smith at first chose to remain neutral because of his family and friends in the Mexican community. He returned to San Antonio one day in October 1835 from a hunting trip to find the town occupied by General Cos's soldiers and under siege by the Texans. The Mexicans refused him entry to visit his family and even fired upon him. Greatly angered, Smith forsook his neutrality and offered his military services to General Austin, who gave him a commission immediately.

Smith was highly valuable to the Texan army, being thoroughly familiar with the countryside and cool and courageous in the face of danger. As a highly skilled scout, he gleaned information on enemy movements, often at great personal risk. He was involved in the battle of Concepcion (near San Antonio) in October 1835, won by the Texans. In the battle of San Antonio in December, he led Texan troops to a rendezvous. Fierce bombardment by the Mexicans ensued a few days later during which Smith was wounded.

At Gonzales, Smith met General Sam Houston, who was en route to help the Texans at the Alamo in San Antonio. He volunteered his services and was made first in command of recruits in the calvary, and soon became Houston's chief scout and spy. Distressed by news of the Alamo defeat, Houston sent Smith and Captain Henry Karness, a fellow scout, to get more information. Smith brought back Mrs. Almeron Dickerson and her baby daughter, the only survivors of the massacre at the Alamo.

The battle of San Jacinto on April 21, 1836, was Smith's crowning moment of glory. His strategy was a major factor leading to victory for the Texans. Smith suggested to General Houston that they tear down the only bridge over a stream, Vince's Bayou, to rob Santa Anna's army of an escape route in case the Texans succeeded in turning them back; the battlefield itself would offer little opportunity for a quick escape due to the presence of geographical barriers. The lost bridge, however, would also imperil the Texans' escape if the enemy prevailed. Houston decided to take the risk, and early on April 21 he sent Smith and several men with axes to destroy the bridge. They returned just in time to participate in the battle of San Jacinto later that day. Caught by surprise during their siesta, the Mexican soldiers lost the battle in less than an hour. Santa Anna, still dressed in a robe and slippers, was captured at the destroyed bridge the next day. This battle assured Texas of gaining its independence from Mexico.

Smith was sent to catch up with General Filisola and deliver a message to him from Santa Anna; Filisola agreed to obey the terms of the surrender. In his report to the Texas provisional government about the battle and the surrender, Houston had special praise for Smith.

Withdrawal of the defeated Mexican troops to Laredo on the Rio Grande caused a border disagreement between Mexico and the Republic of Texas. In February 1837, Smith and his company of rangers, whom he recruited and trained himself, went to Laredo with the intention of taking it for the Republic of Texas. Met by a larger unit of Mexican calvary, they fought a brief battle, after which the Mexicans retreated. Smith decided not to proceed against Laredo, where he might be outnumbered. This show of patriotism is one of the events in "Deaf" Smith's life that earned him a legendary niche in Texas history.

Smith entered the land business, and moved to Richmond in Fort Bend County. He became a partner with Joseph Borden in surveying and land transactions. Ill with a recurrence of the lung ailment of his earlier years in Texas, he died in Richmond on November 30, 1837, at the age of 50, and was buried in a simple grave there. A monument to "Deaf" Smith now stands in Richmond, with the inscription: "So valiant and trustworthy was he that all titles sink into insignificance before the simple name of 'Deaf' Smith." Deaf Smith County in the panhandle of Texas is named in his honor.

Bibliography

Gannon, Jack R.: *Deaf Heritage: A Narrative History of Deaf America*, 1981.

Huston, C.: *Deaf Smith: Incredible Texas Spy*, 1973.

Swain, R. L., Jr.: "The Hero Who Gave His Name to Texas' Deaf Smith County," *The Deaf American*, December, 1969.

Melanie Yager Williams

SOCIAL SECURITY ACT

The Social Security Act establishes the major federal benefit programs that affect the deaf and hearing-impaired communities. These major benefit programs are Old Age, Survivors, and Disability Insurance (OASDI—Title II of the Social Security Act), Supplemental Security Income (SSI—Title XVI), Medicare (Title XVIII), and Medicaid (Title XIX). The OASDI and Medicare programs operate as public insurance funds. Premiums are paid into the federal Social Security Trust Fund in the form of FICA payroll taxes and are distributed at the time that eligibility for benefits is established. In general, blind, aged, and disabled persons who meet a means test or who are found to be medically needy are eligible for SSI and Medicaid benefits. It is possible to be eligible for both OASDI and SSI if the income from OASDI does not exceed the means test requirements for SSI. In 35 states, the state Medicaid plan confers automatic eligibility for SSI recipients. All persons over 65 who have established eligibility for OASDI and all recipients of disability insurance who have been disabled for two years are automatically eligible for Medicare.

HISTORICAL BACKGROUND

During the era of the New Deal, considerable debate centered upon involving the government in matters of federally mandated retirement benefits, a role previously assigned to private insurers. Appointed by President Roosevelt, the Committee on Economic Security played a key role in recommending legislation dealing with the insecurities of old age. However, because of the administrative difficulties associated with protecting against lost earnings due to permanent and total disability (such as making disability determinations) and the pressing needs of political expediency, the Committee on Economic Security did not recommend a disability insurance program, even though models of such programs existed in foreign countries.

Retirement benefits were first provided by the Social Security Act of 1935. The amendments of 1939 provided benefits for dependents and survivors. In 1954 eligibility for retirement and survivors benefits was modified so that periods of disability would not adversely affect the amount of monthly benefits to which one was entitled. In effect, benefit levels were frozen to the level of entitlement at the time of disablement.

It was not until 1956 that Congress authorized monthly disability benefits for persons whose disabilities were expected to last indefinitely. Initially such benefits were payable only to disabled workers between the ages of 50 and 64. In 1960 this age limitation was removed. In 1965 the Social Security Act was expanded to provide disability benefits to disabled workers unable to engage in substantial gainful activity for 12 months or more. Two years later, some disabled spouses of insured workers, meeting a stricter disability test, were provided coverage. It is essentially this stricter disability test that is used today.

A claimant is considered disabled if he or she is unable to engage in substantial gainful work that exists in the national economy (taking into account severity of impairment, age, education, and work experience).

In 1972 Congress established the SSI program, with benefits commencing in January 1974. This program was designed to replace prior federal-state welfare programs thought to be unfairly stigmatizing for disabled recipients. Because of allegations of widespread fraud by ineligible recipients, the 1980 amendments to the Social Security Act required the Social Security Administration to review periodically the eligibility of beneficiaries—in most cases, every three years. The Reagan Administration accelerated the process of continuing disability investigations by beginning in March 1981, well before the scheduled 1982 startup date. Between March 1981 and May 1985, the eligibility of approximately 1.2 million recipients was reviewed. Of this number, 491,000 recipients were deemed ineligible and 214,000 recipients regained benefits after appealing. Remedial legislation requiring face-to-face interviews prior to termination and extending benefits during the appeals process to those who are terminated was enacted in 1982.

ELIGIBILITY OF HEARING-IMPAIRED PERSONS

An individual may be eligible for benefits under OASDI or SSI if he or she (1) has earned wages and paid into the Social Security Trust Fund and is 62 or over and wants to retire or work part-time; (2) has earned wages and paid into the Social Security Trust Fund and is unable to engage in substantial gainful activity because of one or more medical impairments; (3) is a dependent of someone in category 1 or 2; (4) is a survivor of someone who has paid into the Social Security Trust Fund; (5) is 65 or over and has a low income; (6) is unable to engage in substantial gainful activity, has a low income, and has one or more medical impairments; or (7) is a child under 18 who has significant medical impairment and whose family has a low income.

The evaluation of whether a person meets the definition of disability is basically the same under the OASDI and SSI programs. It must be shown that the claimant (1) has a medically determinable physical or mental impairment that can be expected to result in death or has lasted, or can be expected to last, for a continuous period of not less than 12 months, and (2) has an impairment or impairments that prevent the performance of his or her prior work or work in jobs that exist in significant numbers in the claimant's region or several regions in the country. The evaluation of these two conditions for a determination of disability involves a sequential evaluation process. First, it must be found that the claimant is not engaged in substantial gainful activity. Second, the claimant must have a severe impairment that limits physical and mental ability to perform basic work activities. The Social Security Administration has published a list of impairments in the Code of Federal Regulations that are deemed to be severe impairments. Anyone who is found to have an impairment that meets the 12-month duration requirement and that is listed, or that is an impairment equal to the listed impairment, will be considered disabled.

With respect to hearing losses, the impairment listing is established by audiometric tests involving speech discrimination scores of 40 percent or less in the better ear or average hearing threshold sensitivity for air conduction, and corresponding levels of bone conduction, of 90 decibels or greater. *See* AUDIOLOGIC CLASSIFICATION; AUDIOMETRY: Pure-Tone Audiogram.

Third, if the claimant meets the "severity" test but not the "listed impairments" test, his or her "residual functional capacity" to perform work activity on a regular and continuing basis will be examined. This examination involves the measurement of physical abilities such as walking, standing, lifting, carrying, pushing, and so on, and mental abilities such as understanding, carrying out and remembering instructions, and responding appropriately to supervision. If the claimant has the residual functional capacity to return to the prior job, then he or she will be deemed not disabled. Finally, if the claimant is unable to return to his or her prior work, and has a "severe" but not a "listed" impairment, it must be shown that given the residual functional capacity, age, education, and other vocational criteria, the claimant is unable to work at positions available in the national economy. An elaborate grid that attempts uniformly to pigeon-hole such medical-vocational guidelines is listed in the Code of Federal Regulations immediately following the description of listed impairments.

According to a census taken by the United States government over the summer of 1978, 314,000 beneficiaries of the Disability Insurance component of OASDI were people who were deaf or otherwise had hearing impairments. Similar information regarding SSI recipients is not publicly available.

George Zelma

Bibliography

Brown, D. J.: *An American Philosophy of Social Security*, Princeton University Press.

Greenston, P., and M. Hagan: "Insuring the Disabled," Urban Institute Press, Washington, D.C.

"Old Age, Survivors, and Disability Insurance Program, 1983," Social Security Bulletin, Annual Statistical Supplement, 1983.

Social Security Act, 42 U.S.C. §§ 301 et seq.

Weinstein, J.: "Equality and the Law: Social Security Disability Cases in the Federal Courts," 35 Syracuse Law Review, p. 897, 1984.

SOCIAL WORK AND SOCIAL WELFARE

The American social welfare system has its roots in England, and in fact, some national policies in the 1980s reflect the philosophy of the English Poor Laws. In both England and the United States, the earliest concern was for the education of deaf children. It was not until the beginning of the nineteenth century in England and the twentieth century in the United States that significant attempts were made to develop services that would make possible deaf people's fuller participation in society. Services for deaf people consistently lagged behind those available to the nondeaf population.

SERVICES IN ENGLAND, NINETEENTH CENTURY

The major educational opportunities available for deaf children, especially from poorer families, were in residential schools known as asylums. During the early nineteenth century, many people felt that the asylums removed deaf children from society instead of preparing them to function in it. Some deaf children grew up in these institutions and remained there until their death, having had little contact with the outside world. Others were placed in workhouses when they reached adulthood because they were incapable of self-support. In 1836 the Charitable and Provident Society for Granting Pensions to the Aged Poor and Infirm Deaf and Dumb was established in response to the harshness of the New Poor Law of 1834. This society was instrumental in assuring that punitive measures intended for the able-bodied poor would not include deaf persons.

In 1840 deaf people began to organize to help themselves for the first time, because they felt that neither the church nor the state made adequate provision for them. In 1861 Sam Smith, a hearing man, was ordained, and gathered funds to erect the first church for deaf people, St. Saviour's in London, which opened in 1873. Queen Victoria's conferring of royal patronage upon this effort led to the establishment of the Royal Association in Aid for the Deaf and Dumb. This organization soon became concerned with national issues and was greatly involved in exposing the ineffectiveness of schools for deaf children.

As other spiritual missions were established for deaf people, missioners (clergy and lay people working in missions and churches for deaf people) realized the inadequacy of government and voluntary assistance to the social needs of deaf people. Thus, missioners became involved in after-care for those leaving asylums, unemployment, indigence, and bridging the chasm between the deaf and hearing world.

Unfortunately, these efforts often fostered dependence. Many missioners became overprotective of "their deaf," a phenomenon that the Royal Association in Aid for the Deaf and Dumb attempted to overcome. One of the Royal Association's goals was to work for deaf people without preventing them from working for themselves. Some deaf people themselves became concerned about failure to involve them in decisions affecting their own welfare. When the Royal Commission for the Education of the Blind and Deaf Children submitted a report in 1888 without consulting deaf people, there was a strong negative reaction that resulted in the reorganization of the old Charitable and Provident Society of 1836 into the British Deaf and Dumb Association in 1890. This organization concerned itself with the welfare of deaf people in general and offered counseling for those who needed help with problems. Charles Gordon, the organization's first secretary, founded the *Deaf and Dumb Times*, the first British newspaper for deaf people.

At the close of the nineteenth century, unemployment among English deaf people was still great. One consequence was the 1897 Petition of Deaf Workers from Oldham asking that employers be excused from paying compensation for injuries received at work if the injury was due to deafness. Not only was the petition unsuccessful in making more jobs available, but it reinforced the fears of many employers that deaf people could be a liability.

SERVICES IN ENGLAND, TWENTIETH CENTURY

In 1911 the first national body concerned with deaf people and deafness was founded by Leo Bonn. This organization, the National Bureau for Promoting the General Welfare of the Deaf [later known as the Royal National Institute for the Deaf (RNID)], had broad concerns including the training of teachers and welfare workers for deaf people, research and publication, retraining of people who were deafened, social and spiritual welfare, care and training of people who were both deaf and blind, prevention of deafness, vocational training, higher education, and home training of deaf children. *See* UNITED KINGDOM.

The mission movement initiated in the middle 1800s flourished, and by 1929 there were 60 organizations concerned with the spiritual welfare of deaf persons. The dearth of other resources led these organizations to become social service delivery systems involved with employment, legal issues, health, planning for aged and infirm deaf persons, sports, and clubs.

A major development occurred in 1964 with the establishment of the College of Deaf Welfare by the Royal National Institute for the Deaf. In 1975 other significant developments were North London Polytechnic's acceptance of deaf people into social work courses and the employment of deaf social workers by several social work agencies. The National Council of Social Workers Serving the Deaf, an organization of hearing and deaf social workers, seeks to enhance the quality of social work with deaf persons.

SERVICES IN THE UNITED STATES, TWENTIETH CENTURY

In contrast with England, during the nineteenth century virtually nothing was published in the United States concerning social welfare services for deaf people. As was true with England, education of deaf children was the first and most intense area of concern.

In 1896 the founding of the Ohio Home for the Aged and Infirm Deaf marked the beginning of what was to become a model facility. The Ohio School for the Deaf Alumni Association operated the home and, through extensive planning and fund raising during the late 1970s, was able to erect a modern new facility, Columbus Colony. This has made available rent-subsidized apartments, a nursing home, and family cottages. Although it is not the only facility for older deaf persons in the United States, it has a special history and mission.

As recently as the 1940s, there were few social welfare services, public or private, and their scope was very limited. Such organizations as did exist were primarily educational, interested in the dissemination of information, and they advocated oral methods (for example, Volta Bureau, Coolidge Fund

of the Clarke School in Northampton, Massachusetts, and parent associations located in a few large cities). Although organizations such as the YMCA occasionally provided a meeting place, their programs did not reach out to deaf people. Most of the few homes for aged and infirm deaf persons at that time were established by organizations of deaf people with little or no governmental assistance. *See* ALEXANDER GRAHAM BELL ASSOCIATION FOR THE DEAF; CLARKE SCHOOL; EDUCATION.

The foregoing is not meant to suggest that nothing was done, but developments were behind those in England. In 1911 the New York Society for the Deaf was founded—the oldest multifunction social welfare agency in the United States established specifically to provide services for deaf people. The agency is in operation today and provides counseling, training, interpreting, and referral.

Persons who themselves were adventitiously deafened were the first to enter the field of social work for people with acquired deafness. In 1912 the Nitchie Service League was established for this purpose, with Annetta W. Peck as its first president and first professional social worker. This organization was followed by the New York League for the Hard of Hearing, Inc., in 1914. In 1915 a group of hearing-impaired adults organized volunteer social workers and sought to help others with hearing impairments.

Well into the twentieth century, services available to hearing people through social service agencies and social workers were not available to deaf people. Consequently, social services either were not provided or were offered by clergy who ministered to congregations of deaf people. Among the religious groups and denominations with such ministries were Assembly of God, Baptist, Episcopal, Jewish, Lutheran, and Roman Catholic. This movement paralleled the missions that began in England during the middle of the nineteenth century and which continued into the twentieth. *See* RELIGION, CATHOLIC; RELIGION, JEWISH; RELIGION, PROTESTANT.

During the late 1960s the few social workers providing social services to deaf people were still commenting upon the paucity of services and social workers in the field and the very few publications by social workers. In 1967 a survey of the three major groups of professional organizations serving deaf people (educational facilities, rehabilitation and related facilities, speech and hearing clinics) found that only 29% of the respondents employed a social worker.

Since it was apparent that the major obstacles to providing services to deaf people were communication barriers and lack of understanding of deafness, some programs began to prepare deaf people to enter the field of social work. In 1970 the

Department of Sociology of Gallaudet College initiated a sequence of courses and field work under the direction of a social worker knowledgeable about deafness and skilled in sign language. The objective of the sequence was to provide preprofessional social work training. The social work sequence was expanded into a full major preparing students for entry-level social work practice, and by 1977 the Social Work Program was accredited by the Council on Social Work Education. Since 1971, deaf students at the National Technical Institute for the Deaf have been able to earn a degree in social work at the Rochester Institute of Technology, whose social work program was accredited in 1974. These programs have trained a core of deaf social workers prepared to work in a variety of programs serving deaf people, such as family service agencies, public welfare agencies, community service programs, rehabilitation programs, halfway houses, group homes, and residential schools. *See* GALLAUDET COLLEGE; NATIONAL TECHNICAL INSTITUTE FOR THE DEAF.

In 1977 the School of Social Work and Community Planning at the University of Maryland secured a five-year grant which funded a Center for the Hearing Impaired. This center provided interpreting and other supportive services which made it possible for deaf people to study for a master's degree in social work. Deaf graduates of that program have assumed positions of leadership in social work practice, supervision, administration, and teaching throughout the United States. At the expiration of the grant, the services for hearing-impaired students continued in modified form, allowing deaf students to continue to expect the school to be accessible to them. Other graduate schools in social work such as the University of Utah have made special efforts to be accessible to deaf students.

In May 1979 the American Society of Deaf Social Workers (ASDSW) was organized by a small group of deaf social workers. Regular membership is limited to deaf social workers, with hearing social workers welcome as associate members. Goals of the organization include promoting accessibility of quality human services for deaf persons, identification of hearing-impaired social workers in the United States, and promoting recognition of hearing-impaired social workers as qualified professionals. The American Society of Deaf Social Workers has been instrumental in making conferences, symposia, and workshops sponsored by the National Association of Social Workers (NASW) accessible to deaf social workers. In November 1981 interpreters were provided for the National Professional Symposium in Philadelphia; three of the presentations were related to social work and deaf-

ness; and two of the presenters were hearing-impaired.

SOCIAL SERVICE DELIVERY SYSTEM

As indicated earlier, the major obstacles to provision of social services to deaf people are communication and lack of understanding of deafness. Thus, most services are inaccessible unless special efforts are made such as employing professional staff who themselves are deaf, employing hearing professionals with knowledge of deafness and sign language skills, utilizing interpreters, arranging for some staff members to study sign language and psychosocial aspects of deafness, and purchasing telecommunication devices for deaf persons (TDDs). To a limited extent, these kinds of efforts were being made in the 1970s and 1980s in the United States. *See* TELECOMMUNICATIONS:.Telephone Services.

In the voluntary sector, a number of sectarian and nonsectarian agencies are beginning to employ a social worker or set up a special unit of social workers qualified to provide services to the deaf population. Some of these agencies employ deaf social workers.

As is true for social work with hearing persons, services are not confined to social service agencies and organizations. Social workers have provided individual, group, and family therapy in psychiatric inpatient and outpatient programs such as the pioneering Mental Health Unit for the Deaf at St. Elizabeth's Hospital in Washington, D.C.

In some areas, social workers have been involved in the health-care delivery system, functioning as counselors, educators, and advocates within the system, to make it more accessible and responsive to deaf people. Strong Memorial Hospital in Rochester, New York, and Cleveland Metropolitan General Hospital (CMGH) in Ohio are two notable examples. At Cleveland Metropolitan by 1980, as a result of the work of a committee, interpreters were being provided for patient visits, several TDDs were available, sign language classes were offered for hospital staff, a physician on the faculty of the Case–Western Reserve University School of medicine was offering an elective course for medical students about deafness (including psychosocial aspects), and a communication nursery program had been conducted for deaf children and their parents. In addition, the committee chair and another social worker, both of whom were knowledgeable about deafness and had sign language skills, offered training and consultation to hospital staff and provided counseling services to numerous deaf children and adults, and families. Although efforts such as this are impressive, they are not typical of what hospitals are doing, especially outside large urban areas.

A major area in which social services are provided to deaf children, adolescents, and their parents is in residential and day schools. A survey conducted in 1977 found that in schools with 100 or more children enrolled, half employed a social worker who typically provided counseling in relation to the student's behavior and attitudes, peer relations, and family problems.

Although it is apparent that social services are increasingly available to deaf persons, this is true mostly in large urban areas, and even there, services lag behind what is available for hearing persons.

USE OF SOCIAL SERVICES

One survey of deaf people found that they most frequently were concerned about concrete matters such as management of finances, legal matters, employment problems, and health problems, and that they tended not to express a need for help with social or emotional problems. Conversely, some social workers have found that although deaf people frequently do come to an agency with requests for concrete or tangible services, once rapport is established, they often seek help for other problems such as marital conflict and parent-child relations. Still others in some family service and mental health programs have found that deaf people come with the same range of requests as hearing people—tangible services as well as problems of a personal or interpersonal nature.

Frequently, a determining factor in whether help is sought at all is the reputation of the practitioner and agency both in terms of competence (which includes competence in sign language) and in scrupulous regard for confidentiality. Confidentiality within the professional relationship is of greater significance and concern when the client is deaf because of the relatively small size of the deaf community, the rapidity with which "news" travels within the community, and the greater likelihood that the professional (especially if deaf) and client will know some of the same people.

DIRECTIONS FOR THE FUTURE

The social welfare system has made considerable progress since the early 1900s in providing services for deaf people, but despite the existence of some model programs and services, most are available only in selected, large urban areas. There continue to be major gaps in services in many urban and most rural areas. Deaf people themselves have supported the development of many of the services that do exist and, assuming that such efforts and commitments continue, the future should be better, even though resources for human service programs have become increasingly scarce. The key to

success is in the cooperative efforts of deaf people and concerned hearing people.

Bibliography

Best, Harry: *Deafness and the Deaf in the United States*, Macmillan, New York, 1943.

Chough, Steven K.: "Social Services for Deaf Citizens: Some Proposals for Effectiveness," *Deafness*, vol. 3, Professional Rehabilitation Workers with the Adult Deaf, Silver Spring, Maryland, 1973.

Christiansen, John B., and Dorothy P. Polakoff: "Characteristics of Social Workers and Social Work Programs at Residential and Day Schools for the Deaf," *American Annals of the Deaf*, June 1980.

Hurwitz, Sidney N.: "The Contribution of Social Work Practice to the Mental Health of the Hearing Impaired," *Mental Health and the Deaf: Approaches and Prospects*, U.S. Department of Health, Education, and Welfare, 1969.

Marchant, Catherine J.: "Are Social Workers Turning a Deaf Ear? A Study of Social Services to the Deaf," *Health and Social Work*, vol. 4, no. 3, August 1979.

National Institute for the Deaf: *All About the Deaf*, Hanbury, Tomsett, London, 1929.

Peck, Annetta W., Estelle E. Samuelson, and Ann Lehman: *Ears and the Man: Studies in Social Work for the Deafened*, F. A. Davis, Philadelphia, 1926.

Sydenham, Roger: *The Education and Welfare of the Deaf in Britain*, Royal Institute for the Deaf, London.

Janet L. Pray

SOCIALIZATION

The three sections of this article focus on the socialization process, each analyzing how deaf people attempt to learn the values, norms, and language of the culture of which they are a part, and consequently, how they develop a personality.

The first section discusses the family, the initial and most important agent of socialization. It is apparent that deaf children of deaf parents have significantly different socializing experiences than deaf children of hearing parents. The second section looks at schools and examines how different educational settings and philosophies have influenced the socialization of deaf children. The final section examines personality development, one of the outcomes of the socialization process. It is clear that the very experience of being deaf has a significant impact on personality development.

Families

Socialization may be defined as the process whereby individuals in a particular society or culture internalize the rules and symbols of that group and learn to participate as members. The term has been applied most often to children, but it is now recognized that the socialization process occurs throughout the life cycle and can be viewed as interactional and bidirectional. It is through the socialization of its members that society maintains order and that individuals develop personalities. The development of language, or communicative competence, is a major result of the socialization process, as is the achievement of personal and social identities in relation to various groups. Socialization, sometimes called enculturation, is cumulative, so that new skills and new orientations to society build upon those previously acquired. While a variety of social institutions play a part in the socialization of individuals, the family is the most important.

Families in which early childhood deafness occurs may be composed of various combinations of deaf and hearing members. Most deaf children, however, are the only deaf members of their families. Only 7 or 8 percent have deaf siblings, and only 9 percent of all deaf children have one or two deaf parents. The following discussion is concerned with socialization in two types of families: those in which the parents have normal hearing and at least one child is deaf, and those in which both parents and a child are deaf.

Deaf Children with Hearing Parents

The socialization process occurs primarily through direct interaction. Communication between parents and children through a common language constitutes the major part of this interaction. Usually, then, children acquire language and are socialized simultaneously. In fact, since so much of a society's culture is encoded in its language, the child necessarily acquires cultural knowledge as he or she acquires the linguistic system. When a deaf child is born to parents with normal hearing, these usual, taken-for-granted processes of language acquisition and socialization are disrupted because the deaf child does not have access to the spoken language of the home.

Furthermore, the earliest parent-child communication that is not necessarily dependent on a shared linguistic system is disrupted by parental anxiety. Hearing parents do not expect their child to be deaf and often have no experience with or knowledge about deafness. Nevertheless, as their infant grows older, they may begin to feel something is wrong. They may suspect a problem for many months, even a year or more, before deafness is confirmed by a medical doctor or audiologist. Thus, the first years of the deaf child's life usually occur within an atmosphere of parental fear, frustration, self-doubt, confusion, and anger as family members attempt to cope with and understand the deaf child. As the deaf infant becomes a toddler, the lack of a shared linguistic system becomes a more obvious and more critical aspect of the communication difficulties between parent and child.

Over 90 percent of all deaf children in the United States are born to hearing parents. While many of these children are from ethnic minority groups, are from single-parent homes, live in foster homes, or come from a family in which a language other than English is spoken at home, very little is known about the impact of deafness on socialization in these families. In white middle-class families in which both parents are in the home, most of the socialization information available is from or about the mother. Very little is known about the deaf child's interaction with his or her siblings, although in some cases siblings communicate more effectively with the deaf child than the parents do. In this case, siblings may serve as vehicles through which the socialization of the deaf child occurs.

Diagnosis When hearing parents first learn that their child is deaf, they usually experience several emotions: denial, anger, depression, guilt, fear, and frustration. It is often difficult to get a positive diagnosis of deafness in the first months or even the first years of the child's life. When told by a medical doctor, for example, that there is nothing wrong with their child in spite of the parents' suspicions, most parents deny their own feelings and believe the professional, at least until they can no longer ignore their own observations and feelings. Or, once a diagnosis of deafness has been made, parents will often go from one doctor to another hoping that the diagnosis is wrong. Similarly, after the child is enrolled in a school program, the parents might try several educational programs, hoping to find one that promises to eliminate the problems of deafness. Once parents begin to accept the fact that their child is deaf, they often experience guilt, anger, and depression. These emotions are accompanied by the frustration of trying to communicate with and socialize a child who cannot hear and speak.

Education At the time of diagnosis, the parents may receive some information from the pediatrician, hospital, or speech and hearing clinic about educational programs available to them. They may also begin to read about deafness, and soon learn about the oral-manual controversy among educators. This controversy has a long history and is fundamentally an argument about the role of sign communication in the education of deaf children. When deaf children are educated orally, sign communication is not used. Instead, the emphasis is on lipreading, auditory training, and speech development. When children are educated through total communication, sign communication is incorporated into the educational program, usually in the form of simultaneous communication, that is, simultaneously spoken and signed English. If parents of a deaf child live in a community offering both alternatives (or some variation of each), they must choose which educational path to take. Typically, the professionals with whom the parents are in contact are committed to one educational philosophy or the other, and arguments about methodology are emotionally charged. Education in both oral and total communication programs, however, emphasizes the importance of early intervention and urges the parents to enroll their child immediately. Parents then find themselves responsible for making a critical decision about their child's future that they feel unprepared to make. This situation adds stress to an already tense family atmosphere. *See* EDUCATION: Communication.

Educational programs have an impact on the early socialization of the deaf child in the family to a much greater extent than do early education programs for hearing children. Early intervention is intensive and can begin as soon as the child's hearing loss is identified. As of 1984, nine states had passed legislation mandating education from birth for hearing-impaired children. Parents look to the schools or clinics as the authorities on such things as communication, play, discipline, and toilet training. Such intervention programs may or may not recommend that the parents learn to sign in order to communicate with their child, but all educational programs for deaf children emphasize the importance of early parent-child communication and the need for parents to modify their usual way of communicating in specific ways to meet the visual needs of the deaf child. When confronted with deafness, parents who might normally feel confident in their parenting abilities lose their self-confidence and view the professionals as the experts on every aspect of parenting the child.

Communication Because deafness results in a communication problem between the deaf child and other family members, its effect on the family and the socialization process is a pervasive one. During the early years of the deaf child's life, in an environment of frustration and stress, family life frequently becomes centered on the deaf child and the usual patterns of family interaction are disrupted. As parents become more accepting of their deaf child and develop effective communication strategies, the frustration begins to lessen. Communication, however, remains the central issue for most hearing parents and their deaf children. Parents look to the schools for help in communicating with their child and for emotional support. Most hearing parents know nothing about deafness from personal experience and have never met a deaf adult. They do not know what to expect as their child grows older. Often they wonder whether their child will be able to drive a car, to hold a job, to get married and have a family.

If parents decide to use some form of sign communication with their young deaf child, it is likely that they will enroll their child in a school program that utilizes total communication. If they are to communicate with their child at home according to this philosophy, they must learn to sign. Very often parents feel inadequate and awkward when they begin to sign. Furthermore, school programs usually emphasize the importance of the parents' signing at all times when their deaf child is present. Hearing parents of deaf children then are faced with a challenging and difficult task—they must socialize their child and conduct their family life by means of a communication system that is foreign to them and that takes much time and energy to master. The alternative, in most cases, is to have little or no communication with their child because proficiency in speech or speechreading is extremely problematic for children who are profoundly deaf from birth. *See* SPEECH; SPEECHREADING.

If parents decide against the use of sign communication with their deaf child, the task of parenting and developing effective interaction among family members is even more difficult. The home environment must be structured in specific ways to accommodate the child's auditory and speechreading abilities. The auditory environment cannot be too noisy, or the deaf child will not be able to make effective use of his or her hearing aid; the lighting must be appropriate and adequate so that the deaf child can speechread; family members must be certain that the deaf child is attending visually to them before beginning to communicate, or the child will miss part or all of the message. Many school programs encourage parents to teach their deaf children at home, working on speech and speechreading skills daily through structured lessons.

Interaction The mother is usually the family member who is most involved with the deaf child. She becomes the deaf child's teacher at home and the child's link to others, especially those outside of the home. When sign communication is used, mothers learn to sign more frequently than fathers, so that even within the family the mother is the intermediary between the child and significant others. Often the father withdraws, leaving the special education and most communication with the deaf child to the mother. Little is known about the effect of the presence of the deaf child on the socialization of the other children in the family. The birth of the deaf child into a family with no history of or experience with deafness affects relationships with extended family members. Frequently, parents report difficulties with their own parents. For example, as parents face the reality of their child's deafness daily and begin to move from denial toward acceptance of their deaf child, they may encounter the continuing denial of the problem on the part of the child's grandparents, especially if there is infrequent contact between the child and grandparents. In addition, as the parents are learning more about deafness and what it means for their child's present and future life, the grandparents may remain uninformed and isolated from their grandchild. If the grandparents do not learn to communicate with their deaf grandchild, as is frequently the case, the child does not have access to the socializing influence of such extended family members to the same extent as their normally hearing counterparts. Pressures exerted by the grandparents on child-rearing practices in general can make the integration of the deaf child into the family even more stressful.

When hearing parents of deaf children are asked what is most problematic for them, most say communication. Second, and also related to communication, is discipline. Parents often express concern that they cannot effectively communicate what they expect of the child. Frequently they feel guilty about disciplining the child if he or she cannot understand. Such uncertainty about discipline can make parenting more difficult and add to tensions in the family. Communication difficulties and related behavior problems often result in isolation of the deaf child from his or her family. The child misses most of the incidental learning accessible to hearing children through such things as participation in dinner table conversations, television programs, conversations overheard in the everyday interactional life of a family, and in-depth conversations with parents and siblings. It is likely that the majority of childhood socialization occurs in exactly these kinds of interactional contexts. Even parents who have good communication with their deaf child cannot assume that the child is being exposed to the same kinds of incidental learning experiences as hearing children. Instead, they must make an effort to teach explicitly such things as social skills and empathy which hearing children absorb naturally in the course of everyday life.

The interactional exchanges between the deaf child and other family members are shaped by the behaviors of each of the participants. Since deaf children lack hearing and are therefore visually oriented, their communicative capabilities and behaviors are strikingly different from those of normally hearing family members. Studies have indicated that these differences on the part of the deaf child tremendously influence the interactional style of the mother. Hearing mothers of deaf children are more inflexible, controlling, didactic, intrusive, and disapproving in their interaction with their deaf children than hearing mothers of normally hearing children. Hearing mothers and their deaf children appear to enjoy interaction with each other less than hearing mothers and hearing children do, and their interaction is also less mature. The interaction is less complex, less elaborated, and less often initiated by the child.

Concept Most children are socialized by adults whom they can expect to model when they mature. Most deaf children, however, are different from their parents in a fundamental, pervasive, and unalterable way. Their parents' lives are organized and shaped by two primary senses, audition and vision. The deaf child's life must be structured around vision alone. The resulting difference between parent and child in the way each comprehends, organizes, and interacts with the world is similar to a major cultural difference. It is not only that parent and child are physically dissimilar; it is also that they perceive the world in basically different ways. Unlike purely cultural differences, however, these dissimilar world views are due to physical attributes over which parent and child have little or no control. Deaf children cannot become like their hearing parents through any amount of effort, nor can hearing parents experience their deaf child's perspective on the world. Each is barred from full participation in the other's world. This situation creates a problem for the child's developing sense of identity and self-esteem.

The deaf child may first come into contact with deaf adults and with deaf children who have deaf parents when the deaf child begins attending school, especially if the school program is at a residential institution or a day school for deaf children. At this time, the child will learn that there are other people, including adults, who are deaf, and that there are some deaf children who have deaf parents and perhaps deaf siblings. These deaf children live in environments in which all members communicate with each other through the same visual-gestural medium in a comfortable fashion. The deaf child begins to realize the fundamental differences between deaf and hearing people, differences that had been experienced in his or her own family but that had not been seen against an alternative experience until daily interaction with other deaf people began to occur. At the same time these realizations are beginning to take shape, the deaf child may also be acquiring some form of American Sign Language from peers who have deaf parents and learned the language at home and perhaps from deaf adults who work at the school. Deaf children acquire the language of their peers rapidly and are able to engage in fluent conversational interaction in a way never experienced in their own families. See SIGN LANGUAGES: American.

While the deaf child learns about other deaf people and acquires their variety of sign language, most hearing parents do not have similar experiences.

Even if the parents attempt to meet and interact with deaf adults, they do not feel the same affinity for them and for their communication environment as their deaf child. Interaction with deaf people is labored and stressful for the parents. No amount of good will, commitment, or effort on the part of the hearing parents to learn about the deaf community and its culture and to learn its language can change the fact that deaf and hearing people interact with the world in fundamentally different ways. As hearing parents learn more about deaf people and their own deaf child, they begin to see their separation from their deaf child in a larger perspective and with implications for the future. This new knowledge can bring comfort and encouragement to the parents as well as pain. They see happy, well-adjusted, successful deaf adults, many of whom are married and have children of their own. While some early fears about their deaf child's future prospects are allayed, new fears emerge. They see deaf people who usually prefer the company of other deaf people communicating with skill and comfort in a language the parents feel they can never hope to master. They notice their child's sign language skills surpassing their own. Sometimes the deaf child expresses a preference for the company of deaf people.

Socialization of a deaf child with hearing parents within the family is complex from the point of view of both the child and the parents. The developing child has neither the knowledge and experience nor the cognitive tools with which to confront and understand his or her special status in the family and in the world. The parents may have an intellectual understanding of deafness and its impact on their lives, but it is unlikely that they have reached an emotional acceptance of its ramifications. Furthermore, professionals who work with deaf individuals do not agree upon how best to advise parents with respect to the goals and processes of socializing the deaf child within the family. Ultimately, parents are the ones who must decide upon the goals to pursue and how to do so, usually amidst conflicting advice from professionals involved in the education of their child.

Deaf Children with Deaf Parents

When a deaf child is born to deaf parents, especially deaf parents who have a history of deafness in one or both of their families, the parents often expect the child to be deaf, or at least are aware that it is a possibility. Some may hope their child will be deaf so that communication and family relationships can be built upon a common foundation. Other deaf parents express ambivalence with respect to the hearing status of their child. They would like the closeness of the deaf child-deaf parent relationship, but hope their child will have normal hearing and thus be spared the difficulties they experienced growing up in a world structured by and for people who can hear. Regardless of their hopes for their child prior to birth, deaf parents usually adjust to the diagnosis of deafness rapidly. In fact, the parents frequently diagnose the hearing loss themselves within the first days or weeks of their child's life. For them, in contrast to hearing parents, deafness is a known quantity. It is the way they have experienced life, and they do not feel uncertain about how their child will be incorporated into their family.

In general, the case of the deaf child born to two deaf parents (3 to 5 percent of all deaf children) presents a very different picture with respect to early communication. If the deaf parents communicate with each other and with their infant by means of sign language, the child has access to language from birth, and parents and child come to share a common language in much the same way parents and children with normal hearing do. The majority of deaf parents who have deaf children appear to fall into this category. In these families, communication which is so integral a part of the socialization process is not lacking, since the parents use sign language which is visual-gestural and completely accessible to the child.

In addition, early communication with the deaf infant is probably not impeded by fear and anxiety about deafness, since the parents themselves are deaf and know from their own experiences how deafness will affect their child's life and the life of their family. If the parents themselves have parents who are deaf and use sign language, the deaf child born into this family has the opportunity to communicate and interact fully with his or her grandparents and perhaps other members of the extended family. The socialization process, then, for this deaf child occurs in a way similar to the way it occurs for normally hearing children with normally hearing parents, although the content of the socialization might be different in some important ways.

Interaction Studies have shown that the social and linguistic interaction between deaf mothers and their deaf preschool children is comparable to the interaction of normally hearing mothers and children. Deaf mothers are able to have enjoyable, sustained, interactions with their deaf children that are reciprocal and elaborated. These developmentally more mature interactional patterns contrast with those described above for hearing mothers and their deaf children. In addition, when deaf children were separated from their deaf mothers for a few minutes, the children's behavior was comparable to that of children with normal hearing. These children were also similar to deaf children with hearing parents when the latter children were evaluated as having good communicative skills. The deaf mothers who participated in these research studies expressed positive attitudes toward sign language, deafness, and their deaf children. Some evidence suggests that when deaf parents express negative attitudes toward sign language and deafness the resulting interaction between parent and deaf child is more problematic. Some deaf parents may refrain from using sign language with their child even if they use it with each other, because they fear it will have a negative effect on their child's development. Interaction between these deaf parents and their deaf children may be similar to the disrupted interactional patterns of hearing mothers and deaf children.

For deaf parents, the task of socializing their deaf child is twofold. First, there is the process of incorporating the child into the family unit and into the deaf community. This process is as unproblematic for deaf parents as it is problematic for hearing parents of deaf children. Communication between parent, child, deaf family members, and the deaf community is available. It is the vehicle through which this socialization takes place. Second, there is the process of socializing the deaf child to the world at large, a world often inaccessible to both parents and children but one that must be reckoned with for physical and economic survival. In this aspect of socialization, deaf parents are likely to feel less comfortable. They do not have easy access to the larger society, yet they must prepare their deaf child to live in a rapidly changing, increasingly demanding world. Although most deaf parents do not wish for their child to be like a hearing child, they do want their deaf child to acquire the skills necessary for a successful life among hearing people, as free from difficulty and stress as possible. Thus, they usually want their child to acquire speech and auditory skills, because they know from experience that these skills are helpful in daily living. Deaf parents expect schools to help prepare their child to live and work among hearing people. They may also call upon hearing family members for assistance.

It is likely that parent-child interaction, as well as the content of socialization within families with deaf parents and deaf children, will vary with the differential experiences of each family. For example, deaf parents who themselves had deaf parents will have had different early socialization experiences from those of deaf parents who themselves had hearing parents. They will thus have different models of the socialization process from which to take guidance to the socialization of their own deaf children. Similarly, in families having both hearing and deaf members, the socialization process is likely to differ in important ways from that process in families with only deaf members. Even in the latter

case, characteristics of family members such as extent of hearing loss, age at onset, and attitudes toward deafness and language are likely to have important influences on the family climate and the nature of the interaction among family members.

CONCLUSION

Early childhood deafness drastically alters socialization processes within the family. When parents have normal hearing, a deaf child changes their expectations for family life. Parents find that their inability to communicate with their deaf child presents problems in almost every aspect of daily life. Socialization occurs within a family environment where frustration, tension, guilt, and grief may be present. When parents place their child in an educational program, they find they must make a choice between communication methods that incorporate sign language and those that do not. Regardless of the choice, there is some degree of delay in the establishment of even minimally effective communication between parent and child. During the period of early childhood, hearing parent-deaf child interactional patterns through which the socialization process occurs are disrupted. As the deaf child grows older, attending school and interacting with other deaf children and perhaps deaf adults, the child and parents become more aware of the basic differences between them. The deaf child begins to understand the differences between interaction shaped by the needs of deaf people and interaction within his or her hearing family, being pulled toward the former because of its relative comfort and ease and toward the latter despite its awkwardness and inefficiency because of the child's attachment to the parents. These complex and conflicting influences in the lives of deaf children and their hearing parents help to shape the processes of socialization within the family.

Attitudes toward the deaf child as well as interaction patterns within the family are more likely to be positive when the parents are deaf. When the parent and child are similar in such a basic characteristic of identity as hearing status and when communication through sign language is available from birth, socialization processes can proceed without difficulty. In fact, studies comparing personality and social development of older deaf children with deaf parents suggest that earlier parent-child interaction patterns were positive. Deaf parents socialize their children to participate in the life of the deaf community as well as in the larger society. At least in this way, the content of the socialization process in deaf families is different from the content of the process in families where the parents are hearing. In addition, deaf parents are likely to interact with their children primarily through American Sign Language, whereas hearing parents are likely to interact through communication that is shaped by their spoken language. Insofar as the society's culture is embodied in its language, deaf children of deaf parents will acquire cultural knowledge from their parents that will differ from that acquired by deaf children of hearing parents. Similarly, the cultural knowledge of deaf children will differ from that of hearing children who have acquired the spoken languages and cultural categories of the larger society from their parents.

Bibliography

Erting, C., and R. Meisegeier: *Deaf Children and the Socialization Process*, Sociology Department, Gallaudet College, Washington, D.C., 1982.

Freeman, R. D., C. F. Carbin, and R. Boese: *Can't Your Child Hear?*, University Park Press, Baltimore, 1981.

Meadow, K. P.: *Deafness and Child Development*, University of California Press, Berkeley, 1980.

——— et al.: "Interactions of Deaf Mothers and Deaf Preschool Children: Comparisons with Three Other Groups of Deaf and Hearing Dyads," *American Annals of the Deaf*, 126(4):454–468, 1981.

Murphy, A. T. (ed.): "The Families of Hearing-Impaired Children," *Volta Review*, vol. 81, no. 5, 1979.

Schlesinger, H. D.: "The Effects of Deafness on Childhood Development: An Eriksonian Perspective," in L. Liben (ed.), *Deaf Children: Developmental Perspectives*, Academic Press, New York, 1978.

Carol Erting

Schools and Peer Groups

Socialization is defined herein as the process an individual goes through to become a member of a social group. The term has been used most frequently by sociologists to refer to the manner in which children learn the behavior patterns acceptable to the culture of which they are a part.

The socialization patterns experienced by deaf persons are considerably different from those that affect the general population. These experiences are influenced by a number of factors, which include the hearing status of the child's parents, the method of communication used in the home, the type of education program in which the student participates, the child's exposure or lack of exposure to other deaf individuals, the age at onset of hearing loss, and the degree of hearing loss.

This section addresses the socialization influences of the various types of school programs attended by deaf children and the peer relationships among deaf children. The importance of school and peer influences have been increasingly recognized in recent years.

HISTORICAL PATTERNS

During much of the nineteenth century, most deaf children who were able to attend school were sent to one of the state residential schools for deaf students. Many of these children entered schools with no functional language capability. Deaf children who entered school with language skills had lost their hearing after attaining linguistic competence, were moderately hearing-impaired rather than profoundly deaf, or had deaf parents.

The influence of the schools on socialization was clearly far greater for deaf children than it was for hearing children. Most deaf children attended residential schools and were separated from their families most of the time. When transportation was slow, expensive, and inconvenient, children tended to stay at school throughout the year, only returning home for summer breaks or long holidays such as Christmas.

Teachers and other staff members at the schools had more influence than parents did in instilling moral, ethical, and political values and attitudes, as well as in providing the linguistic structure and academic underpinnings to help the children interact effectively with the world around them. In the very early days of deaf education in the United States, schools employed many deaf people as teachers and residential houseparents. Those deaf professionals were probably the first contact most deaf children had with deaf adults; their peers in school were probably the first deaf children they had met. Most schools of this time utilized sign language as the method of communicating with and instructing deaf children. The entry into school for most deaf children with hearing parents marked their first exposure to sign language. Because these children entered school without a formal symbolic communication system, American Sign Language (ASL) was their first language.

In 1880 the Milan Conference on Education of the Deaf passed a resolution discouraging the teaching of deaf children via manual means and encouraging the teaching of speech and speechreading in deaf schools. This began a long process of decline in recognition of ASL by professionals in the field. Increasingly, children were not allowed to use their hands to communicate or even to gesture for purposes of communication. *See* HISTORY: Congress of Milan.

Theoretically, this rule was enforced in the dormitories and during afterschool activities, which led to restrictions on the hiring of deaf people by the schools except for janitorial or related unskilled work, and some vocational teaching. Deaf people were generally not hired as classroom teachers or dormitory supervisors. Parents were advised by professionals that they should not allow their children to learn signs or to use gestures, and that every opportunity to learn and practice speech and speechreading should be taken.

This did not mean, however, that deaf children did not learn to sign; the influence of their peers who could sign took on even greater importance in the processes of socialization. It has been said that deaf children are the only group who learn most of what they know about society and its rules from other children, rather than from adults; that is, children socialize children. This occurs among children generally, but it is founded upon a basis established by the interactions between parents and children through a common linguistic system.

MODERN TRENDS

Since the mid-1960s, sign language has experienced a strong renaissance in schools in the United States and elsewhere. Educators have learned that very few deaf children learn to speak clearly and easily and that few learn to speechread even half of what is spoken to them.

Preschools all over the country now begin teaching deaf children via sign language from the time deafness is identified. Hearing parents are provided with sign language instruction and classes on deafness, as well as necessary counseling opportunities. Local, state, and national associations, focused on the needs of parents, serve as resource and information centers on deafness.

Deaf persons in increasing numbers are being employed in a variety of positions by schools and programs for deaf children. Deaf people are now found in the ranks of teachers, dormitory counselors, social workers, psychologists, counselors, and administrators. In these positions, deaf adults are able to serve as role models for deaf children, demonstrating to the children the possibilities available to them as adults.

MAINSTREAMING

As discussed above, most deaf children used to attend state or private residential schools. In the 1970s, this proportion began declining. A 1975 federal law (Public Law 94-142, the Education for All Handicapped Children Act) mandates that school districts must educate handicapped children in the "least restrictive environment" to the extent possible, in order to receive federal funding assistance. *See* EDUCATION OF THE HANDICAPPED ACT.

The law resulted in the establishment of many local school district programs for deaf children. Some of the programs emphasize full or partial mainstreaming, in which deaf children are integrated with hearing children. Other programs emphasize separate classes for deaf children within public schools, and some provide resource rooms for deaf children to go to for special help or tutoring. Data indicates that 74 percent of hearing-impaired children are educated in day programs and only 26 percent are educated in residential schools. Of the students in day programs, 15 percent are fully mainstreamed and 21 percent are partially mainstreamed. *See* EDUCATIONAL PROGRAMS.

For deaf children, this kind of educational programming often creates educational and interactional problems greater than those imposed by the hearing loss itself. From discussions of the importance of deaf peers in the socialization of deaf children, it is clear that deaf children who do not have these opportunities are deprived of a significant source of socialization input. This is particularly true for children who are profoundly deaf because of the severe communication and language problems they experience.

In addition, the deaf children of hearing parents have limited opportunities to learn ASL in mainstream programs. Few hearing people are fluent in ASL, and ASL is generally not utilized in mainstream programs. Few deaf persons are hired to teach in local public school programs, although this is beginning to change. ASL is not generally taught in residential schools either, but children do have a greater opportunity to learn it from peers and deaf adults in those settings.

Loneliness and isolation are perhaps the two most devastating emotions experienced by a deaf child in a hearing environment. This is particularly true when the deaf child does not have regular opportunities to interact with other deaf children. Many deaf persons who were mainstreamed as children have written about their isolation from the social and academic life of the school. They recall nodding and smiling while not understanding a thing going on around them, playing games when they did not understand the rules, being called upon in class to answer questions they had not been able to lipread, and being the butt of ridicule from other children. Yet the deafness that made them different from their peers was invisible unless they wore hearing aids.

There are, however, positive aspects of mainstream education for socialization purposes. Particularly in the larger cities, hearing parents of deaf children can usually obtain an early diagnosis of their child's disability, assistance in learning sign language, and help in finding an appropriate educational program for the child. Preschool programs are found in increasing numbers throughout the country, and many states have begun providing services to deaf children from the age of identification of the handicap, even if that is as young as a few months of age. Programs that provide assistance to parents in learning about their child's disability are helping parents retain control of the socialization of their deaf children by providing skills that parallel the skills of hearing parents with hearing children.

In the larger metropolitan areas that have large populations of deaf students, school systems have been able to establish magnet programs that bring all of the hearing-impaired students of similar ages together into one school, which also serves hearing students. This makes it possible for deaf students to attend classes with their deaf peers in subjects that require special communication skills, as well as with their hearing peers where such skills are less important. With a large enough deaf population, programs can be developed to meet the needs of individual students for mainstream and non-mainstream experiences. It is also possible to facilitate appropriate social experiences with both deaf and hearing students.

Contact with Deaf Adults

Another critical factor in the socialization of deaf children is the extent to which they have contact with deaf adults in their formative years. Early interactions with deaf persons from all walks of life are critical to help deaf children realize their potential as adults and to become aware that, although deafness imposes some lifelong difficulties, it does not present insurmountable problems. Deaf persons often report that deafness is more of a nuisance than a handicap in daily functioning. Deaf adults can help deaf children to find ways to surmount the "nuisances" that accompany the disability of deafness.

Deaf children of hearing parents need early and sustained contact with deaf adults and with deaf children of deaf parents in order to prepare themselves for adulthood as members of the deaf culture. If culture is defined, in part, as a shared language, then deaf persons who use ASL form an identifiable culture within American society. The group of ASL users has been referred to as a Deaf ethnic group, capitalizing Deaf as is done with Black and Hispanic cultural groups. As they approach adulthood, young deaf people have an array of choices to make: whether to attempt to assimilate into the hearing culture, whether to attempt to function as a member of both cultures, or whether to integrate fully with the deaf culture. Their socialization experiences as children help to determine whether they have the requisite skills to make these choices, or whether their cultural affiliations are preset by the decisions made for them early in life by their parents and teachers.

Conclusions

It is evident that little research has been published on the manner in which schools and peers influence the socialization of deaf children. The key to socialization is communication via a common linguistic system. Where that common language is absent, as is often the case with hearing parents and their deaf children, socialization cannot occur in the same manner as it does when a common language is present. In such situations, the role of the school takes on vastly greater significance in providing the children with a set of social rules to follow, and the role of peers becomes even more critical in providing children with daily interactional guidelines.

Bibliography

Denzin, N.: *Childhood Socialization*, Jossey-Bass, San Francisco, 1977.

Meadow, K.: "The Effect of Early Manual Communication and Family Climate on the Deaf Child's Development," unpublished doctoral dissertation, University of California, Berkeley, 1967.

————: *Deafness and Child Development*, University of California Press, Berkeley, 1980.

————: "Socialization Theories: Implications for Research with Deaf Children," in Carol Erting and Richard Meiesegeier (ed.) *Social Aspects of Deafness*, monograph series, vol. 1: *Deaf Children and the Socialization Process*, Gallaudet College, Washington, 1982.

Moores, D.: *Educating the Deaf: Psychology, Principles, and Practices*, Houghton-Mifflin, Boston, 1978.

Youniss, J.: *Parents and Peers in Social Development*, University of Chicago Press, Chicago, 1980.

David R. Updegraff

Personality Development

Personality is a term used by social scientists to refer to the patterns of behavior and ways of thinking and feeling that are distinctive for each individual. The concept of personality has its origin in the consistency one observes in an individual's behavior over a period of time as well as in different situations. Thus, a person may be characterized as shy (an introvert) or outgoing (an extrovert), as secure or insecure, as dependent or independent, and so on. While it is no doubt true that most individuals exhibit personality traits that appear to be consistent over time, it is also true that what people think, feel, and do may depend on the specific conditions in which their behavior occurs. In addition, research shows that although certain traits and characteristics tend to persist to some degree from childhood into adulthood, personality does continue to change as a result of new experiences and modifications of the environment.

For hundreds of years, there has been an interest in attempting to group the vast differences among people into simple categories. It is not surprising that physical characteristics have long been felt to influence personality development. Although classifications based on body measurements developed by William Sheldon and others are no longer favored by social scientists, interest in the effects of sensory loss on personality development remains.

The first studies of deaf children appeared in the late nineteenth century and focused on physical and mental development. One of the earliest such studies appeared in the *American Annals of the Deaf* in

1889. In the decades following, investigators began to evaluate objectively the intelligence, emotional adjustment, personality traits, and social maturity of deaf children. The early studies of personality development used inventories and rating scales. These studies were followed by others using psychiatric interview techniques, such as the Rorschach. *See* AMERICAN ANNALS OF THE DEAF.

A great deal of controversy surrounds the use of personality tests on deaf persons that have been designed for hearing people. This issue will be discussed more fully below. *See* PSYCHOLOGICAL EVALUATION.

The effects of deafness on personality development may be viewed from at least two perspectives. The first is to consider the influence of deafness from childhood through adulthood. The second is to consider the effects of age at onset of deafness, degree of hearing loss, the school setting (whether the deaf child was educated at a residential school and thus lived away from home and family, or in a nonresidential type of program making it possible to live with the family), and whether the deaf child had deaf or hearing parents.

PRESCHOOL
Prior to two or three years of age, evidence of social immaturity is somewhat difficult to determine, and the studies available are inconclusive. As deaf children's failures to respond normally become obvious, socialization difficulties may appear in the form of gradual withdrawal, continued tantrums, and solitary play. When deaf children are observed in groups, their rapport may be weak and their activities may consist mostly of pointing, showing, and pulling. Bids for attention and boasting actions have also been observed frequently. When deaf children lack verbal language, they are more inclined to use physical means to express emotions, protests, criticisms, and wishes.

ELEMENTARY SCHOOL
The evidence is somewhat more conclusive concerning the effects of deafness on personality development for children within this age group. They are generally found to be emotionally immature and unstable but not overly aggressive. While neither characteristics of introversion nor extroversion predominate, tendencies have been noted toward shyness and the absence of leadership qualities. Children of this age group have been observed to have a "drilled personality" characterized by concrete thinking, a relative lack of initiative, and an absence of natural, adaptive flexibility in new situations. This type of personality is thought to originate in overdependence in early parent-child experiences and in the teaching methods that are frequently adult-dominated and categorical.

HIGH SCHOOL
The picture of deaf adolescents that appears fairly consistently is one in which mental concepts and emotional life are immature, defenses are rigid, thinking is stereotyped, and there is inadequate flexibility in everyday functioning. The deaf adolescents' Rorschach test responses are similar to those given by hearing children of a younger age, and they indicate that deaf children are not so much abnormal as they are subnormal, that is, merely slower, in their personality development. Deaf adolescents are frequently described as impulsive. This trait has been observed not only among deaf American youth, but also among deaf adolescents in Yugoslavia and Japan. Although some researchers have concluded that greater impulsivity is unavoidable with early total deafness, other research indicates that when age, socioeconomic status, and IQ test scores are controlled for, deaf children with deaf parents consistently obtained scores that reflected greater impulse control than the deaf children of hearing parents.

COLLEGE
Deaf students in college are consistently found to be rigid and constricted both emotionally and intellectually. Male deaf college students appear to be anxious and insecure, to have constrictive and withdrawal tendencies and an overemphasis on emotional control. Restrained expression of aggression was also characteristic of the male deaf students. The findings for female deaf college students lack consistency. One study showed deaf college women to be less anxious, less mature, to have less bodily concern, and to be less emotionally repressive than hearing college women. Another study using the same test found the deaf college women to be immature and to show tendencies toward withdrawal, constriction, schizoid adjustment, and depression. In spite of these inconsistencies, a fairly consistent picture of an overemphasis on control is presented by the college groups, especially in the display of emotions.

STUDIES COVERING WIDE AGE RANGES
With few exceptions, comparisons of deaf children and young deaf adults with normal hearing groups or normative data indicate deafness has a negative impact on personality development. The differences tend to occur in the areas of social and emotional growth. Deaf individuals tend to exhibit immature or subnormal, as opposed to abnormal, patterns of behavior. Two exceptions to these findings involved deaf students in grades 1 through 12. In the first study, deaf students were consistently judged higher in intellectual functioning, appeared to have developed greater ego strength, exhibited a lower degree of compulsivity, and had a somewhat

better capacity for organized thinking than did their hearing peers. The second study compared the self-concept of hearing-impaired and hearing students. The study found no differences between the two groups of students. It should be noted, however, that hearing-impaired was defined as a hearing loss greater than 20 decibels. The profession usually classifies a 40- to 55-decibel loss as mild to moderate and a 10- to 25-dB loss as normal.

DEAF ADULT
There has been relatively little research on deaf adults. The general picture that does emerge is that deaf adults are self-sufficient but less dominant, less extroverted, and less stable emotionally than hearing adults. When compared with blind and nondisabled adults, those prelingually deaf (deafened before two or three years of age) were found to be far more authoritarian, to be more alienated, and to have somewhat less ego strength. These differences seem to be related to the communication barriers associated with deafness.

Other studies have attempted to assess the influence of deafness on personality development by focusing on certain factors associated with deafness and their effects. While there is some obvious overlap between these studies and those just discussed, the difference in perspective broadens our understanding. *See* DEAF POPULATION: Deafened Adults; PSYCHOLOGY: Psychosocial Behavior.

AGE AT ONSET
In general, studies of children and very young adults (conducted in the 1930s and 1940s) indicated there was an increase in maladjustment and behavioral problems when the onset of deafness occurred after three or four years of age. Studies done in the 1970s indicate little relationship between emotional and behavioral problems and the age at onset. However, there is some evidence that there is greater ego identity in those deaf adolescents who were congenitally deaf. There is substantial agreement that sudden onset of deafness in adults is associated with the stereotyped picture of loneliness, anxiety, depression, and seclusiveness. Gradual onsets of deafness that become severe in adulthood are associated with feelings of inadequacy, damage, anger, and depression.

DEGREE OF HEARING LOSS
The degree of hearing loss seems to be unrelated to emotional and behavioral problems. How the deafness is perceived and experienced by the individual is more crucial than the physical fact of a decibel loss. If the hearing loss is seen as a stigmatizing condition, that is, as making the individual feel defective or inferior, this perception can lead to emotional and behavioral problems. If the

hearing loss is not seen as a stigmatizing condition, the degree of loss per se does not seem to be related to emotional and behavioral problems. The findings are equally divided on the effects of being able to lipread and use speech. Half of the studies found and half of the studies failed to find, better adjustment among those able to use lipreading and speech in communicating.

SCHOOL SETTING
Although there are a variety of school settings for deaf children, including residential schools, day schools, day classes, and special classes, a major distinction is whether the school or program is residential or nonresidential. In residential programs the child lives away from home and family most of the school year. In nonresidential programs the child lives at home with the family. The findings related to this factor are mixed. Early studies showed contradictory evidence, but in general indicated nonresidential settings, or residence of less than four years in a residential school, to be associated with greater social maturity and fewer behavioral problems. Later studies indicate little or no relationship between residential and nonresidential settings and social and emotional maturity. The findings of these later studies can no doubt be explained in part by the fact that residential schools have taken increased steps to improve the quality of residential living and to mitigate the effects of separation from the family during the school year by scheduling opportunities for students to go home more frequently and by arranging for the parents to be more actively involved in the total school program.

DEAFNESS IN THE FAMILY
The evidence is fairly clear that deaf children of deaf parents tend to be better adjusted than deaf children of hearing parents. This seems to be true for at least two reasons. The first is the ability of deaf parents to communicate with their deaf children. The second is that deaf parents may have more realistic expectations for their deaf children.

It is important to recognize the interdependence of communication and personality development. It is through language that individuals become a part of society; they learn its values and expectations. It is also through language and communication that the ability to express feelings and desires is learned. Language and the ability to communicate are essential for the development of personality. For deaf or hearing children, good communication between parent and child is associated with a well-adjusted personality. Deaf parents already have a language system in place to communicate with their deaf children; most hearing parents do not. There is strong support for using manual (sign language) communication with deaf children. However, regardless of the mode of communication, manual or oral, if there is good communication between parent and child, the child is more likely to be well adjusted.

Parental aspirations and expectations for their child are also important influences on the development of personality. There may be a tendency for hearing parents to place greater emphasis on oral skills than would deaf parents. Hearing parents may also be less certain than deaf parents of what to expect academically from their deaf child. Deaf parents have a ready frame of reference in which to place their deaf child.

In both of these areas, ability to communicate and aspirations and expectations, deaf parents have an initial advantage over hearing parents. With proper guidance, however, hearing parents can be helped to overcome their initial disadvantage.

Conclusion

In spite of the relative consistency of the above information, it is highly questionable whether standard personality inventories are applicable to deaf persons. Deaf subjects do not always understand all the items used in their inventories. Researchers indicate a general vagueness as to exactly what their personality tests show. In short, any conclusions about the effect of deafness on personality must be viewed with caution. *See* PSYCHOLOGY: Mental Health.

Bibliography
Altshuler, K. Z., et al.: "Impulsivity and Profound Early Deafness," *American Annals of the Deaf*, 121: 331–345, 1976.

Bolton, B., J. Cull, and R. Hardy: "Psychological Adjustment to Hearing Loss and Deafness," in R. Hardy and J. Cull (eds.), *Educational and Psycho-Social Aspects of Deafness*, Charles C. Thomas, Springfield, Illinois, 1974.

DiCarlo, L., and J. Dolphin: "Social Adjustment and Personality Development of Deaf Children: A Review of Literature," *Exceptional Children*, 111–118, January 1952.

Greenberg, D.: "Doubtful Cases," *American Annals of the Deaf*, 34: 93–99, 1889.

Hess, D. W.: "The Evaluation of Personality and Adjustment in Deaf and Hearing Children Using a Nonverbal Modification of the Make a Picture Story (Maps) Test," unpublished Ph.D. dissertation, University of Rochester (New York), 1960.

Levine, E.: "Psychological Tests and Practices with the Deaf: A Survey of the State of the Art," *Volta Review*, 76: 298–319, 1974.

———— and E. Wagner: "Personality of Deaf Persons," *Perceptual and Motor Skills*, 39: 1167–1236, 1974.

Meadow, Kathryn P.: *Deafness and Child Development*, University of California Press, Berkeley, 1980.

Myklebust, H.: *The Psychology of Deafness*, Grune and Stratton, New York, 1960.

Richard Meisegeier

SOCIOLINGUISTICS

Sociolinguistics examines the relationship between language and society. It differs from more traditional linguistic methodology by normally investigating quantitative differences in a relatively large number of users of a language who vary according to social background factors. It differs from other subdivisions of linguistics, such as psycholinguistics, by almost never focusing on research in an experimental laboratory situation; rather, it concentrates on field observations of language use. *See* PSYCHOLINGUISTICS.

Since sociolinguistics involves both language and society, researchers in sociolinguistics come from the fields of anthropology, sociology, and linguistics. From the perspectives of these three disciplines, three major subfields of sociolinguistics have emerged: the ethnography (anthropological description) of communication, the sociology of language, and linguistic sociolinguistics (generally referred to as sociolinguistics).

The topics studied by sociolinguists can generally be classified under one of the following headings: multilingualism, diglossia, language planning and standardization, language variation, pidginization and creolization, and the ethnography of communication. While each of these major topics can be studied from each of the three subfields, most sociolinguists would agree that topics such as multilingualism, diglossia, and language standardization and planning belong to the sociology of language, while language variation is included under linguistic sociolinguistics. Pidginization and creolization are often discussed under both the sociology of language and linguistic sociolinguistics. Some sociolinguists consider the ethnography of communication to be a separate field, while others consider it to be a part of linguistic sociolinguistics.

Multilingualism

Most nations have populations that use more than one language. For example, over 200 different languages are used in India. Multilingualism can be officially recognized (as it is in India, which has 14 official governmental languages), or it can be semi-officially recognized (as in Paraguay, with Spanish as the official governmental language and Guaraní recognized as a national but unofficial language). Some governments, for example that of the United States, officially ignore minority group languages despite the large numbers of people who use them.

There is also a great deal of multilingualism at the level of societies. The United States deaf community is multilingual, since both American Sign Language (ASL) and English are used. As with many other societies, not all members in the deaf community are equally fluent in both languages. Those who are somewhat bilingual do not use both languages for all purposes—signers often switch from one language to another. *See* SIGN LANGUAGES: American.

DIGLOSSIA

A specific form of code switching that is common to many bilingual communities is diglossia. The notion of diglossia was first developed to apply to variations between what was considered to be two varieties of the same language, for example, Classical and Colloquial Arabic in Egypt or Standard French and Haitian Creole in Haiti. Later research has shown, however, that it is also helpful to apply the notion of diglossia to bilingual situations such as between Spanish and Guaraní in Paraguay; between English and Swahili and between Swahili and Bantu vernaculars in Tanzania; and between English and ASL in the United States. (Diglossia has also been reported for a number of other sign languages and oral languages, but only in those situations where there is a deaf community and some hearing people sign.)

Ironically, additional support for the notion of bilingual diglossia comes from the original study of monolingual diglossia. At the time of the original study, Haitian Creole and French were considered to be dialects of the same language. Linguists now consider them to be separate languages. Similarly, other linguists have suggested that there is no true diglossia between ASL and English since they are two separate languages, but this may not be valid.

In all diglossic situations, there is an asymmetrical relationship between two language varieties. One variety of a language, generally a standard literary variety, has a special relationship to another colloquial variety. The formal variety is used in more formal situations with more formal topics and participants, while the conversational variety is used in less formal situations. Native users generally consider the formal variety to be publicly superior to the conversational variety, which is sometimes said not to exist. Privately, however, the conversational variety is important for intimate interactions and social identity. The conversational variety is generally learned at home, the initial place of enculturation, whereas the formal variety is studied at school. Most people, however, are never as comfortable in the formal variety, and many do not achieve a high level of proficiency in the formal language (an exception to this is in Switzerland). The literary variety is generally studied formally in the schools; the colloquial is not. Diglossic situations are very stable, since each variety serves important but different functions.

When the concept of diglossia is applied to the relationship between English and ASL in the North American deaf community, it is clear that English serves many of the functions of the literary language variety described above, and ASL serves many of the functions of the colloquial language variety, especially those functions for intimate interaction. While it should be understood that more people are recognizing the intrinsic worth of ASL, ASL is still considered inferior to English. There are many people who advocate English-only education, some who advocate some ASL and English bilingual education, but few who would advocate ASL as the primary method of education for deaf individuals. Although English is a written language, ASL is not. Quantitative studies of classroom communication by hearing and deaf teachers show that the vast majority of both groups use English-like signing in the classroom, especially at the elementary level. *See* EDUCATION: Communication.

While it may seem that diglossia is a negative force, it should be pointed out that diglossia has traditionally played a very positive role in the American deaf community, despite the fact that diglossia has reinforced some negative attitudes toward ASL. Negative attitudes that occur in the deaf community toward ASL have only involved public interaction with the hearing world. The majority of deaf people feel much more comfortable using ASL than using English and feel a special attachment to ASL. This love-hate relationship with the colloquial language variety is typical of diglossic situations, although the intensity may vary considerably from community to community and even from individual to individual.

Diglossia specifies that the appropriate language to use with hearing people (outsiders) is English and with deaf people (insiders) is ASL; thus, diglossia acts as a buffer between hearing and deaf communities. It allows hearing people to be identified as outsiders and to be treated very carefully before allowing any interaction that could negatively affect the deaf community. Hearing outsiders are stereotyped negatively until they prove themselves to the deaf community. At the same time, diglossia serves important functions inside the deaf community by maintaining the social identity and group solidarity of deaf people, and thus it is a positive force in the deaf community. It is apparent that both English and ASL are important in the North American deaf community's interaction; diglossia serves as a helpful model for describing the relationship between ASL and English. *See* DEAF POPULATION: Deaf Community.

PIDGINIZATION AND CREOLIZATION

When languages and cultures come into contact, there is a need for cross-cultural communication. When the languages are equal, the communities may become multilingual. If asymmetrical relations between the cultures are the norm, the subordinate group is normally expected to learn the language of the dominant group. Sometimes, because of factors such as social separation, it is not possible for many members of the subordinate group to become bilingual, and what results is often a continuum of language varieties from the subordinate language to the dominant language.

If there are only two languages involved, and if there is the possibility of eventual acquisition of the dominant language, the language varieties along the continuum are said to be hybridized. The hybrid varieties are only intermediate stages on the road to second-language acquisition. Thus, as time progresses, an individual will actually move toward the standard language.

If there are more than two languages involved, and if there are distinctive social or linguistic barriers to the acquisition of the dominant language, the language varieties are often said to be pidginized. If the sociolinguistic situation remains stable for some time, linguists classify this as a pidgin. Sometimes, native users of the subordinate group will acquire the intermediate varieties as their native language, thus creolizing the language into a totally separate language from the original languages in the contact situation. (Pidginization and creolization as well as stable pidgins and creoles can also develop under other conditions than those described above.)

The variation between ASL and English cannot truly be described as hybridization, even though there are only two languages involved, since hearing impairment and negative attitudes of hearing people make it impossible for most deaf individuals to acquire English and to become assimilated into the majority culture. Also, deaf individuals do not progress from one variety to another but shift back and forth between varieties. Since deaf individuals have not given up ASL to acquire these intermediate varieties, creolization and creole are also not appropriate terms.

There are two explanations for the variation between ASL and English: pidginization, and foreigner talk and learners' grammar. Foreigner talk and learners' grammar is a useful explanation for the type of signing that occurs between deaf signers and nonskilled hearing signers. Deaf signers basically alter their language to accommodate themselves to hearing signers (foreigners) who have not mastered ASL. Unskilled hearing signers attempt to produce ASL but have significant interference from English and make errors (learners' grammar). Thus, instead of analyzing the resultant sign varieties as a separate language or languages, they are analyzed as the linguistic accommodations that skilled ASL users make when communicating with

foreigners, and as the syntactic and semantic errors of unskilled signers.

Foreigner talk meshes nicely with pidginization, since processes similar to pidginization often occur in foreigner talk situations. Moreover, there are other situations in the North American deaf community that cannot be explained solely by foreigner talk. Sometimes skilled hearing signers are misidentified as deaf. When a deaf person discovers that a skilled signer is actually hearing, the deaf individual often switches to English-like signing. This cannot be explained through foreigner talk, since the hearing person is already fluent in ASL. It can, however, be explained by assuming that the deaf person is using a pidginized signing variety to reestablish cultural boundaries that have been violated by the hearing individual.

LANGUAGE PLANNING AND STANDARDIZATION

Language planning and standardization deals with the application of sociolinguistic theory and descriptions to concrete language situations. Often this application occurs at the national level, for example, in deciding on which language to use in national government documents, courts, education, and so on. Language standardization attempts in these situations involve setting up a standard variety of the language or languages involved in the society. It does not involve (as in the standardization attempts in the deaf community) imposing one language on another. Language standardization would normally be seen as setting up national standards for vocabulary, grammar, and phonology based on the already existing framework of ASL and would not be seen as using English as a goal for standardizing ASL.

Failures in language standardization and planning greatly outnumber the successes. Languages are intimately tied to ideology, social structure, and technology. Many times attempts to legislate language are seen as broader attempts at legislation of freedom. This seems to be the case on the Indian subcontinent where riots related to language (and culture imposition) are common. Equally unsuccessful attempts at language planning with less violent reactions have occurred in Ireland. However, probably the greatest example of success in language standardization and planning is Israel.

One of the most important elements in success of language standardization and planning is positive attitudes toward and motivation for learning the new standard variety. One obvious factor mitigating against widespread acceptance of manual codes for English in the deaf community is the ambivalence toward language standardization and especially toward language imposition in the deaf community due to the diglossic language situation.

The love-hate attitude toward ASL of a number of signers seems to perpetuate this ambivalence.

Very little research has been done on sociological-attitudinal problems of manual codes for English. The political, economic, social, and attitudinal atmosphere in the deaf community, not the schools, will determine the acceptability of such codes. The relatively unidentified atmosphere of the deaf community puts attempts at language standardization and planning in the deaf community on a very weak foundation. *See* Manually coded English.

Language planning and standardization can also occur at the local level. Sociolinguistic theory would suggest that some sort of bilingual education would be appropriate for the bilingual diglossic continuum in the North American deaf community. However, attitudes toward signing in general and toward ASL in particular are barriers to establishing bilingual education programs for deaf individuals.

Bilingual education has a long history in the United States. In the late 1700s there were private German-English bilingual schools in a number of states. In the early 1800s there were a number of other types of private bilingual schools and also public tax-supported German-English bilingual schools in Pennsylvania and Ohio. Beginning about 1910, however, and peaking shortly after World War I, strong antiforeign sentiment resulted in negative attitudes toward bilingual education. These negative attitudes persist despite the passage of such legislation as the Bilingual Education Act in 1967.

There are a number of different types of bilingual education programs in the United States, including transitional, bilingual maintenance, bilingual-bicultural maintenance, restorationist, and culturally pluralistic.

The majority of bilingual education programs in the United States today are transitional. This means that the native language is used only long enough for the children to acquire sufficient competence in English. Once English competence is acquired, the use of the native language is dropped from the curriculum. This is strictly a remedial-compensatory orientation to bilingualism. In fact, some transitional bilingual programs in the United States do not teach in the native language but only teach English as a second language.

Bilingual maintenance programs are designed to give the student fluency in English while maintaining fluency in the native language. Bilingual maintenance does not necessarily include information on the native culture and history. This is done in bilingual-bicultural maintenance programs that integrate not only language but native culture as part of curricular content and methodology.

Restorationist programs are bilingual-bicultural programs designed to give students the opportunity to learn a native language and culture that was lost when their ancestors gave up their traditions while becoming assimilated into American culture.

Culturally pluralistic programs attempt to provide two-way bilingual education. Students who do not speak English are exposed to their native language and culture in addition to English language and American culture. Students who are already members of American culture are exposed to another language and culture.

LANGUAGE VARIATION

In addition to the possibilities of multilingualism and diglossia within a social group, there is the distinct probability of variation within each language used. This variation is commonly called dialects; however, a number of sociolinguists prefer to use the term lectal varieties, since dialects traditionally was used to discuss relatively stable regional language varieties. In fact, language variation can occur because of factors of region, social class, ethnicity, age, gender, or a combination of any of these.

All linguists agree that languages vary and are constantly changing over time. However, traditionally linguists believed that while language variation and change were interesting, they were basically peripheral to the scientific study of language. Many linguists thought that by studying the language use of one or two native users of a language, a relatively complete grammar could be written for that language. In addition, most linguists believed that it was impossible to study language change in progress, since phonological change, though constant, is too slow to monitor; and grammatical change, while rare, occurs too suddenly.

Sociolinguists, on the other hand, believe not only that language is constantly changing, but that these changes can be noted by observing the variation that occurs in language between generations and between social, regional, and ethnic groups that retain older forms and those that have adopted newer forms. Traditionally this variation was ignored because it was not noticed by linguists, who limited their studies to one or two informants.

The change in ASL from two-handed signs on the face to one-handed signs provides an excellent example of the difference between a linguistic and sociolinguistic approach to language description. Traditional studies of historical change in ASL state that two-handed signs on the face become one-handed. Signs previously made with two hands, like CAT, are now made with one hand. Other signs, like DEER, are still generally made with two hands.

One sociolinguistic study examined this change in detail with 75 consultants from the southeastern United States. This study found that all signs that had supposedly changed to one hand were still made with two hands by some consultants in the South. Moreover, the study revealed that there was a predictable order for the change of all signers. Thus, by studying these 75 signers, it was demonstrated that the change is on-going, and it was possible to reconstruct how the change is occurring. From this information, it is possible to reconstruct the change for all signers and to show where the change began and how it is spreading. The sociolinguistic approach offers a great deal more information than is possible from a traditional linguistic approach to language change.

TYPES OF VARIATION

Variation in language can occur at the phonological (formational), grammatical, and lexical (vocabulary) levels. Lexical variation, like historical change in vocabulary, is most frequent, followed by phonological variation. The most resistant level to variation and change is the grammatical level.

Each of the three language levels can be influenced by factors of region, ethnicity, social class, age, and gender, or a combination of these factors. For example, the two-hand-to-one-hand change is related to the variables of region, ethnicity, and age. Signers in the southeastern United States use significantly more of the older two-handed forms than other people. In the South, blacks use more of the older two-handed forms than whites, and older signers use more of the older two-handed forms than younger signers.

Regional variation probably occurs in almost all of the world's languages, since geographical boundaries are widespread. Geographic boundaries may take different forms. For example, in the United States, residential schools for deaf children serve as geographic boundaries, rather than states or natural boundaries such as rivers.

Other sociolinguistic factors that influence language variation are not constant, but depend on the specific society. In ASL, ethnicity and social class seem to be much more important than gender or age. Other languages, like Biloxi, an Amerindian language previously spoken in Mississippi, had no ethnic or social class variation but great variation due to gender. For example, in Biloxi there were sometimes four different sets of grammatical endings depending on whether there was a male talking to a female, a male talking to a male, a female talking to a male or female, or a male or female talking to a child.

Ethnic variation in ASL is a result of a difference of social identities of blacks and whites. This difference in social identity is partly due to segregated schools and clubs for deaf people in some regions of the country, but it also is due to the positive influence of the interaction of black deaf people who share the same goals and values.

Social class variation in the North American deaf community is determined not only by education, type and source of income, and residence, but also by parentage and age at sign language acquisition and resultant enculturation into the deaf community. Signers who have deaf parents and signers who learned signs before the age of six use more ASL rules than signers who do not have these characteristics.

STUDYING VARIATION

It is important to understand language variation for three reasons: (1) it increases the understanding of language; (2) various groups are often unjustly stigmatized by the majority culture for their language use; and (3) an understanding of variation in language is important for teachers of students from different backgrounds.

The first reason allows that the more people study human language in its various manifestations, the more they will understand the nature of it. For example, historical changes, such as the two-to-one-hand change, can be explained more clearly through studies of variation. Much of this information would have been overlooked if the study had been limited to white northern signing.

The second reason relates to social progress. Even after reading about the systematic nature of ASL varieties such as black southern signing, some people have continued to believe that blacks were backward because southern blacks tend to use historically older forms more often than southern whites of the same age. This demonstrates a naive and dangerous attitude. That one signing group uses a historically older form does not mean they are backward. Blacks using spoken English in the United States have been shown in numerous studies to be ahead of whites in language change. Few whites would argue that whites are therefore more backward than blacks. Black southern deaf people, despite severe discrimination against them, have flourishing varieties of signs that are different from whites and serve as a social mechanism for language and social identification.

The third reason points out the need for the sociolinguistic study and understanding of language variation for language instruction. Many language teachers believe that their form of language is superior to all others and often attempt to eradicate language differences of students rather than to use the differences to teach students about the intricacies of language behavior. Ignoring regional, social, and ethnic variations may make the student feel that the school does not respect the student's social identity. Moreover, students may not be able to understand the teacher adequately if the teachers' and students' language differences are great.

ETHNOGRAPHY OF COMMUNICATION

The ethnography of communication, sometimes called the ethnography of speaking, draws heavily on the holistic approach of anthropology. Language, the grammatical code, is only one part of the whole communication event. There are also other important influences, such as CHANNEL—the modalities representing the code: for example, speaking, signing, writing; MESSAGE FORM—the type of message communicated: lecture, face-to-face communication, letter; PARTICIPANTS—those individuals involved in the communication: lecturer and audience, one hearing and one deaf person; TOPICS—the information discussed: philosophy, sports; and SETTING—the time, place, and surrounding events: morning in an English classroom, evening at home.

While very few studies of sign languages and deaf communities have attempted to use the framework of the ethnography of communication for analysis, the ethnography of communication offers interesting insights into the nature of language use in deaf communities. Below are two concrete examples of how the ethnography of communication could be applied to language use in the North American deaf community.

The personal-letter message form normally results in a written channel of communication, although videotaped letters are possible. The written channel of communication will predict attempts to represent English, since ASL is not normally written by deaf individuals.

The face-to-face message form allows much more variation. With deaf participants in an informal setting, the code will normally be ASL with a predictable channel of signing. With deaf and hearing participants, the code is usually English, although it could be ASL. English could be written or spoken (for hearing people who do not sign), signed, or simultaneously signed and spoken. Since the sign channel is not an efficient channel for English, some reduction of English structure occurs in the attempt to represent English. Fluent signers often add ASL characteristics to their English-like signing to compensate for the reduction.

The ethnography of communication clearly separates code (ASL vs. English) from channel (signed, spoken, simultaneous, written, typed, and so on) differences. Such a model is crucial in deaf education for an accurate and clear understanding of controversies such as manualism vs. oralism or total (simultaneous) communication vs. oralism. While these controversies need to deal first with the linguistically more important matter of code (ASL or

English), they are often described in the educational literature merely in terms of secondary channel differences (signed, spoken, or simultaneously signed and spoken). *See* HISTORY: Sign Language Controversy.

Bibliography

Bailey, C.: *Variation and Linguistic Theory*, Center for Applied Linguistics, Washington, D.C., 1973.

Cokely, D.: "When is a Pidgin Not a Pidgin? An Alternate Analysis of the ASL-English Contact Situation," *Sign Language Studies*, 38:1–24, 1983.

Fasold, R.: *The Sociolinguistics of Society*, Basil Blackwell, Oxford, 1984.

Hymes, D.: *Pidginization and Creolization of Languages*, Cambridge University Press, Cambridge, 1971.

Leibowitz, A.: *Educational Policy and Political Acceptance*, Center for Applied Linguistics, Washington, D.C., 1971.

Saville-Troike, M.: *The Ethnography of Communication*, Basil Blackwell, Oxford, 1982.

James Woodward

Sign Language Continuum

Linguistic research has demonstrated that ASL and English are two different languages with separate grammatical structures. Many people assume, therefore, that it should always be easy to tell when a person is attempting to sign English and when a person is signing ASL. However, ASL and English are in close contact in a politically unequal situation. This has resulted in a continuum of language varieties between pure ASL and pure English.

Language continua have been reported for British, French, and a number of other sign languages. Language continua also occur frequently between spoken languages, such as English and Spanish in Texas.

The most in-depth research on language continua in sign languages has been done on ASL. Thus, this section will focus primarily on the continuum between ASL and English. Before discussing the specifics of this continuum, it will be useful to examine the following three ways of expressing the meaning of the English sentence "I have gone" (from a specified place). [To simplify the example, none of the face and head movements that occur with the ASL sentence are indicated here.] (1) GO FINISH ME. (2) I FINISH GO. (3) ME FINISH GO.

Sentence 1 is clearly not English. Most users of ASL will report that they have seen people signing ASL use this sentence. Many will also state that they can use this sentence in their production of ASL.

The great majority of signers will identify sentence 2 as English-like signing and will point to the English word order and to "I" as indicators of English. The use of FINISH, even though it is an ASL sign, is rarely commented on by deaf signers.

Sentence 3 presents the theoretical problem. It is identified by some signers as English because of the word order, by other signers as ASL because of the word order and the ME, by still other signers as either ASL or English, and by signers who would not use sentence 3 as neither ASL nor English. It is obvious that sentence 3 cannot easily be labeled as ASL or English.

The classification problems in sentence 3 occur quite often in signed sentences in free conversation. A language continuum is the most reasonable model for describing this in-between variation that is not exactly English and not exactly ASL.

ASL AND ENGLISH

The following are examples of variations of ASL and an example of the manual code for English, each rendition with the meaning of the English sentence "I have gone." [To simplify the example, none of the face and head movements that necessarily occur during the ASL sentences are indicated here.]

ASL: (1) GO FINISH ME. (2) FINISH GO ME. (3) ME FINISH GO ME. (4) ME FINISH GO. (5) I FINISH GO. (6) I END GO. (7) I HAVE GO. (8) I HAVE(V) GO.

Manual code for English: I HAVE(V) GO FINISH.

ASL does not have the same word order as English. The completive marker FINISH tends to go after the verb. Simple subject pronouns when expressed manually tend to go at the end of the sentence. In longer sentences, subject pronouns tend to occur at the beginning and are repeated at the end of the sentence.

In addition to the word order differences noted above, ASL has one form for the subject and object pronoun; English has two. The use of the sign END as a completive marker was very common in English signing before the introduction of artificially developed manually coded English systems. Certain types of English signing, especially those used in educational settings with young deaf children, use an initialized handshape on HAVE(V).

The variation described above is random, but can be described by variation theory in sociolinguistics. One of the easiest methods is to use implications (one-way if-then statements). If people use an initialized completive marker, HAVE(V), then they will also use the sign for "I." The converse is not true, however. If people use an "I," one cannot predict whether or not they will use the initialized completive marker. Another implication that can be derived from the above data is that if people use "I" they will also use English word order, but not the converse.

The previous two implications are not the only ones that can be derived from the examples for "I have gone." They have simply been used for illustrative purposes. Such implications have been found to explain much of the significant variation between ASL and English-like signing. Characteristically, the more like ASL the signing, the less dependence there is on word order and the more dependence there is on nonmanual expressions and internal modifications of signs. ASL-like signing, for example, expresses questions, certain types of negation, conditional clause markers (if), and relative clause markers (who, which, that) totally nonmanually. Relationships between subject and object can be marked on a number of verbs in ASL by direction of movement instead of word order. *See* SIGN LANGUAGES: Facial Expressions.

Because the type of analysis discussed here is not widely known outside the field of sociolinguistics, there has been a great amount of misunderstanding and misinterpretation of this variation. Some educators have concluded that the great deal of variation found in ASL means that ASL has no grammar. Others have suggested that there are in fact many languages between ASL and English, and have given these "languages" names such as Ameslish or Siglish.

As discussed above, it is not always possible to divide sentences unambiguously into ASL and English. It is empirically impossible to attempt to divide further into clear Ameslish, Siglish, and so on. Any attempt to justify these variations as discrete languages would have to be on a case-by-case, ad hoc basis.

The currently acceptable trend in linguistic theory is to recognize ASL at one end of the ASL-to-English continuum and English at the other. The term Pidgin Sign English is sometimes used to discuss those sign varieties that are neither clearly ASL nor clearly English. While it is true that Pidgin Sign English is different from pure ASL and from pure English, it is not a separate language. There is no empirical way to define where Pidgin Sign English begins and ends. The term Pidgin Sign English is merely used to describe the fact that there is not always a clearcut division between ASL and English and allows one to discuss English-like ASL and ASL-like English for deaf people, and ASL-like English for some hearing people and English-like English for most hearing people.

Furthermore, the sign varieties that have been called Pidgin Sign English have more recently been reanalyzed as instances of foreigner talk (how deaf ASL users modify their language when communicating with "foreigners"—hearing people) and learners' grammar (how hearing signers make patterned errors while learning ASL). This analysis demonstrates the folly of labeling these non-ASL, non-English forms of signing as languages.

Continuum Switching

Signers vary considerably in their ability to move along the continuum between ASL and English. Generally, deaf signers of educated deaf parents tend to have the most flexibility. Furthermore, deaf signers tend to use more ASL-like signing than hearing people; deaf people with deaf parents tend to use more ASL-like signing than deaf people with hearing parents; and people who learned signs before the age of six will use more ASL-like signing than people who learned signs after the age of six. Gallaudet College experience is also an important variable in predicting ASL-like competence. Experience at Gallaudet reduces ASL usage for deaf students with deaf parents and increases it for deaf students with hearing parents.

Signers are greatly influenced in their choice of signing by a number of sociolinguistic factors such as participants, topic, setting, message form, and other characteristics of the ethnography of communication. If the topic is formal, English may be used; if it is informal, ASL probably will be used. A formal setting, like a classroom, will often elicit English-like signing, even from a person who is more comfortable in ASL. The presence of an all-deaf audience would shift signing toward ASL; the introduction of hearing strangers would move the conversation toward English.

These factors are mutually interactive. The combination of topic, participants, setting, and so on, help determine the kind of signing a person will attempt to use. Not all elements are equally weighted; some are more important than others. Until there is more research into the ethnography of communication of signing, it will be impossible to predict the type of signing a specific deaf person will tend to use in a given situation.

Bibliography

Baker, C., and D. Cokely: *American Sign Language: A Teacher's Resource Text on Grammar and Culture*, T. J. Publishers, Silver Spring, Maryland, 1980.

Lawson, L.: "The Role of Sign in the Structure of the Deaf Community," in D. Woll, J. Kyle, and M. Deuchar (eds.), *Recent Perspectives on British Sign Language and Deafness*, Billing and Sons, London, 1981.

Woodward, J.: "Some Sociolinguistic Aspects of French and American Sign Languages," in H. Lane, and F. Grosjean (eds.), *Recent Perspectives on American Sign Language*, Lawrence Erlbaum Associates, Hillsdale, New Jersey, 1980.

James Woodward

Sign Language Dialects

Sign languages, like spoken languages, vary in vocabulary, phonology (formational structure), and grammar. This variation can depend on a signer's region, social class, ethnicity, gender, and age, among other factors.

Some type of sociolinguistic variation has been reported for numerous sign languages, such as regional and social variation in British Sign Language; regional, gender, and age variation in French Sign Language; and regional and gender variation in Indian Sign Language. However, the most in-depth research to date on sociolinguistic variation in sign languages has been done on ASL. *See* SIGN LANGUAGES: British, French, Indian.

The sociolinguistic research on ASL demonstrates that virtually all types of sociolinguistic variation that occur in spoken languages can also occur in sign languages. Before discussing the specifics of sociolinguistic variation in ASL, several phonological and grammatical rules in ASL need to be briefly presented.

Phonological Rules

The Face-Hand rule, the Two-to-One rule, and the Elbow-to-Hand rule, among others, describe how the formational structure of certain signs in systematic ways.

The Face-Hand rule involves signs such as MOVIE, RABBIT, LEMON, COLOR, SILLY, PEACH, PEANUT. Some signers make these signs with one hand on the face, while others make these signs (with the same handshape and movement) in front of the body.

The Two-to-One rule concerns signs like CAT, CHINESE, COW, DEVIL, HORSE, DONKEY, DEER, FAMOUS. Some signers use the historically older variants of these signs made with two hands on the face, while other signers use the newer form of these signs made with one hand on the face.

The Elbow-to-Hand rule relates to signs such as HELP, SUPPORT, FLAG, POOR, PUNISH. Some signers use the historically older variants of these signs made with one hand touching the elbow, while other signers use the newer form of these signs made with one hand touching the other hand.

Grammatical Rules

The Negative Incorporation rule, the Agent-Beneficiary rule, and the Verb Reduplication rule, among others, describe grammatical variation in ASL.

In Negative Incorporation, signers negate a limited set of ASL verbs by using an outward twisting movement of the hand(s) from the place where the sign is made, instead of adding a separate negative sign like NOT. Negative Incorporation may be used with signs such as HAVE, LIKE, WANT, KNOW.

In Agent-Beneficiary Directionality, signers begin movement of the sign in the direction of the agent or actor and end the movement in the direction of

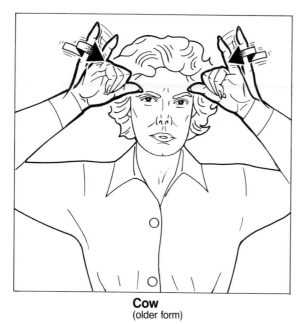

Cow
(older form)

Example of Two-to-One rule. (After C. Baker and D. Cokely, *American Sign Language: A Teacher's Resource Text on*

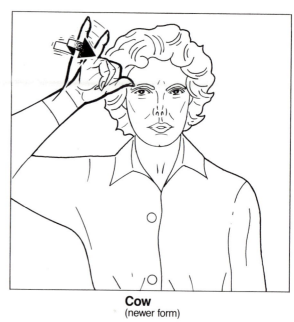

Cow
(newer form)

Grammar and Culture, **T.J. Publishers, Silver Spring, Maryland, 1980)**

the beneficiary or receiver. Agent-Beneficiary Directionality may be used with signs like FINGER-SPELL, HIT, HATE, FORCE, SAY-NO, ASK, TELL, SHOW, GIVE.

In Verb Reduplication, signers repeat the verb to indicate whether the action is continuous or not. Verb Reduplication can be used with signs such as MEET, MEMORIZE, SEE, WANT, STUDY, READ, KNOW, RUN, DRIVE.

REGIONAL VARIATION

There are two types of regional variation in ASL vocabulary: historical (occurring over time) and synchronic (co-occurring during the same time period). Historical variation means that at one time most varieties of ASL used the same sign, while now only certain regions use this form. One example of historical regional variation is the southeastern sign WHAT, which is identical to the com-

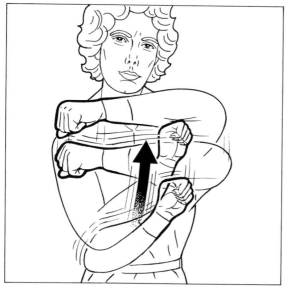

Support
(older form)

Example of Elbow-to-Hand rule. (After C. Baker and D. Cokely, *American Sign Language: A Teacher's Resource*

Support
(newer form)

Text on Grammar and Culture, **T.J. Publishers, Silver Spring, Maryland, 1980)**

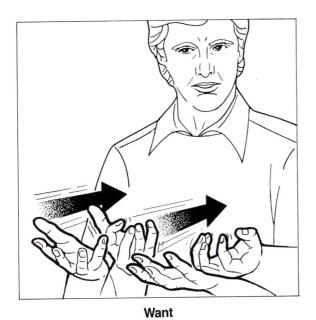

Want

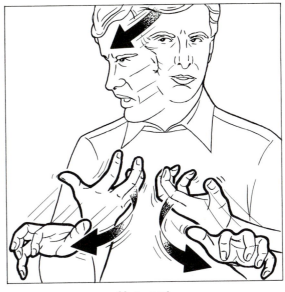

Not want

Example of Negative Incorporation rule. (After C. Baker and D. Cokely, *American Sign Language: A Teacher's Re-*

source Text on Grammar and Culture, T.J. Publishers, Silver Spring, Maryland, 1980)

Me give to you

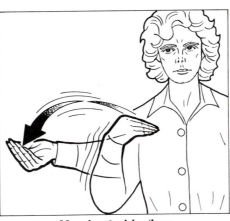

Me give to him/her

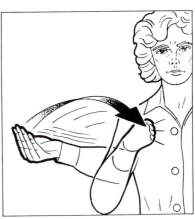

S/He give to me

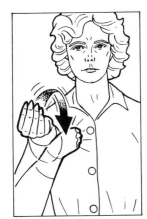

You give to me

You give to him/her

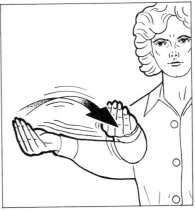

S/He give to you

Example of Agent-Beneficiary Directionality. (After C. Baker and D. Cokely, *American Sign Language: A Teacher's Re-*

source Text on Grammar and Culture, T.J. Publishers, Silver Spring, Maryland, 1980)

Birthday
(Philadelphia)

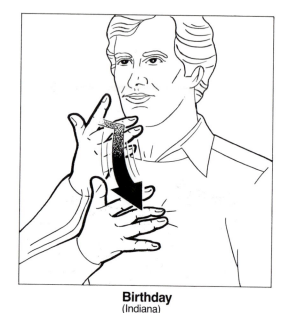

Birthday
(Indiana)

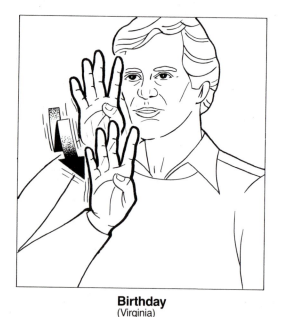

Birthday
(Virginia)

Example of regional variants in ASL vocabulary. (After C. Baker and D. Cokely, *American Sign Language: A*

Birthday
(more conventional)

Teacher's Resource Text on Grammar and Culture, T.J. Publishers, Silver Spring, Maryland, 1980)

monly used sign WHERE. Originally, this sign, which is derived from French Sign Language WHAT, was used in many regions of the United States to mean "what." Now only southeastern signers preserve this form for "what," while most signers from other areas use this sign for "where" and use a different sign for "what."

There are numerous synchronic variations in ASL vocabulary according to region. Very common signs such as BIRTHDAY, SHOES, GOAT, HALLOWEEN

have a number of very distinct regional variants that are not formationally related to each other.

Both the Face-to-Hand rule and the Two-to-One rule vary according to region. Signers in Georgia make signs like RABBIT and LEMON significantly more often on the hands than signers from other areas of the country, who tend to make these signs on the face.

Signers in the southeastern part of the United States use significantly more of the historically older two-handed variants of signs like CHINESE and DONKEY than signers from other areas of the country, who tend to use the more modern one-handed variants of these signs.

Regional variation in ASL grammar occurs in both the Negative Incorporation rule and the Verb Reduplication rule. Deaf signers from the northwest part of the United States use significantly more ASL Negative Incorporation and ASL Verb Reduplication than deaf signers from the northeastern part of the United States.

ETHNIC VARIATION

There are examples of historical and synchronic (nonhistorical) variation in black southern signing. One example of historical variation in black southern signing is PREGNANT, which is identical to the commonly used white sign MOTHER. Black signers in Georgia still use this variant of PREGNANT. White signers in Georgia at one time used this sign, but now use the sign common to many other parts of the country that is made with interlocking hands extending from the trunk.

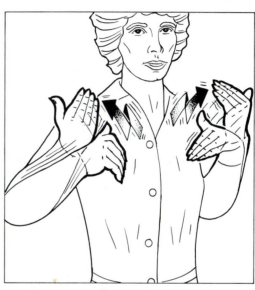

Young
(white signers)

Pregnant
(black southern signers)

Example of ethnic variation in ASL vocabulary. (After C. Baker and D. Cokely, *American Sign Language: A*

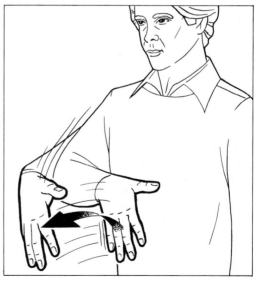

Pregnant
(white signers)

Teacher's Resource Text on Grammar and Culture, T.J. Publishers, Silver Spring, Maryland, 1980)

Young
(black southern signers)

Synchronic variation in black southern signing is more common than historical variation, probably because of the long separation of black and white schools in the South. Examples of synchronic variation among black signers in Georgia include SHOELACE, TRUCK, ZIPPER, WHITE-PERSON, among many others. WHITE-PERSON is a particularly interesting sign because it is used in Georgia only by uneducated black signers, but it is also used by some black signers in Louisiana and on the eastern shore of Maryland, Virginia, and Delaware. This suggests that there may be similarities in certain black signs in a number of southern states.

Both the Face-to-Hand rule and the Two-to-One rule vary according to the signer's ethnicity. Black southern signers use hand variants of signs like RABBIT, COLOR, SILLY significantly more often than white southern and white nonsouthern signers who tend to use more of the face variants of these signs. In fact, the hand variant of SILLY is only used by blacks; no whites have ever been noted to use that variant. Blacks in Georgia use significantly more of the historically older two-handed variants of signs like CHINESE and DONKEY than white signers from Georgia.

At present there are no empirical studies of ethnic variation in grammar. The problems in gathering sufficient syntactic data are enormous, because the only researchers who have done systematic investigations in ethnic variation in ASL have been hearing persons. Almost all of these hearing investigators have also been white. Black southern signers attempt to use more English-like signing when in contact with hearing people and attempt to use more white signing in conversations with outsiders. (The phonology and vocabulary of black southern signing do not change as much as grammar does with outsiders.)

SOCIAL VARIATION

More highly educated signers tend to use more borrowings from English in their ASL. These borrowings may be either through fingerspelling an English word or through an initialized sign, such as a native ASL sign that is modified by using a handshape to represent the first letter of an English word. For example, many ASL signers use the sign meaning "a limited kind of enclosure" (often glossed as BOX) to translate the English words "box" and "room." Some more educated signers use this sign only to mean "box," while they use the same sign with R handshapes (index and midfingers extended and crossed) to mean "room." Gradually, initialized signs change in form to conform to various phonological constraints in ASL.

There have been no studies to date that show a relation between signs and social class.

Negative Incorporation, Agent-Beneficiary Directionality, and Verb Reduplication all vary according to the social class background of the signer. Deaf signers use these rules more frequently than hearing signers. Signers who learned signs before the age of six (a crucial time for first language acquisition) use Agent-Beneficiary Directionality and Verb Reduplication more than signers who learned signs after the age of six. Signers who have deaf parents use Verb Reduplication more than signers who have hearing parents.

GENDER VARIATION

While variation due to gender differences occurs in many languages, there are only a few such variations in the vocabulary of ASL. One of these occurs in greeting behavior. Both males and females can use the standard sign HELLO, made with a B handshape extending outward from the side of the forehead. However, there is another sign for "hello" made with an A handshape that tends to be used only by men when greeting men they know. Women know this sign but rarely use it.

The Elbow-to-Hand rule varies according to the signer's gender. Males in the United States tend to use the newer hand form of signs like HELP and SUPPORT more frequently than females, who tend to use the older elbow form more frequently. The Elbow-to-Hand rule, which also occurs in French Sign Language, exhibited the same gender patterning for French signers.

The Agent-Beneficiary rule varies due to gender. In the northwestern United States, males use significantly more of the ASL Agent-Beneficiary rule as compared with females. No male-female differences in grammar have been found in the northeastern United States.

AGE VARIATION

There are very few documented examples of variation in ASL vocabulary due to age. One example is the older sign for TELEPHONE made with two S handshapes. Used only rarely, this sign is used primarily by older signers.

The Two-to-One rule varies according to the signer's age. Older white signers in the South used significantly more of the older two-handed variants of signs like CAT and COW than younger white signers in the same regions of the South.

Variation in the order of adjectives and nouns in ASL seems to be related to age. The shift from older Noun-Adjective word order to Adjective-Noun word order seems to occur more frequently among younger signers, especially those who are white, middle class, and college-educated.

Bibliography

Croneberg, C.: "Sign Language Dialects," in W. Stokoe, D. Casterline, and C. Croneberg (eds.), *A Dictionary of*

American Sign Language, 2d ed., Linstok Press, Silver Spring, Maryland, 1976.

Deuchar, M.: "Variation in British Sign Language," in B. Woll, J. Kyle, and M. Deuchar (eds.), *Recent Perspectives on British Sign Language and Deafness*, Billing and Sons, London, 1981.

Vasishta, M., J. Woodward, and K. Wilson: "Sign Language in India: Regional Variation Within the Deaf Population," *Indian Journal of Applied Linguistics*, vol. 4, no. 2, June 1978.

Woodward, J.: "Some Sociolinguistic Aspects of French and American Sign Languages," in H. Lane, and F. Grosjean (eds.), *Recent Perspectives on American Sign Language*, Lawrence Erlbaum Associates, Hillsdale, New Jersey, 1980.

——— and S. De Santis: "Two to One It Happens: Dynamic Phonology in Two Sign Languages," *Sign Language Studies*, vol. 10, 1977.

James Woodward

Language Attitudes

Language attitudes are complex. Within the deaf community several questions need to be considered. For example, what are the attitudes of deaf and hearing people toward English and toward American Sign Language (ASL)? How do deaf people feel about hearing people who use ASL or deaf people who use "English-like signing"? How do hearing people feel about deaf people who use ASL as opposed to those who use English-like signing? The answers to these questions are deeply rooted in the history of the education of deaf children and in the culture of deaf people. Before examining them, it is important to review basic information about languages and cultures in the deaf community.

BACKGROUND

Two languages—ASL and English—are used in the deaf community, and deaf people are skilled in each to varying degrees. These languages serve different functions in the deaf community. In general, deaf people use ASL to communicate with each other and use English to communicate with hearing people (via writing, speech, or English-like signing). Deaf people are used to adapting to the communication skills of other deaf and hearing people. Thus, many can switch to more ASL-like or more English-like signing, depending on the skills of the other people involved.

Language is one aspect of culture. ASL is usually associated with deaf culture and English with the culture of hearing people. Although people who are born deaf to deaf parents may develop skills in both languages, they often are members of deaf culture only. Still, there is much variation in the language skills and cultural identities of deaf people because of differences in schooling or in family backgrounds.

SPEECH STUDIES

Most people are not aware that they judge others according to the way they speak, write, or sign. Often their positive or negative evaluations are based on the status of a language variety in their country or on the political views of people who are known to use a language variety. Similarly, the stereotypes of various cultural groups influence people's attitudes when they hear or see the language associated with a particular group.

The classic attitude is that one's own language is better than all other languages. For example, most Americans believe that English is the best language in the world, while many French people think that French, especially Parisian French, is the world's most artful and elevated language.

People who study language attitudes often audio-tape brief speech samples of people from different social classes or occupations, or from different cultural or ethnic groups. Or, they audio-tape the same people speaking more than one language. Listeners are asked to identify those speech samples with different social classes, occupations, cultural or ethnic groups, or personality traits.

Four general categories of conclusions derive from these studies of language attitudes: (1) Listeners tend to associate certain speech features with a particular race or class status (lower, middle, upper). For example, listeners tend to associate the speech feature "ain't" with the lower class and "aren't" with the middle or higher class. (2) Listeners judge personality characteristics, based on speech, that people associate with different cultural or ethnic groups. For example, they tend to use adjectives like "intelligent" to describe people who speak the language of the majority and adjectives like "less intelligent" to people who speak a minority language. (3) Listeners associate particular occupations with people who speak in certain characteristic ways. For example, they believe that they can tell if the speaker is a college professor or taxi driver by the way the person talks on the audio-tape. (4) Teachers evaluate children's background from their speech characteristics. For example, if a black child talks in black dialect on the audio-tape, teachers often judge the speaker as "disadvantaged."

This research on the language attitudes of hearing people shows how prevalent and strong language attitudes are. This, in turn, can help in understanding deaf and hearing people's attitudes toward ASL and English and the people who use these languages.

DEAF COMMUNITY

Ambivalence is a key word in understanding the language attitudes of deaf people. Deaf people have conflicting feelings toward both ASL and English.

These conflicting feelings are a product of their experience of growing up.

Hearing professionals who work with deaf people, especially educators, often value ASL and English differently. These educators are powerful agents in influencing deaf people's feelings toward the languages. ASL is not used as a medium of instruction in academic classrooms or even included in the curriculum. On the other hand, English is taught to deaf children as the language of value, the language of the majority group of hearing people in America, and is emphasized throughout the entire curriculum. Most educators believe that use of ASL interferes with or prevents deaf children from learning English. This belief strongly influences members of the deaf community as well as the families of deaf children. Few educators of deaf children have a positive attitude toward ASL or view ASL as a useful tool for the education of deaf students.

As noted previously, deaf people are skilled in using ASL and English to varying degrees, but many do not take pride in their skills in using ASL and are anxious to improve their English skills. They internally value ASL highly because it enables them to communicate easily and clearly with other deaf people and to enjoy being deaf with them socially. But at the same time, they think ASL does not help them get good jobs or be successful. They believe good English skills are necessary to get a good job and to be successful in a hearing world. Sometimes deaf people who are skilled in using both languages will even deny that they use ASL. Often hearing people, especially those who are not involved in the educational system of deaf children, have a more positive attitude toward ASL than deaf people do. They want to communicate in ASL on deaf people's terms. Deaf people frequently have mixed reactions to these people—feeling good that the hearing people are trying to communicate in their language, or feeling insulted that the hearing people think they have to "lower" their language to communicate with deaf people. Sometimes deaf people resent using ASL with hearing people when they can understand and use English.

However, some deaf people do take great pride in their ASL skills. This pride is related to their self-acceptance as a deaf person. Often, when they accept that English is their second language, their attitude toward English and the learning of English becomes more positive. They then feel more equal with hearing people. In return, they may be willing to teach hearing people ASL as a second language.

These language attitudes are even more complicated for persons who acquired English before they lost their hearing because English is still their first language. These people usually maintain their English skills throughout their lives and often work in top positions in organizations serving deaf people or in the education of deaf children. In fact, they often become spokespersons for the deaf community or "brokers" between the deaf community and the hearing community. They tend to be more ambivalent toward ASL than those who were born deaf and acquired English at a later age. Deafened persons who have acquired English and the cultural values of hearing people may fear they are sacrificing their identity with hearing persons and lowering themselves by learning ASL. Rarely do deafened people view ASL as the language of deaf persons or as a valuable addition to their first language, English, which they are then proud to be able to use. Thus, deaf and hearing people often get mixed messages about ASL and English from those deafened professionals who work with deaf people.

EFFECT ON COMMUNICATION

Deaf people's language attitudes affect how they communicate with hearing people. Deaf people rarely communicate with hearing people in ASL because of their school experiences. For example, as deaf children, when they tried to communicate with their hearing teachers in ASL, they were repeatedly admonished to use their voices or to sign in English.

Because language choice reflects identity choice, deaf persons choose ASL or English depending on whichever identity the system asks of them. When they are with hearing people, they try to communicate in English, either voicing or signing in English or doing both at once.

The words hearing, speech, and English seem equivalent to deaf people. When a deaf person meets a hearing person, the word English is strongly attached to that hearing person, so the deaf person tries to communicate on a hearing person's terms. Deaf people become very skilled in adapting their communication to fit the expectations or skills of different people.

LANGUAGE SUPREMACY

On the other hand, the deaf community can be compared to the majority community of hearing people in terms of language supremacy. Deaf people experience ASL supremacy in the deaf community in a way that is similar to that of hearing people's English supremacy in the majority community. To protect their own identities, deaf people tend to think that hearing people cannot understand ASL; so when they use ASL, deaf people actually are exerting their power.

Paradoxically, deaf people generally have low expectations of hearing people when it comes to the use of ASL. It may be due to their school experiences, when they rarely saw hearing teachers signing in ASL. If a hearing person is very skilled in using ASL, the first question a deaf person will probably ask is if the person has deaf parents. If the hearing person responds affirmatively, the explanation satisfies a deaf person's expectation of why a hearing person uses ASL. Other satisfactory answers are that the ASL skills result from having deaf relatives other than parents, growing up with a deaf friend in the neighborhood, or working at a residential school for deaf children as a houseparent.

Most deaf people find it difficult, however, to accept hearing people who say they are learning ASL for pleasure as a foreign language, similar to Spanish or French. Deaf people expect that hearing people who learn ASL must be involved in some way with deaf people.

Deaf ASL users may avoid deaf persons who use more English-like signing, such as manually coded English (MCE). The MCE signer is often considered snobbish or "college-educated"; thus the person may be rejected by some deaf people. However, the rejection really depends on the attitude of the deaf person who is using the MCE signs. If the person seems to feel that MCE signs are better than ASL signs, or if the MCE person has a condescending attitude, deaf people will reject that person. Sometimes deaf people who have excellent English skills eliminate MCE signs from their vocabulary in order to reduce their social distance from the deaf group and to express their desire to belong to the deaf community.

Ambivalence toward ASL and English is also reflected in the philosophies of the national organizations that serve deaf people. For example, some years ago a professional interpreters organization, the Registry of Interpreters for the Deaf, which mostly consists of hearing people who work with deaf people, wanted to recognize ASL as a language of the deaf community. However, at that time there was not yet any organization of or by deaf people that had recognized ASL as a language. This showed the ambivalence toward ASL of the deaf professionals who were working in national organizations. Not until 1984 did the National Association of the Deaf finally recognize both ASL and English as languages used by deaf people and begin to support bilingual education for deaf children. *See* NATIONAL ASSOCIATION OF THE DEAF; REGISTRY OF INTERPRETERS FOR THE DEAF.

Bibliography

Baker-Shenk, C.: "Experiences of Deaf People in a Hearing World," from a Ph.D. dissertation, "A Microanalysis of the Non-Manual Components of Questions in ASL," chap. 1, University of California at Berkeley, 1983.

Benderly, B.: *Dancing Without Music*, Doubleday, Garden City, New York, 1980.

Higgins, Paul C.: *Outsiders in a Hearing World: A Sociology of Deafness*, Sage Publications, Beverly Hills, California, 1980.

Jacobs, L.: *A Deaf Adult Speaks Out*, 2d ed., Gallaudet College Press, Washington, D.C.

Kannapell, B.: "Inside the Deaf Community," *Deaf American*, vol. 34, no. 4, January 1982.

Nash, J., and A. Nash: *Deafness in Society*, D. C. Heath, Lexington, Massachusetts, 1981.

Neisser, A.: *The Other Side of Silence*, Alfred A. Knopf, New York, 1983.

Woodward, J.: *How You Gonna Get to Heaven If You Can't Talk with Jesus: On Depathologizing Deafness*, T.J. Publishers, Silver Spring, Maryland, 1982.

Barbara Kannapell

Language Policy and Education

The majority of policies established in the educational setting have little direct bearing on the primary business of education—learning and teaching. There are dicta that regulate movement in the hallways ("keep to the right side"), behavior in the lunchroom ("form single lines to enter and exit"), choice of playmates ("primary recess from 12:00 to 12:30, elementary recess from 12:30 to 1:00"), and control of bodily functions ("get a bathroom pass from the teacher"). The main purpose of such policies is, apparently, to ensure the "smooth functioning" of the minisociety that convenes in the school from 9:00 to 3:00. A great deal of energy and time is devoted to developing such policies.

However, in the one area that may be most vital to the "smooth functioning" of the minisociety—language and communication—policies are generally established haphazardly. They are often based on the unquestioned (and, one might add, unsuccessful) assumptions of the past. This article will outline some of the major issues in establishing a language policy in an educational setting and will offer a procedure that educational institutions can follow in establishing a viable, comprehensive language policy.

In simplest terms, a language policy is a clear statement of desired linguistic behaviors that one expects from a specified group of people. Defining these desired linguistic behaviors is part of a process of language planning. The purpose of a language policy is to identify deliberate changes in a language system; the purpose of the language planning process is to ensure that the proposed changes are valid and can be reliably implemented. The language planning process imposes a series of checks on any proposed language policy. These checks are designed to ensure that the resulting language policy is linguistically efficient, linguistically adequate, and sociolinguistically acceptable.

Linguistic efficiency refers to the specifications and applications of a proposed set of linguistic rules or principles. By examining the "ease of use" of proposed rules or principles, it is possible to identify those that are cumbersome or overly complex and thus likely to be ignored or misused. Linguistic adequacy refers to the degree of precision with which a proposed rule or principle can convey specific linguistic information. By examining the "goodness of fit" of proposed rules or principles, it is possible to identify gaps or deficiencies in the proposed policy that will inevitably cause problems for the individuals expected to adhere to the language policy. Sociolinguistic acceptability refers to the effects of any proposed change on the attitudes and behaviors of the users of the language that is to be changed. By examining the attitudes of the individuals expected to adhere to the language policy, it is possible to identify potential resistance to, or rejection of, proposed changes. This set of checks is essential to the development of a valid language policy that can be reliably implemented.

The overwhelming majority of institutional and commercially published language policies, however, bypass this essential set of checks. They ignore the process and focus only on the end product. In residential and day programs for deaf students, the "process" of developing a language policy generally consists of a decision about which sign vocabulary textbook will be selected as the official text. The choice is generally made by selecting a commercially published vocabulary text or by selecting a commercially published "sign system" text. However, none of these texts represents the result of a language planning process. In fact, there is no evidence that the issues of efficiency, adequacy, or acceptability have been appropriately addressed by any commercially published vocabulary texts or by any commercially published "sign system" text. Ironically, when a program attempts to implement the linguistic behaviors recommended in such texts, these unresolved issues generally result in a greater degree of random variability in the linguistic behavior of the participants than existed before the "policy." See SIGN LANGUAGE TEXTBOOKS.

In order to develop an informed, viable language policy, the policy-maker must consider at least the following issues. The language policy itself, or more likely the supporting policy rationale, should lead to an objective discussion of each.

SOCIOLINGUISTIC SITUATION

Those charged with developing language-related policies must attempt to understand the often complex relationships that exist between the spoken languages and the signed languages in any given locale. Often it is assumed that either there are only two languages involved [American Sign Language (ASL) and English] or, more frequently, one language with two forms (one form expressed orally and one form expressed gesturally). While the lat-

ter is usually an erroneous assumption that fails to describe reality, the former assumption, although apparently more "enlightened," may also fail to describe reality. Consider the languages involved in the following situation:

A family has relocated to New York City from Mexico. They have four children, two of whom (ages 9 and 11) are deaf. The two deaf children attended a school for deaf students in Mexico and are quite fluent in the variety of signing used at that school. Neither of the parents is fluent in English, and both are illiterate in Spanish. Neither of the deaf children knows English, nor have they had the opportunity to acquire ASL or any of its varieties.

An accurate understanding of the sociolinguistic situation in this case not only would recognize that there are at least varieties of four languages involved, but would also consider the role, function, and value of each. While this example may seem atypical, it simply reflects the more complex end of a continuum. Even in situations where it is clear that "only" two languages are involved, however, there may be varieties of each language that must be considered. For example, in an urban school setting, it is likely that there are at least two varieties of spoken English (one used by white parents and teachers and one used by black parents and teachers) and at least three varieties of ASL (one used by deaf teachers and parents, one used by students, and one used by hearing teachers and parents).

An accurate and objective understanding of the situation must attempt to determine the relative importance of each language and each variety of a given language. Among other areas, the policy-maker must examine the social importance of each language or variety of language both at school and at home. The social importance of any language or variety of a language certainly must be viewed from the perspective of the wider society. However, such a perspective cannot ignore the minisociety of the students and of the educational setting, nor can it ignore the society that many students will want the option of joining—the deaf community. If the history of educating deaf students and of minority groups has shown anything, it is this: to attempt to dictate how friends and playmates communicate with each other is absurd; to ignore how friends and playmates communicate with each other is folly.

The relative importance of each language or variety of a given language must also be viewed from the perspective of its political importance. Although this generally means that the language of the majority is almost automatically accorded greater import, the political perspective of the minority group must not be ignored. Thus it is necessary to involve deaf adults who are not employees of the educational institution. These deaf adults, because they are not insulated by the educational institution, are able to provide insights into life after school. Their observations on the role and importance of language and communication in the social and internal and external political activities of deaf adults are crucial if educational institutions are to be successful in educating students for life.

Finally, the importance of each language or variety of a given language must be viewed from the perspective of economic importance. Again, it is generally the langauge of the majority that is accorded greater import. However, according the language of the majority greater economic import does not automatically translate into language policy. Thus, while the economic importance of a language may be justification for setting fluency in that language as one of the goals of the educational institution, such a determination does not address the means of achieving that goal, nor should it automatically exclude other languages or means of communication.

DISSEMINATING INFORMATION

Assuming that an accurate and objective description of the sociolinguistic situation is available, it must be shared with those groups that have a vested interest in the language policy of the educational institution. Certainly the parents, students, teachers, staff, and administrators must be involved in the process of describing the sociolinguistic situation. However, since much of the language policy will be based on the sociolinguistic description of the situation, this description must be shared with the relevant groups named above. The reason for this is obvious—these are the groups that are directly affected by the language policy and will ultimately determine whether the policy is successful or not. The descriptive information also provides the background information necessary for these groups to better understand the resultant language policy and how their needs and wishes are integrated into the overall policy.

Obviously the information must be disseminated in a manner that is accessible to the various groups. For example, it may be inappropriate (and certainly is insensitive) to rely solely on a written description if portions of the relevant groups are unable to read the material. Thus, the policy-maker must identify a number of dissemination strategies that can be used (for example, small group meetings, videotaped materials, audiotaped materials, written materials), and the material must be presented in a way that allows for modification and adaptations.

Failure to disseminate this information can only result in negative or apathetic reactions to the resultant language policy. Without sufficient explanation of the rationale for the policy, it will be viewed as another administrative fiat that need only be followed when officials are watching. It is also crucial that the dissemination of such information not be viewed as post-factum rationalization. The relevant groups must have confidence that the policy-maker is acting equitably and objectively. In order to gain the confidence of the various groups, ample time must be devoted to this phase of the development process. Once this time-consuming but essential step has been taken, the policy-maker is in a position to begin to develop a language policy that is sensitive to the sociolinguistic situation.

Unfortunately (and perhaps without realizing it) many institutions and individual educators have allowed "sign language" textbooks to determine their language policies. The selection of a specific textbook influences the way in which teachers, for example, can and cannot sign. (The fact that there is an overconcern for selecting a basic textbook may be a reflection of the communication skills of the faculty.) Rather than develop and adopt a language policy and then, if necessary, select textbooks that support and complement the policy, a textbook is selected and by default it becomes the "language policy." Often the decision about which textbook to adopt is based on the "-est" principle—the newest, cheapest, or biggest textbook available. Unfortunately it is often the case that authors of commercially available "sign language" texts do not have an accurate understanding of the language contact situation between ASL and English. Certainly there are some texts that provide excellent starting points for language policy development. However, even these texts should be validated against the local sociolinguistic situation. Even the best textbook cannot claim to provide an adequate sociolinguistic description that is complete enough, accurate enough, or specific enough for a given educational institution to use in policy development.

PROGRAM GOALS

It is apparent that before a language policy can be developed, the policy-maker must accurately understand the local sociolinguistic situation. It is also necessary that the policy-maker understand the perceived and actual goals of the educational program. In some cases, these goals have not been clearly articulated. However, they must be clearly stated before a viable language policy can be developed. Otherwise the policy may only reflect the goals of the educational program as the policy-maker perceives them. The importance of clearly and comprehensively articulating program goals cannot be understated—they have a direct bearing on the scope of communication strategies that may be sanctioned, and they indicate the extent to which the institution or program is sensitive to the needs and wishes of parents, students, teachers, staff, and administrators. In articulating the educational program goals, at least the following questions must be addressed.

Competence in English First, it is necessary to determine the operational parameters of the term English. What does the institution or program mean by "competence in English"—the ability to read and write English? the ability to speak and lipread English? the ability to use some manually coded form of English? all of these? a combination of these?

Certainly a universally accepted goal would be that the students in the program acquire competence in reading and writing English. While there is no opposition to such a goal, obviously there is much disagreement about the most effective means of achieving that goal. The well-documented failure of educational programs to achieve this goal should not be taken as an indication that the goal of literacy in English is misplaced, nor that deaf students have inherent limitations. Rather, it should be taken as an indication that the appropriate methods for achieving this goal have not yet been identified or implemented.

Defining competence in English to mean the ability to speak and lipread English is, in the context of educating deaf students, especially problematic. While there are some educational programs that report success in achieving this goal, the reality is that such a goal may be impractical for the vast majority of programs or, in some cases, may be partially attained only at great educational expense. Assuming that a program sets this as one of its operational parameters, the program will need to determine what it means by the ability to speak and lipread English. Is the goal that the students' speech will be intelligible to teachers and speech therapists, or is the goal that the students' speech will be intelligible to bankers, doctors, and store clerks who likely are unaccustomed to the speech of deaf individuals? If the former, such a goal is shortsighted and does not make best use of limited instructional time in preparing students for life. If the latter, this may represent an insidious form of oppression because it establishes a set of expectations for the student that cannot be readily met. In any event, it has yet to be shown that the universally accepted goal of competence in reading and writing English depends upon competence in speaking and lipreading English.

Defining competence in English as the ability to use a manually coded form of English is also problematic. Not only is the adequacy and ability of such codes to represent English questionable, but the extent to which they can be accurately and consistently used is highly suspect. If, despite this, a program wishes to define competence in English in this manner, there are several basic issues that

will need to be resolved: (1) Since all existing manual codes are based on written English, and since there are considerable differences between written English and spoken English, what difficulties will parents, students, and teachers encounter when they attempt to use the code for face-to-face communication? (2) Since existing manual codes are based on a variety of written English that reflects white, middle-class usage, what difficulties will parents, students, and teachers encounter when they attempt to use the code? For example, to what extent do parents who speak Black English have to learn to speak a white middle-class variety of English before they can use the coded form of English? (3) What difficulties will the students encounter when they attempt to communicate with deaf adults who do not know the code? (4) Given that there is little or no documentation to demonstrate that the use of coded forms of English facilitates reading and writing English, what difficulties will students face when, having learned the code, they are beginning to learn to read and write?

ASL Use Here the institution or educational program has several options. The option selected should certainly reflect the local sociolinguistic description. However, the institution or educational program must realize that the option selected may also have definite consequences for instructional methodology. Minimally, the institution or educational program must determine: whether ASL is to be used as a medium of instruction for certain academic content areas (that is, whether the institution wishes to adopt some form of bilingual program); whether ASL is to be taught as a separate academic subject; whether ASL (or the variety of ASL used by the students) is to be used only for recreational and social, and not academic, purposes; whether students who do not have skill in ASL will be given a formal opportunity to acquire it (other than from their peers and playmates); whether the teachers and staff will be expected to have receptive and expressive competence in ASL; whether the institution will assume any responsibility for providing formal instruction to parents, faculty, and staff who wish to learn ASL.

Even if the institution or educational program determines that ASL has no place in its educational program, this must be clearly stated. Further, the documented rationale for such determination must be provided to the parents, faculty, staff, and students. In other words, the institution must be able to document and support those language and communication areas that are not addressed by its policy as well as those areas that are addressed.

Academic Goals The institution or educational program must determine whether it wishes the students to attain competence in academic subjects regardless of which language is used for instruction or whether competence in academic subjects is to be attained by using only a specified language. For example, is it more important that the students learn history, or that the history they do learn is acquired by using English? Support for the former position comes not only from spoken-language bilingual programs in the United States but also from the educational experiences of a number of multilingual countries, while support for the latter position comes from traditional practices in the field of educating deaf students.

Cultural Awareness The institution or educational program will undoubtedly want its students to develop an understanding of and sensitivity toward the majority (hearing) culture. This would seem to be a rather universally accepted goal for deaf students. However, the institution must address the issue of whether it wishes its students to have the formal opportunity to develop an understanding of and sensitivity toward minority cultures, including the culture of deaf people. Indeed, it is difficult to imagine how an institution could expect its students to develop a healthy attitude toward the majority culture if the institution ignores or rejects the culture of deaf people. However, if, even in the face of an accurate description of the sociolinguistic local situation, an institution decides to ignore the minority cultures, then at least the rationale for such a decision must be clearly articulated.

DESIRED LINGUISTIC BEHAVIORS

In the language policy development process, of central importance is the stage at which desired linguistic or communicative behaviors are identified. This stage is frequently the most problematic for institutions and educational programs. However, it is far less problematic for institutions and programs that have a clear description of the local sociolinguistic situation, have clearly articulated their educational goals, and have effectively disseminated this information. For such programs, identifying the desired linguistic or communicative behaviors that will best achieve stated educational goals is simply the logical next step.

Unfortunately, this single stage of the overall process is often equated with developing a language policy. Institutions and programs have historically established committees to undertake this task. These committees (often misleadingly called standardization committees or sign selection committees) are generally ill-equipped to handle the task, not only because the members of the committee lack the necessary language planning background and expertise, but also because they do not have accurate or comprehensive descriptive sociolinguistic information with which to work. Nevertheless, these committees forge on and, in their enthusiasm and naiveté, perceive their task as one of determining what will be chosen as the standard reference text. In some instances, more ambitious (but equally naive) committees determine that they must develop their own standard reference text. The reality is that all members of such a committee bring their own descriptions of the sociolinguistic situation and their own perceptions of the educational goals. These unarticulated descriptions and perceptions greatly influence the workings of the committee. In the end, a text may be chosen or developed without a clearly stated rationale or, worse, with an unstated rationale that is fraught with internal contradictions. Then the primary affected groups have little or no assurance that their concerns were addressed. The result is a stated language policy toward which no one feels any sense of ownership, investment, or responsibility.

Clearly the specification of desired linguistic behaviors must flow from the sociolinguistic description and the articulation of educational goals. Although those are time-consuming steps, they are necessary if the primary affected groups are to feel that the policy is reasonable and workable. Specification of the desired linguistic or communicative behaviors will involve several considerations.

One consideration is comfort. Will the faculty, staff, students, and parents be able to achieve a reasonable level of comfort in using the desired behaviors? If they are unable to do so (either because of the complexity of the set of linguistic behaviors or because the desired set of linguistic behaviors requires them to segment their communication in unnatural ways), they will not adhere to the desired behaviors. Then what transpires in the educational setting will be far removed from the stated language policy.

A second consideration is consistency. Will the faculty, staff, students, and parents be able to achieve a reasonable level of consistency in their use of the desired linguistic behaviors? Otherwise, the language and communication models presented to the students will be haphazardly inconsistent and will preclude or seriously impair achievement of stated educational goals.

A third consideration is cohesiveness. Does the set of desired linguistic behaviors make sense in light of the sociolinguistic description of the local situation and in light of the stated educational goals? If the desired behaviors are in opposition to the sociolinguistic environment (and if they are, the deviation should be clearly explained), then it is likely that internal and external social pressures will erode the stated language policy.

A final consideration is communication. Does the set of desired linguistic behaviors have the flexibility to allow individuals to communicate freely and naturally about a range of topics and needs? If the desired behaviors are restrictive, individuals are faced with a choice—either avoid communicating about certain topics or in certain ways, or use some other means of communication. The first option is clearly impractical, and the second renders the stated language policy meaningless.

EDUCATIONAL PROGRAM IMPLICATIONS

Assuming that the stages outlined above have been followed, an institution or educational program then has a language policy that includes an accurate sociolinguistic description of the local situation, a clearly articulated set of educational goals, and a set of desired linguistic behaviors with a cohesive, relevant rationale for these behaviors. However, there are certain program parameters that must be reviewed in reference to the language policy. Again, whatever the outcome of the review, it should be clearly articulated and disseminated. Among the program parameters that must be reviewed are at least the following.

Grouping Criteria   Traditionally accepted grouping criteria (for example, audiometric test results) may be inappropriate in consideration of the language policy. For example, within certain limits, students perhaps should be grouped on the basis of the extent to which they match the desired linguistic behaviors set forth in the language policy. Traditionally, approximately 10% of the students entering an educational program have deaf parents. Presumably, these students already have a level of competence in some variety of sign language. The remaining 90% of entering students (whose parents are hearing and use a spoken language to which the child has had little or no access) are essentially alingual—that is, they have no first language. Since the former group needs language enrichment opportunities and has a linguistic base with which to begin learning or acquiring English, and since the latter group needs first-language acquisition opportunities, it may be inappropriate to mix them together.

Additionally, one could argue that provision of first-language acquisition opportunities should at least acknowledge that these students become fluent in the language (or variety of language) used by their peers much more rapidly than they become fluent in the means of communication used by their teachers—often despite the repressive attempts of educators. However, generally the level of competence attained by these students in the language of their peers is ignored or denied by educators. The reasons undoubtedly have to do with unconditional acceptance, comfort, and naturalness. It is at least worth considering that the first language that alingual students would be exposed to (and expected to acquire) should be like that used by their peers. This language would then become the solid foundation needed to achieve stated educational goals.

Teacher Competencies and Qualifications   Certainly one would expect that the desired linguistic behaviors specified in the language policy would be reflected in the future hiring practices of the institution or program. It is reasonable to expect that the institution would actively seek out those applicants who were able to demonstrate competence in the desired behaviors. Failure to do so means that the institution or program is faced with a constant retraining problem. Obviously it may not be possible to fill every vacancy with individuals competent in the desired linguistic behaviors. However, it is in the best interests of the institution or program to make the effort.

A more difficult programmatic issue concerns the existing faculty and staff. Certainly the institution has a responsibility to provide instructional opportunities for them to gain competence in the desired set of linguistic behaviors. The level of competence to be attained should be related to the specific responsibilities of the position and to the amount of student interaction. However, retraining opportunities cannot be provided indefinitely. There must be a time limit within which existing faculty and staff either will achieve a specified level of competence or will be replaced or reassigned. Such a step is necessary if the language policy is to have any force and meaning. There must be a clearly stated, functional, job-related assessment of the communication competence of the faculty, staff, and administrators. The assessment must be administered regularly so that individuals have the opportunity to demonstrate growth toward competence and so that job-related decisions are not based on a single assessment. In brief, the policy must be perceived as a positive one, and one to be taken seriously.

Family Learning Opportunities   In addition to the retraining opportunities offered to the faculty, staff, and administrators, the institution or program has a responsibility to offer instructional opportunities to the family members of its students. Such opportunities should be afforded to family members on an ongoing basis. Special consideration should be given to the instructional needs of, for example, siblings, parents, grandparents, neighbors, relatives, and playmates. Also, special consideration may have to be given to those family members who are not fluent in English. Access to the instruction is also a consideration—time, locale, and cost. In short, the instructional program that is offered to the faculty and staff cannot simply be offered to family members.

SUMMARY

A language policy should be developed that is reasonable, sociolinguistically sensitive, and has a high probability of success. This development process is dynamic and cyclical. Once the policy has been in place for a period of time, the sociolinguistic situation changes accordingly. New information must be considered as possible changes are contemplated and as adjustments are made. This information and the altered situation must be accounted for and reflected in the policy. The cyclic nature of the process can be seen in the major steps of the policy development process: Describe the current sociolinguistic situation of the deaf students in the program and of the local deaf community. Disseminate this sociolinguistic information to parents, students, teachers, staff, and administrators. Articulate the perceived and actual goals of the educational program. Determine the linguistic behaviors that will most effectively enable the institution or educational program to achieve its goals. Identify the implications of the desired linguistic behaviors for educational program decisions. Provide training and growth-toward-competence assessment opportunities. Reexamine the sociolinguistic situation periodically and regularly.

Clearly the decision to undertake development of a language policy involves a major commitment on the part of an institution or program. The steps outlined above ensure that the vital area of language and communication receives an appropriate amount of institutional time.

Bibliography

Abrahams, R., and R. Troike (eds.): *Language and Cultural Diversity in American Education*, 1972.

Baker, C., and D. Cokely: *American Sign Language: A Teacher's Resource Text on Grammar and Culture*, 1980.

Cobarrubias, J., and J. Fishman (eds.): *Progress in Language Planning*, 1983.

Cokely, D.: *Pre-College Programs: Guidelines for Manual Communication*, 1979.

————: "Program Considerations in a Bilingual ASL-English Approach to Education," *Proceedings of the 1978 National Symposium on Sign Language Research and Teaching*, 1980.

————: "Sign Language: Teaching, Interpreting and Educational Policy," *Sign Language and the Deaf Community: Essays in Honor of William C. Stokoe*, 1980.

Fishman, J. (ed.): *Advances in Language Planning*, 1974.

Jernudd, B., and J. Rubin (eds.): *Can Language Be Planned?*, 1971.

Rubin, J. (ed.): *Language Planning Processes*, 1977.

Tucker, R.: "The Linguistic Perspective," *Bilingual Education: Current Perspectives*, 1977.

Stokoe, W.: "The Use of Sign in Teaching English," *American Annals of the Deaf*, vol. 120, no. 4, 1975.

Dennis Cokely

Total Communication

Total communication is a term that has been used to describe two very different but related concepts concerning communication with deaf people. In its broad and philosophical sense, the term refers to the right of the deaf individual to have easy access to a wide spectrum of useful forms of communication. However, most people who use the term mean the method of communication used by deaf students that combine both speech and sign (or fingerspelling).

ORIGIN IN THE UNITED STATES

During the 1960s, educators in the United States questioned the way in which deaf children were being taught. A number of research studies had brought attention to some educational limitations for severely congenitally deaf children in which the emphasis was placed upon oral teaching methods. In contrast, studies of some young deaf children of deaf parents indicated that early use of signing and fingerspelling had a beneficial effect on social and educational development. Experimental studies carried out in some schools suggested that teaching by methods including manual communication helped English language development.

The concern about the shortcomings of exclusively oral communication for some deaf children, together with a growing awareness of the potential value of manual communication, gave rise to an attitude that encouraged the use of combined oral and manual teaching methods. While such an approach developed on a wide front in American schools, it was in California that a descriptive term emerged. Dorothy Shifflett, a teacher and parent of a deaf child, combined signing and fingerspelling with speech and lipreading in her teaching, and described this as a total approach to communication. In 1968 Roy Holcomb became supervisor of a program for deaf students in Santa Ana and introduced combined communication at all age levels, which he called total communication.

This term was adopted for the educational approach at the Maryland School for the Deaf. David Denton, superintendent of the Maryland School, outlined the methodological options of total communication as comprising "the full spectrum of language modes: child devised gesture, sign language, speech, speechreading, fingerspelling, reading and writing."

The term total communication caught the imagination of deaf and hard-of-hearing people, and its use soon spread. As a liberal force that encouraged an openness to all forms of communication that could be of assistance to deaf children, it did not take easily to precise definition, but by 1976 widespread interest and use led to a definition of an official nature. The Conference of Executives of American Schools for the Deaf (CEASD), at their Forty-Eighth meeting, agreed upon a definition of total communication as "a philosophy incorporating the appropriate aural, manual, and oral modes of communication in order to ensure effective communication with and among hearing impaired persons." *See* CONFERENCE OF EDUCATIONAL ADMINISTRATORS SERVING THE DEAF.

In 1979 D. Cokely took the argument one step further, stating that total communication is a philosophy that is child-centered, not method-centered. He added ASL, art, gestures, pantomime, and drama to the list of potential strategies for communication, noting that the selection of a particular strategy should depend on the student's most effective receptive and expressive means of communication, the goals and constraints of the situation, and the communication skills of the other people involved.

These and other descriptions of the nature of total communication emphasize that it is a philosophy (an attitude toward communication) rather than just a method (a precise way of communicating or teaching). But the total communication movement had a powerful influence on actual teaching methods in schools. A survey conducted in a large sample of American schools in 1978 gave a picture of the change to combined (speech with sign) teaching methods. Within a period of 10 years nearly four-fifths of the schools had changed their communication practice; two-thirds of the classes were reported as using a total communication approach.

DEVELOPMENTS IN EUROPE

The developments in the United States were paralleled by events in Great Britain. Growing dissatisfaction with the quality of communication, English language ability, and educational attainment of deaf children in the predominantly oral climate of British schools in the 1960s led to the setting up of a government committee of inquiry to consider the possible place of fingerspelling and signing. The report in 1968 of the committee—popularly known as the Lewis Report—strongly upheld the need for oral communication and for improved conditions for teaching oral skills, but also recommended that research should be carried out to determine whether the use of manual media of communication would lead to improvements in the education of deaf children. This influential report—which revealed that manual communication was in fact being used quite widely, albeit in an unplanned manner—opened the way for the scientific study of communication in British schools in the 1970s, including the evaluation of the results of teaching by mainly oral means and also the introduction of combined teaching methods. *See* ENGLAND, EDUCATION IN.

Following this report, a major study was carried out jointly by the Northern Counties School for the Deaf and the University of Newcastle upon Tyne. This led to the development of a teaching method that combined speech and lipreading with signing and fingerspelling. Through links with American

schools, notably the Maryland School for the Deaf, the influence of the total communication approach was fairly direct. By the mid-1970s a number of other schools in England had introduced combined methods of teaching, including some of the older schools with past experience of using signing and fingerspelling but also some of the more recently opened schools that were introducing manual forms of communication for the first time. In Scotland there had been research into the effects of combining speech with signing, and this influenced the teaching methods in schools and the wide use of total communication in Scotland. In 1980 a survey of practices in schools for deaf children in Great Britain indicated that a majority were by then using combined teaching methods.

The growth of combined teaching methods in schools brought demands for new teaching skills, as the majority of teachers of deaf pupils in Britain had trained on courses that did not include systematic study or instruction in manual communication. In 1983 the British Deaf Association cooperated with the National Deaf Children's Society in organizing a seminar to consider this problem, together with other implications for the implementation of total communication. The recommendations in the report of this seminar gave priority to the development of facilities for training teachers in the theoretical and practical aspects of total communication, for counseling and training parents and families of deaf children, and for the production of teaching materials.

Also in 1983 teachers in schools came together to consider ways of improving their work. By 1984 they had formed the North of England Total Communication Group, which gained support from teachers and other professionals concerned with the assessment and education of deaf children and support of their families.

Sweden   In Sweden in the 1960s, there was concern about levels of educational attainment for deaf children and pressure for manual communication to be brought back into use in schools. A change of outlook led to the introduction of sign language as a subject for study in Swedish schools for deaf students. The Swedish National Association of the Deaf encouraged the acceptance of signing by parents of deaf children and the use of total communication. This was supported by the government, and a law passed in 1969 recommended the use of signing and fingerspelling in schools. *See* SWEDEN.

Denmark   In Denmark there was a rapid and wide acceptance of total communication. This was helped by the work of the Total Communication Center in Copenhagen, an organization that offered training to parents and professionals, and produced resource materials to support teaching. By 1980 the special schools for deaf people, the national college of continuing education, and most of the special units for hearing-impaired children had adopted total communication. *See* DENMARK.

Belgium In Belgium the oral tradition was changed at first through the introduction of cued speech in French-speaking schools. This in turn led to the use of total communication, including use in some Flemish-speaking schools. *See* BELGIUM; MOUTH-HAND SYSTEMS: Cued Speech.

Netherlands The Netherlands has a strong oral tradition, but the audiological centers for early assessment of young children have acknowledged the need for manual communication from an early age. The Dutch Foundation for the Deaf and Hard of Hearing, in its center at Amsterdam, provides full training in communication for parents. With the support of the University of Groningen, the Groningen School for the Deaf set up a research project to study and guide the practice of total communication. *See* NETHERLANDS.

WORLDWIDE TREND

As total communication became established in the United States, so it became accepted in Canada. The concept soon gained recognition in other countries, and has developed into a worldwide trend. *See* CANADA.

Australia and New Zealand In Australia there had been a history of less extreme difference of educational opinion than in some European countries, with some schools using oral methods and some using combined methods. By the close of the 1970s, all of the Australian states had a major school practicing total communication. *See* AUSTRALIA.

In New Zealand the oral tradition of education was challenged by total communication. Teachers, psychologists, and parents pressed for a change, and this led to choice of teaching method. In 1979 the New Zealand Department of Education made a clear statement on total communication which prescribed that a standard sign system should be used (the Victorian sign system from Australia) with two-handed fingerspelling. It also gave parents the right to have their views considered. *See* NEW ZEALAND.

Other Countries. As in Australia and New Zealand, the education of deaf children in Malaysia had been influenced by the British oral tradition. The Federation School for the Deaf at Penang was originally set up as an oral school, but in due course concern with educational attainments led to a change to a combined approach.

Knowledge of total communication has also influenced practice in such countries as Sri Lanka, Thailand, South Africa, Nigeria, the Philippines, and Brazil. The People's Republic of China has a vast number of deaf children in special schools, who are taught through speech, signing, and fingerspelling. There is also an increasing use of total communication in schools in Japan. See BRAZIL; CHINA, PEOPLE'S REPUBLIC OF; JAPAN; NIGERIA; PHILIPPINES; SOUTH AFRICA, REPUBLIC OF; SRI LANKA; THAILAND.

By the 1980s the term total communication was used widely in countries throughout the world, both as a philosophical attitude toward the communication needs of deaf people and to describe the way deaf children are taught in schools. With few exceptions (for example, Sweden and Denmark), communication methods in schools supporting total communication have not included the use of indigenous sign languages such as American Sign Language.

LINGUISTIC STRUCTURE

The concept of total communication, by its all-embracing nature, comprises a wide network of linguistic forms. It places value on oral communication through speech, including speechreading and aural reception of speech with suitable hearing aids for individuals with usable residual hearing. Essentially, however, total communication includes the use of manual media of communication, particularly signing and fingerspelling. These various forms of communication may be used independently or in combination, according to the needs and preferences of individuals concerned or to the circumstances in which they are used.

The essence of total communication, particularly in situations involving both deaf and hearing persons, is simultaneous communication in speech and signing. The form of signing used will usually follow the pattern of the spoken language (for example, signed English), and varies in different countries. The advance of total communication did much to popularize the use and study of sign languages.

Some schools using total communication regard cued speech as one possible form of communication. In Denmark, which had its own early form of cued speech, total communication includes the use of Danish Sign Language, signed Danish, and the mouth-hand system of supplementing speechreading with handshapes.

Bibliography

Cokely, D.: *Pre-College Programs Guidelines for Manual Communication*, Gallaudet College, Pre-College Programs, Washington, D.C., 1979.

Denton, D.: "A Rationale for Total Communication," In T. J. O'Rourke (ed.), *Psycholinguistics and Total Communication: The State of the Art*, American Annals of the Deaf, Silver Spring, Maryland, pp. 53–61, 1972.

Evans, L.: *Total Communication: Structure and Strategy*, Gallaudet College Press, Washington, D.C., 1982.

Jordan, I. K., G. Gustason, and R. Rosen: "An Update

on Communication Trends and Programs for the Deaf," *American Annals of the Deaf*, 124:350–357, 1979.

Lionel Evans

Simultaneous Communication

Simultaneous communication (also called simcom) is a method that is often used by hearing and deaf people when talking with each other. When using this method, a person will speak or mouth English words and, at the same time, use signs that are supposed to convey the same meaning as the English words. Occasionally, words are fingerspelled (using the manual alphabet) instead of signed.

Simultaneous communication is often confused with total communication. Many people, especially educators, use the term total communication when they mean speaking and signing (with fingerspelling) at the same time. However, the original meaning of total communication is a philosophy of deaf education advocating the use of a variety of communication methods, whereas simultaneous communication is simply one of those methods.

HISTORY

Historically, within the field of deaf education, simcom has also been called the simultaneous method of communication and has been defined as a combination of the oral method plus signs and fingerspelling. This method first appeared in deaf education in the twentieth century as oralism began to take greater hold on the thinking and policies of American educators.

Before the spread of oralism, most schools in the United States were manual—both teachers and students signed in the classroom without speaking. As some educators, notably the wealthy and prestigious Alexander Graham Bell, began to argue more and more strongly about the importance of speech training, many schools began to use the combined method. *See* BELL, ALEXANDER GRAHAM.

In general, the combined method meant that both the manual method and the oral method were used within a school or educational program. Sometimes signs were used part of the time and speech and lipreading were used the rest of the time. A student's day might be divided this way. Sometimes, an institution would divide its students according to their age and degree of hearing loss and then communicate with one group manually and with the other, orally. Later, especially in the twentieth century, students' primary education might be totally oral, whereas their secondary education might be totally manual.

This belief in the importance of speech and lipreading in deaf education eventually led most American educators to the decision that teachers should speak all the time. By 1950 most programs for elementary-age children were officially completely oral, as were many programs for older students. For the minority of schools and teachers who still believed that signing was also important in deaf education, this decision often resulted in the use of simultaneous communication.

However, the use of simcom began to spread rapidly in the late 1960s and early 1970s as educators became disappointed with the negative results of oral-only educational methods. Studies during that period showed that deaf children of deaf parents who used manual communication were academically superior to other students. By 1978 some 481 programs for deaf students had abandoned oral-only methods and 538 programs had begun to use simcom (calling it total communication).

USAGE

Simcom is now used by most teachers in most schools for deaf children across the United States. It is officially endorsed as the standard method of communication at Gallaudet College and is the most frequently used method at the National Technical Institute for the Deaf in Rochester, New York. It is also rapidly being adopted by teachers and schools in many other countries that are moving away from a strictly oral method of instruction.

In addition to the classroom, simcom is frequently used in interactions between hearing and deaf people, especially if one or more of the hearing persons is not a fluent signer. In these situations, the hearing person's lip movements (and sometimes voice) may help the deaf person understand parts of the information that the hearing person does not sign intelligibly or does not communicate at all in signs. Similarly, the deaf person's lip movements (and sometimes speech) may help the hearing person understand parts of the message that might be missed if the deaf person used signs alone.

Sometimes both the hearing and deaf signers in a group choose to use simcom when there is a hearing or hard-of-hearing person present who does not know sign language. Speech will be produced for the benefit of the hearing or hard-of-hearing person, and signs will be for the benefit of the other signers.

With the exception of mixed deaf-hearing situations like those described above, deaf people almost never use simcom when signing with each other. In fact, it seems to be a rule of deaf culture that deaf people should not use their voices in deaf-deaf interactions. When deaf people are asked if they talk while signing with other deaf people, the typical response is negative. Carol Padden, a deaf linguist, gave a reason for this cultural rule by explaining that traditionally speech was forced on deaf people and it represented confinement and denial of the need of deaf people to communicate in their own language. The written records of the practices of deaf Americans from the early 1800s into the late twentieth century show that the deaf people who sign have generally preferred not to use their voices when communicating with each other.

STRUCTURE

When people sign and speak at the same time, their signs generally follow the word order of the spoken language. Thus, a person speaking English will try to use signs that in some way correspond to the English words and will make the signs in the order in which the words are said. It is not possible to speak one language, such as English, and sign another language, such as American Sign Language (ASL), simultaneously. This is because the structures—the word-sign orders and the way the languages express meanings—are very different.

However, there are many different ways in which individuals as well as whole educational programs sign in English word order. These differences can be categorized into three groups: (1) signing that tries to follow the rules of one of the new (1970s) manual codes for English; (2) an older form of signing that is modeled after English but generally does not use any of the new signs and tends to use much more fingerspelling; and (3) a form of signing that has been called Pidgin Sign English and that may involve using some of the grammatical features of ASL.

Manual Codes for English The manual codes for English refer to systems invented in the early 1970s with the goal of helping deaf students learn English by exposing them to a supposed, signed form of English. These systems include Signed English, SEE (Signing Exact English) I, and SEE II. Most of the people who use these systems always speak while they sign.

A person using a manual code for English generally tries to make a sign for each word and affix (such as -ing, -ed, -s) that the person says. These codes include many signs that were invented to represent English affixes. The codes have also taken many signs from ASL, but often have changed their meaning and the way they are made.

For example, suppose a person wants to say the sentence "She is running for the office of President" and, at the same time, sign the sentence following the rules of SEE II. The person would use an invented sign for "she," then a sign that looks like the ASL sign TRUE but has a different handshape for "is," then a sign that means "go fast by foot" in ASL for "run," then an invented sign for "-ing," then a sign that sometimes means "for" in ASL, then an invented sign for "the," then a sign for "office" that looks like the ASL sign ROOM but has a different handshape, then a sign for "of" that

means "connect to" in ASL, and then the ASL sign for "President." People who use this kind of simcom try to synchronize their signs with their words, producing each corresponding sign and word at the same time.

Modeling English A much older attempt to model English "on the hands" can still be seen in the signing of many older Gallaudet graduates, especially in formal situations. People who sign in this way sometimes use their voices (simcom) and sometimes do not. Since this form of signing was developed among people who were often fluent ASL signers as well, it generally does not change the meaning or form of ASL signs (unlike the newer manual codes). And instead of inventing new signs for English affixes, it either omits them or fingerspells those words that do not have direct ASL equivalents.

For example, to sign the sentence "She is running for the office of President," the person might point with the index finger to a place for "she," then use the ASL sign TRUE for "is," then use the ASL sign COMPETE for "running" (with no separate sign or fingerspelling of "-ing"), then make the ASL sign that means "for," then fingerspell "the office of," and then use the ASL sign PRESIDENT. People who use this kind of signing in simcom also tend to synchronize their words with their signs.

Pidgin Sign English The third way of signing that often is used when people are also speaking has been called Pidgin Sign English because it involves features from both sign (ASL) and English and because some linguists in the 1970s thought it looked like a "pidgin" language. However, a more recent study of this kind of signing has determined that it is actually "foreigner talk" (a way that deaf people sign when they are trying to sign more like English) and "learners' grammar" (a way that hearing people sign when they are not yet fluent in ASL).

This kind of signing has a lot of variation. A person's signing can change as the individual becomes more skilled in ASL or English, so people with different skills may sign in different ways. However, if they are speaking at the same time (using simcom), they will almost always follow English word order (and not ASL sign order).

For example, in the sentence "She is running for the office of President," a person might say those words while making the following signs: point with the index finger for "she," then use the ASL sign VOLUNTEER that can mean "to run for (a position)," then use the ASL sign that sometimes means "for," then fingerspell "office" or use the ASL sign WORK, and then use the ASL sign PRESIDENT. In this example, the words "is," "the," and "of" were not signed or fingerspelled. In this case, there are no rules for how a person will sign, but it often seems that people do not sign the unnecessary words—the words that can be dropped without losing the meaning of the sentence.

Similarity of Methods These three ways that people sign in English word order are, in practice, not really separated. For example, hearing people who are not yet fluent in ASL may be using the kind of signing described in the third category but may also use some of the invented signs from the manual codes because they do not know that these signs are not ASL signs. Or, deaf people who are using the older form of modeling English while they speak may neglect to fingerspell or sign some of the small words, which then makes their signing look more like the third category.

RESEARCH

Studies of simcom have focused on the questions of (1) whether it helps deaf students to learn English; (2) whether it is an effective way to communicate in the classroom; and (3) what happens to speech and signs when both are performed together.

Different studies of the first two questions have had different, conflicting results. The methods used in many of these studies have also been criticized. For example, most of the studies that say that simcom (using a manual code for English) helped deaf students improve their English skills actually showed that the students improved in their use of the manual English code, but did not measure any improvement in their English reading and writing skills. Since the manual codes for English are unlike the English language in many important ways, a student's skill in using a manual code is not necessarily related to the student's knowledge of English. Most of the studies have not controlled for the socioeconomic status of the student's parents; but this is a major factor influencing academic performance.

Studies of the effectiveness of simcom—for example, on how well deaf students understand and learn from teachers who use simcom—have had conflicting results. Several studies have compared the test results of students whose teachers used simcom, an interpreter, or sign only (without speaking). Some studies found that simcom gave the best results, some that sign only was best, and some that using an interpreter was best. Most of these studies involved fairly unnatural testing situations, and the reports of the studies do not provide much information about how they actually were done.

Unlike the studies mentioned above, studies of the third question have had very similar results and have revealed a number of major problems that arise when people use simcom. Some of these are that people's spoken English often becomes much

less grammatical; the meanings of the signs often do not match the meanings of the English words; and the rate at which hearing people communicate with simcom is much slower than when they only speak or only sign.

Another serious problem is that hearing people often do not sign everything they say. In fact, they often do not sign important things such as nouns and verbs so that what they sign often does not make sense. Most hearing people are not aware that this is happening, and as a result, deaf people often have difficulty in understanding hearing people when they use simcom.

Most linguists who have studied simcom say that these problems are primarily caused by how difficult it is to speak and sign simultaneously. Although some people, especially deaf people, are better at it than others, even the best simcom users find that it requires a great deal of energy and attention, which limits their ability to communicate comfortably.

Bibliography

Baker, C. L.: "How Does 'Sim-Com' Fit into a Bilingual Approach to Education?", in F. Caccamise and D. Hicks (eds.), *Proceedings of the Second National Symposium on Sign Language Research and Teaching*, National Association of the Deaf, Silver Spring, Maryland, pp. 13–26, 1980.

Caccamise, F. (ed.): "Sign Language and Simultaneous Communication: Linguistic, Psychological, and Instructional Ramifications," *American Annals of the Deaf*, November 1978.

Cokely, D. R.: "The Effectiveness of Three Means of Communication in the College Classroom," Linguistics Research Lab manuscript, Gallaudet College, Washington, D.C., September 1982.

————: *Pre-College Programs: Guidelines for Manual Communication*, Gallaudet College, Washington, D.C., 1979.

————: "When Is a Pidgin Not a Pidgin? An Alternate Analysis of the ASL-English Contact Situation," *Sign Language Studies*, 38:1–24, Spring 1983.

Gallaudet, E. M.: "Report of the President on the Systems of Deaf-Mute Instruction Pursued in Europe," *Tenth Annual Report of the Columbia Institution for the Deaf and Dumb*, Gallaudet College Archives, Washington, D.C., 1867.

Johnson, R. E. (chair): *Sign Language Use and Evaluation*, report to the collegiate faculty of Gallaudet College by the Simultaneous Communication Advisory Board, Gallaudet College, Washington, D.C., December 1983.

Kluwin, T. N.: "The Grammaticality of Manual Representations of English in Classroom Settings," *American Annals of the Deaf*, pp. 417–421, June 1981.

————: "A Rationale for Modifying Classroom Signing Systems," *Sign Language Studies*, 31:179–188, Spring 1981.

Marmor, G., and L. A. Petitto: "Simultaneous Communication in the Classroom: How Well Is English Grammar Represented?", *Sign Language Studies*, 23:99–136, Spring 1979.

Padden, C. A.: "The Deaf Community and the Culture of Deaf People," in C. Baker and R. Battison (eds.), *Sign Language and the Deaf Community*, National Association of the Deaf, Silver Spring, Maryland, pp. 89–103, 1980.

Charlotte Baker-Shenk

Bilingualism

Bilingualism—the regular use of two or more languages—remains a poorly understood and controversial topic in the language sciences. It is surrounded by a number of myths and misunderstandings which are often amplified when one deals with the bilingualism of deaf people. Yet practically every deaf person is bilingual, to some extent at least. In the first part of this article, bilingualism will be characterized in general: the difference that exists between societal and individual bilingualism will be examined; bilingualism and cognitive development will be touched on; and the bilingual's different speech modes will be described. The second part of the article will examine the bilingualism of deaf people: the language rights of deaf people will be evoked; the types of bilingualism that can be found among deaf people will be described; and the differences that exist between the bilingualism of hearing and deaf people will be stressed.

CHARACTERIZATION

One of the many myths that surround bilingualism is that bilinguals are equally fluent in their two languages. In fact, such people are rare exceptions. People become bilingual because they have to interact with the world around them in two or more languages, and they develop their competence in these languages to the extent needed. This can sometimes mean speaking both languages in all domains of life, but more often it means using these languages in specific domains, speaking one language and only reading or writing the other language, and so on. Seen in this way, bilingualism becomes an extremely widespread phenomenon: it is found in all classes of society, in all age groups, in all countries. It has been estimated that half the world's population is bilingual. When the definition is extended to the use of dialects and language varieties and styles,—then practically everyone is bilingual.

Societal Bilingualism A distinction is often made between societal (group) bilingualism and individual bilingualism. Societal bilingualism—where a whole group uses two or more languages in its everyday life—can be due to a number of factors, such as the movement of peoples for political, economic, or religious reasons, nationalism and political federation, intermarriage, education, and deafness. Whenever two groups with different languages come into contact, it is usually the minority group that learns the majority group's language. The minority language will sometimes be recognized officially, thus leading to official bilingualism, as in Canada or Finland. More often, however, it will be neglected, as are the minority languages in the United States, or actually repressed, as was Catalan in Spain under the Franco regime and as are many sign languages throughout the world.

The official policy of a nation toward its languages bears no relation to the number of bilinguals it contains: Canada is officially bilingual but has few bilinguals; Tanzania is officially monolingual but has many bi- or trilinguals.

The language used in education best exemplifies the policy of a nation toward its minority languages. In most cases, the majority language is the only language used in schools, and minority children are forced to become bilingual. Sometimes the minority language is used concurrently with the majority language until the children have acquired enough of the latter to be educated in it (this form of transitional bilingual education is the most widespread in the United States, for example). Only rarely are the two languages employed throughout the school years (true bilingual education).

The status that the majority group gives to the minority language has important consequences for the minority group's attitudes toward it and on how they use it. If the attitude is negative, some may refuse to teach it to their children; others will not use it in particular situations; still others will report they do not know the language well. The coexistence of two or more languages within a speech community and the status and use of each language are studied by sociolinguists under the topic of diglossia.

Societal bilingualism usually evolves over time. The bilingual group may retain its bilingualism, as when it uses two languages for its own internal needs (as do the Paraguayans with Spanish and Guaraní, or the Swiss Germans with Swiss German and standard German) or when political federalism demands the use of a lingua franca (as in the use of Swahili in east African nations). It can also shift to monolingualism in the majority language (as in the language evolution of immigrant groups in the United States), revert to monolingualism in the minority language (as in the case of many Hungarians after World War I), or it can develop a new language by combining two or more languages in the form of a "creole" (as in Haitian Creole or New Guinea's Tok Pisin).

Bilingualism is not coextensive with biculturalism. Although the two are often linked, one also finds bilingualism without biculturalism (as in the case of Swiss Germans or users of a lingua franca) and biculturalism without bilingualism (as in the case of many American Jews, French Basques, and Bretons).

Individual Bilingualism   The study of individual bilingualism concentrates on how people become bilingual, how they separate their languages or let them interact depending on the speech mode they are in, what it means to have a bilingual language competence, the effects of bilingualism on a person's psychology and cognitive development, and so on. Bilingual children acquire their two languages either simultaneously (in infancy) or successively (usually when they first go to school). Although the stages of bilingual development will depend on the age at onset of bilingualism, all children will acquire their second language to the extent needed in everyday communication, and will forget it as quickly as they learned it if it is no longer of any use. Despite decades of research on the effects of bilingualism on a child's intelligence, linguistic skills, and personality and cognitive development, no definite and uncontroversial conclusion has been reached. No study has been able to isolate the sole effect of the regular use of two languages from other factors such as socioeconomic status, cultural and educational background, or family environment. These are the factors that are usually responsible for the so-called advantages or disadvantages of bilingualism, and not bilingualism as such.

Emphasis is slowly shifting from studying adult bilinguals as two separate monolinguals (which they are not) to examining their communicative competence as bilinguals in their different speech modes. Bilinguals, in their daily lives, find themselves at various points along a situational scale (continuum) that trigger a particular speech mode. At one end of the scale, they are speaking to monolinguals and thus in a totally monolingual mode. They have to deactivate their own language as best they can so that it does not interfere with the language being used. Total deactivation is usually quite rare, however, as shown by the interferences (mistakes) bilinguals sometimes make when they communicate with monolinguals.

At the other end of the scale, bilinguals are speaking to other bilinguals with whom they normally mix languages. (Intermediary stages also exist along the continuum.) Here bilinguals first choose which language to use with one another according to a complex set of situational, communicational, and interpersonal factors, and then choose whether to use various elements of one language when speaking the other. One way of doing this is to code-switch, that is, to shift completely to the other language for a word, a phrase, a clause, or a sentence. For example, an English-French bilingual may be speaking French to another bilingual but may switch into English at two different points in the sentence: "Va chercher Marc *and bribe him* avec un chocolat chaud *with cream on top.*" (Go get Marc . . . with a hot chocolate . . .) Considerable research has been done on the factors that explain code-switching, the constraints that govern it, and the way it evolves in different language environments. The other way of bringing in the other language is to borrow a word from that language and to adapt it (integrate it) into the base language, as in "Il faut *mixer* cela." (One has to mix that.) Here "mix" is taken from English and adapted phonologically and morphologically into French. (These types of idiosyncratic speech borrowings are at the source of the better-known language borrowings.)

Analyzing bilingual behavior according to the speech mode that the bilingual is in helps explain certain aspects of bilingualism that were formerly misunderstood, such as the semilingualism of adults and children who were simply in a bilingual speech mode when tested. Bilinguals, like monolinguals, are by nature people who have to communicate; and depending on the situation, the speakers, the topic, and the function of the interaction, either or both of the languages are used. Although their language output may often be quite different from that of monolinguals, it is in every way as efficient once they have attained a stable form of bilingualism.

BILINGUALISM AND DEAF PEOPLE

Very little is known about the bilingualism of deaf people, either at the group or the individual level. Although some deaf people are probably monolingual—those who have received a strictly oral education and who have never learned to sign, or those few who have only learned to sign—most are bilingual. Most deaf people use both the majority language (in one modality or another) and one or several forms of the minority language in their everyday life. The origin of bilingualism among deaf people is their hearing impairment; the outcome of this bilingualism is its maintenance. One important difference with hearing bilingual minority groups, who often shift to monolingualism, is that deaf people will always retain some form of bilingualism despite the educational and social policy that is imposed on them. Rare are the deaf people who never use the majority language in one form or another, but rare also are those who do not use a form of sign language. More than 100 years of sign language repression in many western European countries and in North America have not been able to do away with this natural means of communication for deaf persons. This is because the hearing impairment of deaf people has created and maintained a need for an alternate means of communication to speech. As long as deafness exists, sign language will also, alongside the majority language.

Types of Bilingualism At least two types of bilingualism can be found among deaf people: a sign-sign bilingualism and a sign-speech bilingualism. Sign-sign bilingualism involves a number of varieties of signs, the two best known being the variety used by the deaf among themselves and the variety used with hearing people. Numerous researchers have studied this diglossic situation and have shown when the two varieties are used and with whom, what attitudes deaf people have toward them, and how they are characterized linguistically. Less well known is how deaf people actually use these two varieties depending on the language mode they are in: monolingual or bilingual. There are no answers to how complete the deactivation of one signing variety is when the signer is in a monolingual mode requiring the other variety; how, when, and why deaf people code-switch and borrow from one variety to the other when they find themselves in a bilingual mode; how their production, perception, and memorization processing systems deal with these different varieties in the differing modes; or when and how children acquire these varieties and learn to code-switch and borrow between them.

Little is known about the sign-speech bilingualism that is found among deaf people. There is little information, for example, on the communicative (as compared to formal) competence of deaf people when they use one or a combination of modalities of the oral language—fingerspelling, speaking, writing, signing. It would appear that many deaf people never attain the mastery in oral language skills that they need, and this often leads them to curtail their contact with the hearing world. This is an example of bilingualism where the level of fluency attained in one language—in this case the spoken language—is not based on communicative need but a physical factor, hearing impairment. This should not be confused with the totally false premise that knowledge of sign language hinders the acquisition of spoken language. On the contrary, much of the recent literature on childhood bilingualism shows that a child with a good foundation in one language is better prepared linguistically and cognitively to learn the other language, and will do so with greater ease. A good foundation in sign language can only help the development of oral language skills, given that there is a communicative need for these skills.

In sign-speech bilingualism a distinction must be made between shifting between modalities within a language (for example, going from speaking or writing English to signing it) and shifting between languages (shifting from speaking English to signing American Sign Language, for instance). Very little is known about the psychosocial factors that explain these shifts and the underlying linguistic operations that allow them. In addition, more research is needed on the impact of this type of bilingualism on sign language change in the form of language borrowing and creolization at the level of syntax, morphology, phonology, and so on. More research also is needed on the bilingualism of hearing children of deaf parents who acquire both the spoken majority language and the parents' sign language in infancy. Many serve as interpreters and cultural intermediaries at a very early age and remain fluent bilinguals throughout most of their lives. This type of sign-speech bilingualism is exceptional, however, and does not characterize the bilingualism of deaf people in general.

Minority Status As a minority group, deaf people meet many of the language problems encountered by other minority groups, but these problems are often amplified. Deaf people are rarely recognized as a linguistic and cultural minority, and hence do not benefit from the rights given these minorities, such as formally acquiring and maintaining their minority language or of receiving some form of bilingual education. Hearing minority groups have the implicit right, in fact the duty, to become bilingual so as to be able to take part in the life of the majority group. Deaf people do not have this right (or duty); their potential bilingualism is not recognized. The hearing society expects them to be monolingual in the majority language. Transitional bilingual education is often used by the majority group to integrate minority children into the majority. But even this approach, which ultimately leads to majority language monolingualism, is rarely used with deaf children. Yet it is these very children, because of their hearing impairment, who need bilingual education the most—not just a transitional form but a true and sustained form of bilingual and bicultural education which will reinforce their need to communicate in both the sign language of their group and the language of the majority. Deaf people are often potential bilinguals who have never been given the chance to develop much-needed skills in their various languages; this in turn has cut them off from social interactions in which these skills can be maintained and reinforced. Deaf people who master fully the two types of bilingualism mentioned above are rare.

Unlike oral language minority groups that can shift from being bilingual to being monolingual (in the minority language or more often in the majority language), the deaf communities throughout the world are destined to be bilingual. Only when this fact is recognized and accepted by deaf educators, language planners, speech therapists, the hearing world in general, and deaf people themselves will research on the bilingualism of deaf people become a necessity. In return, it not only will help in understanding which aspects of bilingualism are specific to deaf persons and which are common to all minority language groups, but will also have implications on how deaf people develop and maintain the communicative skills they need in their different languages.

Bibliography

Baetens-Beardsmore, Hugo: *Bilingualism: Basic Principles*, Tieto, Clevendon, England, 1982.

Battison, Robbin: *Lexical Borrowing in American Sign Language*, Linstok Press, Silver Spring, Maryland, 1978.

Bouvet, Danielle: *La Parole de l'Enfant Sourd*, Presses Universitaires de France, Paris, 1982.

Grosjean, Francois: *Life with Two Languages: An Introduction to Bilingualism*, Harvard University Press, Cambridge, Massachusetts, 1982.

Stokoe, William: "Sign Language Diglossia," *Studies in Linguistics*, 21:27–41, 1969.

Woodward, James: "Some Sociolinguistic Aspects of French and American Sign Languages," in Harlan Lane and François Grosjean (eds.), *Recent Perspectives on American Sign Language*, Lawrence Erlbaum Associates, Hillsdale, New Jersey, 1980.

François Grosjean

SOCIOLOGY

To appreciate the contributions sociology can make to the study of deafness, sociology must be understood. Sociology is a diverse intellectual enterprise, and two of its many definitions are basic for an understanding of deafness.

First, sociology involves study of recurrent patterns of social interaction. Consequently, matters such as the degree of hearing loss and age at onset for a particular individual are of secondary importance. Instead, sociologists place individual variation within larger, more inclusive social categories or groups. For example, sociologists frequently group hearing-impaired people by income, occupational type, and the number of years of school they have completed in order to assess the effects of various social forces in their lives. Other studies may classify deaf people according to categories they actually use in their everyday lives. Some of these categories are not part of how deaf people think about themselves. C. Layne, for instance, discovered that in one deaf community there were several ways deaf people evaluated each other's status ("high deaf" or "low deaf"), and these categories reflected the social organization of that particular community.

Second, sociology is methodological. Sociological studies are scientific in that they follow procedures which make public the precise ways in which studies are carried out. They are also neutral because they are conducted so that the personal values of the sociologist do not influence his or her obser-

vations. Sociological studies of deafness also frequently try to link the study of deafness and deaf people to more general concerns in the field of sociology. They range from survey research based on very large numbers of people to studies where the sociologist is on the scene, observing firsthand the activities of relatively small numbers of deaf people.

SOCIAL ORGANIZATION OF DEAFNESS

A sociological understanding of deaf people frequently focuses attention on the group affiliations of deaf people and on the relationships deaf people have with the larger society. For example, A. Boros and R. Stuckless suggested that a "lagging" relationship exists between deaf people and the larger, hearing society because social change is so rapid and the task of adjustment so dependent on being aware of new technological developments that any group of people with limited access to this new knowledge continuously lags behind those who are better informed. Most individuals in a society try to conform to what they perceive to be appropriate social norms. However, when such uniformity becomes difficult, as it is for many people with limited access to new knowledge, one can begin to feel out of "sync" with the times.

The social predicaments faced by deaf people resemble those faced by late-nineteenth- and early-twentieth-century immigrants in America, particularly those from countries outside western Europe. Many immigrants felt trapped between two very different social worlds. The term marginality refers to this state.

Deaf people may also be marginal in a fundamental sense. They are generally not considered completely normal, even if they speak and lipread well, and their culture may be in perpetual tension with the demands of the wider society. The sociological perspective does not stop with this observation, however, but continues to show how adaptations to marginality are possible and how these adaptations must be explained with reference to the social organizational features of the larger society.

The lack of complete integration into larger society does not mean that all deaf persons suffer adversely. The social lives of some deaf people are examples of how conditions of isolation offer opportunities for building a viable, independent social organization.

The strength of the deaf community, the vitality of its language, and the scope of the services it renders to deaf people depend to a great extent upon the relationship the community establishes with the larger society. Under this logic, the vigor and activity of the deaf community is directly proportional to the larger society's lack of response to the needs of its deaf citizens. In some other societies, however, deaf people simply do not have many opportunities to associate with one another and are not able to develop the kind of collective adaptations to the larger society commonly found in the United States.

MEANINGS OF DEAFNESS

Meanings of deafness are ways deaf people try to understand their social existence. The sociologist attempts to reconstruct and convey to a larger audience the ways in which the experiences of people with a hearing impairment are organized into significant and enduring patterns. The work of P. C. Higgins represents this type of sociological understanding. In a study of peddling among deaf people, Higgins shows how peddling is almost universally regarded as deviant by the deaf community. By severely condemning peddlers who are clearly showing disrespect for if not actually violating the norms of the deaf community, the community itself gains a measure of legitimacy.

Other studies have described how the hearing world is perceived from the vantage point of deaf people. J. Nash and A. Nash suggest that deaf and hearing people may have misinformed ideas about one another. Since the conceptions people have of one another can be the basis for social interaction, it is clear that an auditory barrier is not the only thing that separates deaf people from hearing people.

The connections between the social lives of deaf people and their use of sign language is another interesting area of sociological inquiry. Here, sociologists use concepts and knowledge gathered from studying ethnic and linguistic minorities to further their understanding of how deaf communities relate to the larger society. Of course, deaf communities differ from other ethnic and linguistic minorities in several significant ways: only a very small percentage of the deaf community is intergenerational; the community does not have geographical boundaries; and while deaf people must achieve their status as members of the deaf community, tribal and racial identities are primarily ascribed at birth. Still, the analogy with ethnic and linguistic minority groups has been useful. C. Erting, for example, has suggested the appropriateness of the concept of ethnicity for showing the necessity of special policies promoting bilingualism in the classroom. *See* SIGN LANGUAGES; DEAF POPULATION: Demography.

Attention to the meanings of deafness has also resulted in descriptions of the ways deaf children define social situations. K. Meadow has examined the self-concepts of deaf children, discovering that they vary according to the socialization experiences of the child. In general, deaf children of deaf parents appear to have more positive self-concepts than deaf children of hearing parents.

SOCIAL BEHAVIORS OF DEAF PEOPLE

Some sociologists attempt to predict and explain the behavior of deaf people. Their work is closely related to that of psychologists, but it differs in the greater emphasis placed on sociological variables. The primary concern of such studies is to examine the degree to which the actions of deaf people are distinctive, and the features of the larger social environment with which these activities can be linked.

An example of such an approach is S. Ouellette's study in which she examined the interaction between deaf and hearing subjects, giving special attention to nonverbal behavior. She suggests that stimuli such as the animated facial expressions that hearing people see deaf people exhibiting may produce apprehension on the part of the hearing person. However, with actual interaction, fears probably will lessen and may even be replaced with a feeling of satisfaction.

Families, schools, and peer groups are seen as important parts of the environment in which deaf people live. The ways in which parents express intentions to their children, the distance between people in conversation, and the ways deaf people process information are relevant research questions. The answers to these and similar questions may make it possible to explain the behavior of deaf people by using the same general sociological principles used to describe the behavior of people in the larger society.

CONCLUSION

While linguists study signs and anthropologists study the culture of deaf people, sociologists stress the interrelationships between the social organization of deafness and the larger society. Hence, most sociological research on deafness is comparative in the sense that it starts with knowledge about the organization of the larger society and describes the ways in which deafness as a social condition has consequences for the lives of deaf people.

Some sociologists focus on the distinctiveness of deafness as reflected in mental health rates, employment figures, socioeconomic factors, and rates and types of deviancy within society. Others examine the actual processes of organizing the experiences of deafness by discovering how deaf people interpret their world. Finally, some sociologists study deaf people because they afford a unique opportunity to conduct a controlled study, the results of which can sometimes provide strong support for general sociological theories.

The sociology of deafness requires a general view that tries not to overlook any aspect of being a deaf person. This means that sociologists must try to learn the secrets and special views of the people they study. Hence, sociological knowledge with its attention to unanticipated consequences of organized social life has potential to conserve and to change the worlds of deaf people.

Sociology promises the broadest possible interpretation of the actual everyday experiences of deaf people. A sociological perspective should help in judging the impact of current social trends on the lives of deaf people, identifying the core attributes of deaf communities, and assessing the place of deaf people in society.

Bibliography

Erting, C.: "Language Policy and Deaf Ethnicity in the United States," *Sign Language Studies*, 19:139–152, 1978.

Higgins, P.: "Deviance Within a Disabled Community," *Pacific Sociological Review*, 22(1):96–114, January 1979.

————: *Outsiders in a Hearing World: A Sociology of Deafness*, Sage, Beverly Hills, California, 1980.

Jacobs, L.: *A Deaf Adult Speaks Out*, Gallaudet College Press, Washington, D.C., 1974.

Meadow, K.: "Self Image, Family Climate and Deafness," *Social Forces*, 47:428–430, 1969.

————: *Deafness and Child Development*, University of California Press, Berkeley, 1980.

Nash, J., and A. Nash: *Deafness in Society*, D. C. Heath, Lexington, Massachusetts, 1981.

Jeffrey Nash

SOUND AND VIBRATION

Sound and Vibration is a business publication that provides practical technical information on noise and vibration control and related topics. *Sound and Vibration* is published monthly by Acoustical Publications, Inc., and although it publishes editorial material from a number of scientific and professional organizations, it does not have a formal relationship with any of them.

Acoustical Publications, Inc. (an Ohio corporation) was established in 1966 by Jack K. Mowry for the purpose of publishing *Sound and Vibration* and related activities. At that time there were no publications, business or scientific, that served the practical engineering aspects of noise and vibration control. *Sound and Vibration* was first published in January 1967 and was sent to a circulation list of about 8000. This initial circulation was developed from mailings to the memberships of a number of scientific organizations and to a number of company mailing lists. The publishing staff of Acoustical Publications consists of five people employed at the Bay Village, Ohio, office and a group of outside contributing editors. The contributing editors are all self-employed or employed by other firms. Their selection is based on their expertise in the fields covered by *Sound and Vibration*.

In addition to the primary field of coverage (noise and vibration control), *Sound and Vibration* also serves the fields of hearing conservation, architectural acoustics, structural analysis, dynamic measurements, and dynamic testing. Readers' occupations include occupational safety and health, plant engineering, design engineering, acoustical consulting, research and development, and other job functions related to the fields served. Job titles of readers concerned with occupational safety and health include otolaryngologists, industrial hygienists, hearing conservationists, audiologists, audiometric testing technicians, industrial nurses, safety engineers, and consultants. The circulation list includes approximately 21,300 individuals in the United States and a number of foreign countries.

The editorial purpose of *Sound and Vibration* is to provide information on the fields served through technical articles and news on subjects of current interest; tutorial articles; and commercial assistance through advertising, buyer's guides, and new product publicity. The publication addresses industrial hearing conservation programs; the fitting, evaluation, and performance of hearing protection devices; the measurement and control of noise exposure in the workplace; the rating and control of environmental noise outside the workplace; and the effects of excessive noise exposure on hearing-impaired individuals.

Sound and Vibration is circulated without charge to qualified individuals who are concerned with one or more of the fields served. Application for a free subscription may be made by filling out a subscription application form obtainable from the publisher. Others may subscribe for a fee.

Sound and Vibration accepts articles from outside authors, and there are no restrictions on authors' affiliations with other organizations. Scientific and research-oriented articles are rarely published in *Sound and Vibration*. Articles present practical engineering information and are generally one to six published pages in length. Prospective authors should request editorial guidelines from the publisher before preparing a manuscript.

Jack K. Mowry

SOUTH AFRICA, REPUBLIC OF

The Republic of South Africa is a geographically vast nation (over 471,400 square miles or 1,225,600 square kilometers) with a relatively small (over 21,000,000 people) but diverse population. Great variations in culture, from the traditional to the westernized, characterize the country. Deaf South Africans form a very small minority, and through the years have achieved an astonishingly strong bond of unity. This unity is deeply rooted in their ardent desire to support one another as they struggle for recognition of their human rights and as they adjust to the hearing community.

DEMOGRAPHY

The exact number of deaf people in South Africa is unknown. According to a survey conducted in 1978, more than 10,000 children suffered from an auditory disability, while approximately 3000 attended schools for deaf students.

The causes of deafness in South Africa have been investigated. A study of children attending schools for deaf pupils showed that 76 percent had a specific syndrome associated with deafness; 11 percent had undifferentiated familial deafness; 25 percent had acquired deafness; 11 percent had deafness of unknown etiology and other handicaps; and 46 percent had deafness of unknown etiology without other disabilities. Among those studied, 30 percent were believed to have deafness due to genetic factors, a rate perhaps explainable by the fact that 90 percent of married deaf people in South Africa have deaf spouses. See DEAF POPULATION: Demography; HEARING LOSS.

EDUCATION

In the mid-nineteenth century the Dominican Sisters of the Catholic Church of Ireland became involved in training programs for deaf people in South Africa. Their objective was to establish a form of communication with deaf persons in order to christianize them. Through the efforts of the Dominican Sisters and with the assistance of the Reverend Grimley of Cape Town, the first South African school for deaf pupils was established and named after him. In 1874 the school officially opened in a building on the present Garden Square. Two other schools followed before the turn of the century, while the majority of the remaining 21 schools have been established since the 1960s. The founding of schools for deaf children was the first effort in South Africa to formally educate disabled persons.

SOUTH AFRICAN NATIONAL COUNCIL FOR THE DEAF

In 1928, at a conference held in Bloemfontein for teachers of deaf pupils, the idea of establishing the National Council for the Deaf was conceived. By this time, the need for the coordination of services for deaf persons was recognized. On April 4, 1929, the council was officially founded, and in 1940 it appointed the first qualified social worker for deaf clients; the council now has 26 social workers in its service.

The South African National Council for the Deaf (SANCD) is the only nationally organized institution coordinating the activities of local associations and schools for deaf students in southern Africa. Eleven associations and twenty schools are affiliated with the council. Another four schools in independent neighboring states are linked to SANCD's activities. Some 37 organizations providing related services are also affiliated with the council.

The main functions of the SANCD are: to initiate and mantain projects for the welfare of deaf persons; to study the general conditions of deaf people in order to take action in their interest and to investigate the feasibility of educational and training projects geared to their occupational training; to disseminate information about these projects; to research the causes of deafness and to take preventive measures wherever possible; and to coordinate work among deaf people in South Africa.

The SANCD is affiliated with the World Federation of the Deaf and has links with other organizations for deaf persons throughout the world. The *Silent Messenger* is the SANCD's official mouthpiece. See WORLD FEDERATION OF THE DEAF.

COMMUNICATION

In the history of the education of deaf students, differences of opinion with respect to the best medium of communication have long existed. Basically two lines of thought are found: those in favor of sign language and those in favor of oral methods. See EDUCATION: Communication; HISTORY: Sign Language Controversy.

Research in regard to both methods has been done in South Africa. Speechreading is favored by the Departments of National Education and of Coloured and Indian Education in schools under their control. Although other possibilities are being investigated to improve teacher-pupil communication in these schools, sign language is not officially permitted.

In schools under the jurisdiction of the Department of Education and Training, the combined method (total communication) is being used. Signs, fingerspelling, body language, speechreading, and writing are all employed. See SOCIOLINGUISTICS: Total Communication.

Communication between deaf adults is usually by way of sign language and fingerspelling, but lack of a uniform teaching method has resulted in a number of dialects which cause considerable confusion. The need for a uniform communication system has been felt for many years, and for that reason a one-person commission was appointed in 1974 by the SANCD to investigate the feasibility of a uniform sign language system and to compile a manual. This manual, produced in conjunction with the Department of Education and Training, is used in the department's schools as a part of the combined method. See SIGN LANGUAGES: South African.

The combined method is warranted for those

children whose deafness is not identified and treated at an early stage. Even in cases where children's deafness is recognized early, not all possess the full potential to acquire a language by means of modern technological aids. Such children must be helped by other methods, such as the combined method. *See* SPEECH.

When deaf children leave school, they are confronted by the world of hearing people. Their previous association with the school has allowed them only limited contact with the hearing world. Thanks to modern teaching methods, many are now in a position to make fuller use of their speech organs. The incidence of deaf persons without intelligible speech is therefore on the decline.

HIGHER EDUCATION

At present there are no higher educational institutions for deaf South Africans. Due to the efforts of the Human Sciences Research Council, however, arrangements have been made to train deaf people at the Technical College at Worcester. They will receive instruction identical to that of their hearing colleagues.

Deaf people also can register with any university in South Africa to further their studies, but due to their limited vocabulary, deaf students have great difficulty in following the courses. Very few deaf people have acquired post-secondary school qualifications, although some have obtained collegiate training at Gallaudet College in Washington, D.C. *See* GALLAUDET COLLEGE.

EMPLOYMENT

Relatively few problems are encountered with employment of deaf people. To provide employment is a simple matter, as most deaf persons are known to be good and reliable workers. Problems do arise, though, mainly when deaf employees are unsuitably placed, without due recognition of their abilities and talents. The majority of deaf workers can be found in skilled, semiskilled, and unskilled occupations, with some representation in the clerical and professional areas. Most of the occupations practiced by deaf employees require no more than a junior certificate (10 years of schooling) level of education and consequently provide no challenge to the deaf person of advanced intelligence and ability.

Deaf workers have difficulty in venting frustrations when limitations are placed upon them, with the result that job fluctuation is encountered to a great extent. This problem could be overcome through better understanding from employer and colleagues alike. Deaf workers, through in-service training and promotion opportunities, can achieve great heights.

SPIRITUAL CARE

Although the majority of schools for deaf pupils are governed by churches, the spiritual care of adult deaf persons has, until recently, been much neglected. Often there is difficulty in following regular church services, because few churches are arranged so as to enable a deaf person to lipread the minister.

There is a tendency to establish separate congregations for deaf people. Several denominations—for example, the Dutch Reformed Congregation De la Bat for the Deaf, Bellville; the Dutch Reformed Congregation for the Pretoria Deaf; and the Deaf Christian Fellowship, Rosebank—hold special services, while the Roman Catholic Church has an itinerant deaf priest who conducts services for deaf Catholics.

In schools, religious instruction is included in the normal curriculum in conjunction with the churches, and special church services for deaf pupils are held at the residential schools.

Father C. B. Axelrod, a deaf person, who ministers to deaf people, is chairperson of the SANCD Committee of Spiritual Care of the Deaf. Together with one other deaf minister and two hearing ministers, he is responsible for investigations into ways of improving church services for deaf people and of assisting volunteer workers in spiritual care.

SOCIAL WORK SERVICES

As a welfare organization, the SANCD is responsible for the provision of professional welfare services to South Africans. SANCD social workers, who are specially trained to communicate with deaf clients, are stationed in Johannesburg, Port Elizabeth, Klerksdorp, Pretoria, Durban, Worcester, Cape Town, and East London.

With the exception of the Johannesburg Association for the Deaf, which employs two social workers, none of the other societies for deaf people employs social workers. A healthy interrelationship exists between the SANCD and the societies and schools with respect to social work services, which are available free of charge to the members of the societies. *See* SOCIAL WORK AND SOCIAL WELFARE.

The social workers normally visit only those deaf persons who require intervention. They guide the parents of preschool deaf children in the matter of the child's acquisition of language, and they train volunteers to work more effectively with deaf persons. The social workers also play a role in community education by addressing gatherings on various aspects of the welfare of deaf individuals.

ASSOCIATIONS

The following deaf associations which are affiliated with the SANCD operate in South Africa: the Association for the Deaf (Johannesburg), Western Transvaal Society for the Deaf (Johannesburg), Western Transvaal Society for the Deaf (Klerksdorp), Northern Transvaal Society for the Deaf (Pretoria), Port Elizabeth Association for the Deaf (Port Elizabeth), East London and Border Society for the Deaf (East London), Cape Town and District Association for the Deaf (East London), Natal Association for the Deaf (Durban), Free State Society for the Deaf (Edenville), Eastern Transvaal Society for the Deaf (Bethal), Society for the Deaf (South West Africa), and the Letaba Association for the Handicapped (Letaba).

Apart from the East London and Border Society for the Deaf and the Port Elizabeth Association for the Deaf, whose objective is to perform clinical services for the young deaf child and which have no deaf persons in their management committees, all the other associations render, in cooperation with the SANCD, welfare services for deaf people. Deaf members serve on the management committees, and their services are invaluable as voluntary workers among their deaf fellows.

Deaf individuals play an active role in promoting telephone devices for the deaf (TDD) as part of the telephone network in South Africa, and in distributing other aids such as flashing alarms. Although two of the eleven associations for deaf people in South Africa are composed of deaf members only, with a deaf chairperson and secretary, no restriction is placed by the remaining nine associations on the election of deaf people to their management committees.

The SANCD, as the parent body, established a committee of deaf persons with a view to elevating the status of deaf individuals to executive level. A deaf person can be elected as a full member of the executive committee of the council, and a deaf person has served as vice-chairperson of the council.

The Committee for Communication Skills of the SANCD appointed three deaf members to assist in the research project into sign language systems, while seven deaf subcommittees, consisting of deaf members representing seven regions in the country, act as liaison between the Committee for Communication Skills and the different deaf communities of South Africa. Without the participation of these deaf leaders the research project would have been aimless.

A strong sports federation constituted only of deaf persons exists in South Africa, and deaf men and women represented South Africa in the Olympic Games for the Deaf. A number of deaf rugby players appeared in international rugby football games. The South African Deaf Sports Federation is subdivided into four provincial divisions: Natal, Orange Free State, Cape, and Transvaal. Regular competitions on the provincial level in badminton, rugby football, cricket, swimming, tennis, and athletics are arranged. A Summer Games and a Winter Games for the Deaf are arranged on an alternating basis each year, and include all the above sporting activities. *See* COMITÉ INTERNATIONAL DES SPORTS DES SOURDS.

Bibliography

Department of Health and Welfare: *Deafness in Children*, Government Printer, Pretoria, 1980.

Du Toit, C. J.: *Pre-School Treatment of Hearing Impaired Children in South Africa*, SANCD, Jubileum Publication, 1979.

Engelbrecht, G. K.: *Die Dow: Die Maatskaplike en Ekonomiese Posisie van die Dowe in Suid-Afrika, met besondere verwysing na hulle rehabilitasie*, HAUM, 1961.

————: "Die Rol van die Oorerwinsfaktor in die Veroorsaking van Doofheid," *Silent Messenger*, SANCD, October 1957.

Gouws, M.: *Onderwys en Skoolvoorligting vir Dowe Leerlinge*, HSRC Report o-37, Pretoria, 1957.

Human Sciences Research Council: *Careers for Deaf Persons with Post School Qualifications*, Research Finding M-R-60.

Jubileum Publication of the South African National Council for the Deaf.

Neider-Heitmann, N.: "A Survey of Modern History of Deaf Education," *Silent Messenger*, SANCD, March 1973.

Report of the Committee of Investigation on the Injudicious Use of Hearing Aids, Department of Health and Welfare, 1970.

Sellars, S. and P. Beighton: "Childhood Deafness in Southern Africa," *Journal for Laryngology and Otology*, 47(10):885–889.

Sutcliffe, T. H.: *Deafness, Let's Face It*, RNID, Oxford 1971.

Van der Poel, J.: "Die Etiologie van Doofheid by Kinders," *Silent Messenger*, SANCD, March 1974.

J. M. Herbst

SPAIN

Spain's tradition of assisting deaf people reaches back 400 years. Pedro Ponce de León, a sixteenth-century Spanish monk, is considered to be the universal pioneer of "the art of teaching the deaf to speak." Today there are 20,000 members of local associations of deaf persons endeavoring to advance the cause of deaf Spaniards. *See* PONCE DE LEÓN, PEDRO.

EDUCATION

At the outset of the twentieth century, Spanish schools combined the teaching of blind children and deaf children, but this system has changed. There now exists a broad network of special schools and institutions dedicated to teaching deaf pupils at the primary, elementary, and secondary levels.

These schools may be public or private, secular or religious. There is no uniformity of teaching methods in Spanish schools; some are exclusively oral, others use sign language, and total communication is gaining in popularity. Integrated classes have been established for hearing and deaf pupils, but these are opposed by deaf adults and by some parents and teachers who favor the oral methods. Hard-of-hearing students, with considerable residual hearing, are integrated successfully and are assisted by modern technology. *See* EDUCATION.

Generally, deaf children begin school at the age of 4 and finish their formal education at 18. There are both day and boarding students, and the national government grants scholarships for free education in cases of financial need. In addition to regular academic courses, students may take vocational classes at many schools. Vocational training is provided most often in electronics, photography, printing, drawing, drafting, jewelry making and repair, carpentry, bookbinding, and computer programming and related areas. There are no subsidized work centers or factory schools for professional training, although the National Institute of Social Services (INSERSO) in the Ministry of Labor handles a few individuals.

Spain lacks university centers specialized for deaf people. To be accepted by the regular universities, deaf students must prepare on their own. Once enrolled in the university, they face many difficulties in competing with hearing people, for they do not have the assistance of interpreters. Consequently, very few deaf people succeed in higher education.

A number of problems exist in the deaf education system. There are not enough schools or educational centers. The schools have a shortage of textbooks prepared especially for deaf students; most such books that are available are translations from other nations. The National Federation of the Deaf of Spain (FNSE) is the only organization carrying out projects in this area. Another problem is that postlingually deaf persons do not have separate educational centers. They are integrated either with prelingually deaf people or with hearing people. Due to such educational deficiencies, the cultural development of deaf students generally is low.

One means of improving this situation is through continuing-education classes for deaf adults. Usually evening classes offered free, these are held in the local associations of deaf people.

EMPLOYMENT

A number of serious obstacles confront deaf workers in Spain. There are no special factories, departments, or sections for deaf workers. Competitive examinations for staff positions are based on written and spoken language skills in which most deaf people, no matter how capable, are deficient. Even though Spanish law grants tax exemption benefits for every deaf worker in a factory or company, companies are ignorant of the aptitudes and problems of deaf individuals and reluctant to hire them. Handicapped people are supposed to constitute a minimum of 1.5 percent of the personnel in factories and companies, but this quota is rarely met. Furthermore, the larger problem of layoffs and unemployment in Spain has repercussions for deaf workers.

Employment problems are especially acute for the small number of deaf people with college degrees; jobs for them are few. The most accessible jobs are in the field of education.

A small number of deaf people have set up businesses of their own—an effort supported by INSERSO. Most deaf workers have jobs in companies owned by others. Usually they get these positions through the assistance of friends, relatives, or the local associations of deaf people.

Little by little, the employment situation for deaf workers is changing as various companies exhibit more flexibility in their hiring practices. Cultural activities of the local associations and the FNSE reach the public through the press, radio, and television. Publicizing of these activities shows the true dimensions of deaf people. Campaigns by the associations and the FNSE emphasize the capabilities of deaf people and their great ability to concentrate on their work.

COMMUNICATION

Sign language is the means of communication that is used by the majority of prelingually deaf Spaniards. Variations are found in different provinces, but a Spanish Sign Language dictionary (*Diccionario Mímico Español*) was published in 1981 to try to standardize the language. *See* SIGN LANGUAGES: Spanish.

Fingerspelling is used by prelingually deaf Spaniards only as an aid to sign language to designate proper names, people, and geographic places. Also, it is used by postlingually deaf people. *See* SIGNS: Fingerspelling.

Interested hearing persons—parents, teachers, interpreters—are learning sign language. Sign language courses are offered in almost every city, and the FNSE has produced sign films and video tapes to assist learners. The first course specifically for interpreters was established in 1982 by the FNSE under the auspices of the Ministry of Education.

Newer technological developments are beginning to assist deaf people in using telephones. The telephone device used by most local associations is TELESCRIT. The FNSE has assisted the associations in getting these machines, and the Generalidad of Cataluna has helped the association in that region.

Only a small number of deaf individuals have the TELESCRIT phone system. *See* TELECOMMUNICATIONS.

ORGANIZATIONS

Two important national government agencies serve the deaf population: INSERSO and the National Fund of Social Services (FNAS). Both are part of the Ministry of Labor and Social Services. INSERSO is responsible for such tasks as the provision of school scholarships, development of early childhood programs, educational and professional development, prevention of deafness, medical assistance, distribution of hearing aids, and dispersion of information about deafness. The FNAS works with the local associations and the FNSE, subsidizing some organizations and supporting their cultural, vocational, and educational activities.

The local associations of deaf persons, numbering about 70, are integrated into one nationwide association for all deaf Spaniards, the FNSE. Founded in 1936 by Juan Luis Marroquin, and restructured in 1976 by Felix-Jesús Pinedo Peydró, the FNSE serves a multitude of functions. It is administered by an assembly and board with representatives from the regional federations and local associations. Representatives serve without remuneration and are chosen by election every four years. The FNSE is supported by membership fees from the local associations, donations, and profits from the sale of its own publications and video tapes.

The FNSE publishes and distributes several works for and about deaf people in Spain. It also supports competitive cultural activities: National Week of the Theater of the Deaf; National Days of Mime and Pantomime; National Film Competition; Exposition of Painting, Photography, and Sculpture; Regional Folklore Dance Competition; and National Communal Camping. All of these are competitions between the local associations, made possible by financial aid provided by the Ministry of Culture. Cash prizes and trophies are awarded. The objective is to demonstrate to hearing people the culture and skills of deaf people.

Of these FNSE-sponsored cultural activities, the Theater Week in particular enjoys high status and fame. More than a thousand people, including deaf foreigners, gather in the organizing city (determined by the FNSE on an alternating basis). They attend theatrical performances of classical works rendered in sign language with simultaneous oral translations for the hearing public. The participating theater groups are amateurs, with the cash prizes going to the treasuries of the associations to which the groups belong.

The FNSE is a source of information for and about deaf people in Spain, collaborating with other organizations when appropriate to diffuse knowledge that will benefit deaf people. It produces sign language video tapes for the local associations. With voice dubbed in, these tapes can be used by hearing people, deaf persons, or mixed groups during conferences or meetings. The subjects cover a wide range of topics, from studies of classical literature to discussions of the cultural activities of the FNSE. Classes for deaf adults (supported by INSERSO) and courses for sign language interpreters are arranged by the FNSE. The FNSE also represents the Spanish deaf population in international meetings of the World Federation of the Deaf. *See* WORLD FEDERATION OF THE DEAF.

In addition to the government agencies and the FNSE, Spain has three other significant organizations interested in deaf people: the Spanish Association of Educators of the Deaf, the Association of Parents and Friends of the Deaf, and the Foundation of Promotion and Assistance to the Deaf. The last is a general Mediterranean-area foundation that promotes good labor and social relations for deaf people and publishes a monthly magazine, *PROAS*, intended primarily for a hearing readership. All three groups are dominated by hearing individuals; they have no formal connection with the deaf associations nor can they speak for the deaf population.

CONCLUSION

Several major concerns remain for deaf Spaniards. For example, there are severe restrictions on their driving privileges. They are limited to operating automobiles only, not trucks or motorcycles, and to maximum speed of 48 miles (80 kilometers) per hour. To obtain a driver's license, they must pass a written examination, which many find difficult due to their limited facility with the Spanish language. Education remains a significant problem, and deaf adults are especially concerned by attempts to integrate deaf and hearing children. The elimination of discriminatory employment practices, the addition of subtitles to television news programs, and changing the paternalistic attitudes are goals of Spanish deaf leaders.

Bibliography

Colin, D.: *Psicolgía del niño sordo*, Toray Masson. Barcelona, 1978, reprint 1980.

Diccionario Mímico Espānol, FNSE, Madrid, 1981.

Faro del Silencio (Beacon of Silence), FNSE, Madrid, monthly.

Historia y Leyendos de España (History and Legends of Spain), FNSE, Madrid.

Marchesi, A.: "El lenguaje de signos," *Estudio de psicología*, pp. 155–184, 1981.

Perello, J., and F. Tortosa: *Sordomudez*, Científico Médica, Barcelona, 1978.

Pinedo, F. J.: *Diccionario mímico*, Ministerio de Trabajo, Madrid, 1981.

———: *El Sordo y su Mundo*, FNSE, Madrid, 1981.

Ramirez Camacho, R. A.: *Conocer al niño sordo*, CEPE, Madrid, 1982.

Suria, M. D.: *Guia para padres de niños sordos*, Herder, Barcelona, 1982.

Felix-Jesús Pinedo Peydró

SPEAR, ANSON RANDOLPH
(1860–1917)

Anson Randolph Spear was an inventor, administrator, government worker, and staunch advocate of deaf training and employment through the aid of state and national government agencies. A somewhat controversial character, he never completed college and became a successful business person in Minnesota. Like many others of his generation, he was a believer in the combined system, which uses sign language and speech to educate deaf children. Because of the late onset of his deafness, Spear used his voice when communicating with hearing people but at other times did not speak. Largely responsible for the beginnings of a deaf school in North Dakota, he continued his educational efforts after his tenure ceased at the state school. An energetic and versatile man, Spear also contributed to the National Association of the Deaf, hoping to reform it and make it more responsive to the deaf community throughout the United States.

There is some controversy about Spear's date and place of birth. The generally accepted date is January 10, 1860, but the United States Census of 1900 lists June 1859. His birthplace was near the United States–Canada border, either in northern Vermont or in Quebec. The family moved to an Iowa farm in 1869, and the next year to Minneapolis.

At the age of 11 Spear contracted spinal meningitis, which left him totally deaf. He attended the Minnesota School for the Deaf from 1874 to 1878. After graduating he worked at the tailoring trade in St. Paul for a brief period and entered Gallaudet College in 1879. He completed one academic year, but was dismissed in 1880 for various infractions of College rules. *See* GALLAUDET COLLEGE.

Spear found employment in the United States Census Office, but his problems with Gallaudet College did not cease as he appeared on campus intoxicated at least once. He received a sharp rebuke from Edward Miner Gallaudet and was forbidden campus entrance. Because of his difficulties, Spear held unfriendly feelings toward Gallaudet College. *See* GALLAUDET, EDWARD MINER.

In 1882 Spear returned to Minneapolis where he remained until 1889, working as clerk and then head clerk in the post office. In 1889 Congress decided to split the Dakota Territory and set aside 40,000 acres of land to be sold at $10 an acre for the benefit of establishing a deaf school in the sec-

ond area. The old school, located in Sioux Falls, became the South Dakota School for the Deaf. The new one, established at Devils Lake, appointed Spear as its first superintendent.

He resigned his post office position and assumed his new duties in 1890. His first wife, Julia Halvorson, a graduate of the Minnesota school where Spear had met her, became the matron of the North Dakota institution. Spear later married Frances Bell Merriman, a graduate of the Indiana school. He was the father of five children.

Spear hired Alto Lowman, the first woman graduate of Gallaudet College under the co-ed system, as a primary teacher. He remained a superintendent for five years, resigning in 1895 because of some unstated controversy. He returned to Minneapolis, where he established a day school for deaf children. It survived for two years.

Spear not only was involved in the education of deaf people but was a tinkerer and inventor as well. In 1890 he patented a leakproof merchandise mailing envelope. In 1893 he secured another patent, later selling the first one. By 1895 Spear had acquired a hearing partner and begun manufacturing the "Spear envelope" under the firm of Spear-Heywood Envelope Company (later changed to the Spear Safety Envelope Company). Apparently quite successful, the envelopes were designed to be leakproof for mailing samples of flour, grain, seeds, and other merchandise, and they needed no fasteners.

Spear continued to work with and for the deaf community. He proposed a reorganization of the National Association of the Deaf (NAD), which became known as the Spear Plan. Spear desired to make the individual the basis for membership in the NAD, with the membership fee including a subscription to its official publication. He felt that a permanent headquarters should be established for the NAD with a full-time secretary. He envisioned a small representative executive committee that would control the affairs of the group and a large advisory committee and a president who would serve, but not dominate, the organization. Although the plan was not accepted during Spear's lifetime, its major elements became the basis for a rejuvenated NAD in the 1960s. *See* NATIONAL ASSOCIATION OF THE DEAF.

In his private endeavors, Spear gave of his time and money to needy deaf persons, but his major preoccupation was the employment of deaf individuals. In 1913 he was instrumental in helping to establish a Division for the Deaf in the Minnesota State Bureau of Labor and Industries.

In 1917 Spear suggested Congress enact a law that would provide for a department of the deaf to be included in the Bureau of Labor. Although Congress never established such a division, the concept was part of Spear's philosophy in aiding deaf individuals to secure training and employment.

On December 10, 1917, on the way to a Gallaudet Day celebration, Spear suffered an apoplectic stroke from which he died. Largely self-educated, Spear, "in intellectual attainments" and "in the grasp of business intricacies," one observer noted, "was the equal of the best educated deaf men."

Bibliography

Gallaudet College Archives, Washington, D.C.

Gannon, Jack R.: *Deaf Heritage: A Narrative History of Deaf America*, National Association of the Deaf, Silver Spring, Maryland, 1981.

Barry A. Crouch

SPEECH

Speech is a complex process in which the eating and breathing mechanisms are used to generate patterns of sound, which represent words and sentences, which in turn represent concepts, ideas, and messages. The generation of speech requires control of abdominal and chest muscles to produce a sustained flow of air; control of the muscles of the larynx and vocal cords so that the airflow can generate voice; control of the muscles of the velum (soft palate), tongue, jaw, and lips either to modify the sound of the voice or to generate other sounds by the partial or full interruption of airflow; and, above all, the coordination of all these various muscles so that the patterns produced correspond with those used by people communicating in their native language.

Hearing plays a key role in speech development, since it is through hearing that the young child experiences the speech patterns of others and compares them to his or her own speech efforts. It follows that a congenital impairment of hearing will interfere with the development of speech. If the impairment is severe enough, speech does not develop spontaneously, and special training is required. Even with this training, the results may sound very different from the speech of normally hearing people. This section describes these differences, and is organized around the audible characteristics of speech which are grouped under three major headings: voice, temporal patterns, and speech segments. For each characteristic there is an outline of the acoustic and movement patterns associated with typical errors, and comments on their possible causes and consequences. The section ends with a discussion of the differences of speech ability among deaf people.

Voice

The speech of deaf people sounds different from normal speech, regardless of how understandable

it may be. Many features contribute to the characteristic quality of so-called deaf speech, but one of the more important is the quality of the voice, that is, the sound produced by the flow of air between the vocal cords. In normal voice production the vocal cords are brought together gently but firmly, and sufficient pressure is produced in the windpipe to cause the air to push its way through. As the air escapes, it causes the vocal cords to vibrate and consequently the air is released in brief puffs. These puffs follow each other at a rate of 100 or more per second. Between each puff the cords come back together and airflow is temporarily stopped. The resulting sound is a musical tone rich in overtones that cause resonance in the cavities of the throat, nose, and mouth. These resonances combine with the original sound, thus affecting the audible quality of the voice. The process is one of relaxed control, and it is highly efficient, since one or more sentences can be produced on a single breath. Voice production by deaf persons can deviate from this pattern in several ways:

1. Breathiness. A common problem is that the vocal cords vibrate along only part of their length, leaving a space through which air can escape. This weakens the sound of voicing and adds a turbulent hissing noise heard as breathiness.

2. Falsetto. Another common problem is that the vocal cords vibrate in an inappropriate way, barely stopping the airflow between puffs and generating a sound that is deficient in overtones. Such a voice sounds hollow and weak, and is usually high-pitched. This is often referred to as falsetto, in singing.

3. Chest resonance. Associated with the previous two problems is the coloring of the voice by resonances within the chest. This occurs because the vocal cords do not close firmly as they vibrate. Sound escapes back into the windpipe, where it resonates and then escapes back into the mouth. This diminishes the strength of the mouth resonances because they too can escape into the windpipe. The resulting voice sounds deep and hollow.

4. Pharyngeal constriction. The pharynx, the space above the larynx, is usually fairly relaxed during speech. Some deaf people, however, tighten the pharyngeal muscles and constrict the pharynx, thus changing the resonant frequencies of the nose and mouth and imparting a tense, reedy, or nasal quality to the voice.

5. Hypernasality. In normal speech, the velum, the flap at the back of the palate, is held in a raised position for most of the time. This has the effect of minimizing the flow of air and sound into the nose and ensuring that mouth resonances are the most important source of voice coloration. Deaf talkers very commonly hold the velum in a lowered position, thus allowing sound into the nose and

coloring the voice with prominent nasal resonances. The resulting voice is often described as nasal, but the problem is very different from that of pharyngeal constriction.

6. Pitch. The speech of deaf talkers is often characterized by an abnormal pitch, one that is usually too high. The primary acoustical correlate is an abnormal frequency of vibration of the vocal cords. The average frequencies of resonance in the vocal tract can also influence perceived pitch, however, and an abnormally high-sounding pitch can sometimes be traced to pharyngeal constriction.

7. Loudness. The voices of deaf talkers are sometimes louder or softer than is appropriate. Moreover, whereas normal talkers raise their voices in noisy surroundings, deaf talkers are usually unaware of the noise and continue to talk at the same level. *See* SPEECH PRODUCTION: Anatomy and Physiology.

Absence of hearing is the primary reason for errors of voice quality. The speaker is simply unable to distinguish good voice from defective voice since there are no visual or tactile cues for comparison. Even moderate hearing losses can be sufficient to interfere with the development of normal voice quality. In the case of a hearing loss acquired in adult life, voice quality is one of the first features of speech to be noticeably affected. It may be that a defective voice is easier to feel than is a normal voice, and that a deaf person naturally gravitates to speech that is breathy, falsetto, high-pitched, and tense and produces resonance in the chest simply to get a sense of control over the voice. Additional causes can be found, however, in the methods by which speech skills are taught. If the primary attention in the early days of training is on the articulation of vowels and consonants, bad habits of voice production may be established. It is also possible that a teacher who allows the student to become anxious about speech production will promote a general muscular tension that is incompatible with the production of a natural voice. *See* SPEECH TRAINING.

Even when defective, the voice of deaf individuals can serve to define the lengths of sounds, can serve as the sound source for vowels, and can differentiate voiced from voiceless consonants assuming that voice production is properly coordinated with other speech activities. There are, however, some adverse consequences to the typical defects of voice quality found in deaf people. One is the use of excessive airflow, which requires frequent breaths and interferes with the rhythm and timing of speech. Another is the relative weakness of those harmonics, or overtones, that are required to stimulate resonance in the oral cavity and thus help differentiate the various vowels and consonants. A

third is the weakness of those resonances when they do occur because of the loss of sound back into the windpipe through the partially open vocal cords. Yet another problem is that people unfamiliar with deaf speech are distracted by the unusual voice quality and may find it hard to concentrate on what is being said.

TEMPORAL PATTERNS

Speech, like all sounds, is a pattern in time. Each language has a characteristic way of distributing the components of speech in time, giving rise to identifiable rhythms and intonation patterns. When speech is learned without benefit of hearing, these patterns are usually distorted.

Rate The rate at which deaf people talk is often lower than normal, sometimes by a factor of two or three. The motor activities and the acoustic patterns occupy more time than is usual. Slow speech, however, is not necessarily bad; the listener may be helped by having more time to process the speech patterns. One of the causes of slow speech is the care taken by some deaf talkers in the execution of the coordinated movements required for the production of vowels and consonants. The teaching of single syllables as the unit of speech also may lead to slow speech since syllables produced in isolation are naturally longer than syllables spoken in context.

Rhythm More serious than slow rate is the abnormal rhythm found in the speech of many deaf talkers. Normal speech is characterized by a shortening of unstressed syllables and a lengthening of stressed syllables. Pauses, if they occur, are placed between phrases and sentences, and stressed syllables immediately before a pause receive an extra lengthening. For example, in the sentence "Water the fern and feed the cat," "fern" may take as much as eight times as long as "-ter," and a pause, if it occurs, would only make sense after "fern." This all helps to convey information about phrase and sentence boundaries and to show the relative importance of syllables in words, and of words in sentences.

Pauses within phrases are frequently encountered in the speech of deaf talkers. In addition, there is a tendency for all syllables to have the same duration. Research has shown that this comes from a failure to shorten the duration of unstressed syllables rather than a failure to lengthen stressed syllables. In effect, every syllable is stressed.

The perceived distortions of rhythm are reflected directly in the relative durations of acoustic and motor events. One reason for the introduction of inappropriate pauses is traceable to the need for frequent breaths, this being due to the inefficient production of voice described earlier.

Deviant speech rhythm can seriously interfere with the intelligibility of speech by confusing the listener about the location of phrase and sentence boundaries and the relative importance of syllables and words. Its primary cause is the speaker's inability to hear the rhythms of normal speech. An additional problem, however, may be found in teaching methods. For example, if deaf children use the printed word as their primary model for language, they may be putting gaps between words and making all their syllables more or less the same length because this is the way speech appears in print.

Intonation Intonation is the pattern of variation in fundamental voice frequency over time. It is used along with rhythm to mark syntactic boundaries, stressed syllables in words, and important words in sentences. It also is used to express the emotional content of a message and sometimes to convert statements into questions. The intonation patterns of deaf people are typically abnormal. Sometimes the variations of fundamental frequency are very small (monotone speech); sometimes they are large but the rises and falls occur at the wrong times. Sometimes the voice switches erratically between different modes of vibration (which results in erratic changes of fundamental frequency); sometimes these switches are induced by the movements required to produce specific vowels and consonants.

At a motor level, deviant intonation patterns result from a failure to change vocal cord tension appropriately during speech, a failure to develop independent control of the voicing and articulating mechanisms, and a failure to introduce compensatory changes of vocal cord tension for those articulatory movements that directly affect the larynx.

Abnormal intonation patterns, like abnormal rhythm, can have a devastating effect on the intelligibility of speech. The listener is not just deprived of information about syntactic boundaries and the location of stresses; quite frequently a speaker is misled into believing that phrases and sentences end where they do not or that importance should be attached to syllables and words that are unimportant. In the worst kind of abnormal pattern, every syllable is spoken as though it were a complete sentence.

The primary cause of abnormal intonation is the inability to hear intonation patterns, and the absence of tactile or visual cues that might substitute for hearing. Excessive reliance on the printed word as a source of information about language may also be a source of difficulties since intonation is not represented. In addition, the rules for planning intonation contours are not well understood, leaving teachers and clinicians at a loss as to how to induce appropriate patterns in the speech of deaf children.

Speech segments are the vowels and consonants used to construct the words. Their production requires careful control and fine coordination of the breathing, voicing, and articulatory mechanisms.

Vowels There are 16 vowels in English. Voicing is the sole sound source, and the sound is colored by resonances within the mouth cavity. This coloration depends on the shape of the mouth cavity, which is determined by the positions of the tongue, jaw, and lips. Duration is used to differentiate the long vowels such as "ee" in "feet" from the short vowels with similar qualities such as "i" in "fit," and a special class of vowel, the diphthong (as in "cow"), is made by gliding between two mouth shapes.

Deaf talkers frequently fail to differentiate vowel qualities sufficiently. They also may fail to differentiate long from short vowels and may convert diphthongs into pure vowels. Additionally, they are frequently inconsistent in their production of a given vowel. The acoustical correlates of these errors are not hard to identify. Sound spectrographs (voice prints), for example, show that the resonant frequencies of the mouth cavity do not vary as much as they should from their neutral or rest values. This occurs because the tongue does not move as much as it should from one vowel to the next. Lip movements are usually appropriate; however, they are often exaggerated. Unfortunately, lip shape is of only secondary importance in determining vowel quality. Additional acoustic characteristics are a weakness of the mouth resonances caused by the voice problems mentioned earlier, and the addition of excessive nasal resonance caused by inappropriate positioning of the velum.

The production of a restricted vowel system is not a serious problem if the vowels are produced consistently. Unfortunately, the variability from one production of a given vowel to the next may be as great as the difference between two different vowels. In this case the listener will have difficulty identifying the intended vowel, adding to comprehension difficulty. However, the listener is frequently watching the talker and may be helped considerably by the appropriate lip movements.

The primary cause of poor vowel production is the deaf person's inability to hear the changes in voice coloration that are produced by changes of mouth shape. In addition, the fact that the shape of the lip opening is clearly visible tends to shift emphasis from the tongue, the primary controller of vowel quality, to the lip opening, the secondary controller.

Consonants There are 23 consonants in English that, together with the vowels, are used to construct words. These fall into four major groups: the vowellike consonants (such as "w" in "we"), in which the sole sound source is the voice, and coloration is produced by appropriate shaping of the mouth; the nasals (such as "m" in "me"), in which the sole sound source is voicing, but coloration is produced by resonance in the nasal cavity instead of the mouth; the fricatives (such as "s" in "sue"), in which sound is produced by forcing air through a narrow space made by bringing either the tongue or the lower lip into contact with the palate, the upper teeth, or the upper lip; and the stop-plosives (such as "p" in "pea"), in which sound is produced by a temporary blockage of the vocal tract followed by release of the pressure that builds up in the mouth. For most of the fricatives and stop-plosives, there is both a voiceless version and a voiced version, the latter involving a combination of two sound sources (for example, "sue"/"zoo" and "pea"/"bee"). The consonant system is often described in terms of phonetic features. For example, the four ways of making consonants are referred to as different manners of articulation; the presence or absence of voice in the fricatives and plosives as voicing; and the region in the mouth cavity at which the greatest narrowing occurs as place of articulation.

Studies of the consonant production of deaf people have shown numerous errors. Sometimes a consonant is simply omitted; sometimes it is distorted beyond recognition; sometimes an extra consonant or vowel is added; sometimes an error causes one consonant to be replaced with another. Omission occurs more commonly at the ends of words or within consonant clusters (for example, in "strengths"). Distortions are most frequently a matter of incorrect articulation or inappropriate shaping of the mouth cavity. Additions occur most commonly in consonant clusters (as when "play" becomes "puhlay"). Substitutions occur because of errors in all features. The most common error is in voicing—voiceless consonants becoming voiced, and vice versa ("pie" becomes "buy"). The second most common is in manner of articulation—stop-plosives becoming nasals ("buy" becomes "my"), fricatives becoming stop-plosives ("sand" becomes "tand"), and so on. The least common error is in place of articulation ("take" becomes "cake").

Acoustical examination of incorrectly produced consonants shows not only the errors expected on the basis of a phonetic analysis but also serious errors in the relative timings and durations of the various components of the acoustic signal. The errors are directly traceable to failure to coordinate the numerous muscle groups that are involved in consonant production. Sometimes a particular part of the speech mechanism is simply doing the wrong thing, as when the velum remains lowered causing "bee" to emerge as "me." More often, however, it is a matter of doing the right thing at the wrong time, as when the velum is raised too late causing "bee" to emerge as "mbee." Often there is considerable variability among repeated productions of the same consonant. In some cases, there are serious problems in the control of the breath stream and the larynx that interfere with the production of consonants to the extent that the sounds produced are not recognizable. For example, if the vocal cords are held tightly together during the production of a plosive, there is a sudden inrush of air that produces a smacking sound instead of the desired burst of air outward.

Since the consonants play such an important role in the construction of words, it follows that their omission, distortion, addition, and substitution will have devastating effects on the intelligibility of speech. The initial cause of consonant errors lies in the absence of hearing and the fact that so little of the speech mechanism is visible. However, in the case of consonant production, the specific errors can often be traced to particular teaching strategies that fail to take into account the complexity of the coordination required when consonants are produced in running speech, and the need for intensive drilling so that the coordinated movements become automatic.

DIFFERENCES AMONG DEAF TALKERS

Not all deaf talkers exhibit all of the errors described. There are marked differences of speech ability among deaf people. At one extreme are those whose speech sounds basically normal, but with some errors or distortions of consonant articulation and a trace of hypernasality in the voice. Their speech is highly intelligible, even to strangers. At the other extreme are deaf talkers whose voice sounds grossly abnormal, whose rhythm and intonation patterns bear no relation to those of their native language, and whose vowels and consonants are seriously and inconsistently misarticulated. Their speech is unintelligible to strangers and not very intelligible to family and friends. Between these two extremes are deaf talkers whose speech, though full of errors, is highly consistent and is intelligible to family, friends, and colleagues, though not to strangers. A rarer situation is one in which there is good voice quality and carefully articulated segments but abnormal rhythm and intonation. Such speech is often intelligible to strangers after a brief period of exposure. There are several reasons for these differences:

1. Degree of hearing loss. The term "deaf" has been used to describe persons with hearing losses as low as 75 to 80 decibels (dB) as well as persons who totally lack a sense of hearing. Within this range of hearing impairment, however, there are

enormous differences in the ability to hear the details of speech patterns and in the extent to which hearing can play its natural role in the development of speech. Research has shown consistently a direct correlation between the degree of hearing loss and both the accuracy and the intelligibility of the resulting speech. *See* AUDIOMETRY: Speech Discrimination.

2. Training. Deaf children who have a lot of residual hearing (assuming that they use suitable hearing aids) can often acquire speech skills spontaneously. Those with little or no residual hearing, however, are completely dependent on training. In such cases the quality of speech will be directly related to the quality of training. Even children with a lot of residual hearing may not use it to their full potential unless given appropriate training. It has been suggested that much of the research carried out on the speech of deaf persons tells more about training than it does about deafness.

3. Use. Speech, like all motor skills, must be used if it is to develop properly. Those deaf persons who have the best speech skills will almost always be the ones who use spoken language regularly as a medium for interpersonal communication.

4. Age at onset of deafness. This section has been concerned mainly with individuals who were born deaf. It is important to note, however, that when deafness is acquired after speech skills have been developed, the quality of speech, even though it deteriorates over time, is always better than in cases of congenital deafness.

5. Aptitude. Although a lot is known about the speech of deaf persons, and the factors accounting for differences among individuals, exceptions to the rules do exist. It must be assumed that some deaf people simply have a greater aptitude for the development of speech, and spoken language, than others.

In addition to their separate effects, the factors just outlined interact with one another. For example, the influence of good training increases with the degree of hearing loss; the appropriate method of training changes with degree of loss; and neither good hearing nor good training can compensate for an environment in which speech is simply not used.

CONCLUSION

The aim in this section has been to present a coherent description of the speech characteristics of deaf persons and to consider perceptual, acoustic, motoric, and causative factors. Some of the information is factual while some is inferential. The data on the acoustical properties and the intelligibility of the speech of deaf people, for example, are well substantiated, but information on the motoric characteristics is fairly sparse. The issues of

underlying causes (in particular, the roles of training) and the exact nature of aptitude need systematic, objective research.

Bibliography

Boothroyd, A.: *Hearing Impairments in Young Children*, Prentice-Hall, Englewood Cliffs, New Jersey, 1982.

Calvert, D. R., and S. R. Silverman: *Speech and Deafness*, A. G. Bell Association for the Deaf, Washington, D.C., 1975.

Hochberg, I., H. Levitt, and M. J. Osberger (eds.): *Speech of the Hearing Impaired: Research, Training, and Personnel Preparation*, University Park Press, Baltimore, Maryland, 1983.

Ling, D.: *Speech and the Hearing Impaired Child*, A. G. Bell Association for the Deaf, Washington, D.C., 1976.

Osberger, M. J., and N. S. McGarr: "Speech Production Characteristics of the Hearing Impaired", in N. Lass (ed.), *Speech and Language: Advances in Basic Research and Practice*, vol. 8, Academic Press, New York, 1982.

Arthur Boothroyd

SPEECH, ACOUSTICS OF

There are three basic sources of sound in speech: periodic, random, and transient. The distinguishing characteristic of a periodic sound is that the acoustic waveform repeats cyclically. Periodic sounds typically have a tonal or muscial chordlike quality. A good example of a periodic speech sound is a sustained vowel sung at constant pitch, the steady vibration of the vocal cords serving as the periodic sound source. Everyday speech is spoken rather than sung, however, and because of the continuous variations in voice pitch during speech there are few if any sounds that are truly periodic in normal speech. There are, nevertheless, many speech sounds that are approximately periodic, such as the vowels, diphthongs, and nasal consonants. The waveforms of these sounds have a repetitive periodiclike structure, but they are not perfectly periodic in a mathematical sense. In discussing the acoustics of speech, it is convenient to classify these sounds as having a periodic or quasi-periodic source.

The distinguishing characteristic of a random sound source is that the acoustic waveform is entirely unpredictable—that is, it fluctuates randomly over time. Even when the same sound is repeated several times, the acoustic waveform will differ on each production, although the intensity-frequency spectrum will remain the same. Speech sounds produced by a random sound source have a noiselike quality. The fricative consonants are produced in this way, the source of sound being random turbulent airflow through the vocal tract. *See* SPEECH PRODUCTION.

The third basic source of sound is transient in nature, such as the plosion that occurs when a champagne bottle is opened. Speech sounds known as plosives are typically produced by temporarily blocking the flow of air in the vocal tract. When the blockage is removed, a burst of air is released, thereby exciting the vocal tract acoustically. The sequence of articulatory movements involved in the production of plosive consonants is quite complex, and this burst of aspiration is only one of several acoustic manifestations of the plosive consonants.

SOUND TRANSMISSION CHARACTERISTICS

The sounds of speech are characterized not only by the nature of the sound source (periodic, random, or transient) but also by the sound transmission characteristics of the vocal tract. This factor is illustrated here by a waveform and spectrum representation of the components of the vowel /i/. It shows that the intensity-frequency spectrum of a periodic sound source is modified by the resonances of the vocal tract. The pressure waveform of an idealized pulse train entering the vocal tract at the glottis is a characteristic regular, periodic shape (diagram *a*).

The intensity-frequency spectrum of the periodic pulse train at the glottis takes the form of a line spectrum, that is, the spectrum is made up of a large number of harmonic components, each represented by a vertical line at the harmonic frequency (diagram *a*). Note that the lowest frequency component (the fundamental, F_0) has a value of 100 Hz, which is the reciprocal of the period, T, of the pulse train ($F_0 = 1/T = 1/0.01 = 100$ Hz). Of particular interest is the envelope of the line spectrum, which is shown by a broken line in a spectrum representation.

The pulse train and associated intensity-frequency spectrum change when the glottal pulses are passed through a resonance centered at 300 Hz (diagram *b*). The pressure waveform is still clearly periodic, but the shape of the waveform is quite different. The intensity spectrum on the right-hand side shows that the harmonic components in the vicinity of the resonance frequency, 300 Hz, have been preserved, but components at some distance from 300 Hz have been severely attenuated.

When the pulse train and associated intensity spectrum pass through a resonance at 2300 Hz, the shape of the periodic waveform again is altered (diagram *c*). The intensity spectrum shows very little attenuation at the resonance frequency, 2300 Hz, but the spectrum decreases on either side of the resonance frequency.

If the pulse train and associated intensity spectrum pass through a pair of resonances, for example at 300 and 2300 Hz, the resulting waveform is quite complex, containing both low (300 Hz) and high (2300 Hz) frequency components (diagram *d*). The intensity spectrum is similarly quite complex, with two major concentrations of acoustic power, the harmonics centered on 300 Hz and those centered on 2300 Hz, respectively. These concentrations of acoustic power are known as formants.

The waveform of a male voice producing the vowel /i/ will not be perfectly periodic, the second period being very slightly longer than the first (diagram *e*). The shape of the waveform also changes slightly from one period to the next, and the associated intensity spectrum will have at least five formants. In addition to the concentrations of acoustic power at 300 and 2300 Hz, the spectrum envelope also will show peaks at 3300, 3900, and 4700 Hz.

The two most important characteristics of the frequency-intensity spectrum of a speech sound are the formant structure (that is, the peaks in the spectrum envelope) and the spacing of the harmonic components. Most voiced sounds are identified in terms of their formants, particularly the frequencies of the first two formants. The pitch of the voice is determined primarily by the spacing (diagram *e*) between the harmonic components. In the example of the male voice the harmonics are spaced 100 Hz apart, corresponding to a low-pitched male voice. The spacing between harmonics is equal to the fundamental frequency of the voice ($F_0 = 100$ Hz), but there need not be any signal power at the voice fundamental frequency for the voice pitch to be heard. Speech transmitted over the telephone, for example, contains no frequency components below about 300 Hz, yet the pitch of the voice is clearly heard even when the voice fundamental frequency is well below 300 Hz.

Of particular importance is the link between the shape of the vocal tract and the formant patterns that are produced, as shown on page 198 by the vocal tract configurations and diagrams of idealized formant patterns for four key vowels. Only the first two formants need be shown, since the frequency ratio of the first two formants is the primary acoustic cue in the identification of vowels.

VOWELS

For the vowel /i/, as in "seen," the arch of the tongue is placed high up and forward in the mouth; the teeth are also close together. The first two resonances corresponding to this vocal tract configuration are widely spaced. Formant 1 (F1) is low in frequency (about 300 Hz), whereas Formant 2 (F2) is relatively high (about 2300 Hz). For the vowel /u/, as in "soon," the front of the mouth is nearly closed and the lips are rounded, thereby extending the effective length of the vocal tract in the region of this constriction. The arch of the tongue is pushed upward toward the upper, back part of the mouth. This vowel has the lowest two formant frequencies, F1 being about 300 Hz and F2 about 900 Hz. For

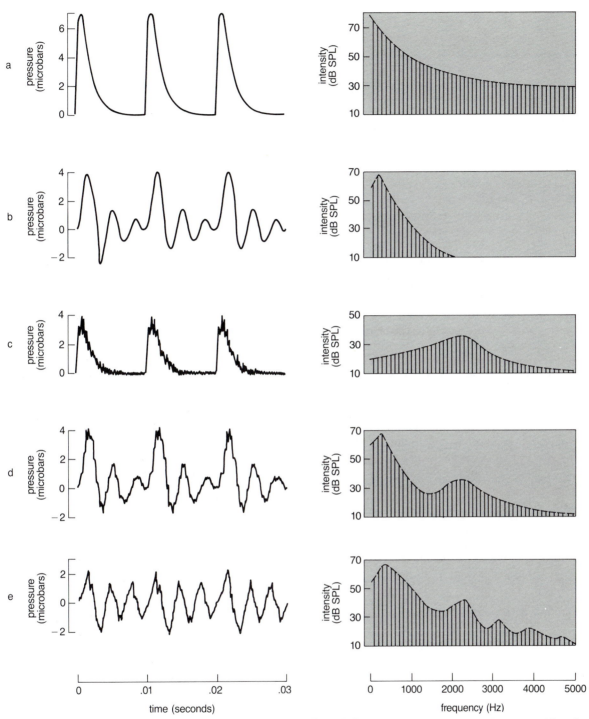

Waveform and spectrum representation of the components of the vowel /i/. **(a) Idealized periodic pulse train + intensity spectrum of glottal pulse. (b) Glottal pulses passed through a resonance of 300 Hz and (c) 2300 Hz, and (d)** through the resonances of 300 Hz and 2300 Hz. **(e) Male voice producing the vowel /i/ (as in "see"). (After Ross and Giolas, 1978)**

the vowel /a/ as in "father," the mouth is wide open with the blade of the tongue low down toward the back of the mouth. This configuration produces relatively little obstruction to the flow of sound through the vocal tract, which is now acoustically similar to an open pipe. The first two formants have intermediate frequencies, 700 and 1300 Hz, respectively. For the vowel /æ/, as in "sat," the mouth is again wide open but with the blade of the tongue toward the front of the mouth and low down. This

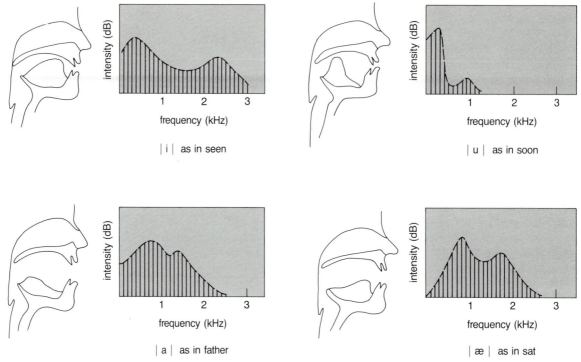

Vocal tract configurations and approximate power-frequency spectra for four key vowels. (After Ross and Giolas, 1978)

vocal tract configuration produces a similar first formant frequency (F1 about 800 Hz) but a somewhat higher second formant frequency (F2 about 1750 Hz) as compared to the preceding vowel.

Vowels are typically classified in terms of tongue position. The vowel /i/ is a high, front vowel whereas /u/ is a high, back vowel. Similarly, /æ/ is a low, front vowel whereas /a/ is a low, back vowel. Another important classification is whether a vowel is tense or lax. Acoustically, a tense vowel is longer in duration than its lax counterpart. The vowels /i/ and /I/ (as in "beet" and "bit," respectively) form a tense-lax pair. The two vowels have similar formant values, but /i/ is longer in duration than /I/. Note that the lax vowels are always terminated by a consonant, whereas the tense vowels can occur with or without a terminating consonant (for example, as in "bee" or "beet"). These are the so-called free vowels. A free vowel, especially one at the end of a phrase or sentence, is characterized by much longer duration than a corresponding checked vowel. There is also some movement of the articulators during a long, free vowel leading to a gradual variation in formant values. This effect is known as diphthongization.

Another factor that affects vowel duration is stress pattern. Stressed vowels are substantially longer than unstressed vowels. The intensity of the vowel and the voice fundamental frequency are typically also increased when a syllable is stressed. Some typical figures are very revealing. The vowel /I/ in "bit" is about 130 milliseconds long when the word is pro-

duced in isolation without emphasis. In contrast, the /i/ in "beet" is about 190 milliseconds long when produced under the same conditions. If, however, "beet" is produced with added stress its duration can exceed 300 milliseconds.

Since vowels are voiced sounds, their spectra have a harmonic structure. If, however, the periodic sound source is replaced by a random sound source (for example, turbulent airflow), then the resulting frequency-intensity spectrum will be continuous rather than discrete. The spectrum of a whispered vowel has approximately the same spectrum envelope as its voiced counterpart. The major difference between the two spectra is that the acoustic power in a voiced vowel is concentrated at the harmonic frequencies, whereas the spectrum of a voiceless vowel is continuous with acoustic power distributed over all frequencies. Note that although it is possible to produce whispered vowels these sounds are not normally used in everyday English.

FRICATIVES

Speech sounds that are normally produced by a random sound source are known as fricatives. There are five fricatives in English: /f/ as in "fin," /θ/ as in "thin," /s/ as in "sin," /ʃ/ as in "shin," and /h/ as in "him." Frication is produced by turbulence in the air stream that is usually caused by a narrow constriction in the vocal tract. The fricatives differ from each other primarily in terms of the location of this constriction. The constriction for the /f/ sound, for example, is at the front of the mouth, whereas, for /s/ and /ʃ/ the constriction is in the middle region of the mouth. Associated with each place of constriction is a different spectrum shape.

The fricative with the highest frequency content is the /s/. The /ʃ/ also has substantial high-frequency components, but the spectral peak for /ʃ/ is lower in frequency than that for /s/. The spectra for /f/ and /θ/ are very similar. In both cases the spectral power is distributed over a wide range without any major peaks in the spectrum envelope, as in the case for /s/ and /ʃ/. Because of the similarities in their spectra, /f/ and /θ/ are often confused with each other in speech reception, even by normal-hearing persons. The fricative /h/ differs from the other fricatives in that it is produced without a major constriction in the vocal tract. As a consequence, the turbulence in the air stream is less than that for the other fricatives, and the /h/ is thus a relatively weak sound.

The voiced fricatives combine both a random and a periodic sound source. In addition to the vibration of the vocal cords, there is turbulence in the air stream. The voiced fricatives have a line spectrum (produced by the periodic vibrations of the vocal cords) that is combined with the continuous spectrum produced by the turbulent airflow. The voiced and voiceless consonants are paired according to their place of constriction. For example, the constriction for /f/ and /v/ is at the front of the mouth and is formed in the same way for both sounds (by placing the lower lip against the upper row of teeth). The /h/ does not have a voiced cognate in English, although it does occur in other languages.

NASAL CONSONANTS

Speech sounds that can only be produced in voiced form are the nasal consonants /m/, /n/ and /ŋ/ (as in "sum," "sun," and "sung," respectively). The acoustic spectra of the nasal consonants are very similar to each other and resemble that of the vowel /u/—that is, the spectrum has a harmonic structure with the major formant peaks in the low-frequency region. The reason for the concentration of acoustic power in the low frequencies is that in producing a nasal consonant the oral cavity is blocked (at the lips for /m/, in the midregion of the mouth for /n/, and toward the back of the mouth for /ŋ/) while the entrance to the nasal cavity is opened by lowering the velum. The latter maneuver effectively extends the length and volume of the vocal tract by a substantial amount, hence lowering its resonant frequencies.

SOUNDS WITH TIME-VARYING SPECTRA

The sounds discussed thus far can all be produced without moving the articulators. As a result, the intensity-frequency spectra of these sounds may be shown as if they were invariant over time. This is not the case in normal speech where the articulators are in constant movement. The spectra shown in diagrams *a–e* should thus be considered as gross, steady-state simplifications. In normal speech the spectra of these sounds will vary with time. There will also be important modifications in spectrum shape depending on the preceding and following sounds. In addition to the above, there are three groups of speech sounds that require articulatory movement for their production and cannot be represented by simplified, steady-state spectra. These are the diphthongs, glides, and stops.

Sounds with time-varying spectra are typically represented in terms of their spectrograms. A sound spectrogram is essentially a three-dimensional representation of sound in which the frequency-intensity spectrum is measured over a short time window and is shown as a function of time. In a spectrogram the horizontal axis shows time, the vertical axis shows frequency, and the degree of grayness shows the relative intensity of the sound. In a spectrogram of the word "see," for example, the early part of the spectrum (from time 0 to about 0.15 second) will show the fricative /s/. Most of the acoustic power of this sound is in the high frequencies, and thus the spectrogram will be relatively dark in the vicinity of 6000 Hz. The remainder of the spectrogram will show the vowel sound (from time ≈ 0.15 second to about 0.5 second). Since the vowel is a voiced sound with a periodic source, this region of the spectrogram will be characterized by vertical striations, each narrow vertical striation corresponding to the sound energy of a single glottal pulse. Dark horizontal bars are the formants of the vowel. Since the vowel is diphthongized, starting with an /I/-like vowel that is gradually transformed into an /i/ vowel, the formants vary with time. The lowest dark bar is the first formant that remains relatively steady at about 300 Hz. The second formant, however, will show a fairly large transition, from about 1800 Hz at the start of the vowel to about 2300 Hz during the later steady-state portion of the vowel.

The vowel in "see" is diphthongized in that the formant values change with time but not by an amount sufficient to produce a separate, distinct sound—that is, the word "see" is heard whether it is produced as /si/ or /ʃIi/. If the effect of diphthongization is to change the meaning of what is said, then the resulting vowellike sound has a separate identity and is known as a diphthong.

Examples of diphthongs are the /aʊ/ as in "sow" and /ɔI/ as in "soy." Note that if only the first part of the diphthong is produced, such as the /ɔ/ in /ɔI/, then the meaning of the word is changed (for example, from "soy" to "saw").

The diphthongs /aʊ/ and /ɔI/ show a fair amount of formant movement over time. This movement, however, is not substantially greater than that manifested by a diphthongized vowel, and it is difficult to distinguish between these two types of speech sound from the acoustic signal only. Context plays an important role in the identification of speech sounds.

The glides, in contrast to the diphthongs, show very rapid formant movements. The amount of movement depends on the following vowel. The glide /w/, for example, begins with the articulators in roughly the position for the vowel /u/, immediately after which the articulators move into positions appropriate for the following vowel. The amount of formant movement for the glide-vowel sequence /wi/ (as in "we") is thus very large, the second formant moving from about 900 Hz (as for an /u/ vowel) to about 2300 Hz for the /i/ vowel. In contrast, the formant movement in the glide-vowel sequence /wu/ (as in "woo") is barely discernible since the articulators are already roughly in the position for the /u/ vowel at the start of the glide.

The glide /j/ begins with the articulators in roughly the position for the vowel /i/. As a consequence, there is minimal formant movement for the glide-vowel sequence /ji/ (as in the word "ye"), but substantial second formant movement for the glide-vowel combination /ju/ (as in "you").

Plosives

The acoustically most complicated speech sound is the plosive or stop consonant. Stop consonants involve a series of articulatory maneuvers, each of which has a distinct acoustic manifestation. The first step is to block the flow of air through the vocal tract. As a consequence, there is usually a break in voicing. When the blockage is removed, a turbulent burst of air is released. The spectrum of this burst of aspiration depends on the location in the vocal tract where the blockage occurred. A blockage at the front of the mouth, as in the production of /b/ or /p/, produces a burst of aspiration that is primarily in the low frequencies. A blockage in the center of the mouth, as in the production of /t/ or /d/, produces aspiration that is primarily in the high frequencies.

Voicing typically begins soon after the release from closure. The time period between the release and the onset of voicing is known as the voice onset time and is an important cue as to whether the stop consonant is voiced or unvoiced. A voiced stop has a much shorter voice onset time than an unvoiced stop. Another important acoustic cue is the duration of the preceding vowel. The vowel preceding a voiced stop is longer than that preceding its unvoiced cognate. Not all stop consonants are released. Unreleased stops are quite common at the end of a word or phrase, and for these sounds the duration of the preceding vowel is a particularly important acoustic cue.

The production of stop consonants involves rapid movements of the articulators as the blockage in the vocal tract is formed and then released. These articulatory movements manifest themselves acoustically as formant transitions. The direction and size of these transitions vary from values typical of the blocked vocal tract to values appropriate for the following (or preceding) speech sound. For example, /ba/ and /ga/ differ significantly in terms of their second formant transitions. Formant 2 for /ba/ begins well below 1300 Hz, moving rapidly toward a steady-state value typical of the vowel /a/. In contrast, Formant 2 in /ga/ begins well above 1300 Hz and falls rapidly toward its steady-state value.

Suprasegmental Structure

Speech has both a segmental and suprasegmental structure. The segmental structure relates to the articulatory and acoustic characteristics of individual speech sounds (sometimes referred to as phonemes). The discussion thus far has dealt primarily with these segmental components. The suprasegmental structure of speech takes into account the way in which individual segments of speech interact as well as the way in which sound sequences are modified so as to convey prosodic and other nonsegmental information.

There is a hierarchy of suprasegmental interactions. At the lowest level (the level closest to the segmental level), neighboring sounds interact depending on the articulatory maneuvers involved in each sound. That is, the articulation of one sound is dependent on the articulatory mechanisms used in the preceding or following sound. This effect is known as coarticulation.

Coarticulation   There is as yet no general theory of coarticulation, but there are general trends that manifest themselves acoustically in various ways. The most common coarticulatory effects involve movement of the articulators. Typically, articulatory movements into and out of a sound produced in the context of everyday speech are less than when the sound is articulated very clearly to emphasize its distinctive characteristics. Acoustically, the reduction in articulatory movement is manifested by smaller formant transitions or, in the case of vowels (or other continuant sounds), there are formant movements toward the steady-state values characterizing the intended sound, but these target values are not always reached before movement toward the next set of target values is initiated.

A particularly common form of coarticulation involves anticipatory movements of the articulators, a consequence of which is that the acoustic characteristics of one sound may appear during the preceding sound. Consider, for example, the words "see" and "soy." During the /s/ in "see," the lips and teeth adjust to the positions needed for the

/i/ vowel. Similarly, there is rounding of the lips during the /s/ in "soy" in preparation for the following diphthong. Spectrograms will show that the /s/ in "soy" has some of the acoustic characteristics of the />I/ diphthong. There are resonances in the /s/ spectrum that are identical in frequency to the higher formants of the diphthong. These resonances are not evident in the spectrum of the /s/ in "see." The overall spectral balance of the latter fricative also shows a greater high-frequency content than for the /s/ in "soy." This difference in spectral balance is similar to that between /i/ and />I/.

Another common form of coarticulation is absorption. This often occurs when adjacent consonants have the same place of articulation. For example, the burst of aspiration during the /t/ in "tar" is absorbed by the friction of the /s/ in "tsar." This absorption also occurs when the /s/ precedes the /t/, as in "star."

Stress Pattern Superimposed upon the complex of coarticulatory effects are durational, intensity, and pitch adjustments imposed by the stress pattern appropriate for a given word. For example, the word "refuse" has two distinct meanings depending on which of its two syllables is stressed. If the first syllable is stressed, the word is a noun meaning "garbage"; if the second syllable is stressed, the word is a verb meaning "to reject." Acoustically, a stressed syllable is typically longer in duration than its unstressed counterpart. Concomitant acoustic correlates of stress are increased intensity and a higher voice fundamental frequency.

The stress pattern of a word or phrase is, in turn, subjugated to the prosodic requirements of the entire utterance. A sentence, for example, often begins with a rising fundamental frequency contour and is usually terminated by a falling contour, except in the case of a simple yes-no question, which may end with a rising intonational inflection. Another important prosodic cue is juncture, in which there is a break in the flow of speech. A common form of juncture is a pause. A pausal juncture is typically accompanied by a prolongation of the preceding syllable and a fall in the voice fundamental frequency just before the pause. Another form of juncture is a sharp change or discontinuity in the voice fundamental frequency.

Nonlinguistic Information In addition to prosody, there is yet another overlay of suprasegmental characteristics. These provide nonlinguistic information such as who is talking (man, woman, or child), the emotional or physical state of the speaker, and other cues that are not indicative of what is said but rather of how it is said. Cues such as average voice pitch, overall vocal effort, rate of talking, hoarseness, and breathiness are very effective indicators in this regard and are often used to convey nonlinguistic information.

A source of great difficulty in describing the suprasegmental characteristics of speech is that the same physical parameter is often used to convey many different cues. For example, a common coarticulatory effect is the lengthening of a vowel before a voiced as opposed to a voiceless consonant. Vowel lengthening is also used to convey stress, as well as to signal the end of a phrase or sentence. At the same time a speaker in a hurry will speak more rapidly by shortening vowel durations.

All of the above effects involve changes in vowel duration, yet in each case the information being cued is quite different. It is thus not surprising that the suprasegmental characteristics of speech are not well understood and there is much ongoing research on the acoustic and articulatory aspects of suprasegmental structure.

Bibliography

Flanagan, J. L.: *Speech Analysis, Synthesis and Perception*, 2d ed., Springer-Verlag, New York, 1972.

Ladefoged, P.: *A Course in Phonetics*, Harcourt Brace Jovanovich, New York, 1975.

Lass, N. J., et al. (eds.): *Speech, Language, and Hearing*, W. B. Saunders, Philadelphia, 1982.

Lehiste, I.: *Suprasegmentals*, MIT Press, Cambridge, Massachusetts, 1970.

Levitt, H.: "The Acoustics of Speech Production," in M. Ross and T. G. Giolas (eds.), *Auditory Management of Hearing Impaired Children*, University Park Press, Baltimore, 1978.

Peterson, G. E., and H. L. Barney: "Control Methods Used in a Study of the Vowels," *J. Acoust. Soc. Amer.*, 24:175–184, 1952.

Harry Levitt

SPEECH, ANALYSIS OF

Complex signals such as speech can be thought of as comprising many simpler, basic units. The elemental unit most commonly used for this purpose is the sine wave. A sine wave is a periodic signal that repeats cyclically (see illustration, page 202). Three parameters are required to specify a sine wave completely: frequency, amplitude, and phase. The frequency, f, specifies the number of times per second that the sine wave goes through an entire cycle (for example, from time t_1 to t_2, or from time t_3 to t_4, and so on). The amplitude, A, is the highest value reached by the sine wave. This peak is reached periodically, and the time difference between successive peaks is equal to the period, T, of the sine wave where $T = 1/f$. The phase, θ, represents the proportion of a cycle completed by a sine wave at time $t = 0$. Each full cycle of a sine wave is subdivided into 360 degrees.

The power of a sine-wave signal is proportional to the square of its amplitude. Since the ear is sensitive to power and relatively insensitive to phase,

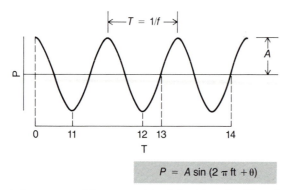

$$P = A \sin (2 \pi ft + \theta)$$

A sine wave and its parameters. (After H. Levitt, "Speech Acoustics," in Larry J. Bradford and William G. Hardy, eds., *Hearing and Hearing Impairment*, Grune and Stratton, 1979)

it is a common practice to specify speech and other complex signals in terms of the power of the component sine waves and to omit the phase information. This form of specification, the power-frequency spectrum, is incomplete but adequate for many practical purposes.

SPECTRUM ANALYSIS

The process whereby a complex waveform can be represented by a sum of sine waves is shown as a–g in the diagram. Row a shows a single sine wave. The power-frequency spectrum of this signal, shown on the right-hand side of row a, consists of a single bar. The location of the bar on the horizontal axis identifies the frequency of the sine-wave component; the height of the bar represents the power of the signal. Note that the phase of the signal is not shown. For those situations in which phase is of interest, the phase spectrum (θ vs. frequency) would also be shown.

Row b of the diagram shows a second sine wave. The frequency of this sine wave is twice that of the sine wave shown in row a, but its amplitude and hence its power is less. Row c shows the sum of the sine waves in rows a and b. Note that this waveform is not sinusoidal in shape but is periodic with a period equal to that of the low-frequency component ($T = 1/f = 1/100 = 0.01$ second). The power-frequency spectrum of this signal is made up of only two components as shown by the two vertical bars in the spectrum diagram. Row d shows what happens when the phase of the second sine wave is advanced by 90 degrees. The resulting waveform is quite different from that of row c, although the power-frequency spectrum remains unchanged. Auditorily, the two waveforms will sound much the same since the ear is relatively insensitive to phase.

Row e shows the waveform and power-frequency spectrum for a signal made up of four sine-wave components. The component sine waves have

been chosen so as to make the composite waveform resemble a periodic pulse train. Note that the periodicity of this composite signal is the same as that of the lowest-frequency component ($T = 1/f = 1/100 = 0.01$ second). Note also that the three remaining sine-wave components have frequencies that are exact integer multiples of the lowest-frequency component (200, 300, and 400 Hz, respectively). The lowest-frequency component is known as the fundamental, and the three higher-frequency components are known as harmonics.

Row f shows the waveform obtained with a very large number of harmonic components. Most of these components have a power that is too small to be visible in the power-frequency diagram. The ear, however, can hear the difference between the signals represented by rows e and f.

In order to provide a representation of the power-frequency spectrum that reflects more accurately the sensitivity of the ear, it is common practice to show signal power on a decibel scale. By definition, power (in dB) = $10 \log_{10}$ (power in absolute units/reference power). The choice of the reference power depends on the specific application of the measurements. A common reference in acoustics is the power required to generate a pressure of 20 micronewtons per square meter (or 0.0002 dyne per square centimeter). The power-frequency diagram in row g is identical to that in row f except that a decibel scale is used and, as a consequence, the higher-frequency harmonics are now visible. For convenience, the power-frequency diagram shown in row g is often referred to simply as the power spectrum.

The power spectrum in row g has a distinct pattern. The power of the harmonics decreases systematically with frequency. The way in which the harmonics vary in power with frequency is known as the spectrum envelope and is shown by the broken line in the diagram. The spectrum envelope is a particularly important consideration in speech analysis. A vowel sound, for example, is characterized by a spectrum envelope having several major peaks known as formants. *See* SPEECH, ACOUSTICS OF.

A major effort in speech analysis is that of determining the spectrum envelope of the speech signal and, for voiced sounds, also determining the harmonic structure of the signal, the most important component being the fundamental F_0. From this information it is possible to determine the resonances of the vocal tract that would give rise to the measured spectrum envelope and, by implication, the shape of the vocal tract. In many practical applications, particularly in the development of speech-training and other sensory aids, derivation of the voice fundamental frequency is of great importance.

Spectrum analysis is the preferred tool for most of these applications, although for limited appli-

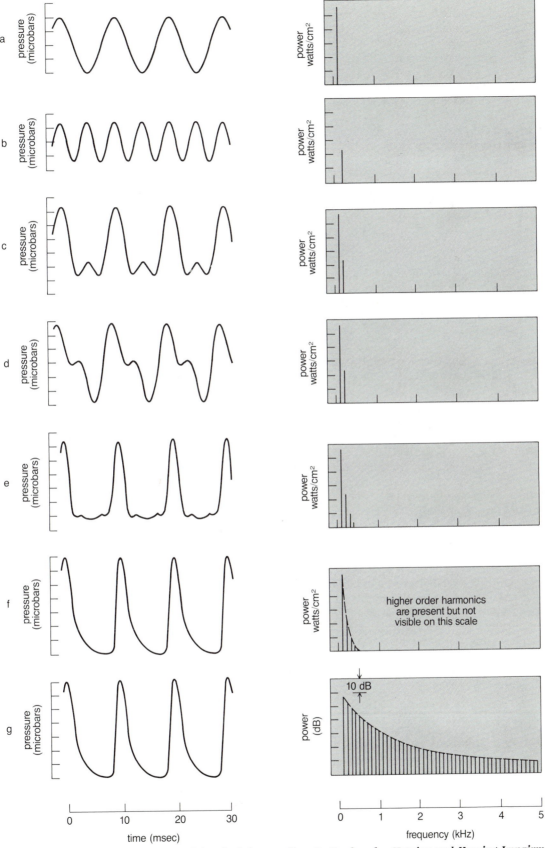

Waveform and spectrum representation of signals. (After H. Levitt, "Speech Acoustics," in Larry J. Bradford and Wil- liam G. Hardy, eds., *Hearing and Hearing Impairment,* Grune and Stratton, 1979)

cations, such as obtaining instantaneous estimates of voice fundamental frequency, the shape of the speech waveform is sometimes analyzed directly without deriving the spectrum. There is also a special form of analysis known as linear predictive coding in which the resonances of the vocal tract are estimated from the speech waveform by using a spectrumlike transformation.

The most common tool in speech analysis is conventional spectrum analysis. Two practical problems, however, need to be addressed in using this technique. The first is that of nonperiodic signals; the second, more difficult problem is that of dealing with signals having time-varying spectra. The speech signal is typically made up of sequences of different sounds (vowels, diphthongs, glides, fricatives, stops, and so on), each of which has distinctly different spectral characteristics. It is important in analyzing the speech signal to be able to track these changes in spectrum shape over time.

NONPERIODIC SIGNALS

The problem of nonperiodic signals is handled simply by treating the signal as if it were periodic but with a period of almost infinite duration. By making the period very large, the harmonic components of this hypothetically periodic signal will be extremely close together and, for all practical purposes, will merge into one another to form a continuous rather than a discrete power-frequency spectrum. Consider, for example, the periodic pulse train in row g of the diagram. If the pulses were to be repeated every 10 seconds rather than every 10 milliseconds, the harmonics of the power-frequency spectrum would be densely packed; that is, the harmonics would be spaced 0.1 Hz apart. However, the spectrum envelope (the broken line in the power-frequency diagram of row g) would remain unchanged. If the pulses were repeated once every 1000 seconds, the harmonics would be even more densely packed (one harmonic every 0.001 Hz), but the spectrum envelope would be unchanged. In the limit, that is, for the period of the pulse train approaching infinity, the harmonics would be so densely packed that the power-frequency spectrum would be effectively a smooth curve taking the form of the spectrum envelope.

TIME-VARYING SPECTRA

Time-varying spectra can be analyzed with a technique known as short-term spectral analysis in which a series of spectral analyses is performed on only a portion of the waveform at a time. A free parameter, to be set by the observer, is the length of time over which each spectral analysis is performed. This time window should be short relative to the time-varying spectral characteristics of the speech signal. The use of a short time window, however,

reduces the resolution with which the speech spectrum can be measured.

The reduction in frequency resolution produced by the use of a short time window is equivalent to that obtained when measuring the power-frequency spectrum with an analyzing filter of broad bandwidth. Consider, for example, what would happen if the power-frequency spectrum shown in row g of the diagram were to be measured with an analyzing filter having a bandwidth of 300 Hz. The harmonics of the spectrum are spaced 100 Hz apart, and thus two to three harmonics would fall within the bandwidth of the analyzing filter as it scanned the frequency spectrum. As a result, the output of the analyzing filter would show the average power contained in the two or three harmonics captured by the analyzing filter. The power of individual harmonics would thus not be measurable with this system. In contrast, if the bandwidth of the analyzing filter were relatively narrow, say 45 Hz, then individual harmonics could be measured. The disadvantage of a narrowband analyzing filter is that its time resolution is relatively poor and individual temporal events within the time window of this filter would be averaged out. The time window of a 45-Hz filter is roughly 2/45 second (about 44 milliseconds), whereas the time window of a 300-Hz filter is roughly 2/300 second (about 6.7 milliseconds). The latter time window is small enough to track individual pitch pulses in the speech signal.

Three dimensions are required to specify the result of a short-term spectral analysis: time, frequency, and power (or intensity). To represent this, time is shown on the horizontal axis, frequency on the vertical axis, and relative intensity by the degree of grayness on a typical diagram. Such a diagram is known as a sound spectrogram. A spectrogram obtained with a relatively broad analyzing filter (300 Hz) is referred to as a broadband spectrogram. A spectrogram with a relatively narrow analyzing filter (45 Hz) is referred to as a narrowband spectrogram.

The broadband spectrogram averages out the effect of individual harmonics, thereby showing the spectrum envelope. Horizontal dark bars in the broadband spectrogram correspond to major peaks in the spectrum envelope known as formants. Since the short-term spectrum analysis is repeated continuously, temporal variations in the frequency and intensity of the formants can be tracked.

The broadband spectrogram also has relatively good time resolution. The vertical striations in this spectrogram correspond to individual pitch pulses in the speech signal. The striations may be very frequent at the start of the utterance, gradually falling off in frequency during the course of the utterance. It is possible to estimate the voice fundamental frequency by measuring the rate at which these pitch pulses occur. A more convenient estimate, however, can be obtained from the narrowband spectrogram.

In a narrowband spectrogram obtained with an analyzing filter of 45-Hz bandwidth, the bandwidth is much less than the harmonic spacing of the speech signal and, consequently, individual harmonics are resolved by the filter. The harmonics appear as narrow, slightly downward-sloping bars in the spectrogram. The formants of a vowel may also be partially visible in that the harmonic bars are darker within the region of a formant (for example, in the vicinity of 300 and 2300 Hz).

The frequency of the fundamental component can be measured directly from the spectrogram, but the accuracy of the measurement will be poor because of the low resolution of the spectrogram in the region of the voice fundamental frequency. A more accurate measurement can be obtained by measuring one of the higher harmonics. A convenient technique is to measure the frequency of the tenth harmonic and then divide by 10 to obtain the frequency of the fundamental.

The sound spectrogram is the most widely used method of speech analysis. Other, more advanced methods use computers to model the speech production mechanism and then to estimate the parameters of these models.

Bibliography

Atal, B. S., and M. R. Schroeder: "Adaptive Predictive Coding for Speech Signals," *Bell System Technical Journal*, 49:1973–1986.

———— and ————: "Predictive Coding of Speech Signals," *Proc. 1967 Conf. Commun. Process.*, pp. 360–361, 1967.

Blackman, R. B., and J. W. Tukey: *The Measurement of Power Spectra*, Dover Publications, New York, 1958.

Flanagan, J. L.: *Speech Analysis, Synthesis and Perception*, Springer-Verlag, New York, 1972.

Markel, J. D., and A. H. Gray, Jr.: *Linear Prediction of Speech*, Springer-Verlag, New York, 1976.

Harry Levitt

SPEECH DEVELOPMENT

Investigators of the process of speech development attempt to describe the ways in which both normally developing and disabled children learn the system of pronunciations for words and sentences. Speech development is concerned with acquisition of a phonetic or "speech sound" system, with special emphasis on speech production and lesser emphasis on speech perception. Nonmeaningful speechlike vocalizations of infancy are currently considered to be precursors to development of a meaningful speech sound system. Researchers generally treat the learning of nonphonetic aspects of the linguistic system (for example, word meanings or syntax) as part of the development of "language" rather than "speech."

ERROR PATTERNS IN NORMALLY DEVELOPING CHILDREN

Normal development of fully intelligible speech, pronounced without errors, is a process that spans the period from age 1 to 5 years. The first meaningful words of childhood usually occur at around 12 months. Early words are characteristically pronounced with certain systematic imperfections. Normally developing children in the age range of 24–30 months usually manifest a stable pattern of errors, favoring syllables that consist of a single consonant followed by a single vowel (called a CV syllable). The consonant is commonly a stop (usually *b* or *d*), nasal (*m* or *n*) or glide (*w* or *y*). The vowels vary from child to child, but most two-year-olds use a limited vowel repertoire. Children of this age often replace or delete sounds that are not favored or do not fit the favored pattern. An example of replacement of less favored (or "avoided") sounds by favored ones occurs when singleton fricative or affricate sounds (*s*, *z*, *f*, *v*, *th*, *sh*, *ch*, or *j*) are replaced by stops (*b* or *d*), as in the pronunciation of "do" for "zoo." Similarly, liquids (*r* and *l*) are often replaced by glides (*w* or *y*), as in "wabbit" for "rabbit" or "yight" for "light." Children may reduce the number of elements in a syllable to accommodate their preference for the CV pattern. For example, consonant clusters may be reduced, as in the pronunciation "top" for "stop," and final consonants may be lost, as in "bah" for "ball." In general, the syllable simplifications indicate the same preferences for particular sound types as the replacements—thus in reduction of fricative-stop (for example, *st*) or stop-liquid (for example, *bl*) clusters, it is the favored stop consonant (*t* or *b*) that is preserved and the fricative (*s*) or liquid (*l*) consonant that is deleted.

The systematic errors of young children usually reduce the total inventory of speech segments or syllables the child will pronounce. Mature languages normally include both singleton and clustered consonants, but the child tends to produce only the singletons; adult languages normally include syllables both with and without final consonants, but the child tends (especially when very young) to produce only syllables without final consonants; adult words include both *r*'s and *w*'s, but the child tends to collapse the two categories together, producing only *w*'s. Since so many of the systematic speech errors of childhood tend to simplify the speech inventory, investigators suspect that the pattern of errors represents, at least in part, a method to make the task of acquiring the phonetic system of the target language more manageable.

It is not true that all the speech errors of childhood systematically simplify the speech sound inventory. Some errors are not made consistently (that is, a particular word may be imperfectly pronounced in a variety of different ways). Other errors are consistent, but do not produce simplification. Such errors are less common and tend to occur mainly at later stages of phonetic development, when much of the error pattern of early childhood has already been overcome.

There is a variation from child to child in particular error patterns during acquisition of speech. Some normally developing children appear easily to acquire, and occasionally individuals show an outright preference for, certain sounds that are usually avoided. Still, an examination of fairly large numbers of children, acquiring a variety of languages, shows an unmistakable predominance of the favored sound types. The childhood favorites are the most commonly occurring mature language sounds, stop, nasal, and glide consonants in CV syllables. The avoided sounds of childhood (fricatives, affricates, aspirated consonants, retroflex liquids, clustered or final consonants, and so on) are often missing in mature languages. The similarity in the sounds favored by young children, and by languages in general, suggests that organismic factors (perhaps ease of production or perception) may account for the pattern of favored sounds.

SPEECH PERCEPTION AND SPEECH ERRORS

Until the 1970s it was commonly believed that speech sound errors of childhood were substantially caused by perceptual insufficiencies of the child. Speech sound confusions were thought to be caused by lack of discrimination. Two kinds of evidence have contributed to a more recent view that rejects a major role for discrimination in the pattern of speech errors. One kind of evidence concerns the fact that systematic speech sound errors in normally developing children are virtually always unidirectional, that is, the favored sound is substituted for the avoided sound, but not vice versa. If only discrimination was involved, one would expect bidirectional substitution, that is, sometimes sound X would be substituted for sound Y, and sometimes Y would be substituted for X. Unidirectional substitution must be attributed, at least in part, to a preference for one sound over another, independent of possible difficulties of discrimination.

The other evidence that has tended to limit the purported role of perception in speech errors comes from direct studies of discrimination of speech sounds in infancy. Beginning in the early 1970s, a variety of studies using instrumental techniques that monitor infant sucking, heart rate, EEG, or head turning in response to experimentally presented sounds have shown that many syllable pairs differing in a single phonetic feature are discriminated by hearing infants of 1 to 9 months old. The experiments on perception were thought particularly important because they showed that infants can auditorily discriminate many sound pairs that are confused in speech production (for example, the English *ba-pa* or *sa-ta* pairs).

Experimental demonstrations of this surprising auditory ability have led some researchers to conclude that infants are innately predisposed to discriminate any speech sound contrasts that occur frequently in languages. However, the experimental studies do not warrant such a conclusion. Only a small number of such contrasts have been considered, and some of those have not been discriminated. Furthermore, the test setting greatly simplifies the discrimination task for the infant when compared to the real task of speech recognition. The infant is presented with one brief (usually one-syllable) utterance at a time in a repeating format. This utterance is contrasted with another single brief utterance in a repeating format. Normally only one exemplar of each utterance type is used. Moreover, each syllable presented to the infant is meaningless; it is not a word. Such a pattern of presentation of speech sounds to infants is much less complex than the real pattern of speech. In real speech every pronunciation of a syllable is slightly, or sometimes substantially, different; repetition is the exception; syllables usually occur in long, highly variable strings; and every syllable is meaningful and must be decoded for its semantic as well as phonetic value. Because the experimental work on speech perception in infants has involved these methodological limitations, the role of perception in the speech sound errors of young children has not been resolved.

Recent studies on meaningful recognition of words by young children at 2 and 3 years of age are also clouded by methodological problems, and provide support only for the idea that some speech sound errors (for example, the childhood confusion of *f* and *th* in English) may involve speech discrimination problems. Most sound pairs investigated have not provided evidence of perceptual difficulties in children. Consequently, knowledge of the role of speech perception in young-child speech errors remains very limited.

ROLE OF INFANT VOCALIZATIONS

Until the 1970s it was widely believed that infant vocalizations of the first year of life were not related to speech development. Investigators did not study infant vocal sounds, because they had been taught that infants produced a morass of acoustic confusion including all possible human speech sounds. These beliefs were unfounded empirically. The first systematic investigations of the relationships of speech sound preferences in infant vocalizations and young-child speech showed unmistakable and widespread similarities. In fact, the preferences for particular sounds or sound sequences in young childhood could easily be discerned in infants' premeaningful vocalizations at 8 to 10 months of age.

Even the sounds of younger infants show unmistakable evidence of the emergence of a linguistic capacity. Infant patterns of exploratory speech-like vocalization show a systematic progression across the first year of life from isolated vowellike sounds and presyllabic articulations to sequences of canonical syllables (for example, "baba," "nana," "dede").

Even though normally developing infants appear always to produce canonical babbling within the first year of life and although such babbling is intimately related to speech phonetically, it is not clear that such babbling is actually necessary for the development of speech. Infants that are largely prevented from vocalizing during the first year by surgical intervention (tracheostomy) to combat respiratory anomalies often show no long-term speech deficits after the respiratory problems are solved. Research does not make clear whether such children may have important short-term deficits in speech development, and it is usually hard to determine how much vocalizing has been possible for the tracheostomized child. Thus, it is not known whether canonical babbling is necessary for the normal development of speech.

General Disorders of Speech

The process of correcting the systematic speech errors of childhood varies from child to child. A particular pattern of error (for example, the *r* problem) may persist for several years in one child but be overcome after only a few months by another. Because of the variation from child to child (all of whom eventually speak flawless mature language), it is difficult to establish a cut-off age after which to categorize the child as speech-handicapped. In general, children who reach elementary school still showing systematic speech sound errors may be considered for speech therapy, especially if the pattern of errors persists beyond the second or third grade. If the child's errors do not substantially impede intelligibility, therapy is sometimes considered to be a matter of choice, since such errors may have only minor social consequences and rarely persist beyond adolescence in any case. For children with errors that do impede intelligibility, treatment should begin earlier and should be especially vigorous. The conditions that contribute to

disorders of the speech sound system include hearing impairment, mental retardation, cleft lip or palate, and motor handicaps such as those attributable to cerebral palsy.

In general, the particular speech sounds favored by normally developing children are also favored by speech-handicapped young children. For example, mentally retarded children without motor handicaps usually show speech errors similar to those of younger normally developing children, except when vocal anatomical or motor anomalies (cleft lip or palate, Down's syndrome, or cerebral palsy) produce deviant patterns of sound that can be directly attributed to the physical anomalies.

Some children show delayed language or speech development even though they are not hearing-impaired or mentally retarded and have no obvious anatomical or motor disability. Such children are said to have functional articulation disorders and, in general, manifest favoritism toward the same class of speech sounds as normally developing children. Occasionally such children show deviant patterns, favoring notably odd elements (for example, VC syllables or unusual consonants). Whether such patterns are due to undiagnosed physical or mental anomalies remains a question for further research.

Hearing-Impaired Children

Speech development in hearing-impaired children is similar to that of hearing children in some ways but differs in others. The differences are magnified in cases of more severe hearing losses, but even those profoundly deaf show many of the features of speech sound preference found in hearing children. For example, both hearing and deaf children tend to favor single initial consonants in syllables. Furthermore, both hearing and deaf children show a preference for stop, nasal, and glide consonants. These common preferences produce substantial commonalities in the patterns of error in the two groups.

Differences in the patterns are, however, quite discernible. Many of the errors of deaf children can be attributed to a reliance on speechreading. Sound elements that are not easily seen tend to be lost. For example, deaf children reduce consonant clusters involving velar stops and liquids (*kr*, *kl*, *gr*, *gl*) by eliminating the velar stop, an element that is very difficult to speechread, while hearing children almost always eliminate the more visible liquid. The vowel errors of deaf children often show correct lip shapes but incorrect tongue positions, a pattern not found commonly in hearing children. *See* SPEECHREADING.

Another difference in speech development between deaf and hearing children is that deaf children tend to produce more bidirectional substitutions. Deaf children may produce *m* in place of *b* or vice versa, a pattern of error that almost never occurs in hearing children. The bidirectionality of this and other common substitution errors of deaf children suggests that the sounds are not discriminated by the children. In general, deaf children's errors tend to be far more unstable than those of hearing children. The same word is pronounced differently on different occasions (with different substitutions, deletions, and additions each time). Such instability of production is usually short-lived in hearing children, but it tends to persist in hearing-impaired individuals.

Errors involving intrusive elements (additions of sound elements) are also more common in deaf children. Unnecessary consonants, vowels, or whole syllables are sometimes added to words by deaf children, a pattern that occurs only in the most circumscribed situations in the hearing child.

Deaf children show a variety of suprasegmental problems with their speech—hypernasality, monotonic or high pitch, and extended segmental durations. Errors of rhythmicity are considered to be among the most characteristic patterns of deaf speakers. Of the rhythmic errors, one of the most difficult to correct is incorrect timing of transitions between vowels and consonants. Such transitions should be smooth and should occur within a time frame of 25–120 milliseconds. Deaf speakers often produce syllables that violate the timing requirement or have breaks in the transition. The rhythmicity problems in speech of deaf children are noticeable as early as the first year of life. Deaf infants commonly do not produce canonical (well-timed) syllables during the first year of life, while hearing children begin canonical babbling by 10 months of age.

The early appearance of speech development deficits in the deaf child, along with the many unique speech error patterns of deaf children, suggests that special speech therapy approaches should be used. These approaches should consider the pattern of errors that deaf children hold in common with hearing children and the patterns that are unique to deaf individuals. There are many empirical indications that early, intensive speech therapy with deaf children can produce substantial improvements in speech capability. *See* SPEECH; SPEECH TRAINING.

Bibliography

Hudgins, C. V., and F. Numbers: "An Investigation of the Intelligibility of the Speech of the Deaf," *Genetic Psychology Monographs*, vol. 25, 1942.

Ingram, D.: *Phonological Disability in Children*, Elsevier, Amsterdam, 1974.

Locke, J.: *Phonological Acquisition and Change*, Academic Press, New York, 1984.

Stark, R. E. (ed.): *Language Behavior in Infancy and Early Childhood*, Elsevier, Amsterdam, 1981.

Yeni-Komshian, G., J. Kavanagh, and C. Ferguson (eds.): *Child Phonology*, 2 vols., Academic Press, New York, 1980.

D. Kimbrough Oller

SPEECH EVALUATION

Speech evaluation is a fundamental part of the educational program of many hearing-impaired persons, and provides information that is the basis for recommending an appropriate intervention program. Subsequent evaluations may be conducted at regular intervals to assess progress.

During speech evaluations, an experienced listener presents appropriate materials to the hearing-impaired person in order to judge several aspects of speech production. The tester evaluates the articulation of phonemes or segmentals comprising vowels, diphthongs, and consonants in American spoken English. In addition, an evaluation is made of suprasegmental production or prosodic features, such as changes in loudness, voice pitch, or duration that together convey syllable or word stress. Prosodic features also include the appropriate use of pauses at the end of a phrase, a thought unit, or a sentence, and changes in intonation or voice pitch to differentiate a statement from a question. The tester must also consider the use of spontaneous vocalizations, vocal intensity or loudness, rate, and pitch control. The evaluation of suprasegmental production and the assessment of voice quality overlap. The listener must judge if the overall level of the voice pitch or fundamental frequency is appropriate for the speaker's age and sex, if there are inappropriate breaks in voice pitch, or if there is inappropriate nasalization throughout an utterance. Segmental and suprasegmental production taken together with appropriate voice quality contribute to the speaker's overall intelligibility.

Speech evaluations are perceptual in nature, since it is the listener's ear that is the ultimate judge of the correctness of the production. Several factors may affect the test scores. For example, even among highly experienced listeners, results may differ if the listener can see the speaker rather than only hear a tape recording. Scores may also vary if the speaker, and more specifically the speaker's particular pattern of speech errors, is well known to the tester.

The speech evaluation usually results in a profile of correct productions as well as error patterns, which then form the basis for speech training. However, the speech evaluation made by the experienced listener may not reflect the intelligibility of the deaf talker to persons unused to the speech of deaf people. Factors that account for the differences between experienced and inexperienced listeners have been studied in some detail, with particular attention given to the type of evaluation material (such as single words versus sentences).

Objective measures of speech produced by hearing-impaired speakers also have been obtained. These evaluative data address specific research questions rather than immediate educational challenges, although such basic information ultimately leads to better diagnostic and intervention programs. Instrumentation studies include acoustic analyses of the speech output of hearing-impaired persons and physiological studies of respiration, phonation, and articulation. These analyses are not yet part of the basic educational speech program, because the instrumentation is often highly specialized and prohibitively expensive, and the analysis of the test results is frequently very time-consuming. As technology becomes more sophisticated and as costs decrease, many procedures once considered experimental will become part of the educational evaluation.

The discussion below focuses on the common perceptual tests currently used to evaluate the speech of hearing-impaired people and describes some of the factors that influence test results. Objective measures used in research studies are also considered, since these methods may form part of the evaluative procedures of the future.

Perceptual Tests

Most speech evaluation depends on perceptual tests of speech production skills. Perceptual tests are of four broad types: segmental production, suprasegmental production, voice quality, and speech intelligibility.

SEGMENTAL PRODUCTION

Articulation testing is a method of systematically assessing the production of vowels, diphthongs, and consonants in varied word positions (initial, medial, or final place). While there has been considerable effort devoted to identifying typical segmental errors in speech produced by deaf people, there are surprisingly few evaluative measures that are both valid and reliable for this population. Further, in these research studies, a variety of test materials (nonsense syllables, words, and sentences) were used, and intelligibility scores varied depending on whether the stimulus was produced as an isolated word or in a sentence. The cognitive and linguistic skills required to produce a word in response to a picture or printed stimulus are quite different from those needed to generate spontaneously an intelligible oral word.

Articulation tests, originally developed to assess speech skills in hearing children, are often adapted for deaf children. However, the tests tend to be inappropriate for the deaf child, since they are based on the developmental sequence of phonemes that emerge in hearing children. This underlying test philosophy may not reflect the sequence in which the hearing-impaired child acquires phonemes. Further, the test may be insensitive to the particular articulation errors of the deaf child that would not be expected in a misarticulating hearing child. In addition, these tests do not assess phoneme production in a variety of phonetic contexts. For example, /d/ in the stimulus word "Dad" would not be articulated the same way as /d/ in the word "do." Thus, little information can be obtained about the effect of phonetic context or of coarticulation of speech sounds for the deaf talker. The validity of these adapted articulation tests as assessment tools for deaf children's speech production remains to be demonstrated.

One test that considers some of these objections was promulgated by D. Ling. His Phonetic Level Speech Evaluation measures articulation of vowels and diphthongs in isolation, as well as consonants in combination with vowels in simple and more complex nonsense syllables. The test assumes a developmental sequence whereby speech sounds acquired earlier by the deaf child occur at the beginning of the test. It also assumes that the child has acquired some mastery of suprasegmental production. At a higher level, the Phonological Level Speech Evaluation examines these skills in spontaneous speech. The test, both the phonetic and phonologic parts, is meant to be a diagnostic teaching instrument in which the results are used in a specific speech-training program. As with the adapted tests, there are no data on test validity and reliability; however, the test is in widespread use.

Articulation tests measure the rate at which improvement in articulation skills is noted over time. For each student, progress is charted in the child's Individualized Educational Plan (IEP) or speech file. However, there are little data on the growth of articulation skills in large groups of deaf children. Changes in articulation skills of approximately 125 hearing-impaired children who were enrolled in 13 schools for deaf pupils in New York State are illustrated. These students were evaluated in a longitudinal study of language, speech production, and speech reception skills of deaf children. The data show little change in performance for any decile. The slight differences (either an increase or a decrease in performance) are not statistically significant, with the exception of decile 1, the poorest group. Unfortunately, the number of phonemes that this group articulated correctly remained rather low overall.

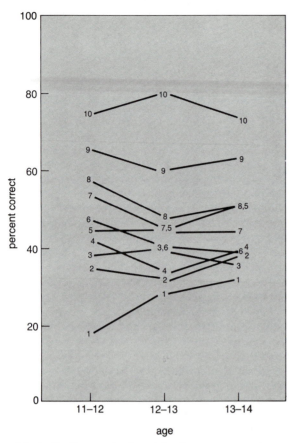

This decile diagram is plotted for the percentage of segmentals produced correctly on the articulation test. The decile plot is obtained by subdividing the speakers into 10 groups according to their relative performance in the first year of the study (age 10–11 years). The first decile contains the scores of speakers whose test performance was in the lowest 10 percent; the second contains the scores of speakers whose performance made up the second-lowest 10 percent, and so on until the highest decile (10). Each decile group contains the same set of children for each year of the study. There is little change in any group's performance during the three years of the study.

Two common errors in deaf children's speech—errors of omission (leaving out a phoneme) and errors of substitution (articulating one phoneme for another)—are also shown. In this illustration the decile groups are inverted, with the highest decile (10) plotted near the bottom of the figure because this decile shows the lowest error score. Decile 1 (the poorest group) had the greatest number of omission and substitution errors. This decile group is distinguished from all others because both error categories showed a statistically significant decline in percent of errors. On the whole, the percentage of errors remained about the same for each decile group during the three years of testing.

These data are discouraging in that group performance did not increase. This should not be interpreted to mean that deaf children cannot achieve better articulation skills. However, it does demonstrate the need for better teaching techniques, as well as better test instruments to evaluate articulation skills and to measure progress.

SUPRASEGMENTAL TESTS

Current theories on speech production in normal-hearing and hearing-impaired children note the importance of suprasegmental production. Correct stress, intonation, and rhythm are crucial to intelligible speech, and the articulatory movements that produce these prosodic features have a direct bearing on articulation skills and also on voice quality. While hearing children develop suprasegmental skills at an early age, deaf children do not. Unfortunately, there is a shortage of standardized tests to examine systematically these important aspects of speech production.

Tests of suprasegmental production may take two forms. The first is a rating scale to assess prosodic features. For example, at the National Technical Institute for the Deaf, prosodic features are rated on scales from 1 (poor) to 5 (good), in one-level increments. Each level on the scale has a different description of the rating. These rating scales, including ones for speech intelligibility and voice quality, have been tested for validity and reliability. However, one problem with rating scales is interrater reliability—given the same set of recordings, different ratings may be awarded by different listeners, even among highly trained judges. While differences between raters may be only one scale apart, an average of several ratings over several listeners is recommended. *See* NATIONAL TECHNICAL INSTITUTE FOR THE DEAF.

A second approach to assessing prosodic feature production is to evaluate specific contrasts, for example, the child's ability to produce a difference in word stress, sentence intonation, or pause. In one experimental form (see first illustration, page 212), deaf children read simple sentences that varied in prosodic forms; the subject's responses were tape-recorded and presented to listeners for evaluation. The listeners were asked to identify if the feature was correct or, if not, which error type had occurred (such as, stress in the wrong location, or a statement produced for a question). The percent of correct productions was then calculated. There were large gains in scores from the first year (ages 11–12) to the second year (ages 12–13), and even children in the lowest deciles (1–3) showed significant improvements.

These results are encouraging, because the evaluative approach seems to be a viable one and because the children showed considerable improvement in prosodic feature production. However, this test assessed only the simplest prosodic contrasts

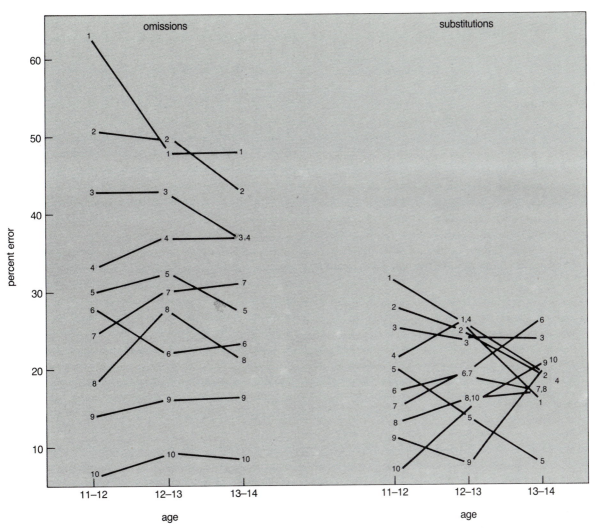

The decile diagram shows the percent omissions (left) and substitutions (right) on the test of segmental production. Decile groups are inverted with decile 1, evidencing the most errors, plotted at the top of the figure, and decile 10, **evidencing the fewest errors, at the bottom. Error patterns remain about the same for each group during the three years of study.**

in read speech, and production of correct suprasegmentals for spontaneous speech is dependent on much finer aspects of speech production.

To summarize, since there are no standardized clinical tests, suprasegmentals or prosodic features are usually assessed by using listener judgments to rate the productions, or they may be evaluated as part of a test of articulatory skills.

VOICE QUALITY

In conventional voice examinations, vocal quality is assessed during phonation of sustained vowels and during production of a continuous speech sample (a read passage or spontaneous conversation). Specifically, voice quality refers to those characteristics that are generated by the voice at the level of vocal-fold vibration. In the broader sense,

however, voice quality refers to the way in which the voice is filtered acoustically by the shape of the vocal tract. Thus, the layperson speaks of a nasal voice quality. It is well known that an abnormal voice quality is a distinguishing charactertistic of the deaf population's speech production. Terms such as breathy, flat, tense, throaty, and nasal are frequently used by teachers to characterize deaf voices, and the deaf voice can be readily distinguished from normal speakers, voice disordered groups, and those feigning deafness when a speech sample consisting of a consonant and vowel is presented to experienced listeners. *See* SPEECH.

These considerations suggest that articulation plays an important role in the listener's perception of voice quality. Yet assessment of voice quality per se is a difficult task. The primary assessment test

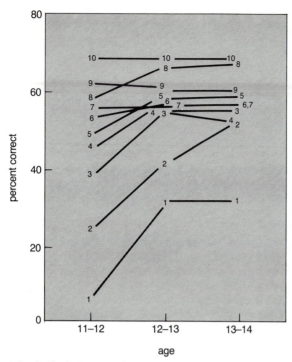

The decile diagram is the percent correct scores obtained by speakers on the test of prosodic feature production. Scores improved considerably with age for many of the decile groups.

is a rating scale judgment of aspects of voice quality such as pitch register (whether the voice pitch is appropriately high or low with respect to the speaker's age and sex), pitch control (whether the speaker can sustain phonation successfully), control of air expenditure, breathiness of voice, and nasal resonance.

SPEECH INTELLIGIBILITY

This measure may be obtained in three distinct ways. In the first, a score, or a percent of intelligible speech, is obtained. The speaker reads a list of words, phrases, or sentences; a listener transcribes the responses; and a ratio of the number of intelligible utterances to the total number of utterances produced is calculated. This is the method of choice in many research studies, although a large sample of speech and a sizable number of listeners are required to obtain reasonable results. This approach was adopted in educational evaluations by M. Magner, who developed a set of 600 sentences within the vocabulary range of young deaf children. However, only a subset of sentences is read at each evaluation. Magner's test has both practical problems (for example, a group of listeners is needed) and methodological ones (the sentence subsets are not balanced for vocabulary, grammatical difficulty, or phonetic or suprasegmental context).

In a second approach, speech intelligibility measures are also made as a descriptive rating reflecting overall speech production performance. Again, the subject reads a selected passage, the subject responds to questions or describes a picture, and listeners rate the sample on a scale similar to, or part of, the National Technical Institute for the Deaf profiling system previously described.

In a third approach, speech intelligibility is assessed by using a forced-choice test. The listener must decide which of several closely related items the talker has produced. Items in the test are selected according to typical error patterns that detrimentally affect speech intelligibility (such as errors of vowel height, vowel place, or consonant voicing). Proponents of this method argue that this speech intelligibility test is objective and analytical, and that it avoids factors such as listener experience and context, which interact with intelligibility.

As in other aspects of special evaluation, developmental data on overall performance are lacking. Intelligibility ratings based on the National Technical Institute for the Deaf rating scales of a large group of school-aged deaf children described above is illustrated. A rating of 1 is given for "speech that is completely unintelligible" and a rating of 5 for "speech that is completely intelligible." The data

The decile diagram is ratings of speech intelligibility for the speakers during four years of evaluation. A rating of 1 indicates "speech that is completely unintelligible," a rating of 5 indicates "speech that is completely intelligible."

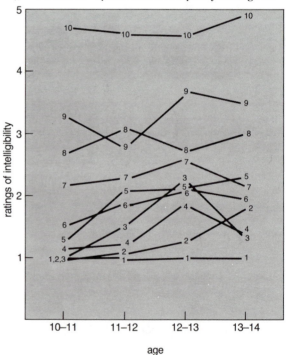

are plotted in deciles as in the preceding figures. A striking feature of the plot is the relatively large proportion of children with low ratings. Nearly two-thirds of the children received ratings of unintelligible (1) or barely intelligible speech (2). The patterns remain essentially the same across the four years of testing.

FACTORS THAT AFFECT EVALUATION SCORES

Perceptual speech tests are to some extent subjective and dependent on factors other than the individual's speech. Two significant factors influencing perceptual speech evaluations are listener experience and context.

Listener Experience One of the most critical factors in the evaluation of speech is the experience of the listener. Speech that is judged relatively intelligible in the classroom may still be virtually unintelligible to the occasional listener. The experienced listener's advantage has been noted for words in sentences, words produced in isolation, and for segmentals such as vowels.

Several explanations have been offered for the experienced listener's advantage, but none has been substantiated in careful study. Experienced listeners do not obtain higher scores simply because they are more familiar with typical segmental errors in deaf speech production and thus recode the speech to compensate for these error types. Furthermore, experienced listeners and inexperienced listeners alike make use of linguistic context to improve the intelligibility of the speaker. The fact that the experienced listener understands deaf speech is not related to personal knowledge of the speaker; once familiar with deaf speech, the experienced listener is able to generate higher intelligibility scores to deaf speakers in general. Both groups of listeners who can see the speaker will perform better than when there are only auditory cues. The differences between groups then, is due to fairly complex aspects of deaf speech production that are not immediately apparent to the listener but that must be learned.

Even within a group of experienced listeners, an important factor is the skill of the evaluator. Many tests require special knowledge on the part of the rater. The test results are meant to be diagnostic and prescriptive in nature, and thus a skilled judge conducting the evaluation will be critical. The detailed analysis that results from the listener's evaluation forms the basis for the subject's remedial training.

Context For both the experienced and the inexperienced listener, words produced in sentences are more intelligible than words produced in isolation. This is known as the context effect and generally refers to the environment in which a key word is produced. However, some sentences may also be higher in linguistic context than others (for example: Get your ball and ___; I ate bacon and ___). Furthermore, knowledge of the test material (such as the test word in the articulation test) can also influence judgments of accuracy. Each of these context effects must be accounted for in speech evaluation testing. Measures of speech intelligibility are particularly sensitive to context effects. Thus, a forced-choice speech intelligibility test may be the best choice since semantic, syntactic, and lexical cues are unavailable to the listener.

Objective Measures

The tests of segmental and suprasegmental production, of voice quality, and of speech intelligibility rely on the listener's ear and are thus perceptual in nature. However, valuable information concerning either perceptually correct or perceptually incorrect productions can be obtained from study of the acoustic speech signal and the underlying physiological activities of speech production.

These events cannot be directly recovered from the listener's perception. Thus, research employing a combined perceptual, acoustic, and physiological approach has been used to study speech produced by hearing-impaired persons. Moreover, the long history of sensory aids research has produced instruments that provide objective feedback of certain parameters of the speech signal. While these sensory aids are used more often in speech training than in speech testing, the potential for such application of these devices should not be overlooked. For example, deaf speakers may not distinguish a declarative sentence, a question, or a word with emphatic stress by changing inflection, or the intonation contour. A computerized visual display of the intonation contour of this production can provide an objective record that the listener can use to confirm the perception. The record also can be retrieved for objectively assessing pre- and posttraining progress. In another example, segmental tests of vowel production reveal substitutions of closely related vowels. Acoustic studies of the format patterns of these vowels shows a tendency for some deaf speakers to produce vowels in a very reduced frequency range. A visual display of the format frequencies could be incorporated as an objective record into the evaluative process. *See* SPEECH TRAINING.

At the physiological level, there exists such noninvasive devices as the laryngograph that, when coupled to an oscilloscope, provides a display of the opening and closing phases of the vocal folds. This device has been used in research and as a sensory aid, but not in the educational evaluation of certain voice quality problems. *See* SENSORY AIDS.

There is always a developmental lag between technology and clinical or educational application.

Initially, the technology may be expensive, the equipment may require the user to have special training, and the analysis may be time-consuming. All these preclude use in the educational setting. There may also be reluctance on the educator's part to relinquish any part of the evaluative process to a machine. But always, in the development of speech evaluation tests such as those described above, the educational goal has been to provide a meaningful record of speech production and to note changes in production over time. The immediate challenge—to couple the listener's perception with objective acoustic and physiological records of the speech performance—may be one of the most interesting directions that speech evaluation research will take in the near future.

Bibliography

Boothroyd, A.: "Evaluation of Speech Production of the Hearing Impaired: Some Benefits of Forced-Choice Testing," *Journal of Speech and Hearing Research*, 28:185–196, 1985.

Calvert, D.: "Some Acoustic Characteristics of the Speech of Profoundly Deaf Individuals," unpublished doctoral thesis, Stanford University, 1961.

Hudgins, C. V., and M. Numbers: "An Investigation of the Intelligibility of the Speech of the Deaf," *Genetic Psychological Monographs*, 25:289–392, 1942.

Levitt, H.: "Speech Assessment: Intermediate and Secondary Levels," in J. Subtelny (ed.), *Speech Assessment and Speech Improvement for the Hearing Impaired*, pp. 30–44, A.G. Bell Association, Washington, D.C., 1980.

———, N. S. McGarr, and D. Geffner: *Language and Communication Skills of Deaf Children*, ASHA Monograph Series, Rockville, Maryland, in press.

Ling, D.: *Speech and the Hearing-Impaired Child: Theory and Practice*, A.G. Bell Association, Washington, D.C., 1976.

McGarr, N. S.: "Evaluation of Speech in Intermediate School-Aged Children," in J. Subtelny (ed.), *Speech Assessment and Speech Improvement for the Hearing Impaired*, A.G. Bell Association, Washington, D.C., 1980.

———: "The Intelligibility of Deaf Speech to Experienced and Inexperienced Listeners," *Journal of Speech and Hearing Research*, 26:451–458, 1983.

Magner, M.: "A Speech Intelligibility Test for Deaf Children," Clarke School for the Deaf, Northampton, Massachusetts, 1972.

Monsen, R.: "A Usable Test for Speech Intelligibility of the Deaf Talker," *American Annals of the Deaf*, pp. 846–852, 1981.

Rubin, J.: "Static and Dynamic Information in Vowels Produced by the Hearing Impaired," doctoral dissertation, City University of New York, Indiana University Linguistics Club, Bloomington, 1984.

Smith, C. R.: "Residual Hearing and Speech Intelligibility in Deaf Children," *Journal of Speech and Hearing Research*, 18:795–811, 1975.

Subtelny, J., N. Orlando, and R. Whitehead: *Speech and Voice Characteristics of the Deaf*, A.G. Bell Association, Washington, D.C., 1981.

Nancy S. McGarr

SPEECH PERCEPTION

Speech perception refers to a person's correct identification of the contents of spoken messages. Similarly used expressions are speech discrimination (in audiology), speech intelligibility to a listener, speech understanding, and speech recognition. This article discusses the scope and general effects of deafness and hearing impairment on speech perception, as well as benefit from hearing aids, types of speech sounds affected, noise, reverberation, and aging.

TESTS

The speech message is made up of a hierarchy of units: a stream of consonants and vowels that form words, and words that form phrases and sentences. Tests of a person's performance in speech perception may focus on any level of this hierarchy, depending on the purpose of the tester. Tests focusing on the auditory factors in hearing individual sounds usually employ one-syllable words. Sentences and meaningful discourse are used when the tester wishes to include the language factor, or simply to assess performance related to everyday speech communication.

SPEECH COMMUNICATION PROBLEMS

Hearing impairments cause deficiencies in speech perception that range from mildly to drastically debilitating. The degree of deficiency depends primarily on two general factors: the severity or degree of hearing loss, and the age at which impairment began.

There is a wide range of severity in the hearing-impaired population. Sometimes there is only a slight loss in hearing for tones and no readily noticeable reduction in speech perception. In many other cases there is a more substantial loss, making communication difficult, even with a hearing aid, but manageable with care and effort. In still other cases there is profound deafness which presents a nearly insurmountable barrier to speech communication.

About half of the approximately 14 million hearing-impaired persons in the United States are elderly, typically with only moderate deficiencies of hearing and speech perception. Only a small part of the total population, about 0.2%, are afflicted with profound or total deafness, usually early in life. *See* HEARING LOSS: Incidence and Prevalence.

Viewing the hearing-impaired population as a whole, there is a very large number of persons, especially among the elderly, who can benefit from suitable communication aids. Many of these people get sufficient help from wearing a hearing aid. However, while most hearing-impaired persons can hear more sound with an aid, more is not always better, and many find they cannot benefit. This is not due to the hearing aid but to abnormal conditions in the auditory system: the impaired ear often has reduced capacity to discriminate one sound from another; the impairment serves to jumble together sequential speech sounds, or to make the sounds seem similar. *See* HEARING AIDS.

SENSORINEURAL HEARING LOSS
This discussion will be limited to hearing impairment of the sensorineural type because impairments that are conductive are well compensated by hearing aids if they are not correctable by surgery. Persons with sensorineural hearing impairment typically experience distortions of sounds that are heard due to the abnormal conditions in the cochlea or the VIIIth nerve. These distortions may consist of abnormal representation of frequency (pitch or timbre), abnormal time-patterning of sounds, and abnormal loudness relations. Thus, when speech sounds are made optimally audible, their correct perception often suffers because of the inherent distortions imposed by the abnormal auditory system. Specific distortion processes are not well understood, although interesting correlations have been found between auditory resolution measures (of frequency, time, and loudness differences) and some aspects of deficient speech perception. At this time, however, it is not possible to make accurate predictions of the speech perception capacity of the impaired ear. *See* EAR: Pathology.

LOUDNESS AND TOLERANCE PROBLEMS
Speech sounds, that is, the different consonants and vowels, vary over a rather wide range of loudness (30 decibels). However, the sensorineural impaired ear often has a very limited range of acceptable sound intensities from barely audible to intolerably loud (small dynamic range or tolerance problem). Thus some hearing aid models incorporate a "compression" function to attempt to fit both the weakest and strongest sounds within the limited range of the user. However, it should be appreciated that compression procedures introduce distortions and may reduce the contribution of differences in speech-sound loudnesses to correct perception.

SOUND FREQUENCIES AND HEARING LOSS
The science of acoustics describes sounds in terms of components characterized by their frequencies of vibration. The strength or amount of each component is measured along with its frequency measured in hertz (cycles per sound). Examples of sounds with strong components in the low frequencies are the rumble of auto traffic, the roar of jet aircraft, and the lower frequencies of the human voice. Examples of sounds that are strong in the midrange of frequencies, say between 1000 and

3000 hertz, are sirens and certain vowel sounds, such as *oh* and *ah*. Examples of high-frequency sounds are the hiss of air released from a compressor and certain consonant sounds, such as *s* and *sh*. *See* ACOUSTICS.

Sensorineural hearing loss often exhibits an imbalance of hearing over the frequency range. Sometimes the hearing is sloping in frequency: relatively good in the low frequencies, worse in the midfrequencies, and worst in the high frequencies. Other types of configuration are also found, including flat losses of nearly equal degree at all frequencies. Thus, in terms of speech sounds, the hissing sounds such as *s, f, z*, and *v* and the noise bursts associated with *p, t*, and *k* may be rendered inaudible or indistinguishable. Differences in timbre among many of the vowel sounds depend on composition in their higher frequencies; thus a sloping loss may result in confusion between certain pairs of vowels, as in the word pairs *beet-boot, backs-box, boat-bait*, and *soot-sit*.

Compensation for frequency imbalance is commonly available in hearing aids; frequency compensation usually results in appreciable or even considerable benefit to the user. Unfortunately deficiencies of frequency distortions in the impaired ear are not yet sufficiently understood and measurable to be incorporated in hearing aids. Research toward this end has received considerable impetus due to the availability of microcomputer circuits capable of carrying out "clarifying" operations on incoming sounds. A better knowledge of each ear's distortion properties and related diagnostic methods is needed before speech-clarifying hearing aids can be effectively prescribed.

As an example, suppose that the rapidly changing sound patterns that distinguish some consonants are not differentiated by an impaired ear. If, however, the changes are either slowed or enhanced by some exaggeration of the patterns, then they can be distinguished. Special sound-processing in a hearing aid could perform such enhancements.

AGING
Aging is often accompanied by loss of hearing. Aging loss is usually sensorineural and thus involves a residual deficit in speech perception after the best amplification of sound. In addition, in some elderly persons standard measures of hearing sensitivity show no loss relative to a young normal person, but speech perception is noticeably deficient under noisy or reverberant conditions. *See* PRESBYCUSIS.

NOISE, REVERBERATION, AND HEARING IMPAIRMENT
Most daily environments for speech reception are somewhat noisy, and some may be extremely so.

Sensorineural impairment makes the auditory system much more susceptible to noise interference with speech perception. Noisy situations that may be negligible or tolerable for normal-hearing listeners may be extremely difficult or impossible for hearing-impaired listeners.

Reverberation of speech signals also causes an abnormal deficit in speech perception for hearing-impaired persons. Reverberation is long and strong in large hard-surfaced spaces like cathedrals and amphitheaters. Modern electronic sound-reinforcing systems are intended to alleviate these effects.

Bibliography

Bergman, M.: *Aging and the Perception of Speech*, University Park Press, Baltimore, 1980.

Boothroyd, A.: "Speech Perception and Sensorineural Hearing Loss," in M. Ross and T. G. Giolas (eds.), *Auditory Management of Hearing-Impaired Children*, pp. 117–144, University Park Press, Baltimore, 1978.

National Academy of Sciences, *Report of CHABA Working Group 93: Speech Understanding and Aging*, 1977.

Pickett, J. M.: "Theoretical Considerations in Testing Speech Perception Through Electroauditory Stimulation," in *Cochlear Prostheses: An International Symposium*, Annals of the New York Academy of Sciences, vol. 405, pp. 424–434, 1983.

Studebaker, G. A., and F. H. Bess (eds.), *The Vanderbilt Hearing-Aid Report*, Monographs in Contemporary Audiology, Upper Darby, Pennsylvania, 1982.

J. M. Pickett

SPEECH PROCESS

The process of communicating by speech involves several distinct stages. The formulation of the message in the mind of the talker, generation of neural signals to control the vocal apparatus production of the acoustic speech signal, transmission of the speech signal from speaker to listener, reception of the speech signal at the listener's ear, processing of the speech signal by the auditory system (and by the visual system if speechreading cues are used) and, finally, understanding of the message by the listener.

This sequence of events is known as the speech chain. An important feedback link in the chain is that speakers normally listen to their own voices. In this way, speakers are able to monitor their own speech production and, in the case of ambient background noise, to raise their voices to an appropriate level so as to be heard. This feedback link is also of critical importance in the normal acquisition of speech and oral language.

LINGUISTIC LEVEL

The speech chain operates at several levels. Generation of the message occurs at the linguistic level. A message may consist of no more than a single word, or a sequence of words forming a phrase or sentence. Longer messages may consist of several sentences or even a lengthy discourse consisting of many sentences.

A basic linguistic unit in all of these messages is the word. It can be subdivided into smaller linguistic units known as phonemes, each corresponding to a basic speech sound. For example, the word *seed* consists of three phonemes, the initial consonant /s/, the vowel /i/, and the final consonant /d/.

Phonemes convey meaning. If a phoneme is changed, the meaning of what is said is changed. There is a big difference in meaning between a rat and a cat, although these words differ by only one phoneme. Changes in meaning can also be produced by changing the stress pattern of an utterance—for example, the word *refuse* with stress on the first syllable is a noun meaning "garbage"; with stress on the second syllable it is a verb meaning "to deny." Other changes in meaning can be obtained by raising the voice pitch so as to signal a question as opposed to a statement, or by introducing breaks in the flow of speech so as to affect phrasing, such as a *light housekeeper* as opposed to *lighthouse keeper*.

There are other aspects of speech that tell the listener something about the speaker, such as who the speaker is, whether the speaker is upset or annoyed or in a hurry, and so on. This information is conveyed not by the phonemes of the language but rather by nuances in the way the phonemes are produced or linked.

PHYSIOLOGICAL LEVEL

The next stage of the speech chain is physiological. The linguistic units of the message generated in the mind of the speaker are converted to motor commands that control the vocal apparatus. This is a complex process that is not fully understood. The vocal apparatus, once activated, produces sound that in turn is modified by the shape of the vocal tract so as to produce the desired sounds of speech. The shape of the vocal tract is continually being changed by movements of the articulators synchronously coupled to changes in the sound source. The resulting acoustic signal is heard as speech. *See* SPEECH PRODUCTION.

ACOUSTIC LEVEL

The next stage in the speech chain is at the acoustic level. The speech signal generated by the vocal apparatus is typically transmitted through air until it reaches the ear of the listener or, alternatively, the microphone of an electrical speech-transmission system (for example, telephone or radio). In the case of face-to-face communication (or television), there is a parallel transmission path in which visual cues are transmitted in addition to the acoustic cues. Visual cues are used in speechreading. These cues are particularly important for hearing-imparied persons because of the reduced acoustic information available via the auditory channel. *See* SPEECHREADING.

Measurement   The sound transmission stage is the one stage of the speech chain that is readily amenable to measurement. Although physiological and psychological measurements have been obtained of the other stages, these measurements cannot match the detail or the precision of acoustic measurements. There is now a substantial body of literature on the acoustics of speech and on acoustical methods of analysis. The corresponding area of video measurement has not yet received the attention it deserves. Advances in video and computer technology allow for the precise video measurement of lip and other articulatory movements but, thus far, there have been only a few studies along these lines. It is anticipated that as the technology advances and both the difficulty and cost of such measurements are reduced, the emerging field of video phonetics will grow rapidly. *See* PHONETICS.

Modification   The acoustic stage is also the stage that is most easily modified. Two common, and important, modifications to the acoustic speech transmission path are the telephone and the hearing aid. In the case of the telephone, the sounds generated by the speaker are transmitted by air until they reach the microphone in the telephone. The acoustic signals are then converted into electrical signals that are transmitted over the telephone network until they reach the receiving telephone, where these electrical signals are converted back into acoustic signals. The transducer is known

as a telephone receiver, although the name belies its function. The regenerated acoustic signals are transmitted by air to the ear of the listener.

The insertion of a telephone link between speaker and listener changes the characteristics of the sound transmission path in several important ways. The bandwidth of a telephone circuit is much less than that of the ear. Typically, telephone circuits transmit sound frequencies between 300 and 3500 Hz. This frequency range covers the most important frequencies of the speech signal for intelligibility, but is only a fraction of the bandwidth of the ear. For a young, normal-hearing person, sound frequencies up to 20,000 Hz can be processed by the ear.

In order to transmit electrical speech signals over vast distances, telephone systems also amplify and process the speech signals in various ways. As a consequence, speech signals received over the telephone are often distorted with an audible background noise. Most telephone companies limit the amount of noise and distortion so that the speech signals are intelligible to normal-hearing listeners. For hearing-impaired people, the background noise and distortions can be particularly deleterious to communication.

The hearing aid represents another type of modification to the sound transmission path which, in this case, is designed to improve the intelligibility of speech for hearing-impaired listeners. As in the telephone, the acoustic speech signal is first converted to electrical form, after which it is processed, usually by amplification and frequency shaping, so as to increase the amount of the speech signal that is both audible and comfortable to the hearing aid user. The amplified, electrical speech signal is then

Diagram of the speech chain.

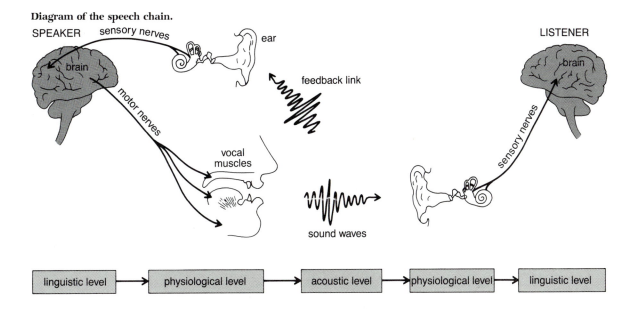

converted back to an acoustic signal that is then transmitted to the ear. *See* HEARING AIDS.

Hearing aids work quite well for persons with mild hearing losses and moderately well for persons with moderate hearing losses, but are unsatisfactory for persons with severe or profound losses. For the latter two groups, experimental speech processing sensory aids are being developed that may add substantially to their ability to communicate by speech. The sound transmission path for these devices is likely to be very different from that of a hearing aid in that the signals received by the user will involve other modalities, such as taction, vision, or direct electrical stimulation of the auditory nerve. *See* COCHLEAR IMPLANTS; SENSORY AIDS.

Conversion to Vibration In the normal speech chain, the acoustic signal reaching the eardrum is converted to mechanical vibrations that are then transmitted through the middle ear to the cochlea. The key components of this mechanical transmission path are three tiny bones in the middle ear known as the ossicles. The ossicles act as a chain of levers that help transform acoustic vibrations in a low-density medium (air) to hydrodynamic vibrations in the relatively dense fluids of the cochlea. The ossicles are controlled by two tiny muscles, the stapedius and tensor tympani, which by means of a reflex action help protect the ear against very intense sounds. Activation of the acoustic reflex may also occur during one's own speech production which, because of the short transmission path, may result in intense sound reaching the ear. *See* EAR: Anatomy.

Mechanical vibration reaching the cochlea is converted to hydrodynamic vibration in the cochlea fluids. These vibrations are filtered hydrodynamically along the length of the cochlea, different regions of the cochlea receiving different frequencies of vibration. The basal end of the cochlea is most sensitive to high-frequency stimuli, whereas the apical end is most sensitive to low-frequency stimuli.

Running the length of the cochlea is the basilar membrane which divides the cochlea into two parallel chambers. Mounted on the basilar membrane is the organ of Corti. Hydromechanical vibration in the cochlear fluids causes a mechanical displacement of the basilar membrane, which in turn triggers the hair cells in the organ of Corti. The pattern of firings forms a neural representation of the speech signal that is transmitted along the neural pathways to the auditory cortex where the speech is recognized.

The most severe forms of deafness involve damage to the hair cells or neural pathways connecting to the organ of Corti. If the hair cells are destroyed but the neural fibers are reasonably intact, then it may be possible to stimulate the auditory nerve

directly by an electrical field. Experimental prostheses of this type have been developed. The most common forms of hair-cell or neural damage affect the basal end of the cochlea more severely and, as a consequence, the high-frequency components of the speech signal are lost. This type of loss is typical of most sensorineural hearing impairments. Even in cases of profound deafness, some low-frequency components of the speech signal may be audible with appropriate amplification.

COMPREHENSION

The last stage of the speech chain, understanding the spoken message, is once again at the linguistic level. There are various theories on how speech is perceived and which linguistic units are being processed. Of great practical importance is that not all of the speech signal need be received for speech to be intelligible. Speech is a highly redundant, complex code, and the human listener employs a variety of strategies for filling in whatever is not heard. For example, on hearing the incomplete sentence "The ship sailed across the . . . ," the average listener is very likely to identify the missing word as *sea*.

Context is particularly important for deaf listeners since it provides the missing cues that allow for the understanding of the speech message although only a fraction of the speech signal may have been perceived. It also facilitates the integration of incomplete sets of cues, such as those received from speechreading, coupled with the residual low-frequency auditory cues resulting from a severe high-frequency hearing loss.

Contextual cues can take many forms. These can range from situational cues (for example, asking for the time when one is late), to semantic cues (such as a missing cue that will render a sentence meaningful), to syntactic cues (for instance, sentences with gross syntactic errors are less likely to be heard correctly) to probabilistic constraints between words, syllables, or phonemes. These cues are not mutually exclusive, and an important area of research is concerned with identifying and quantifying the effect of contextual cues in the understanding of speech by both normal and hearing-impaired individuals.

FEEDBACK LOOP

As noted above, the feedback loop whereby speakers monitor their own speech production is particularly important. This loop, which consists of both the acoustic pathway and kinesthetic feedback (that is, feeling the movements of one's articulators), is constantly being used in speech. For example, one typically raises one's voice when talking in a noisy room by an amount dependent on the perceived loudness of one's speech. Similarly, people who begin to mispronounce a word or phrase typically will try to correct the problem by subsequent compensatory movements of their articulators.

For deaf people, the lack of an auditory feedback loop produces problems in speech production. For the postlingually deafened adult, greater weight is imposed on memorizing learned speech gestures since there is no ongoing auditory feedback. Kinesthetic feedback also plays a much more important role than in speech production by normal-hearing people. For the child who is born deaf or who is deafened prior to the acquisition of speech, the lack of this acoustic feedback is particularly damaging. Not only is speech difficult to understand, but the lack of exposure to one's own speech and to the speech of others severely limits the child's ability to learn speech during those critical early years when speech development is most rapid. As a consequence, prelingually deafened individuals have very poor speech skills.

Harry Levitt

SPEECH PRODUCTION

The discussion of speech production is divided into two major sections. The first describes a theory of speech production, relating the articulatory system and its motor functions to the output acoustics. The second explains the anatomy and physiology of speech production.

General Theory

Different ways of describing speech have coexisted for some time. On the one hand, a person can transcribe speech. Thus, if someone says to another "My name is Mary," the listener not only understands that the speaker has a common given name, but can also, with a little training, make a notation indicating the vowel usage is [ei] or [ε] and infer something about the speaker's geographical origins as well. Turning to deaf speech, a listener may still be able to perform the same sort of operation— "She said [bʌ] instead of [m eI rI]"—but very often one is left with an uneasy feeling that the fault in the articulation has not been well captured by the transcription. This is because transcription is an extremely complex and poorly understood process by which a time-varying acoustic signal is transformed by a listener into some static shapes on a left-to-right sequence on the paper, with many of the signal's characteristics unrepresented. Thus, the deaf speaker, if considered just from the transcription, might be said to have made /b/ for /m/ substitution, denasalized the bilabial lip consonant,

centralized the vowel, and omitted the final syllable. But this description may not adequately represent the fact that the speaker made some articulatory gestures in an unskilled and poorly coordinated way, whose acoustic consequences are spread over the whole signal. The deaf speaker has not done something that a hearing speaker would have done if making the same substitution. To be sure, a skilled phonetician can make a narrow transcription, that is, use a more refined symbol system with diacritics that will perhaps enable the generation of a credible imitation of the speaker. However, it is still true that the phonetician is supplying information about how to move articulators from experiential knowledge, rather than recovering it directly from the symbolization.

Attached to the phonetician's description of speech is a description of place of articulation. The latter is based primarily on a long history of introspection, rather than on direct measurements, and its use historically antedates a theory of speech production relating anatomical structures to speech output, or a theory of speech perception relating the acoustic signal to the perceived sound. *See* PHONETICS.

SIMPLE VOWEL PRODUCTION

One way of representing the acoustic signal that results when a speaker says the three vowels /i/, /a/, and /u/—the vowels of "heed," "hod," and "who'd" as prolonged vowels—is the spectrogram. This way of viewing signals is produced by a spectrograph, a commonly used instrument for analyzing complex acoustic sounds. The spectrograph represents a complex sound as the sum of a number of simple component sounds, and presents the changing mixture as a function of time. Any spectrogram has three dimensions. Time and frequency appear on the horizontal and vertical ones, respectively. The intensity of a given frequency component is indicated by the darkness of the frequency-time region.

If the three vowels are compared, it will be noticed that the dark bands in the spectrogram are in different places. These dark bands, called formants, correspond to the frequency regions in which the vowel has most of its energy. It is customary to number the formants; for any vowel, F_1 is the lowest-frequency formant, F_2 is second-lowest, and so forth. It can be shown that listeners perceive the differences among the vowels on the basis of frequencies of the first three formants. Measurement of a number of spectrograms would reveal that F_1 is low-pitched (and about equal) for the vowels /i/ and /u/, while for /i/, /a/, and /u/, F_2 ranges from relatively high to relatively low.

Examination of the spectrogram reveals that the

dark formant bands are striated. These striations are farther apart at the ends of the three vowels. This characteristic corresponds to the fact that the vowels were produced by the speaker with a falling pitch, which is common when speakers are asked to repeat short words in a list. Thus, by looking carefully at a spectrogram, one can see that the complex vowel sounds have two kinds of frequency associated with them: overall frequency, which might be called pitch in singing, and the formant frequencies, which correspond in this case to vowels. While most people have never seen a spectrogram, they know that different words can be sung to the same melody in speech; that is, different words can be produced with the same intonation; furthermore, the same words can be sung to different melodies, or by different singers with very different overall pitch ranges. One can recognize a word spoken at high pitch by a child or at low pitch by the child's father.

These observations are related to the source-filter theory of speech production. It states that the output vowel sound is the product of a sound source, located in this case at the glottis, or vocal folds, and a filter, provided by the upper vocal tract. The pitch of the vowel thus depends on the vibration rate of the vocal folds, while the relative frequency of the formants depends on the relative shape of the vocal tract.

Typical shapes of the vocal tract for the vowels /i/, /a/, and /u/ may be considered. For /i/, the tongue is raised toward the palate and forms a narrow construction there; for /a/, the tongue is low and back. If one were to uncoil the vocal tract, these shapes would correspond to a tube that is narrow at the front end and wide at the back, or a tube that is wide at the front end and narrow at the back. Tubes of these two characteristics will have formants that differ in the way that /i/ differs from /a/. A tube with a large back cavity and a small front cavity has a relatively low first formant and a high second formant; a tube with a small back cavity and a large front cavity has a high-frequency first formant and a low second formant.

Two other points might be noted: first, the more or less right-angle bend in the human vocal tract does not have very much effect on its characteristics as a resonator; and second, it is *relative* shape, resulting in relative formant frequency, that listeners interpret as vowel difference. Differences in overall vocal tract length, as in the difference between a child and an adult, will result in differences in the scaling of the formants. The description of vowel differences in terms of tube-shape differences is similar, but not identical, to the conventional phonetic description of vowels.

Any complex acoustic wave, like a vowel sound, has many components. In the case of repetitive sounds, these components are related to each other in that they are multiples of a common frequency, the fundamental frequency, perceived as pitch. It is this complex array of simple components, generated acoustically at the glottis, that acts as the input to the upper vocal tract filter. For the relations between source and transfer (filter) functions in producing vowel sounds, the acoustic signal can be represented in two dimensions, amplitude and frequency. The transfer function is different if the vocal tract shape is different. The source function depends on two characteristics of the way that the vocal folds vibrate: their vibratory frequency determines pitch; and the shape of the opening and closing movement of the vocal folds determines the overall shape of the source function.

Vibration The vocal tract is used to produce an acoustic speech output. Within the larynx, the vocal folds may be viewed as two fleshy shelves that intervene between the trachea, which connects to the lungs, and the upper vocal tract. When these fleshy shelves are brought into an appropriate position and exhaled air reaches this bottom surface, the fleshy shelves will vibrate. The essential mechanism of this vibration is known as the myoelastic-aerodynamic theory of vocal fold vibration.

The rate at which the vocal folds vibrate is determined in large part by the properties of the vocal fold tissue. Depending on the activity of the intrinsic and extrinsic muscles of the larynx, the fleshy vocal fold shelves will be thick or thin, positioned appropriately over the exhaled air stream to varying degrees and, since the shelves are made up partly of muscle fiber, of varying elasticity. Obviously, if the shelves are not appropriately positioned, they will not vibrate properly for their entire length.

The lungs act as the energy source in this system. In persons with normal speech, the vocal folds are moved into the air stream during exhalation, and the exhaled air is converted by the opening and closing of the vocal folds into the acoustic source for vowel phonation. The pressure of exhaled air on the bottom of the vocal folds must exceed a critical value to set them into vibration. The extent to which the lungs are inflated sets the outer bounds on how long the vibration of the vocal folds can be sustained. Subglottal pressure determines the amplitude of vocal fold vibration and hence, the vowel amplitude, perceived as loudness.

The muscles of inspiration are used to fill the lungs. Since the lungs are an elastic structure, they will tend to recoil to a resting level after they are distended by inhaled air. In addition, the muscles of exhalation can be used to force air from the lungs. If the vocal folds are appropriately positioned over the exhaled air stream, they will be set into vibration. The output speech sounds will depend primarily on the shape of the upper vocal tract. However, the suprasegmental characteristics of the utterance depend mainly on the interactive characteristics of laryngeal and lung behavior.

Suprasegmental Characteristics A study can be made by preparing the subglottal pressure and fundamental frequency contours for two versions of the same sentence—for example, the statement "Joe ate his soup" and the question, "Did *Joe* eat his soup?" In comparing the fundamental frequency contour of the two utterances, it is seen that the fundamental frequency is higher for stressed "*Joe*" than for unstressed "Joe"; it rises for interrogative "soup?" and falls for statement "soup." An illustration of the acoustic intensity levels for the two utterances shows a much higher acoustic intensity for stressed "*Joe*" than for unstressed "Joe," but very little difference in the overall intensity between the two "soup's." The corresponding subglottal pressure curves demonstrate that there is a subglottal pressure difference between the two "Joe's" corresponding to the difference in acoustic intensity and, in a minor way, to the difference in fundamental frequency. A display of vocal fold tension would reveal higher peaks in tension both for the stressed utterance and for the word corresponding to the interrogative. Pitch rises are accompanied by increases in tension, caused in part by the activity of the cricothyroid muscle, which acts to increase tension in the vocal fold by stretching it. Of course, the overall pitch range of a given speaker is determined by the tissue mass of the folds. Since women and children have smaller vocal folds on average than men, their pitch ranges on average will be higher. However, it is possible, by keeping the folds in a habitually tensed state, to produce an abnormally high pitch. It should be noted that anatomical differences in vocal tract length between men and women are separable in their effects from differences in vocal fold size. The characteristic distinctive vocal effect of the countertenor is caused by the combination of sounds produced by a large male vocal tract combined with a pitch range more characteristic of the smaller female vocal apparatus.

There is a further aspect of overall suprasegmental production that deserves mention. During ordinary conversational speech, only about a half liter (half quart) of air is used; to inhale and exhale much larger volumes of air requires disproportionally large amounts of muscular effort. The easily available air reservoir will sustain appropriate subglottal pressures for phrases of the order of five to seven words in length, without a pause for inspiration. (Of course, singers customarily exceed the respiratory bounds of conversational speech.) The syntactic structure of ordinary conversational speech seems roughly adjusted to these limits. The

syntactic boundary corresponding to the comma in "When I urged my friend Joe, he ate his soup" is thus a convenient place for a breath intake. Speakers who produce speech with prolonged vowels, as many deaf speakers do, will run out of air before the syntax calls for a break and will inhale; thus, the usual relationship between syntax and intonation will be disturbed, making the output difficult to listen to, whatever its other characteristics.

RUNNING SPEECH PRODUCTION
The discussion above has described the statics of vowel articulation and overall intonation as a reflection of the way that the larynx and lungs interact. The following will examine articulation in more detail by making a somewhat arbitrary distinction between articulatory statics and articulatory dynamics.

Articulatory Statics The above discussion of the source filter theory of speech production assumed that the source is always vibratory and that it rests at the glottis. Neither of these characteristics needs to apply. First, consider a whispered vowel, which is made with the vocal tract in the same position as in a normal one, but with the vocal folds somewhat adducted rather than being close enough together to vibrate. In such a semiadducted position, the folds act as an obstruction in the exhaled air stream and cause turbulent flow, which is noise acoustically. This turbulent air thus serves as a source, filtered by the vocal tract in front of it. Whispered vowels have the same formant structure as the corresponding voiced vowels, however, it is possible to form a narrow passage at many places in the vocal tract above the glottis. When this happens, the turbulent flow of air at the narrowing provides the source, which is filtered by the cavities in front of it. This is the general mechanism for the production of the sound /s/ (although here the barrier formed by the teeth has a special role). Since the cavity in front of /s/ is quite small, the noise is relatively high in frequency.

A final manner of producing a sound is to release an occlusion in the tract suddenly. Here, the source energy is provided by the release of air pressure; again, filtering action is provided by the cavities in front of the occlusion. For this reason, the acoustic characteristics of the burst that accompanies a /t/ occlusion release, caused by a tongue-tip release at the alveolar ridge, are similar to the characteristics of /s/ friction, caused by the formation of a narrowing of the vocal tract in the same region.

It is possible to combine tract sources—for example, for the sound /z/, a voiced fricative, there is a sound source at the larynx in that the vocal folds are sufficiently adducted to vibrate, and a secondary source at the alveolar ridge occlusion.

The descriptions to this point have assumed that

a source function is modified by the vocal tract, a tube extending from glottis to lips. It was also assumed that the velum was closed. However, if the velopharyngeal port is open, air can flow down the bifurcated nasal tract, as well as in the oral tract. The presence of an open velum has a positive effect—it changes the acoustic output of the transfer function—as well as a negative effect—it prevents the flow of sufficient air in the oral tract to produce certain effects, such as the buildup of air behind an oral occlusion, as in fricatives like /s/.

In English, some consonants (/m/, /n/) require nasal resonance. Additionally, vowels in the vicinity of a nasal are commonly produced with an open velopharyngeal port; there is no contrast for English between oral and nasal vowels, as there is in many languages. However, a failure to coordinate velar closure with vocal tract occlusion, characteristic of many pathological speech conditions, including deaf speech, has the effect of destroying the mechanism for the creation of supraglottal sound sources, in the oral tract, because the necessary air flows out the nose.

Articulatory Dynamics A full theory of speech production must deal, in addition to accounting for shape-sound correspondences, with the dynamic organization of speech, and motor equivalence. All motor systems show the phenomenon of motor equivalence. In general, any effector organ, such as the arm-hand combination, can reach a given target by using the available muscles in any one of innumerable combinations. Furthermore, the gross muscles themselves are made up of large numbers of motor units, consisting of individual nerve fibers and the muscle fibers each innervates. On any given production, a different subset of motor units may contract for about the same output shape. Motor equivalence in the vocal tract is, in some ways, even more complex than for the arm. While the acoustic theory of speech production will allow one to predict the acoustic output of a given vocal tract shape, the reverse does not hold: a given acoustic output could be produced by an infinite variety of shapes (not all of them physiologically plausible). Even if one considers only ways of producing the same tract shape, there are many equivalent maneuvers. For example, the narrow front-cavity vocal-tract shape appropriate to producing an /i/ sound can be produced by raising the jaw with the tongue lying on it in a bunched and fronted position, or by leaving the jaw low and contracting the muscles of the tongue much more strongly. If the jaw is held open by mechanical means, the tongue will compensate.

An interesting example of motor equivalence has been identified with respect to the respiratory system. The lungs are held in place within a cylinder with the respiratory muscles lying around its circumference, and the abdomen and its contents lying at the base. In order to change lung volume, a speaker can use the chest-wall part of the system, or the abdomen, each with its separate muscles. However, the role of muscle forces changes radically when body position is altered. In particular, the force of gravity on the abdominal wall acts to reduce lung volume when a speaker is lying down, but to increase lung volume when the speaker is standing up. However, speakers can produce the appropriate subglottal pressures for speech without regard to body position change.

Bibliography

Borden, G., and K. S. Harris: *Speech Science Primer: Physiology, Acoustics, and Perception of Speech*, Williams and Wilkins, Baltimore, 1980.

Harris, K. S., B. Tuller, and J. A. S. Kelso, "Invariance and Variability in Speech Processes," in J. S. Perkell and D. H. Klatt (eds.), *Invariance and Variability in Speech Processes*, Lawrence Erlbaum Associates, Hilldale, New Jersey, 1986.

Hixon, T.: "Respiratory Function in Speech," in F. Minifie, T. Hixon, and J. Williams (eds.): *Normal Aspects of Speech, Hearing and Language*, Prentice-Hall, Englewood Cliffs, New Jersey, 1972.

Pickett, J. M.: *The Sounds of Speech Communication*, University Park Press, Baltimore, 1980.

Stevens, K. N., and A. S. House: "Development of a Quantitative Description of Vowel Articulation," *Journal of the Acoustical Society of America*, 27:484–493, 1955.

van den Berg, J.: "Myoelastic-Aerodynamic Theory of Voice Production," *Journal of Speech and Hearing Research*, 1:227–244, 1958.

Katherine S. Harris

Anatomy and Physiology

Human speech production results from the action of numerous anatomical mechanisms. It has been suggested that speech is an overlaid process because the organs and structures used for speech, which include the mechanisms for respiration, mastication, and deglutition, have a primary biological purpose to sustain life. However, human beings have adapted these organs and structures for the secondary purpose of speech production.

Following is a general overview of the anatomy and physiology of speech production. The speech production mechanism will be discussed in terms of the respiratory system, the phonatory system, and the resonance and articulatory systems.

RESPIRATORY SYSTEM

The primary purpose of the respiratory system is to supply oxygen to the blood and to remove excess carbon dioxide from the body. This process is automatic and controlled by the respiratory centers within the central nervous system. However, respiration also is capable of modification so that it can serve as the generating mechanism for sound production.

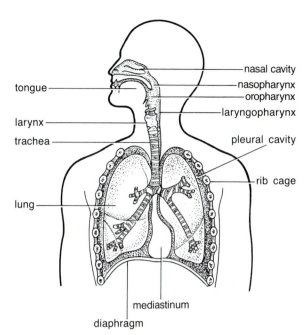

tongue

nasal cavity
nasopharynx
oropharynx
laryngopharynx

larynx

pleural cavity

trachea

lung

rib cage

mediastinum

diaphragm

Upper and lower respiratory tract.

The respiratory system is traditionally divided into upper and lower parts, with the upper tract composed of the nasal cavities, oral cavity, pharynx, and larynx. Since these structures will be discussed later, the present section will address only the lower respiratory tract.

The lower respiratory tract is contained within the thorax or chest cavity of the body. The framework of the thorax is composed of 12 pairs of ribs attached posteriorly to the vertebrae, with 7 of the 12 pairs attaching anteriorly to the sternum. Three of the remaining ribs attach anteriorly to the adjacent superior rib rather than the sternum, while the final 2 pairs of ribs do not have an anterior attachment. Adjacent ribs are attached to each other by two sets of muscles, the internal and external intercostals. The rib cage is attached superiorly to the clavicle (collarbone), the scapula (shoulder bone), and the neck by numerous sets of muscles. These muscles serve as stabilizers and contribute to raising the ribs and sternum, thus assisting in expanding the rib cage during inhalation.

The floor of the chest cavity is composed of a dome-shaped muscle, the diaphragm, which is attached, peripherally, to the lower edge of the rib cage and which separates the thoracic cavity from the abdominal cavity. The diaphragm has a parabolic shape and is concave on the abdominal side during rest. When the circular muscle of the diaphragm contracts, as in inspiration for breathing, it flattens and thus enlarges the volume of the thoracic cavity. The diaphragm contains three openings, one each for the major artery and vein for the lower body and one for the esophagus.

The thorax is connected with the upper respiratory tract, and thus the outside air, by the trachea. The trachea consists of 16 to 20 C-shaped cartilaginous rings, with the most superior ring attached to the base of the larynx. At the lowest tracheal ring, the trachea divides into two smaller tubes, the bronchi, each entering a lung. The bronchi then further divide, followed by further pathway divisions, until they terminate into microscopic areas, alveoli, where the actual gas transfer occurs.

Within the thoracic cavity are three primary structures, the two lungs, each within a pleural cavity, and the mediastinum, which is a broad partition separating the two pleural cavities and which contains structures such as the heart, esophagus, aorta, and lower trachea. The lungs are elastic and airtight, and since they contain no muscle tissue, they are inert bodies that must be acted upon by adjacent structures in order to expand (draw air in) and contract (expel air) during respiration. The lungs are attached to the lining of the thoracic cavity by means of a serous membrane, the pleura, and a fluid-filled area, the pleural space. Through such a linkage, chest wall forces may be directly transmitted to the lungs, thus allowing them to expand and contract according to changes in the thoracic cavity.

The act of inhalation involves increasing the internal volume of the pleural cavities, which in turn creates a condition that requires air to rush into the lungs through the trachea. There are numerous muscles that act to increase the size of the thoracic cavity. These include the diaphragm, whose contraction increases the vertical dimensions of the thorax, and the external and internal intercostal muscles, which are instrumental in raising the rib cage and thus increasing the anteroposterior diameter of the thorax. Other muscles of inspiration include the scalenes, which are long neck muscles that attach to the upper two ribs, and the sternocleidomastoids which course from the sternum to the clavicle (collarbone) to the mastoid process of the occipital bone of the skull. These groups of muscles elevate the upper portion of the thoracic cavity, thus increasing its vertical dimensions.

For speech production, the exhalation phase of the respiratory cycle is initiated by retarding the activity of the inspiratory muscles. The elastic recoil of the lungs and gravity cause the thoracic cavity to decrease in size, and thus air to be expelled. In addition, the inspiratory muscles serve to brake the recoil forces, thus checking the rate of the descent of the rib cage in order to provide sufficient controlled airflow for sound production. As the thoracic cavity decreases in size, the muscles of exhalation may gradually come into play by further lowering the rib cage and compressing the abdominal viscera, which maintains the appropriate amount of airflow and air pressure for speech. The primary expiratory muscles are composed of the abdominal muscles—the internal oblique, rectus abdominis, and transversus abdominis—which course from either the lower vertebrae or pelvic girdle to the lower half of the rib cage.

The central nervous system control of respiration when quiet or resting is known as the Hering-Breuer reflex. The respiratory center is located within the medulla of the brainstem and is affected by stimuli from stretch receptors within the alveoli. When the alveoli are inflated during inspiration, nerve impulses travel to the medulla, inhibiting the respiratory center's stimulation of the muscles of inspiration, thereby terminating inhalation. When expiration is complete, as evidenced by the level of carbon dioxide in the blood and the reduced stimuli from the alveolar stretch receptors, additional impulses from the stretch receptors are sent to the medulla to signal initiation of the next inhalation.

PHONATORY SYSTEM

The larynx consists of a system of cartilages, muscles, and ligaments attached superiorly to the hyoid bone, which is at the approximate level of the root of the tongue, and inferiorly to the first cartilaginous ring of the trachea. The larynx is suspended from the hyoid bone by several muscles, ligaments, and membranes, which allows it to move extensively as it works in conjunction with the tongue and mandible during swallowing and speech pro-

Larynx: (a) anterior view; (b) lateral veiw; (c) posterior view; (d) top view of the vocal fold mass.

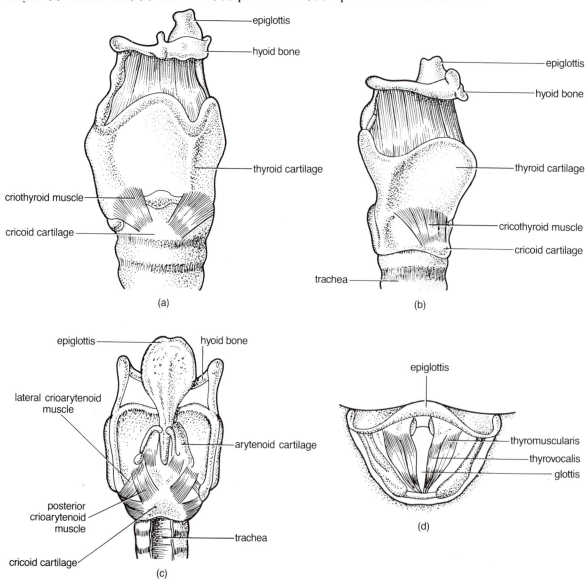

duction. The hyoid bone is U-shaped and is suspended by muscles and ligaments that are attached to the mandible and tongue. Some speculate that the chief purpose of the larynx is to serve as the sound- and voice-generating mechanism in humans, while others contend that it is primarily a sophisticated valve that keeps food from entering the lungs.

The framework of the larynx consists of four cartilages (fibroelastic substances) that lend rigidity to the structure and serve as points of attachment for the muscles, membranes, and ligaments. The largest of these is the thyroid cartilage, which appears to surround the inner structures of the larynx in a protective manner. The thyroid cartilage consists of two sides or wings (alae) that converge anteriorly to form the thyroid notch, or Adam's apple. Inside the cartilage, just below the thyroid notch, is the point where the vocal folds have their anterior attachment. The cricoid cartilage, sometimes identified as the signet ring cartilage because of its shape, is the part of the larynx that attaches directly to the uppermost cartilaginous ring of the trachea. The enlarged portion of this cartilage lies to the posterior, approximately 1 inch (2.5 centimeters) behind the thyroid notch. Situated on top of the enlarged portion of the cricoid cartilage are the two arytenoid cartilages, which are pyramidal in shape. The arytenoids are attached to the cricoid cartilage and to each other by several muscles that allow them to rotate and move laterally and medially to facilitate abduction (opening) or adduction (closing) of the vocal folds. The vocal processes, or anterior projections, of the arytenoids serve as the posterior attachment of the vocal folds. The epiglottis is a leaf-shaped cartilage which rises above the other components of the larynx so that its superior border is near the root of the tongue. It is attached to the thyroid cartilage of the larynx just beneath the thyroid notch, and its action is generally considered to assist in closing off the larynx during swallowing.

The muscles of the larynx are conventionally divided into intrinsic and extrinsic groups. The intrinsic muscles have both their point of origin and their point of attachment (insertion) within the laryngeal structure, while extrinsic muscles have either their origin or insertion external to the larynx.

The intrinsic muscles of the larynx may be categorized according to the way they affect the shape of the glottis (the area between the vocal folds) and the vibratory pattern of the vocal folds; there is abductor, adductor, tensor, and relaxer musculature. The thyroarytenoid muscle, which courses from the thyroid cartilage to the arytenoid cartilages, is a very complex muscle composed of two primary bundles, the thyromuscularis and thyrovocalis. The

thyromuscularis portion assists in adducting the vocal folds and reducing tension. The thyrovocalis portion, which constitutes the main vibrating mass of the vocal folds, serves to shorten the vocal folds and increase their tension. Another intrinsic laryngeal muscle group is the interarytenoids (transverse and oblique) which tract from one arytenoid to the other and serve to adduct the vocal folds. The lateral cricoarytenoid, also a muscle of adduction, runs from the lateral margins of the cricoid cartilage to the arytenoids. The criothyroid, which tracts from the cricoid cartilage to the thyroid cartilage, lengthens and tenses the vocal folds. The posterior cricoarytenoid is the only muscle of abduction; it courses from the arytenoids to the signet portion of the cricoid cartilage and serves to rotate the arytenoids laterally, thus widening the glottis.

The extrinsic laryngeal muscles are divided into the groups of suprahyoid and infrahyoid. The suprahyoid muscles (digastric, geniohyoid, mylohyoid, stylohyoid) course between the skull or the mandible and the hyoid bone. These muscles may either assist in opening the mandible or in elevating the hyoid bone and larynx during swallowing. The infrahyoid muscles consist of a deep layer of muscles (sternothyroid and thyrohyoid) and a superficial layer of muscles (sternohyoid and omohyoid). The sternothyroid lowers the thyroid cartilage–larynx, while the thyrohyoid raises the thyroid cartilage–larynx. Thus, these muscles assist in regulating the length and tension of the vocal folds, thereby affecting pitch.

Neurophysiologically, the larynx is connected with the brain by the tenth cranial nerve, the vagus. Two branches of the vagus, the superior laryngeal nerve and the recurrent laryngeal nerve, provide the principal innervation to the larynx. The superior laryngeal nerve serves the cricothyroid muscles whose contraction lengthens and tenses the vocal folds. All of the other intrinsic laryngeal muscles are served by the recurrent laryngeal nerve, which courses down the neck, under the aorta on the left side of the body, and under the subclavian artery on the right side before returning up to the larynx. This routing of the recurrent laryngeal nerve makes it particularly susceptible to disorders and pathology of the upper mediastinum, as well as to surgical procedures in the posterior neck region, such as thyroidectomy.

RESONANCE AND ARTICULATORY SYSTEMS

While one source of sound used for speech by humans occurs at the level of the larynx, other cavities and structures are used to modify the laryngeal sound or to modify the exhaled air to produce additional sound.

Pharynx The pharynx is a tube of membranes and muscles that extends from the base of the skull to

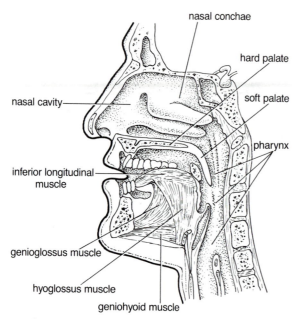

nasal conchae

hard palate

soft palate

nasal cavity

pharynx

inferior longitudinal
muscle

genioglossus muscle

hyoglossus muscle

geniohyoid muscle

Vocal tract; including several muscles of the tongue.

the lower border of the cricoid cartilage of the larynx. The pharynx is important for respiration, for swallowing, and for resonance during speech production. Basically, the muscles of the pharynx are arranged in an inner and outer layer. The outer layer comprises three muscles, the superior, middle, and inferior pharyngeal constrictors. The right and left portions of each of these muscles form the lateral walls of the pharynx, while the union of the two portions forms the posterior pharyngeal wall. The anterior portion of the pharynx is open and communicates with the nasal cavity, the oral cavity, and the opening into the larynx. The inner layer of pharyngeal muscles consists of stylopharyngeus, which originates at the temporal bone, and salpingo pharyngeus, which originates at the eustachian tube. Their respective functions are to increase the diameter of the pharynx and to elevate the superior portion of the pharynx. The pharynx is divided on the basis of the openings in its anterior wall. The uppermost division, above the soft palate, is the nasopharynx; the middle division, between the soft palate and epiglottis, is the oropharynx; the lowest division, between the epiglottis and lower border of the cricoid cartilage, is the laryngopharynx. The primary biological function of the nasopharynx is for respiration and for drainage of the middle ear via the eustachian tube, the nasal cavities, and the sinuses. The oropharynx and laryngopharynx are important for respiration and for peristalsis, the sequential constriction of the pharyngeal musculature which drives a bolus (mass of chewed food) to the esophagus. *See* EAR: Anatomy.

Nasal and Oral Cavities   The nasal cavity extends from the floor of the cranium to the roof of the oral cavity. Anteriorly, the nasal cavity communicates with the exterior by way of the nostrils and, posteriorly, communicates with the nasopharynx. The nasal cavity consists of portions of the nasal, frontal, ethmoid, and sphenoid bones of the skull, while the floor is composed of the palatine process of the maxilla and the horizontal plates of the palatine bone. The lateral walls of the nasal cavity consist of a labyrinthinelike structure, the conchae (shell-shaped), which are covered with mucous membrane and serve to filter and moisten air that is inhaled through the nostrils.

The oral cavity, or mouth, like the other structures used in speech production, has biological as well as nonbiological functions. The mouth aids in establishing communication between the digestive and respiratory tracts and the external environment. Posteriorly, the oral cavity communicates with the pharyngeal cavity and, anteriorly, communicates with the external environment by way of the mouth slit. The mouth also serves as an initiator in the digestive process by chewing and swallowing. Structures in the mouth area are instrumental in modifying the laryngeal sound source (resonance) for the production of speech sounds such as vowels, as well as in interrupting the expelled air to create other speech sounds such as fricative or plosive consonants. The anterior and lateral portions of the oral cavity consist of the teeth, which are embedded within the alveolar process of the maxillary bone, and the mandible (lower jaw). The teeth are important in speech production, particularly the two central incisors and the two lateral incisors in each jaw, which when used in conjunction with the lower lip or tongue create fricatives such as /f/ and /th/. The roof of the oral cavity consists of the hard palate and the soft palate. The tongue can articulate with the hard or soft palate to produce, by means of expelled air, such plosive consonants as /k/ and /g/. The lower boundary of the oral cavity consists of a floor formed primarily by the mylohyoid muscle, which is a troughlike sheet that originates from the inner surface of the mandible and joins together at a midline raphe (seam), which in turn is connected to the hyoid bone. The tongue lies in the floor of the oral cavity.

Velum   The soft palate, or velum, is a muscular structure that originates from the posterior border of the hard palate and extends posteriorly to terminate in the uvula, a midline pendulous structure of the soft palate easily visible when looking into the oral cavity. When the velum is relaxed, its posterior portion hangs in the oropharynx. The velum consists of epithelial surfaces, connective tissue layers, and muscular layers that make it both strong and highly mobile. The muscle structure of the velum consists of five muscle pairs: tensor veli palatini, levator veli palatini, uvulae, palatoglossus, and palatopharyngeus. The bulk of the soft palate is composed of the levator palatini muscle, which runs from the temporal bone and Eustachian tube to the velum and, upon contraction, lifts the soft palate upward and backward to aid in closing off the oropharynx and nasopharynx. The palatoglossus muscle courses from the posterior surface of the velum downward to the sides of the tongue, while the palatopharyngeus runs from the sides of the velum and blends into the sides of the pharynx. Both of these muscles lower the velum. The tensor veli palatini is a ribbonlike muscle that runs from the Eustachian tube to the anterior portion of the velum and serves to tense and flatten the anterior portion of the velum. Since the levator palatini and tensor palatini muscles both have connections to the Eustachian tube, their function helps to equalize air pressure within the middle ear. The uvulae muscle courses from the hard palate posteriorly through the velum to the uvula and acts to shorten and lift the velum. The primary function of the soft palate is to close off the portal between the oral and nasal cavities during swallowing, blowing, and vomiting, and when producing vowels and nonnasal consonants. Conversely, the velum also acts to open the oral-nasal port during production of nasal consonants as well as during quiet breathing.

Tongue The tongue is one of the most versatile organs in the human body and is important for speech and mastication. The tongue lies in the floor of the oral cavity within the body of the mandible. It has been functionally divided into four regions based on the relationship of the dorsum (top) of the tongue to the roof of the oral cavity. The apex (tip) is closest to the teeth, the blade is beneath the alveolar ridge, the front is beneath the hard palate, and the back is beneath the soft palate. The muscles of the tongue, like those of the larynx, are divided into extrinsic and intrinsic groups. The genioglossus muscle forms the bulk of the tongue tissue and is the strongest of the extrinsic muscles. It originates from the front of the mandible and radiates fanlike into the dorsum of the tongue from the root to the tip, with some fibers blending into the sides of the pharynx and others coursing downward to attach to the hyoid bone. Depending on which fibers predominate, the genioglossus muscle may retract and depress the tip of the tongue, or draw the tongue forward and lower the middle of the tongue. The styloglossus muscle originates from the temporal bone of the skull, attaches to the sides of the tongue along its entire length, and serves to retract and elevate the tongue. The hyoglossus muscle runs from the hyoid bone and inserts into the sides of the tongue, thus lowering the tongue and drawing it backward. The final extrinsic mus-

cle is the glossopalatini, also considered to be a muscle of the soft palate, which assists in elevating the back of the tongue.

There are also four intrinsic muscles of the tongue. The superior longitudinal muscle originates from the root of the tongue and courses anteriorly to terminate at the edges to shorten the tongue and turn the tip and sides upward. The inferior longitudinal muscle runs from the undersurface of the tongue to blend with fibers of the genioglossus and hyoglossus muscles and serves to shorten the tongue as well as lower the tongue tip and sides. The transverse muscle arises from the midline and courses laterally to terminate in the sides of the tongue, and is used to narrow the tongue and increase its height. The vertical muscle originates from the mucous membrane of the dorsum of the tongue, runs vertically down to insert into the inferior surface of the tongue, and serves to flatten and widen the tongue.

Facial Muscles The muscles that make up the facial region are numerous and complex; this discussion will focus primarily on those muscles that act upon the mouth. Although not strictly a muscle of the mouth, the orbicularis oris muscle is the principal muscle that acts upon the lips. An oval ring of muscle located within the lips the orbicularis orbis encircles the mouth slit and closes the mouth and puckers the lips when it contracts. The quadratus labii superior muscle is a flat, broad, triangular muscle that is situated above the upper lip and lateral to the midline. It comprises several

Some of the facial muscles.

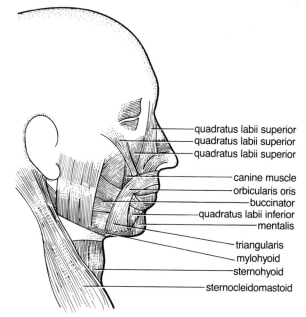

quadratus labii superior
quadratus labii superior
quadratus labii superior
canine muscle
orbicularis oris
buccinator
quadratus labii inferior
mentalis
triangularis
mylohyoid
sternohyoid
sternocleidomastoid

sections that arise from portions of the maxilla and the cheekbone and inserts into the orbicularis oris. Contraction of this muscle elevates the upper lip and angle of the mouth and protrudes the lip. The buccinator muscle is the principal muscle of the cheek, and arises in part from the lateral surface of the alveolar processes of the maxilla and mandible at the approximate point of the last molar and courses forward to join with the muscles of both the upper and lower lips. Contraction of the buccinator compresses the lips and cheeks against the teeth. The canine muscle is a flat, triangular muscle that originates near the canine fossa of the maxilla, inserts into the angle of the mouth and aids in drawing the corners of the mouth upward and in closing the mouth. The mentalis muscle is a small bundle of fibers that arises from the anterior portion of the mandible and runs upward to insert into the orbicularis oris. This muscle protrudes the lower lip. The triangularis muscle is a flat, triangular sheet that arises from the mandible and courses upward to insert into the orbicularis oris near the angle of the mouth, with some fibers continuing on to the upper lip. This muscle may either depress the angle of the mouth or compress the lips against each other. The quadratus labii inferior is a small, quadrangular-shaped muscle that arises from the anterior portion of the mandible and inserts into the lower lip. Upon contraction, it draws the lower lip downward and laterally.

These facial muscles, as well as others, are important for a number of activities that involve the face and mouth regions. Some of them act to assist in speech production by compressing the lips for consonants such as bilabial plosives and nasals, while others assist in producing facial expressions such as smiling or frowning. Other muscles work in coordination with the muscles of the jaw to open the mouth, for both speaking and nonspeaking purposes.

Bibliography

Borden, G. J., and K. S. Harris: *Speech Science Primer: Physiology, Acoustics and Perception of Speech*, Williams and Wilkins, Baltimore, Maryland, 1980.

Daniloff R., G. Schuckers, and L. Feth: *The Physiology of Speech and Hearing: An Introduction*, Prentice-Hall, Englewood Cliffs, New Jersey, 1980.

Denes, P. B., and E. N. Pinson: *The Speech Chain*, Bell Telephone Laboratories, 1968.

Judson, L. S., and A. T. Weaver: *Voice Science*, Appleton-Century-Crofts, New York, 1965.

Kaplan, H. M.: *Anatomy and Physiology of Speech*, 2d ed., McGraw-Hill, New York, 1971.

Negus, V. E.: *The Comparative Anatomy and Physiology of the Larynx*, Hafner, New York, 1949.

Robert L. Whitehead

SPEECH TRAINING

Unlike a child born with normal hearing who acquires speech effortlessly during the first years of life, the child with a profound, congenital hearing loss must be taught how to speak. The practicality of teaching speech to profoundly hearing-impaired individuals has been a source of controversy throughout the history of deaf education. The literature on this topic dates back to 1620 with the first book on deaf education, *Simplification of the Letters of the Alphabet and Method of Teaching Deaf Mutes to Speak*, written by Juan Pablo Bonet. The label "deaf mute" has long been abandoned, and it is widely accepted that deaf children can learn to speak. Controversy still exists, however, regarding the extent to which profoundly hearing-impaired persons can be taught to speak and the procedures that are most effective to help them develop speech. The ultimate goal is the acquisition of speech that can be understood by everyone, even people unfamiliar with deaf speech. The majority of deaf speakers, however, do not attain this performance level, indicating a lack of knowledge of the speech development in deaf children, the variables that affect this process, and the training programs most effective in promoting it. *See* Pablo Bonet, Juan.

History

Historically, speech training was performed by classroom teachers as an academic subject within the school day. The teachers' skills usually were acquired in an apprentice or inservice setting in a school for deaf children. Formal course work in teacher-training programs generally was taught by educators who based suggested methodologies on their direct teaching experiences.

There is no clear-cut chronological demarcation for many speech-training methodologies, and the roots of most existing approaches can be traced back to those in existence in the late 1800s and early 1900s. There appear, however, to be three major areas of technological advances that have made a significant impact on modifying teaching approaches. First, the development of sophisticated processing and analysis techniques in speech science and related areas increased knowledge of normal speech production. It is now recognized, for example, that the speech signal changes rapidly over time in a complex manner. Thus, early training procedures that focused on teaching speech sounds as static events, eventually to be combined like beads on a string to form syllables and words, are no longer in evidence. Further, awareness that there is not a one-to-one correspondence between speech sounds and written symbols has eliminated the use of orthographic symbols as a primary technique to teach speech to deaf persons. *See* Speech production.

Second, early identification and initiation of management programs also has had a major influence on speech-training procedures. New techniques permit the majority of profoundly hearing-impaired children to be identified during infancy and the preschool years, and the approaches to training these younger children differ from those used with school-aged children. Parent-centered activities are used with infants, and often the distinction between speech and language training during these early years is blurred. With young children, the majority of training occurs during the course of everyday activities rather than during structured therapy sessions.

Third, advances in the assessment of auditory capabilities and the development of electroacoustic amplification systems has highlighted the role of residual hearing in the speech development process. Today, most programs incorporate speech training through the auditory channel, although the degree of dependence on residual hearing varies among different progrms.

Today, the general trend is toward development of training strategies based on scientific knowledge and objective data. With the exception of infants and young children, most speech training is performed in individual therapy or tutoring sessions, often by a speech-language pathologist. The classroom teacher is responsible for promoting use of speech, monitoring each child's productions, and helping him or her maintain a specified level of speech production performance. Ideally, there is close interaction between the classroom teacher and the person who performs the individual training to provide a comprehensive program in the development and maintenance of speech skills.

Teaching Methods

Speech teaching methods are organized according to the size of the speech unit emphasized during training and the sensory channels used to promote speech development. Analytic methods emphasize the use of small units of speech (speech sounds and syllables), whereas synthetic methods emphasize the use of speech units no smaller than the syllable, often stressing the role of connected speech during training. Prior to the 1940s, almost all structured teaching programs were multisensory. That is, they used all sensory channels (auditory, visual, tactile) to promote speech development. During the 1940s, when advances in hearing aid technology began to occur, a distinction between programs in terms of sensory channel emphasis became apparent, as the unisensory or auditory-oral progams began to emerge. Some training programs, however, incorporated both analytic and synthetic techniques and a multisensory approach with heavy emphasis on the use of residual hearing.

ANALYTIC TEACHING METHODS

The symbol systems and the elements method focused first on teaching the production of speech sounds as individual units, and then on progressing to combining the sounds into sequences to form syllables and words. The sounds generally were taught by using a system of written symbols. The first attempt to systematize speech training using this approach was performed by Alexander Melville Bell, who developed the Visible Speech system, described by his son Alexander Graham Bell, in 1872. This system, first used with deaf persons by the younger Bell in London in 1869, consisted of groups of symbols intended to express in graphic form the movements of the articulators for the individual speech sounds. Bell claimed great success with the method, although he did acknowledge that it was limited to teaching only articulation of speech sounds. Other techniques had to be used to teach the rhythmic aspects of speech. In 1871 Bell introduced the system to educators in the United States at the Horace Mann School in Boston and at the Clarke School for the Deaf in Northampton, Massachusetts. The system was used for 10 years at the Clarke School, after which, the symbols on the charts were replaced by the characters of the English alphabet. *See* BELL, ALEXANDER GRAHAM; CLARKE SCHOOL; VISIBLE SPEECH.

In 1915, Alice Worcester further modified Bell's system because all English sounds could not be represented by using only the 26 characters of English. In 1925 the system again was revised and organized by Carolyn Yale into systematic charts, which became known as the Northampton Charts and are still in use today. The system classifies the sounds of English into primary and secondary spellings, which are divided further into consonants and vowels. The primary spellings reflect the alphabet letters or combination of letters used to represent a particular sound in writing. The secondary spellings reflect the irregular relation between sounds and the written letters. The consonants are grouped by manner of production: breath, voice, or nasal emission. The vowels are arranged according to the position of the tongue. A system of diacritical markings indicates secondary spellings and identifies those symbols occurring for more than one speech sound. Early use of this system, like the Visible Speech system, emphasized teaching children to associate a specific movement of the articulators with its written symbol.

In 1948 Enfield Joiner of the North Carolina School for the Deaf advocated an elements-type teaching approach which emphasized "tongue gymnastics" to achieve habitually accurate positions for correct production of speech sounds. The Northampton Charts also was an integral part of her program, but Joiner recognized the importance of developing smooth movements to combine sequences of sounds to form syllables and words. Other unique aspects of her program included production of syllables in both a whispered and a normal voice, development of good breath control, use of appropriate accent (stress patterns), phrasing and grouping of words, and speaking at a natural rate.

One of the most recent applications of the elements teaching approach is the association phoneme-unit approach, based on the work of Mildred McGuiness in the early 1950s at the Central Institute for the Deaf. Unlike earlier analytic teaching approaches, this one was intended to be used with students for whom other types of procedures were unsuitable. Traditional techniques were unsuccessful with these students because they appeared to have learning problems in addition to those imposed by their hearing handicap. All sensory systems (visual, auditory, tactile) were used to teach the individual speech sounds, with emphasis placed on memory of the motor act involved in the production of each sound. The written symbol, which was always taught with the sound, was used to prompt the child's production of the corresponding sound. Once the child achieved near-perfect production of a number of consonants and vowels, blending of two or more sounds to form syllables, words, and finally phrases and sentences was performed. *See* CENTRAL INSTITUTE FOR THE DEAF.

A visual-tactile system of phonetic symbolization for teaching speech to the deaf was described in 1954 by A. Zaliouk, director of the Institute for the Deaf in Haifa, Israel. The fingers were used to indicate the most salient visual and tactile components of each sound. The system consisted of static symbols used to denote the articulators (palate, tongue, teeth, lips) and dynamic symbols used to represent movement of the articulators.

In 1942 Mary Numbers of the Clark School for the Deaf raised some astute criticisms of the elements teaching method. She argued that this approach focused only on articulation of speech sounds, ignored the rhythmic aspects of speech, and failed to teach deaf children how to coordinate phonation and articulation. Further, she argued that the elements method assumed by the very nature of its teaching approach that speech consisted of a sequence of sounds, similar to letters in a printed word. Research over the years has shown Numbers to be valid in these criticisms of the elements method. There is no one-to-one correspondence between a speech sound and its written form. Speech is a series of complex events that overlap and change rapidly over time. The approach recommended by Numbers emphasized syllable production, with articulatory movements taught in connection with the syllables in which they were to function.

Even with the convincing arguments raised by Numbers for a more synthetic teaching approach, the emphasis on production of isolated speech sounds persisted for many years. Today, the dynamic, time-changing aspects of speech have been well documented, and are well known to most educators of hearing-impaired persons. Work on isolated sounds might be employed as a teaching strategy during some stages in the teaching process, but this approach is generally not used as the foundation for an entire speech training program.

This situation also is true for written symbol systems, which now are used most often as phonic symbols to help the child learn to sound out words when reading. Written symbols might also be used at various stages in speech training to elicit production of a target sound from children. Color codes and various pictured representations which change in length (to represent long and short speech sounds) or size (to represent loudness changes) also are used for this purpose. There are few, if any, programs today that rely exclusively on the use of written symbols to teach speech to children. Not only does the use of written symbols fail to capture the fleeting events of speech, but it requires the child to be able to read and write before any intensive speech work can begin. Education of deaf children often begins in infancy, and it is generally agreed that children should receive some form of speech instruction long before training on reading and writing skills is begun.

SYNTHETIC TEACHING METHODS

In contrast to the elements approach, synthetic teaching methods emphasize the use of speech units larger than individual sounds. Some of the approaches begin speech training with syllables, gradually working toward the production of words and phrases, whereas others focus on the use of connected speech throughout the stages of speech development. Another distinction between approaches in this category is the number of different sensory channels used to stimulate speech development. A multisensory approach uses all available sensory channels (auditory, visual, tactile-kinesthetic) for speech instruction, whereas an auditory-oral approach teaches the child to rely almost exclusively on input via the impaired auditory system to perceive speech and to monitor his or her own productions.

Multisensory Teaching Methods An underlying assumption of these methods is that information perceived by the impaired auditory system is inadequate for the development of speech. Consequently, other sensory systems are used for speech instruction, notably the visual and tactile systems. Emphasis is placed on production of syllables, gradually progressing to production of words and phrases. Ideally, speech instruction is conducted in individual sessions with the child. The task often required of the child is imitation, wherein the teacher first produces the speech unit being taught and the child is expected to repeat what has been said. The teachers' utterances are produced so children can both see the mouth movements, sometimes with the aid of a mirror, and hear the speech being produced. Additional cues may be provided tactually by having children place their hands on the teacher's face or neck to feel the vibrations associated with particular speech movements.

Early proponents of the synthetic method emphasized the use of frequent, repetitive syllable drills in speech training. One of the most comprehensive systems of syllable drills, known as the Babbling Method, was described in the United States in 1918 by Josephine Avondino. She used syllable drills because they paralleled the babbling behavior of infants with normal hearing. Imitation and repetition were essential features of the drills, which began with single syllables in groups of three (for example, faw, faw, faw), progressing to two-syllable words with the stress (accent) on the second syllable, and finally moving to two-syllable words with the stress on either syllable and each syllable beginning with a consonant. There is an indication of the influence of the elements teaching approach in Avondino's program as she advocated that each sound had to be developed separately because overlapping movements of sound sequences prevented the child from getting the correct idea of the formation needed for the component sounds. It is recognized today, however, that achieving this overlapping movement, or coarticulation between speech sounds, is a characteristic feature of normal speech.

In 1933 a text on speech teaching by G. Sibley Haycock, a renowned educator of deaf people in England, was first published and contained one of the most comprehensive coverages of speech training for hearing-impaired individuals. Although syllable drills were an important part of his program, he emphasized more than just the development of articulation skills. The early stages of training focused on breathing exercises, both with and without phonation, and on controlling pitch and loudness changes in the voice. Haycock stressed the importance of developing "automaticity" of movement, avoiding heavy practice of fixed speech positions. His book also contains a series of systematic exercises to develop proper rhythm, timing, phrasing, stress, and intonation patterns. The suggested teaching order of speech sounds was determined by their ease of production and their visibility on the face of the teacher. Attention to consonants was directed first toward the voice-voiceless and

nasal distinction, beginning with the sounds within these categories with a labial place of production. Vowel training began with the long vowels and diphthongs.

The training program developed largely by Marjorie Magner at the Clarke School for the Deaf incorporated two parallel avenues of teaching. The natural (synthetic) component emphasized the spontaneous use of meaningful oral communication. It was viewed as a fundamental part of every academic lesson and activity throughout the day, requiring continuous, functional use of speech in all situations. This avenue of teaching was introduced as soon as the child's hearing loss was discovered, and continued throughout his or her life. During the preschool years, this type of training was parent-centered, where the parents, under the guidance of professional personnel, learned skills in talking, playing, and working with their infants and young children. This stage of training emphasized the use of techniques that paralleled the developmental stages of speech acquisition in children with normal hearing. Speech input to the child was multisensory, with large units of speech (sentences) preferred to smaller ones (words). During this stage, the child's own vocalizations were encouraged through imitation and reinforcement. Once the child had begun to indicate in expressing his or her thoughts orally and had begun to approximate words and phrases spontaneously, the other avenue of teaching, which involved a more analytic approach, was introduced.

The analytic approach consisted of structured, systematic training techniques, geared toward helping the child acquire specific speech skills that had not developed naturally. This approach was referred to as analytic by Magner because it involved structured training and speech drills. Her use of the term analytic, however, should not be confused with an elements teaching approach. The smallest unit of speech recommended by Magner for use during training was the syllable. Once the analytic training was initiated, the child was encouraged and expected to use the skills acquired during this training in functional communicative situations. Thus, the two teaching approaches were applied in parallel to one another.

In Magner's program, analytic training focused on only one of three general aspects of speech at a time: voice quality, articulation, or speech rhythm. Voice control was achieved through a series of exercises involving coordination of breathing and phonation, and control of nasal resonance, production of syllable strings with different pitch levels, intonation patterns, or changes in loudness. Instrumental to Magner's development of these exercises was the research of Clarence V. Hudgins, also at the Clarke School, who was a leading scientist in experimental phonetics in the United States.

Articulation training was an integral part of Magner's speech program, again with speech units no smaller than the syllable forming the body of the training material. Techniques, including imitation, analogy of production (having children produce a sound they are capable of producing that has features similar to the one being taught), demonstration with mirrors, videotapes, and diagrams of the articulators during production of the target sounds all were used to help children achieve correct production patterns. Although Magner's program incorporated the use of multisensory training, emphasis always was placed on using residual hearing for speech development. The Northampton Charts were used as a pronunciation guide, with written symbols introduced only after the children had mastered production of the corresponding sounds.

Another area in Magner's program was speech rhythm, which focused on stress (accent) patterns, phrasing, and rate of talking. Teaching first focused on the deaf child's reception of these speech features in the speech of adults with normal hearing, gradually progressing to the child's own production during oral readings of passages.

A similar approach to speech teaching was employed at the Lexington School for the Deaf in New York City. The program was based on the work of Mary New and reflected the Natural Language Method developed by Mildred Groht, also of the Lexington School. The program stressed the link between speech and language, and had the underlying philosophy that teaching and learning speech was an ongoing process which must pervade all social and academic experiences. Emphasis was placed on teaching speech at the most natural level possible. Speech instruction began informally during the early school years and became more structured, if necessary, later.

The program consisted of two major levels of instruction. One level, corrective speechwork, was conducted as an integral part of all classroom experiences. Successive stages of correction through which the teacher was to guide a child consisted of: (1) the child's correction with specific help from the teacher; (2) the child's repetition of the teacher's pattern; (3) cueing the child to the specific correction needed; (4) self-correction after the teacher indicated the need for self-improvement; (5) the child's self-correction independent of the teacher.

The second level of speech work was referred to as developmental, where specific training techniques were used to develop or improve those aspects of speech that did not emerge through the use of ongoing corrective speech. Developmental

speech teaching usually involved individual sessions with the student, directed toward improving aspects of voice production, rhythm, articulation, and correct pronunciation of the units of oral language. Primary teaching strategies of the Lexington program consisted of: (1) relating the target speech behavior to the child's own personal experience and to the proper linguistic context; (2) practicing in whole units, not the component parts; (3) understanding the child's dominant sensory modalities and using them to their fullest extent; (4) appropriately demonstrating and reinforcing speech attempts; (5) relating speech work to pleasurable experiences; (6) using exercises and drills only when necessary to develop needed motor coordination; (7) using diacritical markings and written symbols to be supportive of speech without fostering dependency. Although this was clearly a multisensory approach, emphasis was placed on developing as many aspects of spoken language as possible through the auditory channel.

Auditory-Oral Teaching Methods This type of training also has been referred to as aural-oral, the auditory approach, acoupedic, unisensory-auditory, and auditory-global. Its development can be traced primarily to the work of a nineteenth-century Viennese otologist, Urbantschitsch, who advocated helping each child make optimal use of residual hearing. The method was introduced in the early 1900s in the United States by another otologist, Max Goldstein, at the St. Joseph School for the Deaf and the Central Institute for the Deaf, both located in St. Louis, Missouri. The underlying premise of the approach is that use of residual hearing is the most efficient and satisfactory way to develop speech skills. Proponents provide several rationales for this approach. First, hearing impairment is seldom total, and most children have some residual hearing and auditory capabilities. Second, the entire speech signal need not be detected for the perception of many of the features of speech. Third, electroacoustic amplification of speech through a hearing aid can compensate for some of the loss of auditory sensitivity and render certain speech features audible to the listener. Because the auditory channel is the natural one for learning speech by the child with normal hearing, advocates of the auditory-oral approach believe it is the most effective channel for teaching speech as well. Emphasis is placed on helping children learn to perceive the speech of others through audition alone, as well as to monitor their own productions on the basis of the auditory feedback they perceive. Some programs rely on the use of residual hearing nearly exclusively for teaching speech, irrespective of degree of loss. Other proponents of this approach supplement auditory stimulation with visual information when necessary. *See* GOLDSTEIN, MAX AARON.

The general approach to teaching is eliciting speech from children on the basis of only auditory input. Thus, speech training is performed so children cannot see the teacher's mouth. This method of training is intended to help children become dependent on the acoustic speech signal, thereby increasing their attention to it, and helping them improve the use of hearing for speech. Early intervention and the acquisition and maintenance of appropriate hearing aid amplification are important components of the approach. The initial instructional procedure consists primarily of directing spoken language to children, ensuring that they receive as much acoustic information from the speech signal as possible. Once children learn to attend to spoken language, speech may be presented with the mouth hidden. At this time, the teacher can emphasize certain speech sounds or prosodic aspects of speech.

Structured drills are used to elicit, develop, and improve specific speech skills. Elicitation of target speech sounds and patterns is achieved through imitation on the basis of an auditory-oral model only. That is, the child must listen to the teacher's production and then try to imitate the model without the use of visual cues. If the child is unsuccessful, cues other than auditory might be introduced. Once successful production is achieved with multiple cues, imitation is again required on the basis of only auditory information. This type of training is usually not initiated with very young children.

Emphasis is always placed on delivering connected speech to children so that they can learn to take advantage of the prosodic and linguistic information it contains. Expansion and modeling strategies are employed to foster the child's development of connected speech. In the former, the adult imitates what the child has said, and adds to it something to form a complete and grammatical sentence. For example, if the child says "Girl fall," the utterance might be expanded to "Yes, the girl is falling." To model an utterance, the adult makes a relevant comment on what the child has said. For example, the adult might say "Yes, her roller skate fell off" in response to the child's utterance of "Girl fall." Central to this approach and the development of the child's spoken language skills is an environment which supports and reinforces auditory-oral communication.

Ling Method   The best-known speech-training program in this area was developed by Daniel Ling. Ling employs a systematic approach to speech training, based largely on his own teaching experiences with deaf children and the scientific literature. Two major principles underlie his speech training program. The first is that speech skills should be developed in the deaf child in the same order in which they develop in the child with normal hearing. The second is that speech should be taught within a dynamic framework, focusing on the rapid and precise movements required to produce intelligible speech.

The program is viewed as a developmental process spanning the following seven sequential stages: (1) undifferentiated vocalizations; (2) nonsegmental voice patterns varied in duration, intensity, and pitch; (3) a range of distinctly different vowel sounds; (4) consonants contrasted in manner of production; (5) consonants contrasted in manner and place of production; (6) consonants contrasted in manner, place, and voicing; and (7) consonant blends. Each stage requires the development of target behaviors, some of which may be developed simultaneously rather than sequentially. A range of subskills, which must be mastered by the child, underlie the target behaviors.

Teaching and evaluation strategies are developed at the phonetic and phonologic levels. At the phonetic level, emphasis is placed on the child's production of only orosensory-motor speech patterns. Drill work with nonsense syllables is the major teaching strategy at this level. To promote development of smooth, coarticulated speech, repeated syllable drills (for example, ba-ba-ba-ba) and alternated syllable drills (such as ba-bee-ba-bee or ba-ma-ba-ma) are performed. At the phonologic level, the child learns to use the production patterns in a systematic and meaningful way. Training incorporates practice with words, phrases, and sentences. Although Ling contends that there is automatic transfer of skills from the phonetic to phonologic level, experience has shown that this does not always occur, particularly when the child has a profound hearing loss. Some teachers and clinicians have started using systematic drills with words, phrases, and sentences to promote the transfer of phonetic to phonologic skills.

Ling advocates that speech training should occupy short units of time (two to three minutes) four or five times a day, rather than one longer training period, which is the structure for most school programs. The more frequent practice permits the child to have experience with speech throughout the day. An important aspect of his approach is the development of the auditory-kinesthetic feedback loop. That is, the child learns to understand the speech of others as well as to monitor his own productions via his or her residual hearing. Although some techniques in Ling's program can be found in earlier teaching methods (nonsense syllable drill, nonsegmental voice patterns), he was the first person to systematize the techniques and develop a teaching order for the training. The introduction of his speech training program brought with it a renewed interest in teaching speech to deaf people among professions in all types of educational settings. Since the time of Alexander Graham Bell, no single individual has had a greater impact on speech training for deaf people.

Implications for the Future

To date, the relative effectiveness of the various teaching methodologies has not been established. However, research is being conducted in this area. In fact, the development of well-defined training strategies, notably the work of Ling in Canada, has spirited a renewed interest in developing speech skills in profoundly hearing-impaired individuals. In addition, the rigors of scientific method have been applied to study the speech of deaf people and to evaluate the effectiveness of training strategies. Even though knowledge is far from complete in this area, continued research and technological advances should assist many more profoundly hearing-impaired persons to realize their speech potential. *See* SPEECH; SPEECH, ANALYSIS OF.

Bibliography
Calvert, D., and S. R. Silverman: *Speech and Deafness*, Alexander Graham Bell Association for the Deaf, rev. ed., 1983.

Connor, L. (ed.): *Speech for the Deaf Child: Knowledge and Use*, Alexander Graham Bell Association for the Deaf, 1971.

Haycock, G. S.: *The Teaching of Speech*, Alexander Graham Bell Association for the Deaf, 1953.

Ling, D.: *Speech and the Hearing-Impaired Child: Theory and Practice*, Alexander Graham Bell Association, 1976.

Osberger, M. J., et al.: "The Evaluation of a Model Speech Training Program for the Deaf," *Journal of Communication Disorders*, vol. 11, no 2/3, April 1978.

Polack, D.: *Educational Audiology for the Limited-Hearing Infant*, Charles C. Thomas, 1970.

Vorce, E.: *Teaching Speech to Deaf Children*, Alexander Graham Bell Association for the Deaf, 1974.

Mary Joe Osberger

SPEECHREADING

Speechreading is understanding a speaker by watching the movements of the speaker's tongue and mouth and the speaker's facial expressions. The more established term for speechreading is lipreading, which was used almost exclusively up to the mid-1950s. Since then, there has been a conscious effort to change the generic term to speechreading. The newer term is meant to connote the communicative process of speech perception via the visual channel. That is, the observer watches the facial expressions made by the speaker, as well as lip, jaw, and tongue movements. The term lipreading implies observation of just the lips.

Information about speechreading can be found in the literature dating back to the seventeenth century, when it was discussed as a major component in the oral education of deaf children. It has become recognized that information perceived via the visual channel assists the adult with an acquired hearing loss in understanding speech. In fact, there is a distinction between the speechreader who has a congenital hearing loss and one who has an acquired hearing loss. In the latter case, speechreading can be viewed as the process of understanding an already learned language through a sensory channel (visual) that differs from the one used first to learn the language (auditory). In contrast, the child born deaf depends on input via the visual channel as the primary means of first learning the language. It is largely because of this situation that speechreading has been the subject of numerous investigations over the years. This discussion of speechreading will focus on three major areas: (1) visual and audiovisual perception of speech sounds; (2) assessment and teaching procedures; and (3) factors affecting speechreading performance.

PERCEPTION OF SPEECH SOUNDS

Not all phonemes or sounds of English can be distinguished visually from one another. Viseme is the term used to describe a group of speech movements, or lip shapes, that are usually indistinguishable from one another. There is disagreement, however, concerning the number of visemes that exist. For the consonant sounds, there are at least four major categories of visemes, and some studies have shown that observers perceive as many as nine or ten distinct categories of lip movements. The four major categories are: (1) /p, b, m/; (2) /w, r/; (3) /f, v/; and (4) /t, d, n, l, θ, ð, s, z, tʃ, dʒ, ʃ, ʒ, j, k, g, ŋ, h/. The four categories are referred to as bilabial, rounded labial, labiodental, and nonlabial, respectively. Typically, observers can distinguish consonants between viseme groups but not within a group. For example, the lip movements used to make /p/ can be visually differentiated from those used to make /f/, but not those used to make /b/.

Consonants that fall into one group, such as /p, b, m/, are said to be homophenous and to constitute a single viseme. For example, the lip movements used to make /m/ in the word "mop" cannot be distinguished visually from those used to make /p/ in the word "pop." In general, the place of articulation moves progressively backward in the mouth from group 1 to group 4. Group 1 consists of the bilabial consonants. The movement for group 2, consisting of the /w/ and /r/, requires the lips to be constricted and protruded. The group 3 consonants require approximation of the lower lip and the upper front jaw. Some of the consonants in group 4 are produced in the back of the mouth (/k, g, ŋ, h/), which reduces their visual distinctiveness. Other consonants in this group are produced with highly similar movements of the articulators (/t, d, n, s, z, l/), which makes them difficult to distinguish visually. Good lipreaders, however, are sometimes able to distinguish some of consonants in the the fourth group.

The lack of agreement regarding the number of visemes probably reflects fundamental differences in experimental design among speechreading investigations. In addition, there is no general agreement as to the statistical criterion which should be applied to determine when two consonants are contrastive.

Attempts have been made to categorize vowels into homophenous groupings (visemes), but these have been largely unsuccessful. Unlike consonants, which form homophenous groupings because of identical lip movements, no two vowels are produced with exactly the same articulatory movements. There are, nonetheless, typical visual confusions involving the vowels. Vowels are usually confused with vowels adjacent to the target stimulus in articulatory configuration. Vowels produced with the lips spread (such as /i/) can be distinguished from those made with the lips rounded (/u/), but vowels within each of these categories are not visually distinct. Tense vowels (/i, u/) are generally more intelligible than the lax vowels (/I, ʊ/). It also has been found that the visual intelligibility of a consonant is affected by the vowel environment in which it occurs. In general, performance is highest when the consonants occur with a vowel produced with a wide mouth opening (/a/) than with vowels with a more closed mouth opening (/i/, /u/). Also, increasing the distance between the observer and the speaker has less effect on lipreading vowels than on consonants.

Linguistic effects on speechreading performance have been noted. For example, the stress pattern of a word can affect its visual intelligibility, with bisyllabic (two-syllable) words having equal stress being more intelligible than bisyllabic words with the first syllable stressed which, in turn, are more intelligible than monosyllabic words. Isolated words are more intelligible visually than words in sentences, and animate nouns have been found to be more intelligible than inanimate, at least for deaf children with congenital hearing loss. Further, speechreading scores have been found to vary as a function of talker. That is, some talkers are easier to speechread than others.

The foregoing discussion illustrates that the lack of visual distinctiveness among many of the sounds of English limits the usefulness of lipreading by itself. Most hearing-impaired people, however, have some residual hearing, and they are able to perceive some speech cues acoustically. Research has shown that the cues available via visual and auditory channels supplement one another. In general, large increases in understanding occur when the auditory signal is added to the visual signal. Visually, a consonant's place of articulation is distinct, but manner features (voicing and nasality) are not. Auditorily, distinctions between place of articulation are most seriously affected by a sensorineural hearing loss, whereas manner contrasts are least affected. Thus, hearing-impaired people can use both visual and auditory cues to enhance their ability to understand speech.

One system employs a set of hand cues, together with the speechread form, to attempt to resolve the ambiguities in visual speech reception. That technique, caled cued speech, was developed by Orin Cornett of Gallaudet College. Cued speech is a system of hand movements that provides information relating directly to the articulation of sound patterns. Consonants are cued by eight hand configurations and the vowels by four hand positions. Diphthongs are cued by gliding from the position of the initial vowel to the final vowel nucleus. Once mastered, it can be used without affecting the rate and rhythm of running speech. The hand movements from one sound to the next can be executed smoothly so that they flow together as does coarticulated speech. Experiments with cued speech have shown that it can significantly improve speech reception. The system is primarily used with deaf children. *See* MOUTH-HAND SYSTEMS.

ASSESSMENT AND TEACHING METHODS

A number of tests have been developed over the years to assess some speechreading skills. The tests may vary in type of stimuli used (words or sentences), the age group for which the measure is intended (adults or children), the response format (open set or closed set), and whether the test is administered live or on a film. The Utley Film Test, "How Well Can You Read Lips?", is perhaps the most widely used measure. It consists of three parts: a sentence test, a word test, and a story test. The tests require vocabulary skills comparable to a third-grade reading level. The sentences are common colloquial and idiomatic expressions, and the words were selected from Thorndike's list of the 1000 most frequently used words.

The Children's Speech Reading Test is a measure developed by Dolores Butt, intended for use with children who have not yet learned to read. One portion of the test is for children under three years of age, and is composed of an informal checklist. A second portion is for children over three, consisting of objects and picture cards that the child must identify. Another measure is the Craig Lipreading Inventory, which requires word and sentence recognition. The test is administered face to face, and it employs a four-alternative pictured format.

Informal measures may be used to assess speechreading skills. These might consist of a question-answer interchange between the clinician and the hearing-impaired individual, interview techniques, or use of short stories. It is generally preferable to use voice, although the loudness level may be reduced so that it is lower than that typically used in conversational situations. When assessing the speechreading skills of hearing-impaired children, particularly those with profound hearing losses, the clinician should have knowledge of the language abilities of the child. Specifically, the clinician should attempt to determine if the vocabulary used in any measure of speechreading is known to the child.

Historically, methods developed to teach speechreading have been highly structured and have emphasized drill work, although there has been disagreement as to the type of speech material that should be used for the drills. The basic approaches to speechreading training are usually classified as analytic or synthetic. aThe analytic approach assumes that the recognition of speech components in isolated or reduced contexts is necessary for the recognition of those same elements when they occur in connected discourse. Analytic training procedures emphasize eye training, geared toward helping the lipreader learn the articulatory movements associated with individual speech sounds. The training procedures stress syllable recognition rather than the recognition of words or sentences. The synthetic approach emphasizes recognition of thoughts and ideas through vision rather than identification of individual speech components. These procedures advocate the use of sentences as the primary instructional unit, with emphasis placed on using situational and linguistic context to understand what has been said.

The two methods that are traditionally considered analytic are the Muller-Walle method, described by Martha Bruhn in her book *Elementary Lessons in Lipreading* (1927), and the Jena method, described by Anna Bunger in *Speech Reading—Jena Method* (1952), which is the method developed by Karl Brauckmann, a German. The Muller-Walle method was developed for use with children and adults, whereas the Jena method was developed primarily for adults, although suggestions for adapting the procedures for children are described. The Muller-Walle method employs rapid syllable drills with the most visible sounds presented first and the less visible ones later. Syllables always are produced with other syllables. Training progresses from syllable to sentence practice. The syllables are produced naturally and as fluently as they occur in running speech. Voice is always used when the training material is presented to the speechreader. Bruhn's rationale for the heavy emphasis on syllables is that the individual only has to concentrate on recognizing movements rather than attempting to derive meaning from the movements.

The Jena method begins by giving the individual information about the shaping movements of the vowels and articulatory movements of the consonants. Emphasis is placed on helping the student develop kinesthetic awareness (learning how the movements feel) of speech sounds. To emphasize the rhythmic aspects of syllable drills, bodily movement such as clapping, tapping, and ball bouncing are encouraged. In addition to syllable exercises, the Jena method includes drill on grammatical forms, and incorporated work in the later stages of training on conversation and stories.

There are two well-known synthetic approaches, one developed by Edward Nitchie, *Lipreading: Principles and Practices* (1912), and the other by the Kinzie sisters (Rose and Cora), *Lipreading for Children* (1936) and *Lipreading for the Deafened Adult* (1931). Nitchie, who became interested in the area because of his acquired deafness at age 14, initially advocated an analytic approach but eventually stressed the importance of being able to synthesize what the speaker said. Eye training is employed through practice with lists of words and sentences in which only one word or movement is changed from sentence to sentence. For synthesis or mind training, emphasis is placed on understanding the speaker's thought rather than on word-for-word identification accuracy. Nitchie's training procedures are designed for use with adults. The Kinzie sisters developed their training method for use with children and adults. A distinctive feature of this method is the graded lesson materials, designed so students can progress from one level of attainment to the next and, in time, achieve maximum skills. The graded material consists of words, sentences, and stories.

Controversy still exists today regarding the most appropriate approach for teaching deaf people to speechread, and increasingly researchers and clinicians have questioned whether speechreading can be taught. Research findings suggest that systematic speechreading practice in the discrimination of consonants and vowels in nonsense syllables leads to finer resolution of homophenous groupings. Further, there is evidence from one study to suggest that training with syllables improves recognition of sentences. Other studies have shown negligible changes in speechreading tests following training, although participants have reported improvements in their overall communication behavior after training. Specifically, they reported greater confidence in their communication skills and improved ability to manipulate those aspects of communication that make speechreading easier, such as proper illumination of the speaker's face.

There appears to be a consensus that speechreading does not have to be taught, although an individual's skill can usually be improved through instruction. Most approaches used today are eclectic, and there appears to be a trend away from systematic instruction with drills. When drill work is incorporated, it is largely to make the individual aware of the visual distinctions that exist among speech sounds, particularly the consonants. Most suggested training procedures, such as those advocated by Janet Jeffers and Margaret Barley, emphasize the use of sentences and stories geared toward helping the individual perceive the gist or main ideas of the material. Training is generally performed audiovisually with the observer using appropriately fitted hearing aids. An approach which is gaining widespread acceptance is called speech tracking, developed by Carole De Filippo and Brian Scott of the Central Institute for the Deaf. With this procedure, a talker transmits (reads) conversational textual material to a receiver (the speechreader) who is required to repeat the information verbatim. Performance is calculated as the number of correct words per unit of five. Often, the technique is used to compare a hearing-impaired person's performance in a speechreading-alone condition with performance when speechreading is supplemented by information from another sensory channel such as auditory or tactile. The advantage of this technique is that it approximates the speech-perception demands encountered in everyday communicative situations and at the same time permits quantification of performance. *See* CENTRAL INSTITUTE FOR THE DEAF.

FACTORS AFFECTING PERFORMANCE

Attempts have been made to identify what characterizes a good speechreader, presumably because this information could lead to defining optimal strategies to train others. Today, it is still not clear what skills are needed to be a good speechreader. Clearly, visual acuity is important. Speechreading should not be adversely affected if the person's visual acuity is no poorer than 20/80 and the distance between the speechreader and the talker is no greater than 5 feet (1.5 meters). Visual processing skills found to be significantly correlated with speechreading include visual synthesis, visual-spatial processing, visual closure, and visual sequential memory. No association has been found between full-scale tests of intelligence and speechreading, at least in adults with acquired losses. In children, speechreading sentence material has been found to be significantly associated with receptive language abilities.

Environmental factors also may affect speechreading performance. In a number of classic investigations by Norman Erber of the Central Institute for the Deaf, efficiency of speechreading as a function of angle, distance, and illumination was examined. These studies showed the highest speechreading scores were obtained for 0 or 45° observation levels and for distances no greater than 10 feet (3 meters) between the speechreader and the talker. Frontal illumination resulted in higher speechreading performance than facial illumination or high background brightness. These studies also showed that visual identification of vowels was less dependent on distance than consonant identification scores.

THE FUTURE

Advances in computer technology are beginning to influence speechreading research. One technique, employed at the Central Institute for the Deaf, involves the synthesis of lip and mouth shapes to permit determination of the relation between physical characteristics and perceptual data. With this approach, it may be possible to determine which lip and mouth movements contribute to a viewer's perception of specific visual distinctions. Another technique employs digital picture processing in which two-video sequences that differ only in the consonant produced by the speaker in a vowel-consonant-vowel (VCV) context are interleaved. The interleaved sequence results in a video recording with areas of jitter in those regions of the same utterances. This technique has been used to determine if there are visible differences between the homophenous sounds /p/, /b/, and /m/. The results showed there were visually distinct differences for the three sounds in the lower lip and cheeks when the consonant appeared in a /u/ context. Other computer applications consist of development of training aids for speechreading instruction. As technology advances, knowledge of the speechreading process probably will continue to grow.

Bibliography

Jeffers, J., and M. Barley: *Speechreading (Lipreading)*, Charles C Thomas, Springfield, Illinois, 1971.

O'Neill, J. J., and H. J. Oyer: *Visual Communication for the Hard of Hearing*, Prentice-Hall, Englewood Cliffs, New Jersey, 1961.

Summerfield, A. Q.: "Audio-Visual Speech Perception, Lipreading, and Artificial Stimulation," in M. E. Lutman and M. P. Haffard, *Hearing Science and Hearing Disorders*, pp. 132–182, Academic Press, New York, 1983.

Mary Joe Osberger

SRI LANKA

Sri Lanka is a tropical island of about 25,000 square miles (65,000 square kilometers) off the southern tip of India. It is an independent democratic socialist republic, with a population of 14.85 million consisting mainly of three ethnic groups—Sinhalese (74 percent) Tamils (18 percent), and Moors (7 percent). The national languages are Sinhalese and Tamil with English serving as a second language. About 78 percent of the population live in rural or estate sectors. Sri Lanka has a literacy rate of 86 percent.

HISTORICAL DEVELOPMENTS

Work with deaf persons began as a Christian missionary undertaking when the Ceylon School for the Deaf and Blind was established in 1912. This remained the only institution that gave form and direction to the education and welfare of deaf children and adults until long after the island gained independence from the British in 1948.

There are now 14 other schools for deaf persons, most of which were established in the 1960s and 1970s by welfare societies, religious organizations, or social service organizations. Many of these schools also include a smaller section for blind people. Each school operates independently, and no effort has been made to form common objectives or share experiences for the common good. All schools are managed privately.

In the 1970s a special education branch was set up by the Ministry of Education with the objective of direct involvement. This branch began with integration of blind students in regular schools and has extended the same program for deaf pupils, but only on an experimental basis. There are about 300 deaf or partially hearing children in 17 units in regular government schools.

The Ceylon School for the Deaf and Blind at Seeduwa began the vocational training of adults. This function was taken over by the government's Social Services Department in 1948. Four other training centers have been established by the department.

There has been very little increase in public awareness of the problems related to the handicap of deafness since about 1912. There has not been any serious effort toward group action either by interested bodies or by deaf persons themselves to better their prospects. The universities do not offer courses in special education; the only teacher-training course in Sinhalese began in 1973; and there are no professional societies, literature, periodicals, or research in Sri Lanka specifically devoted to deafness.

SOCIAL ATTITUDES

Handicapped people are invariably regarded as objects of pity and charity in Sri Lanka—the more so with regard to deaf people, owing to the communication barrier. Parents of deaf children tend to hide them in the hope of some future cure. In the absence of medical specialists, except in the major cities, parents seek the advice of general medical practitioners and traditional village doctors. Usually, long-term medication is prescribed and hope is given for a cure. Even if the appropriate diagnosis is given, the parents are unwilling to accept the stigma attached to deafness, and so they go to a different doctor.

Also, parents may consult an astrologer, who characteristically predicts that a change in the planetary influences on the child's life (at the age of anywhere up to about 10 years) will result in the child's beginning to speak normally. Often the astrologer also claims that for the changing planetary influences to be effective the parents must make vows at various places of worship or observe certain regular religious rites. Thus, the parents try to keep their faith and live in hope.

INCIDENCE OF DEAFNESS

The 1901 census recorded 3233 "deaf and dumb" people, of whom 1103 were under 15 years of age. In 1981 the census recorded the hearing- and speech-impaired population under three categories—deaf, dumb, and deaf and dumb—as including 3459, 11,845, and 9341 persons respectively. The census also stated that only totally deaf, dumb, or deaf-and-dumb persons were included in the count. It is not clear what definition of total deafness was used or how the information was extracted, or whether the census takers were adequately informed about how to confirm deafness. Therefore, the figures may not be reliable. Large percentages in each category (45, 88.47, and 92.4 percent, respectively) are reported as having been born with their defects. If all the enumerated individuals were totally deaf or dumb, as stated in the report, then there must be many more with less severe hearing and speech problems. *See* DEAF POPULATION: Demography.

CAUSES OF DEAFNESS

In the absence of proper records, causes of deafness cannot be ascertained. However, marriages between cousins are fairly common, suggesting consanguinity as a major cause. The large number of people reported as deaf at birth suggests the same. Only 21.4, 5.3, and 3.3 percent, respectively, in the three categories reported acquiring their disability as a result of illness, the rest of the cases were due to accident, violence, or unknown cause. *See* HEARING LOSS: Genetic Causes.

EDUCATION

There are two types of programs available: residential schools, and special units in regular day schools.

Residential Schools Deaf children may be admitted to schools and hostels for resident students after the age of 4½. However, there are no organized procedures, medical or otherwise, for early detection, remedial treatment, referral, or parent guidance, and the dissemination of information regarding availability of educational services is grossly inadequate or nonexistent. Parents usually learn of a school for deaf children in the course of their long search for cures. Often they bring the child to school as a last resort years after the appropriate age of admission.

Schools for deaf children form a part of the national school system and are expected to adapt to all the codes governing regular schools. There are no special national codes or guidelines for education of handicapped pupils. The deaf schools are academic schools trying to teach the subjects offered in regular schools. There are no instruments specially designed to measure the achievement levels of deaf children. No school has entered a deaf child for the General Certification of Education (Ordinary Level) examination in any subject (the G.C.E. is a required step toward national certification in certain subjects), and the achievement levels generally are very limited.

Academic schedule requirements leave little time for career preparation. However, in the residential schools, students receive some basic experience in trades requiring manual skills. A list of residential schools is given in the table.

Maintenance School's do not charge fees. Voluntary donations from parents and well-wishers are accepted, and the Social Services Department provides funds for each child on a monthly basis for board and lodging, but this represents only 20–25 percent of the actual cost. Some children also need clothing. Thus, the schools must subsist on the income from the Social Services Department, voluntary donations and legacies, bequests, and endowments. The foster parents look for help from people in the developed countries, and grants from funding agencies abroad have become a major source of income for a few schools since the 1970s.

The schools are classified as Grade III assisted schools under the education code, with special provision for a teacher-student ratio of 1:10. The Ministry of Education gives a salaries grant based on the number of teachers employed at this ratio. The teacher requirement for any one year is calculated on the average attendance of students in the previous year. A high rate of absenteeism and a much larger number of new admissions compared to school-leavers each year adversely affect the num-

Sri Lanka Residential Schools for Deaf Students

School and Location	Established and Controlled by	Medium of Instruction	Year Established
School for the Deaf, Ratmalane	Ceylon School for the Deaf and Blind	Sinhalese	1912
St. Joseph's School for the Deaf, Regama	Sisters of Our Lady of Perpetual Help—Belgium, Sri Lanka	Sinhalese	1935
Nuffield School for the Deaf and Blind, Kaitady	Ceylon School for the Deaf and Blind	Tamil	1956
Sivarajah School for the Deaf and Blind, Mahawewa	All Ceylon Buddhist Congress	Sinhalese	1958
Sri Chadrasekera School for the Deaf, Horetuduwa	National Council for the Deaf	Sinhalese	1960
Yasothara Deaf and Blind School, Balangoda	All Ceylon Buddhist Congress	Sinhalese	1960
Senkadagala School for the Deaf and Blind, Kandy	Senkadagala Society for the Deaf Ltd.	Sinhalese	1963
School for the Deaf and Blind, Anuradhapura	Welfare Society for the Deaf and Blind	Sinhalese	1964
Rohana School for the Deaf and Blind, Matara	Rohana Welfare Society for the Deaf and Blind	Sinhalese	1964
Sandagalla School for the Deaf and Blind, Kurunagala	Welfare Society for the School for the Deaf and Blind	Sinhalese	1968
Tangalle School for the Deaf and Blind, Tangalle	Special Education Service Society, Polanmaruwa, Tangalle	Sinhalese	1976
Lions School for the Deaf, Trincomalee	Lions Club of Trincomalee	Tamil and Sinhalese	1979
Sri Sutharshi School for the Deaf and Blind, Ella	Special Education Society, Tangalle	Sinhalese	1979
Sambodhi Deaf and Blind Home, Wattegama	Sambodhi Welfare Society, Ltd.	Sinhalese	1982
School for the Deaf and Blind, Koswane, Matale	Matale Social Service Society Ltd.	Sinhalese	Not available

ber of teachers granted by the Ministry of Education. Thus, most schools employ more teachers than the allotted number, and these teachers are paid out of the limited funds available. Most of the teachers have received special training in the education of the deaf children; teachers in Tamil schools have received only in-service training.

Most schools do not have sufficient individual or group hearing aids. Some schools have received educational aids as tax-exempt gifts from donor agencies.

Communication Methods The school that was established in 1912 began with the pure oral method. The medium of instruction was English, with Sinhalese and Tamil introduced on an experimental basis in 1943. The introduction by the government of free education and the Swabasha concept in 1945 put a permanent stamp of approval on what began as an experiment; all schools now teach English as a second language. By 1949, the pure oral system had been replaced by the combined method, which uses lipreading and signs; today every school uses this method. However, no school debars the use of signs by the children, and no school teaches formal signs; new children learn the signs from their peers. The importance given to lipreading and speech, and the encouragement and opportunity afforded to the children to learn oral communication, vary widely from school to school. It is only the exceptional student that acquires both sufficient language ability and oral communication skills, the average student is not able to communicate orally when leaving school. *See* EDUCATION: Communication.

Sign Language Since the signs used by deaf people in Sri Lanka have evolved around each school community according to its particular needs, signs are not uniform, though there may be similarities. The signs used have not been codified by any school and are thus still primitive. Some deaf persons use (British) English fingerspelling to spell proper names and key words they know in English. There is no method of fingerspelling in Sinhalese or Tamil, probably because these languages have a large number of vowels and consonants and different characters for vowel-consonants (that it, single letters that represent the vowel and consonant sounds together; the two sounds are written as a single unit), making too many letters to spell with the fingers. Deaf persons who have attended schools use more signs than those who never attended. Such varied use of signs creates many social problems, such as when the testimonies of deaf witnesses have to be interpreted in the courts. *See* SIGN LANGUAGES.

Special Units in Regular Day Schools These units were formed by identifying those children in regular schools who had special education needs. When a few children with hearing and speech problems are discovered in a school, a special class is formed. The stress in these special units is on academic achievement and oral communication, although signs are accepted in class. Some handicapped children with higher communication and language ability are fully integrated in regular classes. It is expected that this program eventually will give maximum opportunity for full integration.

GOVERNMENT PROVISIONS

There is no legislation recognizing the rights of or granting privileges to handicapped individuals. However, through administrative provisions some assistance has been given to benefit those with handicaps. The first school (1912) received token grants from the state. Then, with the introduction of the Universal Free Education Scheme in 1945, it became possible for schools for handicapped students to receive state aid for teachers' salaries. The Social Services Department undertakes to maintain children in schools through grants; however, the amount of the grant is not commensurate with the rising cost of living.

The Social Services Department also provides 50 percent of the cost of construction of new living accommodations (hostels) plus the cost of equipment. The availability of funds allocated to the department is a limiting factor in meeting all the demands. The Free Education Scheme and the grant given by the Social Services Department have made it possible to set up many more institutions for handicapped children.

ADULT REHABILITATION

The first school for the deaf and blind, located at Ratmalane, assumed total responsibility for the children admitted. Thus, sheltered workshops were established within the school itself. In 1942 sheltered workshops were set up away from the school at Seeduwa, and students were sent to these workshops for vocational rehabilitation after their school career. After the Social Services Department was set up in 1948, adult rehabilitation was taken over by the state. The Social Services Department was made responsible for this program. Four more centers at Katawela, Wattegama, Hambantota, and Moratuwa were established by the department.

Vocational training in the following trades is available in these centers; textile weaving, carpentry, tailoring, leather work, rattan weaving, coir work, ornamental handicrafts, motor mechanism, spray painting, welding, sheet metal work, lathe work, tinkering, electrical wiring, mask making, radio repair, and agriculture. All these trades are not available in all centers.

EMPLOYMENT

There is no legislative requirement for the employment of handicapped workers. On the contrary, one has to undergo a full medical examination and be found perfectly sound to obtain employment in the state sector. Many deaf persons are denied employment in the state sector even as manual workers, although some state institutions overlook the medical requirement.

PLACEMENT

Placement of handicapped persons is one of the many functions of the social service officers. Personal contact and persuasion are the only instruments used to accomplish this task. However, according to the assistant director of Social Services Rehabilitation of the Handicapped, the department does not find it difficult to place trained deaf workers. The schools also report that most of their former pupils find reasonably good jobs. It should be noted, however, that only a small percentage of the deaf population in the country complete their education in school, and a still smaller percentage are enrolled in vocational training. It could be presumed that since Sri Lanka is predominantly an agricultural country, many have joined the agricultural work force without schooling or training.

NATIONAL COUNCIL FOR THE DEAF

This is an independent body which has its own school and also provides additional services. Receiving state assistance, the council provides audiometric services; fabricates ear molds; imports, sells, and repairs hearing aids; conducts a preschool; operates a sewing center; does parent counseling; and undertakes sample surveys. Many of these services are free.

Bibliography

Census of Population and Housing, Sri Lanka, 1981, Population Tables, Preliminary Release no. 1, and Statistics on Physically Disabled Persons, Department of Census and Statistics, Ministry of Plan Implementation, November 1981.

David, J.S.: "Perspectives and Prospects of the Education of the Tamil Deaf in Sri Lanka," unpublished paper, Smith College, Northampton, Massachusetts.

Dewendre, T. O.: "Education of the Handicapped," in *Education in Ceylon*, pt. 3, pp. 913–922, Ministry of Education and Cultural Affairs, Ceylon, 1969.

Education in the Commonwealth, no. 5, *Special Education in the Developing Countries of the Commonwealth*, pp. 27–29, 151–157, Commonwealth Secretariat, London, 1972.

Welikala, J. L. O.: "Founding of Deaf Education in Ceylon," *50 Years 1912–1962 Jubilee Souvenir*, Ceylon School for the Deaf and Blind, Ratmalane, pp. 43–64, 1962.

J. S. David

STATE STATUTES

The United States has a federal form of government. Each of the 50 states is a sovereign entity, but each has ceded to the federal government some of its substantive sovereign powers. Some ceded powers may be exercised only by the federal government; for example, only the federal government can declare war or coin money. In the case of other ceded powers, each state may adopt laws that pertain to its local domain if the central government has not insisted upon exclusive jurisdiction and if the state laws do not conflict with any laws of the central government. For example, the Constitution assigns to the central government jurisdiction to regulate interstate commerce. However, each state may regulate commerce within its borders as long as the regulations do not interfere with laws or regulations of the central government. Telecommunications is also a branch of interstate commerce, but each state may regulate telecommunications within its borders.

Substantive powers not ceded to the federal government are retained by each of the states, including laws involving criminal activity, commercial transactions, human relations, and everyday affairs. Laws dealing with guide dogs for hearing-impaired individuals and equal opportunity are representative of this area.

The United States and each of the individual states maintain their own court system, and each jurisdiction has laws to regulate practices and procedures in its courts. Laws providing for the appointment of interpreters for hearing-impaired individuals are examples of procedural laws. State laws on the appointment of interpreters are discussed below.

Michael A. Schwartz

INTERPRETERS IN JUDICIAL PROCEEDINGS

Each state has some form of interpreter laws requiring that qualified or certified interpreters be provided for hearing-impaired individuals in various types of judicial and nonjudicial proceedings held within the state. It was not until the late 1960s that states enacted laws requiring interpreters in judicial proceedings; prior to these laws, it was customary for friends or family members to interpret for a deaf party or witness involved in a judicial proceeding. Not all of the laws are satisfactory; many state associations of the deaf and interpreter associations are endeavoring to improve their respective state laws requiring provision of interpreters for deaf and hearing-impaired persons in various local, state, and governmental proceedings at all levels.

State Law The first state interpreter laws for deaf individuals were very simple and covered only judicial proceedings; some of those laws are still in effect. For example, Hawaiian law merely states that courts and administrative judges may appoint interpreters when "necessary." The law is unclear as to who or which agency will pay for the services of the interpreter; the necessary qualifications for the interpreter are also unstated.

The majority of states now have laws that require appointment of qualified interpreters in judicial proceedings, specifically criminal proceedings, at the time of arrest as well as during the interrogation of the deaf person. Georgia provides an example of this more comprehensive requirement. Its interpreter laws require that an interpreter be provided when a hearing-impaired person is in a custodial arrest. This is a great improvement over the former Georgia law which had allowed an arresting officer to interrogate a deaf person in writing. Georgia law now states that a qualified interpreter must be present when an arresting officer either interrogates or administers the "Miranda warning" to a deaf or hearing-impaired suspect.

Qualifications of the Interpreter In a judicial proceeding, the judge has the discretion to determine the qualifications of interpreters. Some states require the judge to consult with the National Registry of Interpreters for the Deaf (NRID) or the state's own chapter of the Registry, as well as either the state association of the deaf or the State Commission of the Deaf/Hearing Impaired, when developing a list of interpreters in the state who are qualified to interpret for the deaf person as well as to translate sign language into speech. The interpreter must be able to communicate effectively with the hearing-impaired person; if unable to do so, the court must appoint another interpreter. Some states allow the use of an intermediary interpreter who can assist the certified interpreter in situations where the deaf person in the proceeding has only minimal language skills and can communicate only with another deaf person. The deaf interpreter will communicate with the minimal-language hearing-impaired person and translate for the certified interpreter, who will then voice into English what is being said. *See* INTERPRETING; REGISTRY OF INTERPRETERS FOR THE DEAF.

Scope of Interpreter Laws Some states, like Alaska, do not define when an interpreter is to be appointed, while other states have very comprehensive laws that outline when qualified interpreters are to be appointed.

Louisiana, Texas, Connecticut, and North Carolina have comprehensive interpreter laws which require that qualified interpreters be appointed for hearing-impaired people: (1) in all civil cases; (2) for the preparation of depositions; (3) in criminal trials; (4) in mental commitment proceedings; (5) before grand juries; (6) for any state examination that is a prerequisite for state employment or licensing; (7) in proceedings within the legislative bodies, before administrative agencies, or before a licensing commission; (8) in juvenile proceedings;

and (9) at the time of arrest. Most comprehensive state laws provide that communications between the interpreter and the hearing-impaired person are privileged and confidential, unless the hearing-impaired person agrees to waive the privilege and allows the communication to be shared with others.

The judicial proceedings can be videotaped to evaluate the accuracy of the interpreter's translation of the proceedings.

Payment The procedure for paying interpreters varies from state to state. In some states, the judge decides whether the fee will be paid by the parties involved as part of the court costs or paid by the losing party. The court can also decide to pay the interpreter out of court or county funds if authorized to do so by state law. In Connecticut, payment is made by the State Commission of the Deaf/Hearing Impaired with reimbursement made to the commission by the hiring authority.

Federal Law In those states where it is unclear if state law covers a particular situation, such as providing an interpreter at the time of arrest, federal law may govern. Section 504 of the Rehabilitation Act of 1973 forbids discrimination on the basis of handicap by programs or activities that receive some federal financial assistance. The Department of Justice promulgated regulations for law enforcement agencies and courts that receive federal financial assistance when they are working with hearing-impaired persons. The rules of the Department of Justice state that qualified interpreters must be provided for hearing-impaired individuals who are defendants, witnesses, parties, or the subjects of investigations by law enforcement agencies.

Bibliography
Interpreter Chart Compilation, National Center for Law and the Deaf.
"New Justice Department 504 Regulations," National Center for law and the Deaf Newsletter, September 1981.

Sheila Conlon Mentkowski

GUIDE DOGS

Almost every state has a body of laws that deals with guide dogs for hearing-impaired individuals. For many years, those laws pertained only to guide dogs for visually impaired individuals, but since the mid-1970s state legislatures have amended those laws or enacted new laws to deal with guide dogs for hearing-impaired individuals. Generally, the laws fall into three categories: access to public transportation and facilities, housing accommodations, and licensing fees.

Access to Public Transportation and Facilities Hearing-impaired individuals are guaranteed full and equal access to planes, trains, buses, boats, hotels, lodgings, public accommodations, and other places where the public is invited. This access encompasses the right of the hearing-impaired individual to be accompanied by the guide dog. In several states, trainers of guide dogs are permitted to be accompanied by a dog in any public place for the purpose of training. Moreover, the hearing-impaired person does not have to pay an extra charge for the dog. However, some states require that the dog be harnessed and muzzled and that the person be able to produce papers certifying that the dog is trained and serving as a guide. Some states further require that the dog wear a bright orange collar. Additionally, the dog's master remains liable for any damage that the animal might cause.

Anyone who interferes with a hearing-impaired individual's access to public transportation or a public facility because the guide dog is not welcome is guilty of a violation of law. The punishment ranges from 25 to 500 dollars and from 10 to 60 days in jail.

Some states give hearing-impaired individuals accompanied by guide dogs the right to full and equal use of streets and public buildings. Drivers of motor vehicles must take all reasonable precautions to avoid inflicting injury on hearing-impaired individuals accompanied by guide dogs. Failure to do so renders the driver liable to the hearing-impaired individual for damages. However, failure by the hearing-impaired individual to be accompanied by a guide dog does not constitute contributory negligence.

A few states, such as New York, allow hearing-impaired individuals to be accompanied by their guide dogs when they are on the job. Employers are forbidden from barring a guide dog if it is with its master for legitimate purposes.

Housing Accommodations Many states have statutes that assure hearing-impaired individuals the right to full and equal access to all housing accommodations open to the public. Hearing-impaired individuals cannot be denied leases because their guide dogs are unwelcome. Moreover, the dog cannot be the basis for a charge of additional rent. However, in several states the owner of the property is not under a legal obligation to make physical changes in the property to accommodate the dog. Further, the owner may adopt reasonable regulations governing the presence of the dog, and the hearing-impaired tenant remains liable for any property damage.

Generally, the regulation of guide dogs for hearing-impaired individuals is a responsibility of the states. However, federal law forbids that the owner or manager of federally assisted rental housing for elderly or handicapped persons prohibit or prevent a tenant from owning a common household pet, subject to reasonable guidelines that consider such factors as density of tenants, pet size, type of pets, potential financial obligations of tenants, and standards of pet care.

Licensing Fees and Miscellaneous Items Some states, such as Maine and Connecticut, waive the licensing fee for the guide dog, but require that the hearing-impaired individual file a certificate as proof that the dog is a trained guide dog. The individual will be issued a special card or papers and an orange tag or collar that identifies a guide dog for the hearing-impaired.

A few states, like California, will permit the hearing-impaired individual to deduct from his or her taxes all expenses incurred for the care and maintenance of the guide dog, including veterinary fees. A few states, like New York, specially exempt the guide dog from the scope of personal property that may be seized because of a money judgment obtained against the hearing-impaired individual. Finally, a few states, like Texas, forbid the improper use of a guide dog; if a hearing-impaired person attempts to pass off an untrained dog as a trained guide dog, the person commits a misdemeanor punishable by a fine.

Michael A. Schwartz

EQUAL OPPORTUNITY

Due in great part to the civil rights movement of the 1960s and 1970s, most states have included disability among the traditional categories of race, creed, color, national origin, and sex that are guaranteed equal opportunity. The majority of states have enacted civil rights or human rights legislation that articulates and protects the rights of disabled persons in employment, housing, education, and financial credit. The legislation also guarantees to all disabled people equal opportunity to the benefits, advantages, and rights of society. While certain laws guarantee equal opportunity, they are to be distinguished from affirmative action, which attempts to remedy past discrimination by taking positive steps such as quotas and favorable hiring and firing practices.

Declaration of Policy Some states grant all their citizens freedom from discrimination on grounds of physical handicaps. Other states recognize a special responsibility for the care, treatment, education, and rehabilitation of and advocacy for their handicapped citizens, and articulate a policy that provides for coordination of services for disabled individuals among the state agencies charged with that responsibility. Other states declare it their policy to encourage the participation of disabled people in the social and economic life of the state and to promote the remunerative employment of disabled people. Generally, most states prohibit the deprivation of constitutional-civil rights of any individual because of physical disability. Such deprivation is classified as an offense punishable by state criminal law.

Prohibited Discriminatory Practices States like New York prohibit the denial of equal opportunity to obtain and maintain employment on the basis of deafness or any other disability. Among several examples of unlawful discriminatory practices are: an employer refusing to employ, attempting to discharge, or failing to promote a person on the basis of deafness; an employment agency failing to assist an individual because of deafness; and a labor organization excluding or expelling anyone on the basis of deafness. Some states require that all parties to a public contract refrain from unlawful employment discrimination. Some states also mandate their own agencies and political subdivisions to grant equal employment opportunity to disabled people. Moreover, no employer, employment agency, labor organization, or anyone engaged in an activity covered by the statute may discriminate against a deaf person because of the use of a guide dog on the job. Many states have established a legal procedure by which aggrieved individuals may pursue a remedy for unlawful discrimination. Sometimes this procedure is a prerequisite for a private lawsuit, but if the state does not have such a procedure, an aggrieved individual may commence a lawsuit without having to fulfill any other requirements.

It is illegal to deny a disabled person admittance to, or the equal use and enjoyment of, any public facility. A public facility is defined as including, but not limited to, all modes of public and private transportation; all public and private housing accommodations; all educational facilities; restaurants, theaters, and all other places of public accommodations, convenience, resort, or business. Disabled people may fully and freely use the streets, highways, sidewalks, public places, and public conveyances. Denial of equal access to public facilities is an offense, which can be the basis for civil as well as criminal prosecution.

Some states bar housing discrimination on the basis of disability. It is unlawful to refuse to rent or lease publicly assisted housing accommodations, to discriminate in the terms, conditions, and privileges of such accommodations, and to solicit information regarding the applicant's disability. The sale, exchange, rental, or lease of real property must be free of discrimination, and it is a civil rights violation to refuse to engage in a real estate transaction because the other party is disabled.

Many states have made it a civil rights violation to refuse to issue a credit card because of the person's disability. It is also a violation for a lending institution to refuse credit for the purchase, construction, or repair of housing accommodations, land, or commercial space on the basis of disability.

Michael A. Schwartz

TELEPHONE DEVICES

A few states have enacted laws that address the role of telephone devices for the deaf (TDDs) in the life of the deaf community. Illinois and New Mexico, for example, provide for the installation of a telecommunication device for deaf individuals in police stations, sheriffs' offices, or public safety agencies. Maryland has a similar provision, providing TDDs in state and local government agencies, public facilities, and services such as police, fire, and rescue. Calls to these numbers are toll-free, and any state agency issuing a telephone number for public service must also provide a TDD number.

In Washington and Wisconsin, the laws regarding placement of TDDs take into consideration the size of government units. Washington requires each fourth-class or larger county and each city with a population in excess of 10,000 to provide a TDD within their jurisdiction. Moreover, fifth-class or smaller counties are required to consider whether they need a TDD, and reconsideration of a negative determination is mandatory if a deaf individual indicates a need for a TDD. In Wisconsin, the size of a given county determines whether a TDD is placed in the sheriff's department, the police department, or the fire department.

Texas has an elaborate scheme, which vests in the Texas Commission for the Deaf the power to establish and administer a program for the placement and use of TDDs in selected state agencies and the provision of TDDs for certain emergency services. The commission must establish rules for this program and consult with other state agencies and state organizations of and for deaf individuals in determining which agencies will receive the TDDs. The commission is also responsible for the cost of the TDDs and the training of personnel to operate them.

California, Connecticut, and Michigan laws require telephone companies to participate in providing telecommunication services to deaf people. Each California telephone corporation must provide a dual-party relay system that utilizes third-party intervention to connect deaf people with TDDs to nondeaf people without TDDs. The California Public Utilities Commission must initiate an investigation, conduct public hearings to determine the most cost-effective method of providing this dual-relay system, and solicit advice and counsel from state consumer groups representing deaf individuals.

Connecticut telephone companies must provide TDDs for rental or sale to deaf persons, and must be responsible for maintenance and repair of all TDDs that they lease or sell. The public utility department has the responsibility of establishing conditions of service and rates for the companies. Also, each company having over 100,000 customers must pay $100,000 annually until January 1, 1987, into a special telecommunications equipment fund, and this fund must be available to deaf persons for the purchase, rental, maintenance, and upkeep of TDDs. Connecticut also exempts from state tax all gross receipts of monies from the sale of TDDs.

Michigan has a similar system to Connecticut's in that the telephone company must sell or lease TDDs to deaf people, and the public service commission must establish a rate recovery mechanism. Additionally, Michigan allows its deaf consumers who lease TDDs to apply their lease payments toward the purchase price of the equipment.

In Massachusetts, the Office of Deafness rents, leases, or sells TDDs to deaf persons at a reasonable price, and the schedule of fees for such rental or sale is based on the circumstances, need, and annual income of the deaf person seeking the equipment. Monies from the sale or rental of TDDs goes into a revolving fund, which is used to buy more TDDs for distribution to deaf individuals.

A few states, like Georgia, Virginia, and Mississippi, have a statutory scheme that governs telecommunication devices such as telephones, radios, televisions, and other electromagnetic systems, but do not include TDDs in their scheme. Tennessee has established an Emergency Medical Service Area Telecommunications system to provide rapid emergency medical service to the general population, but it has not included TDDs. Pennsylvania provides for the erection, operation, and maintenance of a county police radio fire network and other public safety radio and telecommunications networks, and Montana has established a telecommunications network to fight crime by connecting all law enforcement agencies in the state by teletype. These two states have not included TDDs in their telecommunications systems, yet there is enormous potential in these systems for the inclusion and utilization of TDDs for deaf persons.

Some states, such as California, Connecticut, Michigan, Minnesota, and Wisconsin, provide for the free distribution of TDDs to deaf individuals within their borders. The statutes of these states vary in their stipulations, ranging from the distribution of TDDs to all deaf persons, to the distribution to deaf persons below a designated economic level.

Each state has a commission to regulate public utilities within its borders, including intrastate telephone service provided by local telephone companies. The local telephone companies draft and file tariffs, which the state public service commissions approve, showing the cost for each service provided by the companies. In most states, the telephone companies provide discounts to deaf individuals using TDDs for intrastate calls, ranging up to 75 percent in Connecticut. In several states, more substantial discounts are offered for evening intrastate calls, and even greater discounts for night calls. The discounts are offered because calls made using a TDD take substantially longer than comparable voice calls. The American Telephone and Telegraph Company (AT&T) is one of the carriers providing interstate telephone services, which are regulated by the Federal Communications Commission. AT&T provides discounts to deaf individuals making interstate calls on a TDD. *See* TELECOMMUNICATIONS.

Bibliography

California Public Utilities Code §2881.
Connecticut General Statutes Annotated §§12-412, 16-2556.
Georgia Code Annotated §50-5-160 et seq.
Illinois Revised Statutes, chapter 111 ½, paragraph 420 et seq.
Maryland Annotated Code article 78A, section 51A.
Massachusetts General Laws Annotated chapter 6, §84 I.
Michigan Comp. Laws Annotated §484.103.
Mississippi Code Annotated §31-7-201 et seq.
Montana Code Annotated §44-2-301 et seq.
New Mexico Statutes Annotated §28-11A-1.
Pennsylvania Consolidated Statutes Annotated §1944.
Tennessee Code Annotated §68-39-201 et seq.
Texas Human Resources Code Annotated §81.011.
Virginia Code Annotated §2.1-563.1 et seq.
Washington Revised Code Annotated §70.54.180.
Wisconsin Statutes Annotated §59.07.

Michael A. Schwartz

SWEDEN

Hearing-impaired individuals in Sweden are divided socially and educationally into two discrete groups, those who are hard of hearing and those who are prelingually, profoundly deaf. The former group comprises about 200,000 individuals out of Sweden's total population of 8 million, while there are only about 8000 in the latter. Approximately 200 babies with hearing impairments are born in Sweden annually; of these, about 50 are profoundly deaf. Most hard-of-hearing people strive toward an identity as hearing persons, communicating primarily with speech. Technical aids and other oral-communication support systems are used to augment their residual hearing. Profoundly deaf persons, however, stand out as a separate entity. They use sign language as their major communication method, and they are recognized as having needs comparable to those of members of ethnic minority groups. *See* DEAF POPULATION: Demography.

When Swedish society began to show interest in the situation of its deaf members, the primary concern was education. Through teaching deaf children the language, it was expected that they would improve their life situation and be accepted as worthy members of society. Schools for deaf pupils played a prominent role in the social life of the deaf community, and they constituted the only special provision for deaf persons. Deaf children typically spent eight years in special residential schools where they were separated from their parents and where their lifetime relationship to the hearing world was defined.

Today, however, changing attitudes toward all handicapped persons have had a tremendous influence on the daily life of hearing-impaired people. Important developments have been recognition of Swedish Sign Language and the proliferation of services in addition to education. The welfare system of Sweden comprises a variety of services delivered through audiology centers, vocational guidance offices, religious care, and various other programs designed to lessen the isolation of deaf persons and to facilitate the communication of deaf people with a hearing environment. *See* SIGN LANGUAGES: Swedish.

EDUCATIONAL HISTORY
The first school for deaf children in Sweden, the Manilla School for the Deaf in Stockholm, was opened in 1809 by Per Aron Borg. The Manilla School was influenced by other European schools, especially those of France, Austria, and Germany. The training of teachers of deaf pupils began at the Manilla School when a special college was opened in 1874. The teachers admitted to the program were already certified to teach in Sweden's public schools for hearing children.

Official recognition of the importance of educating deaf children did not come until 1889, when the first law related to deaf education was signed. Based on the Manilla School's experience, the law provided education for deaf children seven years of age or older. It was amended later to require eight years of school attendance. In 1902 private preschools were established for deaf children, and in 1915 special classes for hard-of-hearing pupils were organized in the regular community schools.

Beginning in the Manilla School in 1861 and continuing until the 1970s, Swedish schools emphasized oral methods. Unlike some of their European counterparts, Swedish schools never completely abandoned sign language and fingerspelling. From the outset, the deaf schools employed special curricula in which language learning was based on reading and writing, while speech and lipreading were recommended for pupils who showed talent in these skills. Teacher training emphasized preparation in oral methods until 1967, when a variety of methods was accepted. *See* EDUCATION: Communication.

In the twentieth century, Swedish schools pioneered in the use of modern audiological equipment and the development of special curricula and guidelines for hearing-impaired students. During an especially fruitful period from 1950 to 1970, a complete regional service system was established employing medical, technical, and educational experts. Emphasis was placed on early diagnosis of hearing loss and rapid intervention to encourage natural language acquisition. Medical-technical hearing centers opened, where consultants, usually qualified teachers of deaf pupils, helped parents to utilize their children's residual hearing. These efforts were based on the hope that a strong, technologically, medically, and educationally based program—centered on the auditory-oral approach—would conquer the language problems associated with deafness.

One result of this attempt was the integration of many hard-of-hearing children in the regular community schools. Many children acquired sufficient language competence to participate successfully in ordinary schools. Today, hard-of-hearing pupils are taught in special classes or in mainstream programs, as are other handicapped persons.

SCHOOLS TODAY
Education of hearing-impaired children in Sweden is divided between the community school system and a few state schools exclusively for deaf students. Ten years of education is compulsory for deaf children, compared with nine years for hearing children. School attendance is required for hearing-impaired children seven years or older, but there is a comprehensive voluntary preschool program as well and programs for continuing education, including vocational training and advanced study of academic subjects. The federal government bears all expenses related to school attendance, and provides low-cost loans to both hearing and deaf students who pursue university studies.

In 1969 the Swedish Board of Education issued guidelines to clarify the division of responsibility between the community schools and the special schools for deaf students. The board decided that determination of which program individual hearing-impaired children would attend should be based on the student's communication method. Degree of hearing loss and age at onset of deafness are factors influencing communication method. Thus, persons with sufficient audition to comprehend speech, with or without the use of hearing aids or lipreading, and to develop their own speaking skills are placed in the community schools; their language acquisition is through hearing, though sometimes with visual support.

The special schools for deaf pupils, on the other hand, serve those students for whom language acquisition is through vision. Profoundly deaf students—those who cannot be assisted by hearing aids and who have not developed spontaneous speech and lipreading skills—need sign language to communicate.

This division of hearing-impaired pupils has increased the influence of hearing-handicapped organizations on the school system. The National Association of Deaf Persons and the National Association of Hard-of-Hearing Persons make contrasting claims and demands. Therefore, politicians must try to resolve the conflicts caused by the two factions: the manualists, who tend to be profoundly deaf from an early age and who attend the deaf schools; and the oralists, who tend to be less deaf or postlingually deaf and who have backgrounds in the ordinary public schools. See HISTORY: Methods controversy.

The choice of methods to be used in the education of hearing-impaired children is influenced by many factors. Sweden officially recognizes the value of allowing immigrant children to develop competence in their native language; immigrant children constitute about 13 percent of the Swedish school population. Still, Sweden recognizes the importance of a common language to facilitate communication and to socialize children to a common culture. Bilingual education, which attempts to serve both purposes, seems to be one solution.

There are sufficient similarities between deaf children, whose native language might be thought of as Swedish Sign Language (SSL), and immigrant children to justify the application of the bilingual model to schools for deaf pupils. While the 1969 law recommended the use of fingerspelling and signing in deaf schools, SSL was not officially recognized as a true language until 1982. Subsequent amendments to the public education laws reflect this new consciousness and indicate that a bilingual (SSL and Swedish) approach is the preferred method of language development in the deaf schools.

The recent reevaluation of sign language and the focus on first developing a child's home language have had a major impact on the deaf schools. Previously, the emphasis was placed on structured methods of teaching words, syntax, speech, and lipreading. Today, emphasis is purely visual and on developing a strong basis in manual communication first.

This method is expected to lead to bilingual language competence among deaf pupils, and is supported by the government. However, there are problems. Knowledge of SSL grammar is very limited; a complete analysis of SSL has yet to be carried out. Also, it is difficult to teach sign language to hearing people; parents and teachers are likely to have a less complete command of sign language than deaf children. Further study is needed before bilingual education for deaf students can be thoroughly evaluated.

Many educators support a compromise between the auditory-oral approach and the bilingual method. There is great interest in discovering a means to use visual communication to teach Swedish. Teachers of deaf pupils are studying combined signed-oral methods and the curriculum experiments in schools in the United States. The use of residual hearing, tactile senses, speech, and lipreading are advocated as means of improving children's learning of speech.

The lack of consensus about the best means of educating deaf Swedes and the widespread dissatisfaction with educational results are not surprising. The issues involved are often highly emotional, and it is difficult to set realistic goals. The great hope of deaf people is that their own language, when used the way they themselves desire, will improve greatly with social situation. Following the educational guidelines established in 1980, it is hoped that better curriculum development, teachers' teamwork, and closer cooperation between school and home will yield better results.

SERVICES FOR YOUNG CHILDREN

The Swedish Ministry of Social Affairs carries the ultimate responsibility for the well-being of all handicapped Swedes. Other authorities, such as the Ministry of Education and the Ministry of Labor, also cooperate, and parents, organizations of deaf people, and labor unions contribute to societal decisions. The tendency is to decentralize social activities, so that recipients can have more opportunities to develop their own life styles. Private institutions are relatively insignificant.

The government's social welfare organization is responsible for the detection and measurement of deafness and the development of appropriate remediation for preschool-age (under seven years) children. High-risk infants are checked immediately after birth, and local child-welfare centers provide continuous health monitoring and assistance to all children. The local centers refer handicapped children to special regional centers. County councils have organized hearing clinics open to any person with a hearing problem. Special units for hearing-impaired children are part of the county system. See AUDITORY DISORDERS, EVALUATION AND DIAGNOSIS OF.

Sweden has no profession analogous to the audiologist found in the United States. Instead, the hearing clinics employ a team of specialized doctors, technicians, psychologists, social workers, and educators. Services, including provision of hearing aids, amplifiers, and home visual-warning devices, are free. In addition, there are special family allowances to parents of handicapped children. *See* AUDIOLOGY.

The creation of optimal home conditions for all hearing-impaired children is an important aspect of Sweden's program. A home visitor from the regional center is assigned to look after the family and observe the child's development as soon as a hearing loss is detected. Usually a kindergarten teacher, the home visitor encourages parents to communicate with their hearing-impaired children and teaches them how to do so. Although early use of hearing aids and direction from the home visitor usually allows natural development of speech and language, parents are encouraged to use sign language when auditory training is unsuccessful. Such a drastic change in usual communication methods and parental expectations for their children often causes great anxiety in the family. Every effort is made to acquaint parents with the meaning of deafness and to introduce them to deaf adults to help alleviate this situation. To this end, Sweden is training and certifying nursery and preschool teachers who are themselves deaf. *See* PARENT EDUCATION.

Profoundly deaf children often are diagnosed earlier than those with less severe losses, and special efforts are directed toward their needs. Deaf teachers and sign language are especially important to help establish their identities and to begin their language learning as quickly as possible. They are placed in segregated classes of profoundly deaf children, where both deaf and hearing teachers communicate in signs.

Preschool-age hearing-impaired children can be placed in community day-care centers to the same extent as other children. Depending on several variables, hearing-impaired children are offered training in community or regional nurseries or kindergartens, most of which are integrated but offer access to specially trained staff. Even in integrated preschool programs, signs and fingerspelling may be used.

One of the most difficult tasks facing hearing-clinic staffs is to plan for each child's education. In annual regional conferences, experts from social and educational programs determine the best possible educational placement for every child. Parents, too, are involved, and no placement is made against their wishes. For most hearing-impaired children, the decision is for their integration in local schools so that they may live at home. Profoundly deaf children, especially those from rural areas, often attend special state residential schools for deaf pupils.

CONTINUING EDUCATION

More than 90 percent of Swedish students continue their education beyond the compulsory 9-year min-imum in the "gymnasium," a two-to-three year program open to the graduates of the compulsory schools. The costs of the gymnasium are borne by the government to the same extent as the costs of compulsory programs. There are no special provisions for hard-of-hearing pupils, who tend to enroll in the programs in their local community, but there is a special gymnasium in Örebro for deaf persons.

The Örebro gymnasium offers a wide range of training and educational choices employing teachers specially prepared for deaf education. Deaf students in Örebro may prepare for most vocations common in Sweden, or they may take preuniversity studies. Although deaf students traditionally have been trained for only a few deaf vocations, this is not true at Örebro, where vocational guidance consultants thoroughly plan an appropriate sequence of courses and training for each pupil.

In addition to the gymnasia, continued education is carried out through Sweden's "folk high schools" and through reeducation programs that are established when necessary. The Swedish Association of the Deaf is primarily responsible for the folk high schools for deaf adults. Using visual communication exclusively, these schools offer deaf persons over 18 years of age a variety of educational options, from short courses to three-year study programs.

Hard-of-hearing adults attend both the folk high schools for deaf persons and those that are open to the general population. Sometimes people with a severe hearing loss but full command of speech join programs at the folk high schools. *See* EDUCATIONAL PROGRAMS: Continuing Education.

SOCIOECONOMIC CONDITIONS

The social security and welfare system is part of a thorough service program for all members of Swedish society, and it gives special consideration to handicapped people. Most medical and dental care is covered by health insurance. Audiological services, including the fitting and distribution of hearing aids, amplification devices, and signals, comprise part of the total service program. Deaf persons also receive telecommunication devices (TTY phones) at no cost. *See* TELECOMMUNICATIONS.

Unemployment of deaf persons is low. Labor-exchange bureaus have special consultants familiar with deafness and sign language who work closely with the schools for deaf students to assist graduates in finding appropriate employment. The state church and the Salvation Army also have long traditions of training deaf workers. All handicapped individuals receive special income allowances from the government. Deafness is considered sufficiently serious to warrant a relatively high financial subsidy.

The mass media in Sweden have contributed in assisting deaf people directly and in improving awareness of and attitudes toward hearing-impaired persons. In recent years, many programs about sign language and the communication problems associated with hearing loss have appeared in the media. Swedish television programming provides daily news with captions and a comparatively rich group of other captioned programs.

ASSOCIATIONS

The organizations of handicapped persons in Sweden are well administered and politically influential. Hearing-impaired persons are represented by two associations, Sveriges Dövas Riksförbund (SDR) and Hörselfrämjandets Riksförbund (HfR). That SDR has about 4000 and HfR 40,000 members reflects the fact that deaf people are a small minority of all handicapped persons in the country. Both organizations receive considerable government support and are important sources for information to the public. Both organizations advocate the same philosophy which is expressed in their programs.

SDR was founded in Stockholm in 1868 and has published its journals since 1893, while HfR was established in 1921. The program of SDR comprises topics related to the benefit of profoundly, prelingually deaf persons and is divided under the following headings: language, culture, clubs, work, service and care, technical equipments, family, care of children, and education. The dominant plea concerns the place of manual communication, and there is an emphatic demand that sign language should be used by all who work with deaf people.

The concentration on questions related to the acceptance of the sign language of deaf individuals has no correspondence in the program expressed by the HfR. This organization maintains a close relationship with the health and welfare system of the country. Local and other clubs attached to either of the two organizations arrange a number of activities for the members, but the executive boards carry the responsibilities of cooperation and negotiations with the government and other authorities. There is a close cooperation between SDR and HfR.

RESEARCH

Research on deafness has a long tradition in Sweden. Beginning in the 1950s, Swedish research was especially significant in the areas of audiology and speech. This research has been augmented by studies of pedagogy, psychology, and sociolinguistics related to deaf people. Annually, the government supports a number of deafness research projects of a multidisciplinary character as well as more specialized studies of areas such as sign language. Despite the work of various research institutes and universities and substantial expenditures, teaching methods for deaf people remain limited in effectiveness, and a great deal more attention needs to be directed toward the education of profoundly deaf persons. On the other hand, most hearing-impaired people have been helped in achieving a life style similar to that of their hearing fellows.

Bibliography

Ahlgren, I.: "Döva barns teckenspråk," *Forskning om teckenspiråk VII*, Stockholms universitet, Institutionen för lingvistik, 1980.

———: "Projektet tidig språklig kognitiv utveckling hos döva och hörselskadade, Arbetssätt och erfarenheter," *Forskning om teckenspråk IV*, Stockholms universitet, Institutionen for lingvistik, 1980.

Basilier, I.: *Hörseltap og egentlig døvhet i socialpsykiatrisk perspektiv*, Universitetsforlaget, Oslo, 1973.

Bergman, B.: *Studies in Swedish Sign Language*, University of Stockholm, Institute of Linguistics, 1982.

Crafoord, E., and M. Axelsson: *Personlighetsutveckling vid dövhet*, Stockholms universitet, Department of Psychology, 1975.

Government reports: SOU 1955:20, *Det döva barnets språk—och talutveckling*. SOU 1976:20, *Kultur åt alla*. SOU 1978:14, *Arbete åt handikappade*. SOU 1979:50, *Huvudmannaskapet för specialskolan*. SOU 1980:34, *Handikappad Integrerad Normaliserad Utvärderad*. SOU 1981:27, *Omsorger om vissa handikappade*. SOU 1981:23, *Tekniska hjälpmedel för handikappade*. SOU 1982:19, *Handikappade elever i det allmänna skolväsendet*.

Kommunikation trots handikapp, Riksbankens jubileumsfond, Stockholm, 1980.

Nordén, K.: "Learning Processes and Personality Development in Deaf Children," *American Annals of the Deaf*, vol. 26, no. 4, 1981.

Periodicals and journals: *Auris*, HfR, Stockholm. *SDR—Kontakt*, Stockholm. *Scandinavian Audiology*, Almqvist och Wiksell, Stockholm. *Nordisk tidskrift för hörsel—och dövundervisning*, Bloms tryckeri, Lund.

Preisler, G.: *Deaf Children in Communication*, University of Stockholm, Department of Psychology, 1983.

Research and Development Concerning Integration of Handicapped Pupils in the Ordinary School System, National Swedish Board of Education, Stockholm, 1980.

Rut Madebrink

SWITZERLAND

Because of the decentralized political system of Switzerland, a confederation of 23 cantons, the situation of deaf people varies from one canton to the other. Four languages are spoken and officially recognized: German, French, Italian, and Romansh (listed in descending order of the number of speakers). The linguistic map reflecting the diversity does not coincide well with the political map, so there are bilingual cantons and even a trilingual one (Graubünden). This situation creates special difficulties for deaf persons in their everyday life and complicates traveling or moving to other linguistic areas. In addition, there is an enormous gap between the spoken German language and the standard official German as it is taught in school and used in all written documents. Furthermore, great dialectal diversity characterizes the German-speaking parts of the country. Romansh also has problems since there are a number of different dialects and no unified writing system. The canton of Graubünden thus has to publish its schoolbooks in five different versions of Romansh (in addition to German and Italian); in the first three grades of elementary school, teaching is in Romansh. The diversity of German and Romansh dialects creates difficulties for deaf people in Switzerland beyond the main one of learning an oral language.

EDUCATIONAL SYSTEM

The educational system varies greatly between cantons. However, certain general principles are respected throughout the country. First, children equipped with auditory aids and capable of following a normal curriculum frequent the same schools as hearing students. Speech therapy is provided, if needed. Second, when integration into ordinary schools is impossible, the main educational objective is to teach deaf children to speak and to lipread. Third, when hearing loss is accompanied by other handicaps, it is usually the hearing loss that determines the type of educational establishment.

Different types of schools are devoted to the education of deaf people. Some are public; others are subsidized by private foundations or associations concerned with deaf persons. The schools cater to a total of about 1500 students. They offer primary and secondary education to children from 6 to 16 years of age (the obligatory schooling period), and most of the cantons have kindergartens or nursery schools for younger deaf children; the other half are day schools. Most of them also offer speech therapy, psychomotor and psychological assistance, or therapy. *See* EDUCATIONAL PROGRAMS.

Schools teach the language of their area—German, French, or Italian. In the bilingual canton of Fribourg/Freiburg, two sections exist in the institution for deaf students (French and German). In the German-speaking parts of the country, standard high German is taught to profoundly deaf children, while the local Swiss-German dialect is used for less impaired children. Only standard German is used for writing, since Swiss-German dialects have no official status and no standard writing system.

PRESCHOOL

Before schooling, and as soon as deafness is suspected, the child and his or her family will be placed in the charge of a team that may include a physician, a psychologist, a speech therapist, an audio therapist, a psychomotor therapist, and others.

Medical and hearing examinations, speech and psychomotor sessions, and hearing aids are free of charge when they are necessary.

ADULTHOOD

The choice of a profession is generally limited to manual and clerical work, and the level of professional achievement is rather low. A certain number of "silent" clubs exist, mainly oriented toward sports, social games, and group activities. There are few newssheets for deaf people.

The telephone is accessible through telescrit, a combined telephone and keyboard, which may replace an ordinary home telephone (reimbursed in most cases); public telescrits are found in every main post office and railroad station. A program for people with impaired hearing is transmitted on the national television, and the news is translated into sign language at certain hours of the day.

SIGN LANGUAGE

Though sign language is generally not used or specifically taught in the school system, it is used among deaf individuals. However, there are important dialectal differences between local sign languages. Since about 1980, in the French-speaking part of the country, efforts have been made to introduce sign language in the schools. The school of Montbrillant in Geneva is applying a new approach to deaf children; since 1981 the French Sign Language (LSF) has been used in the classroom as a first language and French is presented as a second language. During language lessons, French is initially presented in its written form and correspondences are established between signs and written words, without the intermediary of the oral form. Oral language is taught later with the collaboration of a speech therapist. Teachers avoid turning all the lessons into French lessons, and several subjects (mathematics, geography, history), are taught mainly in sign language. The general philosophy of the school is to consider the deaf child as a bilingual person, with French as his or her second language. All teachers are fluent in sign language and some of them are deaf. Montbrillant also offers a sign language course for adults, especially for parents of deaf children.

In January 1983 a training program for interpreters for deaf individuals was set up in Lausanne. Students are taught simultaneous translation from French into either sign language or the signed form of French, with the cooperation of the Geneva School of Interpretation. They are offered a three-year curriculum of part-time study, and most of them attend sign language classes held weekly in their home towns. Videotapes of sign language are also available so that they can practice at home. The courses cover four areas: (1) "deaf culture" throughout the world as well as in the French-speaking part of Switzerland; (2) studies of sign language, including practical skills in all forms of the language, linguistic analysis, and theory; (3) public speaking skills in oral French, and (4) the theory and techniques of interpretation. An official diploma is delivered to those who pass the final test.

The Association of Sign Language Teachers and a Franco-Swiss association for the promotion of bilingual education for deaf children (Deux Langues pour une Education) have also recently been founded.

The use of a standard sign language, LSF, makes these initiatives possible. In the German-speaking part of the country, there is no such standard form of the language. However, existence of different dialects does not seem to be considered a problem by deaf persons. On the contrary, they are rather proud of this diversity, just as Swiss-German speakers are proud of their dialectal differences. On the practical level, deaf people from different areas succeed in communicating; only hearing persons learning sign language as a second language feel uncomfortable.

Until recently, no research was done on the different forms of sign language used in Switzerland. In 1983 a center for sign language research (Forschungszentrum für Gebärdensprache), based in Basel, was founded by Penny Boyes-Braem, whose main research theme is the study of Swiss-German sign dialects. Boyes-Braem has already observed some of the pecularities of these dialects, for example, the use of lips articulation when signing, which is one of the means used by deaf individuals from different areas to communicate. No use of a manual alphabet has been observed and accordingly no sign deriving from manual spelling. Proper nouns are articulated on the lips, generally without any sound. On the grammatical level, dialects do not seem to differ but individual signs may from one dialect to another. The linguistic analysis of these differences has only just begun and is still at a preliminary stage. *See* SIGN LANGUAGES: Swiss.

Bibliography

Boyes-Braem, Penny: "Zur Erforschung der Dialekte der Gebärdensprache in der Deutschsprachigen Schweiz," in *Erste Bericht des Forschungszentrums für Gebärdensprache*, pp. 16–30, Basel, 1983.

Die Einrichtungen für die Erfassung und Schulung hörgeschädigter Kinder und Jugendlicher in der Schweiz, Schweizerischer Verband für das Gehörlosenwesen, Bern.

"L'enfant sourd et l'école; réalités et perspectives," in *Cahier N 2*, Service Médico-pédagogique, Geneva, 1981.

Malé, Anne, and Francoise Rickli: "Introduction du bilinguisme: langue des signes française-française oral, à l'école de Montbrillant," in *Cahier Spécial N 4*, pp. 87–96, Service Médico-pédagogique, Geneva, 1983.

Mémento des Institutions pour Sourds da la Suisse Romande, Association Suisse pour les Sourds Démutisés, Lausanne, 1981.

Josselyne Gérard

T

TEACHING ENGLISH TO DEAF AND SECOND-LANGUAGE STUDENTS

Teaching English to Deaf and Second-Language Students (*TEDSL*) is a journal aimed at educators, teachers, and researchers who are seeking practical methods and innovative strategies of teaching the English language in the deaf or second-language classroom. Articles selected for their original and unusual approaches to teaching problems range from "guided" sentences to dialogue journals. Other features in the journal are: the "Grammar Corner," a regular column on teaching fundamentals of grammar and structure; printed interviews with noted teachers and researchers concerned with language development; and the "Resource Room," which includes letters and subsequent comments from readers on practical or theoretical material describing problem areas in language teaching, stating the readers' research and/or development in progress.

The journal was begun in 1974 by the English Department at Gallaudet College, and was originally titled *Teaching English to the Deaf*. The first few issues carried the printed goal: "to promote the study and discussion of the practical problems confronting today the educators of the deaf in general and the teachers of English to the deaf in particular." However, in 1981 the editorial board voted to change the title in order to include a growing number of teachers in the English as a second language (ESL) field who found themselves teaching deaf students as well as hearing second-language students. There was also a growing awareness on the part of the national organization of ESL teachers, called Teachers of English to Speakers of Other Languages (TESOL), that there is a relationship between teaching English to foreign students and teaching English to deaf students. Still, the journal's primary goal is to provide practical information on teaching language arts skills to deaf people. *See* GALLAUDET COLLEGE.

Since 1977 the journal has been the official organ of the Section of English Teachers of the Deaf, which is affiliated with the Convention of American Instructors of the Deaf. Through this Section and the Teachers of English to Speakers of other Languages, the journal's circulation has increased to 1000 copies. *See* CONVENTION OF AMERICAN INSTRUCTORS OF THE DEAF.

Teaching English to Deaf and Second-Language Students is published three times a year, and members of the Section of English Teachers of the Deaf receive the journal as part of their dues. However, to be a member of the Section, one must be a member of its parent organization, the Convention of American Instructors of the Deaf.

Contributors may send manuscripts dealing with classroom methods and techniques, materials development, or approaches to second-language acquisition to the editor in chief of the journal at Gallaudet College. Manuscripts submitted for publication should follow sections 1, 4, and 7–9 of the "TESOL Quarterly Style Sheet," which appears in the December issue.

Nancy E. Kensicki

TEACHING PROFESSION

Universal recognition of teachers as professionals by the general public has been a slow evolutionary process. Raising the image of teachers from the level of the practitioner of a skill or craft to that of a professional came about as a result of the work of organizations formed by teachers and educators of teachers.

Attention to the special educational needs of deaf individuals had its beginnings in the Middle Ages. The records of these events were widely dispersed in Europe, and they span several hundreds of years. These events were instigated by individuals who were interested in the plight of deaf people and who undertook to do something educationally constructive for them. *See* EDUCATION: History.

Governmental interest in sponsorship, governance, and management of special schools and facilities followed private and church efforts to do the same. The first of these sponsored by government occurred in France in the late 1700s. This was followed by work in Germany and then in England in the early 1800s.

Individuals who found success in their efforts to educate deaf persons often made teaching deaf pupils their profession. The earliest teachers, as individual entrepreneurs, tended to keep their methods shrouded in secrecy in order to protect their unique livelihood. This attitude worked against deaf individuals by delaying the growth and development of organized programs for deaf education.

Interest in the education of deaf people in the United States began in the early nineteenth century. The American development was greatly influenced by what was being done in Europe. American schools prepared their teachers informally by using in-service training techniques. Observing the teaching done by others was initially the basis for helping to prepare others to teach deaf children.

Preparation for teaching soon developed as an apprentice-type activity which involved learning from and consulting with well-known, successful masters of the art. More formalized programs for training teachers followed as the demand and need for teachers increased. These programs were generally school-based and were located in established, well-known schools for deaf children. The leadership for such teacher preparation programs was totally dependent upon the work of recognized master teachers in the schools.

Professional organized efforts to raise the standards of teachers began in the United States in the 1920s. One of the leading organizations of educators of this period was the Association to Promote the Teaching of Speech to the Deaf, which produced the first set of standards for the training of teachers. These later became the basis for the first program for granting certificates to individuals who completed recognized teacher training programs. The program initiated by the association was later adapted and administered by the Conference of Superintendents and Principals. *See* ALEXANDER GRAHAM BELL ASSOCIATION FOR THE DEAF; CONFERENCE OF EDUCATIONAL ADMINISTRATORS SERVING THE DEAF.

Today teachers who are involved in many types of programs and a wide variety of service delivery systems are required by most states as well as by their profession to have received their preparation for teaching in institutions of higher education. In most instances, graduate-level preparation or a master's degree is required before recognition of professional-level teaching ability is granted.

The teacher of deaf students is unique because of the special skills required to work with deaf children. Special techniques are significantly different from those required to teach children with normal hearing. Preparation for all teachers of deaf children include such studies as the anatomy and diseases of hearing and speech organs, the use of hearing in learning language, and the techniques of teaching language.

Specialization beyond the basic preparation and study requires more precise attention to the needs of deaf children at different ages and different levels of hearing impairment. These levels of specialization usually include infants and early childhood, children in elementary school, and those in middle or upper school. Within the upper or high school levels, teachers specialize further in skill and training to teach academic subject matter areas or a variety of vocational or career interests.

The teacher of deaf students, as an identifiably distinct specialist, is recognized today by the general field of education. University programs have been developed to focus research, curriculum development, and special teaching techniques and methods on the special needs of these children.

The uniqueness of the teacher of deaf students is best defined in a quote from a conference publication on the subject of the preparation of teachers of the deaf: "The teacher of the deaf is one who is concerned with the development and conservation of language and communication in children whose hearing impairment is great enough to preclude the establishment or retention of language and communication through normal and developmental means. In addition, he is also a teacher like any other, in that he must develop within the child the understanding of content normally acquired by most children in our culture."

Bibliography

Bender, Ruth E.: *The Conquest of Deafness*, Interstate Printers and Publishers, 1981.

Davis, H., and S. R. Silverman: *Hearing and Deafness*, Rinehart and Winston, 1978.

Frisina, Robert (ed.): *Bicentennial Monograph on Hearing Impairment*, Alexander Graham Bell Association for the Deaf, 1976.

Quigley, S.: *Preparation of Teachers of the Deaf*, Report of a National Conference, U.S. Department of Health, Education and Welfare, 1964.

Scouten, Edward L.: *Turning Points*, Interstate Printers and Publishers, 1984.

Ralph L. Hoag

History of Changes

The teaching profession as it relates to the education of deaf people has undergone many changes. In more recent years, the rate of change for the teacher and the programmatic impact on students have been especially great. It is too early to know whether the most recent changes affecting the profession will be better or more influential and productive than earlier changes.

BACKGROUND

The first documented records of teachers of deaf persons are from England in the eighth century, the Netherlands in the fifteenth century, and Spain in the sixteenth century. Records of the work done by these pioneers and the achievements of their deaf students make very interesting reading. They illustrate what was involved in teaching deaf persons, often referred to as "dumb," to speak, to read, and to communicate with others. Before the eighteenth century, these efforts invariably involved a teacher and only one or two deaf students. There were no classes or schools and no efforts made to educate poor deaf persons.

Early methods for developing basic reading and language skills included the teaching of writing by associating objects with the printed word. The teaching of movements of the vocal organs in association with letters and printed words was the earliest method used for teaching speech and articulation. An early Spanish teacher was the first to introduce the use of a one-handed manual alphabet in the process of educating a deaf child.

The divergence of methodologies later in history led to bitter disputes between and among proponents of one method or philosophy over another. The most intense dispute, arising in the 1700s, was between what were identified as oral and manual methodologies.

Educators in France and Germany in the 1700s began to view deaf people as a group, rather than as isolated individuals. They saw the plight of the collective population of individuals suffering a life without hearing in a world that did not understand or appreciate them and tended to treat them as subhuman. These educators soon became concerned about programming for large numbers of deaf pupils and they were instrumental in establishing the first schools. Governmental support for the education of these children followed the efforts of early educators to serve the existing populations of deaf children in their respective countries.

TUTOR IN THE CLASSROOM

The first changes in the approaches to educating deaf children moved from the tutorial model to meeting the needs of larger numbers and groups of deaf individuals. This involved the development of skills and strategies for working with groups of similarly aged children in the classroom settings of a school or institutional environment.

These early schools and programs, because of the low incidence of deafness and the need for bringing numbers of children together into one facility, became residential facilities. This then required that further adaptations be made in the training of personnel and in construction of school buildings. People also had to be trained to work with children at different age levels and with different education needs in 24-hour residential educational setting.

Newer teaching methods were developed and introduced in the early programs. As communications developed between the professionals involved with different programs and schools, disputes over philosophies and the approaches used became very intense. The French introduced and promoted the use of sign language and gestures, believing this to be the natural language of deaf persons and that the education of deaf children should be based on it.

The Germans, on the other hand, felt very strongly that in order for deaf individuals to become a part of a hearing society they must be taught exclusively through the use of speech and speechreading (lipreading). The Germans considered spoken language to be the foundation of education. They felt that teaching deaf children had to involve the teaching of oral language through the use of speech. Speechreading was taught first; the student had to learn to associate ideas with the lip movements of the speaker. The teaching of reading and writing followed a firm foundation of knowing how to speak. *See* L'EPÉE, ABBÉ CHARLES MICHEL DE; HEINICKE, SAMUEL.

During the period when the German and French teachers argued over their differences, the English moved ahead and became well known for their success in the teaching of speech to deaf people in their school programs. *See* BRAIDWOOD, THOMAS.

The French philosophy of educating deaf students was adopted by the earliest American educators. The first school for deaf pupils in America, the American School for the Deaf, was established in Connecticut in 1817 and used the French method of manual instruction. During the next 50 years many schools were developed in other states, and their programs were modeled after the American

School for the Deaf. *See* AMERICAN SCHOOL FOR THE DEAF; CLERC, LAURENT; GALLAUDET, THOMAS HOPKINS.

Meanwhile, a series of independent and intensely interested individuals went to Europe and sought first-hand information to verify what they had heard about the German oral method. Preference for the oral philosophy by those who witnessed programs in Germany influenced the development of the first major oral school for deaf students in the United States. This was the Clarke School for the Deaf, which opened in 1867 in Northampton, Massachusetts. Later, oral schools were established in other locations in the United States. *See* CLARKE SCHOOL.

Controversy raged over these two basic methods to such an extent that an eventual amalgamation of methods, called the combined system, developed. The newer philosophy became a somewhat generally used approach for educational programs in most state-supported and -operated schools of the period. By the early twentieth century almost all private and residential schools and public day schools for deaf students had adopted oral methods of teaching. This approach was considered by most educators of the day to be the best approach for teaching deaf children, especially in their early years.

State-operated residential schools for the most part did not fully adopt the policy for the entire school. While they used the oral method in the lower school and in beginning classes, they used manual methods of teaching for older students in upper classes. *See* HISTORY: Sign Language Controversy.

Teachers during these years received their training in programs located within these schools. The type of school, whether an oral or a combined system school, determined the type of training received and where graduates might successfully find employment.

PROFESSIONAL ORGANIZATIONS

As the numbers of schools and programs grew, teachers and administrators looked to personnel in other schools for new ideas. This kind of interest on an informal basis led to the development of professional organizations. These organizations, established to serve persons in the field of deaf education, were among the first to be developed in education in the United States. Instructors in residential schools established in 1850 an organization of teachers which became known as the Convention of American Instructors of the Deaf. *See* CONVENTION OF AMERICAN INSTRUCTORS OF THE DEAF.

Teachers, supporters, and advocates of oral education moved to form their own organization. The first was known as the American Association to Promote the Teaching of Speech to the Deaf and was established in 1890. This organization later became known as the Alexander Graham Bell Association for the Deaf.

Administrators and principals formed their own organization, known today as the Conference of Educational Administrators Serving the Deaf. The original organization, the Conference of Superintendents and Principals, was established in 1868.

These organizations moved in separate directions to promote their special interest in the improvements of programs for deaf children.

The Convention was organized primarily to serve teachers in residential schools. The leadership, however, came from administrators of programs in the organizations' earlier years. The Conference later allied its organization to the Convention in order to share information and hold concurrent meetings at similar locations. The focus of the attention of the Conference, though, was broader than that of the Convention, for it was concerned more with the administration, programming, staffing, financing, and construction of buildings for schools. The membership of the Conference included administrators of both combined system and oral schools.

The members of the Bell Association in its beginning was made up primarily of administrators and teachers of oral schools and programs. Still, teachers in combined system schools were encouraged to become members. Many did join the organization and strongly supported its philosophy for educating children.

The primary focus of interest of the Bell Association was to promote the use of speech in all schools for deaf students. The emphasis in this approach was to assure that no child be denied the opportunity to develop speech or to learn to read lips.

TEACHER PREPARATION

The Conference, the Convention, and the Association all had a common concern related to the preparation of teachers and the eventual development of standards for training. Some sharing of ideas between the committees of each organization took place in the late 1920s. The first concerted action occurred when the Association announced a plan for the registration and certification of teachers through its own offices. A discussion ensued among the three organizations with an attempt to determine which organization would be best suited to administer such a program.

Standards that were proposed in the beginning of this effort recommended that a two-year program be developed for the preparation of teachers of deaf pupils. This was later considered to be impractical, since the two-year program was required in addition to a prerequisite two-year normal school program.

Finally, a series of courses were defined and developed as the basis for an adoptable program. The responsibility for administering both a program approval process for training programs and a certification program was mutually agreed to be that of the Conference. The first peer review process for evaluating programs for the preparation of teachers of deaf students was adopted by the Conference and got underway in 1931.

All centers for the preparation of teachers at the time were school-based in-service-type programs. The move to higher education sponsorship of teacher preparation programs developed gradually during the following 30 years. Today all programs are run, managed, and supported by colleges and university departments.

DAY SCHOOL MOVEMENT

The first schools in the country were residential schools. Justification for this, as for the earlier schools in Europe, was based on the incidence or numbers of cases. Only 7.5 per 1000 children were found to have deafness or severe hearing loss as an educational problem. Schools served a wide geographic area and therefore had to be residential. *See* EDUCATIONAL PROGRAMS: Residential Schools.

Larger cities such as Boston, New York, Detroit, and Chicago had concentrations of population large enough to be reasonably able to develop day school programs. Support for this new concept came from parents of deaf children who very vocally expressed the need to move schools for deaf children into closer proximity to the home and to schools for normal or hearing children. The attempt here was to provide more opportunity for normalization of relationships with the home and with students in regular public schools. *See* EDUCATIONAL PROGRAMS: Day Schools.

The teacher in this kind of program had to adapt to the change and be able to fit curriculum and program activities that would take advantage of the new environment and the closer contact with parents and other children. This movement took place in the early 1900s and continued to develop over the years at an accelerated pace.

FEDERAL LEGISLATION

Perhaps the largest factor influencing change in the delivery of educational services to deaf children was Public Law 94-142, the Education of All Handicapped Children Act of 1975. The law provided for the equalization of the educational rights of all handicapped children. As a result, parents demanded that local public schools provide appropriate programs for their children. Mainstreaming became a new word in the lexicon of education language, and meant the inclusion of handicapped children in classrooms and activities of all children in public schools.

In many instances, this philosophy spelled educational disaster for deaf children. Those first thrust into mainstream education were further isolated socially and encountered considerable difficulty in getting trained help that was sorely needed in order to make any attempt to keep up educationally. Later, many deaf children, with proper preparation and continuing support services, were able to succeed and do well in mainstream situations. For those children who needed more support, programs of itinerant teaching and part-time mainstreaming developed. The real impact of P.L. 94-142 for the deaf child is yet to be realized, and whether these changes will be beneficial needs to be evaluated. *See* EDUCATIONAL LEGISLATION.

Teachers involved in mainstream situations are faced with a whole new set of needs and skills. Adjustment to prepare teachers for serving as a resource teacher, a tutor, and often as an administrator had to be made by training programs, and is still going on.

TOTAL COMMUNICATION

In 1973 the term total communication was introduced to identify the method of instruction that had been in common use in many schools for deaf children for quite a number of years. The Conference of Educational Administrators Serving the Deaf in 1976 adopted a formal definition for the term: "Total communication is a philosophy requiring the incorporation of appropriate aural, manual and oral modes of communication in order to ensure effective communication with and among hearing impaired persons."

Total communication as a teaching tool and a means of communication in education spread during the 1970s to many schools. The schools adopted the term to describe their program, and disseminated it in their publications.

This movement affected programs for the preparation of teachers as well. Courses in fingerspelling and manual communication began to appear in college curricula of teacher training programs as well as in programs for rehabilitation counselors, interpreters, and other related professional and paraprofessional training programs.

The true and lasting effect of this on possible improvement of instruction, acceleration of academic learning, overall social and emotional adjustment, and eventual successful involvement of deaf people as participating members of community and society in general is yet to be measured and reported. *See* SOCIOLINGUISTICS: Total Communication.

IMPACT OF CHANGE

The social, governmental, and technological changes cited here, and others not noted, continuously influenced the process of education for deaf pupils. Revisions had to be made in all aspects of programming, classroom structure, curriculum materials, subject matter content, and methods and techniques for working with children.

During all of these adjustments, deaf students had to work along with the system, hoping that what was being done for them educationally would help them achieve the newly discovered goals and opportunities opened as a result of changes made in education. More recently, deaf individuals have taken much more active roles in the process. As educators and professionals, they have made significant contributions to what is now being done on behalf of deaf children everywhere.

Bibliography

Babbidge, H. D.: *Education of the Deaf*, Report by the HEW Advisory Committee on Education of the Deaf, 1965.

Bender, R. E.: *The Conquest of Deafness*, Interstate Printers and Publishers, 1981.

Brill, R. G. *Administrative and Professional Developments in the Education of the Deaf*, Gallaudet College Press, 1971.

Davis, H., and S. R. Silverman: *Hearing and Deafness*, Holt, Rinehart, and Winston, 1978.

Frisina, R. (ed.): *A Bicentennial Monograph on Hearing Impairment*, Alexander Graham Bell Association, 1976.

Scouten, E. L.: *Turning Points in the Education of Deaf People*, Interstate Printers and Publishers, 1984.

Ralph L. Hoag

Training

Major programmatic changes in American schools for deaf students occurred following World War II. These changes resulted from several factors: advancing technology, including equipment for hearing aids and classroom amplification; an expanding population; the lowering of entry age for children beginning educational programs; and a steadily increasing number of children with multiple handicaps. Programming for the educationals needs of deaf children was complicated by these changes, which forced educators and administrators to examine and evaluate existing teaching practices and techniques. Moreover, the preparation of teachers was made complex due to the effects of population mobility, the proliferation of new programs, and new technology, and the effects of new research in language and linguistics.

By the 1950s most programs for the preparation of teachers were located in or administered by colleges and universities. However, a number of the original or older established programs were still basically school-centered with administrative and support links to institutions of higher education.

FEDERAL LEGISLATION

Between 1950 and 1960 the number of students enrolled in schools for deaf children increased as dramatically as it did in all schools throughout the country, reflecting the impact of the postwar baby boom. Similarly, the number of schools and programs increased. This growth in school population and increase in the number of classes caused a severe shortage of teachers. The 30 or more teacher training programs then in existence could not produce enough teachers to meet the rapidly expanding need. Only 300 to 400 new teachers were graduating each year from these programs. The crisis faced by school administrators led to an attempt to solve the problem.

In response to this need, the newly established coalition of organizations, the Council on Education of the Deaf, took action to gain the attention of the U.S. Congress in an effort to provide financial support for the training of more teachers. Their efforts resulted in the passage of Public Law 87-276 in 1958. This legislation authorized and financed the funding of a student scholarship aid program and a grant-in-aid program for the establishment of new programs.

RESULTING CHANGES

Within five years of the passage of P.L. 87-276, the number of programs increased dramatically to more than 60, with well over 1000 students graduating annually. Previously existing programs also benefited from the federal aid, which allowed them to make improvements in staff, curriculum, and facilities.

Prior to the advent of federal assistance, most programs for training teachers of deaf students were very limited in resources. Typically, one person taught most courses; assigned, managed, and supervised practice teaching; recruited, selected, and counseled students; maintained contact with schools that served as observation and student teaching resources; and in general administered the program as a branch within a department in a college or university. The number of students in these programs varied from 10 to 50, depending upon the size of the university, the staff, the resources available, and the demand for its graduates.

The earlier programs were typically one-year programs requiring about 30 units of work. Most were in undergraduate schools. Some were administered by colleges or schools of education. Others were managed by departments of speech sciences, audiology, or speech pathology within a college or university setting.

During the first 10 years after the program of federal aid started, many programs were upgraded from undergraduate programs to graduate programs. Course work and curriculum requirements advanced from 30 units of study to as much as 40 or 50 units. The result was a gradual but noticeable increase in the quality of programs and their graduates.

COUNCIL ON EDUCATION OF THE DEAF

The program standards of 1930 established by the Conference of Educational Administrators serving the Deaf, although improved and upgraded in 1952 and again in 1959, were rapidly becoming outdated as guidelines for programs in the 1960s. The general trends in education toward teacher competence and skills created the need for program change. Additionally, government funding required accountability for the funds provided to support programs. This involved site visits and program evaluation. Standards in use at the time, therefore, needed considerable updating.

The federal government in 1964 assisted in this process by sponsoring a National Conference on the Preparation of Teachers of the Deaf. This was the first time in the history of deaf education that a meeting was held involving the representatives from virtually all the diverse interests in the field. All who attended focused their attention on the problem of preparing teachers.

Recommendations were many and were all directed at the need for updated program standards. One of the more important and significant recommendations was to move the jurisdiction of program evaluation and certification of teachers from the Conference of Educational Administrators Serving the Deaf to another organization. There was general agreement that the Council on Education of the Deaf would be a more appropriate organization to take on this work, since it represented a coalition of all three of the organizations concerned with the education of deaf children.

The debate within and among the member organizations of the Council went on for another five years before final steps were taken to make the change. The Council officially took over the teacher certification program and undertook the project to upgrade the standards and requirements for both teacher certification and the training of teachers in college and university programs.

New standards, written by committees serving the Council, were adopted in 1974. Two years after the new program got under way, the program for the certification of teachers exploded from 250 applicants a year to 1500 or more.

TEACHER PREPARATION TODAY

The need for additional teachers in the mid-1980s was not as great as it was from the 1950s through the 1970s. The problem of teacher specialization to meet the individual needs of children and to serve in the variety of programs has become more critical. There are about 80 individual college or university programs currently training teachers of deaf pupils. Approximately 55 of these function under the standards for programs offered by the Council. These programs graduate over 1000 students annually.

Bibliography

Frisina, R. (ed.): *A Bicentennial Monograph on Hear-* *ing Impairment*, Alexander Graham Bell Association, 1976.

Hicks, D. E.: *Current Issues and Trends in the Education of the Hearing Impaired Persons*, Proceedings of 45th Meeting of the CEASD, 1982.

Hoag, R. L. (ed.): *Standards for the Evaluation of Programs*, Council on Education of the Deaf, 1980.

Quigley, S. P. (ed.): *Preparation of Teachers of the Deaf*, a report of a national conference, U.S. Office of Education, 1964.

"University Programs Training Personnel in Deafness," *American Annals of the Deaf*, vol. 129, no. 2, April 1984.

Ralph L. Hoag

Certification

The professional certification of American teachers of deaf students began in 1931. Much work had been done during the preceding decade to develop a set of program guidelines or criteria that could be used by schools involved in training teachers to work in schools for deaf children. The initial work had primarily been done by an organization known as the American Association to Promote the Teaching of Speech to the Deaf (now known as the Alexander Graham Bell Association for the Deaf).

In 1926 the administrative organization known as the Conference of Superintendents and Principals (now known as the Conference of Educational Administrators Serving the Deaf) worked somewhat independently on their own set of program guidelines and teacher certification requirements.

The two plans that had been developed were administered separately by the two organizations as a registry of teachers and a certification program. In 1935 they were merged into a single program, and the Conference was selected as the more appropriate organization to administer it. Today, the program is administered by the Council on Education of the Deaf (CED), a body composed of representatives from the Conference and from the Convention of American Instructors of the Deaf.

The certification of teachers by states and local schools is a legal responsibility required by laws that govern and monitor those who serve within specific political boundaries. Generally, in the development of state and local standards for teacher certification, officials look to standards developed by professional organizations as guides to developing their own. In this instance, the existing CED standards for teachers of deaf pupils still are the most widely accepted standards for this purpose, providing the basis for many state certification regulations and licensing activities.

CED STANDARDS

The trend in CED certification of teachers today is toward specialization. Current standards provide specific requirements for specialization in parent-infant education, early childhood education, elementary education, secondary education, vocational education, and education of multihandicapped deaf students.

In addition to the certification of teachers at these different levels of teaching, the CED has expanded its program to include the certification of supervisors of instruction, administrators, and psychologists. The program requires these people to develop special skills and abilities in order to be able to serve deaf school children more effectively.

The standards require that teachers of hearing-impaired children, in order to be certified by CED, have specific skills enabling them to provide appropriate educational services in at least one special area or level of teaching. This implies having the knowledge and ability to identify and evaluate general educational needs of all hearing-impaired children as well as special ability as a teacher in at least one level or area of specialization.

Certificates are awarded by the CED for two different levels of preparation in each area of specialization. The first is the provisional level; the second is the professional level.

Provisional Level

For professional-level certificates, the applicant should have completed coursework generally required for state public school teaching credentials in early childhood, elementary, or secondary education. In addition, the applicants must complete a core program of at least 30 semester hours of coursework plus 6 semester hours of student teaching with hearing-impaired children in their area of specialization

The core program of 30 units of study must include work in the following general subject areas: foundations in the education of hearing-impaired children, audiology and speech science, language and communication, curriculum and instruction, and supervised observation and student teaching with hearing-impaired children.

In order to receive a CED provisional certificate, the candidate must have attended a program that had been reviewed and endorsed as an approved program by the CED.

Professional Level

Required coursework for professional certification must be at the graduate level and must follow the completion of provisional-level preparation. Persons who have already completed a master's degree as part of their provisional-level training must take an additional nine units of study related to their area of specialization. Applicants who previously completed a program at the bachelor's level must take an additional 30 units of study at the graduate level.

After completion of the above coursework and

three years of full-time successful teaching experience, the candidate may be eligible to apply for professional-level certificate.

Program Approval

The CED has been involved since 1969 in the review and evaluation of college programs for the preparation of teachers. Program approval by the CED is granted to sponsoring institutions after an intensive self-study of the program is conducted and a site visit under CED sponsorship is made by a team of competent educators.

Fifty-five institutions since 1969 have been through this process and have been recognized as approved programs. As required by the CED many of these have been subjected to second and third program update reviews that are repeated every five years.

About 1000 new teachers graduate from these programs each year. Most of the graduates serve in schools and classes for deaf children all over the nation. This program has enabled the profession to maintain high standards for the preparation of teachers and thus has assured better programming in schools for deaf children.

Bibliography

Brill, R. G.: *Adminstrative and Professional Developments in the Education of the Deaf*, Gallaudet College Press, 1971.

Frisina, R. (ed.): *Bicentennial Monograph on Hearing Impairment*, Alexander Graham Bell Association for the Deaf, 1976.

Hoag, R. L. (coord.): *Certification Standards for Professionals Involved in the Education of Hearing Impaired Children and Youth*, Council on Education of the Deaf, 1985.

———: *Standards for the Certification of Teachers of the Hearing Impaired*, Council on Education of the Deaf, 1974.

Ralph L. Hoag

Resource Specialists

The resource classroom or resource specialist program may be a service for individuals with various handicaps. Robert Irwin started such a program for children with visual problems in the early 1900s. Resource programs for hard-of-hearing students were developed shortly after Irwin's initial program. Many states in the nation have had resource or remedial programs to help regular students in reading or mathematics, but it is only recently that handicapped students have had an option that would enable them to obtain an individual educational program in a free and appropriate setting within the least restrictive environment, as is now required by the federal government.

Students placed in this type of program must be in regular classes at least 50 percent of the time. Therefore, students benefit from the support found in the resource program while remaining integrated with their peers in their home-based school.

Extra costs are minimal, as no special form of transportation is needed. Pupils usually walk to the school or are transported by the system. Students work in small groups or individually with a teacher and instructional aide. Flexible scheduling and careful planning for each student is critical. The student has an individualized program, while the resource teacher acts as a consultant to the regular teachers and assists in modifying the regular instruction program. The resource teacher works with eligible pupils in all of the grades the school serves. At the current time, the majority of students found in this setting are learning-disabled, although a few hard-of-hearing and deaf students are being placed in this setting.

The resource specialist program is an attendance-area-based service. Pupils in one geographic area attend their local school. The resource teacher is a member of the local school staff serving pupils who are identified as eligible under state and federal guidelines but who are able to receive the majority of their instruction from a regular classroom teacher.

Although the resource specialist teacher is usually required to possess a special education credential and training in both regular and special education, there is seldom a requirement for special preparation for teaching hearing-impaired children.

Children served by regular education and resource specialist teachers may also receive the assistance of other itinerant special education services. Speech and language therapy is by far the most common service. Audiologic counseling, psychological counseling, and adaptive physical education are other services extended to pupils with special needs whose instructional program can be provided in a regular classroom with nonhandicapped pupils under the direction of a regular education teacher. Pupils can be scheduled to attend class for a specific time each day to use special equipment, participate in a small group instructional program, or receive tutorial assistance from a classroom aide or paraprofessional.

The focus of the resource teacher is to assist the pupil in maintaining progress with the regular education class. Tutoring for mathematics problems, individual reading instruction, and drills on spelling lessons followed by individual spelling tests given in a modified environment are examples of services provided by the resource teacher to a hearing-impaired pupil.

Bibliography

California Education Code, Sect. 56362.

Title 45 Code of Federal Regulations, 121a.750–121a.754.

Weiderholt, J. Lee, Donald D. Hammill, Virginia Brown: *The Resource Teacher*, Allyn and Bacon, Boston, 1978.

Brenda S. Sorenson; Harriet Flynn Daford

Itinerant Teachers

An itinerant teacher provides supportive services to school-age hearing-impaired students that enable the student to function in an assigned classroom. Individual tutoring sessions typically offer assistance in academic skills, communication development, and socialization. These sessions, which may be scheduled for one or more times each week, are provided at the student's school. Itinerant teachers are found in both public and private schools.

STUDENT POPULATION

Pursuant to the Education for all Handicapped Children Act and its provision to supply a full spectrum of related services for handicapped students, itinerant teachers serve students with hearing losses ranging from mild to profound. The majority of students receiving itinerant teacher assistance are those considered to have hearing loss as their primary handicap and who receive their instruction in regular education classes. In addition to this group are students whose primary handicap may be physical, developmental, emotional, or communicative and who also have a secondary handicap of hearing loss, and thus, under the guidelines of the Education for All Handicapped Children Act, may also be eligible for itinerant teacher assistance. *See* EDUCATION OF THE HANDICAPPED ACT.

QUALIFICATIONS

Professional organizations affiliated with the education of hearing-impaired students strongly recommend that the itinerant teacher have credentials in deaf education. However, in some areas of the United States, itinerant services are provided by the speech and language specialist or special education resource teacher.

RESPONSIBILITIES

Itinerant teachers participate in the preparation and implementation of the hearing-impaired student's Individual Education Plan. They assess the student to determine current levels of functioning, suggest annual goals, and provide instruction for the student's achievement of these goals.

For hearing-impaired students who are fully mainstreamed in regular education classes, the itinerant teacher confers with the student's classroom teacher, provides academic tutoring for the mastery of class material, and assists the student with study and test-taking skills. The itinerant teacher may arrange for a classroom notetaker and may confer with the student's parents and with other support personnel. To assist the student with continuing communication development, the itinerant teacher monitors the student's amplification (hearing aid or auditory trainer) and provides instruction in language and speech development. To assist the student with socialization in a regular school setting, the itinerant teacher may confer with the administrator about class selection and scheduling and may provide in-service training about hearing impairment for the school staff.

For those students with mild to moderate losses who are in regular or special education classes (not classes for hearing-impaired students), the itinerant teacher conducts assessment and provides instruction in auditory training and speech reading to enable the student to function in a classroom. The itinerant teacher helps the student and the teacher to understand the implications of the student's hearing loss, monitors the student's amplification, and may confer with the teacher about preferential seating.

CASE LOAD

The number of students that constitute an itinerant teacher's case load varies across school districts and is determined by the number and grade level of students at each site, the travel time between sites, and the amount of time allocated to each student according to the student's Individual Education Plan. In urban school districts with large numbers of hearing-impaired students, itinerant teachers may serve 10 to 20 students at a number of relatively close sites. In rural districts, an itinerant teacher may serve as few as five students at five sites located within a large geographical area. Individual tutoring sessions of 30 minutes to over an hour are scheduled.

Bibliography

Hearing-Impaired, vol. 9 of *Resource Manuals for Exceptional Children*, State Department of Education, Georgia, 1981.

Karchmer, Michael A., and Raymond Trybus: "Who Are the Deaf Children in Mainstream Programs?", *Directions*, 2:13–17, 1981.

Moores, Donald F.: *Educating the deaf: Psychology, Principles and Practices*, Houghton Mifflin, Boston, 1978.

Nix, Gary W.: *Mainstream Education for Hearing Impaired Children and Youth*, Grune and Stratton, New York, 1976.

Northcott, Winifred H.: *The Hearing Impaired Child in a Regular Classroom*, Alexander Graham Bell Association, Washington, D.C., 1973.

Sandy Sanborn

TELECOMMUNICATIONS

Two telecommunications advances since the 1960s have had a major impact on the deaf community of the United States: telecommunications devices for the deaf (TDDs), which permit deaf people to use regular telephones with relatively small, portable, and inexpensive auxiliary equipment; and considerably more expensive television captioning systems and decoders.

These technological innovations have helped to bring many more deaf people into contact with each other and with the hearing community. At the same time, however, neither device has had the complete success predicted by proponents. Both rely on the ability of users to transmit and receive information in written English, a task that some deaf individuals find difficult and unpleasant. Nevertheless, particularly among more educated and affluent members of the deaf population, TDDs and captioned television have become essential factors in their private and professional lives.

Telephone Services

The telephone needs of the American deaf people have always been similar to the needs of nondeaf people. Yet the telephone, invented in 1876 by Alexander Graham Bell, set deaf individuals back in their struggle for full citizenship rights. The irony is that Bell, who was a teacher of deaf persons, married to a deaf woman, and interested in promoting the welfare of deaf people, was responsible for this technological impediment to persons who cannot hear. It was not until 88 years after Bell's invention that the telephone gap was finally bridged by an enterprising deaf ham radio operator. *See* BELL, ALEXANDER GRAHAM.

EARLY DEVICES (1876 TO 1963)

Since the original telephone was of no use to deaf people, a series of devices entered the market for deaf people, all with negligible benefits to the average deaf person; all failed to achieve widespread usage.

The volume control handset, enabling the voice to be raised to a desired level, helped hard-of-hearing callers but not deaf people. The watchcase receiver required the assistance of a third party, either one whose lips could be read easily or one adept with the language of signs. A deaf person, who had good speaking skills, could talk on the telephone while the third party would interpret the returned messages. A picture phone, akin to the television phone, cost several dollars per minute and required an appointment for use at a special booth at the telephone center. However, it was too costly and inconvenient to use, since it was necessary to make advance arrangements with another party and then to make a trip to the telephone center. If one party did not know sign language, or was not able to lipread, then the picture phone conversation would be very difficult. The telewriter, a "writing machine," was used by deaf professors at Gallaudet College in the late 1960s. It had to be either leased or rented. Penmanship skills were required, and equipment was compatible only if the manufacturer was the same. The facsimile machines, which sent prepared messages across the phone lines, required preparation of the message in advance, preventing instant communication. The voice meter indicated only yes or no responses and severely limited the conversation. The Code-Com sets contained flashing lights to indicate Morse code letters and required users to know Morse code. The commercial teleprinters were very expensive to use, akin to the teletype (TTY) machines that deaf people use today.

WEITBRECHT MODEM

Robert H. Weitbrecht, a deaf physicist and a licensed ham radio operator, used a radio TTY machine (RTTY) to talk with other RTTY operators on the air all over the world. He was coaxed by several deaf acquaintances to adapt this RTTY device for use over telephone lines. He succeeded in his efforts, and the first public demonstration of a machine was held at Salt Lake City, Utah, in 1964. All that was needed was a specially modified modem (developed by Weitbrecht), on which to place the telephone, and a modified teleprinter machine, with some mechanical changes to the gears. This acoustic/inductive modem converts typed letters into tones which are then transmitted over the telephone line to a receiving handset. This receiver reconverts the impulses into signals which enter the teletypewriter, and the message is printed out.

It took Weitbrecht several years to perfect the modem (later named the Weitbrecht Modem) for the marketplace. The two national organizations of deaf people, the Alexander Graham Bell Association for the Deaf (AGBAD) and the National Association of the Deaf (NAD), worked together to arrange for the distribution of surplus teleprinters by AT&T and other carriers. However, both organizations were afraid that the paperwork associated with the distribution of these machines would overwhelm their resources and therefore encouraged the formation of a new national organization, called Teletypewriters for the Deaf Distribution Committee, based at Indianapolis, Indiana. *See* ALEXANDER GRAHAM BELL ASSOCIATION FOR THE DEAF; NATIONAL ASSOCIATION OF THE DEAF.

Three abbreviations comprise the TTY communications protocols: GA, meaning go ahead, designating the other user's turn to communicate; SK, meaning good-bye, acknowledging readiness to sign off and to hang up; and HD, meaning to hold or to wait. All became a universal part of household language in the TTY user homes.

TTY NETWORK

Even though the first TTY was developed in 1964, for all practical purposes the TTY network started in 1968. The deaf TTY network grew slowly, but faster in some areas than in others. St. Louis, for example, buoyed by its aggressive deaf leaders, became the leading locale in the numbers of TTY machines installed. The Washington, D.C., metropolitan area was close behind St. Louis. Much resistance, however, was felt in other areas. Many deaf people resisted investing a considerable amount of money in a piece of equipment when there were few people with whom to use it. Also, toll call rates were another major expense.

Resistance gradually broke down across the United States. Abetting this development was a growing alliance of deaf TTY technicians, repairers, and agents who received donated machines, often by truckloads, reconditioned them, and then distributed them to more and more households. The telephone company Pioneers, an organization of retired telephone personnel, conducted classes in machine reconditioning.

In 1971 the Internal Revenue Service ruled TTYs to be a tax-deductible medical expense, the first major breakthrough achieved by the deaf community in getting their legitimate communication needs recognized by the government. *See* INTERNAL REVENUE CODE.

TDD

By the mid-1970s, easy access by the deaf community to donated surplus machines ceased to exist. The machines and the spare parts became very scarce. However, sleek electronic portable machines soon came on the market. These units were very light and could easily fit into a handbag. Because of this development, the term teleprinter became a misnomer. A new name was coined and accepted universally—telecommunication device for the deaf (TDD). The acronym is claimed by some to have another derivation—telephone device for the deaf.

During this period of change from TTY to TDD, AT&T undertook to assess the needs of deaf people in telecommunications in terms of TDD Operator Assisted Services, reduced toll call rates, low-cost TDD rental programs, technical compatibility standards, 24-hour relay services, free TDD for low-income households, and so on.

Computer Age and Telephone Equality The advent of computers in American society caused a considerable controversy among the manufacturers, the advocates, and the futurists concerning the most appropriate design on which to base the TDD. The options relate to the codes comprising combinations of bits which correspond to each printed character. The Baudot code is considered obsolete, but is the foundation of the deaf TDD network with about 100,000 users. The ASCII code is the basis for computer telecommunications and is the code of the future. However, the two codes are incompatible with each other, unless a special "black box" converter is used to marry them. ASCII, developed in the 1960s, is more convenient, but since every TDD in the country is Baudot-based, the costs of such a changeover could be staggering.

With the continued demand for parity in toll call rates, New York and Connecticut became the first states to enact reduced intrastate toll call rates for TDD users. Within a few years, every state except California followed suit. AT&T contributed by reducing interstate toll call rates.

Even though California did not offer reductions in intrastate toll call rates, it mandated that every deaf resident receive a free TDD, regardless of income or social status; of the remaining states, only Rhode Island and Connecticut followed California's lead. Only about 25,000 free TDDs were given out, which raised questions as to why deaf people would refuse to use a TDD even when it was given free. The resistance reflects a combination of factors: the high cost of one-time telephone installation; the expense of monthly toll call rates in states that did not enact reduced intrastate rates; the difficulty of using the device without typing skills; low language skills; and personal resistance. *See* STATE STATUTES: Telephone Rates.

Another breakthrough presented itself in 1980 when AT&T established a nationwide toll-free Operator Assistance Center. This enabled deaf people to receive operator services on the same basis with the rest of the nondeaf population.

The computer age has influenced the deaf TDD network in three ways. The first was the electronic bulletin board, with which a user could theoretically send one message to many private electronic mail boxes, or simply post it on the open electronic bulletin board, thus saving the time and expense of mailing each letter or telephoning each person. The earliest TDD electronic mail prototype was developed by Robert Bruninga. Bruninga called the project the Virginia TTY Message Center. Preceding Bruninga's efforts was the Hermes project, which operated for a short time as a local deaf-only network in Framingham, Massachusetts. Hermes was not TDD-compatible, while Bruninga's project was.

Two government grants in 1979 pushed the electronic mail concept to a larger scale. The Deafnet, which offered full TDD/ASCII compatibility, was operative in the Washington, D.C., area for three years until funding expired. On a smaller scale is the Handicapped Educational Exchange (HEX), also developed by Bruninga and his group, the Amateur Radio Research and Development Corp. (AMRAD), an organization of amateur radio and computer enthusiasts. HEX has been refined and expanded and is still operative, even though federal funding expired, and it enjoys the status of being the oldest and most successful private electronic mail system for deaf people.

The second influence of the computer age on TDDs was the programming of personal computers into TDDs.

The third influence was the incorporation of ASCII terminal features into TDDs. A prime example is the Porta Printer 40, which offers the option of using it as a TDD, as an ASCII-only TDD, or as a portable computer terminal complete with a paper printout.

One hope of the deaf community for telephone equality was met in many cities by the TDD relay service. It enables the TDD-user to get in touch with a nondeaf person with the assistance of a third party—the answering relay service. Two privately run national toll-free TDD relay services were established but lasted only a short time.

More and more businesses, government agencies, and public facilities have installed TDDs to communicate with deaf people, but the results have been mixed. Depending on the attitude and expectations, some of the installed business numbers were taken out of service, while others have continued with scaled-down expectations.

Other Services To help deaf-blind persons, I. Lee Brody developed the Braille-TTY. Unfortunately, very few are used due to their high cost.

The Pennsylvania School for the Deaf in Philadelphia developed the Radio TTY Center. News transmitted by radio subcarrier frequencies could be printed out on TDDs in homes with the help of special receivers. A telephone connection was not necessary; this was an advantage in that users were not bothered by busy telephone signals. Another name for this innovation is "captioned radio," and perhaps this term provides a more accurate description of this system. Unfortunately, like other federally funded projects, the center closed when funding stopped.

To communicate with those not having a TDD, a touchtone device was developed. At one end of the telephone line, the user, with the required touchtone telephone, transmits letters by using the telephone touchtone pad as a "keyboard." At best, communication is very slow, and not as efficient as with TDDs. This device has not been supported by the deaf community, but it is actually aimed at the hearing-impaired market.

Barry Strassler

Captioned Television

Television captions are subtitles that appear on a television screen and correspond to the audio portion of the program, thus enabling viewers to read what they may not hear. Television captions may be transmitted in two different forms: open and closed.

OPEN CAPTIONS

Open captions are superimposed over a portion of the television picture and appear on all television sets showing the program. They are created by the same equipment that generates most writing seen on television programs. Open-captioned programs became nationally available in the early 1970s when the Caption Center at television station WGBH in Boston began to offer a few open-captioned programs to stations affiliated with the Public Broadcasting Service (PBS). Later, PBS itself added captions to several of its programs. Typically, the first airing of one of these programs was noncaptioned while a subsequent rebroadcast was open-captioned. The general consensus was that the hearing audience would find the captions distracting if they accompanied all broadcasts. In a collaborative effort, *Captioned ABC News*, a late-night rebroadcast of the news program that aired earlier that day on the ABC television network, premiered on a few PBS stations late in 1973, and later was shown nationwide.

When PBS began to broadcast programs with closed captions in 1980, it first reduced, then eliminated, its open-captioned programming. For a while, some programs on PBS were broadcast in both open- and closed-captioned formats, and some individual PBS stations continued this policy for a longer period.

A few open-captioned programs still air on some local stations and regional networks, and educational institutions continue to make open-captioned programs for their own use.

CLOSED CAPTIONS

Closed captions appear only on televisions that are specially equipped to receive them. They are invisible (or closed) on sets lacking this equipment. The technology uses that part of the television signal that appears as a black bar which rolls up or down the television screen when the set is not properly adjusted. This black bar, the vertical blanking interval, consists of 21 lines. (The television signal, on American television, is made up of 525 lines, including both the picture and the vertical blanking interval.) Digital information placed (or encoded) on one or more of these 21 lines can be transmitted to television receivers where it is interpreted (or decoded) and displayed on the television screen.

Line 21 System In December 1971 the National Bureau of Standards, in cooperation with ABC television, demonstrated that this technology could be used to provide captioning. About a year later, PBS, under a contract from the Bureau of Education for the Handicapped, then part of the Department of Health, Education and Welfare, began work to make the technology practical. The system that was developed used only the twenty-first line of the vertical blanking interval (the bottommost line of the

black bar) for closing captioning. Thus, it is known as the Line 21 system.

A closed-captioned program is broadcast in the same way any other program is broadcast, except special caption codes are added to line 21. In a noncaptioned program, there are no such codes on this line. A decoder attached to the television reads the codes, creates the captions, and superimposes them on the television screen. Without a decoder, or if the decoder is turned off, there is no way for the television set to interpret the codes, and the captions do not appear.

The nationwide closed-captioning service began in March 1980 with programs on ABC, NBC, and PBS. The captioning work was performed by the newly founded National Captioning Institute (NCI). Since that time, the number of closed-captioned program hours has significantly increased, and closed captions have even been added to videocassettes for home use. CBS began showing some of its programs with line 21 closed captions in 1984. *See* NATIONAL CAPTIONING INSTITUTE.

The line 21 system is capable of giving the viewer a choice between two types of captions during a single program (such as two different languages), though this feature so far has been used infrequently. Also, the system may provide full-screen text information. A viewer may switch the decoder to "text," and the television picture is replaced by written material (news summaries, program information, and so on) which scrolls up the screen. The viewer has a choice of two text channels.

Teletext Closed captions are also broadcast on a system known as teletext, for which a separate decoder is needed. Teletext works in much the same way as the line 21 system, but it uses several lines of the vertical blanking interval, not just one. In appearance, teletext captions are similar to line 21 captions, but the captions may appear in either of two type sizes. In addition, special symbols (called icons) may be employed to indicate sound effects, such as a small telephone to signify that a telephone is ringing.

The text capabilities of teletext are more elaborate than those of the line 21 system. Teletext offers several hundred "pages" of information which can be selected individually by the viewer and which do not move up the screen.

There are several different teletext systems. In the United States, CBS has adopted the NABTS (North American Basic Teletext Specification) system for both text services and captioning. Only CBS has broadcast teletext captions. NABTS teletext decoders became available, with extremely limited distribution, in 1984, and the audience for teletext captioning has been quite small so far. Given current technology, teletext cannot be used with home video recorders, and it requires excellent television reception in order to work properly. In the fall of 1984 CBS began to offer dual-mode captioning, broadcasting each captioned program with both line 21 and teletext captions.

CAPTION CONTENT

Captions on nationally broadcast television programs today are usually edited to control the speed at which they appear. Captions for most programs are presented at a rate of about 120 words per minute, though for some children's programs the rate may be lower.

In the case of live programming, there is usually little or no time available to edit the captions, so they are verbatim—that is, word for word—or nearly so, and may appear at a faster rate.

Captions may be edited by eliminating words that the captioner feels are not essential to the meaning of an utterance, restructuring the sentence in a more compact form, or sometimes adjusting vocabulary not to exceed that of a certain school grade level.

CAPTION PRESENTATION

Captions, whether open or closed, may appear in two basic forms, roll-up and pop-on. Roll-up captions are in continuous motion, the words actually being written out letter by letter on the screen. To make room for a new line of type, the top line disappears, each remaining line moves up, and a new line forms on the bottom. Roll-up captions have been used, in particular, for news and live events where caption editing is not possible.

A pop-on caption remains on the screen for a short time and is instantly replaced by any following caption. Pop-on captions appear in different parts of the screen, normally to identify who is speaking.

Teletext captions may appear in yet another fashion. They may be quickly written out, letter by letter, until the caption is complete, remain on the screen for a while, then disappear, to be replaced by the following caption, which takes form in the same manner.

TYPES OF CAPTIONING

Depending on the nature of the program, any of several procedures may be used to create captions.

Prerecorded Captions For programs on videotape, captions are normally prepared ahead of time and made part of that tape. Thus, whenever the tape is broadcast, the captions are broadcast as well.

To create prerecorded captions, after viewing and listening to a videotape of the program, a captioner writes the captions and types them into a computer, along with information about when each one should appear and disappear, where it should appear on the screen, and so on. After proofreading, the captions are made part of a videotape by playing a tape of the program on one machine, the captions on another, and recording a new tape which contains the audio and video of the program along with the captions.

Live-Display Captions Sometimes it is possible to prepare captions in advance, but not possible to add them to the videotape. This is the case, for example, with live television programs for which a script is available, such as a presidential address.

Live-display captions are typed into a computer and stored. Later, when the program is broadcast, a captioner sends the captions from the computer to a device that adds them to the television signal.

Real-Time Captions For live programs for which no script is available, such as news conferences and some special events, captions may be created as the program is actually being broadcast. Such captions are written on a stenotype machine such as is used by court reporters to record legal proceedings. The operator of the stenotype machine, or shorthand reporter, does not spell out each word letter by letter but uses a special shorthand system. A computer converts the shorthand into regular English words and organizes the words into captions. Then, as with live-display captions, the captions are sent to a device that adds them to the television signal.

There is a delay of a few seconds between the time a word is uttered and the time it appears in a caption. This is caused in part because the shorthand reporter cannot enter the word until after it is spoken, and in part because the computer needs a certain amount of time to operate. To diminish the delay somewhat, real-time captions are always roll-up captions. This allows each word to appear on the screen as quickly as possible. Because they are created live, real-time captions are close to verbatim rather than edited, and thus appear at a somewhat faster rate. Also, since there is no way to proofread real-time captions before they are broadcast, they occasionally contain errors.

Commentary Captions For some sports programming, captions have been used that give information about an event but do not follow the program audio. Such captions give play-by-play, scoreboard, and background information. For the last, the captions are prepared in advance in the manner of live-display captions. For play-by-play and scoreboard captions, the information is entered into a computer when a play occurs (such as "out 3"), and the computer generates the exact phrasing of the caption (such as "That's the third out and the Yankees are up next.").

Combination of Types For some programs, several different types of captions may be used. In a news program, for example, those portions for which a script is available or which can be previewed are usually captioned with the live-display method, while those portions for which no script is available are captioned with the real-time method.

Bibliography

Block, M., and M. Okrand: "Real-Time Closed-Captioned Television as an Educational Tool," *American Annals of the Deaf*, vol. 128, no. 5, September 1983.

Braverman, B., and B. J. Cronin (eds.): *Captioning: Shared Perspectives*, 1980.

Cronin, B. J.: "Closed-Captioned Television: Today and Tomorrow," *American Annals of the Deaf*, vol. 125, no. 6, September 1980.

Hutchins, J.: "Real Time Closed Captioning at NCI," *Broadcast Engineering*, vol. 25, no. 5, May 1983.

Marc Okrand

TELECOMMUNICATIONS FOR THE DEAF, INC.

The irony of Alexander Graham Bell inventing a device to aid deaf people that developed into the telephone and placed them at great social and economic disadvantage was somewhat alleviated in 1964 by the invention of the acoustic coupler. Robert Weitbrecht, a deaf engineer, conceived of the system that enabled deaf people to use the telephone, though requiring a complex arrangement of equipment. Originally the set-up utilized teletypewriters (TTYs) and later more sophisticated electronic instruments generically referred to as telecommunication devices for the deaf (TDDs) to generate audible signals that were transmitted by the telephone lines via the acoustic coupler. *See* BELL, ALEXANDER GRAHAM.

The TTYs were originally obsolete equipment donated by American Telephone and Telegraph (AT&T) to deaf people. A means had to be found to distribute the surplus TTYs equitably and to service them efficiently. Volunteer efforts, such as had been given by AT&T's Telephone Pioneers (service personnel who contribute their time for community projects), could not adequately meet the demands from the deaf consumers, and the resulting unfilled needs led to the founding of Teletypewriters for the Deaf Distribution Committee in 1968. It then became Teletypewriters for the Deaf, Inc. In 1979 the organization changed its name to Telecommunications for the Deaf, Inc., reflecting the altered electronic state of the art while retaining the organization's well-known acronym—TDI.

TDI emerged as a result of the joint efforts of the National Association of the Deaf (NAD) and the Alexander Graham Bell Association for the Deaf (AGBAD). The two associations worked through a committee that was headed by the National Association of the Deaf's Jess Smith and the Bell Association's Latham Breunig. The latter was the first chairperson of the Oral Deaf Adult Section of the Bell Association, a division formed in 1964 to give greater visibility to its deaf members. Together, the two leaders established TDI as a membership organization. First chartered in Smith's home state of Indiana as a nonprofit corporation, TDI moved to Washington, D.C., in 1975, initially into the Bell Association's headquarters, then in 1978 into Halex House, the building owned by the National Associaiton of the Deaf. *See* ALEXANDER GRAHAM BELL ASSOCIATION FOR THE DEAF; BREUNIG, H. LATHAM; NATIONAL ASSOCIATION OF THE DEAF.

PURPOSES

The original purpose of TDI was to coordinate the acquisition and distribution of surplus teletypewriters to deaf people. To that has been added 13 objectives: to establish compatibility standards for TDDs, to work with government agencies and legislative bodies on TDD matters, to encourage installations of TDDs in public places, to answer inquiries from individuals and organizations on TDD matters, to publish an annual directory and newsletters, to sponsor a biennial convention of members and interested friends, to encourage the use of computer communications, to bridge the gap between existing Baudot (five-level) and upcoming ASCII (eight-level) devices, to set up product evaluation guidelines, to oversee functions of agents, to advise manufacturers and electronic engineering personnel on TDD matters, to deal with captioning on the line 21, Teletext, and cable TV systems, and to sell special devices at reduced prices.

ACTIVITIES

As a membership organization, TDI maintains a roster of those who have joined, out of which has grown the *International Telephone Directory of the Deaf (ITDD)*. This document provides names and addresses of people who have TDDs, listed geographically and by type of installation (residential, business, governmental, and so on). The directory also contains the TDD numbers for national organizations of and for deaf people, social clubs, listings for emergency and travel information, key federal government agencies, medical, legal, and interpreter services, hotlines, news and electronic message systems, alcohol treatment and counseling facilities, financial and real estate brokers, public utilities, TDD sales representatives, relay and answering services, and toll-free TDD numbers. The lists are updated annually.

The directory carries a few TDD listings from Canada, France, Israel, New Zealand, South Africa, and the United Kingdom. TDI also has been involved in international communication: it participated in the first intercontinental TDD call (between the United States and the Philippine Islands) in 1970, and the first transatlantic call (between the United States and England) in 1975.

The directory contains yellow pages that feature advertisements of goods and services directed solely to deaf consumers. While other publications by deaf organizations have a few commercial advertisements designed to sell things to deaf persons, no other publication has them to the extent found in the directory.

Publications   Since 1970 TDI has distributed a newsletter called *GA-SK* (the abbreviations of "go ahead" and "stop keying" used to initiate and terminate TDD conversations) to all subscribers to the directory. It is published quarterly and contains information of interest to deaf persons, particularly TDD users. TDI also publishes materials directly relevant to their purposes. In 1974 it sponsored and distributed *Teletypewriters Made Easy*, a booklet instructing agents and service personnel on how to rewire, clean, and adjust TTYs.

Conventions   TDI also holds biennial conventions. The first TDI national meeting was held in Chicago in 1974; since 1977 conventions have been held every two years. They bring together the members and representatives of electronic manufacturers who have an opportunity to gain first-hand reactions to their products, while the consumers are able to become acquainted with and compare the full array of available equipment. In addition, lectures and discussion groups enable the participants to update their information about matters of concern to deaf users of electronic equipment, especially in the regulatory arena. Such factors as the breakup of AT&T are of great consequence to TDI and its constituents. The conventions also provide the occasion to present the H. Latham Breunig Humanitarian Award to a distinguished deaf person who has made major contributions to the welfare of the Deaf Community. Among those honored have been Gordon L. Allen of Minneapolis, Minnesota, in 1979, Paul Taylor of Rochester, New York, in 1981, Lester Zimet, also of Rochester, in 1983, and Robert W. McClintock of St. Augustine, Florida, in 1985. The first recipient of the award was H. Latham Breunig in 1977, and it has borne his name since then.

Electronic Communications   TDI has taken a leadership role in securing governmental actions to improve electronic communications for deaf persons and, at the same time, to reduce the costs that they must bear. As the supply of surplus TTYs has been exhausted, deaf persons who desire TDDs have been forced to purchase commercially available equipment, often at five and more times the cost of the donated machines. This change in the market has placed increasing burdens on TDI to work with manufacturers and consumers to improve the quality of equipment, lower its initial cost, and reduce its operating and maintenance costs. One strategy favored by TDI is for the states to provide deaf persons with TDDs at either no cost or for a modest annual fee. In 1980 California made TDDs available without charge to its deaf citizens. In 1983, Connecticut became the second state to distribute TDDs at no initial cost to deaf persons. Another approach that TDI has been fostering is to make more TDDs available in public places, much as telephones are now placed. TDI also urges that more government agencies have TDDs, so that deaf persons can contact them. Especially needed are TDDs in public transportation facilities. *See* STATE STATUTES.

TDI has joined with various states to secure special long-distance telephone rates for TDDs. Twelve states made such concessions to deaf TDD customers in 1980, and 30 more followed suit in the next year. AT&T filed with the Federal Communications Commission to develop uniform tarrifs throughout its jurisdictions. In those regions not served by AT&T, TDI offered to work directly with the independent telephone companies.

Following representations by TDI and other deaf consumer organizations, the Internal Revenue Service ruled in 1971 that deaf taxpayers may deduct the cost of TDDs as a medical expense. That ruling, while favorable, does not have the tax benefits that would accrue if the costs of TDDs could be deducted against income because IRS regulations attenuate the deductions for medical expenses. *See* INTERNAL REVENUE CODE.

In 1977, with the urging of TDI, AT&T agreed to review the needs of handicapped telephone users. That same year saw the inception of a radio-TDD center in Philadelphia. A subcarrier on a radio frequency was used to transmit signals that drove specially equipped TDDs in the same way that an acoustic signal sent over a telephone line did. The Philadelphia experiment lasted a little over four years, during which time it did not capture much interest outside of that city. The AT&T study has resulted in the company installing TDD operators to service long-distance calls by deaf customers. However, the dissolution of AT&T has created new difficulties for TDI because it must now deal with many companies in order to secure services and reduced rates for deaf persons.

Computer Network   TDI has participated in experimentation to integrate computers into TDDs. One such effort was Project Deafnet that TDI undertook to implement in the Washington, D.C., area in 1980 for Stanford Research International, which had been funded for that research by the Department of Education. As a result of that and related studies, deaf people can expect to benefit from the development of electronic mail, the use of computers to store messages that can be retrieved at will by those who are addressed. TDI has also worked with others (for example, Amateur Radio Research and Development Corporation) to advance technology and develop standards for TDDs. A serious constraint on the integration of TTYs into the computer network is that they use different electronic codes. As an accommodation to the telephone company, which was concerned about devices that might interfere with telephone service, Weitbrecht designed the acoustic coupler to use Baudot, an electronic code that has now been superseded by the much faster ASCII code. All modern computers "talk" to each other in ASCII, not Baudot. The equipment used by deaf people, therefore, is not compatible, and deaf people cannot purchase computer terminals for use in communicating with other deaf people or with computer centers. TDI has been addressing this problem and is seeking solutions such as urging manufacturers to provide both codes on the TDDs they are now building so that users can switch from Baudot to ASCII without buying new equipment.

Telecommunication Devices From TTYs, TDI has broadened its products to embrace any device that is intended to give deaf persons access to telecommunications. Among the products that TDI markets in addition to telephonic aids are telecaption decoders and Braille teletypewriters. The latter were first made available for deaf-blind persons in 1974. With respect to the former, the National Captioning Institute has acknowledged TDI to be the leading organizational distributor of telecaption adapters. Almost all of the sales of the devices marketed by TDI are discounted in keeping with TDI's objectives to encourage the use of TDDs by deaf people and to sell special devices at reduced prices. *See* NATIONAL CAPTIONING INSTITUTE; TELECOMMUNICATIONS.

GOVERNANCE AND MEMBERSHIP

Latham Breunig was the first executive director of TDI. Since he stepped down from this position in 1979, his successors have all been, like him, deaf persons with professional-managerial backgrounds. The executive director serves with the approval of the TDI board, which is made up of a president, vice-president, secretary-treasurer, and nine directors, each representing one of the regions of the United States. Prior to 1973 the board consisted of only three members. TDI had established an ad hoc committee to study its reorganization in 1972, and the committee recommended including the directors.

While the majority of the members are deaf consumers, TDI also accepts TDD dealers and hearing persons as members. Dealers, manufacturers of electronic equipment, and others are also encouraged to make tax-deductible contributions to TDI. TDI has agents in 38 states and Canada who sell

and repair TDDs and provide it with some modest income to help the organization defray its operating expenses. TDI is a tax-exempt, nonprofit corporation.

For administrative purposes, TDI divides the United States into nine regions; each region elects one director to the board of TDI. In addition, TDI has chapters in 24 states and cities (listed in order of establishment): Georgia, Minnesota, Florida, Arizona, Des Moines, Missouri-Kansas, Rochester (New York), Delaware Valley, Mobile Bay (Alabama), Wisconsin, New York–New Jersey, Central Illinois, Chicago, Syracuse, St. Louis, Mid-Kansas, Frederick (Maryland), Southeast Texas, Jefferson County (Alabama), Acadiana (Louisiana), Fones (Washington), Cincinnati, Ohio, and Northeast Louisiana. Through these individual chapters, TDI can provide immediate contact with a sizable proportion of the TDI membership. Such easy access by deaf persons to the organization accounts in part for the fact that TDI is now one of the three largest membership groups of deaf people in the United States.

Jerome D. Schein

TELEVISION AND MOTION PICTURES

The years since 1970 have seen a phenomenal increase in the influence of deaf people on motion pictures and television. To better understand the impact of deaf participants and spectators on these media, a simple model of television and film communication with three parts must be considered: (1) a subject to be transmitted, such as a story, play, or nonfiction presentation; (2) a transmitting medium, such as broadcast or cable television, home video equipment, or movies at the theater; and (3) an audience that receives the transmission. With their cultural perspective based on American Sign Language, deaf people have transformed the formerly hearing model of television and film communication. *See* SIGN LANGUAGES: American.

For example, the films of Peter Wolf and productions by such groups as DEAF Media, Silent Network, and Beyond Sound, and the addition of deaf characters to hearing television programs and films, have generated a deaf perspective. The addition of captioning and sign language interpreting, as well as the presentation of sign language versions of musical and dramatic entertainment, have transformed a medium previously based on the spoken word. As a result, the audience has expanded to include deaf spectators. *See* WOLF, PETER.

This section will explore three major types of television and film programs that appear to be the most developed at present: (1) Deaf Access Programming—a hearing program is made accessible to deaf audiences by adding captions or sign language to the medium. (2) Deaf-Hearing Cross-Cultural Programming—a cross-cultural program dealing with deaf and hearing relationships is transmitted through a mixed medium to a primarily hearing audience (although the addition of closed captions in recent times has allowed access to deaf people). (3) Deaf Cultural Programming—the program is developed from a deaf cultural perspective and transmitted primarily through American Sign Language with voice narration to audiences of deaf and hearing people.

Deaf Access Programming

This can take the form of captioned films, captioned television, signed or interpreted programs, or signed performances of songs and plays.

CAPTIONED FILMS

The early silent films with their exaggerated gestures and intertitles (separate title cards that displayed information and dialogue) were accessible to deaf and hearing audiences alike until the introduction of sound in 1926 shut the door of the movie industry on the deaf community. Even desperate measures such as plot summaries in the *Silent Worker* or efforts by hearing friends, such as the Reverend C. Roland Gerhold who interpreted a showing of *The Ten Commandments* using white phosphorescent gloves in the darkened theater, were at best stopgap measures that could not satisfy the needs of deaf people.

In 1947 Emerson Romero, a deaf Cuban actor who had performed in several silent movies, purchased a number of sound films, spliced in intertitle cards for the dialogue, and rented them out to deaf clubs, churches, and other organizations. While this method lengthened the film considerably, it led to efforts three years later by the Conference of Executives of American Schools for the Deaf to set up a similar library of films for deaf people, this time with the captions superimposed on the film scenes. When the library project proved too expensive to operate, the conference turned to the federal government, and in 1958, with the support of the National Association of the Deaf, the Alexander Graham Bell Association of the Deaf, the Vocational Rehabilitation Administration, and other organizations, Congress passed Public Law 85-905, which established Captioned Films for the Deaf as a federal program. *See* ALEXANDER GRAHAM BELL ASSOCIATION FOR THE DEAF; NATIONAL ASSOCIATION OF THE DEAF.

Under the leadership first of John Gough, then Gilbert Delgado and Malcolm Norwood (who is himself deaf), Captioned Films expanded and diversified its operations. By 1976 it maintained three distribution centers that loaned out approximately 500 feature films to schools, clubs, churches, and other organizations. It also operated more than 50 depositories for almost 800 educational films and funded numerous programs including four regional media centers for training and production of new educational materials. During 1975–1976, almost 5000 groups representing 1.7 million deaf people made use of the services of Captioned Films for the Deaf. The program was so successful that the federal government expanded the role of this agency to include other disabilities and changed its title to Media Services and Captioned Films Branch.

CAPTIONED TELEVISION

The efforts of Malcolm Norwood and Media Services and Captioned Films Branch to create captioned television programming ran into problems: (1) Unlike film, television was broadcast to a wide audience of deaf and hearing people. (2) Studies had shown that a significant number of hearing viewers reacted negatively to captions, and broadcasters were reluctant to risk loss of advertising revenue caused by lowered ratings. (3) The sheer volume of broadcast programming and the need to quickly caption individual programs was overwhelming compared to the relatively small numbers and slower turnaround time of captioned films.

A period of experimentation and research resulted in two solutions to these problems. First, open captions were displayed directly with the program material and were visible to all viewers. To counter negative reactions from hearing viewers, this system was used with programs that were aired more than once a week on the Public Broadcast System (PBS) network, giving viewers a choice of a captioned and noncaptioned version of the same program. Second, closed captions were hidden within the broadcast signal and visible only to people who had a special device to decode the signal.

In Boston, television station WGBH led the way when it open-captioned several segments of *The French Chef* in 1972 with funding from Media Services and Captioned Films. This was followed by an open-captioned version of President Nixon's Inaugural Address in 1973. The success of these two ventures led to funding and development of an ambitious project: the broadcast of the *Captioned ABC News* weekdays on the PBS network. An extraordinary level of speed and coordination were required to begin this series in December 1973. Each program was taped from the ABC system at 6:30 P.M., the narrative was reedited to a sixth-grade reading level and shortened to fit time and space limitations, captions were prepared from the edited narrative and fed into the videotape, and special filler material was inserted to take the place of advertisements. All had to be completed in time for rebroadcast at 10:30 or 11:00 that same evening. Syndication of the *Captioned ABC News* by as many as 120 stations in 1976 opened up news coverage to deaf people in almost every major city. With the success of this program, WGBH expanded its captioning operations to include "The First Signs of Washoe" from the *NOVA* series, two half-hour reports on the Eighth World Winter Games of the Deaf, and such regular programs as *The Adams Chronicles* and *Zoom*.

Because the open-caption system was only feasible for programs aired more than once a week on the PBS network, Media Services and Captioned Films and PBS continued their research and development of a closed-captioning system. From 1970 to 1976, they established the feasibility of encoding the captions on the twenty-first line of the standard 525-line grid on American televisions. Although this line would be masked by the frame of a regular television receiver, a special decoder could be used to convert the information on the line into readable captions. In 1976 the Federal Communications Commission agreed to reserve line 21 to be used for captions for deaf people. That same year, the National Captioning Institute was established with funding support from the Department of Health, Education and Welfare. Its purpose was to caption programs using line 21 technology that would then be decoded by special devices. Of the four major networks, ABC, NBC, and PBS agreed to sponsor up to 20 hours of captioning per week. By early 1980, closed captioning for deaf people had become a reality.

The increasing prime-time captioned programming and advanced techniques enabled the National Captioning Institute (NCI) to create real-time captioning. On October 11, 1982, captions were added to *ABC'S World News Tonight* after only a few seconds of delay. NCI had developed a system by which a court stenographer, listening to the newscasters, typed a shorthand version of the narration which was then converted by a computer into captioned text. It became possible to live-caption news programs and special events. *See* NATIONAL CAPTIONING INSTITUTE.

The single hold-out to the line 21 captioning system was CBS, which went ahead with its own captioning system, called Teletext. Already widely used in Europe, Teletext made use of a different portion of the broadcast signal and offered not only captions but as many as 100 pages of textual information which could be called up by a calculator-like device. Since Teletext could offer up-to-the-minute information about news, weather, sports, freeway conditions, and so on, CBS felt that it could be marketed to a much larger group of consumers than the line 21 decoders, and at a much lower cost. There were some drawbacks to the system,

especially the fact that captions could not be recorded on home video recorders (VCRs).

The decision by CBS to pursue an alternative closed-captioning system and to delay transmission of captioning generated a great deal of controversy and several demonstrations sponsored by groups such as the National Association of the Deaf. The confusion also caused NBC to withdraw much of its support for the line 21 system, forcing NCI to obtain funding for captioned NBC programs from nonnetwork sources. Eventually a dual-mode system, compatible with both Teletext and line 21 decoders, was developed, and promises to resolve some of the conflicts between the two systems. *See* TELECOMMUNICATIONS: Captioned Television.

SIGNED OR INTERPRETED PROGRAMS
The use of sign language through interpreting or direct presentation has provided another means of making television accessible to deaf people, particularly for locally produced news programs. The tradition for interpreted news programs began in May 1959, when John Tubergen, who was concerned about lack of warnings for deaf people during emergencies, persuaded Zenith television and later NBC to sponsor a five-minute interpreted version of the news. It was not until the 1970s, however, that this type of program became more widely accepted.

One stimulus for this acceptance was *Newsign 4* of KRON-TV in San Francisco, a direct presentation of the news in sign language by two deaf newscasters, Jane Norman and Peter Wolf, with the assistance of off-camera narrators. The five-minute program, broadcast each weekday morning, consisted of a summary of the current news along with special items of interest to the deaf community. As the first program to present news directly in American Sign Language rather than by means of an interpreter, it won an Emmy Award and inspired several other deaf people to establish their own news programs. In Los Angeles, Gregg Brooks used a similar format to establish *Deaf Community News* on Theta Cable, and his program also won an Emmy. In Washington, Cynthia Saltzman opened an early morning news program each weekday, and Tim Medina inaugurated *Total Communication News*. Medina's show was unusual in that he both signed and spoke for himself and also added special visual and graphic displays in line with a total approach. In Portland, Oregon, Henry Stack presented a five-minute news program. The response to the pioneering efforts of these deaf newscasters was an increase in interpreted programming across the country until, in 1977, a survey reported a total of 43 weekday news programs that provided signed interpretation or presentation. However, with the wearing off of the novelty of these programs and the increasing reliance on captioning, all of the deaf newscasters were cut from the schedule, as were many interpreted news segments.

Nonnews programs have also experimented with the use of sign language interpreters, although captioning has proven a far more popular alternative. *Watch Your Child/The Me Too Show*, a daily television program of activities for children, featured Maureen Collins, a 16-year-old deaf student, in a corner insert as the interpreter. Religious programs such as *Light unto My Path*, Jerry Falwell's *Old Time Gospel Hour*, and *Christopher Close-up*, a Christian-oriented talk show, all feature sign language interpreters inserted on the screen. It is much cheaper to use an interpreter than it is to caption a program, but captions provide access to a larger group of hearing-impaired peopel, some of whom are not familiar with sign language.

Signed Performances of Songs and Plays

With the establishment of professional sign language theaters such as the National Theatre of the Deaf and the Fairmount Theatre of the Deaf and the increasing popularity of sign language as an artistic medium, television has made theatrical works and musical entertainment accessible to deaf people through performance in sign language. Programs in this category differ from deaf cultural programming in that the material presented is based on theatrical or musical entertainment for hearing people. There is little effort to add a deaf cultural element other than the fact that sign language is used—and the signing itself is often Pidgin Sign English rather than American Sign Language. *See* Fairmount Theatre of the Deaf; National Theaters of the Deaf: United States.

Probably the earliest example of a signed performance of muscial entertainment was *Rock Gospel*, aired in Washington, D.C., during Christmas 1973. An all-hearing group of performers signed religious songs to the music of a live band, the Sons of Thunder. The popularity of this entertainment medium led several hearing-impaired groups to stage their own versions of musical entertainment. One popular show of this type was *Good Vibrations*, staged by the Hughes Memorial Theatre in Washington. The deaf director of this group, Cynthia Saltzman, later collaborated with Stephen Howard to produce an Emmy Award–winning program, *Song, Sung, Signed*, aired in 1974. This program experimented with video effects, which enhanced the artistry of the signed presentation. Several performers from this pioneering show went on to professional work in television and theater, including Rita and Ed Corey, who, with Bob Hilterman, formed *Musign* 10 years later and taped a series of song-interpreting programs with Silent Network Productions.

Theater groups have also been able to share their works through television. The National Theatre of the Deaf had several sign language productions broadcast, including *A Child's Christmas in Wales* and the *Festival of Hands* series, with some segments directed by Edmund Waterstreet, who is deaf. The Fairmount Theatre of the Deaf won two Emmys for *Beauty and the Beast* and *The Miser*, the latter scripted by deaf writer Don Bangs. Spectrum: Focus on Deafness, a Texas-based organization of deaf artists, collaborated with a television station to produce an exotic version of *Beauty and the Beast*, originally directed by Elizabeth Quinn, who is deaf. Through the efforts of Richard Gibbe, a hearing producer-director, the signed performances of the all-deaf cast were enhanced by the use of special effects such as glowing hands and mirrors that could sign.

Not only have these programs made musical entertainment and theater accessible to deaf audiences, but they have also expanded the artistic and technical possibilities of American Sign Language as a television and film medium.

Deaf-Hearing Cross-Cultural Programming

The conflicts between deaf people and hearing people who cannot sign have formed the basis for several films and numerous special episodes of regular television series. Unfortunately, in the 1950s and 1960s, because of poor technical advice and because of the need to create a dramatic situation, most of these programs portrayed deaf characters in highly unrealistic and stereotyped ways. These characters were presented as sentimentalized and pathetic figures deserving of the sympathy of a mostly hearing audience. A recurring theme, especially in the films *Johnny Belinda* and *The Heart Is a Lonely Hunter*, is loneliness and isolation. While deaf audiences might sympathize with the frustration of the deaf heroine and hero in their efforts to communicate with hearing people, they would also wonder why the films never bothered to show the existence of a deaf community where the characters could certainly communicate quite comfortably.

In addition to stressing isolation, television programs have also portrayed deafness as an unwanted attribute that is amenable to cure, either by surgery or by development of superhuman lipreading ability skills so that the deaf character meets with a "happily-ever-after" ending. This is contrary to the real world of deaf people, many of whom are not unhappy to remain deaf and who cannot lipread well. *See* Speechreading.

As long as these programs were produced and performed by hearing people, the stereotyping continued despite complaints from deaf community leaders. However, as a result of urgings from the

National Theatre of the Deaf, network film producers began to offer deaf character roles to deaf professional performers. The work of these performers as well as the efforts of deaf technical consultants resulted in more realistic portrayals of deaf characters and situations. Audree Norton, from the National Theatre of the Deaf, was the first deaf person to act on television when she portrayed a deaf character in an episode of *Mannix* in 1968. This was followed by a number of other roles, and Norton and other deaf performers and technical advisers exerted their influence on the deaf image on television. Linda Bove, as the first deaf regular on *Sesame Street*, introduced television audiences to a positive deaf character who interacted effectively with both her hearing and deaf friends. Bove was also the first deaf performer in a daytime soap opera, and her portrayal of a deaf character carried a much greater degree of realism than would have been accomplished otherwise. Bove, Phyllis Frelich, Seymour Bernstein, and Peter Wolf all played deaf characters in situation comedies, offering a badly needed alternative to the recurring tragic view of deaf people found in other programs. *See* Bove, Linda; Frelich, Phyllis.

Perhaps the culmination of this increasingly positive and realistic portrayal of deaf people came in the made-for-TV movie *And Your Name is Jonah*. The movie starred Sally Struthers, young deaf newcomer Jeff Bravin, and a large group of other deaf performers, and had technical assistance from Barnard Bragg and Gregg Brooks. Like many other programs of this genre, the theme was isolation due to deafness. However, it was the hearing protagonist who suffered a greater degree of isolation in her attempts to break through the communication barrier and in her confusion and frustration with an oral education establishment. Her salvation came when she met the deaf parents of one of Jonah's deaf classmates and through them a deaf club and the wider deaf community—the first time such a community had been portrayed on a major network feature film. And it was a young deaf member of that community who pointed the way by teaching Jonah sign language in one of the most moving scenes of the film.

There have been some setbacks in the movement of deaf-hearing cross-cultural programming toward a more positive and realistic deaf portrayal. The film *Voices* cast a deaf character with a hearing performer and lost thousands of dollars in sales as the result of deaf pickets in several cities. Officials of one Academy Awards program were confronted by a group of angry deaf community leaders when it turned out that a group of "deaf" children who sang for the program were actually hearing. But in 1985, with plans underway for the three films *Children of a Lesser God*, Sesame Street's *Follow That Bird*, and Hallmark Hall of Fame's *In This Sign*, all with deaf performers and deaf technical consultants and the third with a deaf executive co-producer, Juliana Fjeld, the future can look forward to a true portrayal of deaf people in their conflicts with the nonsigning majority.

Deaf Cultural Programming

While programming that reflects a deaf cultural perspective has appeared only since the late 1970s, there were several educational programs produced in the 1960s and 1970s that provided some cultural information within the format of an interpreted educational program. *Hearing Eyes*, a weekly program broadcast in 1964 in Oklahoma City, provided information on a variety of subjects of interest to deaf people. Similarly, *Now See This*, a series of 26 programs broadcast in St. Paul, Minnesota, during the 1968–69 season, featured appearances by Bernard Bragg, Francis Crowe of the Minnesota Association of the Deaf, and other deaf professionals and community leaders. *See* Bragg, Bernard.

But deaf cultural programming could not appear until there were deaf producers, writers, and directors to create the television programs and films, and lack of training and opportunities prevented this. Peter Wolf made a breakthrough when he was selected to receive training at Cinemalabs, and from this training he was able to direct the first feature-length films with a deaf cultural perspective, *Deafula* and *Think Me Nothing*. Gregg Brooks was selected as a fellow at American Film Institute, and Don Bangs and Toby Silver completed master's degrees in radio-television-film at the University of Texas. But for most deaf people there were few training opportunities in producing, directing, and writing television and film programs.

To resolve this problem, several training and production organizations were established during the 1970s. New York University sponsored training workshops in several cities in the east in 1973 and also produced, in cooperation with NBC-TV, a 30-minute program series titled *Speaking with Your Hands*, which taught introductory American Sign Language using special topics on deaf culture. At about the same time, the Deaf Media Council, based at the University of Maryland, provided workshops in television production for the deaf community of metropolitan Washington, and these workshops led to the development of a visual intercom system that enabled deaf directors in the studio control room to communicate directly with camera persons, floor managers, and other production people in the studio itself. The system used a camera in the control room that picked up the signed instructions of the director and relayed them to tiny television monitors atop each camera as well as to a floor monitor for other production crew members.

At the same time a floor camera picked up communications from the floor crew and relayed them to the director via a television monitor in the control room. This visual intercom system has been used by other institutions, such as the National Technical Institute for the Deaf and Gallaudet College.

Also in the early 1970s, a group of deaf and hearing people at KCSM-TV in the San Francisco Bay area teamed up to produce a weekly television variety show about deaf people titled *Silent Perspectives*. Using a format of interviews with deaf personalities, the series offered a rich potpourri of deaf cultural information. *Silent Perspectives* won an Emmy in 1975 and led to the formation of Deaf Artistic and Educational Frontiers Media—DEAF Media, Inc., the first production company devoted primarily to deaf cultural programming.

While *Silent Perspectives*, operating entirely through volunteer effort, continued its weekly broadcasts for the next five years, a more ambitious program, *Rainbow's End*, was developed to meet the needs of deaf children. Eight episodes of *Rainbow's End* were produced from 1978 to 1985 by a mostly hearing production crew. Early programs, developed within the setting of a wacky television studio, presented short segments about deaf history, creative uses of American Sign Language, language skills in both English and American Sign Language, and other aspects of deaf culture. Later episodes involved an extended story line that continued the adventures of Supersign, Olivia the Octopus, and other characters that are now a part of deaf children's literature. DEAF Media received Emmys for *Rainbow's End* and for *Eye Music*, a special deaf awareness program, both broadcast by a San Francisco station and the PBS network.

Until 1979 most deaf cultural programs were broadcast through the PBS network or through network affiliates, perhaps because the other broadcast networks felt that such programming was not commercially viable. In 1979 Sheldon Altfeld and Kathleen Gold established Silent Network, a production company that developed deaf community programming aimed at the commercial market. One of its first programs, *The Sign of Our Times*, a sign language entertainment program, generated some interest and support from the networks. Altfeld followed this with several series, including *Say It with Sign*, a sign language teaching series; *Off-Hand*, a deaf talk show featuring Herb Larson and Lou Fant, which won an Emmy Award in 1983; *Handle with Care*, a program series for deaf teenagers, hosted by Kevin Mills and Julianne Gold, which explored issues such as puberty, venereal disease, drugs, pregnancy, lifestyles, and relationships; *Aerobisign* and *Aerobics in Motion*, two exercise

programs employing sign language; and *Its a Good Sign*, a series of short-form programs for teaching sign language to hearing children, which won Silent Network its second Emmy in 1984.

In 1983 Silent Network Satellite Service (SNSS) was launched, and two hours of programming were beamed by satellite all over the country one evening each week. This satellite system created an alternative network for deaf community programming, and it enabled many deaf Americans to view Silent Network's coverage of the World Games for the Deaf, held in Los Angeles in 1985. Silent Network completed taping of more than 300 programs by 1983, and continues to be the leading producer of deaf community and cultural programming.

While these deaf cultural programs provided career opportunities for many deaf performing artists, no training program had yet been developed for deaf professionals on the other side of the cameras, that is, producers, directors, writers, and other technical staff. For this reason, Beyond Sound was established in 1981 to provide professional training, employment opportunities, and production of programs for hearing-impaired people. The two codirectors of this production company, Saul Rubin and Gregg Brooks (Brooks later resigned and was replaced by Larry Fleischer), were themselves hearing-impaired, and the organization has been run by a staff composed almost entirely of hearing-impaired people.

Initially, Beyond Sound developed a training program aimed at developing producers, directors, production managers and assistants, writers, researchers, production crew, editors, and other professionals. More than 50 hearing-impaired and deaf people received training for this program until funding cuts made it necessary to curtail the scope of the program. One feature of the training program was a deaf talent showcase at a local nightclub, The Horn, where deaf performers appeared before an audience of deaf and hearing patrons.

Beyond Sound also conducted two major conferences that examined the role of deaf people in television and film. The first conference brought together leading deaf thinkers and artists from around the state of California to meet with their hearing counterparts. A second conference drew deaf artists from across the country to share their ideas and programs with each other and with a panel of representatives of major television networks and production companies to sensitize them to the needs of deaf people.

With an increasing pool of deaf professionals, Beyond Sound was able to begin producing a weekly half-hour news program, *Beyond Sound News Review* (later called *The World of Beyond Sound*) in 1982. This program presented news through four deaf newscasters along with short interview segments hosted by Gregg Brooks. Beyond Sound also produced three documentaries: *GLAD–By, Of and For Deaf People*, about the Greater Los Angeles Council on Deafness; *Los Angeles Club of the Deaf*, about the history of this organization; and a short feature on the National Theatre of the Deaf. *See* GREATER LOS ANGELES COUNCIL ON DEAFNESS, INC.

In November 1984, Beyond Sound was honored by the city of Los Angeles for producing its one-hundredth program almost entirely by deaf professionals, both in front of and behind the television cameras.

Bibliography

du Monceau, Michael P.: "A Descriptive Study of Television Utilization in Communication and Instruction for the Deaf and Hearing Impaired," dissertation, University of Maryland, 1978.

Gannon, Jack: *Deaf Heritage*, pp. 261, 266–69, 384–89, NAD Publications, Silver Spring, Maryland, 1981.

"Section Updates," *Visual Media*, NAD Publications, 1:1, 1981, and 3:10, 1983.

Don Bangs

Silent Films

The silent film era (1893–1929) represents a benchmark in the cultural history of the American deaf community. Even though the substance of the movies themselves often reflected insensititivity to both deafness and deaf people, as well as to other minorities such as Blacks and Indians, silent films through their technological limitation permitted the hearing and deaf audience to become one. Deaf people watched and participated in the movie theater, with no need for a third-party interpreter, special captions, elaborate sound systems, or other added-on devices. For a comparatively brief time, deaf people could share in a public entertainment event on a nearly equal basis with their hearing peers. However, ever since the industry converted to talking motion pictures, deaf people have not had the same equality of access to this form of entertainment. Thus, the older members of the deaf community view the period from the turn of the century to 1929 as a high point of cultural equality.

The substance of the films, too, was important. Prominent leaders in the deaf community expressed an early interest in the movies and understood their potential importance for education, cultural preservation, and development of public image, in addition to their general entertainment value. Moreover, a few deaf persons saw the burgeoning movie industry as a place of employment.

All of this potential was destroyed when the advent of the talkies in 1929 began to exclude most profoundly hearing-impaired persons from the audience. Thereafter, the deaf community sought alternate forms of entertainment or technological and government aid to bridge the gap created by the demise of silent films.

EDUCATION

Teachers and schools for deaf students quickly recognized the pedagogical value of the visually oriented medium. It might be assumed that the special virtue of silent films was the use of captions, but this is not true. Since silent movie captions were printed in standard English, they were not always effective with poor readers, including large numbers of deaf people. Hearing audiences of the silent films regularly commented upon the good "acting," or lack thereof, of particular actors and actresses. In contrast, deaf audiences of talking motion pictures often comment on the lack of "action," meaning that the films have too much emphais on talking or speech. While the audiences of the silents were commenting upon the regular and expected use of facial and body expressions for communication, this aspect has largely been dropped in favor of speech in today's films. Deaf audiences today simply have accepted action—large motion such as fights, chases, and sight gags—as a poor substitute for the sometimes subtle nuance of, say, a raised eyebrow that was a part of the acting of the silents.

The true value of the silent films was that they tried to tell their story or to make a point visually with little or no dependence on the use of words. When a particular film achieved this level of communication with an audience, it provided a substantial base of information from which a teacher could develop and make a transition to the English language with deaf children. This is why current captioned foreign films are not the equivalent of the old silent films. These foreign films are simply talking movies in another language.

During the heyday of the silents, most profoundly deaf children attended residential schools in their home states. As evidenced by accounts in school newspapers, these schools provided substantial film programs. The published viewing schedules of the films included both educational and entertainment films. Attending film presentations two or three times a week, students would typically see vocationally oriented films on manufacturing and industry. Although newsreels such as *Pathe News* included a great deal of propaganda, especially during World War I, they represented an excellent opportunity for classroom discussions of current events. Appropriate entertainment films would be shown in the evenings or on the weekends. It was common practice for teachers to require students to keep journals about the movies they viewed. School newspapers often included student letters and essays that mentioned movies in their content. With the demise of the silent films in 1929, it would not be until the 1960s that movies again became widely used in educational programs for deaf children through the creation of the federally sponsored captioned films program.

CULTURAL PRESERVATION

The early years of the development of motion pictures coincided with an escalating pedagogical and linguistic controversy which engaged the attention of most deaf citizens. Many hearing educators, termed oralists, were arguing that sign language should be banished from the schools in favor of the exclusive use of speech and speechreading; yet the willingness and ability to use American Sign Language (ASL) was a key test of membership in the American deaf community.

Enraged by this assault on their language, the adult deaf community perceived these oralist educators, who were taking over the administration of schools for deaf students in the United States, as the enemy. Moving pictures became a means of preserving ASL from oralists, who continually counseled the public as well as parents of deaf children that its use would produce "dumb" children who could not function in the real world of speech and hearing. *See* HISTORY: Sign Language Controversy.

Prior to World War I, the chief deaf consumer organization, the National Association of the Deaf (NAD), collected money to create a fund that supported the production of a series of special-purpose films using ASL. These films of plays, poetry, and stories, the earliest of which date back to 1913, were signed by masters of sign language in order to preserve their skills for the future. Through the payment of rental fees, they were then exhibited throughout the United States at local deaf clubs. These films are today maintained at both the Library of Congress and Gallaudet College, in Washington, D.C.

Deaf individuals also used the new film medium to preserve images of life and events in the deaf community. Newspapers in the deaf community routinely reported special shows that featured films of sports contests between deaf schools as well as meetings of state and national organizations of deaf people. After the demise of silent films, some deaf persons produced amateur movies designed for deaf audiences. Only a few of these films still exist, but they represent a valuable resource of the cultural history of deafness.

PUBLIC IMAGE

Although they understood the cultural significance and the community news value of their own ama-

teur films, deaf people continued to look to Hollywood for entertainment. They monitored commercially produced silent films very carefully, and recognizing the importance of public awareness of deafness, they examined the image portrayed when deaf characters did appear in films. Most films that portrayed deafness used the handicap as a gimmick. Typically, a person feigning deafness caught a crook or foiled a villain when the supposedly deaf hero heard a secret message or conversation; or a deaf person fingerspelled a message of help over long distances or with their hands tied behind their back.

Deaf people had mixed reactions to these stereotyped portrayals. Many were simply flattered to see any deaf character portrayed on the screen, but most were disturbed by the blatant inaccuracies. In particular, they viewed the communication issue with increased consternation. Through letters to the editor of local newspapers, deaf writers constantly admonished moviemakers to distinguish between types of deafness: profoundly deaf, postlingually deaf, or hard-of-hearing. Profoundly deaf people endeavored to persuade the general public that the problems of the different hearing-impaired groups were not the same. They viewed negatively oralists' contentions that deaf people could speak and lipread clearly as unrealistic propaganda. Persons who were hard-of-hearing or who became deaf later in life could lipread and speak, but profoundly deaf adults knew that very few of them could speak or lipread with much success. Most deaf persons preferred to communicate with hearing people through the use of notepad and pencil.

The American Film Institute (AFI) catalog of feature films for the period 1921 to 1930 lists 12 films that include deaf-mute characters or deafness. Five scripts include characters who feign deafness or deaf people who are cured, usually by a blow to the head. Two of these films, plus an earlier one, are good examples both of the public image of deafness presented by the silents and of exceptions to it.

The Silent Voice (1915) starred a prominent leading man, Francis X. Bushman, in an adaptation of the Beethoven theme, where a talented musician becomes deafened but continues to write his music. In this version, the hero musician not only adjusts to his hearing loss but then proceeds, unlike the historical Beethoven, to become an expert lipreader. Since the character performed magical feats of lipreading over distances and under conditions that could not be replicated by any real deaf persons, the film resulted in negative commentary in deaf community publications. Alexander Pach, a prominent art critic for a national deaf magazine, the *Silent Worker*, dismissed the movie as ridiculous. Unfortunately, the obscenity factor clouded the lipreading controversy. In the early period of silent films, some actors jokingly mouthed obscenities on the assumption that their audiences would not understand. But some hearing-impaired persons could interpret them and reported the utterances to the newspapers. It is ironic that those deaf persons who can lipread seem to have particular success with obscene words. Unfortunately, repeated episodes of lipread obscenities reinforced the public view that most deaf people were expert lipreaders. Shortly before World War I, the Board of National Moving Picture Film Censors responded to the obscenity controversy by selecting an expert lipreader to monitor the movies regularly. It was even more ironic that the board's choice for an expert lipreader was a hearing woman, opera singer Irene Langford. *See* BEETHOVEN, LUDWIG VAN.

When the industry converted to talking pictures in 1929–1930, the deaf community pointed to their inability to lipread as an argument for the continuation of captions. Even those who opposed the use of sign language came to the aid of deaf people on this issue. The national conference of Superintendents of Schools for the Deaf established a committee to obtain captions. Oral deaf adults who opposed ASL joined the fray, and in 1929 the speechreading club of Philadelphia organized a limited effort by clubs of hard-of-hearing persons to protest the talkies. Petitioners requested the use of captions. In contrast, sound engineers of the day reported that only a comparatively few number of deaf persons could not hear or benefit from the new talkies. Even though amplification through the use of individual headsets never developed into general use, a few of the new talking movie theaters used them and invited both blind and hearing-impaired patrons to attend well-publicized events. Hence, for reasons of economy and technology, Hollywood did not take the complaints seriously and the petitions did not succeed with the film producers. Subsequent talking pictures also continued to feature the fantastic lipreading skills so graphically but erroneously portrayed in *The Silent Voice*.

A second film, *Bits of Life* (1921), was an exception to most of the films described in the AFI catalog. Although there are no known surviving copies of this film, there is a synopsis of the script in the catalog. In addition, there are publicity still-photographs from the film at the archives of the Eastman House in Rochester, New York. The script develops the theme of the good samaritan gone wrong and includes several discrete episodes with separate casts. One of the episodes includes a deaf character who is helped to hear through an assistance device given to him by a good samaritan. The deaf character is a self-employed barber who is happily

married and surrounded by good friends. Once cured, he discovers through his ability to hear that his wife has been unfaithful and that his friends are villains. In anger, he throws away his assistance device and becomes deaf again and presumably happy.

When one understands that most deaf persons are well adjusted to their deafness and do not want to be cured and that early hearing aids for hard-of-hearing individuals were cumbersome and considered to be an anathema by most profoundly deaf persons, the realistic deaf perspective of the film is clear. However, it is improbable that hearing people in the audience would be sensitive to it. More puzzling is the question of how this particular perspective came to be incorporated in the film. The explanation is most clearly attributable to the presence of Lon Chaney.

Chaney was a member of the cast in one of the other episodes of *Bits of Life*. Since both of his parents were deaf, Chaney was fluent in ASL and privy to the attitudes of deaf people. Also, his father had been a barber. The fact that Chaney was a popular Hollywood star and thus able to influence the story provides strong circumstantial evidence of why *Bits of Life* was the only film of the 12 films listed in the AFI catalog to include a deaf perspective.

The third film, *You'd Be Surprised* (1926), was also an exception to the usual stereotypes, but for different reasons. A well-known comedy star, Raymond Griffith, played the lead role of a coroner who investigates the theft of a diamond necklace and two accompanying murders. Central to the plot is the presence of a deaf-mute servant who witnesses the crime and contributes to the climax of the film when he turns out to be the coroner's hearing deputy, feigning deafness in order to capture the murderer. The film received positive reviews in the *New York Times*, which commented favorably on the deaf-mute concept. This film has been preserved and is a part of the AFI collection at the Library of Congress.

The film is unique because a deaf person, Granville Redmond, actually played the role of the supposedly deaf-mute character. The script is also unique because both Redmond and Griffith communicated through the use of fingerspelling and occasional signs. The few signs that appear, such as break, swear, who, and deaf, are used correctly, and while one would expect the deaf man, Redmond, to fingerspell well, the hearing actor, Griffith, also does a credible job with his fingerspelling. In fact, there are some fingerspelling scenes without captions that can only be understood by a deaf audience. Unfortunately, the film also portrayed some of the stereotypical features. For example, Griffith shoots off a gun behind Redmond's head as a test of deafness. Unlike the real deaf person that he is, who would have felt the shot blast, Redmond makes no response and thus convinces everyone that he is deaf. *See* REDMOND, GRANVILLE.

There are several sight gags that take advantage of the deafness motif. In one, Redmond fingerspells "I saw it," but the caption reads, "He saw everything from the skylight and wore out three fingers yelling for help." In another, Griffith fingerspells his summary of the crime to a jury while he simultaneously consumes a hotdog with mustard and sauerkraut and drinks from a bottle of milk. In another, the murder suspect confesses when he is confronted by the now hearing Redmond who has feigned deafness; in the scene, Redmond mouths "Did you call me, chief?" to a hearing person.

Given that Redmond was a character actor with only limited influence, and the desire for sight gags, it is not surprising that the stereotypes persisted even with the presence of a deaf actor. It is also consistent with the treatment of other minorities in the films of the day. The fact that in the film Redmond was able to get some accurate information, primarily through correct fingerspelling and signs, represented a tremendous achievement for the period. Other than the two films linked to Lon Chaney or Granville Redmond, the deaf characters and deafness depicted in the movies were the result of hearing persons unfamiliar with or insensitive to the deaf community.

DEAF ACTORS

Granville Redmond was not the only deaf person to appear in silents. Brief descriptions of the achievements of other deaf actors appeared in newspapers and magazines from the deaf community in the 1920s, such as the *Deaf Mutes Journal*, *Silent Worker*, and the *California News*. In addition to Redmond, they included Emerson Romero (stage name Tommy Albert), Louis Weinberg (stage name David Marvel), Carmen de Arcos, and Albert Ballin.

Granville Redmond played small roles in *A Dog's Life* (1918), *A Day's Pleasure* (1919), *The Kid* (1921), and *A Woman of Paris* (1923), all with Charles Chaplin, in *The Three Musketeers* (1921) with Douglas Fairbanks, and in *He's a Prince* (1925) and *You'd Be Surprised* (1926) with Raymond Griffith. Profoundly deaf, Redmond graduated from the state residential school in Berkeley, California, where he had studied art. Later, achieving prominence as a landscape artist, he became well known in the California art community. Several contemporary accounts identified Redmond further as a nonspeaking deaf person who was a master of sign language. Initially, he took part in some amateur films produced by the Bohemian Club in San Francisco, where he was brought to the attention of Chaplin. Chaplin then hired the deaf artist and provided him with studio space to paint at his movie lot in Hollywood. There is no direct explanation of why Chaplin kept Redmond at the studio. The Hollywood actor Adolph Menjou in his autobiography, *It Took Nine Tailors*, observed that Chaplin liked to have characters, including an artist, around the lot. Menjou never referred to Redmond by name, but they both appear in *A Woman of Paris* and in a group photograph carried by the *Silent Worker* magazine.

Among Redmond's several films, *You'd Be Surprised* is the most interesting to the deaf community. Because he played in films with major Hollywood stars, his movies survive in various archival collections. The only exception is *He's a Prince*, which has been lost. Despite his connection with the stars, Redmond still had only limited exposure and consequently has received no recognition from movie publications or film histories.

Emerson Romero's film name was Tommy Albert. Born in Cuba, he received his education at the Wright Oral School in New York City. His brother Dorian produced Spanish-captioned silent movies in Cuba for the Pan American Picture Corporation, and Romero starred in several comedies for the company. While there, he came to the attention of American director Richard Harlan, who convinced Romero to move to California. In Hollywood for approximately one year, Romero starred in the short films "Beachnuts," "The Cat's Meow," "Sappy Days," "Great Guns," and "Hen-Pecked in Morocco."

Unemployed because of the talkies, Romero returned to New York, where he continued his training and experience. He became very active in efforts to establish a professional deaf repertory company and to produce captions for the now inaccessible talking movies. Another relative, cousin Cesar Romero, became a popular male star. It is ironic that many persons in the deaf community know that Cesar Romero had a deaf relative but did not realize that this deaf relative had also performed in the movies.

Louis Weinberg also came from New York, where he had attended the Lexington School for the Deaf. Weinberg worked in show business before he acted in the movies. Known as the Russian toe dancer, Weinberg performed on the vaudeville circuit under his stage name, David Marvel. Hollywood tried to build upon the fame of operatic star Geraldine Farrar and produced several movies for her. Weinberg played the role of the Indian prince in one of these films, *The Woman God Forgot* (1917). Thereafter, Weinberg returned to his dance career in vaudeville.

Two other deaf persons performed in silent films. One was a Cuban woman, Carmen de Arcos, who Emerson Romero described as a mute and who worked with him for the Pan American Picture Corporation. Most of the references to her work, such as *La Chica y El Gato*, are through Romero.

Little else is known of her career. The other deaf actor was Albert Ballin.

Ballin's acting career primarily consisted of jobs as a movie extra. Attracted to Hollywood in 1924, Ballin sold a movie script, "Sardanapolus," to the Palmer Photoplay Corporation. Although no one produced his script, Ballin stayed in California and supported himself as an extra and portrait painter. Continuing his writing, Ballin penned several articles about the movies for deaf community publications and eventually produced a book, *The Deaf Mute Howls* (1930), which included a section on how the movie industry could benefit from the use of sign language.

It is ironic that his most prominent film never was distributed. *His Busy Hour*, which starred Ballin as a hermit, was the product of the popular notion that deaf people were natural actors because of their skills of expression and mimicry. In 1918 a movie editor for the *New York Times*, James O. Spearing, brought together a group of deaf actors to make *His Busy Hour*, which Spearing had written. Although he later worked as a scriptwriter for Paramount Studios on Long Island, New York, Spearing turned to the deaf community for the financial capital to distribute the film. Exhibiting the film to a deaf audience at the Lexington School for the Deaf in 1926, he explained that his goal was to establish a stock company "of and by the deaf." The film, designed for a general movie audience, did not use sign language. Since the deaf community did not invest in the film, it never was distributed commercially, and is lost.

Most silent films have been lost. Hence, there are very limited opportunities to see these deaf actors in their films. The early film industry was not motivated to maintain an archival record of its products because it was both expensive and dangerous. Nitrate-based film stock has inevitable chemical decay that can result in spontaneous combustion. The American Film Institute estimates that only 50 percent of the more than 21,000 feature-length films produced in the United States between 1900 and 1951 exist today. The surviving films that have been copied onto modern acetate film stock are held by American archives or private individuals and corporations and, hence, are generally only available for limited public viewing.

SUMMARY

At the opening of the twentieth century, entrepreneurs blended technology and art to establish a movie industry anchored in Hollywood. The silent movies created the largest mass audience for public entertainment in the nation's history, and for a brief time the deaf community participated fully in the mainstream of this popular cultural form.

The movies provided both pedagogical and entertainment value for deaf patrons. Films also pro-vided employment for a small band of deaf actors, and even though the public image of deafness portrayed on the movie screen usually was erroneous, film technology facilitated the preservation of American Sign Language. The deaf community views the silent movie era as a cultural highmark, a time when they truly had equal access to a public entertainment event.

Bibliography

Bergman, Eugene: *A Report from the National Endowment for the Arts: Arts Accessibility for the Deaf*, National Endowment for the Arts, Washington, D.C., 1981.

Everson, William: *American Silent Film*, Oxford University Press, New York, 1978.

Munder, Kenneth W. (ed.): *American Film Institute Catalogue of Motion Pictures Produced in the United States, 1921–1930.*

Schuchman, John. "Silent Movies and the Deaf Community," *Journal of Popular Culture*, 17:4, 1984.

Walker, Alexander: *The Shattered Silents: How the Talkies Came to Stay*, William Morrow, New York, 1979.

John S. Schuchman

George W. Veditz Film Collection

The George W. Veditz Film Collection, established in 1982 as part of the Collection on Deafness at the Gallaudet College Archives in Washington, D.C., represents an effort to preserve the cultural history of the deaf community. Even though many profoundly deaf persons use a visual form of communication, the Collection on Deafness consists primarily of traditional print materials. However, the collection also includes photographs, videotapes, and motion picture films. The videotapes and films together constitute the Veditz Film collection. *See* GALLAUDET COLLEGE.

NAD FILMS

The collection is named in honor of Veditz because its core consists of films produced by the National Association of the Deaf (NAD). Veditz, a deaf teacher, taught for many years at the Colorado School for the Deaf and Blind and was the seventh president of the NAD. Identifying American Sign Language (ASL) as "the noblest gift God has given to deaf people," Veditz led the NAD's effort to preserve the deaf community's language. As oralist educators took over the administration of an increasing number of residential schools at the turn of the century, NAD leaders expressed concern that ASL would be lost. Under the Veditz presidency, the NAD collected funds to produce films that recorded several old masters of sign language for future generations. This collection of poems, lectures, and memories produced from 1910 to 1920 used 35-mm film shot with a stationary camera. This technique was comparable to many of the commercially produced movies of this silent film era. In order to reduce the danger from fire and decay inherent in the unstable nitrate-cellulose film, these original films were reduced to 16-mm modern acetate film and copies were given to the Library of Congress and Gallaudet College. *See* VEDITZ, GEORGE WILLIAM.

Depicted on these films are both hearing and deaf signers: Edward M. Gallaudet (founder and first president of Gallaudet College), Edward A. Fay (vice-president and Gallaudet College faculty member), John B. Hotchkiss and Amos G. Draper (both Gallaudet College faculty members), Thomas F. Fox (principal of Fanwood School, New York), Robert P. McGregor (Ohio teacher and deaf leader), Mary W. Erd (Michigan teacher), Willis Hubbard (Michigan teacher and leader), George T. Dougherty (chemist and leader), the Reverend James H. Cloud (teacher and missionary to the deaf community), Winfield E. Marshall (master performer of signed poems and recitals), as well as Veditz himself, who made an impassioned plea for the "Preservation of Sign Language" which still evokes emotion and tears from audiences who see it today. The Veditz film is the only one that is captioned for persons unable to read sign language. A complete citation of these film titles is listed in the *Gallaudet Media Distribution Service Catalogue*. However, of special note is the film *Memories of Old Hartford*, signed by John Hotchkiss. Speaking about his recollections of the first permanent public school for deaf students in the United States, the American School for the Deaf located at West Hartford, Connecticut, Hotchkiss signs and mimes stories, which include references to Laurent Clerc. This film is of particular interest to students of ASL, linguistics, folklore, and history. *See* AMERICAN SCHOOL FOR THE DEAF; CLERC, LAURENT; FAY, EDWARD ALLEN; GALLAUDET, EDWARD MINER.

DRAMA PRODUCTIONS

With the transition in 1929–1930 of the commercial movie industry from silent films to talking motion pictures, the excluded deaf community turned to its own resources. Deaf thespians sought to produce plays of and for their own special audience. Through the leadership of the former deaf silent film actor Emerson Romero, New Yorkers established a theater guild in 1934 owned and operated by deaf people. Many urban centers with large deaf populations replicated these efforts to create theater groups. Although these performers earned their living at other employment, they continued to practice their dramatic skills. These efforts eventually resulted in the creation of the National Theatre of the Deaf in 1967 and the recognition of deaf actors on the commercial stage in the Broadway production *Children of a Lesser God*.

From time to time, enterprising deaf individuals with cameras filmed these productions, some of which are now a part of the Veditz Collection. The core of these films are plays performed by Gallaudet College students. The earliest play is *The Mikado* (1947) supplemented by several adaptations of Greek and Shakespearean drama such as *Oedipus Rex* and *Hamlet*. These plays were produced on 16-mm film and usually photographed by faculty members. In addition to classical selections, there are contemporary plays from the 1940s through the 1980s. This part of the collection includes filmed highlights of the sign language version of *Arsenic and Old Lace*, which was a hit on Broadway in the early 1940s. Gallaudet students, led by Eric Malzkuhn, decided to produce this contemporary hit. Much to their surprise, in 1942 the play's producers not only gave permission to the students to perform the play on campus but invited them to come to New York and give their sign language version on the Broadway stage. Amid much excitement in the deaf community, this performance was the first time that a sign language play was performed by deaf thespians in a major public theater. Although poor in quality, the film segments are of the Broadway signed performance.

ERNEST MARSHALL AND MOVIES FOR DEAF AUDIENCES

In addition to filmed plays, some deaf filmmakers created movies for deaf audiences. Although hearing audiences were invited to these movies, the films most often were shown at deaf clubs and thus limited to persons who understood sign language. When they were advertised, the movies always attracted a large deaf audience. Several deaf individuals produced an occasional movie, but Ernest Marshall of New York City stands out as a major film maker in the deaf community.

Marshall faithfully preserved his films and films for which he was responsible. To date, he has given videotape copies of his films, which he has promised eventually to donate, to the collection. He has supplemented this material with copies of his scrapbook of printed materials as well as oral history interviews of his recollection as film maker.

Marshall comes from a deaf family. His parents and earlier generations were deaf, and his uncle, Winfield Marshall, was one of the individuals whose sign was preserved by one of the early NAD films. Graduating from the New York School for the Deaf (Fanwood) in 1931, Marshall quickly became a part of deaf theater groups. He combined his talent for drama with an interest in photography and motion pictures. This interest paralleled developments at the Eastman-Kodak Company which designed the Cine-Kodak 16-mm system in 1923, the Standard-8 system in 1932, and Kodachrome in 1935, all intended for amateur moviemakers like Marshall. Marshall also developed his skills as a projectionist and for years ran films for organizations of the deaf throughout the metropolitan New York area. As a consequence, he obtained access to other films of interest to the deaf community. For example, many schools for deaf students routinely included military drill as part of the educational regimen of male students, who were addressed and organized as military cadets. Among other items of interest, the silent drills of the student military corps of the New York School for the Deaf have been preserved on film. As a projectionist, Marshall had access to these films and obtained permission to make copies that are now a part of the Veditz Collection.

The movies that Marshall produced span the period from 1937 to 1963. With no outside financial aid, Marshall purchased his own equipment and film and relied on deaf actors, who donated their time with only a remote possibility that they would share in profits from ticket sales. The entire enterprise was an act of charity by and for the deaf community that no longer had equal access to the movies. Marshall and his deaf colleagues worked evenings, weekends, and vacations, eventually producing nine feature films: *It Is Too Late* (1937), *The Magic of Magicians* (1938), *The Debt* (1955), *The Confession* (1956), *The Face on the Barroom Floor* (1959), *Ten Barrooms in One Night* (1961), *The Neighbor* (1961), *Sorrowful Approach* (1962), and *A Cake of Soap* (1963). Deaf writers wrote most of the scripts, but some were adaptations of classical dramas by Anton Chekhov and Guy de Maupassant. Marshall directed seven of the plays, Emerson Romero directed *A Cake of Soap*, and a deaf woman, Kathleen Fettin, directed *Sorrowful Approach*.

HOMEMADE MOVIES

In addition to this basic core of NAD films, filmed dramatic productions, and Marshall's movies, there are other visual records of interest to the deaf community. Two groups of 16-mm films deserve mention. The Baltimore Deaf Club displays social events of the club that include picnics, annual banquets, and sports tournaments. Another collection, produced by Ludwig Kennedy, displays social events in the deaf community during the 1930s and 1940s. Both groups of film could be informative for research in such areas as folklife-folklore, social history, and linguistics.

USE OF THE COLLECTION

There is no separate public catalog of these visual materials. Also, almost none of the films includes captions; hence, users require a working knowledge of ASL or the services of an interpreter. Unless an individual personally visits the Gallaudet College Archives, the only information that exists is published as a part of the *Gallaudet Media Distri-*bution Service Catalogue, although the college archivist estimates that only 30 percent of the films are listed. This catalog is periodically updated and is disseminated free of charge through the college library. The college also distributes, for loan or sale, a 34-minute videotape, *Our Priceless Gift*, produced at its television studio in 1982. The videotape provides an introductory overview of sign language recorded on film and videotape using selections of stories, poetry, and plays from the college collection. The selections date from 1910 through the 1980s. Because the creation is so recent, its primary purpose has been to bring attention to the films and to encourage the donation of visual materials from and about the deaf community. Since its creation in 1982, the collection has received several major additions. It is anticipated that the collection, which is already the largest such film collection, will continue to grow and will develop a separate catalog.

Bibliography

Gallaudet College: *Gallaudet Media Distribution Service Catalogue*, Washington, D.C., 1982.

Stewart, Roy J.: "Report of the NAD Motion Picture Fund," *Silent Worker*, 39:371–373, July 1927.

Tadie, Nancy B.: "A History of Drama at Gallaudet College: 1864–1969," unpublished Ph.D. dissertation, New York University, New York, 1978.

John S. Schuchman

TERRY, HOWARD L.
(1877–1964)

The "venerable dean of letters" of deaf people, Howard L. Terry, was born in St. Louis, Missouri, on January 4, 1877. Becoming deaf from unspecified causes at the age of 11, he continued his education in the public schools until, in 1895, he entered Gallaudet College. Presumably, this is where he first became acquainted with sign language. During his second year at the college, however, he withdrew because of eye trouble—a condition which was to bother him throughout his life. Even before entering Gallaudet, Terry had demonstrated a proclivity for writing. He had written two "books": *Cave Diggers* (1891) and *Poems* (1894), published with the aid of a toy printing set. Both were written about in the St. Louis papers at the instigation of his father and brought him much acclaim in his native state. These were followed by *A Tale of Normandy and Other Poems* (1898). *See* GALLAUDET COLLEGE.

CAREER

In 1901, Terry married Alice Taylor, also from Missouri, whom he had met at Gallaudet College. For eight years, the couple lived on Sunset Farm in southwest Missouri and made a living from agriculture. During this sojourn, *Waters from an Ozark Spring* emerged in 1909, and the groundwork for several other books was laid. *Our Celebrities* (1910) was a mild dig at some of the deaf leaders of the day. *A Voice from the Silence*, probably Terry's most important work, was begun in 1912 after he sold the farm and moved to Carthage, Missouri. (During this same year, *The Dream*, a metrical drama in two acts, was finished). This novel was published in *The Ohio Farmer*, a bimonthly magazine, where it ran in serial form for seven months. The publication made Terry well known and resulted in his offering the motion picture rights to the Selig Polyscope Company in 1914. When this company took up his offer, Terry seemed headed for more fame in the burgeoning motion picture industry. Unfortunately, the company never made the movie and was soon eclipsed by other, newer companies.

Despite this setback, Terry had demonstrated that deafness was no barrier to writing well or to being published. He continued to have poems and articles accepted in magazines such as *American Poetry*, *Poetry World*, *Wee Wisdom*, *Social Science*, *The Hesperian*, in various California papers (*Los Angeles Times*, *Santa Monica Outlook*, *San Francisco Chronicle*, *Fresno Republican*); and in *Silent Broadcaster*. Paradoxically, although he advised deaf writers not to let editors become aware of their deafness, he was at the same time promoting deaf writers. Jimmy Meagher, a Chicago writer for many deaf publications and a self-appointed public relations man for Terry in those publications, had organized a small informal group of deaf writers into a club called the Pen Pushers. For several years, Terry tried unsuccessfully to organize this group into a permanent Guild of Deaf Writers. (Even today, deaf writers remain largely unorganized.) Another more successful attempt occurred when, in the 1930s, Terry joined J. H. MacFarlane and Kate Shibley, teachers in various schools for deaf students, in compiling an *Anthology of Poems by the Deaf*; this project had been begun by the late J. S. Long, a well-known educator of deaf pupils. The project was finally brought to completion in *The Silent Muse* (1960) by a board of editors composed of Robert Panara, Taras Denis, and MacFarlane.

WRITINGS

Assessment of Terry's work is difficult. Turn-of-the-century American literature was still circumscribed by the Romantic tradition in both poetry and prose. The influences on Terry's writing undoubtedly date from the late nineteenth century so that, in most respects, he was a creature of the times. According to Terry's foreword to his *Sung in Silence* (1929), he still "hears in his mind's ear the folk song of his childhood days" and he deplores "the new conditions and the new literature, almost all of which is wild and experimental." He says that the deaf writer "grows less sure of his way as times change . . . his themes savor of the old." Thus, Terry appears to have been somewhat appalled by the literary turmoil of the early twentieth century—turmoil brought about by such figures as Ezra Pound, T. S. Eliot, Conrad Aiken, Wallace Stevens, and others who changed the form and texture of American poetry.

The writing of prose also underwent modification with the growth of the motion picture industry and the establishment of numerous periodicals, bringing with them a new generation of writers. Although perhaps dismayed and feeling left out of the main currents of literature, Terry cannot be dismissed from either the main body of literature or the literature of the deaf community. To be sure, he made no significant impact on American literature as a whole, but he was published as a novelist, poet, writer of greeting card verse, and author of feature stories. Although his poetry may have verged on the *fin de siècle* style, certain poems such as "Burns Cottage" and "On Coming upon a Fragment of Meteorite" escape this characterization and are as relevant today as when they were written.

Insofar as there is a separate literature of deaf people, Terry possesses considerable status. He is a role model for the American deaf writer of this and future generations. In the sheer breadth of his work, he has not been equaled in the United States. In 1938, Gallaudet College awarded him the honorary degree of master of letters. In 1940, his name was included by *Who's Who in America*.

Howard L. Terry died on March 3, 1964, in Los Angeles, California.

Bibliography

Klugman, Marjorie: *The Silent Worker*, pp. 3–5, May 1950.

Panara, Robert F.: "The Deaf Writer in America from Colonial Times to 1970," part 2, *American Annals of the Deaf*, pp. 675–676, November 1970.

Terry, Howard L.: *The Modern Silents*, pp. 4–6, February 1940; pp. 4–5, March 1940; pp. 9–10, April 1940.

————: *Sung in Silence*, privately printed, 1929.

Rex Lowman

THAILAND

Thai society only recently recognized the special characteristics and needs of deaf people. On December 10, 1951, the third anniversary of the Declaration of Human Rights by the United Nations, a center was established in Bangkok to experiment with teaching deaf persons. Since then, deaf people in Thailand have received assistance in education, health care, welfare, vocational training, and income-generating activities.

EDUCATION

Early efforts to provide education for deaf people in Thailand were supported by the U.S. Institute of International Education, which provided funds for M. R. Sermsri Kasemsri to study in the United States. Sermsri Kasemsri, an official in the Ministry of Education, studied at Gallaudet College and then returned to Thailand to establish in 1951 the center of special education for deaf children. From a modest beginning of 4 or 5 students, the center quickly expanded to serve 50 students in its second year. *See* GALLAUDET COLLEGE.

The Thai Ministry of Education, with the cooperation of the Sethsatian Foundation and the Foundation for the Deaf of Thailand, opened the first government school for deaf children in 1953. Called the School for Deaf Children at Dusit District, Bangkok, this facility admits both day and residential students aged 7 to 12. Children older than 12 are permitted to study reading and writing, and pursue occupational training as well. There is no tuition fee, but parents or guardians of the residential students pay for meals. The Foundation for the Deaf of Thailand renders assistance to those from genuinely impoverished families.

All schools for deaf children use the normal curriculum as prescribed by the Ministry of Education for any school in Thailand. The old curriculum stressed academic achievement, requiring deaf students to take the same examinations as hearing students to complete their primary education (formerly at grade 7) and secondary education (formerly at grade 10). In 1978, however, the curriculum was altered to allow more flexibility, stressing both academic achievement and career preparation. Most deaf schools provide 10 years of classes for their students: 1 year for preschool, 6 years for elementary education, and 3 years for lower-level secondary education. The schools also have the responsibility for measuring and evaluating their deaf students.

Prior to 1980, when the law was abolished, deaf people, like those with other disabilities, were exempt from compulsory education. Today deaf children have the same rights and opportunities as other children, and those who can communicate well are integrated in regular classes of public schools. Since 1975, hard-of-hearing students have been placed in classes with hearing pupils, beginning in kindergarten. In order to assist children in areas where there are no facilities for special education, the Ministry of Education has provided special schools for hard-of-hearing and for profoundly and severely deaf children. These schools are the Chonburi School for the Hard-of-Hearing and the Sotesuksa Wat Champ School in Bangkok.

COMMUNICATION

There is no overall policy determining communication methods for deaf children in Thai schools. Fingerspelling, Thai Sign Language, oral methods, and total communication are all in use. *See* EDUCATION: Communication.

First attempts toward communication involving sign language and fingerspelling were made at the School for Deaf Children at Dusit District, Bangkok. Kamala Krairiksh, the school's first principal and a graduate of Gallaudet College, initiated these efforts. Krairiksh invented the Thai Manual Alphabet to be used in conjunction with Thai Sign Language. The latter is a combination of indigenous signs used by deaf people in Thailand and American Sign Language. Krairiksh and her colleagues codified these signs to establish a vocabulary sufficient for communication and education. The School for Deaf Children at Dusit District, Bangkok, uses the combined method in instruction, emphasizing the development of both manual and oral communication skills. Since 1975, the total communication philosophy has been followed by schools in Khonkaen, Tak, and Songkla, while Chonburi School for the Hard-of-Hearing and the Sotesuka Wat Champ School in Bangkok are purely oral.

People in Thailand are interested in studying more about communication with deaf people. Books on auditory and speech training and speechreading are available in the Thai language. The first book of Thai Sign Language was published in 1966 with basic words and a written description for each sign. This proved to be inadequate, however, and there have since been various attempts to collect and codify signs and to provide illustrations for them. In 1982, with financial support from several embassies in Bangkok, particularly those of Australia and Canada, a two-week seminar was held which resulted in the strengthening and systematizing of the research on Thai Sign Language conducted by the Center for Deaf Alumni. Teachers from deaf schools expanded the collection of signs, and the signs they collected from deaf adults were published as a dictionary in 1983. *See* AUDITORY TRAINING; SPEECH TRAINING; SPEECHREADING.

EMPLOYMENT AND SERVICES

Employment opportunities for deaf people in Thailand are sharply limited. A principal reason for this is that Thailand has a great supply of labor. Thus, most deaf people work with their families or relatives. Those who choose careers are concentrated in occupations such as drawing, molding, painting, electronics, dressmaking and tailoring, cosmetics and makeup, cooking, photography, and typing. Deaf people in the labor force earn pay equal to that of hearing coworkers.

An important step forward in assisting deaf people to become more independent was the establishment on July 21, 1969, of the Adult Deaf Club of Thailand, with 93 members. Its headquarters was at Sethsatian School for the Deaf in Bangkok. In 1980 it expanded its functions and set up the Center for Deaf Alumni in order to make the most of community work skills and to become a model of deaf self-help activity. In May 1982 the center moved from the school to the east side of Bangkok and dedicated itself to three major tasks: membership and job counseling, running a workshop for deaf people, and Thai Sign Language research. The center is in contact with organizations of deaf people in various countries, and one of its committee members becomes an active board member of Disabled Persons International.

A variety of services have become available to deaf people in Thailand since 1981, the International Year of Disabled Persons by United Nations proclamation. The Thai government has provided more funds for the rehabilitation of deaf people, while public sectors have made available funds and opportunities to allow deaf persons to participate in various activities for the promotion of their cognitive and community growth. The Ministry of Public Health has helped train community workers to assist deaf people in rural areas in obtaining education and health care. The Ear, Nose, and Throat Association of Thailand has a mobile unit to treat those in rural areas who have hearing problems. The Foundation for the Deaf of Thailand, under the patronage of Queen Sirikit, has cooperated with the Departments of General Education, Public Welfare, and Labor in setting up career training and job placement services for deaf adults. The United States International Development Agency, through the International Human Assistance Programs, has assisted Thai organizations in rendering services for both preschool and postschool deaf persons. Colleges and universities and the Ministry of Education have begun training teachers to work with deaf students.

There are indications that deaf people in Thailand will make greater progress in the future. The royal family, for example, has shown interest in deaf people. In 1983 Princess Maha Chakri Sirindhorn arranged for the establishment of an experimental center for deaf children within the school for hearing children in the compound of the Grand Palace. Professionals involved in the rehabilitation of deaf people established this center for profoundly deaf children aged three to six. The three-year curriculum employs the total communication

philosophy, and all teachers' aides are deaf persons. Parents or guardians are encouraged to work closely with teachers in organizing classroom programs. This experiment, greater government commitment, and the further strengthening of international contacts all bode well for the future of deaf Thais.

Bibliography

Board of Directors of the Foundation for the Deaf in Thailand: *Thirtieth Anniversary* (report in Thai of the foundation under the patronage of the Queen), Thammasart University Press, Bangkok, 1983.

Division of Special Education: *Annual Report on Special Education 1983* (in Thai), Department of General Education, Ministry of Education, Bangkok, 1983.

Ministry of Education, Thailand: *The National Education Scheme 1977*, Ministry of Education, Bangkok, 1977.

National Economic and Social Development Board: *The Fifth Economic and Social Development Plan 1982–1986*, Bangkok, 1982.

Sathaporn Suvannus

THEATER, COLLEGE

Theatrical activities involving deaf college students started more than a hundred years ago. As early as 1874 a men's literary society was founded at Gallaudet College with the goal of improving the signing and oratorical skills of its members. To meet these goals, programs featuring pantomimes, stories, monologues, and skits were presented. Following the men's example, by 1892 the female students of Gallaudet had established a literary society, and short theatrical presentations became part of their activities. *See* GALLAUDET COLLEGE.

GALLAUDET COLLEGE

British theater artist and poet Dorothy Miles provides information on theater activities in her unpublished thesis, "The History of Theatre Activities in the Deaf Community of the United States." She notes that the male students formed an organization in 1891, entitled the Saturday Night Dramatics Club, for the purpose of presenting "dramatic entertainments." The club was successful with its initial productions, and by 1895 the female students of Gallaudet had formed their own dramatic organization, the Jollity Club. These two clubs served as the dominant producers of dramatic presentations at Gallaudet until the Jollity Club disbanded in 1928 and the fundamental nature of the Saturday Night Dramatics Club changed with the addition of female participants in 1935.

The selected plays represented various styles, genres, lengths, and authors. However, each of the performances was presented in sign language. By the middle of the 1930s, hearing actors were placed offstage to "voice" the lines of the signing actors.

This practice made the plays accessible to hearing individuals with no knowledge of sign language.

Until the integration of men and women on the Gallaudet stage in 1935, the quality and the scope of the productions depended upon the enthusiasm and skill of the individual students. With the production of Ben Jonson's *Volpone*, the college seemed to commit itself to increased support for the theater. No longer were the productions dependent only upon students, for now faculty became involved regularly. Professors Irving Fusfeld and Frederick H. Hughes advised and assisted the student director and the integrated cast of *Volpone*. During the next five years, faculty members directed several productions, and the number of students participating in drama productions increased. In 1940 this theater activity created a new opportunity for Gallaudet students when the college offered its first dramatics class, taught by Hughes and Mary Yoder.

With the advent of this class focusing on acting and stagecraft, Gallaudet offered consistent support for the study of theater. Along with teaching, Hughes produced and directed many plays. The plays he selected were written for the traditional hearing audiences; he adapted the scripts into sign language.

The most famous production during this time was *Arsenic and Old Lace*. In 1942 the Broadway producers gave permission to Gallaudet to produce their play, even though it was still playing in New York at the Fulton Theater. Gallaudet's sign language performance so interested the Broadway producers that they invited the student cast to perform for one night in place of the New York cast. This performance received considerable publicity and made a much larger audience aware of Gallaudet's efforts in theater.

In the decade following *Arsenic and Old Lace*, the Gallaudet students appeared in productions as varied as R. C. Sherriff's antiwar drama *Journey's End*; Gilbert and Sullivan's operetta *The Pirates of Penzance*; Ferenc Molnar's *Liliom*; and Molière's *The Miser*. Following graduation, the students appearing in these productions became the leaders in establishing theater activity for deaf individuals in many deaf residential schools and in community theaters in major cities. Gallaudet's program permanently influenced the development of theater for deaf people throughout the United States.

Just as Hughes's era was ending in the middle 1950s, new members of the Gallaudet faculty were showing their interest in theater activities. George Detmold, Leonard Siger, and Robert Panara became especially active. *Oedipus Rex*, *Hamlet*, *Othello*, and *The Trojan Women* were among the plays produced by this team. The combined talent and energy of these men enhanced the quality of the productions. After Hughes's death in 1956, Gallaudet hired one of its graduates, Gilbert Eastman, to be an instructor in dramatics. Eastman's responsibilities included assisting with production and teaching a variety of theater courses.

In 1963 Gallaudet formed a Department of Drama with Eastman in charge, and made the school's newly constructed theater its home. The practice of using plays written for hearing audiences and adapting them into sign language continued. For the next several years, contemporary plays such as *Picnic*, *Harvey*, and *The Crucible* shared the schedule with such traditional selections as *Romeo and Juliet*, *Medea*, and *The Inspector General*. However, in 1973 Eastman produced his play *Sign Me Alice*, which was written specifically for deaf theater. The success of Eastman's play stimulated the production of other plays dealing with deafness. As a result, plays with themes relating to deafness appeared almost annually in the Gallaudet theater schedule.

Since 1969 Gallaudet has offered students the opportunity to select drama as a major field of study. The Theatre Arts Department, the new name for the Department of Drama, offers two areas of concentration: production-performance and developmental drama. Creating these opportunities made a larger theater faculty and staff necessary.

As the public became more aware of Gallaudet's theater activities, the demand for performances increased. Between 1978 and 1983 a touring theater company of Gallaudet students performed mostly in the eastern United States. Each year a play for children attracts 5000 young people to the campus. In 1973 Eastman's adaptation of Sophocles's *Antigone* was performed by Gallaudet students for the American College Theatre Festival V at the John F. Kennedy Center for the Performing Arts in Washington, D.C. Also, William Moses' original play *The*

Charles Katz and Marsha Goeken in the Gallaudet College production of *The Kid*, written and directed by William Moses. (Photo by Chun Louie)

Kid reached a wide audience in 1983 when it was selected for the finals of the American College Theatre Festival XV at the Kennedy Center.

NATIONAL TECHNICAL INSTITUTE FOR THE DEAF
At the same time Gallaudet was putting more resources into its theater program, a new college opened for deaf students. In 1968 the National Technical Institute for the Deaf (NTID), in Rochester, New York, enrolled its first students. This new college became one of the nine colleges of a larger and older institution, the Rochester Institute of Technology (RIT), which enrolls hearing students in its other colleges. *See* NATIONAL TECHNICAL INSTITUTE FOR THE DEAF.

The first teacher hired at NTID was the Gallaudet professor, Robert Panara. He brought his love for theater with him and soon establbished an NTID Drama Club. For the next six years, the drama club produced plays and variety shows in different auditoriums on the RIT campus, and Panara taught dramatic literature courses to deaf and hearing students. Panara also developed a plan to start a formal theater program for deaf students. He wanted

Scene from a National Technical Institute for the Deaf production of *The Tempest* by William Shakespeare. (Photo by Mark Benjamin)

this program to give the students an outlet for creative expression; to encourage communication skills; to enhance, through drama, the study of traditional subjects; to create experiences similar to future employment situations; and to provide personal and social growth opportunities.

Panara's plans became a reality when, in 1974, NTID opened a new 500-seat theater designed especially for deaf audience members and theater productions; the Experimental Educational Theatre Department was established. Faculty members in acting, directing, design, and technical directing were hired to run the theater and develop a theater curriculum. For a period of time, Panara continued his activity in the theater. However, as the new faculty, especially Jerome Cushman in directing and Robert Pratt in technical theater and design, became more accomplished in working with deaf students, Panara gradually reduced his involvement to teaching his dramatic literature classes.

By the mid-1970s, theater classes in the new department were filled with deaf students. Each year NTID offers at least three fully mounted productions featuring deaf actors signing and hearing actors voicing the lines. The majority of the productions feature the deaf and hearing actors on stage together. The hearing actors typically are cast in minor roles allowing them to voice for the leading characters who use sign language only. Like Gallaudet, most productions in NTID's theater are sign language adaptations of plays written for hearing audiences. Among these adaptations are Molière's *School for Wives*, Bertolt Brecht's *The Threepenny Opera*, and Elmer Rice's *The Adding Machine*. The NTID theater program does not offer drama as a major field of study. Although the program is extensive, the nature of a technical institution prevents this type of study. However, this has not prevented continued growth for the theater program or successful theater careers for former students.

A Gallaudet graduate and National Theatre of the Deaf veteran, Patrick Graybill, arrived at NTID to act, teach, and direct. Cushman, who is also trained in movement and dance, began offering dance classes. With the arrival in 1979 of Bruce Halverson as the chairperson of the department, other parts of the program were expanded. Another teacher to work exclusively in dance was hired, and the RIT Dance Company was formed. This company features deaf and hearing dancers and presents productions each year. In addition, deaf performers have danced in several musicals, including *A Funny Thing Happened on the Way to the Forum*, *Once upon a Mattress*, and *Oklahoma*.

The theater program expanded into music as Robert Mowers and Diane Habeeb were hired to develop a music program for deaf students. Within five years, deaf students played a wide variety of instruments; performed in their own combo for local, national, and international audiences; joined hearing students in the campus pep band; and played in the pit orchestra for theater productions.

With the addition of programs in music and dance, the Experimental Educational Theatre Department changed its name to the Department of Performing Arts. In 1980 the department also initiated an outreach program, under the supervision of Timothy Toothman. The main part of the outreach program is Sunshine Too. This group consists of three deaf and three hearing performers who tour throughout the United States and Canada presenting theater programs in sign language and voice. They perform for millions of people through special television appearances and for more than 75,000 people annually in live performances. Their material is developed specifically for them and deals with deafness and related themes.

NTID's Department of Performing Arts continues to offer courses, productions, and workshops to its students. Nationally recognized artists perform regularly at the college in an effort to increase appreciation of deafness and the performing arts for both audiences and performers. In 1984 A. Richard Nichols became the chairperson of the department, and he began to establish new areas of growth and exploration.

OTHER COLLEGES

Consistent growth and activity have not taken place on college campuses other than at Gallaudet and NTID at RIT. For a brief time in the mid-1970s, California State University at Northridge (CSUN) involved deaf performers and presented sign language productions. Again, Robert Panara, on leave for a year from NTID at RIT, was in part responsible. He and Dorothy Miles served as visiting professors at CSUN, and during their time *Godspell* and Miles's *For the Love of Seven Dolls* were presented with deaf and hearing performers. Lou Fant, a hearing actor with exceptional skill in sign language; Darlene Allen, a theater graduate student with interest and experience in deaf theater; and Halverson, as Director of Theater, were at CSUN with Panara and Miles at this same time. Deaf students were active in the drama department's classes and occasionally in some hearing productions. For example, professional actor Jon Voight came to CSUN to appear in *Hamlet* and a deaf student appeared with Voight in this production. *See* CALIFORNIA STATE UNIVERSITY, NORTHRIDGE.

College productions adapted into sign language have been presented in several regions since the 1970s. Not all of these productions have had significant numbers of deaf performers and technicians because the respective colleges typically did not enroll large numbers of deaf students. Montana State University's Theatre of Silence, directed by Jack R. Olsen, has toured thousands of miles presenting variety shows in sign language. The Florissant Valley Theatre of the Deaf, directed by John Heidger, is located on the campus of the St. Louis Community College and works with both the college theater program and the local deaf community. The Callier Theatre of the Deaf is associated with the University of Texas at Dallas and involves mostly deaf community members. Also, at various times, Seattle Community College in Washington, St. Paul Technical Vocational Institute in Minnesota, the University of Northern Colorado in Greeley, and the University of Tennessee in Knoxville have had theater groups presenting plays in sign language.

Other colleges also have had productions involving deaf individuals or in sign language on a regular basis for limited periods. However, because of the lack of institutional commitment, theater programs in colleges designed for hearing students have not consistently developed theater opportunities for deaf students; historically, this type of opportunity has depended more upon dedicated individuals. As the individuals move or change priorities, the theater opportunities for participation by deaf students follow.

One important example is at New Mexico State University in Las Cruces. Mark Medoff, a faculty member of the drama department and a nationally recognized playwright, invited deaf actress Phyllis Frelich and her husband, designer and actor Robert Steinberg, to be guest artists in the department. From this association came the award-winning play *Children of a Lesser God*, which features deaf characters. Using the college program as a place for experimentation, Medoff was able to write one of the most influential pieces of literature in the area of deafness. *See* FRELICH, PHYLLIS.

Deaf theater students now have more opportunities to perform and to see accessible performances than ever before. Although the number of college theater programs involving deaf students is not extensive, the programs have helped to make theater a regular part of the lives of many deaf people and have created a new awareness of an exciting art form for all people.

Bibliography

Gallaudet Theatre Department Papers, Department of Theatre, Gallaudet College, Washington, D.C.

Halverson, Bruce R.: "Deaf and Hearing Together," in Ann M. Shaw, Wendy Perks, and C. J. Stevens (eds.), *Perspectives: A Handbook in Drama and Theatre by, with, and for Handicapped Individuals*, American Theatre Association, 1981.

Heidger, John M.: "The Theatre of the Deaf in America: The Silent Stage," unpublished thesis, Southern Illinois University, Edwardsville, 1979.

Miles, Dorothy M.: "A History of Theatre Activities in the Deaf Community of the United States," unpublished thesis, Connecticut College, New London, 1974.

Bruce Halverson

THEATER, COMMUNITY

Community theater of deaf people in the United States may have its origin in the literary society that was until recent times a prevalent and important activity in residential schools and communities of deaf people. Established to encourage expressive and forceful use of sign language, the societies offered their members a means for public speaking or performance, the only opportunity for most of them. Presentations included poetry recitals, songs in sign, monologues, readings, storytelling, skits, charades, and pantomime, as well as debates and discussions. The Clerc Literary Association of Philadelphia dates back to 1865, while the Ballard Literary Society was founded at Gallaudet College in 1874, in honor of the college's first graduate, Melville Ballard. *See* GALLAUDET COLLEGE.

NINETEENTH CENTURY

In New York City during the 1890s, St. Ann's Church for the Deaf, a mission founded by the eldest son of Thomas Hopkins Gallaudet, sponsored an active dramatics group. Regular entertainment was also offered in the city by the Protean Society and the New York Institute for the Deaf and dumb. Meanwhile, in Chicago the Pas-a-Pas Club offered "varied dramatic entertainments" and boasted a large, well-lighted stage, a drop curtain, and a full set of scenery. The All Souls Working Club of the Deaf in Philadelphia presented *The Merchant of Venice* in sign language in 1894. *See* GALLAUDET, THOMAS HOPKINS.

1900–1945

Like their hearing counterparts across rural America, deaf audiences had shown a preference for the vaudeville type of entertainment over the more intellectual classic plays. By the 1920s, vaudeville was regular entertainment at National Association of the Deaf conventions, at National Fraternal Society of the Deaf banquets, and at deaf clubs. A common practice was to call upon the best signers in each community to give lectures or to tell stories and jokes at public gatherings. *See* NATIONAL ASSOCIATION OF THE DEAF; NATIONAL FRATERNAL SOCIETY OF THE DEAF.

As the twentieth century progressed, American theater became more diversified and sophisticated, increasing in verbalism and decreasing in visual expression, even in musical comedies. These changes did not appeal to deaf audiences, and theater fell further away from their scope of experience and interest.

In the mid-1930s, a deaf actor in silent films, Emerson Romero, saw his film career cut short when Hollywood switched to talkies. A multitalented individual, he established the New York Theatre Guild of the Deaf and wrote, directed, and acted in playlets and skits with a minimum of dialogue and a maximum of acting and pantomime. In addition to performing with the group in and out of New York, he gave many one-man shows. *See* TELEVISION AND MOTION PICTURES: Silent Films.

Wolf Bragg, a member of the Romero group, started to direct his own productions, adapting short plays and stories for sign language presentation. Under the sponsorship of the New York Hebrew Association of the Deaf, his troupe performed in Newark, Baltimore, Philadelphia, Hartford, and Boston. It disbanded in 1948.

The Chicago Silent Dramatics Club came into being after local people were asked to put on skits for the reception and banquet entertainment during the National Association of the Deaf convention held in Chicago in 1937. Under the leadership of a talented young woman, Virginia Dries, the club boasted a membership of nearly a hundred.

A dramatics class was set up at Gallaudet College in 1940 by Frederick Hughes, who noticed a large number of postlingually deaf undergraduates on the campus. Skilled in both English and sign language, many of the students joined the Dramatics Club, allowing Hughes to carry out his concept of a sign language adaptation of the spoken theater. Over the years, the club gave a number of outstanding productions, and its members not only influenced their prelingually deaf contemporaries to attempt complete adaptations of classic plays but also carried Hughes's concept to schools for deaf students all over the country. Emil Ladner and Leo Jacobs promoted serious drama at the California School for the Deaf in Berkeley, Joseph Hines and Robert Panara at the Fanwood School in New York, Loy Golladay at the American School, Race Drake in Arkansas, Ralph White in Georgia and Texas, and James Orman and David Mudgett in Illinois. *See* AMERICAN SCHOOL FOR THE DEAF.

Frank Sullivan, Len Warshawsky, and Celia (Burg) Warshawsky joined the Chicago Silent Dramatics Club. Florian Caligiuri worked in Florida and Los Angeles while Eric Malzkuhn gravitated to San Francisco. The Philadelphia Theatre Guild of the Deaf was founded in 1947 by Michael Iannace, who possessed the gift for scenic design and spectacular stage effects. More than a few community theaters, however, failed to thrive when two camps, one of college graduates and the other of noncollege individuals, could not agree on the question of entertainment and production.

POSTWAR PERIOD

Increased mobility and improved communication, such as the revival of the publication *Silent Worker* following World War II, served to encourage cultural exchange between deaf communities. In 1950 the Chicago Silent Dramatics Club performed the play *Alibi Bill* in New York and Indianapolis. Chicago was visited in the same year by a group of Canadians, the Toronto Troupe, led by David Peikoff. A man of great vision and energies, Peikoff envisioned a home office for the National Association of the Deaf (NAD) and, as an endeavor to raise funds for this purpose, he instituted the idea of an "NAD Rally." The idea was an instant success and became an effective outlet for deaf dramatic talent across the country.

The advent of television encouraged rather than decreased theater activities among deaf persons. Its fare of variety shows and panel games proved to be a popular source of material for the NAD Rallies and local gatherings.

New York has always been the theater center of America, be it for the hearing or the deaf communities. The Metropolitan Theatre Guild of the Deaf was founded in 1957 by Richard Meyer and Joseph Hines to continue the tradition of short comedies and variety acts that had always been popular with deaf audiences. This mandate was passed on to the New York Deaf Theatre in 1979.

Founded in 1959, the Dramatics Guild of the District of Columbia Club of the Deaf proved immensely popular with area adults, and its 1962 production of *Lithuania*, directed by Betty Miller, won the Honorable Mention in a one-act play tournament sponsored by the D.C. Recreation Department. Miller's father, Ralph, received the Best Actor award. The Guild was eventually succeeded by the Frederick Hughes Memorial Theatre, which produced *Flower Drum Song* in 1961, the first full-length modern musical attempted by a deaf community theater. The Hughes Theatre also performed *Tales from a Clubroom* to standing ovations at the National Association of the Deaf Centennial Convention in Cincinnati in 1980.

Gilbert Eastman used G. B. Shaw's *Pygmalion* as an inspiration to write *Sign Me Alice*, which premiered at Gallaudet in April 1973. A month later, a new group called the Hartford Thespians presented Dorothy Miles's *A Play of Our Own*. The two productions were the first known examples of deaf theater or work created by deaf persons based on their own deaf experience. Except for the National Theatre of the Deaf's *My Third Eye* in 1971, the deaf community had witnessed only sign language theater, which is essentially "hearing theater" performed in sign language.

While its productions have not always been wholly embraced by the deaf community, the National Theatre of the Deaf has nevertheless shown that, given the right training and opportunity, a deaf person can enjoy the theater experience that has always been available to hearing audiences. Its Professional School, established in 1967, has trained

hundreds of deaf individuals in theatrical arts and offers a playwright program for the aspiring writer. With this acquired knowledge and affirmation, the students return home to help set up, or to become more involved in, community theaters. *See* NATIONAL THEATERS OF THE DEAF: United States.

A theater can exist only as long as the community supports it. Because of its relatively small number of members, a deaf community's demographic makeup is often drastically adjusted with the addition or loss of a few individuals. The loss of but one key individual may cause a community theater to close.

To keep track of all community theaters of deaf people in the United States is difficult. The theaters go as quickly as they come. It is not uncommon for an old theater to reorganize under a new name. Some are identified as theaters of the deaf, yet carry as many or even more hearing members than deaf members. Others specialize in sign-song presentations with music arranged by hearing members, of which many are interpreters for deaf people. Several theaters started with the purpose of arranging interpreted performances of hearing productions for the deaf people in the audience. Theaters have been sponsored by deaf clubs, colleges, community agencies, hearing theaters, and government grants. Most metropolitan areas can claim at one time or another to have had a community theater of deaf people. Groups that have been in existence for a number of years and have staged noteworthy productions include Callier Theatre of the Deaf (Dallas), Stage Hands (Atlanta), Deaf Drama Project (Seattle), Chicago Theatre of the Deaf, Spectrum (Austin), Boston Theatre of the Deaf (formerly Urban Arts Project in Deafness), Pittsburgh Theatre of the Deaf, and Theatre of Silence (Bozeman, Montana).

Bibliography

Miles, Dorothy S.: "A History of Theatre Activities in the Deaf Community of the United States," Connecticut College, New London, 1974.

Shanny Mow

THEATER, PROFESSIONAL

If job opportunities promising security and contentment have for centuries been limited for deaf individuals, the chances of breaking into the highly competitive field of entertainment have been almost nil. For anyone desiring to entertain outside the deaf community, pantomime was the only means for theatrical expression. Sign language carried a stigma. Frenchman Henri Gaillard, for example, failed in 1892 to secure official backing for a "theatre of deaf-mute pantomimists." Skeptics argued that deaf persons could not follow music, which, to their thinking, was essential to a pantomime performance. Yet within half a century a number of deaf dancers followed music as professionals: David Marvel, Louis Weinberg, Charles and Charlotte Lamberton, Maxine Morris, Frances Woods, and later Florita Tellez Corey, whose daughter, Rita Corey, toured nationally and in Japan during the 1980s as a founding member of a professional sign and dance group, Musign. Spectrum's American Deaf Dance Company and Kol Demama Dance Company of Israel came into being during the late 1970s and have performed continuously. *See* PERFORMING ARTS; WOODS, FRANCES.

During the 1930s, Albert Ballin signed in concerts while hearing persons recited. As the first professional deaf mime, Bernard Bragg performed in San Francisco night clubs and appeared on his own television show, *The Quiet Man*, in the 1950s. *See* BRAGG, BERNARD.

In 1962 the Soviet government decided to subsidize the Moscow Theatre of Mimicry and Gesture. As a professionally licensed theater, a group of deaf individuals could now enjoy for the first time a livelihood as performing artists working together and growing professionally. Wide recognition of the deaf artist did not come, however, until near the end of the 1960s. In 1967 a grant from the U.S. Department of Health, Education and Welfare helped set up the National Theatre of the Deaf (NTD) in Waterford, Connecticut. With innovative staging in its productions, NTD exposed the world to the power and grace of sign language and the multitalents of deaf actors. A combination of factors during the 1960s and 1970s speeded up public acceptance: the civil rights movement, the growing militancy of deaf people, the advent of total communication, and the emergence of bonafide research in sign language. Also, federal funding allowed NTD to train hundreds of deaf persons at its Professional School for Deaf Theatre Personnel; Gallaudet College added a drama major; and the National Technical Institute for the Deaf started its Experimental Educational Theatre Department. *See* GALLAUDET COLLEGE; NATIONAL TECHNICAL INSTITUTE FOR THE DEAF; THEATER, COLLEGE.

Across the country, new theaters of the deaf came into being and old ones were given new leases on life. While not professional in the full sense of the word, many theaters and programs are in a position to pay, in varying degrees, their actors and staffs. As the first professional residential theater of the deaf, the Fairmount Theatre of the Deaf of Cleveland, Ohio, staged its first production in 1975. Professional theaters also blossomed in Australia (New South Wales Theatre of the Deaf), Sweden (Tyst Theater), Great Britain (Interim), and Japan (Japan's Theater of the Deaf.) *See* FAIRMOUNT THEATRE OF THE DEAF; NATIONAL THEATERS OF THE DEAF.

The success of Mark Medoff's *Children of a Lesser God* (1980) brought a bonanza of publicity and opportunities for deaf actors. The Broadway production included three deaf actors: Phyllis Frelich in the lead of "Sarah," a deaf cleaning woman who falls in love with a speech therapist; Lewis Merkin as "Orin," and Julianna Gold as "Lydia." The play won Tonys for Frelich as Best Actress, for John Rubinstein as Best Actor, and for Medoff for Best Play. Suddenly, deaf actors were in demand for the three roles in national touring companies and repertory theater productions of the play. More than a dozen deaf women in America and abroad have played "Sarah." In London, Elizabeth Quinn captured Britain's top award, the Society of West End Theater Actress of the Year, for the role. Deaf individuals even got to direct the play, as Edmund Waterstreet did for the Theatre by the Sea in Portsmouth, New Hampshire, and Shanny Mow did for the Fayetteville (North Carolina) Little Theatre. In 1984 Frelich and Medoff teamed up again for a new play, *The Hands of Its Enemy*. *See* FRELICH, PHYLLIS.

Professional experience has given birth to a new breed of deaf individuals: freelance artists. In addition to performing on the professional stage, they can, for a fee, give theater workshops to hearing people, teach deaf children, display their expertise at deaf awareness festivals, or make guest appearances in amateur productions. Deaf actors shared the stage with hearing actors in the Los Angeles Actors' Theatre production of *Trojan Women* (1980). American Theatre Arts offered a special American Sign Language production of Shakespeare's *Twelfth Night*. While still in high school, Bruce Hlibok appeared as a deaf teenager in the Off-Broadway musical *Runaways* (1980). Waterstreet directed *Story Theatre* (1981) and *Wind in the Willows* (1983) for the Empire State Institute for the Performing Arts. Alfred Corrado served as scenic artist for the Metropolitan Opera and Chuck Baird designed and painted sets for several theaters.

From its inception in 1979, the New York Deaf Theatre has led as a producer of deaf theater which focuses on the deaf experience. It has presented, for example, *A Play of 1,000 Words*, *Deaf Pa What?*, *The Traveling Road Show*, and *ASL Festival*, most of which have been written and directed by popular deaf comedian Mary Beth Miller.

At the Fairmount Theatre of the Deaf, Adrian Blue wrote and directed *Circus of Sign*, which won the Outstanding Original Script of 1982 award from the Cleveland Critics Circle. Another Fairmount production, Molière's *The Miser*, won Donald Bangs an Emmy for his Old West adaptation of the play. However, no play with a deaf theme written by a deaf playwright has been produced by a commercial theater. In the 1960s Eric Malzkuhn wrote *The*

Sound of Silence with a central character who was deaf, but he could not find a producer. Gilbert Eastman's *Sign Me Alice* (1973), Dorothy Miles's *A Play of Our Own* (1973), as well as Rico Peterson's *A Play of Our Own, Part II* (1978), Steve Baldwin's *A Play of Our Own, Part III* (1979), and Bernard Bragg and Eugene Bergman's *Tales from a Clubroom* (1980) were all written with a deaf audience in mind. But the basic problem remains of where to find parts for deaf actors. For every part, speaking or nonspeaking, that becomes available in professional theater, there are hundreds of hungry hopefuls.

In the past, hearing actors played deaf characters, but any producer who continues that practice will risk the wrath of deaf actors and the deaf community. Nevertheless, unless plays write in more deaf characters and both the producers and the theater goers accept them as a matter of course rather than as a novelty, most deaf actors will enjoy only limited professional success.

Bibliography

Miles, Dorothy S.: "A History of Theatre Activities in the Deaf Community of the United States," Connecticut College, New London, 1974.

THOMSON, ALFRED REGINALD
(1894–1979)

Alfred Reginald Thomson was born in Bangalore, Mysore, India, in 1894. His father, George Thomson, was an inland revenue paymaster for the British army stationed there and held the rank of major. An army doctor pronounced Alfred born deaf when he failed to respond to his father's voice. During early boyhood Alfred developed a liking for drawing figures, mostly animals, on the white walls that surrounded the family house. The father went to England to choose a school for his son. In 1901 father, mother, and son sailed for England, where Thomson was left at the Margate School for the Deaf. He never saw his mother again—she died soon after her return to India.

Thomson grew into a tall and frequently sick boy. His school record was undistinguished, but he showed some promise in art. When asked by a teacher what he wanted as an occupation when he left school, he mentioned artist. His father, on leave, was dismayed at Thomson's poor school attainment and notable absence of speech, so he had the boy removed to the Barber Oral School in North London. From this school he acquired nothing but unintelligible speech. Fortunately, on the advice of his art teacher at Margate, he was allowed to attend an art school in Central London. His tutor was the son of Sir William Orchardson, a leading artist at that time.

A. R. Thomson in 1938.

George Thomson, on hearing of his son's involvement in art, was furious. He came over from India and forced him to a farm in Kent as a fee-paying agricultural student. Instead of being trained, Thomson was made to work like a slave and was forbidden to have anything connected with art, such as paper, pencil, or paint. He endured this harsh existence for two years before fleeing to Chelsea in London.

In 1916 Thomson set himself up as an artist in Redfern Road, known as the "Road of Hopefuls." As a result, his father disowned him. He sat for the entrance examination for the Royal Academy School of Art but failed. He took up farming, this time working for a pleasant woman farmer in Bedfordshire. Soon the lure of art became far too strong, and he rushed back to Chelsea. He did paintings, earned little money, and soon became destitute, often going without food for days and sleeping in the vaults of St. Martin in the Fields Church, which was used to shelter the homeless.

Thomson's break came when he was befriended by a wealthy woman whom he met at an all-night club. She fed and housed him for a time. His forenames were distasteful to her so she christened him Tommy, a name his contemporaries adopted as well. Her influence enabled Thomson to obtain work as a commercial artist. His drawings advertizing Daimler cars and Tuborg beer later became famous. A sympathetic architect commissioned him to do murals for the walls of the Duncannon, a well-known central London public house. Its four walls displayed Thomson's Dickensian characters in their environments. These paintings made an impact in the art world and were mentioned in the press. He was accepted as a member of the elite Chelsea Arts Club, but with some reluctance because of his deafness. He became friendly with fellow members Augustus John and Sir William Orpen, who were artists of great renown. John found Thomson a teaching post in East London, where he taught by using written notes and by correcting details on students' works. He was welcomed at John's villa at Martigues in southern France, where he painted murals at a house of a wealthy family.

In 1938 the Essex County Council proclaimed an open competition for a painting relating to the Pilgrim Fathers, who were mostly of Essex origin. After spending several days at Plymouth where the Pilgrim Fathers embarked for America and after studying historical records at the British Museum, Thomson entered the contest and won. His painting showing an embarkment scene was hung on the Royal Wall at the following Summer Exhibition of the Royal Academy. The press and critics gave it an overwhelming acclaim, and Thomson was immediately elevated to the status of Associate of the Royal Academy. His father, now retired, made no attempt to recognize his son's astronomical success; nevertheless, Thomson's future was assured and his ambition fulfilled.

Famous people waited to be painted by the famous deaf and dumb artist. During World War II, he served as the official Royal Air Force artist, and while at an airfield failed to hear the challenge of a sentry, who shot him in the shoulder. The bullet remained there, as its removal would have paralyzed his arm. After the war, he became a senior academician and served on the hanging committee for six years. He disliked the position, as it meant rejecting the works of so many aspiring artists.

Thomson was the first painter in history allowed the subject of the interior of the House of Commons and of the House of Lords. He painted both houses in session; this involved visits to his studio of many famous people, including Winston Churchill, Clement Attlee, and Harold Macmillan. These two large pictures branded Thomson as one of the greatest specialists in the difficult art of composite groups. His *Seated Boxer* won him a gold medal in the art section of the London Olympics in 1948. Dogged by ill health, he continued to work till the

last few days before he died at the age of 84 on October 27, 1979. Thomson's works can be found in many art galleries around the world. Queen Elizabeth herself owns about a dozen of his pictures. He married Majorie Horne in 1927, but the marriage was a disaster. In 1940 he made Gertrude Parker his second wife, and they were wonderfully happy. They had two children. Both wives acted as his manager, secretary, and speaker.

Bibliography

Dimmock, A. F.: "Deaf Great," *British Deaf News*, 1959.
————: *Tommy*, 1984.
Holroyd, Michael: *Augustus John* (part 2), 1972.
The Times, Newspaper Library, North London, extracts from 1922, 1928, 1938, 1939, 1959, 1961, 1979.

A. F. Dimmock

TILDEN, DOUGLAS
(1860–1935)

Douglas Tilden was the first native California sculptor to win recognition outside the United States. The acceptance of the plaster model of his *Baseball Player* in the Paris Salon, 1889, was a remarkable achievement for a young man who had lost his ability to hear and to speak following an attack of scarlet fever in early childhood.

Born May 1, 1860, in Chico, California, Tilden was fortunate that his parents, William Peregrine Tilden, a medical doctor, and Catherine (Hecox) Tilden, enrolled him in the California School for the Deaf, Berkeley (CSDB) shortly before his sixth birthday. The school's principal, Warring Wilkinson, believed wholeheartedly that art instruction was a means of teaching broader relationships in the education of his hearing-impaired students. Tilden was a bright student always interested in art. Following his graduation, he passed the entrance exams for the nearby University of California. However, he decided not to attend, and accepted a teaching position at CSDB, where he remained for eight years. During this time he studied drawing and painting briefly at the California School of Design, took one month of private instruction from sculptor Marion Wells, and set up a studio of his own on the grounds of CSDB.

The development of his talent led the board of trustees of CSDB to lend him $500 per year for study in New York and Paris. Tilden first attended classes for eight months in New York at the National Academy School of Fine Arts and at the Gotham Students League.

When he arrived in Paris in 1888, Tilden immediately began work on his monumental *Baseball Player*, with occasional instruction from deaf sculptor Paul Chopin. At the end of the nineteenth century, acceptance and recognition in the prestigious Paris Salon was mandatory for the fame and

Douglas Tilden, about 1895.

den with their first professorship of sculpture. For the first time a deaf man was teaching art to students who could hear and speak. His classroom was unique, with his unorthodox methods of communicating with pencil on paper and with pantomime. Tilden attracted attention in his unusual position where he was always "faultlessly dressed from the crown of his shiny hat to the tips of his patent leather shoes." For seven years he exerted an enormous influence on a young generation of Bay Area sculptors, and his works continued to be exhibited—at the Universelle Exposition, Paris, 1900; the Pan American Exposition, Buffalo, New York, 1901; Louisiana Purchase Exposition, St. Louis, Missouri, 1904; and the Alaska-Yukon-Pacific Exposition at Seattle, Washington, in 1909.

The young civic-minded mayor of San Francisco, James Duval Phelan, a true renaissance man, thought "the great conquering power of the world was art." He spent his personal fortune on the arts, ordering several monuments to commemorate important events in the city's history. Tilden received several of the commissions. Large monuments take many months, sometimes years, to bring to fruition. Although Tilden's total output was small, many of his monuments are recognized today as "the most original and exciting sculptures, based on allegorical or genre themes, ever produced in California." They stand as a testimony to the turbulent and magnificent renaissance of the arts at the turn of the century in San Francisco.

While Douglas Tilden was still a teacher at CSDB, he published several articles about educating deaf people in the *American Annals of the Deaf*. During his stay in Paris, the distinguished *Overland Monthly* magazine published his "Art and What San Francisco Should Do About Her," in which he advocated the building of an art museum in Golden Gate Park. San Francisco had no permanent museum at that time. A few years later, the *Overland Monthly* awarded him first prize for his "Poverty of Fortune," a fictional account of a young sculptor in San Francisco.

Along with his preoccupation with art and his interest in writing, Tilden devoted much of his energies toward promoting a better understanding between deaf and hearing people. He thought this understanding was best accomplished by bringing together these two worlds. Tilden worked long and hard for his credo that art can transcend humanity's diversities and unite all. Feeling that deaf individuals were poorly organized for their own welfare in society, Tilden set up the original California Association of the Deaf, but his quick temper and impatience with his fellows created problems which caused him to drop out of the group. This would be an increasing problem for him the rest of his life.

fortune of a sculptor—practically guaranteeing future commissions for large civic monuments. During the six years Tilden worked in Paris, the Salon accepted five of his monuments, which were praised for their unorthodox subject matter, reflecting a "truly American spirit." He had major exhibits at the Société des Artistes Française and the Société National des Beaux-Arts in 1889, 1890, 1891, 1892, and 1894. His *Tired Boxer*, later destroyed in the 1906 San Francisco earthquake and fire, won Honorable Mention. European success, especially in Paris, was the yardstick by which artists were measured in American art circles.

The influence of the European renaissance in art reached its zenith at the World's Columbian Exposition in Chicago in 1893. Tilden was a European member of the sculpture jury. He joined the National Sculpture Society that year, and four of his monuments were exhibited at the exposition. The artistic impulse of the American renaissance, which led to city-beautiful movements all over the United States, was in full swing when Tilden returned home to San Francisco in 1894. Tilden was soon appointed to inaugurate the first department of modeling on the Pacific coast at the California School of Design, Mark Hopkins Institute of Art (now the San Francisco Art Institute), which was then an affiliated college of the University of California, Berkeley. The regents of the university honored Til-

Tilden's *Mechanics*, dedicated May 1903 in San Francisco; the bronze statue itself is 15 feet high.

In the first two decades of the twentieth century, the era of the wealthy art patron ended, and the public demand for costly monumental statuary diminished. Many artists changed to a more personal vision, but Tilden did not go along with this trend. Despondent, as the World War I years dragged on, he worked as a machinist and as a creator of movie sets in Hollywood, and finally made an unsuccessful attempt at a comeback in sculpture. His deaf wife of 30 years, Elizabeth Cole, who had borne him two children, filed for divorce. He continued to write as well as to be a watchdog for political concerns at CSDB. On August 6, 1935, Douglas Tilden died of a heart attack, alone, in his Berkeley studio.

A number of Tilden's monumental bronze sculptures may be viewed in California: *Baseball Player*

and *Father Junipero Serra*, Golden Gate Park, San Francisco; *Admission Day*, *Mechanics*, and *California Volunteers*, Market Street, San Francisco; *Bear Hunt*, California School for the Deaf, Fremont; *Football Players*, University of California, Berkeley; *U.S. Senator Stephen White Memorial*, Los Angeles; *Twelve Stages of Man*, bronze panels on McElroy Memorial Fountain, Oakland; *Grief*, Valentine Memorial, Cypress Lawn Cemetery, Colma. His *Oregon Volunteers* is in Portland, Oregon.

Tilden's smaller works include *Golden Gate*, bronze statuette, Oakland Museum, California; bronze replica of *Baseball Player*, Baseball Hall of Fame, Cooperstown, New York; *Young Acrobat*, bronze and marble, Monterey Museum, California; miniature *Bear Hunt*, solid gold, Old Orchard Museum, Sagamore Hill, New York; marble bust, *Father Edmund Young*, University of Santa Clara, California, *Joseph LeConte*, bronze plaque, LeConte Lodge, Yosemite Valley, California; *Junipero Serra*, bronze medallion, Mission Dolores Historical Museum, Mission Dolores, San Francisco; *Joaquin Miller*, bronze, private collection.

Mildred Albronda

TINNITUS

The physical disorder tinnitus (literally, ringing) may be broadly classified into tinnitus aurium (ringing in the ear) or tinnitus cerebri (ringing in the head). The preferred term is ear noise or head noise because all sounds experienced by tinnitus sufferers are not ringing. The sounds may be described as buzzing, humming, cricketlike, hissing, or combinations of these, although ringing is the most common description used. There are many theories to explain probable generators (mechanisms) of tinnitus and the possible causes, but none seems to have gained wide professional acceptance.

CLASSIFICATION

In 1950 Victor Goodhill offered a classification system for tinnitus. Under aural noises, he included two broad categories: vibratory and nonvibratory. The vibratory tinnitus was described as any tinnitus that was external to the inner ear and caused by a vibration of the various mechanisms within the middle ear, such as a dislocated ossicular chain, wax resting upon the tympanic membrane, or a vascular bruit emanating from a blood vessel. Because vibratory tinnitus could be heard by another person, this fell under the classification of objective tinnitus. Nonvibratory tinnitus, which was thought to originate from either the inner ear or the auditory nervous system, was called subjective. There are times when objective tinnitus is so loud it may be heard by a person as much as 3 feet away from the affected individual. Tinnitus may also be classified as continuous or intermittent. In evaluating the presence of tinnitus, the clinician must be certain that the affected person does not confuse the intermittent nature of some tinnitus with the possibility that it is continuous and simply rendered inaudible at times by masking, that is, by noise in the environment.

EVALUATION

If an individual experiences a loud ear noise in one ear only, a complete evaluation by an ear specialist (otologist) and hearing specialist (audiologist) is strongly recommended. Unilateral (one-sided) tinnitus can be a symptom for a number of serious auditory disorders. An individual experiencing ringing or noise in one ear, not attributable to noise exposure, requires a complete otologic and audiologic examination to rule out the possibility of an acoustic neuroma or tumor. Sometimes the pitch of the tinnitus gives a clue as to its probable cause. Low-frequency tinnitus may be associated with a conductive (mechanical) hearing loss or with Ménière's disease. The tinnitus associated with Ménière's disease may be constant or intermittent. However, in most cases it is reported either to increase dramatically in intensity or to appear just prior to and during the onset of a vertiginous attack. It is commonly accepted that high-pitched tinnitus accompanies hearing loss caused by exposure to loud noise (shotguns, chain saws, rock music). High-frequency tinnitus also may be associated with high-frequency sensorineural hearing loss brought on by other causative agents. These guidelines are broad, and are only signposts for diagnosis.

Unfortunately, the presence and level of annoyance of tinnitus are almost impossible to evaluate medically. In the case of nonvibratory subjective tinnitus, only the affected individual can be aware of it. The clinician has only the patient's word that tinnitus exists. Consequently, in medical-legal cases, it is difficult if not impossible to demonstrate that the individual is experiencing an ear noise.

Many normal-hearing individuals experience some form of ear noise. It is not uncommon for a clinician to examine an individual with a complaint of ringing in the ear and to give the person a clean bill of health. In this case the clinician cannot find a physical basis to explain the ear noise.

Richard H. Nodar

CAUSES

It is possible to provide a listing of those things that are thought to cause tinnitus, even though it is difficult to state with certainty the specific cause for tinnitus in a given person. There are many different things that can produce tinnitus; each of various maladies does not necessarily have its own distinctive tinnitus, and this complexity has been compounded by the lack of standardized testing procedures for tinnitus.

Acoustic Overload   One of the most common causes of tinnitus is exposure to very loud sounds. A typical example is the individual who has worked many years in a noisy environment, such as the wood products industry, and in addition has engaged in noisy recreational pursuits such as shooting, using chain saws, or driving snowmobiles. These persons show bilateral high-frequency hearing losses and high-frequency tonal tinnitus that is also usually bilateral. However, all persons exposed to very loud sounds do not develop tinnitus. Why some people are more susceptible to noise-induced tinnitus is an area that has not been investigated.

Most people with noise-induced tinnitus have been exposed to noise over a long period of time. There is, however, a subgroup of noise-exposed individuals who have experienced a single episode of great intensity. The latter reveal similar high-frequency hearing losses and high-frequency tonal tinnitus, but their tinnitus tends to be unresponsive to any present-day relief procedure.

Head Injury   Another frequent cause of tinnitus is head trauma. Such tinnitus is highly variable in pattern. It can appear initially days after the injury and can go into spontaneous remission years later. It can be unilateral, bilateral, or localized in the head, probably depending upon the extent and location of the lesion, which is assumed to involve primarily the higher auditory brain centers. Tinnitus that is produced by head trauma is almost always difficult to manage.

Drugs   There are drugs that appear invariably to induce tinnitus with sufficient consumption. Aspirin is one such drug, although the tinnitus is temporary and will disappear after cessation of aspirin ingestion. Quinine is another drug that produces tinnitus, which is usually permanent.

It is commonly held that many aminoglycoside antibiotics produce tinnitus. Moreover, physicians are usually instructed to look for tinnitus as the first sign of an auditory side effect resulting from these drugs. Studies have not supported this claim, however, in that the tinnitus appears to develop only after extensive hearing loss has occurred, and then after a long period of drug treatment.

Disease States   There are many disease conditions of the ear that may have tinnitus as a symptom. Otosclerosis, sudden hearing loss, Ménière's disease, tumor of the eighth cranial nerve, middle-ear infections, as well as simple matters such as wax or foreign material on the eardrum may have some form of tinnitus as a symptom. In some cases, treatment of the disease will remove the tinnitus. For example, otosclerosis is usually accompanied by a low-pitched roaring tinnitus. When a successful stapedectomy is performed, the tinnitus usually disappears. Ménière's disease may be surgically corrected or go into spontaneous remission, only to find later that the tinnitus has shifted from a low-pitched roaring to a middle-pitched tone. Qualitative shifts such as that with Ménière's disease do not usually occur with the other disease conditions; changes that do occur are mostly of a quantitative nature.

Another fairly frequent cause of tinnitus is the common cold or flu. It is not an unusual symptom, and it generally disappears with recovery. However, tinnitus may persist in people who took an airplane flight while they had a cold or the flu. In addition, there are cases of severe and persistent tinnitus for which no cause can be found.

APPROACHES TO RELIEF

The four main approaches to relieve tinnitus that are either in use or under investigation are masking, medications, biofeedback, and suppression by electrical stimulation.

Masking Masking such as is presently used to relieve tinnitus was introduced by J. Vernon in 1975. However, the essence of masking has been known since the work of J. A. Spaulding in 1903. Masking is defined as substituting for the tinnitus an external sound or noise that the patient finds more acceptable. Not all tinnitus yields to masking, and only by appropriate testing is it possible to determine whether masking is worthwhile for a given person.

Gradually over the years, masking has evolved into three main approaches: simple masking, masking by hearing aids, and masking by the tinnitus instrument.

Simple Masking. Tinnitus maskers were developed so as to deliver a band of noise that could be centered at low, middle, or high frequencies. This selection was made available on the assumption that the pitch of tinnitus would be found to be distributed over the audio-frequency range. That expectation has not been borne out, and today a prescribed tinnitus masker is almost always a high-frequency masker.

Hearing Aids. It has been found that 90 percent of the people suffering severe tinnitus also have a hearing loss; only 15 percent of them have tried hearing aids. Hearing aids usually work well to relieve tinnitus when the pitch of the tinnitus is low so as to correspond to frequencies located in the regions where hearing aid amplification works well, say at 3000 Hz and lower. If the tinnitus is bilateral, it is almost always necessary to fit both ears. *See* HEARING AIDS.

When hearing aids do produce relief of tinnitus, it is assumed that they do so by amplifying ambient environmental sounds that in turn serve to mask the tinnitus. Where the tinnitus is high-pitched, even the high-frequency hearing aid does not have much of an opportunity to be effective, since ambient environment noise is primarily below 4000 Hz.

Tinnitus Instrument. At one time, efforts at masking were defeated by the affected individual's hearing loss. The high-frequency tinnitus coupled with the high-frequency hearing loss made it impossible for the person to hear those frequencies necessary to effect masking. The use of a combination of a tinnitus masker and a hearing aid has provided a solution to this problem. The combination unit, termed a tinnitus instrument, is provided with two independent volume controls and is available as behind-the-ear or in-the-ear models.

Use of Medicine Studies done in 1935 showed that injection of a local anesthetic could produce temporary cessation of tinnitus. Today, the impetus for the search for medication to relieve tinnitus is compelling, and it comes from the positive results of intravenously injected lidocaine. Because the effect is temporary and brief, this route of administration does not offer a practical procedure with which to control tinnitus. On the other hand, the fact that it does affect a high percentage of tinnitus patients (87 percent) has motivated the search for a similar drug that can be administered orally.

Tegretol has been administered orally and found to be effective in 62 percent of the persons on whom intravenous lidocaine had worked. Unfortunately, many persons experienced some serious side effects associated with Tegretol. Also, Tocainide is a near oral analog for lidocaine, but when it was tested only 5 percent of the individuals obtained any relief from their tinnitus. Again, there were serious side effects that affected many.

It is not uncommon for tinnitus sufferers to experience bouts of depression, and in such cases the depression is treated with one of the tricyclic antidepressant preparations. In some instances this medication will exacerbate the tinnitus, while in others it will relieve the tinnitus as well as the depression. Other drugs that have been investigated but found to be ineffectual are dilantin sodium, mysoline, sodium valproate, amylobarbitone, praxilene, baclofen, and Valium. Valium does have a tranquilizing effect, but has no direct effect upon tinnitus. A promising study was conducted with glutamic acid and its antagonist glutamic acid diethylester administered intravenously in successive order. Where relief was produced, it lasted from 3 to 18 months.

Biofeedback One rationale for using biofeedback to combat tinnitus is to teach the individuals to use deep relaxation and focus their attention away from the tinnitus. It has been found that many people indicate an exacerbation of tinnitus during periods of tension or stress. Thus, it seems logical that reducing stress through biofeedback may also be a way to reduce tinnitus. One important part of the biofeedback experience is that the individual is given information about tinnitus. Reassurance by a competent professional may also help reduce anxiety.

Electrical Suppression   Electrical stimulation was first used for the reduction of tinnitus in 1893. In more modern times, the positive effects of galvanic current upon tinnitus were noted. Still more recent has been work motivated by suppression of tinnitus in some affected individuals receiving electrical stimulation in the auditory system via a cochlear implant. Investigations have led to the conclusion that tinnitus can be suppressed in some people by use of direct current. The current must be positive to be effective; otherwise the electrical stimulation produces an auditory sensation or pain. It has also been found that a transtympanic electrode could be utilized to produce electrical suppression of tinnitus and that (1) the direct current must be positive to relieve tinnitus; (2) negative direct current produces exacerbation of tinnitus; and (3) sinodal waveforms (alternating current) are essentially ineffective. *See* COCHLEAR IMPLANTS.

In one study, a variable rate of pulse presentation which the subject controlled was utilized. Mostly, pulse rates of 500 to 800 Hz were used; lower rates tended to produce vibrotactile or prickling sensations. Others have utilized direct current in a variety of waveforms, and some degree of success has been obtained from all of them. No cases of exacerbation of the tinnitus and no complaints of vertigo were found. The duration of the positive effect is highly individualistic, lasting in some cases for a matter of several weeks.

It is well established that electrical currents can produce tissue damage; thus the use of direct current to suppress tinnitus encounters this possible risk. If conditions can be found that lead to long-term suppression of tinnitus after stimulation, then the risk of damage would be reduced.

CONCLUSIONS

While tinnitus is a sympton of some auditory malady, it nevertheless takes on an existence of its own and has a high incidence rate. It sometimes seems to persist long after the initiating conditions have ceased to exert any influence.

As described above, a variety of treatments can be offered to the tinnitus sufferer, but each could be improved. In masking, for example, there is a need for a highly flexible masker that can be adjusted to the bandwidth of noise and the slope of the skirts, as well as the center frequency. In some cases, it would be most desirable to make these adjustments available to the affected individual.

There is also need for special controls for the elderly population.

In drug investigation there is need for a more concerted and systematic effort to find effective medications. Investigations in this area would be greatly enhanced by use of an animal model, but work in that area is all but nonexistent.

The electrical suppression of tinnitus is far from ideal because the parameters of stimulation have not been worked out. The reports presently available permit little comparison in such matters as electrode size and placement, stimulus intensity, and stimulus configurations.

Bibliography

Aran, J. M., and Y. Cazals: "Electrical Suppression of Tinnitus," in *Tinnitus: Ciba Foundation Symposium 85,* pp. 217–231, Pitman Books, London, 1981.

Barany, R.: "Die Beeinflussung des ohrensausens durch intravenos injizietate lokalanasthetica," *Acta Otolaryngol.,* 23:201–203, 1935.

Brummett, R. E.: Personal communication, 1983.

Chouard, C. H., B. Meyer, and D. Maridat: "Transcutaneous Electrotherapy for Severe Tinnitus," *Acta Otolaryngol.,* 91:415–422, 1981.

Ehrenberger, K., and R. Brix: "Glutamic Acid and Glutamic Acid Diethylester in Tinnitus Treatment," *Acta Otolaryngol.,* 95:599–605, 1983.

Emmett, J. R., and J. J. Shea: "Treatment of Tinnitus with Tocainide Hydrochloride," *Otolaryngol. Head Neck Surg.,* 88:442–446, 1980.

Field, G. P.: *A Manual of Diseases of the Ear,* Bailliere, Tindall and Cox, London, 1893.

Fowler, E. P.: "Intravenous Procaine in the Treatment of Ménière's Disease," *Ann. Otol. Rhinol. Laryngol.,* 62:1186–1200, 1953.

Gejrot, T.: "Intravenous Xylocaine in the Treatment of Attacks of Ménière's Disease," *Acta Otolaryngol.,* 82:301–302, 1964.

Goodey, R. J.: "Drugs in the Treatment of Tinnitus," in *Tinnitus: Ciba Foundation Symposium 85,* pp. 203–278, Pitman Books, London, 1981.

Graham, J. M., and J. W. P. Hazell: "Electrical Stimulation of the Human Cochlea Using a Transtympanic Electrode," *Brit. J. Audiol.,* 11:59–62, 1977.

Hatton, D. S., S. D. Erulkar, and P. E. Rosenberg: "Some Preliminary Observations on the Effect of Galvanic Current on Tinnitus Aurium," *Laryngoscope,* 70:123–130, 1960.

House, J., L. Miller, and P. House: "Severe Tinnitus: Treatment with Biofeedback Training, Results in 41 Cases," *Trans. Amer. Acad. Ophthal. Otolaryngol.,* 84:697–703, 1976.

House, P. R.: "Personality of the Tinnitus Patient," in *Tinnitus: Ciba Foundation Symposium 85,* pp. 193–203, Pitman Books, London, 1981.

House, W. F.: "Cochlear Implants," *Ann. Otol. Rhinol. Laryngol.,* vol. 85, suppl. 27, 1976.

Israel, J. M. et al.: "Lidocaine in the Treatment of Tinnitus Aurium," *Arch. Otolaryngol.,* 108:471–473, 1982.

Lewy, R. B.: "Treatment of Tinnitus Aurium by Intravenous Use of Anesthetic Agents," *Arch. Otolaryngol.,* 25:178–183, 1937.

Martin, F. W., and B. H. Colman: "Tinnitus: A Double-Blind Crossover Controlled Trial To Evaluate the Use of Lignocaine," *Clin. Otolaryngol.*, 5:3–11, 1980.

Melding, P. S., R. J. Goodey, and P. R. Thorne: "The Use of Intravenous Lignocaine in the Diagnosis and Treatment of Tinnitus," *J. Laryngol. Otol.*, 92:115–121, 1978.

Melding, P. S., and R. J. Goodey: "The Treatment of Tinnitus with Oral Anticonvulsants," *J. Laryngol. Otol.*, 93:111–122, 1979.

Schleuning, A. J., et al.: "Masking and Tinnitus," *Audio. Hear. Ed.*, 6:5–9, 1980.

Shea, J. J., and M. Harell: "Management of Tinnitus Aurium with Lidocaine and Carbamazepine," *Laryngoscope*, 88:1477–1484, 1978.

Shulman, A., and B. Goldstein: "Treatment of Tinnitus," in *Tinnitus: Ciba Foundation Symposium 85*, pp. 257–259, Pitman Books, London, 1981.

Spaulding, J. A.: "Tinnitus, With a Plea for Its More Accurate Musical Notation," *Arch. Otolaryngol.*, 32:263–272, 1903.

Vernon, J.: "Relief of Tinnitus by Masking Treatment," in G. M. English (ed.), *Otolaryngology*, Harper and Row, 1982.

———: "Tinnitus," *Hearing Aid Journal*, 13:82–83, 1975.

———: "Tinnitus Masking: Unresolved Problems," *Tinnitus: Ciba Foundation Symposium 85*, pp. 239–256, Pitman Books, London, 1981.

———: "The Use of Masking for Relief of Tinnitus," in H. Silverstein and H. Norrell, *Neurological Surgery of the Ear*, 2:104–118, 1979.

——— et al.: "A Tinnitus Clinic," *Ear Nose and Throat J.*, 56:181–189, 1977.

Jack Vernon

TSIOLKOVSKY, KONSTANTIN EDUARDOVICH (1857–1935)

The space age passed from the realm of fantasy to reality with the work of a trio of pioneers in rocket dynamics: Robert H. Goddard in the United States, Hermann Oberth in Germany, and Konstantin E. Tsiolkovsky in the Soviet Union. First in time was Tsiolkovsky, a self-educated schoolteacher, mathematician, scientist, author, and visionary.

In the late nineteenth century Tsiolkovsky did both theoretical and technical studies on the feasibility of airships and airplanes before forging ahead of his contemporaries by concluding that liquid-propulsion rockets would make interplanetary travel possible. His influence is traceable through the work of Sergei P. Korolyov, the chief designer responsible for the landmark launchings of both *Sputnik I* and the first cosmonaut in space, Yuri Gagarin. The Soviets view Tsiolkovsky as the patriarch of the space age, crediting him with initiating astronautics.

Tsiolkovsky was born on September 17, 1857, in the village of Izhevskoye, Ryazan Province, Russia. Scarlet fever left him with a hearing impairment when he was about 10 years old. Puzzlement about the sudden silence, confusion due to uncertain communication, and an awareness that he was being ridiculed brought him moments of deep humiliation and depression. The once-lively youth became awkward and constrained among others and dropped out of school. To avoid boredom he read, reread, concentrated, dreamed, wrote, and soon discovered a keen interest in mathematics and physics.

Having learned from his father how to make tools, young Tsiolkovsky experimented and created numerous innovations. Wherever he resided, the experiments of the deaf "crank" became the talk of the community.

Impressed by his deaf son's resourcefulness, the father sent him to Moscow to further his education and provided him with a small monthly allowance. The Moscow stay, from 1873 to 1876, was formative both educationally and in personal development. Unable to enroll as a student, Tsiolkovsky studied in the libraries at a time when Moscow's liberal political atmosphere promoted intellectual ferment and much scholarly production. To save money for precious books and materials needed for experiments conducted at his lodging, he literally lived on bread and water.

These years forced the bewildered rural youth to depend on himself. There were no relatives or acquaintances to look after him in the large city. He got used to being looked at askance because of his shabby acid-stained clothing, uncut hair, and deafness—conspicuous when he used a funnel-shaped, self-made ear trumpet. In time the now-assured youth rejoined his family, undertook private tutoring, and passed the necessary examinations to obtain a teaching certificate when he was 22.

Soon after taking a teaching position in Borovsk, his residence from 1880 to 1892, Tsiolkovsky forwarded his discoveries on the kinetic theory of gases to the Russian Physico-Chemical Society at St. Petersburg, only to learn that the findings were already long known. Nevertheless, the response, prepared by the notable chemist D. Mendeleyev, encouraged the budding scientist to continue. The incident only indicated the appropriateness of his approach and reinforced confidence in his own conclusions. Soon another study earned him membership in the esteemed Society.

About 1885 Tsiolkovsky decided to concentrate on what had always fascinated him: air travel. The decade was to be productive, yet filled with letdowns when his studies did not bring forth the financial support needed to proceed with actual designs. Within two years he had completed theoretical studies concerning maneuverable dirigibles. By 1890 he had specific proposals for the construction of an elongated metallic airship, capable of adjusting its volume to changing altitudes and atmospheric conditions.

In 1892 Tsiolkovsky took a better teaching position at Kaluga and, unable to proceed beyond the dirigible blueprints, focused on the study of the airplane. His typically thorough research and conclusions yielded impressive results. Material published in 1894 included both a description and drawings of a surprisingly modern streamlined metal monoplane, with nose propellers and wheeled undercarriage. His experiments indicated that elongated shapes were the least air-resistant, a concept which he incorporated in all his models and which indicated that the rocket was the means to overcome both the pull of gravity and the retarding air pressure of the atmosphere. In 1896 he began concentrating on what he had considered over a decade earlier: the possibility of travel into space. In so doing, he practically leapfrogged over the airplane stage. His findings consistently showed that the dirigible was more practical, and in 1930 he stated that the days of the propeller plane were numbered, and that the future belonged to jet planes.

Previously in 1883, Tsiolkovsky had written a manuscript entitled "Free Space," describing his conceptualizations of man and vehicle in gravityless space. Significantly, he first mentioned the reaction (jet) principle as the means of space propulsion at this time. These embryonic generalizations were further elaborated in his science fiction novelettes, *On the Moon* (1893) and *Dreams of Earth and the Sky* (1895). In the latter, he considered an artificial satellite and suggested its orbit. In 1896 he began to record data for still another manuscript, *Beyond the Earth*, the final version being published in 1920.

By 1898 Tsiolkovsky had completed preliminary studies of space travel and submitted the results for publication. The conclusions may have seemed too fantastic to the editor, since the work was not to appear in print until five years later.

In the meantime a formula, later termed the Tsiolkovsky formula, was computed, which showed how a rocket could attain the velocity needed to take off into space. The need for precise data about air resistance led Tsiolkovsky to construct a primitive but effective wind tunnel by 1897, the first in Russia. Impressed, he recommended the device for use in the laboratories of all learning institutions. The results of his studies finally brought a grant, and a larger tunnel was built. This enabled him to study the maneuverability and stability of objects of various shapes under controlled conditions. Although no further financial support was forthcoming, the findings advanced his rocket dynamics studies to the point that, 20 years after his ideas had first been recorded, a definitive work was ready for publication in 1903. It was the now-classic article "Investigating Space with Reactive Devices." However, he was to be disappointed again when the periodical in which his article appeared was confiscated by the police and publication ceased. The second installation was not published until 1911–1912, by which time Tsiolkovsky's studies had advanced even more.

As a scientist, Tsiolkovsky was fully aware that his conclusions were tentative and that progress operated by chain reaction. Nevertheless, he was so certain that repeat experiments would substantiate his findings that he published whatever tentative conclusions he had reached, most of them printed at his own expense. He hoped for scientific feedback, but this was not forthcoming. In the area of space travel he simply was ahead of what was considered feasible on the basis of science and technology available at the time.

Following the Russian Revolution of 1917, Tsiolkovsky retired in 1920. The pension granted by the new Soviet government enabled the aged man to devote almost full time to formulating his theories about rocket dynamics, and to writing and correspondence. Always a prolific writer, he now composed the majority of his over 500 works. Although not in attendance, he lived to share in the exuberance when a liquid-propelled rocket finally took off in a 1933 test. His perseverance had been vindicated!

The breadth of Tsiolkovsky's thinking and research is impressive. His studies showed that to overcome the pull of gravity incredible speed had to be attained and maintained. The formula he worked out suggested how rocket performance could be maximized. For the rocket to continue on its way, the speed had to be increased. He arrived at the significant conclusion that liquefied gases had definite advantages over the solid fuels then in use. In airless space the vehicle needed to depend on its own fuel for both combustion and exhaust, the latter controlling movement. To attain greater velocity, he proposed that the vehicle discard excess weight by jettisoning useless parts, such as those that had contained fuel used up in escaping earth's gravity. Two different rocket combinations were designed.

Tsiolkovsky studied all aspects of the feasibility of rocket travel. This ranged from analyzing the nature of gases in various combinations to the psychological effects when a person was confined in such a vehicle. He was concerned with the vehicle's design and its strength estimates, with the effects of extreme temperatures and how to counter these, with the launching angle, with the vehicle's reentry into the atmosphere, and with its landing. He considered various guidance systems, and even thought of an automatic pilot. The needs of a man surviving the dangerous acceleration and his functions in airless space were attended to. Spaceship drawings included ecological hothouses utilizing solar energy to grow plants for food and respiration. He came up with several detailed rocket designs to determine the best overall shape for space travel. A turbofan engine was proposed.

Tsiolkovsky believed that space travel would benefit humankind. People would no longer be at the mercy of natural forces such as earthquakes, fluctuating climate, overpopulation, or cataclysms such as meteorite collision. When the sun's life-giving light finally snuffed out, humankind would continue inhabiting hothouse environments, colonizing space, and getting sustenance from other suns.

With the appearance of Oberth's *The Rocket into Interplanetary Space* (1923), Tsiolkovsky's genius was fully recognized. His "Investigating Space with Reactive Devices" was reprinted, as were many of his other works, and new articles were published. In 1927 an international exhibit on rocket technology was held in Moscow. Prominently displayed were the works of Tsiolkovsky. A nine-volume encyclopedia on space travel devoted an entire volume to this pioneer and his work. By his seventy-fifth birthday he was a national figure. A larger home was offered, and the old one was converted into a museum. Stalin sent him greetings, and the Order of the Red Banner of Labor was awarded at the Kremlin. Tsiolkovsky died on September 19, 1935, in Kaluga.

Had the *Sputnik* been launched in September,

an appropriate "Tsiolkovsky Centennial" would have been marked in 1957. Even so, both he and his hometown of Kaluga have been immortalized. His likeness has appeared on stamps and medals. A feature-length film depicts his life and work. An impressive monument, dedicated to the cosmonauts and portraying a seated Tsiolkovsky in front of a rocket taking off, was erected in Moscow. The Kaluga museum was renovated, and a State Museum of the History of Cosmonautics was built, with Yuri Gagarin laying the cornerstone. In 1967 one of the craters on the far side of the moon was named after the scientist. Regular scientific symposiums have been held to build upon the work that Tsiolkovsky inaugurated singlehandedly.

Bibliography

Braun, W. von, and F. I. Ordway, III: *The Rocket's Red Glare*, 1976.

Clarke, A. (ed.): *The Coming of the Space Age*, 1967.

K. E. Tsiolkovsky: Selected Works, trans. by G. Yankovsky, 1968.

Kosmodemyansky, A.: *Konstantin Tsiolkovsky: His Life and Work*, trans. by X. Denko, 1956.

Parry, A.: *Russia's Rockets and Missiles*, 1960.

Riabchikov, E.: *Russians in Space*, trans. by Guy Daniels, 1971.

Thomas, Shirley: *Men of Space: Profiles of the Leaders in Space Research, Development, and Exploration*, vol. 1, 1960.

Ausma Smits

U

UNITED KINGDOM

The United Kingdom, separated from the continent of Europe by the English Channel, comprises England, Wales, Scotland, and Northern Ireland. The United Kingdom must be distinguished from the British Isles, which comprise the two large islands of Great Britain and Ireland and about 5000 smaller islands. The population of the United Kingdom is slightly less than 60 million.

Hearing-impaired individuals in the United Kingdom are grouped by the Government into three categories: deaf without speech, those who have no useful hearing and whose normal means of communication is by signs, fingerspelling, or writing; deaf with speech, those who (even with a hearing aid) have little or no useful hearing but whose normal method of communication is by speech and lipreading; and the hard-of-hearing, those who (with or without a hearing aid) have some useful hearing and whose normal method of communication is by speech, listening, and lipreading. This entry is primarily concerned with the first two categories.

DEMOGRAPHY

Statistics concerning the number of hearing-impaired children receiving special educational treatment are kept separately by the Departments of Education in England, Scotland, Wales, and Northern Ireland. Representative figures may be those of England in 1982, when deaf and partially hearing children who were receiving education in special schools or analogous institutions made up 3.98 and 5.77 per 10,000 of the total school population, respectively. No statistics are prepared with respect to hearing-impaired children in attendance at ordinary schools and classes. The prevalence rate for profound prelingual deafness in the United Kingdom, however, is thought to be between 0.8 and 1.5 per 1000 live births.

Statistics on the incidence of adult deafness in the United Kingdom are based on estimates rather than a census. In 1947, for example, L. T. Wilkins of the Social Survey Division of the Central Office of Information made a study for the Medical Research Council "To provide a measure of the incidence and prevalence of deafness or hearing defect in the civilian adult population of England, Scotland, and Wales." This study was made primarily for the purpose of ascertaining the number of hearing aids likely to be required for free loan under the National Health Service Acts of 1946 and was based on a stratified random sample of those persons in the three countries who were over the age of 16 years. It concluded that there were about 45,000 totally deaf persons, another 70,000 who were deaf to "all natural speech," and about 1,650,000 more people with hearing impairments.

These figures were updated in 1976 by the Statistics and Research Division of the Department of Health and Social Security to reflect changes in the age distribution of the population. An estimate of the prevalence rates for children was also made. According to this study, by 1975 there were 62,000 people over the age of 16 with very severe hearing impairment and 2,298,000 with other impairments. The preschool-age population contained 6200 children with severe impairments and 41,900 with other impairments, while the school-age population included 15,400 children with very severe impairment and 106,000 children with other impairments. Thus, the prevalence rate for children was 1.6 per 1000 with very severe hearing impairment and 11 per 100 with other hearing impairment.

The Department of Health and Social Security also publishes annually details of the numbers of deaf persons without speech, deaf persons with speech, and hard-of-hearing persons on Local Authority registers. Registration is voluntary; these registers do not include returns for Scotland.

Studies of marriage patterns among deaf people in the United Kingdom confirm the findings of researchers in other countries. In the United Kingdom, as elsewhere, the overwhelming majority of married prelingually deaf persons have deaf spouses. *See* DEAF POPULATION: Demography.

EDUCATION

Since 1944 education in the United Kingdom may be considered at four levels. Primary education includes three ranges: nursery for children under 5 years, infants for children from 5 to 7 or 8 years, and juniors for children from 7 or 8 to 11 or 12 years. Secondary education covers the age period from 11 or 12 to 16 years (the minimum age to leave school) but may be extended to 19 years. Further education technically may cover any period beyond the minimum leaving age of 16, but is generally taken to exclude those who remain at school and those in higher education, that is, the fourth level, studying at universities or colleges.

The legislation for Scottish education is separate from that for England and Wales, and since 1922 the educational system of Northern Ireland has been controlled by the Northern Ireland Ministry of Education. *See* IRELAND, NORTHERN; SCOTLAND: Education.

The first residential institution for the education of deaf persons in the United Kingdom was opened in 1792 on Grange Road, Bermondsey, London. In 1809 this school moved to the Old Kent Road and in 1876 became the Royal School for the Deaf, Margate. The Edinburgh Institute for the Deaf was founded in 1810, the Ulster Institution for the Deaf at Belfast in 1831, and the Cambrian Institution for the Deaf at Aberystwyth (Wales) in 1847. By 1890 there were 16 residential institutions for deaf students in the United Kingdom.

The Elementary Education Act 1870 and corresponding legislation for Scotland provided that all children in each school district should receive elementary education, and did not specifically exclude deaf pupils. Although the example of the London School Board, which established classes for deaf students in 1874, was followed by a few enlight-

ened authorities, the majority of school boards in the nineteenth century ignored the existence of deaf children rather than attempting to solve the practical difficulties of teaching them.

The Royal Commission on the Blind, Deaf and Dumb, which was established in 1886 and reported in 1889, led to the enactment of the Education of Blind and Deaf Mute Children (Scotland) Act 1890 and the Elementary Education (Blind and Deaf Children) Act 1893. These laws made the education of deaf children compulsory between the ages of 7 and 16 and provided grants to educational institutions under the Education Acts rather than the Poor Law. In 1938 the compulsory school age was reduced from 7 to 5, and many deaf children now enter preschool classes at age 2.

The *Report of a Committee of Inquiry into Problems Relating to Children with Defective Hearing*, published in 1938, recommended a fourfold classification of hearing-impaired children: (1) those capable of attending ordinary classes without special arrangements; (2) those more severely affected, who might either attend an ordinary school with the help of a hearing aid and support from visiting teachers of lipreading or be taught in a special school (day or boarding) for partially deaf persons; (3) those whose hearing is so impaired that they need to be educated with deaf persons; and (4) those who are profoundly deaf.

The report published in 1949 by the Advisory Council on Education in Scotland, *Pupils Who Are Defective in Hearing*, accepted the grading system suggested by the English Report of 1938. As a result of the 1938 report, some residential schools for partially deaf persons were opened, and in 1945 deaf children and partially deaf children were listed among the categories of handicapped children for whom Local Authorities were required to make provision. In 1959 the designation "partially deaf" was amended to the more positive "partially hearing." The report, *Ascertainment of Children with Hearing Defects*, issued by the Scottish Education Department in 1967, recommended that this term also be used in the Scottish Regulations.

This change in terminology reflected the developments in audiology and electronic hearing aids which made it easier to ascertain and exploit residual hearing. In consequence, the numbers of "deaf" children declined while the incidence of "partial hearing" rose. There was also greater emphasis on "integration" and the education of hearing-impaired children in ordinary rather than special schools. "Partially hearing units" were first established in four London primary schools in 1947. Today there are about 400 of these in England.

The *Report of the Committee of Enquiry into the Education of Handicapped Children and Young People*, issued in 1978, resulted in the enactment of the Education Act 1981. This legislation replaced the existing categories of handicapped individuals, including those who are deaf and partially hearing, with the concept of special education provision based on the special educational needs of each child. A child has special education needs if he or she has a learning difficulty that requires special educational provision to be made to meet those needs. Declining numbers of deaf children and the implementation of the 1981 act will, no doubt, result in a reduction in the size and number of special schools for deaf children.

Two schools in the secondary sector require special mention. The Mary Hare Grammar School for the Deaf in Newbury, Berkshire, formerly a private school, was recognized in 1946 by the then Ministry of Education, and caters to deaf and partially hearing pupils with an aptitude for academic work leading in some cases to university study. The Burwood Park School in Walton-on-Thames, Surrey, was opened in 1955 in response to the need for secondary technical education for deaf boys. Both schools are residential and admit pupils sponsored by local education authorities on the basis of a competitive entrance examination administered jointly by the two schools.

Further Education   Further education in the United Kingdom, while vocationally biased, may also include the provision of general education and recreational courses. Many schools for hearing-impaired students arrange for their pupils to attend neighboring technical colleges or colleges of further education. A few such colleges offer full or part-time courses exclusively for hearing-impaired students. Limited trade training is offered by some schools for hearing-impaired pupils. The National Study Group on Further and Higher Education for the Hearing Impaired publishes directories of available further education courses and of concessions to hearing-impaired candidates made by public examination bodies.

For older persons, the City Literary Institute, London, has a Centre for the Deaf. Some welfare societies for adult deaf persons also offer classes, and a program of further education is arranged by the British Deaf Association.

Higher Education   A small number of students from the Mary Hare and Burwood Park schools take degree or professional courses at universities or polytechnics. The Open University is doing experimental work in the provision of higher education for hearing-impaired individuals. Facilities for deaf students are available at Sussex University and at the College of St. Hilda and St. Bede of the University of Durham.

Teacher Training   The pioneer institutions for the training of teachers of deaf persons in the United Kingdom were the Association for the Oral Instruction of the Deaf and Dumb, opened in 1872 in Fitzroy Square, London, under the directorship of William Van Praagh, and the Society for Training Teachers of the Deaf and for the Diffusion of the Oral System, which opened a college in Ealing, London, in 1878. The two colleges amalgamated in 1912. In 1916 the Earling Society ceased functioning, and the Fitzroy Square Association carried on the work until 1919, when the students in training were transferred to the newly opened Department of Education of the Deaf at Manchester University.

There is some uncertainty regarding the future of the training of teachers of deaf pupils. This is due to a recommendation by the Advisory Committee on the Supply and Education of teachers that the present mandatory requirement that teachers of hearing-impaired pupils must possess a specialist qualification should be withdrawn because of the present emphasis on the development of integrated schooling for pupils with special education needs.

COMMUNICATION

The Royal Commission of 1889 recommended that "every child who is deaf shall have full opportunity of being educated in the pure oral system." Oralism therefore became general in the United Kingdom schools for deaf students, although the practice was usually modified for pupils who made little progress with this approach. Disquiet about the results of oralism led to the appointment by the Secretary of State for Education and Science of a committee "to consider the place, if any, of finger-spelling and signing in the education of the deaf." This committee reported in 1968, and while reiterating that "every deaf child should have the fullest opportunities of oral education," recommended that research studies should be undertaken to determine "whether or not and in what circumstances the introduction of manual media of communication would lead to improvement in the education of deaf children." *See* EDUCATION: Communication.

Other studies have provided evidence of the communication problems encountered by many prelingually deaf children in postschool life, and they reveal that more than 60 percent of classes in the schools are taught by oral methods while slightly less than 40 percent are using total communication. In England, 19 of the 41 schools reported some use of total communication, while in Northern Ireland 1 of 2 (50 percent) and in Scotland 9 of 11 (82 percent) reported such use. The percentage of classes using total communication in Scotland (46 percent) compared with those in England (35 percent) suggests a difference in communication philosophy between England and Scotland. Studies also show that the trend to total communication is rapidly increasing; workshops for deaf persons are probably accentuating this trend. *See* SOCIO-LINGUISTICS: Total Communication.

Other communication methods in use at schools for deaf persons in England are the combined method, Paget-Gorman Systematic Sign Language, one-handed fingerspelling, and cued speech. A discussion document prepared by the British Association of Teachers of the Deaf (1980) recommended that for children in need of manual methods the oral approach should be supported by either Signed English or the Paget-Gorman System, with a strong preference for the former. *See* MANUALLY CODED ENGLISH: Signed English; MOUTH-HAND SYSTEMS: Cued Speech.

Signed English should be distinguished from British Sign Language. The former is "a specific device for representing the English language grammatically in a manual form based on British regional and national signs and two-handed fingerspelling"; the latter is a "mode of manual visual communication incorporating the natural and regional signs used in Britain within a specific structure." British Sign Language is recognized as a language in its own right, distinct from English. *See* SIGN LANGUAGES: British.

United Kingdom academic research into communication methods used by prelingually deaf persons in adult life is sparse. In general, studies show that most prelingually deaf persons use mixtures of signing, gestures, speech, and lipreading when communicating with hearing people, and British Sign Language when conversing with other deaf people. Difficulties in understanding signs used by deaf persons from different areas of the United Kingdom have been reported and ascribed to the relative lack of mobility among deaf groups and the localization of children in deaf schools. These difficulties become greater as the distance separating groups increases. Thus, residents in Avon were less likely to understand the signing of other deaf people living in Newcastle (285 miles distant) and Scotland (360 miles) than those from Birmingham (90 miles) and Leeds (195 miles). Another factor is the greater use of fingerspelling in Scotland than in the west of England.

EMPLOYMENT

Indications of occupations followed by adult deaf persons in the United Kingdom in the nineteenth century and earlier part of the twentieth century can be obtained from the Census Reports 1851—1911, the Report of the Royal Commission 1889, and from a survey made for the National Institute for the Deaf by Clark and Crowden (1938). A report on juvenile employment prepared in 1958 contains much useful information, as does a further study, the *Hearing Impaired School Leaver*, by Rodda (1970). The Eichholz Report (1932) is still the most comprehensive investigation of the employment of deaf individuals in England and Wales, even though industrial and legislative changes have made this study only of historical interest.

More recent studies give a better picture of the current situation. Just over half of employed deaf persons, for example, have jobs in factories, but only 2 percent have a supervisory role. The employment rate for deaf persons seems to be slightly below that for the general population. Underemployment may be a problem, however, for 82 percent of deaf workers are not involved in planning their work and only 12 percent envision any possibility of promotion; nevertheless, 71 percent of deaf workers interviewed claim to be happy in their work. Most deaf workers studied have manual jobs at the lower end of the wage scale. Even well-educated deaf people are likely to encounter difficulty in obtaining suitable employment, especially in positions involving interpersonal communication.

A 1979 study showed that 50 percent of the public thought deaf people had different jobs than those with normal hearing, and that the most suitable employment was in manual occupations or those requiring no contact with people. Promotion prospects for deaf people were considered to be worse than for hearing persons, employer prejudice and communication difficulties being the main reasons.

Deaf persons are entitled to register under the Disabled Persons Act of 1944, aimed to assist disabled persons to obtain and retain suitable employment. Deaf school leavers may be helped by the Careers Service administered by local education authorities. The Employment Service Agency of the Manpower Services Commission provides facilities applicable to deaf persons, including grants to enable employers to make adaptations to premises and equipment necessary for employing a disabled person; this would include the installation of telephone aids and amplifiers.

HEALTH

The National Health Service Act 1946 and corresponding legislation for Scotland laid upon the Minister of Health a duty "to promote the establishment of a comprehensive health service, designed to secure improvement in the physical and mental health of the people . . . and the prevention, diagnosis and treatment of illness." A number of amending acts have been passed, such as that of 1951, permitting a charge to be made for prescriptions. These acts have modified the original intention of providing a complete health service, mostly free, for every person in the United Kingdom.

Preventive medicine such as rubella vaccination has an important role in preventing hearing impairment. In 1979 and 1980 the Department of Health and Social Security issued circulars urging health authorities to intensify the vaccination program against congenital rubella. *See* HEARING LOSS: Prenatal Causes.

In 1967 the Scottish Education Department issued a report, *Ascertainment of Children with Hearing Defects*, which stated that a child with some degree of deafness should have otologic and general examinations to enable teams to recommend, before the child is 2 years old, the nature of medical, educational, and social care to be given and the most appropriate schooling. In 1981 a Department of Health and Social Security Advisory Committee on Services for Hearing Impaired People recommended screening for hearing defects at the ages of 7–8 months, 2½–3 years, on school entry, and at about 8–9 years. The Education Act 1981 requires health authorities to inform parents and the appropriate local education authority if a preschool child under 5 years has or is likely to have special eduational needs. The application of screening tests is not, however, universal in the United Kingdom, and standards of practice vary. There is also no national pattern of referral after a child has failed the screening test for hearing. *See* AUDITORY DISORDERS, PREVENTION OF: Screening.

Under the National Health Service a range of hearing aids is available on free loan on the recommendation of an otologist. Acoustic aids such as speaking tubes and ear trumpets can also be issued under National Health Service provisions. If, in the opinion of the otologist, there is no suitable instrument available within the National Health Service range, a health authority has discretion to purchase any commercially available aid. Two aids may be prescribed if the otologist considers this desirable. Batteries and repairs of National Health Service aids are free for both children and adults. *See* HEARING AIDS.

The Hearing Aid Council Act 1968 is the only United Kingdom statute exclusively concerned with hearing impairment. The act seeks to prevent the exploitation of hearing aid users and established a Hearing Air Council responsible for the registration and training of hearing aid dispensers and for the regulation of trade practices.

RELIGION

Because the numbers of prelingually deaf persons in any locality are relatively small, any denominationalism in spiritual work other than the broad divisions of Protestant and Roman Catholic is usually impracticable. Protestant work for deaf people in England is almost entirely under Anglican auspices and is coordinated by the General Synod Council for the Deaf, which has its origins in the Central Advisory Council for Promoting the Spiritual Care of the Deaf and Dumb, established by the Convocations of Canterbury and York in 1922. A forum for representatives from each of the 75

churches for deaf people in the country is offered by the National Deaf Church Conference, which endeavors to provide a link between autonomous worshiping communities. The Deaf Christian Fellowship is Pentecostalist and fundamentalist.

In Wales, some spiritual work is undertaken by voluntary societies, especially in Cardiff and Swansea. Protestant work for deaf Scots is either under the auspices of the Church of Scotland or undenominational. The largest congregations are centered in Aberdeen and district Edinburgh, and the east of Scotland. Smaller congregations either have the services of a minister to deaf congregants or are able to obtain the services of an ordained minister and interpreter. In Northern Ireland the main Protestant work is centered in Belfast.

Work for deaf Roman Catholics is coordinated by the Association for the Roman Catholic Deaf in Great Britain and Ireland, established in 1968, and is carried on in all parts of the United Kingdom. Ecumenical activity for deaf individuals in the United Kingdom is undertaken by two bodies. The Chaplains to the Deaf Examinations Board holds examinations for ordained priests and ministers and lay ministers of all denominations. The Ecumenical Council of Christian Workers with the Deaf is closely involved in the provision of training for deaf lay helpers and arranges courses designed to enable deaf people to take leadership roles within their communities.

RESEARCH

The Medical Research Council and the Department of Health and Social Security share the major responsibility for funded research into hearing impairment in the United Kingdom. In 1944 the Medical Research Council established the Otological Research Unit, but in 1970 the Chronically Sick and Disabled Persons Act (Section 24) provided that the Secretary of State "shall collate and present evidence to the Medical Research Council on the need for an institute of hearing research, such institute will have the general function of coordinating and promoting research on hearing and assistance to the deaf and hard of hearing." This act was followed by the report *Deafness: Report of a Departmental Enquiry into the Promotion of Research* (1973). The institute was founded in 1976 and is based at the University of Nottingham, with Welsh and Scottish sections based at the University Hospital of Wales, Cardiff, and the Southern General Hospital, Glasgow. The institute also has clinical sections at Nottingham and Southampton.

The Department of Health and Social Security, either directly or by the funding of regional hospital board research, has supported a number of hospital-based projects, including the psychiatric problems of deaf adults at Whittingham Hospital,

Preston, England, and hearing aids at the Royal National Throat, Nose and Ear Hospital, London. It has also supported research carried out by the Technical Department of the Royal National Institute for the Deaf.

Educational research is largely centered at the Department of Audiology and Education of the Deaf, Manchester University. The British Sign Language Research Group, based in the School of Education, University of Bristol, has issued several important reports and publications. Probably due to the pressure group activities of the national organizations for hearing-impaired persons and a greater public awareness of hearing impairment, funds for research into this field from both statutory services and private trusts are becoming more available.

Bibliography

Deuchar, M.: *Diglossia in British Sign Language*, unpublished Ph.D thesis, Stanford University.

Jones, K. D.: *The Adult Deaf Population of South Humberside*, unpublished Master of Philosophy thesis, University of Nottingham, 1938.

Kyle, J. G., and L. Allsop: *Deaf People and the Community: Final Report to the Nuffield Foundation*, Sign Language Research Unit, University of Bristol.

Lysons, C. K.: *The Development of Social Legislation for Blind or Deaf Persons in England 1834–1939*, unpublished Ph.D. thesis, Brunel, 1973.

———: *Hearing Impairment*, Woodhead Faulkner, 1984.

———: *Voluntary Welfare Societies for Adult Deaf Persons in England 1840—1963*, unpublished M.A. thesis, Liverpool, 1965.

Montgomery, G.: *Alien Communication: Sign Systems Extant in the U.K.*, B.D.A., 1981.

Pritchard, D. G.: *Education and the Handicapped*, Routledge and Kegan Paul, 1963.

Reed, M.: *Educating Hearing Impaired Children*, Open University Press, 1984.

Schein, J., and M. Delk: *The Deaf Population of the United States*, National Association of the Deaf, 1974.

Stevenson and Cheeseman: "Hereditary Deaf Mutism with Particular Reference to Northern Ireland," *Journal of Human Genetics*, 20:177–281, 1956.

Watson, T. J.: *A History of Deaf Education in Scotland, 1760–1939*, unpublished Ph.D thesis, University of Edinburgh, 1949.

Woll, B., J. Kyle, and M. Deuchar: *Perspectives on British Sign Language and Deafness*, Croom Helm, 1981.

C. K. Lysons

Organizations

United Kingdom organizations concerned with hearing impairment can be classified by area of influence, clientele, and specific interests.

The four national organizations for hearing-impaired individuals in the United Kingdom are the British Deaf Association, (BDA; 1890), the Royal National Institute for the Deaf (RNID; 1911), the National Deaf Children's Society (NDCS; 1944), and the British Association of the Hard of Hearing (BAHOH; 1947). Regional organizations for deaf persons covering Scotland and the Midland and northern counties of England were founded in 1928. Associations now cover the Midlands, North, South-East, and West Regions of England in addition to the Scottish Association of the Deaf and the Wales Council for the Deaf. The BDA, NDCS, and BAHOH also have a network of regional and local branches.

The earliest local societies for deaf people were founded in Edinburgh in 1818 and in London in 1840. Before 1960 virtually all local provision in postschool life was under voluntary auspices. Most United Kingdom local authorities now discharge their statutory responsibilities to hearing-impaired persons through directly provided services. Recreational and religious facilities, however, are still largely provided by voluntary effort. The RNID lists 86 local societies for deaf people, distinct from other categories of hearing impairment, in England, 5 in Wales, 10 in Scotland, and 1 in Northern Ireland.

Organizations may be "for" or "of" the hearing impaired—the RNID being of the former and the BDA and BAHOH of the latter categories. The National Union of the Deaf (1976) is run by deaf people for deaf people. The NDCS and BAHOH clearly serve a specific clientele. Similar organizations include the National Deaf Blind Helpers League, the National Deaf-Blind and Rubella Association, the National Association of Deafened People, and the British Tinnitus Association. The Breakthrough Trust Deaf Hearing Integrations aims to promote closer contact between deaf and hearing persons.

The RNID is the only national body dealing with all aspects of hearing impairment. Since 1971 the Panel of Four, comprising the RNID, BDA, NDCS, and BAHOH, meets annually with the Minister for the Disabled to review services for hearing-impaired persons.

Numerous organizations exist for workers in the educational, welfare, medical, research, communication, and religious aspects of hearing loss. Typical examples are the British Association of Teachers of the Deaf; the National Council of Social Workers with the Deaf; the British Association of Audiological Physicians, the British Sign Language Research Group, the Council for the Advancement of Communication with Deaf People, and the Church of England Council for the Deaf.

The British Deaf Sports Council, the Deaf Christian Fellowship, and the Jewish Deaf Association are representative of United Kingdom organizations serving the recreational, spiritual, and ethnic needs of hearing-impaired persons. "Workshops" have also been established in Northumbria, Yorkshire, and Northern Ireland, patterned on the Scottish Workshop with the Deaf. *See* SCOTLAND: Scottish Workshop with the Deaf.

C. K. Lysons

BRITISH DEAF ASSOCIATION

The British Deaf Association (BDA) was founded in 1890 as the British Deaf and Dumb Association and was renamed in 1971. Controlled by deaf people, the association is increasingly active in the public sphere, and committed to self-determination for the deaf community. Today it is one of four major charities—together forming the Panel of Four—working in the field of deafness in Britain. The Panel of Four (the British Association of the Hard of Hearing, the British Deaf Association, the National Deaf Children's Society, and the Royal National Institute for the Deaf) meets frequently and has regular access to the Minister for the Disabled.

History The British Deaf Association was established in the midst of intense controversy over the use of sign language and fingerspelling and over the exclusion of deaf people from national policy making. The cause of the controversy was an 1889 Royal Commission report to Parliament about the needs of deaf people. Coming at a time when manual communication was under attack in Europe, in the United States, and in England, the report was prepared, many deaf persons believed, without input from deaf people and without appropriate consideration of their needs. *See* HISTORY: Sign Language Controversy.

In response to this report, the magazine *Deaf Mute* urged that deaf people hold a meeting to unite and support their interests. A National Conference of Adult Deaf and Dumb Missions and Associations then convened in London in 1890 and proposed that a national society be formed, "the chief objects of which will be the elevation [of the] education and social status of the Deaf and Dumb in the United Kingdom." Thus, the British Deaf and Dumb Association (BDDA) was born.

The BDDA held its first congress in 1890 in Leeds. Reflecting the raging controversy of the period, its first resolution stated that "this Congress . . . indignantly protests against the imputation . . . that the finger and signed language is barbarous. We consider such a mode of exchanging our ideas as most natural and indispensible and that the combined system of education is by far preferable to the so-called oral." *See* EDUCATION: Communication.

Organization and Membership The British Deaf Association has a membership of more than 10,000, with another 8000 affiliated through the British Deaf Sports Council. While most members have been deaf since childhood, a small minority are hearing people. Scattered throughout England, Scotland, and Wales, the members are organized into 162 local branches that, in turn, combine to form seven regional councils. The BDA is managed by the executive council; its members are elected every three years. The rules of the association are such that deaf people are guaranteed majority representation on the executive council.

While the executive council manages the association, resolutions passed at British Deaf Association congresses help to determine its work. The congresses combine business meetings, discussions, and formal decisions with social and cultural activities, such as drama competitions. Deaf people of all ages and from all parts of the United Kingdom attend the congresses.

Since the 1960s the British Deaf Association has grown significantly and its services have expanded considerably. The first full-time field officer, Mark Clydesdale Frame, a deaf minister, was appointed in 1961. In May 1966 Allan Brindle Hayhurst, who had been the honorary secretary/treasurer, was appointed full-time general secretrary/treasurer, and the association expanded, growing from 76 branches in 1970 with 5000 members to 162 branches today with over 10,000 members. At the same time that Hayhurst was appointed, the association set up a small full-time office. By the beginning of the 1970s, however, it was apparent that these quarters were inadequate. Therefore, in 1971 the association bought three adjoining houses in northwest England, at Carlisle, and moved into these offices in the spring of 1972. This growth was made possible through increases in the British Deaf Association's income, which comes entirely from voluntary sources.

Objectives The principal objective of the association always has been "to advance and protect the interests of deaf people." With its growth, however, the association has defined its goals in more specific terms: (1) To unite in fellowship deaf people and those interested in their well-being; (2) to make opportunities for deaf people to express their opinions, and to furnish information to appropriate bodies on issues that concern them; (3) to assist those responsible for the education of deaf children by making available to them the experience that deaf people have gained in adult life; (4) to encourage and facilitate research into any matter concerning deaf people; (5) to further the cultural and educational advancement of deaf people and for this purpose organize appropriate courses; (6) to publish a magazine, literature, and other documentary material in the interests of deaf people; (7) to make grants to missions, centers, and other agencies in order to further the religious, educational, social, industrial, and general welfare of deaf people, and to assist in the training of workers with and for those who are deaf; and (8) to assist aged and infirm or needy deaf people, and to cooperate with and assist organizations of and for deaf people at home and abroad.

Activities In order to meet these objectives, the British Deaf Association has engaged in wide-ranging activities and has changed some of its traditional methods of operation. In the early 1980s, for example, the association established a long-awaited London office to service the south of England, and to ensure that the association is represented in all relevant discussions in London. In February 1983 the association's magazine, the *British Deaf News*, began monthly publication for the first time in a newspaper format. Aware that senior British Deaf Association staff should be deaf, but also that deaf people in England have not had the opportunity to acquire such experience, the association has begun appointing deaf trainee administrative assistants, whose program includes professional management courses.

The British Deaf Association's six major areas of activity are as follows.

1. Sign language. Since the demands of today's BDA membership are not unlike those expressed nearly 100 years ago, the promotion of better communication and an understanding of sign language is an important goal. During the 1970s the association continually publicized current research into British Sign Language and the sign languages of other countries, particularly in relation to the education of deaf children. With the help of a grant from the Department of Health and Social Security, a communication project was established to promote communication between hearing and deaf people. The *Dictionary of Signs* for Great Britain was published in 1983, and the Register of Interpreters was created to facilitate the provision of interpreter services. Similarly, the position of communication and interpreting service officer was created within the British Deaf Association to promote sign language teaching and to help make interpreters available. Finally, the National Deaf Video Service was established with special programs in British Sign Language for deaf adults and children. As local British Deaf Association branches acquire facilities and equipment, this service will expand to exploit the full potential of video.

2. Education. The British Deaf Association supports the concept of total communication, and attempts to advance the educational development of deaf students at all levels. The association's Education Service provides summer schools plus a range of weekend and full-week activities. Special courses for deaf people, arranged by the association, are now an annual event bringing together youngsters from residential and day schools for deaf children and from units attached to ordinary schools. The

association has a long record of involvement in striving to increase opportunities for deaf individuals to obtain higher education, raising money over the years to enable students from England to attend Gallaudet College. In higher education, the Allan Hayhurst Research Fellowship established at Durham University provides the opportunity for a deaf scholar to carry out research for a period of up to three years. *See* GALLAUDET COLLEGE.

3. The aged. Recognizing the special needs of aged deaf persons, the British Deaf Association strives to serve them. In 1947, for example, the association bought Fulford Grange, Rawdon near Leeds, and established there a residential home for elderly and infirm deaf people. The home served as many as 30 people at a time until 1978, when it had to be closed due to a decline in the number of residents. Today the British Deaf Association arranges special economical holidays for deaf senior citizens at seaside resorts.

4. International cooperation. The British Deaf Association believes in the importance of international cooperation among deaf people, and works with the World Federation of the Deaf (WFD). Association representatives have attended all WFD congresses since 1957. The British Deaf Association's publication of *Gestuno: International Sign Language of the Deaf* in 1975 reflects the joint efforts of a commission composed of deaf persons from Italy, the Soviet Union, the United States, Denmark, and England. *See* WORLD FEDERATION OF THE DEAF.

The British Deaf Association Congress of 1980 marked a turning point for the association as it reappraised its activities and began to emphasize the importance of making hearing people in the United Kingdom more aware of deaf people and deafness. The Association used the occasion of the International Year of the Disabled (1981) to promote the Sympathetic Hearing Scheme, according to which service industries, stores, banks, and public authorities display a sticker indicating the willingness of their employees to give extra time and consideration to deaf customers. This program has continued, with the association instituting a training program for those who meet the general public in their daily work.

5. Publications. The British Deaf Association also publishes articles and books on the subject of deafness to help enlighten hearing persons. Publications include such materials as the *British Sign Language Teaching Manual* (for deaf instructors of hearing students), *Deafness: A Teaching Pack for Juniors* (aimed at hearing schoolchildren), and the *Dictionary of Signs*. The 1982 British Deaf Awareness Week, organized by the association, marked a further attempt to bring to the public the issues of importance to deaf people in the United Kingdom;

the effort was supported by unpaid national television spots and media coverage. The issues included recognition of British Sign Language as a language in its own right, the importance of total communication in schools, the attempt to halt the closure of special schools for deaf pupils, the advantages of allowing deaf adults to teach deaf children, the necessity for improved access to television and telephone services for deaf people, the need for increased participation by deaf persons at public meetings, and the importance of improved employment opportunities for deaf adults.

6. Recognition. The efforts of the British Deaf Association and others to develop public and official awareness of deaf people have borne results. Even with high unemployment in the United Kingdom, the association and the government have set up short-term projects in which deaf and hearing people work closely together on a variety of programs. These include a signed reading project, a video project, a community education project, and projects to develop information and training packages.

On February 17, 1983, Buckingham Palace announced that the Princess of Wales had consented to be Royal Patron of the British Deaf Association. This undoubtedly will bring about a greater recognition of the deaf community in the United Kingdom.

Bibliography

"Conference Reports," *British Deaf News.*

Papers of the British Deaf Association.

Arthur W. Verney

ROYAL NATIONAL INSTITUTE FOR THE DEAF

The Royal National Institute for the Deaf (RNID) is a voluntary organization that operates throughout the United Kingdom. Founded in 1911 as the National Bureau for Promoting the General Welfare of the Deaf, in 1924 it was reconstituted as the National Institute for the Deaf; in 1961 the Queen was "graciously pleased to command that the Institute shall be known as 'The Royal National Institute for the Deaf.' " The institute's general aims, "to promote and encourage the prevention and alleviation of deafness and to promote, safeguard and protect the interests and welfare of deaf people," belie its wide program of services for all age groups and covering all degrees of hearing loss.

Organizational Structure   The RNID has a unique position in the sphere of deafness in the United Kingdom. Its governing council comprises people from the fields of medicine, education, and the social services, together with deaf and hard-of-hearing people and the parents of deaf children. This composition allows a vital partnership between the

professions and "consumers" at the policy-making level. As an extension to this formal structure, a consumer group, whose members are all profoundly deaf, work in an advisory capacity in association with the institute's specialist committees and working parties.

For many years six autonomous regional associations have provided a coordinating role within the framework of the RNID. With the appointment (1982) of a full-time RNID regional adviser in the north of England, plans were made for countrywide coverage by RNID's own regional staff.

The institute is a company limited by guarantee and not having a share capital, and is regulated by a Memorandum and Articles of Association. While the RNID has many thousands of supporters, voting rights are held by registered members; they are represented by a balanced mix of deaf and hearing people. The RNID's annual expenditures on services exceed 3 million pounds. The Institute relies upon voluntary contributions, receiving no direct financial support from government sources.

Services   In keeping with its position as the umbrella organization for services for deaf people throughout the United Kingdom, the RNID gives financial support to many independent centers and groups. This means that in some areas new work can go forward, and in others a firmer basis is possible for important existing services. There are links with a number of British universities which are focusing upon many aspects of hearing loss. Financial support is also being given to the British Society of Otolaryngologists Undergraduate Prize Fund with the aim of encouraging more medical students to opt for the specialty of otology.

The services may be described in nine areas as follows.

1. Medical research. The RNID sponsors medical research toward the prevention and amelioration of deafness; tinnitus (a distressing condition of noises in the head), Ménière's disease, vertigo in the elderly, and hearing detection in premature babies are all part of the current program. Involvement with research into tinnitus led in 1979 to the establishment, under RNID aegis, of the British Tinnitus Association, which has local self-help groups of sufferers that are doing much to focus attention on tinnitus among doctors, otologists, and the press. *See* AUDITORY DISORDERS, EVALUATION AND DIAGNOSIS OF: Symptoms.

2. Special services. Residential provision includes long-term care for profoundly deaf and deaf/blind people, special rehabilitation facilities for younger deaf and deaf/blind people, special services for deaf people who have been psychologically ill, and centers for young deaf men with emotional or social disorders. Other special services cover communication programs, education, employment, infor-

mation, and advice and counseling. A library, at the RNID London headquarters, contains one of the world's most significant collections of books on deafness and other communication disorders. The scientific and technical staffs in London and Glasgow work on the everyday problems that confront deaf people.

3. Employment. The closely linked issues of employment, unemployment, and underemployment, as they affect deaf people, are areas where new initiatives have been taken. Research was carried out in association with the University of London into the employment potential of deaf school-leavers. It focused on the transition, from school to work, of the profoundly deaf school-leaver and was the first empirical research to investigate this transition while it was ongoing. The research endeavored to identify those factors that most affect career prospects, and examined job situations in which deaf people are not hindered by their handicap.

4. Education. Methods of education of deaf children have long been the subject of detailed and searching discussion within the RNID. In 1978 the council pronounced in favor of a liberal approach to methods of communication in the education and care of deaf children, since it had found no evidence that the addition of manual methods is likely to inhibit the development or oral skills. However, the variety of signing systems in use in the United Kingdom presented a confused situation, necessitating further study.

5. Communication. In March 1982, with generous sponsorship from Esso Petroleum, the RNID was able to bring a group of specialists together to take a detailed look at the place of manual communication in the education of deaf children. Participants were chosen based on their knowledge of, and long experience with, the difficulties and problems that profoundly deaf children and adults face, either as parents, teachers, psychologists, administrators, or (of crucial importance in a meeting of this kind) as profoundly deaf persons themselves. Much common ground was reached on difficult issues, and the outcome of the meeting provided a sound basis for the establishment of further RNID policy and new initiatives.

Participants considered the several signing systems, with the majority supporting the use of Signed English in the educational process. Thus, there should be a concentration of resources to provide Signed English in some special schools. While not necessarily a long-term solution, this was felt to be a desirable first step. The ongoing assessment of children must not be overlooked, and there was agreement that a growing number of profoundly deaf children do develop satisfactory spoken language.

The RNID administers a Television for the Deaf Fund which provides television sets, free of charge, to deaf people with special needs: those who have other handicaps, who are housebound, who live alone or in isolated rural areas. The television authorities have a firm commitment for subtitled programs, and there is promise of a significant future output. Discussions with the British Broadcasting Corporation (BBC) over many years and financial support for subtitling projects have contributed to these major developments.

6. Hearing dogs. A Hearing Dogs for the Deaf pilot program was launched under the auspices of the RNID in 1982. The scheme followed the model in the United States where dogs, trained by the American Humane Society, are successfully placed as "hearing dogs" for deaf people. This project was funded; no cost has fallen to the RNID.

7. Research. While continuing its basic role of research and development, the RNID Scientific and Technical Department has been involved in contracts for both the government Department of Health and Social Security and the Medical Research Council. These contracts have been concerned with the perception of amplified speech by people with hearing loss and methods of evaluating the effectiveness of hearing aids. A microprocessor-based visual-speech display was developed and put into commercial production. Besides providing a very flexible display of pitch and amplitude for perception studies, the device can be used for hearing aid testing and for keeping audiometric and other types of records. The demand for special aids and other devices developed in the department increased to the point where their commercial manufacture was encouraged.

8. Telephone service. In 1980 a group of deaf people, all with good speech, took part in an experiment to explore the possibility of holding telephone conversations with hearing contacts through a Voice Bureau. This experiment was set up jointly by RNID, British Telecom, and the National Research Development Corporation to evaluate the benefits of such a service and to study the operational problems of instituting it.

9. Public education. The RNID's role goes beyond its program of services, now the largest and most comprehensive in the United Kingdom, to include a continuing campaign to educate the public about problems associated with deafness. Conferences, seminars, and study groups, usually of a professional nature, explore issues of special concern. Links with members of Parliament and government departments afford regular opportunities for important matters to be raised at the highest level, and there is encouragement in the regularity with which many of these now appear in parliamentary de-

bates. The production of information booklets and pamphlets is also an important feature of RNID's support services.

Future Prospects   The Medical Research Council Institute of Hearing Research, in reporting upon preliminary results of a national study of deafness, suggested that one in five persons in the United Kingdom suffers from hearing loss to some degree. There are limitations to what the RNID can do on behalf of so significant a number of people. Assuredly, the future work of the institute will continue very much on the lines of its present services and involvement. It is hoped that other areas of concern will be added, especially in the sphere of elderly people. Hearing loss is a large problem among the elderly, and with increased longevity even greater numbers will be affected in years to come. *See* PRESBYCUSIS.

The RNID is associated with the work of the World Federation of the Deaf (WFD), Rehabilitation International, the International Society of Audiology, and the International Congress on Education of the Deaf. *See* INTERNATIONAL CONGRESS ON EDUCATION OF THE DEAF.

Roger Sydenham

NATIONAL DEAF CHILDREN'S SOCIETY

The National Deaf Children's Society (NDCS) is the only national organization in Britain especially concerned with the needs of deaf children and their families. It is a voluntary organization and a registered charity. It receives no financial support from the British government or other official agencies. The primary aim of the NDCS is to secure that all deaf children "are enabled to live fulfilling lives by promoting and ensuring for them the maximum benefits and happiness for their home environment, educational and medical facilities and the co-operation of the general public."

Organizational Structure   The NDCS was formed in 1958 as a federation of smaller organizations for deaf children, including the Deaf Children's Society in London and the North West Deaf Children's Association in Manchester. The society now has 75 regional associations and 60 smaller branches. Regional associations are autonomous, with their own constitutions, budgets, and activities. They are registered separately as charities. Representatives of the regional associations meet three times a year as the National Council of the Society, and discuss matters of mutual interest and make national policy.

Headed by a director, the NDCS is governed by three honorary officers—the chairman, the vice chairman, and the treasurer—and by a management committee of up to 15 members. The honorary officers and the management committee are elected by a vote of members at the annual general meeting. There are subcommittees composed of parents of deaf children and professionals dealing with education, welfare, and medical and audiological services. The NDCS is administered by a small paid staff. The staff works from a head office in London, and includes experts in the education and welfare of deaf children; these experts provide a unique advice and information service to parents, professionals, students, and others.

Membership in the NDCS is open to all who have an interest in childhood deafness. The founding members were parents of deaf children, and it is from parents that the majority of the membership is drawn. Many teachers of deaf children, social workers, doctors, and audiologists are also members. The society represents the interests of families with deaf children rather than those of any particular professional group. Regional associations are effective as self-help groups and as pressure groups to improve local facilities.

Services   The NDCS has long campaigned for smaller school classes for deaf children, for a fully qualified teaching profession, for weekly boarding facilities in residential schools, and for the establishment of a peripatetic preschool service in every local area in Britain. The society has also been active in promoting the development of the unit system, enabling many children with hearing losses to be educated in ordinary schools with the assistance of a specialist teacher. The NDCS has also sought improvements in National Health Service hearing aids and in audiological services for children. Present concerns include the discovery and identification of deafness in infants, the welfare of deaf children in hospitals, increased involvement of parents in educational assessment and placement, and the development of further and higher educational opportunities for deaf students.

The society's income is derived mainly from donations and from legacies, with a smaller proportion coming from investment income. The society's audited accounts are published in the NDCS's yearbook. The growth of the society's income and active membership has enabled it to provide practical support for many thousands of deaf children. The NDCS gives welfare grants to children and families in need; runs and trains a Home Assistants Service; gives grants for educational, scientific, and medical research; and provides bursaries to help train teachers of deaf people. In 1983 a scholarship fund was launched to provide an annual scholarship for an outstanding student teacher. Through the fund-raising work of the regional associations, nearly every school and unit in the country has been provided with radio hearing aid equipment as well as with other technical aids, and hundreds of deaf children also have personal radio hearing aids for use at home, either as a gift or on loan from the society. *See* HEARING AIDS: Types.

One function of the NDCS has been to provide a forum where parents and professionals may exchange ideas and make known their views. The society arranges regular conferences which attract speakers of the highest standing. Notable conferences have been held on the psychiatric problems of deaf children and adolescents (1962), careers and employment (1976), parents as partners (1979), further and higher education (1981), and discovering deafness (1983). In 1962 the society held its first residential course for child-care staff and teachers' assistants, and thereafter these courses have been held annually. The NDCS also promotes an annual Festival of Mime, now the largest single event involving deaf children in Britain. Over 1000 children annually take part in the seven regional festivals and the national final.

The NDCS publishes the quarterly magazine *Talk*. *Talk* was established in 1956, and now has a circulation of some 15,000 copies distributed to 40 different countries. The society produces a yearbook which contains information about the society's work, about educational provisions, and about other organizations for deaf people. Some 25 booklets and information sheets are available from the NDCS, covering all aspects of childhood deafness. All the society's publications are available from its head office.

Cooperative Activities The NDCS cooperates with other organizations working with deaf children and adults. Representatives of the society meet regularly with the three other major organizations for deaf persons in Britain; together they are known as the Panel of Four. The society is active in the National Council for Voluntary Organizations and the Voluntary Council for Handicapped Children. International contact is maintained with individuals and organizations wherever deaf children exist.

Bibliography

Bloom, Freddy: "Talk In," in Freddy Bloom (ed.), *Talk*, no. 70, 1974.

National Deaf Children's Society: *Yearbook and Annual Report and Accounts*, 1958–

Smith, Gordon: "A Really Worthwhile Job," in Freddy Bloom (ed.), *Talk*, no. 74, 1974.

Harry Cayton

BRITISH ASSOCIATION OF THE HARD OF HEARING
Estimates of the number of people suffering from a hearing handicap in Great Britain vary. Some put the figure as high as 10 million, or one in six of the total population. The majority are elderly, and because the numbers of elderly are growing, provi-

sion for hearing handicaps should increase as a social service.

A registered charity, the British Association of the Hard of Hearing (BAHOH) was formed in 1947 as a self-help group for those who suffer a hearing loss. Through social clubs, national and local magazines, publications, conferences, courses and rallies, and practical personal counseling, the BAHOH promotes the aids available to help those who have lost some or all of their hearing. It also tries to make contact with and build confidence through those who have a hearing handicap.

The BAHOH aims to bring its influence to bear on local and national government to improve provisions for deaf persons. The association also aims to improve public understanding of deafness.

Deafness often is stigmatized, much misunderstood, and the butt of many jokes. It is a handicap that is profoundly isolating, cutting the person off from friends, relatives, and social contact. The BAHOH tries to lessen the loneliness by sponsoring clubs, lipreading classes, and national gatherings for deaf people. The Sympathetic Hearing Scheme also attempts to facilitate communication between deaf and hearing individuals by encouraging deaf individuals to use a "credit card" which explains that they suffer a hearing loss. Participating agencies, which include shops, banks, social services, libraries, various institutions and organizations, and a host of commercial groups, display the international symbol for deafness, showing that they are prepared to take the time and trouble to assist people who have a hearing handicap.

Through the magazine *Hark*, the association has tried to improve diction via a "Clear Speech" campaign—it is hoped that standards of lipreadability may be bettered by highlighting television personalities who speak well and those who speak poorly. Leaflets are also issued to pass on practical advice about clear speech. A series of lipreading films have also been an aid to lipreading skill, and a booklet entitled *Lipservice* sets out changes desired in the range of lipreading classes available. Specialist interpreters, called "lipspeakers," have been trained and are used by the association to help members at meetings by introducing easier lipreading.

Prevention of hearing loss involves monitoring and controlling noise levels, particularly at work. A series of posters and regular briefings offer advice and warnings about the dangers of noise. Practical aids such as inductive loops are installed and catalogued under the auspices of the association, a display of environmental aids is maintained, and queries are answered.

Services for deaf people in Great Britain still demand considerable improvement. Deaf persons lack resources and understanding, but through the increased use of subtitling, interpreters, and specialist broadcasts, this "hidden handicap" is benefitting from a greater awareness.

Paul Hannon

NATIONAL UNION OF THE DEAF

The National Union of the Deaf (NUD) was founded in Wimbledon, London, on March 13, 1976, when deaf people assembled to form an organization exclusively run by themselves. Its aims were "To Restore the Rights of Deaf People," and since that time it has become a pressure group, initiating and involving other deaf people in campaigns, usually focused on the issues of sign language and deaf involvement in decisions that affect deaf persons. Operating with several hundred members and a small, entirely self-financed budget, it consists mainly of grass-roots deaf members and hearing associate members. It has several branches and a biennial convention, and publishes a newsletter and occasional papers.

The NUD began a total communication campaign in the summer of 1976, a time when re-evaluation of deaf education was beginning. By publishing direct appeals to teachers, written in the personal language of deaf experience, the campaign forced a previously academic issue onto a level of humanism and basic human rights. Some teachers and schools responded, and the NUD became involved in helping them create total communication programs. This, together with the British Deaf Association's (BDA) more academic approach and the publication of momentous research, meant that by 1982 more than half the deaf schools in the country and a few deaf units had embarked on total communication programs. There was less success with the campaign for deaf teachers, whose numbers are still minute, although more deaf people became classroom assistants and governors. But the involvement of deaf people in campaigning and reaching hearing people was equally important in raising the self-esteem of the deaf community. The NUD believes, however, that major improvements in the education of deaf children will not occur until the oralist peripatetic service legislation is abolished and deaf people's beliefs control the education system. *See* ENGLAND, EDUCATION IN.

In employment, the NUD was able to prevent deaf car and HGV (heavy goods vehicles) drivers from having their licenses removed by linking enlightened employers, haulage associations, and American statistical evidence. The NUD also worked to awake the conscience of labor unions, where it believed ultimate change lay.

In 1977 the NUD initiated links with other disabled groups to campaign for a government allowance. Although the Thatcher administration ended the campaign, the historical importance of the links remains. NUD also has campaigned on behalf of establishing guiding principles for registered interpreters and in support of better telecommunication devices for deaf people.

In 1978 the NUD began to promote British Sign Language (BSL) and deaf culture as a source of pride and outlined a national program of language planning. Part one was based on dialect sign books, leading to agreement on a national vocabulary that would preserve the United Kingdom's rich dialects. Part two, a BSL/Total Communication National Liaison Centre, was essential in linking parents, teachers, social workers, and other hearing people to the deaf community. Resources to carry out the plan were not available, but the strategy remains crucial to the concept of building a national deaf community.

In addition to launching campaigns directed at specific problems faced by deaf people, the NUD provides help for individuals (members and non-members) and encourages others to fulfill their potential in deaf work. The NUD believes that it is crucial to have grass-roots deaf people involved in activities rather than creating a deaf elite to replace a hearing one.

Perhaps the most successful area of work has been in television. In 1976 proposals for a regular national program were outlined, and by 1979 a pilot program, *Signs of Life*, was aired on a British Broadcasting Corporation (BBC) access slot. Following the success of this program (which was placed in the BBC archives), liaison with the British Deaf Association saw the inauguration of the Deaf Broadcasting Campaign. Pressure was maintained, and by 1981 a nationally networked, twice-weekly, BBC program for deaf people was started. The campaign's success opened the floodgates: several regions started to use news interpreters; three regions started regular deaf programming; and a disabled program started to include deaf items.

The NUD next turned to establishing a charter of rights of deaf people in the world, and focused on what it perceived to be an emerging threat to the deaf community—the mainstreaming of deaf students into hearing schools. The 1981 Education Act gave legal force to the idea of integration of deaf and hearing pupils, and this law provided the means for education authorities to cut spending on deaf education, as well as enabling oralists to work toward the closure of schools converted to total communication. *See* EDUCATIONAL LEGISLATION: Mainstreaming.

The NUD proceeded from the logic that deaf people were a linguistic (BSL-using) minority to see if the United Nation's (UN) Rights of Disabled People protected them. Finding that the Rights did not, the NUD turned to the UN's International Covenant on Political and Civil Rights, and found protection there for linguistic minorities under Article 27. The NUD then detailed the ways that this Article and the UN's Charter of Rights of the Child were infringed by oralism. The NUD also discovered three clauses relating to the destruction of linguistic minorities in the UN's Convention on the Prevention and Punishment of the Crime of Genocide that might be applicable to the situation faced by deaf people in the United Kingdom.

This evidence was sent to the UN's Human Rights Commission in 1982. The significance of the document is as yet unmeasured, but the NUD has suggested that oralist practices throughout the world could be brought to a halt through legal means. Swedish Sign Language legislation seems to reenforce this conclusion, but the worldwide cooperation of deaf organizations will be necessary to counter the arguments of oralist educators and their supporters in government. *See* SIGN LANGUAGES: Swedish; SWEDEN.

Whatever its ultimate success, the achievements of the NUD in its short history have made it impossible for organizations in deaf work to maintain credibility without major deaf involvement and have transformed the possiblities for deaf people in the United Kingdom.

Bibliography

National Union of the Deaf: *Blueprint for the Future*, 1977.

————: *Charter of Rights of the Deaf Child*, 1982.

————: *Epistles to Teachers of the Deaf*, parts 1 and 2, 1976, 1977.

————: *Occasional Papers*, nos. 1 and 2, 1977.

P. Ladd

BRITISH ASSOCIATION OF TEACHERS OF THE DEAF

The British Association of Teachers of the Deaf (BATOD), established October 16, 1976, also known as the Association, is the sole affiliation representing qualified teachers of deaf pupils throughout the United Kingdom. Its antecedents were the National College of Teachers of the Deaf (NCTD) and the Society of Teachers of the Deaf, which was founded in 1959.

History The Society of Teachers of the Deaf owes its existence to the fact that by the 1970s more and more hearing-impaired children were being educated in mainstream programs and the teachers felt that the NCTD did not really represent their interests. The college, for its part, did not desire this split in the profession and made several attempts to gain the society's cooperation. These attempts failed on the grounds that the representation that was being offered was not considered to be fair to teachers working in the External Services. However, the relationship between the two bodies remained good.

Cooperative ventures culminated in 1974 in agreement on a joint submission regarding the status and salaries of teachers of deaf people to the Hougton Committee, organized by the government to review the status and salaries of all teachers in England and Wales. Cooperation on such fundamental issues led to demands for a much closer liaison between the college and the society, and negotiations led to the amalgamation of the two bodies.

Organizational Structure The constitution of the Association reflects it origins. Emphasis was placed on the fact that it is a national body controlled by a National Executive Council (NEC) consisting of 32 elected members. These are chosen from each geographical region—North, Midland, South, Scotland, and North Ireland—and there is a balance between the number of representatives of special schools and representatives of special-education teachers in the regular schools.

To safeguard the interests of both sides, it was agreed that decisions of the NEC required a two-thirds majority if a matter of policy or a change in the rules and constitution was under discussion. In effect, the Association became so tightly knit in the first few years of its operation that demands grew for a fundamental revision of the rules and constitution.

The Association has five honorary officers elected by the full membership to administer its affairs: a president, president-elect, national secretary, assistant national secretary, and national treasurer. The work is carried out through six departments, each consisting of five elected NEC members. The departments are: (1) the Information and External Relations Committee, having responsibility for the Association's journal, which inherited the title *The Teacher of the Deaf* from the NCTD. This department is also responsible for relations with the press and public and for the Association's publications; (2) the Education Committee, which is responsible for the Association's educational philosophy, research, and policy; (3) the Management and Administration Committee, which deals with professional affairs; (4) the Program Committee, which is responsible for the organization of at least two national functions each year in connection with two general meetings and the annual general meeting and for courses and conferences of the Association; (5) the Teacher Training and Training Courses Liaison Committee, which deals with every aspect of the training of teachers of deaf students; and (6) the Examination Board, which is responsible for the examination of candidates for the diploma of the Association.

The government agreed in 1976 that the authority vested in the NCTD to issue a diploma to successful candidates should be transferred to BATOD. This diploma is recognized as having equal standing with the qualifications gained by students who attend a one-year full-time course of training as a teacher of deaf students conducted by the nine training departments situated in England, Scotland, and Ireland.

Like its predecessors, the Association has no permanent office; it operates from the address of its current national secretary. It exists solely on the subscriptions paid by its members, although the cost of administering the examination for the Association's diploma is financed from government funds. Full members of the Association are those who are qualified teachers of deaf pupils engaged in full-time work involving deaf education. Qualified teachers of deaf persons who do not fulfill the foregoing requirements and persons who are not qualified as teachers of deaf people but are involved in the education or welfare of deaf children or young persons may become associate members.

The regions of the Association base their organization on that of the national body, and the National Executive Council is represented on each of the regional committees. Subscriptions are collected on a regional basis, and full membership totals about 400 in the North Region, 600 in the South Region, 300 in the Midland Region, 150 in Scotland, and 50 in Northern Ireland. The total represents about 85 percent of the practicing qualified teachers of deaf pupils in the United Kingdom.

Activities The Association is affiliated with the Special Educational Needs National Advisory Council, and it sends representatives to many organizations concerned with the education of deaf persons. It has established direct links with the Department of Education and Science, the government department that oversees education, and with the local education authorities that administer education throughout the country. The Association is working toward the completion of a full policy document, by which it hopes to influence all the agencies involved in the education of hearing-impaired children in the United Kingdom.

The journal of the Association has a different format from the journal of the National College of Teachers of the Deaf in that it has two sections. One section has articles relating to research and the principles and practice of the education of deaf persons; the other section is a magazine section related to Association affairs. Distribution is worldwide.

The Association also publishes other works, mainly pamphlets about various aspects of teaching deaf children. They are prepared for teachers new to the field of deaf education and for parents of deaf children.

A. Bates

NATIONAL COLLEGE OF TEACHERS OF THE DEAF

The National College of Teachers of the Deaf (NCTD), 1918–1976, also known as the College, was a voluntary body of qualified teachers of deaf pupils that was supported entirely by member subscriptions. It originated from the College of Teachers of the Deaf and Dumb (CTDD), founded in 1885, and the National Association of Teachers of the Deaf (NATD), founded in 1895.

History The CTDD came into existence because the leaders in deaf education at the time were concerned that there was almost no cooperation between the 20 institutions that existed, and there was a desire to raise the standards of teaching and to improve the status of deaf education. Five headmasters were chosen to conduct an examination for a diploma the possession of which was a requisite for membership in the College.

At the end of the nineteenth century, the Government did not accept the need for an extra qualification in teaching deaf children, so many of the teachers working in the institutions were not entitled to membership in the College; hence the new society, the National Association of Teachers of the Deaf, came into existence in 1895. This association at first had three branches: Northern, Scoto-Irish, and Central. These were joined in 1901 by the Metropolitan and Southern Branch, in 1905 by the Midland Branch, and in 1910 by the Western Branch.

Richard Elliott, a leading figure in the establishment of the College, was the first chairperson of the association, and thus the aims and to some extent the membership of the two bodies overlapped. Their greatest achievements in the early years of the twentieth century were the foundation of a professional journal and the procurement of recognition by the Government in 1909 that the diploma issued by the college was the recognized specialist qualification for teachers of deaf pupils. The journal *The Teacher of the Deaf* was established as the organ of the association. The first issue appeared in January 1903, and stated that the journal was "called into existence for the direct purpose of reporting the proceedings of the NATD and forwarding the life work of its members," and it aimed "To devote itself to the many matters of educational interest and value which arise from time to time in the training of the deaf." This journal, published bimonthly, has survived all subsequent changes in organization.

It was only a matter of time before these two bodies would amalgamate. On November 17, 1917, a special resolution of the CTDD was passed, changing its name to the National College of Teachers of the Deaf (Incorporated). This was confirmed on December 15, 1917, and on January 5, 1918, the new name was entered in the Register of Companies. This new body inherited the organization of the association and the right to issue diplomas from the old college. The objects of the College were: to further the cause of the education of the deaf; to afford opportunities for the discussion of professional and educational topics; to promote the professional interests of teachers; to arrange for holding biennial conferences; to render advice and assistance to members in connection with their work; and to form a Register of Teachers and appointments open to them.

Organization and Activities Membership was open to all teachers who held the College diploma or an equivalent qualification. Teachers who were not so qualified were able to join as associate members. The College was managed by an executive committee consisting of 24 members who were elected by the members on an annual basis. There were four branches: Metropolitan and Southern, Midland, Northern, and Scoto-Irish. These branches sent two representatives each to meetings of the executive committee.

One of the first tasks of the new college was to help in arranging for the establishment of the Chair of Education in the Education of the Deaf at Manchester University. In 1922 the College sold the library it had inherited to Manchester University. The College also inherited an award called the Braidwood Medal, which had been inaugurated in 1898. The most outstanding entry for this medal was an essay on speech by Sibley Haycock, submitted in 1928, which is still widely read. In 1930 a new award known as the Eichholz Prize was established to mark the regard of the College for the work of A. Eichholz, who had served as a government inspector in special education for 32 years. The prize was awarded annually to the most outstanding candidate in the diploma examination. In 1959 the Mary Grace Wilkins Travelling Scholarship was established as the result of a bequest from Miss Wilkins, who had retired as headmistress of the Maud Maxfield School in Sheffield in 1936. In 1969 the Herbert Shorrock Memorial Medal was introduced as a tribute to the College's late general secretary. *See* BRAIDWOOD, THOMAS.

In the 1930s the College was very active in seeking to persuade the Government to lower the admission age of children to deaf schools. Success was achieved in 1938 when an education act lowered the admission age from seven to five years. After World War II one of the College's main tasks was to defend the right to administer the diploma, which was continuously under threat of extinction by the national government. The College also became more active in seeking to raise the educational standards for deaf children. To this end, a diploma course was arranged in 1955 for those teachers taking the diploma examination, and a similar course has been arranged annually ever since. In 1964 a diploma subcommittee was formed to help in training teachers for the diploma.

The College was responsible for producing a pamphlet entitled *For the Guidance of Parents of Little Deaf Children* and for *"Seeing Sense,"* a method of teaching language based on the use of color. The Midland Branch produced revised texts of a reading scheme that was very popular in mainstream education, and many children's classics were rewritten and specially adapted by teachers of deaf children. In 1968 the College published the *Guide to the Education of Deaf Children*, in which there were contributions from 20 experienced teachers of deaf pupils. It was issued primarily for use by teachers studying for the College diploma. Biennial conferences were arranged by the branches of the College, and leading educators were invited to speak at alternate annual general meetings.

After World War II there were revolutionary changes in the organization of deaf education in the United Kingdom. This movement tended to diminish the role of the established schools for deaf children, which had been the basis of the organization of the College. Therefore, in 1976 the members of the College voted by an overwhelming majority to end the functioning of the College and to join with colleagues in the Society of Teachers of the Deaf in forming a new professional organization called the British Association of Teachers of the Deaf.

A. Bates

COUNCIL FOR THE ADVANCEMENT OF COMMUNICATION WITH DEAF PEOPLE

The Council for the Advancement of Communication with Deaf People (CACDP) is a national organization made up of representatives from all the major professional and voluntary organizations concerned with deafness and hearing impairment. It was founded in 1980 in Carlisle, Cumbria, for the purposes of promoting training in communication skills with deaf people, conducting a system of examination in such skills, maintaining and administering a Register of Interpreters, and encouraging research and collating information relevant to the improvement of communication skills. Though the CACDP's activities are primarily confined to England and Wales, it has close links with Scotland and Northern Ireland to ensure that comparable standards of training and examination are maintained.

Each of the 12-member organizations has two representatives (at least one of whom should be deaf) who, together with up to six co-opted members, make up the CACDP. The full council meets twice each year, with the committees on general policy, finance, and training meeting more frequently.

Origins During the early 1970s there was increasing concern about the limited number of sign language interpreters in the United Kingdom. While undoubtedly reflecting the growing aspirations of deaf people, it was also a response to policy changes that influenced existing provisions.

In the United Kingdom, most sign language interpreting in formal settings is by the Social Workers for the Deaf. Prior to the 1970s they usually worked from a religious mission or other voluntary organization for the deaf. Their part-time training was within the specialist-work situation, and they took examinations administered by the Deaf Welfare Examinations Board (DWEB), a body representative of the principal organizations with a direct interest in social work for deaf people. The examinations included a test of interpreting skills. *See* INTERPRETING: Interpreter Training.

Over the two decades that followed World War II, social-work services expanded to meet specific needs. Administrative fragmentation and specialist training resulted and were seen as barriers to effective provisioning of services. Changes in government policy in the late 1960s emphasized the need for all social workers to receive full-time training in general social work, and established generic social-work departments within local authorities. As a result, many of the local voluntary societies for deaf people were absorbed within the new departments, the in-service training provision for specialist social workers with deaf persons was severely weakened, and—with its qualifications not being recognized within the new structure—the DWEB ceased to function. Thus ended the only national scheme of interpreter training. *See* SOCIAL WORK AND SOCIAL WELFARE.

During the late 1960s and early 1970s there also was a growing awareness of developments elsewhere, especially in North America and Scandinavia. Research into sign language, and the forming of the American Registry of Interpreters, prompted the British Deaf Association to publish reports and invite first-hand accounts of such progress. *See* REGISTRY OF INTERPRETERS FOR THE DEAF.

In 1976 the British Deaf Association was granted funding by the Department of Health and Social Security (DHSS) to carry out a Communication Skills Project. The project's aims were (1) to encourage hearing people to acquire basic sign communication skills and (2) to train, assess, and register interpreters. Under the auspices of this project, the CACDP was formed as a means of continuing and extending these aims when the project ended in 1981.

Finance and Administration On completion of the Communication Skills Project, the CACDP became a fully independent charitable organization with starter finance from the DHSS and member organizations supplemented by donations from industry, commerce, and charitable trusts. The CACDP believes that its financial support should come from government funding to avoid relying on a minority of its members or appealing for funds to the general public.

Though the CACDP was headquartered at Carlisle, its intention was to move eventually to a college or university where it would be independent of member organizations and of any single method of communication and where there would be easy access to training and assessment facilities.

Training and Examinations Commencing with sign language, the CACDP introduced a scheme of training and examination in communication skills which has provided not only a directive and incentive for both teachers and students, but also the means by which progress can be made from elementary to advanced levels. On completion of the advanced certificate in communication skills, there is a further year of in-service training and assessment before admittance to the Register of Sign Language Interpreters.

While the CACDP is concerned with sign communication, it seeks to improve, through the development of training and examinations, other methods of communication between deaf and hearing people. There are plans to develop a Register of Oral Interpreters, and to initiate training and standards of competence in the use of technical aids (for example, Palantype, a kind of shorthand machine). New courses have been provided by the CACDP, but it is intended that, where possible, future provision whould be within the structure of further education, thus placing greater emphasis on the CACDP's role as a validating and examining body.

The Register of Interpreters When the Register of Interpreters was formed from holders of the DWEB qualification, it was recognized that some members were no longer practicing interpreters, and that since the DWEB's demise, many young and competent interpreters for whom there had been no formal training had emerged. To achieve greater credibility for the Register, membership is granted for a five-year period, at the end of which those who wish to remain on the Register will be assessed. In addition, membership in the Register is offered to other competent interpreters on the successful completion of short training courses and examinations.

In its attempts to develop the Register of Interpreters, the CACDP is in a relatively weak position. Outside of professional social work with deaf people and related activities, there are few opportunities for the payment of interpreters. The development of interpreting services elsewhere has been greatly assisted by the creation of opportunities for deaf people in further education and vocational training often supported by government directives and provision. There is no comparable provision in Britain.

Research and Information Conscious of the need to safeguard the interests of deaf people in vital situations, the CACDP has obtained government funding for research into legal interpreting, especially regarding the training of legal interpreters.

To support its training activities, the CACDP is developing a library of books and video materials, and is currently producing distance learning packages on specific aspects of interpreting.

Potential The CACDP's main achievement is the bringing together of all the professional and voluntary organizations for the common purpose of developing communication between deaf and hearing people. Relatively new and thus financially vulnerable, the CACDP has made progress and has the potential to develop rapidly and gain widespread recognition. Its future success depends not only on support that it receives from government, but also on the social, economic, and education opportunities that are made available to deaf people.

Bibliography

Lysons, C. Kenneth: "Aspects of the Historical Development and Present Organisation of Voluntary Welfare Societies for Adult Deaf Persons in England 1840-1963," unpublished thesis, University of Liverpool, 1965.

———: "The Development of Training for Work with Adult Deaf Persons," reprinted from the *British Deaf News*, British Deaf Association, 1977.

Simpson, T. Stewart: "Council for the Advancement of Communication with Deaf People," supplement to the *British Deaf News*, British Deaf Association, 1981.

———: "The Development of Communication Skills: Time to Register Approval," supplement to the *British Deaf News*, British Deaf Association, 1980.

———: *Report on the Communication Skills Project 1977-1982*, British Deaf Association, 1983.

T. Stewart Simpson

Periodicals

A periodical may be defined as a publication issued at regular intervals longer than a day. While this definition also covers annual reports, updated information material, and other items published periodically, the present article is limited to journals for deaf people or relating to hearing and deafness and published in England. The first part of the article relates to some English journals now defunct; the second part provides information on periodicals currently in circulation.

EARLY DEFUNCT PERIODICALS

Possibly the earliest magazine for deaf readers published in the United Kingdom was the *Edinburgh Messenger*, which appeared in October 1843 under the editorship of Robert Kinniburgh, headmaster of the Institution for the Deaf and Dumb. The last known issue is dated January 1845.

In England the first periodical for deaf people, the *Magazine for the Deaf*, came out in July 1855. Published infrequently, the magazine probably terminated with the fifth issue, sometime in 1857. The third issue, dated February 1856, has the cover title *The Magazine of the Association in Aid of the Deaf and Dumb*.

In January 1873 the Royal Association for the Deaf and Dumb (RADD) published *A Magazine Intended Chiefly for the Deaf and Dumb*. Edited by Samuel Smith, the association's chaplain, the magazine comprised 16 pages and sold for twopence. A semireligious monthly, the magazine featured articles and poetry for deaf authors and comments on contemporary news. In 1879 the title became *Deaf and Dumb Magazine*. Two years later, Smith transferred responsibility to a "Mr A F Strathern and a few deaf and dumb gentlemen," but in June 1883 publication was suspended for lack of support. In January 1884, however, the magazine was resuscitated and continued until April 1885 under the editorship of James Paul. In his last issue, Paul introduced the *Deaf and Dumb World*, an 8-page journal started by a Mr. Abrahams. This expanded to 12 pages, costing a penny in January 1886, and consisting mainly of news articles and stories. The title changed to the *Deaf Mute World*, a 16-page monthly in 1887, but later that year heavy losses caused Abrahams to cease publication. In July 1888 another magazine appeared, the *Deaf Mute*, described as the magazine of the Deaf Mute Association, a short-lived organization which disappeared with its journal in September 1889.

LATER DEFUNCT PERIODICALS

During the latter half of the nineteenth and early part of the twentieth century there were numerous publications similar to those described above, usually of an ephemeral nature and indicative of a deaf subculture based on the missions. Six periodicals, however, achieved more than transient importance.

British Deaf Times In June 1889 appeared the *Deaf and Dumb Times*. A twopenny unsectarian monthly of between 8 and 16 pages containing well-written news, articles, and correspondence on all topics relating to deaf people, it achieved greater popularity than any of its predecessors. The title was changed to the *Deaf Chronicle* in November 1891. Shortly afterward, Abrahams, earlier associated with the *Deaf Mute World*, became editor and part proprietor, and the name was again altered to the *British Deaf Mute*, which continued until October 1896 when it became the *British Deaf Monthly*, which claimed to be "the best known and most widely read publication for the deaf and their teachers in the world." From December 1903 until 1954 the title was the *British Deaf Times*.

Ephphatha   In January 1892 the Reverend F.W.G. Gilby of the Royal Association of the Deaf and Dumb began to publish *Our Quarterly Paper*. Two years later this became *Our Monthly Church Messenger to the Deaf*. When in January 1896 the editorship passed to a Mr. Cuttell, the title became *Ephphatha*. This journal amalgamated with the *British Deaf Monthly* in November 1899. Meanwhile the Royal Association of the Deaf and Dumb news was published in *Our Noticeboard* until Gilby revived the original title of *Ephphatha* in March 1909. Primarily the magazine of the Royal Association of the Deaf and Dumb, it later became a magazine that provided news of missions throughout the country and became a vehicle of Anglican teaching. Publication ceased abruptly with issue number 200 in 1959.

Deaf Quarterly News   The *Bolton, Bury, Rochdale and District Deaf and Dumb Society Quarterly* was founded in April 1905 by Ernest Ayliffe, the superintendent of the Bolton, Bury and Rochdale Society for the Deaf. Ayliffe originally intended his magazine to circulate only within the area of the missions for which he was responsible. The success achieved, however, exceeded all expectations, and in 1908, with the name changed to the *Quarterly News*, Ayliffe went national. The title became the *Deaf Quarterly News* in the following year. Ayliffe continued as editor until 1947. On his death in 1955 it was stated that "the magazine soon became the most widely read periodical in the deaf world and there must have been few deaf homes where its yellow cover was not readily visible." The name was changed to the *Deaf News* in 1950.

Quarterly Review of Deaf Mute Education   The object of the College of Teachers of the Deaf, founded in 1885 by Richard Elliot and William Stainer, was to raise the status of its members by granting certificates of competency on the results of an annual examination. The *Quarterly Review*, the organ of the college, appeared in January 1886 and contained 32 pages. The first editorial committee comprised T. Arnold, D. Buxton, R. Elliott, J. Howard, W. Neill, S. Schöntheil, W. Sleight, W. Stainer, J. Thompson, and W. Van Praagh—some of the greatest names associated with the education of deaf pupils in nineteenth-century England. The *Review* contained valuable technical, historical, and biographical papers and was regarded as the British equivalent of the *American Annals of the Deaf*. In October 1898, however, the editors stated that insufficient financial support on the part of the profession compelled them to discontinue publication. *See* AMERICAN ANNALS OF THE DEAF.

Journal of the Society of Teachers of the Deaf   The Society of Teachers of the Deaf was formed in 1959 to represent the interests of teachers of deaf pupils employed in hospitals, in partially hearing units, or as peripatetic teachers. Duplicated newsletters of the society began to appear about 1966. First published in 1968 and issued three times a year, the *Journal of the Society of Teachers of the Deaf* continued until 1976, when the society amalgamated with the National College of Teachers of the Deaf to form the British Association of Teachers of the Deaf.

Deaf Welfare   *Books and Topics Which May Interest the Missionary to the Deaf*, a typewritten publication, was first issued in November 1947 at the instigation of the General Council of Church Missioners to the Deaf and Dumb and came out three times yearly until it was replaced by *Deaf Welfare*, a printed journal, in November 1955. As the official journal of the National Council of Welfare Officers to the Deaf, it contained many useful articles relating to adult persons and continued until November 1972.

Hearing   The *Silent World*, the organ of the then National Institute of the Deaf (NID), came out in June 1946. The first issue stated that the magazine was "going to be about the deaf and dumb, the deafened and the hard of hearing . . . to put ourselves across to the hearing and—no less—to bring the hearing across to us." The title became *Hearing* in July 1963. *Hearing* and its predecessor provided information relating to communication, hearing aids, and developments in such fields as the education and welfare of deaf persons and ear surgery. Contributions from hearing-impaired persons were welcomed. In the last issue, November/December 1981, the Royal National Institute for the Deaf (RNID) announced that the high deficit incurred in publishing *Hearing* could not be sustained.

CONTEMPORARY PERIODICALS

The four national organizations constituting the "Panel of Four" are the Royal National Institute for the Deaf (RNID), the British Deaf Association (BDA), the National Deaf Children's Society (NDCS), and the British Association of the Hard of Hearing (BAHOH). With the demise of *Hearing*, the RNID had no official journal until 1984, when it published *Soundbarrier*. The magazines of the BDA, NDCS, and BAHOH are respectively the *British Deaf News*, *Talk*, and *Hark*.

British Deaf News   In 1954 the *British Deaf Times* and the *Deaf News* amalgamated under the sponsorship of the British Deaf Association. The "best parts of the 2 titles" were combined in the *British Deaf News*, a bimonthly journal first published in January 1955.

Talk   The *Deaf Children's Society News Letter* came out in September 1953 and was superseded by *Talk* in Autumn 1956. The National Deaf Children's Society stated that the purpose of *Talk* was to remedy the fact that there was "no publication devoted solely to the interests and welfare of deaf children" and promised that the contents would be "articles of direct help to the parents of deaf children and of interest to their teachers . . . It will report international progress and developments in the field and try to increase understanding of the problem among the general public." *Lipreader*, the magazine of the NDCS, North West, commenced publication in May 1958.

Hark A quarterly first issued in Autumn 1959, *Hark* was initially devoted to news of hard-of-hearing clubs affiliated with the British Association of the Hard of Hearing. With the Winter issue of 1982 a new and improved format was adopted.

School Magazines The earliest of these was probably the *Deaf and Dumb Institution (Margate) Pamphlet*. Eight issues appeared subsequent to that for Easter 1883. A new series, issued twice yearly, began in 1899. The *Royal Asylum Magazine*, "printed by the boys of the asylum," began in January 1907, and the present *Magazine of the Royal School for Deaf Children* is a continuation of this publication. *Bluebird*, the magazine of the Mary Hare Grammar School, and the *Boar Journal*, of Burwood Park School, published since 1948 and 1959, respectively, are typical of several other school magazines.

Religious Journals Those currently in circulation include *Joy for the Deaf*, *Hearing Eye*, and *Outreach*, published respectively by the Deaf Christian Fellowship, the Hard of Hearing Christian Fellowship, and the Association for the Catholic Deaf of Great Britain and Ireland.

British Journal of Audiology In 1967 the Royal National Institute for the Deaf published *Sound*, a quarterly technical journal which included reports of the institute's Scientific and Technical Department on hearing aids and audiometric equipment. The contents were soon broadened by the publication of the transactions of the British Society of Audiology, also founded in 1967. The title *British Journal of Audiology* was adopted in 1974. Ownership of the journal was relinquished by the Royal National Institute for the Deaf in 1979 and was then vested in the society.

Teacher of the Deaf The National Association of Teachers of the Deaf was formed in 1895, and in 1918 amalgamated with the College of Teachers of the Deaf to form the National College of Teachers of the Deaf. The journal of the association, the *Teacher of the Deaf*, was first published as a bimonthly in January 1903. This issue hoped that the "reproach" [that] Great Britain, unlike America and Germany had no educational journal especially devoted to the technique of deaf instruction would be removed." Under the joint editorship of S. E. Hull and A. J. Story, the *Teacher of the Deaf* soon established itself as a learned journal with an inter-

national readership. A new run of the *Teacher of the Deaf* commenced in January 1977 following the formation in 1976 of the British Association of Teachers of the Deaf.

Magazine of the Association of Teachers of Lipreading Adults The first issue was Winter 1976. The magazine is published twice yearly.

Look This newsletter has been issued irregularly since 1973 by the National Council of Social Workers with the Deaf, and may be regarded as the successor to *Deaf Welfare*.

Journal of Laryngology and Otology This periodical first appeared in January 1887 as the *Journal of Laryngology and Rhinology* under Morrell Mackenzie and Norris Wolfenden, two London laryngologists. The title was expanded to include "Otology" in 1892, and shortened in 1921 by the omission of "Rhinology."

Clinical Oto-Laryngology This journal was founded in 1976 to meet the need for a European journal dealing primarily with clinical otolaryngology.

British Journal of Disorders of Communication This is the organ of the College of Speech Therapists. First published in 1966, it contains occasional articles of interest to workers in the fields of deaf education and welfare.

Bibliography

Gorman, P. P. (comp.): *List of British Periodicals on Deafness*, 1962.

Lysons, C. K.: "Some Early Magazines for the Deaf," *British Deaf News*, vol. 13, no. 7, January/February 1982.

          C. K. Lysons

Voluntary Societies

In the context of this section a voluntary society means an organization that controls its own policy, is financially supported at least in part by voluntary contributions, and exists to provide services for, or on behalf of, hearing-impaired persons. This definition distinguishes voluntary from statutory organizations. Statutory organizations also provide services but differ from voluntary organizations in that they exercise their functions within the limits prescribed by statutes and administrative regulations and are accountable for the expenditure of their finance, which is almost wholly derived from public funds.

Overview

Voluntary societies for deaf people in England may be classified in at least four ways: by geography, by principal area of interest, by primary membership, and by roles undertaken.

The area covered by a voluntary society may be national, regional, or local, and can usually be deduced from its title. Thus, the Royal National Institute for the Deaf, the National Deaf Children's

Society, the British Deaf Association, and the British Association of the Hard of Hearing are all national in scope. The North Regional Association for the Deaf and the St. Helens Society for the Deaf are, respectively, examples of regional and local voluntary organizations. The Commonwealth Society for the Deaf aims to assist other countries within the British Commonwealth to deal with problems of deafness within their own areas.

Some voluntary societies nationally represent a particular area of interest, such as communication, education, spiritual provision, social welfare, sport and recreation, or particular groups of deaf persons. The Council for the Advancement of Communication with Deaf People, the British Association of Teachers of the Deaf, the General Synod Council for the Deaf, the British Deaf Sports Council, the National Deaf-Blind Helpers League, and the National Association for Deaf-Blind and Rubella Handicapped are typical examples.

Voluntary societies for deaf people may also be distinguished according to whether their membership comprises mainly deaf persons or those (mainly hearing persons) professionally associated with deaf individuals. The membership of the British Deaf Association, the National Union of the Deaf, and the British Association of the Hard of Hearing are predominantly made up of hearing-impaired persons. Examples of clubs or associations that provide a national focus for deaf persons with special interests include the British Deaf Drivers Association, the Deaf Christian Fellowship, and the English Deaf Chess Association.

Professional associations for those who work with deaf people or who are concerned with hearing are found in the fields of audiology, audiological medicine, otology, education, hearing aid dispensing, spiritual provision, and social work. Typical examples from each of these fields would be the British Society of Audiology, the British Association of Audiological Physicians, the British Association of Otolaryngologists, the British Association of Teachers of the Deaf, the Society of Hearing Aid Audiologists, the Chaplains to the Deaf Examinations Board, and the National Council of Social Workers with the Deaf.

The roles undertaken by a voluntary society differ according to whether it is a national, regional, or local organization.

While most national and regional organizations provide some form of direct service to individuals, this is usually a subsidiary activity. National organizations maintain contact with their comparable organizations in other countries and may be affiliated with such international organizations as the World Federation of the Deaf, Rehabilitation International, the International Society of Audiology, and the International Congress on the Education of the Deaf. Another national role is that of intermediary. In this role, the national body liaises between statutory and voluntary bodies concerned with hearing impairment and enables varying interests and disciplines to work together. Other national roles include the promotion of research, the collection and dissemination of information, the representation or protection of the interests of the hearing-impaired persons served, the identification and innovation of services not provided by statutory agencies, and, perhaps most important, political action as a pressure group. In connection with this, the Panel of Four Principal Organisations for the Hearing Impaired, namely the Royal National Institute for the Deaf, the British Deaf Association, the National Deaf Children's Society, and the British Association of the Hard of Hearing, has since 1971 had an annual meeting with the Minister of State for Social Services and the Disabled to keep government policy for hearing-impaired persons under regular review.

The six regional associations for deaf people covering the Midlands, North, South-East, West, Wales, and Scotland also act in an intermediary capacity and provide a forum for various groups including audiologists, otologists, teachers, social workers, and representatives of District Health and Local Authorities within the region served, thus helping to break down the parochialism to which work for deaf people is prone. The associations may also exercise a pressure-group role in encouraging greater uniformity in the provision of services for deaf clients on the part of the Local Authorities.

It is at the local level that voluntary societies provide direct services to the individual, and it is with the local voluntary effort for deaf persons in postschool life that the remainder of this article is mainly concerned. In this context the term "deaf" relates primarily to prelingually deaf people or those who use manual methods of communication, rather than hard-of-hearing persons who form hard-of-hearing clubs generally affiliated with the British Association of the Hard of Hearing.

DEVELOPMENT OF LOCAL SOCIETIES

The first organized effort in Britain to educate deaf people on public lines began in 1792 with the founding of the Asylum for the Deaf and Dumb Poor in Old Kent Road, London. In 1840 some former pupils of the asylum began to meet for worship in Fetter Lane and for social purpose in a coffee room in Aldersgate. These meetings came to the notice of a George Crouch, the father of five deaf children. On January 29, 1841, Crouch and seven others formed a committee to establish a society entitled the Refuge for the Deaf and Dumb. This society, subsequently renamed the Institution for Teaching Useful Trades and Conveying Religious Instruction to the Adult Deaf and Dumb, continued until 1854 when it was reorganized as the Association in Aid of the Deaf and Dumb. "Royal" was appended to the name of the association in 1876 when Queen Victoria became a patron.

In the provinces, local voluntary effort expanded in two ways in the nineteenth century. First, societies established in large centers such as Manchester (1846), Leeds (1860), and Liverpool (1864) extended their activities to neighboring towns by forming branches which often became autonomous organizations. Second, in rural areas "missions" were developed under Anglican auspices on a diocesan basis. After the Royal Association for the Deaf and Dumb and after Manchester, the number of welfare societies for deaf people in England and Wales expanded rapidly, with 34 new societies established by 1900.

Although the general pattern in many localities seems to have been for a school for deaf children to precede the founding of a society for deaf adults, there was formerly much hostility between the schools and societies due to the oral-manual controversy. Thus, in 1889 the *Report of the Royal Commission on the Blind, Deaf and Dumb*, much influenced by the recommendations of the Milan Congress of 1880, stated that "so long as there are adult deaf and dumb who have been educated on the silent system it will be necessary that these societies should hold meetings where services, lecturettes, etc are given to such adults in their own language." With orally taught deaf people, however, the situation was different. The report argued that these individuals should be discouraged from mingling with other deaf persons to prevent them from forming "a class apart," intermarrying, or losing their self-reliance. Fortunately, this antagonism between schools and societies gradually diminished.

Motives for Founding Voluntary Societies

Three main motives inspired the founding of local voluntary societies for deaf people, namely, mutual aid, evangelism, and philanthropy. The initiative for the formation of a society usually came from deaf persons themselves who wished to associate with others sharing a common method of communication and culture. The Liverpool Deaf and Dumb Benevolent Society, for example, was originally "a mutual help club" founded by deaf individuals themselves. At Manchester, the need for "a mutual help society," in addition to religious services, was recognized due to the "misery, privation and want of employment among the deaf."

The evangelistic motive is evidenced by the use of the term "mission" in the title of most early societies. The founders of such missions recognized that deaf people were unable to participate in the ordinary ministrations of the churches. Thus in 1841,

the committee of the "Refuge for the Deaf and Dumb" resolved that deaf people were ignorant "regarding the Word of God" and that the Society would "adopt suitable measures by which they shall be taught in the Scriptures of truth and brought to a sound knowledge of the Christian religion."

Philanthropy did not play the same part in the development of agencies catering to the spiritual and material needs of adult deaf persons as it did in the case of those who were blind or even in the founding of schools for deaf children. Philanthropy seems to have been exercised by persons who were themselves deaf, related to someone deaf, or brought by chance into contact with deaf people. At Southampton, Sir Arthur Fairbairn, himself deaf, raised funds for the erection of a church for deaf parishioners. At Rochdale, an institute was built by Sir J. E. Jones, whose son Ellis Llwyd Jones had been born deaf.

Activities

The range of services that every welfare society for deaf people should aim to provide was set out in a document prepared by the Royal National Institute for the Deaf in 1947, and is still relevant. Six categories of activity were recognized: interpretation, spiritual care, placement and industrial supervision, social services, visiting, and individual welfare. The scheme also suggested that societies with adequate staff and premises might extend their work to include: further education, increased facilities for sport and physical recreation, training in hobbies, handicrafts, housewifery, and so on, cooperation with organizations for blind persons in promoting improved arrangements for deaf-blind individuals; and provision for the needs of hard-of-hearing people.

Since the majority of persons attending the welfare societies for deaf adults have either failed to achieve social competency through the oral system, or, outside working hours, have abandoned the effort to comprehend and share in the nondeaf milieu, it follows that "every aspect of the work of a welfare society for the deaf turns more or less on interpretation."

Current Status

Presently there are in England and Wales over 70 local societies, founded by voluntary effort, to meet the spiritual and secular needs of adult deaf persons. The majority of these call themselves associations, centres, or societies, but there are also committees, diocesan councils, institutes, and missions.

By far the largest of these organizations is the earliest society, the Royal Association of the Deaf and Dumb. The Royal Association has nearly 7000 deaf members, over 30 full-time employees, and operates some 36 centers, mostly in London, Middlesex, Essex, Surrey, and West Kent.

These organizations do not, however, comprise the only bodies serving deaf people on a local basis. Work for Roman Catholic deaf persons is organized in at least 15 dioceses in England and Wales under the auspices of the Association for the Catholic Deaf of Great Britain and Ireland. The Jewish Deaf Association, founded in 1947 "to promote, encourage, provide for and generally organize the religious, moral, physical and mental welfare of members of the Jewish faith who are deaf," has a hostel and Friendship Club in London. A number of independent deaf clubs, such as the Spurs Club started in 1934 and the National Deaf Club founded in 1906, exist mainly in the South and Midlands, catering to orally inclined deaf and deafened persons usually of higher educational or social strata who, for various reasons, do not wish to attend the societies or missions where manual communication predominates. Groups affiliated to the Breakthrough Trust, established in 1971 "to bring deaf and hearing people into continuous contact with each other in such a way as to facilitate better communication, better understanding, mutual respect and friendship," have been established in about 15 centers throughout England. Finally, some deaf persons attend hard-of-hearing clubs where speech is the normal method of communication. Over 200 such clubs are affiliated with the British Association of the Hard of Hearing.

THE FUTURE

For well over a century, local voluntary societies constituted virtually the only provision for deaf persons in postschool life. In 1960 the Minister of Health directed the council of every county and borough to exercise their powers under Section 29 of the National Assistance Act of 1948 to promote the welfare of persons who are "blind, deaf or dumb." A Local Authority is able to provide for deaf clients either directly by establishing a service under the authority's auspices or indirectly by entering into an agency agreement with one or more voluntary societies. At first the Local Authorities were glad to use the expertise of the voluntary societies. In 1962 at least 101 of the 128 authorities that existed in England and Wales prior to the reorganization of local government in 1974 had full agency agreements by which the voluntary society provided all services for deaf people. Of the remainder, 11 and 6, respectively, had a partial agency or directly provided service while information from the 10 remaining authorities was not available.

The future of voluntary work for deaf persons was, however, already under threat as a result of the Younghusband Report, *Social Workers in the Local Authority Health and Welfare Services* (1959). The report made a number of general recommendations regarding the role of Local Authorities in the provision of welfare services for deaf individuals, including: (1) Local Authorities should take a more direct interest in the welfare of deaf people; (2) a proportion of Local Authority welfare officers should learn to make adequate contact with deaf people; (3) where greater understanding and fluency of communication is required, Local Authorities should either continue to use the services of voluntary organizations or employ their own trained and experienced staff for this purpose; (4) the aim of Local Authority provision for deaf individuals should be to "establish a high standard of service without establishing a separate service"; (5) Local Authorities should ensure that spiritual ministration is available to deaf people but should not take over this function themselves; and (6) a casework service should be provided for deaf people who need it even if this service must initially be attempted through an interpreter.

The committee also stated that if their recommendations on future patterns of development were implemented, a proportion of the work then being undertaken by the staffs of voluntary organizations for deaf people would become the responsibility of officers directly employed by Local Authorities. Religious ministrations and a proportion of clubwork and social activities would, however, continue to be undertaken by voluntary effort.

A further impetus to direct Local Authority provision was given by the Seebohm Report, *Local Authority and Allied Personal Social Services* (1968), which recommended the creation of new departments of social services which would integrate responsibility for welfare and social work, at that time diffused among several Local Authority departments. It further recommended that the new social services departments should be staffed by trained social workers, operating on area teams, and dealing with the whole range of social need rather than specializing in any particular field.

As a result of these developments there was a rapid increase in the number of Local Authorities providing a direct service for deaf people. By the early 1980s only about 20 of the Local Authorities in England and Wales still entrusted all aspects of deaf welfare to a voluntary society. Yet most local societies managed to continue. The ability of an individual society to survive the complete or partial cancellation of an agency agreement depends on at least four factors: (1) the extent to which a Local Authority is prepared to continue financial assistance; (2) the amount of income obtained by the society from investments or voluntary sources; (3) whether the voluntary society is prepared to accept a limited role, for example, recreational and spiritual ministration only as distinct from the provision of a comprehensive service; and (4) the capacity of the society to justify its continued existence by initiating and developing new services or amenities.

Further research is needed to determine whether deaf people are better served by a voluntary service or a directly provided service.

Bibliography

Future of Voluntary Organizations, Report of the Wolfenden Committee, Croom Helm, London, 1978.

Eicholz, A.: *A Study of the Deaf in England and Wales 1930–32*, Her Majesty's Stationery Office (HMSO), 1932.

Lysons, C. K.: *The Development of Local Voluntary Societies for Adult Deaf Persons in England*, British Deaf Association, 1979.

———: *The Development of Training for Work with Adult Deaf Persons*, British Deaf Association, 1977.

Report and Minutes of Evidence of the Royal Commission on the Blind, Deaf and Dumb, 1889.

Report of the Committee on Local Authority and Allied Personal Services, Seebohm Report, HMSO, 1968.

Report of the Working Party on Social Workers in the Local Authority Health and Welfare Services, Younghusband Report, HMSO, 1959.

C. K. Lysons

Social Work

There are 133 local authorities in England, Wales, Scotland, and Northern Ireland which have a mandatory duty to provide social work services for deaf persons. The two major acts covering these responsibilities in England and Wales are the 1948 National Assistance Act and the 1970 Chronically Sick and Disabled Persons Act, with similar relevant legislation covering Scotland and Northern Ireland. These authorities mainly provide direct services, using their own staff. In a few instances, however, their responsibilities are delegated, in total or in part, to a local voluntary society which acts as agent and accordingly receives payment from the local authorities.

POTENTIAL USERS OF SERVICE

The Department of Health and Social Security estimated that in 1975 there were 62,000 people over the age of 16 living in England and Wales with a very severe hearing impairment, and a further 2.3 million persons with a hearing impairment of lesser severity. It was also noted that while most of the prelingually deafened persons had registered for assistance from Social Services Departments only a fraction of the hard-of-hearing population had done so.

STAFFING

Although all social workers employed by Social Services Departments may have some contact with hearing-impaired persons, it is the specialist Social Workers with the Deaf who overwhelmingly provide most of the service. In 1975 there were 379 full-time equivalent Social Workers with the Deaf employed by local authorities and local voluntary societies in England and Wales. Of these, only 158 were shown to be qualified, and a number of these persons were in management and supervisory posts. A more limited survey conducted in 1980 in the 37 local authorities in the north of England showed 110 Social Workers with the Deaf operating in the region, of whom only 48 were qualified as social workers. This survey also indicated that there was an estimated average hearing-impaired population per Social Worker with the Deaf in the north of England of 153 persons with severe hearing impairment and 5500 with a less-than-severe hearing impairment. The above figures suggest that the staffing ratios and training opportunities within the corps of specialist workers with deaf persons are extremely low and raise serious doubts about the adequacy of the social services offered to hearing-impaired people in the United Kingdom.

TRAINING

The Council for Education and Training in Social Work is the organization responsible for training social workers. Two formal types of training are available for basic social work skills. The one that is appropriate for Social Workers with the Deaf is a two-year full-time course of study which is available at some universities and colleges and which leads to the Certificate of Qualification in Social Work. University graduates with relevant degrees can usually take this training on certain courses in one year.

A one-academic-year postqualifying course offering specialist training for social work with deaf persons is available at the Polytechnic of North London and Moray House College of Education, Edinburgh. Candidates need to be qualified in general social work and in most instances also need to have had two years' postqualifying professional experience.

FUNCTION OF SOCIAL WORKERS

The functions the Social Workers with the Deaf mainly exercise are assisting deaf people with problems of behavior and relationship, acting as an advocate and interpreter, obtaining material resources for deaf people, and supporting deaf people in achieving greater independence. A variety of roles are filled by the workers in discharging these functions, including adviser, caseworker, group worker, community worker, interpreter, advocate, trainer, and community educator.

The people who are helped by Social Workers with the Deaf are usually hearing-impaired children and their families, prelingually deafened adults preferring total or manual methods of communication, prelingually deafened adults rejecting manual methods of communication, adults who become profoundly deafened with rapid onset due to traumatic causes, deaf-blind persons, and hard-of-hearing persons.

THE FUTURE

Limitations on resources are likely to inhibit any expansion of social work services for deaf people in the foreseeable future. Deaf people are rapidly becoming more independent and are turning to social workers for help less frequently in some spheres. On the other hand, widespread unemployment and the increasing complexity and stress of everyday living are likely to make the most vulnerable sections of the deaf population more dependent upon the social services. It has been suggested that the way ahead rests on the twin objectives of greater discussion and cooperation with the consumers of services, and more support from lay persons in local communities for those who need help because of disability or social problems. It seems likely that social services for deaf people in the United Kingdom will follow this general trend.

Bibliography

Bunting, Claire: *Public Attitudes to Deafness*, HMSO, London, 1981.

Burton, Derek K.: *Survey of the Estimated Hearing Impaired Population per Social Worker for the Deaf in the North Regional Area of the Royal National Institute for the Deaf*, Report to RNID Executive Committee, Manchester, 1980.

Department of Health and Social Security: *Report of a Sub-Committee Appointed to Consider the Role of Social Services in the Care of the Deaf of All Ages*, Advisory Committee on Services for Hearing Impaired People, London, June 1977.

National Institute for Social Work: *Social Workers: Their Role and Tasks*, Bedford Square Press, London, 1982.

Wilkins, Leslie T.: *A Survey of the Prevalence of Deafness in the Population of England, Scotland and Wales*, Central Office of Information, London, 1948.

Derek K. Burton

Psychological Research

Traditionally, research into deafness in Britain has explored similarities and differences in the way deaf and hearing people think. Although this tradition continues, interest has extended to the study of deaf people's everyday lives and to considerations of the contribution that psychology can make to the well-being of deaf people. The Government inaugurated an Institute of Hearing Research in the early 1980s to examine, develop, and evaluate services and aids for hearing-impaired individuals. Furthermore, research into the development of deaf children in their family; the study of teaching techniques and their effectiveness; the problems of training hearing people in sign language to facilitate communication with deaf people; and the nature of translation between sign and speech in such communications have all started to flourish.

FAMILY LIFE

Studies of the development of deaf children in the family have produced a great deal of controversy.

One group of studies suggests that the development of deaf infants in hearing families differs in a number of important respects from that of hearing children and that deaf parents with deaf children are generally more effective in handling such problems. These studies show that deaf babies often do not provide hearing parents with the range of cues and social signals that, in the hearing baby, facilitate the growth of preverbal and verbal communication. Lacking these cues, parents often become more controlling in their interactions with the baby, not only acting out of phase with the stage of development but also leading the baby to become more passive or to reject interactions with the parents. In such cases, both the foundations of communication and the development of autonomy and initiative in the child are at risk.

Others argue that the pathological aspects of parent-child interaction can be normalized, given effective guidance and powerful hearing aids. As yet, the issue is not resolved. It seems clear that the hearing family is unlikely to provide an environment that serves all the deaf baby's needs. Whether effective parental support can overcome these difficulties has still to be proven.

Another aspect of the debate concerns the normality of the child's linguistic development: Some argue that the child is simply delayed, while others believe that the child's development follows a different path. The issue is not simply an academic one—the stance one adopts is likely to influence the teaching methods, and so on, deemed most relevant to the child. The same debate surfaces in studies of older children.

LANGUAGE, LITERACY, AND NUMERACY

Deaf children leave school in Britain at 16 years of age with an average reading age of around 8 to 9 years and a math age of about 13 years. In reading, degree of deafness is a major determinant of achievement; this is not so in mathematics. Studies of reading test performances show that such tests do not measure similar abilities in deaf and hearing children, leading to the questioning of the validity of such test scores for deaf persons. In mathematics, deaf children score normally, though they are delayed, and there is no reason to suppose that deafness itself need prevent children from good performance in mathematics.

Studies of oral linguistic skills in deaf children show that while their ability to communicate with unfamiliar hearing people is poor, they do develop a linguistic system and a limited grammar for English. Some aspects of this grammar parallel those of younger hearing children, but there are specific features of deaf children's language that are not found with hearing children. Why deaf children should be similar in some respects but different in others is not clear. One hypothesis is that learning language by eye (speechreading or sign language) leads to different language structures to learning by ear. Another is that many deaf children do not encounter normal language and communication and that this affects the language they develop. The issue is a complex one and the subject of research.

Observations of teaching styles with deaf children parallel the findings with parents—teachers tend to overcontrol children during interactions. Those who are less controlling, ask fewer questions, and interrupt less frequently to correct the child's speech, facilitate more speech and longer utterances from the child. By helping overcontrolling teachers to change their style, it has been shown that children can be encouraged to speak more and show greater initiative in interactions. Children from different schools are being studied to explore the long-term effects that differences in teaching styles make on their language development. *See* PSYCHOLINGUISTICS: Language Development.

Sign language is being introduced into some British schools, but as yet no systematic evaluations of its effects on teaching and learning have been reported.

ADULT COMMUNICATION

The relationships between poor communication skills and psychiatric problems in deaf adolescents and adults have been explored, and implications for the use of sign language in schools are the subject of debate. Techniques for improving the teaching of sign language to hearing people to facilitate better communication with deaf persons and the evaluation of techniques of simultaneous translation between sign language and speech are also in progress. One feature of this work is a growing involvement of deaf people in the research process.

The changing focus of psychological research into deafness is symptomatic of more than a growing interest in wider aspects of deaf people's lives. The underlying image of deaf people has changed. Where they were once viewed mainly as people with little or no language and as useful subjects for studying the effects of language on thinking, they are now viewed more positively as a population with similar intelligence to the hearing majority and, in many cases, as members of a distinctive cultural group within society. This leads many psychologists to ask about differences rather than deficiencies. The study of deafness offers the promise not only of an improved personal life for deaf people but also a way of understanding the nature of humans, whose intelligence and adaptability survive even such a seemingly fundamental sensory impairment as loss of hearing.

Bibliography

Conrad, R.: *The Deaf School Child*, Harper and Row, London, 1979.

Savage, R. D., L. Evans, and J. F. Savage: *Psychology and Communication in Deaf Children*, Grune and Stratton, Sydney, New South Wales, 1981.

Woll, B., J. Kyle, and M. Deuchar (eds.): *Perspectives on British Sign Language and Deafness*, Croom Helm, London.

Wood, D. J.: "The Linguistic Experiences of the Prelingually, Hearing-Impaired Child," *Teacher of the Deaf*, 6(4):86–93, 1982.

———, A. J. Griffiths, and A. Webster: "Reading Retardation or Linguistic Deficit (II)? Test-Answering Strategies in Hearing and Hearing-Impaired School Children," *Journal of Research in Reading*, 4(2):148–156, 1981.

David Wood

Mental Health

Workers with deaf people in the United Kingdom have been aware of the special needs of such people with mental illness for some time. As long ago as 1923, the annual report of the Royal Association for the Deaf and Dumb recorded a scheme whereby their workers visited deaf patients in mental hospitals. As a result, comment was made upon the need for a special officer with knowledge of mental illness, and in 1926 an officer was appointed to undertake this work. However, it was not until 1965, following a survey of deaf patients in two psychiatric hospitals in the north of England, that a psychiatric outpatient clinic for deaf patients was established at Manchester University. Later a 24-bed unit catering to deaf patients was opened at Whittingham Hospital, Preston, Lancashire. Although the needs of deaf people with psychiatric problems are becoming increasingly recognized, there are no psychiatrists training in this field.

FACILITIES

The residential unit at Whittingham Hospital has a national catchment area and accepts patients from England, Scotland, Wales, and Northern Ireland. It is served by outpatient clinics at the unit, but clinics are also held bimonthly at the Manchester Royal Infirmary and monthly at the Royal National Throat Nose and Ear Hospital in London.

The department at Whittingham Hospital has close connections with a hostel for the rehabilitation of deaf people who have suffered from mental illness. This is situated in Blackburn, some 12 miles from the Whittingham unit, and is run by the Royal National Institute for the Deaf. The medical director of the Whittingham unit is also honorary psychiatrist to the Blackburn hostel.

The only other residential unit in the United Kingdom for the assessment and treatment of deaf people with psychiatric illness is at Springfield Hospital, London, which has 22 beds. In Scotland, Wales, and Northern Ireland there are no residential psychiatric units for deaf persons. However, there is a rehabilitation hostel for deaf patients in Glasgow,

Scotland, which has two visiting psychiatrists, both of whom have facility in manual methods of communication.

MENTAL HANDICAP

Until the early 1970s deaf persons who were also mentally handicapped were almost completely neglected in the United Kingdom. Schools for deaf children adopted a purely oral approach to communication, and in consequence many mentally handicapped deaf children were either not accepted into schools for deaf students or were accepted and then rejected as ineducable. Similarly, deaf people in hospitals for the mentally handicapped were neglected. Fortunately, there was adoption of combined oral and manual methods in many schools for deaf children in the United Kingdom, and as a result fewer children are regarded as ineducable. At the same time, many hospitals for the mentally handicapped have developed schemes for the training of staff in manual communication skills.

Bibliography

Critchley, E.M.R., et al.: "Hallucinatory Experiences of Prelingually Profoundly Deaf Schizophrenics," *British Journal of Psychiatry*, 1981.

Denmark, John C.: "Early Profound Deafness and Mental Retardation," *British Journal of Mental Subnormality*, December 1978.

——— and Raymond W. Eldridge: "Psychiatric Services for the Deaf," *Lancet*, August 2, 1969.

——— and Frank Warren: "A Psychiatric Unit for the Deaf," *British Journal of Psychiatry*, April 1972.

John C. Denmark

Telecommunications

Telecommunications means information transfer by electromagnetic means such as wire or radio waves. Deaf people in the United Kingdom have gained access to these communication modes since the late 1970s through use of telephones, television, and television services.

TELEPHONES

A portable keyboard telephone known as Vistel has been marketed by the Breakthrough Trust, a deaf/hearing self-help group. Vistel has replaced an earlier generation of ex-General Post Office teletypewriters with which Breakthrough Trust began their keyboard telephone venture. Vistel has an acoustic coupler to which any normal telephone handset can be attached. The test is typed on a conventional QWERTY typewriter keyboard and displayed on a 20-character traveling display on the top of the equipment. The same message appears on the display of the person receiving the message. Vistel has a 1000-character memory for storing a message before transmission, thus saving connect time.

A more sophisticated two-way telecommunication system is Prestel. Prestel operates as an interactive information-providing terminal based on a huge central database of commercial and public service information. The Prestel subscriber can access thousands of pages of information with a television, a Prestel decoder, and a telephone line. It is also possible to communicate directly between a Vistel and a Prestel terminal.

Prestel has also been tried in person-to-person communication in conjunction with the Palantype shorthand machine. The experiment involved setting up a central telephone bureau, or Voice Bureau, in which a Palantypist sat waiting to receive messages. A deaf person with speech could talk directly to a hearing person. The hearing person could then reply via the Voice Bureau, and the reply would be relayed by the Palantypist at word-for-word speed to a Prestel terminal in front of the deaf person. The deaf person can then speak again, and so on. The system can also be operated by using an ordinary audiotypist at the Voice Bureau. This results in quite effective communication and may have useful applications, especially in offices employing deaf people.

Another experiment, supported by the United Kingdom's Department of Industry, makes use of computer mailboxes. Each deaf person is allocated a mailbox space in a central computer and is also given a list of mailbox numbers for other people in the system. Using a home terminal (Prestel, Vistel, or certain other computer terminals with telephone interfaces), a deaf person can type a message into another person's mailbox. The message waits until the other person checks the "mail" and takes appropriate action. The system, known as Visicom, allows mailbox users to chat on-line to each other and to provide an alerting signal to indicate that a caller is on-line.

TELEVISION

Teletext is a method of coding information in a digital form in the unused lines of the television picture. These lines are normally invisible, but the information can be decoded and displayed as full-screen text and simple graphics by means of a teletext decoder and a remote control page selector. Hundreds of pages of information are available covering news, sports, weather reports, TV program details, horoscopes, recipes, advertisements, and so on. Teletext decoders are marketed in two forms: either as a separate add-on box, or as part of an integrated teletext television receiver. Add-on decoders are more expensive than teletext that is incorporated into an integrated receiver.

Teletext also offers the opportunity to broadcast optional subtitles superimposed on ordinary television programs. The viewer can choose, by the press of a button, whether to watch the subtitles. This development in information technology is thus providing additional special help for deaf people.

Other teletext subtitling services have been under development. One problem concerns live television programs, where there is little or no time to prepare subtitles. One method for dealing with this involves the use of a Palantype shorthand machine and a specially trained operator. With Palantype it is possible to produce an almost word-for-word transcription of speech at normal television speech rates. The phonetic Palantype codes are converted to English by a computer. However, the English spelling is far from perfect. The alternative method is a rapid input terminal for conventional English subtitles. The output is easy to read. However, typing speeds mean that it is only possible to subtitle about one-third of what is said.

Teletext has the flexibility to provide full subtitling and simplified subtitling on two different teletext pages, which allows viewers to choose the version they prefer. This is potentially of great value to less able deaf readers, who have difficulties with the generally acceptable level of subtitling. An optional reduced level of subtitling also gives the deaf viewer, tired after a day's work, the opportunity to view programs in a more relaxed way, watching with "half an eye"—just as hearing viewers can monitor a program with "half an ear." If a program appears to be worth watching in detail, the deaf viewer could switch instantaneously to a more comprehensive level of subtitling.

Cable television is not widely established in the United Kingdom. However, commercial exploitation is becoming possible, and deaf pressure groups are planning to take advantage of cable television as a way of providing programs for and by deaf people. Widespread availability of coaxial land lines may also open up the possibility of person-to-person video television communication.

Bibliography

Baker, R. G., A. C. Downton, and A. F. Newell: "Simultaneous Speech Transcription and TV Captions for the Deaf," in P. A. Kolers, M. E. Wrolstad, and H. Bouma (eds.), *Processing of Visible Language 2*, Plenum, New York, 1980.

Baker, R. G., A. D. Lambourne, and G. Rowston: *Handbook for Television Subtitlers*, IBA Winchester, 1982.

Grossfield, K., et al.: "A Feasibility Trial of a Bureau-Based Telephone Service for the Deaf," *British Journal of Audiology*, vol. 16, 1982.

Hawkins, W., and L. A. Thomas: "The Economic Preparation of Teletext Subtitles," *Internal Broadcasting Convention*, Brighton, 1980.

Lambourne, A. D.: "Newfor: An Advanced Subtitle Preparation System," *IBA Technical Review*, no. 20, May 1983.

Royal National Institute for the Deaf: *Teletext, Prestel, the Deaf Telephone*, "Hearing" Supplement, 1980.

Robert G. Baker

TELEVISION SERVICES

The television companies in the United Kingdom are split into two major sectors: British Broadcasting Corporation (BBC) and Independent Broadcasting Authority (IBA). The BBC is an organization created by government statute and paid for by the viewer through a license fee. It is split into a number of areas, but its television production is shown on two channels. Programs are made by a number of departments, but its major provision for hearing-impaired viewers is a program called "SEE HEAR." This half-hour show runs for 26 weeks a year and is a compilation of news, views, and light entertainment. It commenced broadcasting in 1981. The program, which is shown throughout the United Kingdom, is produced by two departments, Community Programmes and Educational Television, and is presented by both hearing and deaf people in simultaneous speech and sign language. It also makes use of invision (open) subtitles and, where necessary, interpreters who are inserted onto the screen. Other BBC provisions for deaf viewers include open subtitles of daily news headlines, a 45-minute weekly news roundup on BBC2 called "News Review," and "SIGN ON," a series of educational programs on British Sign Language.

The IBA was also created by government statute and is the watchdog for issuing franchises to a number of independent television companies throughout the United Kingdom. These companies raise income by the use of advertising and will commission or produce programs to be shown on either the Independent Television (ITV) Channel or Channel 4.

While there is no nationwide broadcast, as with "SEE HEAR," some companies are producing programs for hearing-impaired people within their regional viewing area. These include Grampain television, whose production is "SIGN HEAR"; Television South-West, whose weekly roundup of local news and views is presented with an interpreter sitting alongside the resident presenter; Granada television, which selects programs of local interest and educational value that can be interpreted by the insertion of an interpreter; and "LATE CALL," a short religious program presented in sign language and produced by Scottish Television (STV).

Some companies, including STV, Tyne Tees television, and Harlech television, provide an interpreter to interpret the daily news headlines. Thames television presents a program for disabled viewers known as "LINK," which includes either a sign language presenter or an inserted interpreter when the topic relates to deafness. Channel 4's commitment relates to the provision of open subtitles on certain selected programs, usually those that have been shown originally without subtitles.

Schools Broadcasting on both channels has been an area where there has been conspiciously little provision for hearing-impaired children, but there are plans to provide more subtitled programs, and Yorkshire television is presenting a series, "IN-SIGHT," with sign language as an integral part of the series.

The final area of television services is the production, by the British Deaf Association and other interested groups, of videotapes on a variety of materials that the viewer might otherwise never have the opportunity of seeing. These include educational programs where children's stories are presented in British Sign Language.

The outlook for television services in the United Kingdom looks brighter. The involvement of deaf people in presentation and, hopefully, in production, and the developments in advanced television technology can only improve the standard of service the deaf community receive in the United Kingdom. *See* TELECOMMUNICATIONS.

M. Colville

Drama

"Drama" as used herein is a broad term covering educational and creative drama and theater with deaf children and adults. Professional theater of the deaf is excluded except where it is directly involved in educational and recreational areas.

EDUCATIONAL SETTINGS

Creative drama in Britain has been widely accepted as part of the school curriculum for hearing children. Its use in the education of deaf children has been less widespread and its value as a social, educational, and artistic activity less readily recognized. In recent years, however, there have been signs of growing interest not only in theatrical performances in schools but in the use of drama as a learning medium.

Educational drama builds on a child's natural inclination to play. It reinforces and directs play activity into more conscious and therefore more easily understood channels and utilizes the self-motivated learning inherent in play behavior. Play behavior in children is closely linked to the development of symbolic thought and to the acquisition of language, and is therefore of particular importance to the development of the deaf child. As a teaching method, educational drama is unique because it is both medium and message; drama may be used to teach certain information or to develop a particular communicative skill, but at the same time it is an artistic, emotional, and social experience. Educational drama functions on three levels. First, it is a personal experience for each child, allowing psychological adjustments and assimilations to be explored in a secure environment. It may therefore be of therapeutic value. Second, it is a communicative experience and encourages the improvement of expressive skills and social awareness. Third, it is an educational experience, extending a child's understanding of the world in which he or she lives.

One of the events which has encouraged the development of drama with deaf children is the National Deaf Children's Society (NDCS) Festival of Mime. The festival was started by the NDCS in 1971 and is open to all schools for deaf pupils and to ordinary schools that have deaf children attending them. The festival takes place annually in two stages: seven regional festivals held in March of each year, followed by a three-day festival in London in May. The festival includes workshops and demonstrations by professional mimes and evaluation and advice on the children's performances; it is noncompetitive. Associated with the Festival of Mime, the NDCS runs courses for teachers in mime and educational drama.

TRAINING

Courses for deaf and hearing people wishing to work in drama with deaf children and adults are also available at the Interim Theatre Company Summer Schools. Using tutors from both the professional theater and the deaf community, the summer schools are designed for deaf people who wish to improve their skills in drama and stagecraft, and for hearing people who wish to share and learn about drama with deaf people. The Interim Theatre Company also has run workshops for deaf children in schools.

More formal training for drama leaders with deaf drama groups is provided by a two-year part-time course run with the backing of the Royal National Institute for the Deaf at centers at Reading in Berkshire, and at Doncaster in South Yorkshire. The course first ran from 1974 to 1978 and was restarted in 1980. Originally, successful candidates were awarded the Special Diploma of the Associated Drama Board, but since 1982 the course has been validated by the Royal Society of Arts. This course combines written and practical work and requires students to submit for formal assessment.

PERFORMANCES

Many deaf clubs in Britain have their own drama groups. They present mimes, theatrical performances, and plays in sign language or sign mime. Performances are given regularly at the Congress of the British Deaf Association. In London, the "66 Club" for young deaf adults has its own drama group, which has staged full-scale productions.

The Unicorn Childrens Theatre in London has presented plays aimed specifically at an integrated audience of deaf and hearing children, using deaf actors. The Unicorn also has staged events for deaf children, including demonstrations, workshops, performances, and master classes in mime, drama, and dance. Similarly the London International Mime Festival has staged performances by the Electric Light Show for deaf children, using synchronized audiovisual techniques with mime and movement.

Opportunities for deaf children and adults in Britain to participate in creative drama and improve their theater skills remain limited. There is increasing interest, however, and the growing numbers of deaf people involved in professional theater is generating further opportunities. In 1983 a Committee of Enquiry into the Arts and the Disabled chaired by Sir Richard Attenborough was set up by the Carnegie United Kingdom Trust, and a National Study Group on drama and theater with deaf children and adults was established to bring together all people involved in work in this area. Ultimately, however, it is deaf people themselves actively involved in performing or teaching who will develop drama for deaf Britons.

Bibliography

Cayton, Harry: "The Contribution of Drama to the Education of Deaf Children," *The Teacher of the Deaf*, (5)2: 49–54, March 1981.

Keysell, Pat: *Motives for Mime*, Evans Bros., 1975.

Harry Cayton

Sport and Leisure

There is a widespread assumption that able-bodied deaf athletes can compete with and emulate their hearing counterparts in all sports. Unfortunately, this is not the case. Even though coaching has reached a higher level of importance in today's sports, the deaf sports enthusiast competing to achieve a high standard generally fails to reach the desired goal and has to be content with a lower performance level. This is because almost all sports coaches rely upon lengthy talks on methodology to improve the athletes' performances. The great misfortune is that few coaches are conversant with deaf people who strive to excel in sports. Some deaf people have been known to have innate ability, but they were never helped and therefore failed to succeed. However, a small number managed to become successful by sheer dedication and iron will.

CLUBS

Very little is recorded about deaf people's involvement in sport and leisure until 1840, when the first institution was opened for deaf people to gather socially and for spiritual enlightenment. Between then and 1939, 62 societies and missions were established for deaf people's benefit. Basically, however, the missions were for spiritual welfare rather than sport or leisure activities. The instigators found that public contributions came readily only if the missions were helping deaf persons toward religious perception. Consequently they were run by clergymen or educated deaf men of strong religious principles. Church services and bible reading were major activities, and the people were encouraged to practice temperance.

After 1900 there was a notable change. Missions became clubs, and management was taken up by a committee of deaf members. Facilities for indoor games and outdoor sport were provided and paved the way for greater forms of enjoyment among the deaf community. Attendance at church services dwindled until missioners lost their importance and were gradually replaced by welfare workers.

Committees found new sources of revenue; they introduced bars selling alcoholic beverages to pay for the upkeep of their clubs. Many of these clubs enter local leagues for a variety of sports which contribute in a large measure toward the enjoyment of leisure among the deaf individuals today.

INDIVIDUALS

During the era before 1840 there was one legendary figure—James (Deaf) Burke. Born in 1809, he worked as a Thames waterman and was taught to fight by a veteran pugilist. He dominated the prize ring in which fighters used bare fists and continued fighting until one of them fell; sometimes 100 rounds were endured. Burke was of medium height and weight, but he had remarkeable fighting abilities. Fighters of those days were intent on inflicting severe injuries on each other. At the age of 36, only a couple of years after giving up the game, Burke was found dead in a London gutter from tuberculosis.

Another legend of the nineteenth century was Arthur Wilson. Although deaf, he popularized cycling and introduced cycle races, which he won many times. He also edited the *Irish Cyclist*, a magazine for cycle enthusiasts. Later he turned to advertising and built a large firm in London. This made him wealthy and enabled him to become an entrepreneur. He started a number of sporting competitions and gave away many prizes that bore his name. He founded a federation of deaf clubs in London, which led to interclub events between the 10 clubs that existed during the period 1920–1950. This organization introduced a large variety of indoor as well as outdoor sports.

Arsenal, a soccer club, won almost all the major competitions in the English football scene during the latter half of the 1920s and first half of the 1930s. One of its star players was Cliff Bastin, who had a hearing impairment. He earned the nickname of Boy when at the age of 17 he became the youngest soccer player ever selected to play for England. He held the left wing position and was partnered by Alex James, reputedly the greatest forward at the time. To create an understanding with Bastin, James used gestures on the field and during training.

Another leading club, Wolverhampton Wanderers, in 1933 signed William Readman, a deaf person, but coaching problems developed and he was given a free transfer, thus ending his playing career as an undistinguished minor league footballer. It was the Readman case that revealed the problems related to coaching, and since then no deaf player has managed to enter top-class football.

Winning his first classic in 1954, Lester Piggott made an impact in horse racing. Although a former pupil of a school for deaf people in East Anglia, he apparently gained some hearing after leaving school. There was a notable impediment in his voice, causing him to be somewhat taciturn. His winning record of 28 classics led experts to regard him as the greatest jockey of all time.

Three wrestlers, Harry Kendall, Mick Eagles, and Alan Kilby, all profoundly deaf, became well known through their numerous appearances on television. Kendall represented Great Britain in the 1968 Olympic Games but failed to win any medals. Two totally deaf road racing cyclists, Nobby Clarke and Malcolm Johnson, won a number of events, some national, during the 1950s and 1960s. Clarke was a member of the record-breaking team of three, the Becontree Wheelers; two of their records remain unbroken.

The only British deaf person to win an Olympic Gold was the famed painter A. R. Thomson, a Royal Academician and a Royal Painter. The 1948 Olympic Games in London had a competition for artists to depict sporting scenes; Thomson's picture, *Seated Boxer*, won the first prize. He was sent a telegram to appear at the stadium to collect his medal, but he was away on a sailing holiday and could not be reached. For the first time in the history of the Olympics, no winner mounted the rostrum to collect the prize. It was later delivered to him by special messenger. *See* THOMSON, ALFRED REGINALD.

Bibliography

Adamson, W. W.: "Council of Church Missioners to the Deaf and Dumb," *Minute Book*, July 1916.

Baird, W.: "Report of the 1953 International Games of the Deaf at Brussels," *British Deaf Times*, autumn 1953.

Bastin, Cliff: *New Chronicle*, Newspaper Library, North London, April 1933.

Buckley, Frank: *Wolves Topics*, 1958.

Burke, Tom: "Deaf Burke," *ABC of Sport*, November 1973.

Dimmock, A. F.: *Tommy*, (biography of A. R. Thomson), unpublished.

"History of Our Adult Deaf and Dumb Societies," *British Deaf Mute*, January 1895.

Mecredy, R. J.: "What Can Be Achieved by a Man Although Deaf," *Silent World*, about 1923.

Missioners and Welfare Workers to the Deaf and Dumb (pamphlet), 1928.

A. F. Dimmock

Interpreting

British Sign Language is used by about 30,000 people in the United Kingdom. Interpreting is therefore vital if deaf people are to have full access to society.

HISTORY

Interpreting in the United Kingdom grew in much the same way as in other countries, initially through using the relatives of deaf people. Records of court cases in the late eighteenth and nineteenth centuries give historical evidence that sign language interpreters were in use even then. Deaf people were allowed to give evidence in court if "they could communicate by signs, and there was someone in court who could interpret the signs to the court."

The role of the interpreter, however, requires an ability to pass information without bias. In the eighteenth and nineteenth centuries, interpreters were usually relatives of deaf people, and the records show that sometimes the relatives' interpreting was unsatisfactory, with evidence not being repeated, and bias.

This problem was to a certain extent resolved in the late nineteenth century with the formation of local voluntary societies for deaf people. These societies then provided an interpreting and welfare service for deaf people in their area. They were the forerunner of modern-day social services, and many still exist, providing the base for deaf clubs and social services.

Consequently, interpreting work has traditionally been considered the province of chaplains, welfare workers, and social workers for deaf persons. Until the mid 1960s, these people were usually children of deaf parents, who often learned sign language as their first language and who, from early childhood, were bilingual.

In the late 1920s the Deaf Welfare Examination Board was established. The training and examination for welfare workers with deaf people included assessment on interpreting from speech to sign and from sign to speech. This specialist in-service training continued until the early 1970s, when changes in social work practice emphasized more generic social work training and brought about the end of a national system of training and examination in communication and interpreting skills.

A postqualifying one-year specialist course for generic social workers was established in the mid-1970s which included training in communication skills. There was also at that time a change in many areas from a local voluntary society–based service to a direct local authority service as generic social work departments were established. The emphasis was on provision of a social work service, and the training geared to meet this end. Interpreting services continue to be provided by this group of professionals, with many people who have joined the profession being primarily social work-trained and biased.

PROFESSIONALIZATION

Several changes have occured since the 1970s that influenced interpreting in Great Britain. One of these was the emergence of the deaf community. It became more aware of its potential and of opportunities open to it. Another was research into sign language that created more awareness and recognition of British Sign Language as a language in its own right. A third was the acceptance of interpreting as a profession in its own right.

A shortage of suitably trained and qualified interpreters led the British Deaf Association, with funding from the Department of Health and Social Security, to establish a Communication Skills Project in 1976. Part of this project's work was to instigate training and assessment of interpreters and carry out foundation work to establish a register of interpreters. The project's work quickly established a need for more definition of the interpreters' role and understanding of the languages used and the processes involved. When the project ended, the Council for the Advancement of Communication with Deaf People was established, and it now administers a register of interpreters and has introduced a scheme of training and examination in communication skills.

The register of interpreters at first consisted predominantly of people who passed the Deaf Welfare Examination Board diploma and certificate and who were used as a nucleus to establish the register. They were allowed to remain on the register until 1986, when those who wanted to remain had to be assessed. Short courses and assessments were offered to people who had become involved in interpreting work since the Deaf Welfare Examination Board ended. The Scottish Association of the Deaf in 1978 published a paper, "Training and Certification of Interpreters for the Deaf," and subsequently established their own training and register.

The register at this stage cannot be regarded as an effective national list of acting and available interpreters because: (1) the list of names taken from the Deaf Welfare Examination Board includes many retired people—names are only deleted on death; and (2) development of interpreting services has been linked to provision of social work services. This has meant that the local social worker is also the interpreter and largely provides the service only in the immediate area.

Development of an interpreting profession separately from the interpreter–social worker is still in its infancy; there are still only a small number of free-lance sign language interpreters. Furthermore, research in British Sign Language has shown that the sign languages used by interpreters vary from signed English (used to support English), through pidgin English (where signs are used in an English word order but with no supplementary reference for tense, plurals, and so on), to British Sign Language. *See* SOCIOLINGUISTICS: Sign Language Continuum.

The linguistic status of British Sign Language, and the changes in attitude toward the deaf community, have enormous implications for the sign language interpreter. It is not enough to say one can interpret sign language—the definition of one's skills must be wider. Traditionally, terms like "low verbal" were used to describe deaf people who use no speech sounds in conversation; they are now recognized as British Sign Language users. Other deaf people use signed English. Consequently, interpreting skills must reflect the needs of different groups of deaf people, and interpreters must develop more proficiency in interpreting British Sign Language.

The use of sign language interpreters on television, at party political conferences, in theaters, and at public meetings since the 1970s has done much to increase public awareness.

The British Deaf Association's Manifesto in 1982 asked the Government to finance further training and to implement a national program to train more British Sign Language interpreters. Much has been done to allow other physically disabled individuals rights to access; similarly, there will be increasing demands from the deaf community for equal access.

Bibliography

British Deaf Association: *Deaf Discrimination: A Challenge to the Hearing Community*, 1984.

——— Department of Health and Social Security: *A Handbook for Assessment*, Communication Skills Projects, 1979.

Council for the Advancement of Communication with Deaf People: *Annual Report 1983*, 1984.

Hough, Jean: *Legal Interpreting*, 1981.

Kyle, J. G., P. Llewellyn-Jones, and B. Woll: "The Qualities of Interpreters," *British Deaf News*, 1979.

Llewellyn-Jones, P.: *Platform and Conference Interpreting*, 1981.

Jean Hough

VEDITZ, GEORGE WILLIAM
(1861–1937)

George W. Veditz was one of the pioneer institution builders of America's deaf community. Living through the crucial years of the late nineteenth and early twentieth centuries, when deaf people were struggling to maintain their language and cultural autonomy, Veditz was instrumental in establishing organizations of and for deaf people, organizations that would—through the succeeding decades—prove immensely valuable to the deaf community. He also fought vigorously for issues important to deaf Americans, especially employment opportunities in the federal government and the preservation of sign language. Ironically, Veditz was totally bicultural, equally comfortable in either the deaf or the hearing communities, and most of his adult years were spent in occupations that had nothing to do with deafness.

Born on August 13, 1861, in Baltimore, Maryland, Veditz grew up in a bilingual environment. His parents, Anthony and Joanna Veditz, were German immigrants who always spoke their native language at home and sent their son to the Zion School in Baltimore, a private German-English school. Nevertheless, with his sisters and his playmates, Veditz invariably communicated in English until he became deaf.

When Veditz was almost nine years old he contracted scarlet fever, which left him profoundly deaf. Two apparently unsatisfactory years of private tutoring followed, and in 1875, when he was 14, his parents decided to send him to the Maryland School for the Deaf in Frederick in hopes that he could learn to become a shoemaker. There Veditz mastered sign language, becoming, he later wrote, a "triple polyglot."

Veditz's academic career, both at the Maryland School for the Deaf and later at Gallaudet College, was an unqualified success. After one year at the former, he was selected the private secretary and bookkeeper—the steward—for Superintendent Charles R. Ely. After three years at the Maryland School, Veditz passed the entrance examination for Gallaudet College but did not have sufficient money to enter. Undaunted, he learned enough printing skills during the summer in a Baltimore printing office to return to the Maryland School in the fall as foreperson of its new print shop. Two years later, at age 19, he entered Gallaudet College. He graduated in 1884 after earning the highest grade average of any Gallaudet student in the nineteenth century. Veditz was so successful at Gallaudet that he was accepted into the graduate school of Johns Hopkins University (unusual for a deaf person at that time) but he decided to teach instead. *See* GALLAUDET COLLEGE.

Veditz's first teaching position was at the Maryland School for the Deaf. Staying four years, he was the school's first vocational instructor and editor of its newspaper, the *Maryland Bulletin.* In 1888 he moved to Colorado to take a teaching position at the Colorado School for the Deaf, where he again edited the school newspaper, the *Colorado Index.* Veditz taught at the Colorado School until 1905

George W. Veditz. (Gallaudet College Archives)

and then remained as its accountant for five more years. In 1894, while still a teacher, he married Mary Elizabeth Bigler, a colleague at the Colorado School, and began the activities that made him so important to the deaf community.

Veditz established three organizations of deaf people during his career and twice served as president of a fourth. In 1892 he founded the Maryland School for the Deaf Alumni Association; in 1889, the Gallaudet College Alumni Association; and in 1904, the Colorado Association of the Deaf. In 1904 and again in 1907 he was elected president of the National Association of the Deaf (NAD). It was in the last capacity that Veditz became especially well known in the deaf community and among people interested in the welfare of deaf persons. *See* GAL-LAUDET COLLEGE ALUMNI ASSOCIATION; NATIONAL ASSOCIATION OF THE DEAF.

One of Veditz's major goals as president of the NAD was to convince the federal government to change civil service regulations that discriminated against deaf individuals. In 1907 deaf persons were classified with criminals and insane persons as unfit for civil service employment. Veditz pressured

Presidents Theodore Roosevelt, William Howard Taft, and Woodrow Wilson to remove this prohibition. In 1910, after limited progress had been made, Veditz urged deaf people to join the civil service in those positions that had been opened to them to force the government to open still more opportunities.

Veditz was even more concerned about the preservation of sign language, and throughout his life he would be one of the deaf community's most vocal, strenuous, and acerbic advocates of sign language as the best communication medium in schools for deaf children. Becoming NAD president during the years when sign language was under attack by Alexander Graham Bell and various professional organizations, Veditz lashed back. He was particularly critical of Bell, whom he termed "the most to be feared enemy of the American deaf." In 1911 Veditz described the attempt to force deaf children to give up sign language as "wickedness" and "evil," whereas he praised sign language as "the noblest gift God has given to deaf people." *See* BELL, ALEXANDER GRAHAM; EDUCATION: Communication; HISTORY: Sign Language Controversy.

Veditz argued his case wherever possible. In letters to school administrators, in newspaper articles, and in the deaf press, he urged people to recognize the importance of sign language. He insisted that deaf children should be introduced to sign language first, then be taught lipreading and speech. He reasoned that this would be effective because deaf children of deaf parents, who acquired American Sign Language as their first language, "made remarkably efficient articulators and lip readers." Veditz was scathing in his criticism of deaf people who did not acknowledge their preference for sign language, and admonished the NAD to send representatives to the meetings of organizations like the American Association to Promote the Teaching of Speech to the Deaf, the Otological and Laryngological Society, and the National Education Association to proselytize in favor of sign language. He was so fearful that sign language might disappear or become less sophisticated as it was pushed out of public use that he convinced the NAD to set up a motion picture fund to film and preserve the sign language of excellent signers, such as Edward Miner Gallaudet and Edward Allen Fay. *See* ALEXANDER GRAHAM BELL ASSOCIATION FOR THE DEAF; FAY, EDWARD ALLEN; GALLAUDET, EDWARD MINER; SIGN LANGUAGES: American; TELEVISION AND MOTION PICTURES: George W. Veditz Film Collection.

Despite Veditz's preoccupation with sign language and the maintenance of the deaf community, he had other interests as well. After resigning from his teaching position in Colorado, he raised poultry, pigeons, and prize-winning flowers in Colorado. At various times he edited *Western Poultry*

World, was associate editor of the *Western Pigeon Journal*, and was editor in chief of the *Deaf American* in Omaha, the *Optimist* in Atlanta, and the *Silver Courier* in Chicago. He contributed articles and reviews of German-language books for the *American Annals of the Deaf* and was secretary-treasurer of both the Pikes Peak Poultry Association and the Colorado Springs Chess Club, whose tournaments he always won. *See* AMERICAN ANNALS OF THE DEAF.

Veditz lived through the early decades of the twentieth century when deaf people were on the defensive: their language was repressed; schools refused to hire them as teachers; and everywhere there was pressure to force them to accept second-class citizenship. Many people within the deaf community and in educational institutions urged Veditz to moderate his strident tone of protest against these conditions. But until his death on March 12, 1937, he remained adamant.

Veditz contributed greatly to the survival of America's deaf community. As a founder of organizations that help bind deaf people together, as a leader of the NAD, as an example to the hearing community of what a deaf person could achieve, and as an uncompromising advocate of deaf people's right to self-determination, George W. Veditz was important to deaf Americans.

Bibliography

George W. Veditz: "The Sound-Memories of a Semi-Mute," *American Annals of the Deaf*, 44(2):117–126, March 1909.

"George W. Veditz," in James E. Gallaher (ed.), *Representative Deaf Persons of the United States of America*, James E. Gallaher, Chicago, 1898.

"George William Veditz," *Maryland Bulletin*, 57(7) 121–123, April 1937.

John V. Van Cleve

VISIBLE SPEECH

One of the earliest notions in the field of sensory aids was to provide speech signals directly to the visual sense in some manner, permitting visual understanding or interpretation.

OSCILLOGRAPHIC TECHNIQUE

The oscillograph, developed in the late nineteenth century, presented the speech waveform directly on a chart in a left-to-right manner. This display constituted the earliest instrumentally generated form of visible speech and was used extensively for phonetic studies. The invention of the electronic oscilloscope (now commonly referred to as the cathode-ray tube, or CRT) in the 1930s provided a practical means of displaying a speech waveform instantaneously or in real time.

The characteristics of speech that can be identified visually in an oscillographic display are limited to a small number of rather coarse features—whether a speech signal is present or absent; and whether the sound is sustained periodic (voiced), sustained nonperiodic (unvoiced), or a brief burst or plosive pulse type. The spectral characteristics are not easily discerned in an oscillograph. The spectrum of a sound describes how the energy is distributed on the frequency dimension; for example, a sound might consist principally of high-frequency components or low-frequency components. As a result, it is generally possible to identify the type of speech sound in an oscillographic display, but not the specific sound within that type.

SPECTROGRAPHIC TECHNIQUE

A spectrogram represents the speech signal as a time-varying spectrum, that is, a description of how the sound energy distribution varies in time. The speech sound spectrograph was invented in the late 1930s at the Bell Telephone Laboratories. In the mid-1940s an experimental system that operated in real time was developed expressly to explore the basic notion of visible speech. This device was called the Visible Speech Translator (several variations of the basic system were developed) and was used in an extensive study of speech reception by real-time spectrograms. In this study, a group of adults (which included one deaf individual) learned to read spectrographic speech at slow-speech rates and with substantial vocabularies. The deaf subject reached a vocabulary of 800 words. Following this remarkable achievement, there was little further development of real-time spectrographic displays until the mid-1970s, when technological advances made it possible to produce a real-time spectrograph at reasonable cost. Advances in microprocessors and storage technology suggest that complete real-time spectrographic speech displays may become more widely available. *See* SENSORY AIDS.

The principal value of the spectrogram as a visual representation of speech is in its ability to display the formants or resonances of the vocal tract varying in time. The formants of the speech signal, appearing as dark bands, are the direct result of the particular articulatory configuration of the vocal tract. Thus, a spectrogram might be viewed as visible articulation, although its relationship to articulation is not a simple one. *See* SPEECH PRODUCTION.

The principal shortcomings of the spectrogram as a visible speech display are in its inability to exhibit clearly certain characteristics of the speech signal that are obvious and are important to the auditory perceptive sense. Examples are (1) subtle changes in the formant frequencies and amplitudes which are difficult to see but which correspond to an auditory perceptual change of one whole phoneme, and (2) spectral characteristics of brief events in a speech signal, such as a plosive burst, which are distinctive perceptually but are not clearly distinguished in the spectrogram. At this time, however, the sound spectrogram constitutes the nearest thing to a true visible speech display.

PHONETIC DISPLAYS

The term visible speech was coined by Alexander Melville Bell, father of Alexander Graham Bell, as the name of his system of sound writing or phonetic transcription, with which he claimed one could represent all of the distinctive sounds of speech. A major segment of current research in speech is directed at accomplishing such a phonetic representation of speech automatically, which would constitute a complete form of visible speech. The error rates of current efforts are in the range of 20 to 30 percent. However, significant improvements can be expected in the future. *See* BELL, ALEXANDER GRAHAM.

Bibliography
Levitt, H., J. M. Pickett, and R. Houde: *Sensory Aids for the Hearing-Impaired*, IEEE Press, 1980.

R. Houde

VOLTA REVIEW

The *Volta Review* is the official journal of the Alexander Graham Bell Association for the Deaf, used since 1910. From 1899 to 1910 the journal was known simply as the *Association Review*. See ALEXANDER GRAHAM BELL ASSOCIATION FOR THE DEAF.

READERSHIP

The *Volta Review* is directed to teachers of deaf people, speech pathologists, linguists, audiologists, and other professionals concerned with oral or aural rehabilitation of hearing-impaired children and adults. It is circulated currently to a membership of approximately 5500 throughout the United States, Canada, and several other countries. It publishes the findings of research into methodology, technology, and theory affecting hearing-impaired education, rehabilitation, and development of communication with specific reference to hearing, speech, and language development. The journal is a membership benefit of the association.

EDITORIAL POLICY

The *Volta Review* is a refereed journal with a seven-member editorial board. Those who wish to submit articles for publication should write for a copy of "Information for Contributors," which contains guidelines concerning editorial style and publication format. Manuscripts are edited for content, style, and readability. Authors are asked to approve the final version. In most cases, authors transfer copyright to the association. The association is thus free to issue reprints and authorize copying, indexing, and abstracting of its articles.

While the journal has served as an organ of the association throughout the latter's history, it underwent a major change in 1976. Until then the executive director of the Bell Association doubled as the editor of the *Volta Review*. As a result, the journal had evolved into an editorial grab bag, attempting to serve a diversity of interests and audiences, with its editorial identity as the official organ of the association becoming obscured. The board of directors, recognizing the need and opportunity for change, directed that the *Volta Review* become a professional journal while a newsletter, *Newsounds*, took on the role of news dissemination. There would be six regular issues of the *Volta Review*, instead of nine, and one single-topic monograph issue. Wilbert L. Pronovost, a professor in the Department of Special Education of Boston University, became the first editor of the new *Volta Review*, and he selected associates in educational audiology, speech and language, education, parents issues, medical and health factors, and psychosocial factors. In 1979 Richard R. Kretschmer, Jr. assumed the post; and in 1985 Richard G. Stoker, an expert in the field of communicative disorders who himself has a profound congenital hearing loss, became editor.

Gina Doggett

W

WALES

The principality of Wales was incorporated with England by the Acts of Union of 1536 and 1543; since that time it has been governed by the Parliament of Great Britain. With a land area of 8019 square miles (20,850 square kilometers), approximately one-sixth that of England, Wales is much less densely populated, having only about 2.8 million, one-sixteenth as many people. A minority of the inhabitants (about 20 percent) are both Welsh- and English-speaking, and with the exception of a few Welsh language schools, English is the language of education.

EDUCATION

Education in Wales follows exactly the pattern of England. There are eight autonomous Local Education Authorities (LEAs), and each LEA is responsible for meeting the educational needs of all children residing in its area. Acting through the agency of the Welsh Office, the LEAs bear the same relationship to central government and the Department of Education and Science as in England. *See* ENGLAND, EDUCATION IN.

It was not until 1893 that the education of deaf children was made compulsory in England and Wales. As the result of voluntary effort, however, the first school for deaf pupils in Wales was established much earlier, in 1847, at Aberystwyth. The school moved to Swansea in 1850, where it remained until heavy bombing during World War II

forced the evacuation of pupils and staff to mid-Wales in 1941. In 1950 financial difficulties caused the Welsh Joint Education Committee to take over the responsibility of educating deaf children, and a new school was opened with 157 pupils at Llandrindod Wells. A small day and residential nursery-infant school opened 10 years later at Cardiff. Both of these schools are now closed.

Today there are two special schools for hearing-impaired children in Wales—Ashgrove School for 80 pupils at Penarth in the south and a small school for 20 pupils at Mold in the north. Fewer than 150 Welsh children of school age are classified as deaf. In addition to the 100 or so pupils attending the two special schools, approximately 300 hearing-impaired children attend the 40 special units attached to ordinary schools. A further 500, mostly with less severe losses, are enrolled into ordinary classes, where they receive support from the 35 peripatetic teachers of deaf children employed by the eight LEAs.

The great majority of hearing-impaired children in Wales are educated by using an oral approach, manual supportive methods being thought necessary for only a few. Some children in special units attending ordinary schools learn Welsh as a second language, and a number of the more able children transfer to the Mary Hare Grammar School in England for secondary school. It is unlikely that there will be major changes in the established pattern of education of deaf persons in Wales in the foreseeable future, though the Education Act (1981) will in time result in relatively fewer children being educated in the two special schools. *See* EDUCATION: Communication.

TEACHER TRAINING

Wales has never had a course of training for teachers of deaf pupils and, therefore, has used the full-time resources offered in England. Three of the newer English courses (Oxford, Birmingham, and Bristol) are all geographically reasonably near the Welsh border.

Special schools for deaf students in Wales, and more recently units within services, have made considerable use of the part-time in-service form of qualification offered by the British Association of Teachers of the Deaf (until 1976 the National College of Teachers of the Deaf). *See* UNITED KINGDOM: Organizations.

C.A. Powell; David M. Braybrook

WELFARE SERVICES

Work for adult deaf persons in Wales was pioneered by the Glamorgan and Monmouthshire Missions to the Deaf and Dumb established in Cardiff in 1869. The Glamorgan Mission to the Deaf and Dumb with headquarters at Pontypridd was founded later. Today, all eight Welsh counties make provision for the adult deaf either by a directly provided service or under an agency agreement with a local voluntary society.

WALES COUNCIL FOR THE DEAF

The Wales Council for the Deaf was founded in 1950 as the Welsh Regional Association for the Deaf and adopted its present title in 1976. The objects of the council include the promotion of the welfare of the hearing-impaired in Wales and cooperation with other organizations having similar aims. The council acts as a coordinating body for representatives of county councils, social service departments, health and education authorities, and national and local voluntary organizations. The council's journal, *Watch*, appears monthly.

Kenneth Lysons

WASHBURN, CADWALLADER LINCOLN (1866–1965)

Cadwallader Lincoln Washburn was born in Minneapolis, Minnesota, on October 31, 1866, to Elizabeth (Muzzy) and William Drew Washburn. His family was wealthy—from lumber, railroad, and flour-milling interests—and prominent. His father was a United States senator from Minnesota, two uncles were state governors, another uncle was a United States secretary of state, and his great-

grandfather was a signer of the Declaration of Independence. Given his family background, Washburn might have gone into public service or business, but he became deaf from scarlet fever and spinal meningitis at age five.

EDUCATION

Washburn began his education at the Minnesota School for the Deaf. There he learned printing from Olof Hanson, and in 1884 he entered Gallaudet College with hopes of becoming a newspaper printer. During his early college years, he gave no evidence of artistic talent, for his deep love of nature and insects occupied most of his time. One of the many important papers contributed by Washburn during his lifetime was his senior dissertation, "The Working Mind of a Spider," which he read in sign language on commencement day. However, he discovered his interest and talent in art when he needed drawings to accompany his articles about insects. This interest, and perhaps the influence of Hanson, his former teacher and a well-known deaf architect, caused Washburn to decide to study architecture after graduation from Gallaudet College. *See* GALLAUDET COLLEGE; HANSON, OLOF.

Cadwallader Washburn, about 1950. (Gallaudet College Archives)

Washburn began his study of architecture at the Massachusetts Institute of Technology, but after one year he decided to give it up, feeling that the field was too confining for his inquisitive and experimental mind. Instead, he decided to pursue a career in art and went to New York City and joined the Art Students' League.

There, Washburn won a place in the life class under the instruction of William Merritt Chase. Chase was impressed with Washburn's bent for hard work and asked him to accompany him on a trip to Spain to study Velasquez's paintings. On this trip Washburn met the great Spanish master Joaquin Sorolla, who became his next teacher. Sorolla had a deep influence on Washburn, and Washburn remained Sorolla's student for two years. While in Europe, Washburn traveled to Holland and France, studying the great masters and meeting notable artists. In 1898 Washburn's first salon painting *Un Marche de Tanger*, was exhibited at the Salon Champs d'Elysée.

After staying in Africa for a year, Washburn went to London to study with another well-known artist, John Singer Sargent. Unfortunately, Sargent had just received a commission in Boston, so he gave Washburn a letter of introduction to Albert Besnard, the director of the Ecole des Beaux Arts in Paris. Besnard accepted Washburn as his pupil, and Washburn assisted him in painting panels of religious subjects as part of the murals in the Hospital Chapel at Berek-sur-Mer, in Normandy. This same year, 1899, Washburn's *Un Nude* was exhibited at the Salon Champs de Mars in Paris.

CAREER

In 1903 Washburn went to Venice, where he saw etchings by James McNeill Whistler and decided to try his hand at this art form, marking a major change in his art career. Since Venice lacked the facilities Washburn needed to pursue this new interest, he went to Paris and visited an American etcher, observing the etching process from grounding the plate to pulling the print. Then he went back to Venice, and after a month-long series of failures, two months of experimenting, and two trips to Munich to view quality etchings, he produced four plates: *Casa Cecchino*, *Casa d'Oro*, *Grand Canal*, and *Square in Verona*.

Washburn never took formal etching classes, but his experience in learning the tools and equipment of printing, his drawing, and his work with Besnard, who did some etching, probably assisted his transition to this art medium. Washburn was unique in that he did not do preliminary sketches; he was well known for his method of working directly on the copperplate. He also was very concerned about the quality of the prints, sometimes destroying a copperplate after only 30 to 40 prints were made

***The Matriarch*, etching by Washburn. (Gallaudet College Archives)**

from it to prevent the production of lower-quality, imprecise prints. He believed in capturing the "spirit of the subject" in his work.

For the next 35 years Washburn traveled widely with his etching needle. He also served as a war correspondent, beginning in 1904 when he and his brother, Colonel Stanley Washburn, covered the Russo-Japanese War for the *Chicago Daily News*. From 1910 to 1912 Washburn lived in Mexico, recovering from pneumonia, writing a short paper, "Etchings of Mexico," etching, and reporting on the Mexican Revolution, again for the *Chicago Daily News*. As the violence of the Mexican Revolution grew worse, Washburn finally was forced to flee. Unfortunately, the ship he was on, the *Merida*, collided with another vessel and sank with 50 of his precious etchings, representing two years of work.

Undaunted, Washburn continued his etching and traveling. In 1914 he received a commission to make copperplate engravings of buildings of the Panama-Pacific International Exposition in San Francisco. During World War I he again became a war correspondent and was assigned to the Orient. During the 1920s he accompanied a University of Minnesota professor on a field expedition to the Marquesas Islands, where they studied and drew sketches of rare birds and insects.

Washburn never settled long enough to establish a permanent address. He moved to Morro Bay, Cal-

Antonio Viale, **an etching by Washburn. (Gallaudet College Archives)**

ifornia, in 1925, visited Tunisia in 1929, went to Paris in 1934, and traveled to the Canary Islands in 1935. After this last trip Washburn, now 69 years old, had to give up etching because of the strain to his eyes and resume oil painting.

When almost 77, Washburn married Margaret Cowles Ohrt on October 17, 1943. He died on December 21, 1965, in South Livermore, Maine, the family home away from Minnesota.

Washburn received numerous honors, and his works have been exhibited in important art galleries and museums. He is listed in *Who's Who in American Art*, the *Dictionary of American Painters, Sculptors, and Engravers*, and *Biographical Sketches of American Artists*. He received honorary doctoral degrees from Gallaudet College in 1925 and Bowdin College in 1947. He was honored both for his works of art and for his studies of insects. Two papers in particular, "Some Experiments with a Chrysalis" and "Language of the Bees," were important scientific contributions.

Bibliography

Sonnenstrahl, Deborah M.: *Analysis of the Etchings of Cadwallader Lincoln Washburn*, a dissertation submitted to the Graduate School of Arts and Sciences of The Catholic University of America, Washington, D.C., January 1967.

Deborah M. Sonnenstrahl

WILLIAMS, BOYCE ROBERT
(1910–   )

Boyce R. Williams more than any other American was responsible for the development and expansion of the state-federal vocational rehabilitation program of services for deaf and other communicatively disabled people. He has spent all of his adult years in service to deaf people.

Williams was born August 29, 1910, in Racine, Wisconsin. He was totally deafened at the age of 17 by spinal meningitis. A Gallaudet College graduate (1932), Williams quickly learned the grim realities of life for deaf people in the dearth of employment opportunities in the Great Depression. A teaching vacancy at the Wisconsin School for the Deaf in 1933 was his entry into the field of education of deaf people. From 1935 to 1945, he was associated with the Indiana School for the Deaf, first as a teacher and then as vocational training director. His 1937 marriage to Hilda C. Tillinghast, a hearing fellow teacher, produced three sons, Boyce, Jr., John David, and Thomas Edward. During his years at the Indiana school, he attended summer graduate school at Columbia University, receiving his master of arts degree in 1940. *See* GALLAUDET COLLEGE.

In 1945 the Office of Vocational Rehabilitation, Federal Security Agency, in Washington, D.C., was looking for an individual to develop the groundwork for a vocational rehabilitation program for deaf and hard-of-hearing people. The Vocational Rehabilitation Act Amendments of 1943 had broadened the original vocational rehabilitation program established in 1920, authorizing new services to eliminate or reduce disabilities. A requirement that the person hired be able to hear at a distance of at least six feet at first precluded deaf applicants. The concern of a handicapped consumer group over equal employment opportunities for handicapped people worked to remove the requirement. Williams's Indiana experience in vocational training, which closely paralleled the vocational rehabilitation process, strongly recommended him for the position, and he was hired. He began his career in Washington with the then Office of Vocational Rehabilitation (OVR) on August 1, 1945, assuming a role that he was to continue for 38 years. Beginning as Consultant, Deaf and the Hard of Hearing, he advanced through the years to the position of Chief, Deafness and Communicative Disorders Branch, from which he retired in 1983. *See* REHABILITATION.

Boyce R. Williams.

When Williams joined the OVR, it was obvious to him that a vocational rehabilitation program for deaf people could not be built in a vacuum. Accordingly, much of his first work entailed preparation of formal statements of working relationships with organizations and institutions concerned with deafness and deaf people. Separate agreements of cooperative relationship were drawn up between the OVR and the Conference of Executives of American Schools for the Deaf, the Convention of American Instructors of the Deaf, the American Hearing Society, the National Fraternal Society of the Deaf, and the National Association of the Deaf. The agreements provided a framework for cooperative action and mutual understanding between vocational rehabilitation and special education, with voluntary and professional organizations and agencies, and with hearing-impaired consumer groups. Essentially, the agreements laid the groundwork for the hundreds of national, state, regional, and community conferences and workshops addressing issues pertinent to the rehabilitation of deaf people that have taken place since. *See* NATIONAL ASSOCIATION OF THE DEAF; NATIONAL FRATERNAL SOCIETY OF THE DEAF.

Promoting better understanding of deaf adults, their needs, problems, and capabilities was always the single greatest thrust of Williams's work. He repeatedly stressed their normal intelligence, strength, and mobility as considerations in their job placement. He continually emphasized the need for appropriate training opportunities for deaf individuals to enable them to achieve their vocational potential. Also, even though his own speech was good, he acted as a strong proponent of expert manual communication among service delivery professionals.

His constant encouragement to state vocational rehabilitation agencies to hire rehabilitation counselors trained in deafness and able to communicate in sign language achieved results over the years. Every state now has a number of rehabilitation counselors serving deaf clients exclusively. Additionally, most of the state agencies assign one staff person to coordinate the vocational rehabilitation program for hearing-impaired people. The approximately 25,000 deaf persons who are in the case loads of the state rehabilitation agencies on any given day are testimony to Williams's strivings to improve and broaden their access to more and better rehabilitation services.

Two occurrences in the early 1950s combined to aid Williams in advancing rehabilitation program development for deaf people. In 1950 Mary E. Switzer became commissioner of OVR. A great humanist and visionary, she saw that vocational rehabilitation could be the means to implement Williams's far-reaching goals. She became an active partner with Williams in developing the unique rehabilitation services structure that deaf people require, and worked closely with him for over 15 years. During this period many programs emerged, including the National Theatre of the Deaf, the Registry of Interpreters for the Deaf, Captioned Films for the Deaf, the Communicative Skills Program,

Williams (right) meeting with Mary E. Switzer, Commissioner of the Office of Vocational Rehabilitation, and Joseph Hunt, Assistant Commissioner, with the assistance of interpreter-secretary Charlotte A. Coffield (left).

the National Leadership Training Program on Deafness, and a network of postsecondary programs especially for deaf persons including the National Technical Institute for the Deaf. *See* NATIONAL TECHNICAL INSTITUTE FOR THE DEAF; NATIONAL THEATERS OF THE DEAF: United States; REGISTRY OF INTERPRETERS FOR THE DEAF.

The second occurrence was the passage in 1954 of amendments to the Vocational Rehabilitation Act providing for innovative projects to meet the needs of severely disabled people and authority for research, demonstrations, and training activities. A way opened to mount long-needed special projects for severely disabled and low-functioning deaf people, for research on deafness and deaf people, and for short- and long-term training programs to increase the number of professionals and lay persons capable of working with and for deaf individuals.

From 1955, when the first rehabilitation research project on deaf people was funded, Williams became actively involved in promoting, developing, monitoring, evaluating, and furthering the utilization of the more than 100 research projects which formed the backbone of rehabilitation program development for hearing-impaired people. Williams also contributed to research development for deaf people in other countries, notably in Yugoslavia, Poland, Italy, India, Israel, and Egypt. His foreign travels, correspondence, and publications made him an internationally recognized authority on the rehabilitation of deaf people. He participated at World Federation of the Deaf congresses and had a leading role in bringing the 1976 congress to the United States as a rehabilitation project in cooperation with the National Association of the Deaf. *See* WORLD FEDERATION OF THE DEAF.

Another long-time concern of Williams was improving and increasing mental health services to deaf people. He worked actively with New York State mental health experts in the early 1950s in designing the first research project on deafness funded by the Rehabilitation Services Administration (RSA) to demonstrate techniques of in-service and out-service treatment to emotionally disturbed and mentally ill deaf adults. The steady progress in the intervening years in mental health program development for deaf people was a source of constant satisfaction to Williams. The capstone was the funding of a Research and Training Center on Mental Health and the Deaf People by RSA in 1979. *See* PSYCHOLOGY: Mental Health.

Beginning with a historic workshop, Personal, Social and Vocational Adjustment in Total Deafness, held at the New York School for the Deaf in 1957, Williams promoted, designed, evaluated, and actively participated in a majority of the almost 200 short-term training projects on deafness that were funded by RSA. Many of the projects responded directly to legislative mandates for which Williams was responsible in respect to deaf people. Others focused on needs and problems peculiar to deaf people that were long recognized by Williams. Williams saw the emergence of effectively demanding deaf leaders from these workshops as the most important outcome.

Williams also gave his energy, talent, and skills to voluntary service on behalf of his deaf fellows. He served diligently on most if not all of the executive boards of consumer and professional organizations concerned with deafness and deaf people. The Gallaudet College Alumni Association Centennial Fund was his concept and design. He was the first Gallaudet alumnus to be appointed to the college board and served as the first chairman of the college board of fellows. *See* GALLAUDET COLLEGE ALUMNI ASSOCIATION.

Many honors were bestowed upon Boyce R. Williams. They include honorary degrees from Gallaudet College and Carthage College; distinguished service awards from the World Federation of the Deaf, the National Association of the Deaf, the Council of Educational Administrators Serving the Deaf, and RSA; citations of meritorious service from religious, and community organizations. Williams's appointment to the Powrie Vaux Doctor Chair of Deaf Studies at Gallaudet College in 1983–1984 capped an illustrious career. *See* CONFERENCE OF EDUCATIONAL ADMINISTRATORS SERVING THE DEAF.

Bibliography

Garrahan, M.: "Many Helping Hands Find Jobs for the Hearing Handicapped," an interview with Williams, *Between Friends*, vol. 8, no. 1, 1973.

Shafte, M.: "Government Rehabilitation Programs: Is the Hearing Aid Dealer Involved?", an interview with Williams, *The Hearing Dealer*, vol. 21, no. 11, November 1970.

Shaposka, B.: "Boyce Williams: The VR Investment in the Future of the American Deaf," *The Silent Worker*, vol. 16, no. 9, May 1964.

Edna P. Adler

WOLF, PETER
(1945–   )

Peter Wolf is a producer, director, cinematographer, and performer for numerous film, television, and stage productions for both deaf and hearing audiences. In particular, he was the first deaf person to write, direct, and perform in two feature-length films in American Sign Language, *Deafula* and *Think Me Nothing*. To market these films, he devised a unique strategy of using local deaf organizations to sponsor screenings in hearing movie theaters. He is currently the leading deaf professional in film production, whether in American Sign

Peter Wolf.

Language or through conventional hearing film techniques. *See* SIGN LANGUAGES: American.

Wolf was born on January 25, 1945, in London, England, to a theatrically inclined family that later moved to New York. While attending the New York School for the Deaf, he was inspired by several films, including a German film, *The Last Command*, and decided at an early age to pursue a career in film making.

While a student at Gallaudet College, Wolf majored in drama to increase his skill in translating between English and American Sign Language as well as to gain a deeper understanding of acting and directing. He starred in such memorable roles as Actor in *Spoon River Anthology*, Sheridan Whiteside in *The Man Who Came to Dinner*, Pozzo and Vladimir in *Waiting for Godot*, John Proctor in *The Crucible*, and had leading roles in *Everyman*, *Dr. Jekyll and Mr. Hyde*, and *RUR. See* GALLAUDET COLLEGE.

In 1969 he joined the National Theatre of the Deaf (NTD) and for the next two seasons played a variety of roles in *Under Milkwood*, *Sganarelle*, *Journeys*, *Miracles*, and *Woyzeck*. Later Wolf played Menelaus in the Los Angeles Actors Theatre production of *The Trojan Women*. He appeared opposite Phyllis Frelich as the boyfriend-pimp of a prostitute in an episode of the *Barney Miller* tele-

vision series. *See* FRELICH, PHYLLIS; NATIONAL THEATERS OF THE DEAF: United States.

While touring with NTD, Wolf studied books on film making, and with the help of $50 from each NTD company member, he directed a film about the travels of NTD.

In 1971 Wolf was one of 20 people selected from 400 applicants as film-making students at Cinemalabs, a professional training program in San Francisco. His teachers were so impressed with his work that they presented him with the Outstanding Film-maker Award.

After graduating from Cinemalabs, Wolf collaborated with Jane Norman to create *Newsign 4* at KRON-TV in San Francisco, the first news program presented directly in American Sign Language by deaf newscasters. Wolf also produced a half-hour film about deaf people titled *My Eyes Are My Ears*. This film and *Newsign 4* earned Wolf two Emmy Awards in 1972. However, he lost his job in 1973 as a result of staff changes at KRON-TV.

Wolf moved to Portland, Oregon, where Bancorp, a banking organization, were impressed with his credentials and hired him to produce videotapes for their communication design center. Bringing a stack of sign language books to work with him, he quickly trained his coworkers in American Sign Language, and his collaborative video work increased income and productivity for Bancorp.

But Wolf's dreams were about deaf film making, and he resigned in 1975 to form his own company, Signscope, with its goal being the production of films about deaf people. His first film, *Deafula*, was a deaf version of *Dracula*. Wolf had been inspired by the all-black production of *Blacula* then playing in movie theaters around the country. He had originally planned to cast Joey Velez in the title role, but Velez, weakened by cancer, was unable to perform, so Wolf assumed the role. Using amateur performers, he developed a system of acting coaching that produced highly naturalistic performances. *Deafula*, presented in many theaters and at the Eighth World Winter Games for the Deaf in Lake Placid, New York, was well received by the deaf community and later distributed by Captioned Films for the Deaf.

Wolf's second film, *Think Me Nothing*, had originally been intended as a four-hour feature about deaf twin brothers, one the black sheep of the family. However, extensive editing cuts distorted the film and caused problems with audience comprehension, as well as culture shock to the more conservative viewers because of several soft porn scenes. Despite imaginative cinematography and good performances in scenes filmed mostly in southern California, the film did not do as well financially as *Deafula*.

Still, more than most film makers, Peter Wolf has blazed a pathway in a largely uncharted region—feature films for deaf people.

Don Bangs

WOODS, FRANCES
(1907–)

When Robert Ripley, the famous cartoonist and author of "Ripley's Believe It or Not," first saw the dance team of Frances Woods and Billy Bray, he called them the Wonder Dancers. Frances Woods was indeed a wonder because she danced with grace and rhythm, and yet was totally deaf. Frances Woods, whose real name was Esther Thomas, was born in Girard, Ohio, in 1907. She was a premature baby who weighed only 1½ pounds and had no eardrums.

Woods attended the Ohio School for the Deaf and was very active in sports, becoming captain of the women's basketball team. After graduating from the Ohio School, she met a hearing man, Anthony Caliguire, at a dance. In her father's garage, Caliguire taught her to dance by playing the piano so that she could feel the 4/4 time or the 3/4 time of the music, then teaching her the dance steps to follow the particular music. She became so attuned to the rhythm of music that she could feel the vibrations through her fingertips as well as from the dance floor.

Woods and Caliguire married in 1926 and began to dance professionally. First, they called themselves the Dancing De Sondos. Later, while performing in a Broadway nightclub, they were given the stage name of Frances Woods and Billy Bray by the producer C. B. Maddox.

Success did not happen quickly. They had difficulty getting work during the Depression years, but they had faith in themselves and continued to rehearse. They often danced in cheap one-night hotels and lowly taverns, and they depended on people to throw them money on the dance floor.

In 1933 they experienced their first success when R.K.O. Productions arranged for them to dance in vaudeville in the R.K.O. chain of theaters. One of their best acts was the "Adagio," a dance that includes acrobatic twirls and somersaults. Another specialty was the "French Apache," a combination of dance and mine.

Later, Woods and Bray developed a versatile program that was fashioned after the popular dances of the times—the fox trot, the waltz, the tango, the samba, the cha-cha, and the rhumba. For each of these dances, Woods designed and made all her own clothes.

Throughout the 1930s, the 1940s, and the 1950s, the Wonder Dancers performed in many famous nightclubs and hotels. They danced to many of the big bands—Wayne King, Ted Weems, Cab Calloway, Eddie Duchin, Horace Heidt, and Paul Whiteman. At the Edgewater Beach Hotel in Chicago, they danced when Lawrence Welk conducted his band at his first major appearance, and Bray taught Welk how to become a fine dancer.

The Wonder Dancers performed in Europe, often appearing at the famed Palladium in London. Extended engagements at the Shoreham Hotel in Washington made them favorites with the government social set, and their friends and admirers included many prominent persons.

In 1968 Woods was forced to wear a pacemaker because of a heart problem. By age 77 she was wearing her fourth pacemaker; yet in 1984, even after retirement, Woods and Bray were still dancing together. At their own studio in Youngstown, Ohio, they gave dance lessons and often uplifted senior citizens, handicapped persons, and people in nursing homes by giving exhibitions.

Frances Woods was honored many times during her career. Among the awards was a plaque given to her and Bray at the Governor's Awards Banquet in 1978, which recognized Ohio natives whose careers have benefited humankind. Wax figures of Woods and Bray are displayed at the Ripley Museum in St. Augustine, Florida.

Bibliography
Bray, Billy: *The Wonder Dancers: Woods and Bray*, Youngstown, Ohio, 1981.

Panara, Robert, and John Panara: *Great Deaf Americans*, Silver Spring, Maryland, 1983.

Robert Panara

WORLD FEDERATION OF THE DEAF

Prior to the establishment of the World Federation of the Deaf, several international meetings for deaf people were organized in both Europe and the United States. Delegates from different countries, and sometimes diplomats representing their countries' deaf people, reported on but rarely discussed the socioeconomic and educational levels among deaf people. These reports usually focused on the existence of social and job discrimination, limited job and educational opportunities, the public suppression of sign language or the extolment of oralism, and government restrictions of civil rights. These issues have recurred as discussion topics at practically every quadrennial congress of the World Federation of the Deaf.

HISTORY
The number of international meetings of deaf persons is unknown. A French delegate reported at the Fourth World Congress of the Deaf in Buffalo, New

York, in 1930, that his national association of the deaf had participated since World War I in most of the major international congresses of the deaf in seven European cities. As several international meetings were known to have been held prior to World War I, the number of such meetings must have exceeded 10.

Although an international federation of deaf people apparently did not occur to deaf participants at the world congresses on education of the deaf in the United States and Europe, deaf participants did explore different ways to increase their international cooperation and exchange of ideas and experiences. Prior to World War I, deaf people in most European countries had already established local clubs. In 1880 deaf individuals in the United States formed the National Association of the Deaf, which later was reorganized as a federation of state deaf associations. Local clubs in European countries were united under new national federations mostly during the 1920s and 1930s. Although their interest in international cooperation was clearly demonstrated prior to World War II, the low socioeconomic conditions, limited job opportunities, restricted civil rights, and inadequate educational levels among deaf people delayed their establishment of an international organization. *See* INTERNATIONAL CONGRESS ON THE EDUCATION OF THE DEAF; NATIONAL ASSOCIATION OF THE DEAF.

Government grants and a strong encouragement from the Italian government enabled Ente Nazional Sordomuti (the Italian deaf association) to take the initiative to unite the national deaf associations of the world. The first world congress after World War II was held in Rome during September 19-23, 1951. National deaf associations representing 16 countries, including the United States, agreed to send their deaf representatives to the world congress. Other countries were represented by observers (usually hearing) and diplomats. At their first assembly, the representatives reached an agreement to establish an international organization called the World Federation of the Deafmutes (WFD), later replacing "Deafmutes" with "Deaf." During the Congress, invited educators and physicians specializing in deafness, mostly from Italy, discussed their concerns and research problems under the WFD auspices. These professionals then submitted their recommendations to the World Federation of the Deaf for its approval.

STRUCTURE

This kind of congress structure, where professionals, researchers, and other groups of specialists submit their policies, resolutions, and recommendations affecting the welfare of deaf people to the WFD for approval, has continued in all subsequent congresses. A similar involvement of disabled persons and their organizations in the policy-making process was recommended in the United Nations programs for the International Year of Disabled Persons and for the International Decade of Disabled Persons. As potential consumers, disabled persons have the responsibility to examine and, if approved, support policies that can promote their welfare. Many countries have too often failed to consult disabled people and their leaders in making policies or laws.

The World Congress of the World Federation of the Deaf is divided into two parts, the General Assembly and the Scientific Section. The General Assembly is a law-making body composed of two delegates from every national deaf association. One delegate from each nation must be deaf. The General Assembly convenes every four years to elect new board members and to adopt policies and programs for the next four-year term.

The WFD board, more popularly called the Bureau, is composed of a president, four vice-presidents, a general secretary, and five members, each of a different nationality. The Bureau usually meets once a year to review reports and programs submitted by the president and the general secretary. It acts on the admission of new national deaf associations to membership in the WFD and establishes regional secretariats in cooperation with sponsoring national associations. The Bureau also sponsors international conferences or seminars.

COMMUNICATION

While English and French, the official WFD languages, are used for correspondence and written or printed announcements, Gestuno, the international sign language, is employed for communication in the General Assembly and the Bureau. Official interpretation from Gestuno to voice or vice versa has not been available at the past meetings of the General Assembly or the Bureau. Whether all the delegates in the General Assembly are able to understand Gestuno is still an open question. Some delegates have complained, however, that Gestuno is difficult to understand, perhaps because they are inexperienced at international meetings or are unwilling to learn another language. The communication process in the Bureau is far more well defined. Bureau members have been able to discuss anything ranging from the concrete to the abstract in Gestuno, provided that they are skilled in paraphrasing and interpreting meanings and have a broad understanding of cultures in the world. *See* SIGN LANGUAGES: International Gestures.

MEMBERSHIP

Because of budget limitations, the travel expenses of Bureau and General Assembly members must be covered by their national deaf associations. In effect, only "rich" national associations can regularly have their delegates nominated and elected in the Bureau. Both the Bureau and General Assembly are acutely aware of this serious and unfair practice but have not found a satisfactory solution. Still, the General Assembly has been able to find at least one Bureau member from each continent. The distribution of the approximately 70 national deaf associations that are ordinary members of the WFD indicates that European organizations make up nearly 40 percent, while African, Asian, and South American organizations each make up 17 percent. Although members elected into the Bureau are not allowed to promote the interests of their own national associations within the Bureau, the WFD has been dominated by European and North American cultures.

SCIENTIFIC SECTION

The Scientific Section is coordinated by the WFD General Secretary. At the end of every Congress, the Bureau appoints experts to commissions in several different areas, such as audiology, education, psychology, sign language, interpreting, vocational rehabilitation, deaf culture, arts, theater, technical aids, aid to developing countries, social aspects of deafness, and spiritual care. The commissions serve as advisory bodies to the Bureau in its preparation of documents or policies in response to requests from international organizations, governments, and agencies. In addition, they assist in making recommendations and resolutions on the basis of papers presented at the World Congress of the WFD. Historically, the commissions have not been very productive; they have had few or no meetings between the congresses and have tended to work as a team only during the congresses. Even correspondence has been found as an unworkable alternative to meetings among the commission members. The Commission on Communications is an exception, as it has had several meetings between the congresses and has produced three dictionaries in international sign language, including Gestuno.

Financial limitations are the oft-cited but not necessarily only reason for the limited activities of most WFD commissions. Other limiting factors have been the tendency of professionals to work independently of deaf organizations or deaf individuals, the resistance of professionals to accept nonmedical aspects of deafness as legitimate research topics, the tendency of deaf organizations to give special attention to local and national concerns, the scarcity of deaf leaders, and the lack of full-time staff within the WFD. However, UNESCO has urged professionals specializing in disabilities and disabled people and their organizations to work more closely.

WORLD CONGRESSES

The World Congress of the WFD usually attracts over 2000 persons from at least 50 countries. It is an event where deaf and hearing people can interact and share mutual concerns. The opening and closing ceremonies of the Congress are witnessed by officials representing the United Nations, the World Health Organization, the International Labor Organization, and other international agencies and governments. Interpretations from voice to Gestuno or to national sign languages and vice versa, and translations into English or French, are always available to participants at the meetings of WFD commissions during the Congress and during the ceremonies. The number of deaf speakers in proportion to hearing ones is increasing as more and more deaf persons become gainfully employed in the professional area. Papers presented at the commission meetings and recommendations or resolutions are published one or two years after each congress.

The difficulty of establishing permanent regional secretariats in different parts of the world has been caused by the scarcity of deaf volunteers with administrative experiences, which is a chronic problem among deaf organizations in practically every country. Regional secretariats function as extensions of the WFD General Secretariat. The regional secretariats usually are transferred from one sponsoring national deaf association to another, depending on the availability of capable volunteers and government support.

Despite the limitations and the small WFD budget ranging from 15,000 to 30,000 dollars a year (obtained from financial grants from governments, contributions from organizations, and membership dues), the WFD has proved itself an important link among national deaf associations. The annual celebration of the fourth week in September as an International Week of the Deaf helps deaf people to strengthen their local, national, and international solidarity. The purpose of this event is to increase the understanding of deafness by publicizing the problems and achievements of deaf people. As the WFD has successfully maintained Category B status in the United Nations organization, it has served as an important source of information on deafness for many international organizations and national governments.

Bibliography

Brill, Richard: *International Congresses on Education of the Deaf: An Analytical History, 1870–1980*, Gallaudet College, Washington, D.C., 1984.

Confederacion Nationale des Sourds de France: *Proceedings of the 6th World Congress of the WFD* (1971), Paris.

Deutsche Gehörlosen-Bund e. V.: *Proceedings of the 3d World Congress of the Deaf* (1959), Bonn, 1961.

Ente Nazional Sordomuti: *Atti Ufficiali del Congresso Mondiale dei Sordomuti* (1951), Rome, 1953.

National Association of the Deaf: *Proceedings of the World's Congress of the Deaf and the Report of the 4th Convention of the National Association of the Deaf 1893.*

—————: *Proceedings of the 9th Convention of the National Association of the Deaf and the 3d World's Congress of the Deaf—Colorado Springs (1910), 1912.*

—————: *Proceedings—World Congress of the Deaf—Buffalo, 1930.*

—————: *VII World Congress of the World Federation of the Deaf* (1975), Silver Spring, Maryland, 1976.

Polski Swiazek Glychych: *V Congress of the World Federation of the Deaf* (1967), Warsaw, 1970.

Savez Gluvich Yogoslavije: *Proceedings of the II World Congress of the Deaf* (1955), Beograd.

Sveriges Dövas Riksförbund: *Proceedings of the IV World Congress of the WFD* (1963).

Union des Sourds de Bulgarie: *Proceedings of the VII World Congress of the WFD* (1979), Sofia, 1981.

World Federation of the Deaf: *Gestuno*, Rome, 1975.

Yerker Andersson

WRIGHT, DAVID
(1920–   )

Born February 23, 1920, in Johannesburg, South Africa, David Wright became deaf at the age of seven when he contracted scarlet fever. Before he became deaf, he had been educated in a kindergarten, where he learned to read, write, and count, and had attended one term at a church school. A long convalescence ensued after his illness, and was compounded by a mastoid-tonsil operation. A period of going from doctor to doctor in London in a futile effort to regain his hearing then occurred. This ended when the ministrations of a faith healer failed to produce any results.

EDUCATION

Young Wright's education continued with a teacher who specialized in deaf students—a Miss Neville who taught him the pronunciation of vowels and consonants, thereby arresting the deterioration of his speech. When he and his mother went back to South Africa, a Miss Holland (who had worked with Miss Neville) was asked to join them later and to continue working with Wright in subject matter areas common to his age. The onset of the 1930 depression made it necessary for the family to release Miss Holland. Consequently, Wright's education was haphazard over the next three years. A saving grace was his love of reading. The books sent from England by his aunt offset the lack of ongoing regular education. Also, his acceptance as a day student in a preparatory school in Johannesburg provided at least a modicum of preparation in some subjects. However, his parents realized that if he was to go to college, he needed a much more rigorous education. This required taking him to England and enrolling him in the Northampton School for the Deaf, the only school in the British Commonwealth capable of preparing a deaf student for college or university work.

Introduction to the special world of deaf people as typified by the Northampton School was an unsettling experience. It involved gesticulation, pantomime, facial expression, exaggerated mouthing of words, and so on—a sort of unconventionalized sign language. The two-handed alphabet used in some schools was against the rules at Northampton. Among the students, there was wide variation in knowledge, deafness being responsible for gaps in awareness of even rudimentary things. Instruction was not too different from that of the public schools, but constant repetition was necessary since lipreading was far from perfect. Young Wright adapted to this environment and, with a diversion into the nearby grammar school for Latin and French, eventually succeeded in passing the entrance examinations to Oriel College, Oxford.

At the same time, he reacted against the smothering effect of deafness on his social life. He disregarded his aunt's and mother's admonitions not to go far from the school while on holiday, and he forced himself to talk with strangers while on a ship or train. This aided him immeasurably at Oxford. In fact, he said that the tutorials—a direct confrontation requiring speech between student and teacher—were a great aid in helping him get through college. Otherwise, he would have had to depend almost wholly on lecture notes and text—a somewhat hazardous situation, and more time-consuming for a deaf man. At Oxford, Wright continued to force himself to talk with others, to invite other students for social gatherings in his rooms, and in general to emerge from the isolation of deafness. He met Sidney Keyes, Drummond Allison, Keith Douglas, and John Heath-Stubbs, all important Oxford and English poets. His already strong interest in poetry was furthered by these associations, and he began to read Eliot, Joyce, and Pound, as well as other poets to whom he had not previously had access. His literary beginnings, however, he traces in large part to associations formed after college in Soho with the help of John Heath-Stubbs and others.

CAREER

Young Wright had not given much thought to what he wanted to do after college. He had started writing poetry at the age of eight and had somewhat decided that this was to be his life's work, almost without careful scrutiny of the job market. He was definitely not interested in the jobs that attracted his fellow students at Northampton—jobs where deafness was not too much of a liability.

His first professional job was writing a poem for a ballet, *Minster Lovell*; however, it did not get performed until 1966 under a different name, *Ginevra*. Perhaps his most important publication, in the sense that it yielded him an income sufficient to permit him to go on writing verse, was a translation of *Beowulf* into modern English. Later, he gave *The Canterbury Tales* the same kind of translation. With these bread-and-butter books out of the way, he could give more time to poetry. His poems began to appear in various magazines: *Agenda*, *Aquarius*, *Contrast*, *Poetry* (U.S.A.), *The Scotsman*, *Two Rivers*, and various others. His first collection of poems was published in 1949. Winning one of the Atlantic Awards in 1950, he used the prize money to live in Italy for a few months. The following year he married the actress Phillipa Reid.

Altogether, Wright has published eight books of poetry, one book of criticism, three travel books, and five anthologies in addition to editing two literary magazines, *Nimbus* and *X*. He has been included in several anthologies, for example, *The Modern Poets* (McGraw-Hill, 1963) and *The Norton Anthology of Modern Poetry* (Norton, 1973). In 1969, he wrote an account of his life titled *Deafness*. This book discusses his youth, from South Africa through the years at Oxford, and concludes with an account of the present status of the education of deaf persons in England. Presumably, he is saving for a future book the account of his life since leaving Oxford, including a discussion of his tenure from 1965 to 1967 as Gregory Fellow in Poetry at the University of Leeds.

Wright is undoubtedly the best-known of all deaf writers today, and the only one who has made a full-time vocation of the writing profession. He holds a high rank among British poets. His poetry is coldly objective and sardonic at times, without ready classification as to school or style, but colored by his deafness and his Johannesburg upbringing. For deaf people everywhere, the following lines from his "Monologue of A Deaf Man" (published in *To the Gods the Shades*) are among the most significant ever written:

> Talk to me then, you who have so much to say,
> Spectator of the human conversation,
> Reader of tongues, examiner of the eye.
> And detective of clues in every action,
> What could a voice, if you heard it, signify?

Bibliography
Wright, David: *Deafness (A Personal Account)*, Penguin Press, 1969.

————: *Metrical Observations*, Carcanet New Press, 1980.

————: *To the Gods the Shades*, Carcanet New Press, 1976.

Rex Lowman

ZUBIAURRE, RAMÓN DE
(1882–1969)

Ramón de Zubiaurre y Aguirrezabal was a Spanish artist whose most successful paintings reflected themes rooted in his provincial Basque background. Accepting neither the landscape methods of his contemporary Joaquín Sorolla y Bastida nor Picasso's cubism, Zubiaurre often was criticized for being old fashioned and out of step with modern artistic trends. Politics, too, interfered with the acceptance of his works, for in the 1950s, when he returned to Spain after 10 years in Latin America, he was suspected of communist allegiances. During his lifetime he achieved more fame outside of Spain—in Latin America, France, and Italy—than in his native country.

The younger brother of Valentín de Zubiaurre, Ramón de Zubiaurre was born deaf on September 1, 1882, in Garay, a small town in the northern Spanish province of Viscaya. He lived there for his first four years, during which time he was raised by a foster mother. Then he was taken to Madrid, where his father, Valentín de Zubiaurre, was a noted musician and director of the Royal Chapel of Music, to begin his formal education. Recognizing his son's interest and ability in art, the father enrolled the boy in the Academy of Fine Arts of San Fernando. Zubiaurre later worked in the studio of Alejandro Ferrant and Muñoz Degrain and studied anatomy in Madrid before beginning serious painting. He sold his first work for 300 pesetas in 1898

or 1899. In 1899 Zubiaurre also showed his work publicly for the first time, displaying landscapes with figures in the National Exhibition in Madrid. *See* ZUBIAURRE, VALENTÍN DE.

Travel and study abroad broadened Zubiaurre's background and acquainted him with the works and ideas of several European masters. He took his first trip to Paris when he was still in his teens. When 23, he accompanied his family to Paris, studied at the Julian Academy, and then toured Europe. His artistic development was most influenced by the older masters, especially El Greco, the Florentine painters Giotto di Bondone and Fra Angelico, the fifteenth-century German painters Albrecht Dürer and Hans Holbein, the fourteenth-century Flemish painter Jan van Eyck, and the seventeenth-century Spanish artist Velázquez. The ideas of fifteenth-century Italian religious reformer Girolamo Savonarola, who believed that beauty is the result of a synthesis of drawing and color and reflective of a divine spirit, also influenced Zubiaurre. Finally, Zubiaurre studied Japanese color prints and from these developed his method of representing depth perception by using the diminution of masses receding into the background.

Zubiaurre's work can be divided into four periods: 1891–1903, 1903–1915, 1915–1960, and 1960–1969. During the first, his years of apprenticeship, he immersed himself in examination of the Basque country and people, making careful academic studies of their life. This informative period inspired Zubiaurre for the rest of his artistic

Ramón de Zubiaurre's *Los remeros vencedores de Ondárroa,* **exhibited in Paris in 1923, now in the Musée National d'Art Moderne, Paris.**

career. He also began, in the latter years, to show his first works, mainly landscapes, in the national exhibitions of Madrid.

The second period, 1903–1915, marked the evolution of a particular style shared with his brother Valentín, the "Zubiaurre style," that emphasized drawing and careful color technique. In 1911 his

Jugando al Julepe. **(Collection of D. Luis Benito del Valle, Bilbao)**

Picaros y Mendigos (Lazy Ones and Beggars) won a medal at the International Exhibition in Rome and is today on display in Rome's Modern Gallery. In 1915 he produced *Los remeros vencedores de Ondárroa* (The Victorious Rowers of Ondárroa), a work that represented a departure from the style of Valentín. This painting shows Zubiaurre's mastery of composition and predominant verticality achieved by using elongated figures. It also displays his characteristic synthesis of color, design, and drawing. The figures appear static outwardly, but inwardly they teem with dynamism and power, indicating Zubiaurre's impression of the Basques, at once severe and tender, happy and taciturn.

The third period, 1915–1960, marks Zubiaurre's complete independence from his family and the development of his personal life. Married in 1917, Zubiaurre soon after began to gain international fame. In 1918 he became an associate member, and in 1924 a full member, of the Hispanic Society of America in New York City. He made his first trip to Latin America in 1920, and lived there in 1926–1928, in 1930, and in 1940–1950. He was well received in Latin America, especially in Argentina, Uruguay, Chile, and Peru, and received numerous commissions. In 1923 Zubiaurre received the French Legion of Honor for an exhibit in Paris.

Shanti Andia, el Temerario, **first prize winner in the National Exhibition of 1924, Museo Español de Arte Contemporáneo, Madrid.**

A typical painting from this period is *Shanti Andia, el Temerario* (Shanti Andia, the Bold), which won a first prize at Madrid's National Exhibition in 1924 and today is displayed in the Museo Español de Arte Contemporáneo in Madrid. Based on an episode in Pio Baroja's novel *Las Inquietudes de Shanti Andia* (*The Anxieties of Shanti Andia*), the story of a courageous fisherman, Zubiaurre's painting captures the tension of the moment accentuated by gestures and natural movements set against a raging sea.

Another illustrative work from this period is *Jugando al Julepe* (Playing Julepe), currently in the collection of D. Luis Benito del Valle in Bilbao. Here, Zubiaurre chooses the noisiest and most vigorous characters to portray human sentiment. Zubiaurre's bold, humorous exaggeration of expression comes into full play by depicting resignation transformed into apparent happiness on the faces of old people gathered around a table. Though his themes may be archaic, their realism is evident in the long thin arms of the elderly subjects, the somber clothes, taut skin, and triangular faces. Most fascinating to the observer, however, is Zubiaurre's rendering of the penetrating bright eyes of the card game participants.

The fourth period of Zubiaurre's work, 1960–1969, led him in new directions. Concerned with the qualities of color, he took up colored drawing, a medium he had used before, such as in the 1938 work *Madre e hijo* (Mother and Child), now in the collection of D. Carlos D. Estrada. His figures in this last period became more transient, appearing spiritualized, as though existing in another dimension. The colors in his last works were subdued, while he employed lines sensitively and ingeniously.

In addition to his artistic endeavors, Zubiaurre was active in Spain's deaf community. A member of the Deaf Association of Madrid, he prepared the

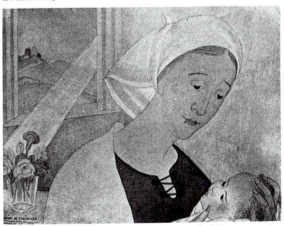

Madre e hijo, a colored drawing. (Collection of D. Carlos D. Estrada)

principal addresses to commemorate Pedro Ponce de Leon and Juan Pablo Bonet in 1920 and 1926. He also represented the Madrid Deaf Association at the International Congress of the Deaf held in Paris in 1912, Belgium in 1924, and Czechoslovakia in 1928. *See* PABLO BONET, JUAN; PONCE DE LEÓN, PEDRO; SPAIN.

Throughout a long professional career, Zubiaurre concentrated on the subjects he knew and loved best: the peasants, fishermen, and landscapes of the Basque area of northern Spain. He died in Madrid on June 9, 1969.

Bibliography

Enciclopedia Universal Ilustrada: Europeo—Americana, Espasa-Calpe S.A., Madrid.

Mochizuki, Takeshi: *Ramón de Zubiaurre, El pintor y el hombre*, Publicaciones de la Diputacion Foral del Señorio de Vizcaya, 1980.

Pantorba, Bernardino de, *Historia y Critica de las Exposiciones Nacionales de Bellas Artes Celebradas en España*, Jesus Ramón Garcia-Rama J., Madrid, 1980.

Elva Fromuth Loe

ZUBIAURRE, VALENTÍN DE (1879–1963)

Born deaf on August 22, 1879, in Madrid, Valentín de Zubiaurre y Aguirrezabel became one of Spain's foremost painters of the twentieth century. His father, also named Valentín de Zubiaurre, was a Basque musician and director of the Royal Chapel of Music in Madrid, and always retained a family residence in the northern province of Viscaya. Zubiaurre's brother Ramón, also deaf from birth, was a well-known artist. *See* ZUBIAURRE, RAMÓN DE.

Zubiaurre began his education in Madrid, where he studied art at the Royal Academy of San Fernando. Later, he broadened his familiarity with painting by studying in Paris and touring Europe's major museums and galleries. The inspiration for most of his work, however, came from his immersion in the folkways of the Basques of Viscaya Province.

Displaying his work for the first time in Madrid's National Exhibitions in 1899 and 1901, Zubiaurre was treated severely by art critics. He rejected the contemporary style of photographic naturalism in favor of a more primitive style that emphasized outline and ignored shadow and underlying structure. His characters often appear serenely naive or sentimental, and they do not seem to recognize each other's presence. The latter characteristic may be due to Zubiaurre's deafness, which can be intensely isolating, or it may be attributed to his desire to convey the self-assured stance of the personages he painted.

Zubiaurre's characters and locations were mostly the peasants and countryside of northern Spain.

Valentín de Zubiaurre's *Versolaris*, first prize winner in a national exhibition; now in Museo Español de Arte Contemporáneo, Madrid.

Depicted most frequently in their daily surroundings—fishermen on the beach or women with their distaffs for spinning, for example—the people Zubiaurre captured on canvas rarely smile or show animation. They appear introverted, melancholy, powerless, and nostalgic; yet they are portrayed with affection.

Despite early criticism, Zubiaurre's work eventually received acclaim. He won awards in exhibitions in Madrid, Brussels, Barcelona, San Francisco, Panama, San Diego, Rome, Venice, and other locations. Today his canvases are on display at museums in Europe, the United States, Japan, and Latin America. He also was honored by membership in Las Palmas Academy in the Canary Islands, the Hispanic Society of New York City, and the Society of the Salon d'Automne of Paris. Zubiaurre received the Legion of Honor award in Paris, and he was the honorary president and founder of the Society of Deaf Artists in Paris. He died in Madrid on January 24, 1963.

Bibliography

Bozal, Valeriano: *Historia del Arte en España*, Madrid, 1972.

Enciclopedia Universal Ilustrada: Europeo—Americana, Espasa-Calpe S. A., Madrid.

Manaut Viglietti, José: "Valentín de Zubiaurre," *Goya Magazine*, no. 14, pp. 129–131, Madrid, 1956.

Pantorba, Bernardino de: *Historia y Crítica de las Exposiciones Nacionales de Bellas Artes Celebradas en España*, Jesus Ramón Garcia-Rama J., Madrid, 1980.

Elva Fromuth Loe

Contributors

Contributors

Catherine Masakwe Abilla
Senior Inspector of Schools—Special Education,
Ministry of Education, Inspectorate,
Nairobi, Kenya.

Dhun D. Adenwalla
Oral School for Deaf Children, Calcutta, India.

Edna P. Adler
Assistant Chief, Deafness and Communicative
Disorders Branch, Rehabilitation Services
Administration, U.S. Department of Education.

Inger Ahlgren
Institute of Linguistics, University of Stockholm,
Sweden.

Mildred Albronda
Research Associate, California School for the Deaf,
Fremont.

William M. Aldrich
Director, Audio-vestibular Laboratory,
Saint Francis Medical Center, Peoria, Illinois.

Jerome G. Alpiner
Taylor Hearing Center, Denver, Colorado.

Barbara M. Altman
Coordinator, Sociology Undergraduate Program,
University of Maryland.

Yerker Andersson
Professor of Sociology, Gallaudet College;
President, World Federation of the Deaf.

Edward L. Applebaum
Francis L. Lederer and Department Head,
Department of Otolaryngology—Head and Neck
Surgery, University of Illinois at Chicago.

Isamu Arakawa
Professor of Joetsu University of Education.

Carl W. Asp
Professor, Department of Audiology and Speech
Pathology, The University of Tennessee, Knoxville.

Gary F. Austin
Professor/Director of Rehabilitation Institute,
Southern Illinois University, Carbondale.

Byron J. Bailey
Wiess Professor and Chairman, Department of
Otolaryngology, University of Texas Medical
Branch, Galveston.

Robert G. Baker
Department of Electronics, University of
Southampton, England.

Charlotte Baker-Shenk
Sign Language Linguist; former Research Associate,
Gallaudet Linguistics Research Laboratory.

John E. D. Ball
President, National Captioning Institute.

Don Bangs
Producer/Director/Writer/Performer, SignRise
Performing Arts Company.

Sharon N. Barnartt
Associate Professor, Department of Sociology and Social Work, Gallaudet College, Washington, D.C.

Arnold Bates
Headteacher, Thomasson Memorial School for the Hearing-Impaired, Bolton, U.K.

Trent Batson
Professor of English, Gallaudet College, Washington, D.C.

Carter E. Bearden, Sr.
Field Consultant on Deaf Ministry, Language Missions Division, Home Mission Board, Southern Baptist Convention.

Daniel S. Beasley
Director and Chairman, Department of Audiology and Speech Pathology, Memphis Speech and Hearing Center, Memphis State University.

Gaylene Becker
Assistant Director, Institute for Research on Health and Aging, University of California, San Francisco.

Kurt Beermann
Professor of History, Gallaudet College, Washington, D.C.

Reverend Otto B. Berg
Missioner to the Deaf, Diocese of Washington—Episcopal Church.

Kenneth W. Berger
Kent State University, Kent, Ohio.

Eugene Bergman
Gallaudet College, Washington, D.C.

Moe Bergman
Professor Emeritus, Hunter College of the City University of New York, and Sackler School of Medicine, Tel Aviv University.

René Bernard
Lauréat de l'Académie française; Professeur honoraire, Institut National de Jeunes Sourds de Paris.

Dennis Berrigan
Instructor, Sign Language Studies Department, Madonna College, Livonia, Michigan.

Pedro Berruecos Téllez
Fundador y Director General, Instituto Mexicano de la Audición y el Lenguaje, A.C.

Bill G. Blevins
Assistant to the President, Clarke School for the Deaf, Northampton, Massachusetts.

John D. Bonvillian
Associate Professor of Psychology, University of Virginia.

Arthur Boothroyd
Professor of Speech and Hearing Sciences, Graduate School and University Center, City University of New York.

Harry Bornstein
Professor Emeritus, Gallaudet College, Washington, D.C.

Alexander Boros
Professor of Sociology, Kent State University, Kent, Ohio.

Ron Bourgea
Editor, "American Rehabilitation," Rehabilitation Services Administration, U.S. Department of Education.

Penny Boyes Braem
Center for Sign Language Research, Basel, Switzerland.

David Braybrook
Oxford Polytechnic, Lady Spencer-Churchill College, Wheatley, Oxford, England.

Richard G. Brill
Retired Superintendent, California School for the Deaf, Riverside.

Patricia A. Broen
Professor, Department of Communication Disorders, University of Minnesota.

Honorable Richard S. Brown
Presiding Judge, New Line Court of Appeals, New Line District II, Waukesha, Wisconsin.

Derek K. Burton
Head of Regional Development Services, Royal National Institute for the Deaf, London, England.

Howard R. Busby
Director, National Academy, College for Continuing Education, Gallaudet College, Washington, D.C.

Anne M. Butler
Associate Professor, Department of History, Gallaudet College, Washington, D.C.

Frank Caccamise
Senior Research Associate, National Technical Institute for the Deaf, Rochester Institute of Technology, Rochester, New York.

Rosemary Calderon
Doctoral Candidate, Department of Psychology, University of Washington.

Donald R. Calvert
Director, Central Institute for the Deaf.

Jane Carlstrom
Clinical Supervisor/Audiology, Department of Communication Disorders, University of Minnesota.

Simon J. Carmel
Rockville, Maryland.

William E. Castle
Director, National Technical Institute for the Deaf at Rochester Institute of Technology.

Francis I. Catlin
Chief of Otolaryngology Services, Texas Children's Hospital, Houston.

Harry Cayton
The National Deaf Childrens Society, U.K.

Marc P. Charmatz
Director, NAD Legal Defense Fund, Washington, D.C.

Michael A. Chatoff
Director and former President of the New York Center for Law and the Deaf.

John B. Christiansen
Professor of Sociology, Gallaudet College, Washington, D.C.

Jean Christie
Professor of History, Emerita, Fairleigh Dickinson University.

B.R. Clarke
Professor and Head, Educational Psychology and Special Education, University of British Columbia, Vancouver, B.C., Canada.

Dennis Cokely
Linguistics Research Laboratory, Gallaudet College, Washington, D.C.

M. Jane Collins
Associate Professor, Division of Communicative Disorders, Louisiana State University, Baton Rouge.

Martin Colville
Lecturer in Communication Methods with the Hearing Impaired, Moray House College of Education, Edinburgh, Scotland.

Sara E. Conlon
Education Program Specialist, Special Education Programs, U.S. Department of Education, Washington, D.C.

R. Orin Cornett
Professor and Director of Cued Speech Programs, retired, Gallaudet College, Washington, D.C.

Robin T. Cotton
Professor, Otolaryngology and Maxillofacial Surgery, University of Cincinnati College of Medicine, Cincinnati, Ohio.

Alan B. Crammatte
Editor, "American Annals of the Deaf," Arnold, Maryland.

Florence B. Crammatte
Arnold, Maryland.

Barry A. Crouch
Associate Professor of History, History Department, Gallaudet College, Washington, D.C.

Harriet Danford
Selaco South Middle School, Southeast Area Office, Downey, California.

J. S. David
Principal, Nuffield School for the Deaf and Blind, Kaitadi, Sri Lanka.

David L. de Lorenzo
College Archivist, Gallaudet College, Washington, D.C.

Michael L. Deninger
Dean for Curriculum and Instruction, Pre-College Programs, Gallaudet College, Washington, D.C.

Taras B. Denis
Consultant to the Headmaster, New York School for the Deaf.

John C. Denmark
Consultant Psychiatrist, Department of Psychiatry for the Deaf, Whittingham Hospital, Preston, Lancashire, England.

Susan De Santis
Model Secondary School for the Deaf, Gallaudet College, Washington, D.C.

Allan O. Diefendorf
Associate Professor, University of Tennessee, Knoxville.

A. F. Dimmock
National Union of the Deaf and British Deaf Association, United Kingdom.

Donald D. Dirks
Professor, School of Medicine, University of California, Los Angeles.

Valerie L. Dively
Free-lance Sign Language Instructor/English Instructor.

James D. Dixon
Vocational Rehabilitation Specialist/Audiologist, Broomfield, Colorado.

Gina Doggett
Former Managing Editor, "Volta Review," A. G. Bell Association for the Deaf.

James A. Donaldson
Professor of Otolaryngology, University of Washington, Seattle.

Marion P. Downs
Professor Emerita, Department of Otolaryngology, University of Colorado Health Sciences Center, Denver.

Sy DuBow
Legal Director, National Center for Law and the Deaf, Gallaudet College, Washington, D.C.

John D. Durrant
Professor of Otolaryngology and Chief, Section of Audiology/Speech Pathology, University of Pittsburgh School of Medicine.

Catherine Elmes-Kalbacher
Associate Professor of English and American Studies, Gallaudet College, Washington, D.C.

R. Greg Emerton
Associate Professor, National Technical Institute for the Deaf, Rochester Institute of Technology.

Karen Emerton
President, Juvenile Detention Association of New York State.

Carol Erting
Center for Studies in Education and Human Development, The Gallaudet Research Institute, Gallaudet College, Washington, D.C.

Sergia G. Esguerra
Chief, Elementary Education Division, National Capital Region, Ministry of Education, Culture and Sports, Quezon City, Philippines.

Lionel Evans
Headmaster, Northern Counties School for the Deaf, Newcastle upon Tyne, England.

Barry G. Felder
Proskauer, Rose, Goetz and Mendelsohn, New York, New York.

James J. Fernandes
Associate Professor, Department of Communication Arts, Gallaudet College, Washington, D.C.

Virginia D. Fickel
President, Acoustic Neuroma Association.

Charles M. Firestone
Adj. Professor of Law and Director, Communications Law Program, School of Law, University of California, Los Angeles.

Della Fitz-Gerald
Human Sexuality Consultant/Therapist, Orlando, Florida.

Max Fitz-Gerald
Human Sexuality Consultant/Therapist, Orlando, Florida.

Alexander Fleischman
Executive Director, The National Congress of the Jewish Deaf, Greenbelt, Maryland.

John C. Fletcher
National Institutes of Health, Bethesda, Maryland.

Mary Florentine
Director of Research, Department of Speech-Language Pathology and Audiology, Northeastern University, Boston, Massachusetts.

John W. Flynn
Executive Director, Victorian Deaf Society, East Melbourne, Victoria, Australia.

Stanislaus J. Foran
National Association for the Deaf.

Charles N. Ford
Associate Professor, Center for Health Sciences, Department of Surgery, Division of Otolaryngology, University of Wisconsin.

Roger S. Fouts
Professor of Psychology, Central Washington
University, Ellensburg, Washington.

George Robert Fraser
ICRF Cancer Epidemiology Unit, Radcliffe
Infirmary, Oxford, England.

Thomas J. Fria
Former Director, Division of Audiology, Children's
Hospital of Pittsburgh, and former Assistant
Professor of Otolaryngology, University of
Pittsburgh School of Medicine.

Nancy Frishberg
Consultant in Sign Languages and Interpreting,
Stamford, Connecticut.

Hans G. Furth
Professor of Psychology, Catholic University,
Washington, D.C.

Jack R. Gannon
Office of Alumni and Public Relations, Gallaudet
College, Washington, D.C.

E. Elaine Gardner
Associate Legal Director, National Center for Law
and the Deaf.

Carol J. Garretson
Assistant Professor in Communication Arts,
Gallaudet College, Washington, D.C.

Mervin D. Garretson
Special Assistant to the President, Gallaudet
College, Washington, D.C.

Janice (Lange) Gavinski
Educational Audiologist, Madison Metropolitan
School District, Madison, Wisconsin.

Isaac Gay
Chairman of ENT Department, Hadassah
University Hospital, and Senior Lecturer at the
Hebrew University.

Sarah S. Geer
Staff Attorney, National Association of the Deaf
Legal Defense Fund.

Josselyne Gerard
Invited Professor, Faculty of Psychology and
Education, University of Geneva.

Robert Goldstein
Professor of Communicative Disorders, University
of Wisconsin, Madison.

Loy E. Golladay
Professor Emeritus, English and General
Education, National Technical Institute for the
Deaf at Rochester Institute of Technology.

Judith N. Green
Physician/Surgeon, Jackson Clinic/Jackson
Foundation, Madison, Wisconsin.

Mark T. Greenberg
Associate Professor, Department of Psychology,
University of Washington.

Sister M. Nicholas Griffey
Director, Courses in Education of the Deaf and
Audiology, University College, Dublin, Ireland.

Nora Groce
Fellow, Family Development Study, Boston
Children's Hospital, and Department of Pediatrics,
Harvard Medical School.

François Grosjean
Professor of Psychology, Northeastern University,
Boston, Massachusetts.

Tan Chin Guan
National Society for the Deaf, Malaysia.

Ruth Gussen
Professor of Pathology, School of Medicine,
University of California, Los Angeles.

Gerilee Gustason
Professor of Education, Gallaudet College,
Washington, D.C.

Bruce R. Halverson
Associate Professor/Performing Arts, National
Technical Institute for the Deaf at Rochester
Institute of Technology.

Paul Hannon
Secretary General, The British Association of the
Hard of Hearing, London, England.

Britta Hansen
Director, The Center for Total Communication,
Copenhagen, Denmark.

J. Donald Harris
Consultant, U.S.N. Submarine Medical Research
Laboratory, Submarine Base, Groton, Connecticut.

Katherine S. Harris
Haskins Laboratories, New Haven, Connecticut.

Cecil W. Hart
Associate Professor of Otolaryngology—Head and Neck Surgery, Northwestern University Medical School.

J. Hatton
Headteacher, Longwill School for the Deaf, Birmingham, England.

J. M. Herbst
Director, S. A. National Council for the Deaf.

Francis C. Higgins
Professor Emeritus, Gallaudet College, Washington, D.C.

Paul C. Higgins
Associate Professor, Sociology Department, University of South Carolina.

Corrine Hilton
Archives/Library Curator, Photographs, Gallaudet College Library, Washington, D.C.

Ralph L. Hoag
Formerly, Superintendent, Arizona School for the Deaf, Tucson.

Harry W. Hoemann
Professor, Department of Psychology, Bowling Green State University.

Robert Hoffmeister
Education of the Hearing Impaired, Boston University, Boston, Massachusetts.

Sister M. Alverna Hollis
O.P.; Executive Director, National Catholic Office for the Deaf.

Gary L. Holman
Superintendent, North Dakota School for the Deaf.

Vicente Honrubia
Professor, Director of Research, Division of Head and Neck Surgery, School of Medicine, University of California, Los Angeles.

Norma T. Hopkinson
Consultant in Audiology; formerly with Audio-Vestibular Laboratory, and School of Medicine, University of Pittsburgh.

Robert A. Houde
President and Director of Research, Speech Recognition Systems, Rochester, New York.

Jean Hough
Interpreter, and Member of Register of Interpreters.

Alrick Huebener
Formerly Executive Director, Canadian Co-ordinating Council on Deafness, Ottawa, Ontario, Canada.

Ivan Hunter-Duvar
Professor of Otolaryngology, The Hospital for Sick Children and University of Toronto, Ontario, Canada.

T. Alan Hurwitz
Associate Dean for Educational Support Services, National Technical Institute for the Deaf.

Catherine W. Ingold
Provost, Gallaudet College, Washington, D.C.

Robert G. Ivey
Assistant Professor, University of Western Ontario, London, Ontario, Canada.

Burton F. Jaffe
Chestnut Hill Ear, Nose and Throat, Chestnut Hill, Massachusetts.

Mary A. Jansen
Dean for Professional Affairs, California School of Professional Psychology, Fresno.

Ray L. Jones
Director, National Center on Deafness, California State University, Northridge.

Jerald M. Jordan
Director, Records Management, Gallaudet College, Washington, D.C.

Eugene F. Joyce
Assistant State Coordinator for the Deaf, N.Y.S. Office of Vocational Rehabilitation, Albany, New York.

Janice H. Kanda
President, Conference of Interpreter Trainers, 1981–1986.

Kazuyuki Kanda
Associate Professor, Tokai Sangyo Junior College, Okazaki, Aichi-Pref, Japan.

Barbara Marig Kannapell
Linguistics Specialist, Gallaudet College, Washington, D.C.

Raymond S. Karlovich
Professor, Department of Communicative Disorders, University of Wisconsin—Madison.

Judy Anne Kegl
Psychology Department, Northeastern University,
Boston, Massachusetts.

Adam Kendon
Research School of Pacific Studies, The Australian
National University, Canberra.

Nancy E. Kensicki,
Professor of English, Gallaudet College,
Washington, D.C.

Doreen Kimura
Professor, Department of Psychology, University of
Western Ontario, London,
Ontario, Canada.

Alan D. Kornblut
Clinical Associate Professor of Surgery
(Otolaryngology), Georgetown University School of
Medicine, Washington, D.C.; Clinical Professor of
Surgery (Otolaryngology), Uniformed Services
University of the Health Sciences, Bethesda,
Maryland.

Art Kruger
Chairman Emeritus, AAAD/USA World Games for
the Deaf Committee, founder and first president of
AAAD.

Rolf Kuschel
Associate Professor, Psychological Laboratory,
University of Copenhagen.

Eva Kwan
Special Education Department, Lee Gardens,
Causeway Bay, Hong Kong.

Jim Kyle
School of Education Research Unit, University of
Bristol, U.K.

Paddy Ladd
British Deaf Association.

Robin Lakoff
Department of Linguistics, University of California,
Berkeley.

Harlan Lane
Professor, Northeastern University,
Boston, Massachusetts.

Helen Schick Lane
Principal Emeritus, Central Institute for the Deaf,
St. Louis, Missouri.

Robert R. Lauritsen
Director, Program for Deaf Students, St. Paul
Technical Vocational Institute, St. Paul, Minnesota.

Barbara C. LeMaster
Anthropology Department, University of California,
Los Angeles.

Ella Mae Lentz
Oakland, California.

Regina Leven
Forschungsstelle Deutsche Gebärdensprache,
Germanisches Seminar, Universität Hamburg,
Federal Republic of Germany.

Harry Levitt
Distinguished Professor of Speech and Hearing
Sciences, Graduate School and University Center of
the City University of New York.

A. Liambey
Athens Centre for Deaf Children, Athens, Greece.

E. Robert Libby
President, Associated Hearing Instruments,
Upper Darby, Pennsylvania.

R. B. Lindsay
Professor (deceased), Portsmouth, Rhode Island.

David M. Lipscomb
Professor, Department of Audiology and Speech
Pathology, University of Tennessee, Knoxville.

Nina Fletcher Little
Honorary Fellow for Research, Department of
American Decorative Arts and Sculpture,
Museum of Fine Arts, Boston.

Glenn T. Lloyd
Professor, Lenoir-Rhyne College.

Elva Fromuth Loe
Associate Professor, History of Art, and Chairman,
Art Department, retired, Gallaudet College,
Washington, D.C.

Filip T. A. Loncke
Neurolinguist, Laboratory for Neurolinguistics,
University of Brussels, and Research Department,
Institute of the Deaf, Gentbrugge.

Jean M. Lovrinic
Professor, Department of Speech, Temple
University.

William S. Lovrinic
Otolaryngologist, Philadelphia, Pennsylvania.

Edgar L. Lowell
Executive Director, John Tracy Clinic.

Rex P. Lowman
Professor, Department of Economics, Gallaudet College, Washington, D.C.

Barbara Luetke-Stahlman
Department of Special Education, University of Nebraska, Omaha.

Samuel F. Lybarger
Acoustical Consultant, McMurray, Pennsylvania.

George E. Lynn
Professor, Departments of Audiology and Neurology, Wayne State University School of Medicine, Detroit, Michigan.

Clifford Kenneth Lysons
Head of Department Emeritus, The St. Helens College of Technology, England.

Brian F. McCabe
Professor and Head, Department of Otolaryngology—Head and Neck Surgery, University of Iowa, and Editor, "Annals of Otology, Rhinology and Laryngology."

Evelyn Zebrowski McClave
Assistant Professor, Gallaudet College, Washington, D.C.

J. G. McClelland
Headmaster of Jordanstown Schools, Newtownabbey, Co. Antrim, Northern Ireland.

Nancy S. McGarr
Center for Research and Speech and Hearing Sciences, Graduate Center, The City University of New York.

Terrence J. McGovern
Assistant Professor of Romance Languages, Alfred University.

Marina L. McIntire
Department of Special Education, California State University, Northridge.

John McKendry
Managing Editor, "Hearing Rehabilitation Quarterly," New York League for the Hard of Hearing, New York, New York.

Tom McLaren
Director, Scottish Association for the Deaf.

Carol C. McRandle
Associate Professor, Audiology, Western Washington University, Bellingham, Washington.

Rut Madebrink
Formerly Manillaskolan, Specialskola för döva och hörselskadade, Stockholm, Sweden.

Julia Maestas y Moores
Continuing Education, Gallaudet College, Washington, D.C.

Russell L. Malone
Director, Public Information Department, American Speech-Language-Hearing Association, Rockville, Maryland.

Judy Mannes
Curator, Office of Fine Arts in Education, Gallaudet College, Washington, D.C.

Robert H. Margolis
Professor, Communication Sciences and Disorders, Syracuse University.

Robert John Mather
Attorney, United States Department of Justice.

Paul H. Mattingly
Professor of History, New York University.

Thomas A. Mayes
Vice President for Public Services, Gallaudet College, retired.

Peter O. Mba
President, Nigerian Association of Special Education Teachers.

Kathryn P. Meadow-Orlans
Senior Research Scientist, Center for Studies in Education and Human Development, Gallaudet College, Research Institute.

Richard W. Meisegeier
Professor of Sociology, Gallaudet College, Washington, D.C.

Maurice I. Mendel
Professor of Audiology, Department of Speech and Hearing Sciences, University of California, Santa Barbara.

Jacqueline Z. Mendelsohn
Executive Director, American Society for Deaf Children.

Sheila Conlon Mentkowski
Staff Attorney, National Center for Law and the Deaf.

Edward C. Merrill, Jr.
President Emeritus, Gallaudet College, Washington, D.C.

Marcella M. Meyer
Executive Director, Greater Los Angeles Council on Deafness, Inc.

Maurice H. Miller
Chief, Audiology, Center for Communication Disorders, Lenox Hill Hospital, New York, New York.

Aage R. Møller
University of Pittsburgh School of Medicine, Eye and Ear Hospital, Pittsburgh, Pennsylvania.

Ernest J. Moncada
Professor, Gallaudet College, Washington, D.C.

Randall B. Monsen
Associate Professor, Department of Communication Arts and Sciences, Howard University, Washington, D.C.

Luisa Montero-Díaz
Technical Consultant for the National Institute of the Child and Family, Ecuador.

George Montgomery
Senior Lecturer, Department of Psychology, University of Edinburgh, Scotland.

Bill Moody
Free-lance Interpreter, New York, New York.

Donald F. Moores
Director, Center for Studies in Education and Human Development, Gallaudet College, Washington, D.C.

Bernard Mottez
Maître de Recherche CNRS, Centre d'Etude des Mouvements Sociaux, EHESS, Paris.

Shanny Mow
Playwright, Chester, Connecticut.

Jack K. Mowry
Publisher, "Sound and Vibration."

Shirley Mubarak
Profesora Especializada en Audicion y Lenguaje, Asociacion Peruana de Profesores Especializados en Audicion y Lenguaje.

Joachim Mugdan
Priv.-Doz. Dr., Arbeitsbereich Linguistik, Westfälische Wilhelms-Universität Münster, Federal Republic of Germany.

Lowell J. Myers
Attorney at Law, Chicago.

Jeffrey E. Nash
Professor of Sociology, Macalester College, St. Paul, Minnesota.

Arlene Neuman
Research Associate, Center for Research in Speech and Hearing Sciences, Graduate School, City University of New York.

Arthur F. Niemoeller
Associate Research Scientist, Central Institute for the Deaf, St. Louis, Missouri.

Gary Nix
Faculty of Education, University of British Columbia, Vancouver, Canada.

Richard H. Nodar
Head, Section of Communicative Disorders, Department of Otolaryngology and Communicative Disorders, The Cleveland Clinic, Cleveland, Ohio.

Jerry L. Northern
Head, Audiology Division, and Professor of Otolaryngology, University of Colorado Health Sciences Center, Denver.

Robert J. Nozza
Director, Division of Audiology, Children's Hospital of Pittsburgh, and Assistant Professor of Otolaryngology, University of Pittsburgh School of Medicine.

Marc Okrand
Manager, News and Text Services, National Captioning Institute.

D. K. Oller
Associate Professor, University of Miami, Mailman Center for Child Development.

Wayne O. Olsen
Consultant in Audiology, Mayo Clinic, Rochester, Minnesota.

Michael J. Olson
Processing Archivist, Gallaudet College, Washington, D.C.

Ynez Violé O'Neill
Professor of Medical History, School of Medicine, University of California, Los Angeles.

Michael Orlansky
Department of Human Services Education, Ohio State University, Columbus, Ohio.

Mary Joe Osberger
Assistant Professor, Department of Communicative Disorders, University of Wisconsin—Madison.

Carol A. Padden
Assistant Professor, Department of
Communication, University of California,
San Diego.

John Panara
Captioning Specialist/Assistant Professor, National
Technical Institute for the Deaf, Rochester Institute
of Technology.

Robert Panara
Professor of English and Drama, National
Technical Institute for the Deaf, Rochester Institute
of Technology.

Alison D. Parra
Educator and Interpreter for the Deaf, Mexico.

Carlos A. Parra
Artist, Educational Materials for the Deaf, Mexico.

Michael Parsons
Inspector Supervising Special Education, Education
Department of New Zealand, and President of
Hearing Association, Christchurch.

Frank Allen Paul
San Diego, California.

Jorge Perelló
Professor of the University of Salamanca, Spain.

Olivier J. Périer
Specialist in Neurology and Rehabilitation of the
Hearing Impaired; Professor, University of Brussels;
Director, Language Center Comprendre et Parler,
Brussels.

Laura Petitto
Department of Psychology, McGill University,
Montreal, Quebec, Canada.

James M. Pickett
Director, Sensory Communication Research,
Gallaudet College, Washington, D.C.

Felix-Jesus Pinedo Peydro
Presidente, Confederacion Nacional Sordos de
España.

Elena Pizzuto
Cattedra di Psicologia Sperimentale,
Universita di Palermo, Italy.

Howard Poizner
Staff Scientist, The Salk Institute for
Biological Studies.

Daniel H. Pokorny
John of Beverley Professor of Deaf Ministry,
Concordia Seminary, St. Louis, Missouri.

C. A. Powell
Head of Department of Educational Development,
Oxford Polytechnic, Oxford, England.

Desmond J. Power
Director, Brisbane College of Advanced Education,
Centre for Human Development Studies.

Helen Powers
Author, "Signs of Silence" (1972), Danbury,
Connecticut.

Maria Isabel Prata
Lisboa, Portugal.

Janet L. Pray
Associate Professor and Director, Social Work
Program, Department of Sociology and Social
Work, Gallaudet College, Washington, D.C.

John D. Rainer
Professor of Clinical Psychiatry, College of
Physicians and Surgeons, Columbia University.

Tamara L. Redburn
Editor, "Communication Outlook," Artificial
Language Laboratory, Computer Science
Department, Michigan State University,
East Lansing.

Stephen J. Regnier
Editor, "Rehabilitation Literature," National Easter
Seal Society, Chicago, Illinois.

Jerry Reichstein
School of Education, Tel Aviv University,
Tel Aviv, Israel.

H. N. Reynolds
Professor of Psychology, Gallaudet College,
Washington, D.C.

R. W. Rieber
John Jay College of Criminal Justice, The City
University of New York.

Terhi Rissanen
Sign Language Researcher, University of Helsinki,
Department of General Linguistics, and Finnish
Research Centre for Domestic Languages.

Martin S. Robinette
Professor and Associate Dean, College of Health,
University of Utah, Salt Lake City.

Michael Rodda
Professor, Hearing Impaired Program, Educational Psychology Department, Faculty of Education, University of Alberta, Edmonton.

Ross J. Roeser
Chief of Audiology and Associate Professor, Callier Center for Communication Disorders, University of Texas, Dallas.

Roslyn G. Rosen
Dean, College for Continuing Education, Gallaudet College, Washington, D.C.

Benjamin Rosenblut
Professor and Head of E.N.T. Department, University of Chile Clinic Hospital.

Kenneth S. Rothschild
Sloatsburg, New York.

Clifford R. Rowley
American Society of the Deaf.

W. F. Roy III
Registry of Interpreters for the Deaf, Silver Spring, Maryland.

Phyllis Rubenfeld
President, American Coalition of Citizens with Disabilities, Inc.

Moshe Rubinstein
Professor, School for Communication Disorders, The Chaim Sheba Medical Center, Tel Hashomer Hospital, Israel.

Kenneth O. Rust
Chairperson, Sign Language Studies Department, Madonna College, Livonia, Michigan.

Mary Ann Salem
Principal, Deaf Multi-Handicapped Unit, California School for the Deaf, Riverside.

Sandy Sanborn
Program Specialist, Los Angeles Unified School District, Deaf and Hard of Hearing Program.

Derek A. Sanders
Professor of Audiology, Department of Communicative Disorders and Sciences, State University of New York at Buffalo.

Jerome D. Schein
Professor of Communication Arts and Sciences, New York University.

I. M. Schlesinger
Department of Psychology, Hebrew University, Jerusalem.

Earl D. Schubert
Professor, Hearing Science, Stanford University, Stanford, California.

John S. Schuchman
Professor of History, Gallaudet College, Washington, D.C.

K. Schulte
Prof. Dr., Forschungsstelle der Pädagogischen Hochschule Heidelberg für Angewandte Sprachwissenschaft zur Rehabilitation Behinderter, Heidelberg.

Sabina (Kurdziel) Schwan
Harper Hospital Division, Harper Grace Hospitals, Detroit, Michigan.

Michael A. Schwartz
Assistant District Attorney, New York County District Attorney's Office.

Edward L. Scouten
Professor, Rochester Institute of Technology, National Technical Institute for the Deaf, Rochester, New York.

Roy K. Sedge
Director, Army Audiology and Speech Center, Walter Reed Army Medical Center, Washington, D.C.

Gary F. Seifert
Chairman/Professor, Philosophy Department, Gallaudet College, Washington, D.C.

Reverend S. Wayne Shaneyfelt
Foreign Missionary to the Deaf, The General Council of the Assemblies of God.

David C. Shepherd
Professor of Audiology, Department of Communicology, University of South Florida.

Hiroshi Shimizu
Associate Professor and Director, Hearing and Speech Clinic, Department of Otolaryngology—Head and Neck Surgery, The Johns Hopkins University School of Medicine.

Stanislaw Sila-Nowicki
The Secretary of Scientific Commission, Polish Association of the Deaf, Warsaw, Poland.

S. Richard Silverman
Department of Otolaryngology, University of Florida, Gainesville.

F. Blair Simmons
Professor of Otolaryngology/Head and Neck Surgery, Stanford University School of Medicine.

Audrey Simmons-Martin
Formerly Director, Early Education Central Institute for the Deaf, and Professor, Washington University, St. Louis, Missouri.

T. Stewart Simpson
Director, Council for the Advancement of Communication with Deaf People.

Jess M. Smith
Indianapolis, Indiana.

Mansfield F. W. Smith
Ear Medical Clinic, San Jose, California.

Wayne H. Smith
Instructor, Department of Foreign Languages, Gallaudet College, Washington, D.C.

Ausma Smits
Assistant Professor of History, Gallaudet College, Washington, D.C.

James B. Snow, Jr.
Professor and Chairman, Department of Otorhinolaryngology and Human Communication, University of Pennsylvania School of Medicine, Philadelphia.

Jorge Soler
Department of Philosophy, Gallaudet College, Washington, D.C.

Deborah M. Sonnenstrahl
Associate Professor, Gallaudet College, Washington, D.C.

Brenda Sorenson
Selaco South Middle School, Southeast Area Office, Downey, California.

Charles E. Speaks
Department of Communication Disorders, University of Minnesota, Minneapolis.

Mauro Spinelli
Coordenador de Program de Disturbios da Communicacao, Secretaria de Pos Graduacao du PACSP, São Paulo, Brazil.

Joe D. Stedt
Department of Speech and Hearing, Cleveland State University, Cleveland, Ohio.

H. J. T. Steyn
Editor and Education Contributor.

Richard G. Stoker
Department of Communication Disorders, Pennsylvania State University, University Park.

William C. Stokoe
President and Editor, Linstok Press, Inc., Silver Spring, Maryland.

Howard E. Stone, Sr.
Executive Director, Self Help for Hard of Hearing People, Inc.

Barry Strassler
President, Deaf Factory Store.

E. Ross Stuckless
National Technical Institute for the Deaf, Rochester, New York.

Frank B. Sullivan
Formerly Grand President, National Fraternal Society of the Deaf.

Patricia M. Sullivan
Director, Psychological Services, The Boys Town National Institute for Communication Disorders in Children.

Allen E. Sussman
Professor of Counseling, Gallaudet College; and Licensed Psychologist.

Sathaporn C. Suvannus
Secretary-General, Foundation for the Deaf in Thailand under the royal patronage of H.M. the Queen, Bangkok.

Mary-Jean Sweeny
Greenbelt, Maryland.

Roger Sydenham
Director, The Royal National Institute for the Deaf.

Bernard T. Tervoort
Prof. Dr., Institute for General Linguistics, University of Amsterdam, The Netherlands.

Juergen Tonndorf
Professor Emeritus of Otolaryngology, Columbia University, New York, New York.

S. Morag Turner
Director, Scottish Centre for the Education of the Deaf, Moray House College of Education, Edinburgh.

David R. Updegraff
Superintendent, Michigan School for the Deaf, Flint.

John V. Van Cleve
Professor and Chair of the History Department, Gallaudet College, Washington, D.C.

Madan Vasishta
Texas School for the Deaf, Austin.

Arthur Verney
General Secretary, The British Deaf Association, United Kingdom.

Jack Vernon
Department of Otolaryngology, Kresge Hearing Research Laboratory, The Oregon Health Sciences University, Portland, Oregon.

Marit Vogt-Svendsen
University of Trondheim, Department of Linguistics, Norway.

Lars von der Leith
Professor, Audiologopedic Research Group, University of Copenhagen, Denmark.

W. Dixon Ward
Professor, Department of Communication Disorders, University of Minnesota, Minneapolis.

Henry Warner
Office of Rehabilitation Services, U.S. Department of Education, Atlanta, Georgia.

W. Bruce Warr
Senior Staff Scientist, Boys Town National Institute, Omaha, Nebraska.

Dora B. Weiner
Professor of Medical Humanities, School of Medicine, University of California, Los Angeles.

Bruce A. White
Assistant Professor, Department of English, Gallaudet College, Washington, D.C.

Josephine White Eagle
Linguistics Department, Massachusetts Institute of Technology.

Robert L. Whitehead
Chairperson, Department of Communication

Research, National Technical Institute for the Deaf, Rochester, New York.

Julius Wiggins
Publisher, Silent News, Inc.

Ronnie Wilbur
Department of Audiology and Speech Sciences, Purdue University, West Lafayette, Indiana.

Terry L. Wiley
Professor, Department of Communicative Disorders, University of Wisconsin—Madison.

Melanie Yager Williams
Burke, Virginia.

Robert Lee Williams
Professor and Chairman of Psychology, Gallaudet College, Washington, D.C.

Richard Winefield
Director of Policy and Planning, Oakland Unified School District, Oakland, California.

M. A. Winzer
University of British Columbia, Vancouver, Canada.

Peter R. Wisher
Professor Emeritus, Gallaudet College, Washington, D.C.

Enid Gordon Wolf
Research Scientist–Psycholinguist, New York State Institute for Basic Research in Developmental Disabilities.

Bencie Woll
Professor, School of Education Research Unit, University of Bristol, England.

David James Wood
Reader, Department of Psychology, University of Nottingham, England.

James Woodward
Research Scientist, The Gallaudet Research Institute, Center for Assessment and Demographic Studies.

Phillip A. Yantis
Professor, Department of Speech and Hearing Sciences, University of Washington.

Yau Shunchiu
Director of Research, Centre National de la Recherche Scientifique, France.

Piao Yongxin
Deaf People and Education, Department of
Education, Beijing Normal University, Beijing,
People's Republic of China.

Annette Zaner
Director, Communication Disorders, Mt. Carmel
Guild, Newark, New Jersey.

George Zelma
Zelma & Grossman, Attorneys at Law,
New York, New York.

Andrija Žic
Lawyer and Editor, "SLUH," magazine of the
Association of the Hearing Impaired of Croatia.

Frank R. Zieziula
Professor, Department of Counseling,
Gallaudet College, Washington, D.C.

Jozef J. Zwislocki
Institute for Sensory Research,
Syracuse University.

Index

Index

Asterisks indicate page references to article titles.

B

C

H

J

O

P

Q-R

S

Y-Z